AN IRISH HISTORY OF CIVILIZATION

Volume One

AN IRISH HISTORY OF CIVILIZATION

An Irish History of Civilization

Volume One

Comprising Books 1 and 2

DON AKENSON

Granta Books
London

Granta Publications, 2/3 Hanover Yard, Noel Road, London N1 8BE

First published in Great Britain by Granta Books, 2005
First published in Canada by McGill-Queen's University Press, 2005

A CIP catalogue record for this book is available from the British Library.

1 3 5 7 9 10 8 6 4 2

ISBN 1 86207 804 1

Typeset by Dynagram Inc.
Printed in Canada on acid-free paper

To the memory of

Sir Walter Raleigh,
who should have known better,

and in honour of

Eduardo Galeano,
who certainly does.

Contents

Preface

As in the case of the two supernal Talmuds, the Yerushalmi and the Bavli, nothing original is proposed in these volumes, only respectful commentary on what Sages have said, or should have. Everything in them I have read, heard from somebody, or talked about to myself; or the reader has creatively imputed new meanings to old words. For all of these voices, I am grateful. Where I have directly quoted someone, it is pretty clearly marked.

Against my inclination, my publishers have insisted that to aid librarians and bookstore owners in putting these volumes on the right shelves I label clearly what they are. Like all human lives, this is a collection of fictive short stories or, if you prefer, of Aggadah: very little in the way of Halachah here.

Some of the stories are accurate; all of them are true. Of course, as Church dogma teaches, if any thing is not true, then no thing is. Still, as far as mere accuracy is concerned, not all seeming errors in the text are accidental. Sometimes even the immortal Homer only pretended to nod.

Taken together, this Irish history of civilization is a micro-Talmud of humankind: for, ultimately, we are all of the one stock, and what we learn of one of us tells us something about each of us. I am confident that Irish readers will be generous and will permit their culture's experience of world history to be presented in this Jewish form. After all, the Irish rarely forget a debt.

DA

AN IRISH HISTORY OF CIVILIZATION

Book One

Downpatrick Is the Butterfly Capital of the Universe

PRELUDE

Is this Really an Irish Problem?

After the annual Presidential Prayer Breakfast, Richard Nixon, thirty-seventh president of the United States, has his friend Dr. Graham visit the Oval Office for a private chat with himself and H.R. Haldeman, his political hitman: tape recorded, but Graham does not know that.

Nixon is considering whether or not to run for a second term, and is leaning strongly towards doing so. He's more asking for Billy's blessing than for political advice.

The President has one problem that constantly bothers him and on this he does indeed desire counsel of America's great evangelist: the Jewish problem. Not Israel. Nixon, Haldeman, and Graham all agree that the best Jews are the Israeli Jews. One hundred percent behind Israel, all three men. No, the problem is the American Jews, and only some of them. Nixon says it's the ones who control the media, all left-wing and anti-Nixon.

Billy agrees: *The Bible says there are satanic Jews and that's where our problem arises.*

Nixon is less scriptural. *The big news sources are totally dominated by the Jews.*

Yes. And it's the Jews who are putting out the pornographic stuff, Billy adds.

Nixon, who likes a good dirty movie, manages to stifle a smile. *Every Democratic candidate will owe his election to Jewish people.*

This stranglehold has to be broken, Mr. President, or this country's going down the drain.

You believe that?

Yes sir.

Oh boy. So do I. I can't ever say that, but I believe it.

*No, but if you get elected a second time, **then we might be able to do something.***

THE DISCUS THROWERS
16–400 CE

Genealogy

"Repeat, repeat, repeat!" Paul's father demanded. And Paul did. Again and again and again. The stripling Paul knew that to curse one's father was a transgression that would cut him off forever from Yahweh's love and, worse, bring him face-to-face with His wrath. So he repeated, time and time again, each time perfectly, or so nearly perfect that he didn't understand why the old man did not let it go.

Why does he have to do all this rigmarole for the Coming-of-Age ceremony, when most of my friends are just learning slabs of Torah? Why do I have to grind all this stuff from Hillel? – our Prince! a Babylonian! – and why all all all, oh it is killing me, all this Oral Torah and why these genealogies that have nothing to do with my family and are just about dead teachers? and why can't I go to the latrine or have a bit of bread and where is all this leading when all I want to do is be a trader in tent cloth and sit in the shade and maybe visit a marble-faced city or two and maybe ...

Ahhhh!! That hurt. Why is the old man being such a beast? I won't mess up the service. I can do the Hebrew bits by heart and all the quotations that the old man's fellow Pharisees demand are easy enough, especially as they are in Greek and why am I looking at that fly walking across the ceiling when I know if I let my eyes wander the old man will ...

Ahh, dear father of the prophets, that stings ... I shall, I now repeat accurately the major sayings of your most blessed Rabbi, the great Hillel ... and ... oh, here goes:

– Great joy to those who weep, for they shall be comforted.

– Do not, unto anyone do, what you do not wish them to do to you. (Yes, father, I will stop singing; this is not a psalm, yes, father, I know that.)

– Be prudent in judgement; raise up many disciples; make a fence around the Torah.

– Great joy to the pure in heart; God will see them.

– On what does the world stand? It stands on the Torah, on the Temple Service, and on deeds of loving kindness.

– Great joy to all who are peacemakers. They are the children of the Almighty.

– On what does the world stand? It stands on faith, on hope, on love. But the greatest of these is love.

Oh thank you father. Yes, the words are balm to my soul. As if, silly old man, my soul needed balm. I could use a good scratch of my arse right now and that's hard to come by.

Yes, yes, father, I will now rehearse how the Oral Torah came down to us – to you and to me and to all the Righteous in the Diaspora and in Eretz Israel and yes, yes, father, I know that the Oral Torah is equal to the Written, and yes, that the two entwine together, and that we have in unbroken tradition the words of the Almighty to Moses, our sage of blessed memory. All right. Just give me a moment to gather myself and here goes our ladder to the stars. (Oh, that was close; wouldn't do to say something like that in the ear of old Hillel's disciple Gripey Guts). The proper order, revered sir, is as follows:

– Hillel, (and God forgive me, I must mention Shammai),
– received Oral Torah from:
Shemaiah and Abtalion
– who had received Oral Torah from:
Judah ben Tabbai and Simeon ben Shetah
– who had received Oral Torah from:
Joshua ben Perahyah and Nittai of Arbela
– who had received Oral Torah from Yose ben Yohanan. Those are "The Pairs."

Yes, father, I know that there are more. And, well, actually, father, why do things become so fuzzy after that? Aiyeee! I apologize father: all is sound, all is solid. Oh dear demons of Sheol, that hurt! Back to business.

Yose ben Yoezer and Yose ben Yohanan who ... who
– received Torah from Antigonus of Soko
– who was given Torah by Simon the Just
– who received Torah from the Great Assembly
– who received Torah from the Prophets,
– who received Torah from the Elders
– and the first of these elders was Joshua
– and Joshua received Torah from Moses
– and Moses received Torah directly from Yahweh at Sinai.

"Well done, son. No errors."

Yes: correct, certainly; it's not hard, just boring: but does the old man actually believe that the source of the things he teaches me goes all the way up the holy mountain? To the mind of the Almighty One? Still, it's something, being part of an unbroken chain.

ANTIOCH-ON-THE-ORONTES. 18CE

The Discus Throwers

"Better to be strong like a willow than strong like a cedar."
Paul's father was forever quoting maxims. "That I learned from the second-greatest teacher of our faith, our Prince, Hillel."

Young Paul, just turned fourteen, was on his first adult journey with his father. He did not like listening to him repeat the same points, especially because they always had a hidden question or pointed comment barbed inside. This time it was merely idiotic – really, of course, father, I know who our truly greatest teacher is, even greater than Hillel: Moses of blessed memory – and, yes, father, I know that I am becoming stout and yes, I know that great cedars snap in the wind, while the lean willows flex like whips, this way and that, and they survive. Yes, yes, yes.

Paul was nettled by the queries and embarrassed by how loud his father talked. They were attending a set of athletic competitions that the local governor put on annually. Paul's father was one of the few Jews who had access to the seats reserved for Roman citizens and every word he said was taken in, with a smirk or a wink, by the goyim. He had gained his Roman citizenship by being a good merchant and he was proud of himself: he frequently bragged that without the canvas he provided to the Roman garrisons, half the legions in Syria would have dropped from rain, sun, or wind.

To be allowed to see Antioch, it was worth putting up with his father, Paul calculated. The third largest city in the Roman world, its heart glistened, for Herod the Great had paved its centre with marble. And on a clear day one could see Cyprus floating on the distant horizon. Paul's father made a trip, following a crescent pattern, from Tarsus to Antioch to Damascus, twice a year. He had his own goods train and he delivered tent cloth to garrisons and to private customers and took orders for his next trip. He was a person of consequence, but he was not a lickspittle: he did business with everyone, but was unembarrassedly Jewish, which did not endear him to his son, not in this arena.

"And, another thing I heard the Great Hillel say ..."

Paul did not turn to look at his father, but concentrated on the athletes. Many of them competed naked and Paul looked at the hanging parts with the attention of a mongoose regarding a cobra. So that's what they look like, the goyim!

Even more interesting, young Paul suddenly caught sight of a discuss thrower, a man he knew was Jewish. He was from Tarsus and yet ... It was all very confusing and he asked his father how that could be; how does somebody circumcised stop being so?

This was a moment of potentially humiliating public embarrassment for the older man, but he overcame it. "Oh," he replied with a laugh that was falsely hearty, "everything good comes to him who waits!"

Everyone around laughed heartily and Paul had the good sense to pretend to be amused. He understood. His father was well enough trained in biblical Hebrew to play with the puns, an inevitable aspect of the scriptures, given that the basic language was made up of three-letter consonants and no vowels. Puns were half the joy of being one of the Chosen People. Whether or not the Gentiles surrounding the canvas merchant and his son actually understood the Jewish verbal game being played is unclear: Paul did.

And by "wait," Paul understood the second meaning, the one his father really had in mind: weight. If a circumcised Jew really wanted to progress in many fields, he had to extend himself, as it were. This was accomplished by weights. Sometimes it took months, occasionally a year or more. The man involved had to wear an ever-increasing set of weights attached to his penis until finally his foreskin became long enough to be Greek or Roman or anything but Jewish.

Paul took that in instantly. It was possible to be both circumcised and, later, if one wished, not.

That was a big lesson.

And the second was like unto it: later, as they left the arena, Paul's father began to talk about the Jewish discus thrower. Not about the athlete's anatomy but about physics.

"Paraphrasis," Paul thought to himself. When will he get to the point? Who cares about how the turncoat hurls the thing?

His father surprised him, for the point had to do with direction and momentum, not with keeping one's self pure.

"Notice how useful it is to be able to change direction."

"Oh?"

"The discus is the best athletic event there is – it's the only one that allows taking one sort of power – circular at that – and turning it into another path, a linear one."

"Yes ...?"

"So, consider what would happen if a relay line of discus throwers was strung out between here and the horizon: any direction you choose, it doesn't matter." Paul and his father stopped and regarded each other as the exiting crowd streamed by them. "They would change all history. From pivoting in one place to covering the entire earth."

Paul halfway understood. "For the moment, I'll wait," he replied.

SEPPHORIS, LOWER GALILEE. 29CE

Slicing Torah

A whack on the side of the head prevented Paul of Tarsus's ever casting eyes on Yeshua of Nazareth, the man whom he later encountered as the transfigured spiritual Jesus-the-Christ. The blow was unexpected and was launched by a Roman legionnaire who stepped up behind Paul and swung his gauntlet-covered forearm in a lazy arc. The response was satisfactory and the soldier permitted himself a smile wide enough to show his ochre-coloured teeth to the miscreant. Paul was stunned, but not injured and he waddled hurriedly down a backstreet.

Paul had been pressing himself to the back of one of Sepphoris's municipal buildings, trying to hear what the man standing in the agora in the city centre was expounding. Sepphoris was the administrative hub of Galilee and a very toney place, with marble-faced municipal buildings, a theatre that seated 3,000, and a small imperial palace. The man whose words Paul was trying to catch moved with a confidence that told his audience that he was at home in such surroundings; he had been here frequently since it was only four miles from his home in Nazareth ...

But what was he saying? Heterodoxy, surely, but of what sort? Paul heard a member of the audience phrase a question suavely, a trick question: "What, teacher, would you have us do to respect Torah? How can we keep all the commandments of the Almighty's Law?"

"Torah teaches us one thing," Yeshua replied, "and all else is detail."

"Yes, please, teacher. What is that one thing?"

"That bread must be sliced carefully, and very very thin."

This was the moment when the legionnaire, whose job it was to keep derelicts, lunatics, and suspicious persons on the move, thumped Paul of Tarsus. Paul had been on the point of sticking his head around the corner of the building that concealed him, just on the verge of seeing this teacher. Then, the ear-ringing clap on the side of his head, and Paul was clearing away, moving quickly back to the Jewish sector of Sepphoris. There he had allies. And, in any case, he needed to take a drop of wine for his head's sake.

Paul, like the man whom he'd been sent to spy upon, was a Pharisee. These were laymen who argued points of law with more scholarship than did most of the priests; they kept themselves ritually clean as any Temple server; and they were zealous on personal purity, and especially dietary law. The Pharisees were not a united front. Some, like Paul, came from the Jewish Diaspora and were slightly different, city by city; others, like Yeshua of Nazareth, were out-country residents of Eretz Israel and they had some peculiar regional twists in their beliefs; and still others were based in Jerusalem: like all the inhabitants of all the metropoli of the world, they looked down on the others and haughtily told the rustics when and where they got it wrong. The various sets collected information on each other, and the hot-heads among them were continually arguing for a bit of physical force when calm reasoning with their rivals failed. Paul was one of those.

The words that Paul had heard – the only words of Yeshua of Nazareth ever to reach directly the man who became Christianity's great missioner – infuriated him. They were a direct insult, a challenge to other Pharisees, a rebuke, an arrogation ... words failed him. Paul, by the time he reached his friends was incandescently furious. "And, so, he has the brass necked pride to as-good-as-say that only his lot honours table-purity. Only his band of scale-covered fishmongers keeps to the full Law."

"Did he say that?"

"He would have, I know. It's what he meant. No doubt there." Paul's compatriots were not inclined to contradict him, for his reputation for violence was considerable and justified. Besides, Paul was confirming something about Yeshua of Nazareth that they already knew: that on some matters he claimed to be not only more rigorous than everyone in the Pharisaic movement, but more pure than Moses himself: this because of his argument that Moses was wrong to permit divorce. All the courts, the *Beth Dinim*, were wrong, Yeshua said. They, the successors of Moses were wrong and even the Man who had talked directly to Yahweh at Sinai was wrong. Too lax!

Years later, when in visions the Apostle Paul talked to Jesus-the-Christ, he learned that Yeshua of Nazareth did not actually mean what Paul of Tarsus had heard him say. He did not demand unthinking obedience to the 613 commandments of the scriptures or scrupulous and detailed, knife-sharp attention to the hundreds and hundreds of halachic rulings based upon those commandments. "You see, what He meant," Paul later would explain with avuncular familiarity, "is that Torah is our bread, our source of life. And that instead of accepting it unthinkingly, we should be very careful and take Torah and its suggestions a little piece at a time, and in a way that fits our own individual needs."

The Apostle Paul was always grateful for this revelation. It was wonderfully flexible. It could be applied to sacred teaching in almost any situation. The revelation gave liberation from the squalid and confining chrysallis defined by the unimaginative, obsessive, argumentative, pilpulistic Yeshua of Nazareth and freed the air-borne, translucent, vertiginously looming figure of Jesus-the-Christ.

Christianity became possible.

THE RIVER EUPHRATES, BETWEEN ALEPPO AND BAGHDAD. 33CE

Heaven Visiting

Luminescent butterflies appeared in the distance. Paul watched them approach, beguiled like a child in a meadow. He hoped they would draw close, so he could touch them and feel their colours. As they grew closer, the sun caught their wings and was split into a thousand rainbows. This, Paul should have thought, is heaven, but when a person is in heaven that is the one thought not permitted. God's funny that way.

As the creatures flitted closer their flight became straighter, more purposive, and Paul recognized them as figures he had read about often and recently seen in frescoes and mosaics. They were angels, and the most important ones at that: Michael, of course, and Gabriel and Raphael, and Phanuel. As they approached he wanted to put out his hand and with just a single finger contact them, gently as feather might touch feather. Their manner though was determined, and not at all inviting. The Archangel Michael scowled and pointed to their flank, where a small cloud was forming on the horizon. Dark, it gave off tiny sparks of St. Elmo's fire and it swirled towards Paul. The four angels placed themselves as guardians before Paul and it is well they did, for he was within an eyelash-breadth of losing his soul forever, so he later recalled. The black cloud spun out into the ferocious forms of the Fallen Angels: Azaz'el, Baragel, Kokba'el, and behind them, directing them as a charioteer would drive a troika, was Satan, or Mastema, or Beelzebub, whatever name he chose to wear this day. Satan, blocked, remained regally silent. His only response was to spit and immediately the air became noisome with sulphur. Then he turned, revealing his naked and pendant nether parts, and led his band away, an ever-diminishing cyclone on a dustless plain.

What was occurring to Paul – he's well on his way at this point to being the Apostle Paul – has been forever made a bollocks by the author of the Acts of the Apostles, a pillock who never met the man, who never read a word of any of his letters and who, when embarrassed by Paul's very Jewish behaviour turns him into something different, a kind of neo-Platonic, Pharisee-hating, Hellenophile.

Take the story in Acts of the Road-to-Damascus conversion of Paul. Great stuff, but the trouble is, old Paul never mentions this in his epistles (and heaven knows, he mentions everything in those letters but the recipe for barley soup): he never even hints at the Damascus lark. And the big blinding light. And all that. Instead, he tells us he was taken up into heaven – actually, the "third heaven" – and there he had a revelation beyond words, although he did a pretty good job, one grants, of getting it part way into words.

Such visions were as natural to first-century Jews as was going to the Temple. They were part of the same game, and there was nothing "Christian "about such visions. Go into any sizeable town in the Diaspora or in Eretz Israel and one could find a custodian of one of the several versions of the Book of Enoch; someone else would have the Book of Jubilees; rarer, but not uncommon, was the War Scroll; and there were scores of other records of roaring, swooping, vivid visions. The invisible world was full of things to be seen, and many faithful worshippers of Yahweh told and retold their own private mysticisms, real, wrenching, all permissible within the faith.

Paul, when he had his own life-transforming vision, was on a journey that would eventually take him to Damascus indeed, but that's a point of intentional misdirection by that Acts guy. Actually, Paul was visiting a place called "Europos," delivering tent cloth and meeting with the local Pharisees. He had never seen this town before, although his father had vaguely told him that there were splendors in its places of worship, and indeed there were. As was usually the case, the local synagogue and its separate mikveh were built to resemble on the outside the everyday homes of prosperous citizens. Inside, however, was a revelation for Paul: both edifices were bedizened not only with the decorative bands and the stylistic representations of the fruits of the earth found in most Diaspora synagogues, but in panel-after-panel of sacred scenes: fifty-eight in the synagogue and another half-dozen around the ritual bath, plus some ceiling and floor pieces that took one from the underworld to the heavens. To someone accustomed to the tiresome Jewish architectural conventions of the era – lintels of carved lentils being the favourite device – it was a walk in the clouds.

For Paul, the key motif in this celestial experience was the figure of Enoch, the father of Methuselah and the man who walked so closely with the Almighty that he did not die, but was taken up alive into heaven. Enoch, as the first person in the religion of Yahweh to forego worldly death, would have been important in any case, but Paul, brooding wrathfully on the reason why the followers of the bent Pharisee, Yeshua-of-Nazareth, refused to accept his death, started to intuit uncomfortable similarities. And, later, as he walked alongside the Euphrates, Paul saw a Torah-like scroll unfurling of its own accord and from it stepped the figure of Enoch. And he was quoting to Paul words that the man from Tarsus well-knew already, for they were the start of the Book of Enoch that circulated so widely among Jewish devotes. "The blessing of Enoch by which he blesses the elect and righteous who will be present when the great world tribulation begins and all the ungodly ones are removed ..."

Paul joins the vision. He sees the god of the universe come forth from his holy dwelling and march to Mount Sinai and then the whole earth is rent asunder. The righteous and unrighteous are judged, the wicked destroyed and then the whole thing circles around again and now in the heavens the good angels and bad angels battle, conduits of good and evil respectively, and heavenly figures of unrepresentable glory appear, the Righteous One and the Elect One and the Ancient of Days and the Before-Time, and their battle whirls every observer into a dervish-like state of demented, intoxicated enlightenment, and the whole vision spins again and Paul sees the Son of Man unlock the hidden storerooms where the earth's treasures are now kept and the cells where all the deposed evil kings are incarcerated and, oh the vision spins yet again and the rooms where the hail, mist and wind are kept are revealed, and again, again, everything revolves and Paul's eyes fix on the universe's ultimate light-refracting structure, a multi-crystal construction built up and up into the heavens, with tongues of living fire issuing forth light from the interstices where one crystal abuts its neighbour and there, in one of those tiny cracks, Paul sees the entire heavens and universe as in a fly's-eye painting and understands that Yeshua of Nazareth was, like Enoch, immortal, and that he was in existence before Time began and would be there after it ended and that he had gained his power, had become Moshiah, by standing at the intersection of earth and heaven, of past and future.

The remainder of Paul's walk to Damascus was uneventful.

JERUSALEM. 50CE

The Jerusalem Conference

The noise of the workmen continually interrupted the negotiations and, because of the construction dust that swirled into, around, and out the house, everyone in the room kept a scarf or sleeve in front of his mouth. Often phrases had to be repeated so they were unambiguous. Cutting a covenant in the house of Yacov, brother of Yeshua of Nazareth, and his mother, Miriam, was no joy. The house, a three-storey collection of boxes, was stacked crazily against a corner in Jerusalem's second wall. The crucial meeting was taking place in the house's largest room, an eating room in the middle storey, and the negotiators lounged on the floor as if they were present at a banquet in which the food was inexplicably missing. It was mid-afternoon and a shaft of sunlight illuminated the bursts of dust that poured in from the workings across the road. There Jerusalem's third wall, begun by Herod the Great, continued by Herod Agrippa, was now being taken further, a total of ninety towers being constructed.

Had a line been drawn down the centre of the room with quicklime, the two halves could not have been any more clearly demarcated. On one side was Paul and his outrider Barnabas, a presentable man of middle-age with an inclination to smile too often and to nod too agreeably. On the other side, unbending in every aspect was Yacov, head of the Jerusalem church and the generally recognized doyen of all who were of what he called "The Family." He was the equivalent of a caliph and everyone on his side of the room sat in ranks behind him: John (always known as "John, the son of Zebedee") and Peter, in a file of their own. Then, a row back, the other brothers of Yeshua of Nazareth, Shimon, Yudah and Yosef. And in a corner, towards which Yacov looked frequently for approval, stood three women in black: two sisters of Yeshua and Yeshua's mother. The placement of the players resembled a giant board game and mirrored accurately the power relationship of the two sides.

For Paul, this was a tough room.

"So, we agree, then: imperial and Herodian coins shall be considered equal. Proconsular coinage, of whatever region, shall be adjudged and discounted by weight." The voice was that of Barnabas and he was smiling and bobbing around as if he had just found the secret entrance to the Pool of Siloam.

Paul's stomach was killing him. If only he dared asked for a little wine to quieten it, but he dared not. He had lost enough face already.

"And, next," Barnabas waffled on, "we needst discuss the silver didrachmas of Tyre. They are the standard for the Temple tax and ..."

"Why do you not simply say a 'half-shekel' and be done?" Yacov interrupted sharply. Paul, who was looking fixedly into the middle distance, managed to catch a quick glimpse of Yacov's face. What a cold man, but at least one to respect. Yacov, just like all of Yeshua's family, had not followed him when he was on earth, but afterwards, when the Yeshua-faith had continued to roll onwards, Yacov had seen the Risen Jesus. Paul had no doubt about Yacov's sincerity. He was as self-denying a man as lived within Jerusalem's walls and he had a will of iron, and without his approval, no branch of The Family was licit.

That's why Paul was in Jerusalem and at some peril to himself: he needed approval for his Gentile mission.

Barnabas continued, smiling unctuously. "... and the, ah, half-shekel will be our collection for each man, woman and child in the synagogues we establish outside of Eretz Israel and ..."

Paul allowed himself to remember his earlier visits to Jerusalem, the ten months he had spent in the city at his father's expense when he was sixteen; he had moved from the fringe of one group of keen Pharisees to another, and even spent a week in the back row of the Beth Hamidrash of Gamaliel I, the son or grandson of the great Hillel (everyone was fairly muddy on this point for reasons that Paul never thought worth pursuing). And then Paul had been back briefly three years after his life-changing Heaven-Visiting, to be instructed by Peter on the acceptable details of belief. Peter, who had smuggled him in and out of Jerusalem so that Paul's old allies, the extreme edge of the Pharisees, would not do him in, dear Peter! now ranged against him!

"... shall be collected and brought to the Holy City, where it shall be used to pay the Temple Tax ..." Barnabas bowed deeply in what he took to be the direction of the Holy Mount.

Shimon interrupted. "And to be used to aid the poor of The Family. The Family of Belief." He stared at Paul in challenge. "Is that not correct, brother?"

Other than the ascetic Yacov, Paul detested the brothers of Yeshua. How he hated the way they travelled like merchant princes while serving as emissaries to scattered congregations. How he despised their taking their wives along, as if they were Imperial administrators. This on the purses of the faithful! But what most burned in Paul's stomach was the undeniable fact that this family had tried to have Yeshua – the future Moshiah! – put away as being out of his mind. And they have the gall to keep reminding me that I was persecutor of the faith! "Yes, Shimon, that is correct. Entirely. You, that is, Yacov, shall be free to decide how much of the Jerusalem Collection that Barnabas and I make shall be allocated to the Temple and how much to the poor of The Family."

"Entirely?" The question was high-pitched. It came from Miriam, mother of The Family's dead founder and, of course, of Paul's crucified Moshiah.

Paul flushed and would have answered sharply, but was saved by a crash from outside where a construction timber had given way and a raft of scaffolding had splintered to earth. A tidal surge of dust filled the room, and by the time sound and grit had settled, Paul had himself back in check. "Yes, most revered Miriam. Yes: entirely." It would not do to get on her wrong side. Here in Jerusalem she was given a place of honour as the mother of Yeshua, but in some distant synagogues – not those Paul founded, to be sure – she was referred to as the Mother of God. That wouldn't play here in Jerusalem, for the place was full of Yeshua's brothers and sisters and their families and they all knew what was bred in the bone had come out in the flesh. The Family, however, was not averse to a little holy mystery when bumpkins-from-beyond were concerned. Mother Miriam one kept sweet; that Paul knew.

So ended the negotiations. A deal had been struck, a covenant cut. It was humiliatingly simple. In return for spending all his spare moments for the next five or ten years badgering his congregations for denarii to schlepp to Jerusalem, Paul would be given a free hand to preach his version of Jesus-the-Christ to the Gentile world. He did not have to have Gentiles circumcised. And he could still keep on accredited terms with the closest spiritual descendants of Yeshua of Nazareth, his physical family, the chief guardians of his memory, and the continuing conduit to the Jerusalem Temple and the Jewish faith.

Jerusalem ruled. But, as Paul explained to Barnabas, sometimes it is better to marry than to burn.

GALATIA. 51CE

The Tools of the Missionary

The missionary leaned back against the rock that provided him with shade. This relieved the pain in his spine and allowed his massive stomach to wander, as if of its own free accord, towards the ground, a goal it never reached but always seemed to be seeking. Carrying this burden from one desolate portion of Asia Minor to another had become almost a holy cause with the missioner: "my collection for the Jerusalem church" he sometimes called it.

"Recitation time," he said with resignation. His companion was a tall, hardened man, perhaps a former soldier, a useful body guard. But that is not why he was paid to accompany the missionary. "Yes. We will recite now."

And for half an hour the Apostle went through a collection of idioms, basic verbs and, especially, nouns relating to religion, getting their pronunciation correct, trying to form full sentences. When he faltered, his companion quietly corrected him. "Done now, Saul," he suggested, using the apostle's birth name. "More road."

The missionary rose slowly, as an ancient volcano rising from a large plateau. "And don't call me Saul! I've warned you often enough of that." This was a point of sensitivity with the colporteur, for "Saul" turned too easily into "Saulos" and in the Aramaic spoken by most Jews in the Land of Israel this meant "slut-arsed" and if there was one thing that the missionary hated it was rent boys. And pushy women. "Always call me 'Paulos.'" Even that was bad enough, because it could mean short-stuff, or little-guy, but that was like calling a bald-headed man "Curley." At least there was irony and, besides, being a big man and denominated small was a lot better than being constantly reminded of these dextrous sexual sins and the sinuous sinners that so often flashed before the mind of the Apostle Paul.

His companion acknowledged the command with a curt nod. "Shall we continue with the local language? As we journey?"

Paul was striving to gain a basic vocabulary of the form of Celtic spoken in parts of Galatia. "Yes, we'll need it in the north, if only to start off ceremonial occasions and to offer the occasional phrase in the middle of one of my orations." Paul was good at languages and had Aramaic, ancient Hebrew, several Greek dialects and some demotic Latin at his call. This, however, was his first brush with a Celtic tongue and he was having a hard time getting the rhythm of the verbs. Everything was backwards from proper Greek, and the way that verbs and pronouns compounded made his head ache.

Less than an hour later, he commanded another stop. "The thorn in my flesh is killing me." He referred to his grotesque stomach, which he had named, with a touch of inverse pride, for the dagger that had been thrust into the obscene belly of Egon, King of Moab, by Ehud, the first recorded professional assassin in history. That thorn, the dagger, because of the obesity of the Moabite, could not be removed.

THE SACRED CAPE (CAPE ST. VINCENT), SPAIN. 56CE

The Ends of the Earth

The Apostle Paul had a curious habit. Whenever he entered a town, village, hamlet, or encountered any inhabited crossroads, no matter how small or derelict, he took off one of his sandals. Then, turning his back to wherever he had been, he raised the object and vigorously made the sign of the cross on which his Lord and Saviour had been put to death. He did the same thing when leaving a place where he had preached or had engaged in some business transaction. Occasionally this was misconstrued as a rude gesture.

When he disembarked from his small sailing ship, the Apostle was crabbit from seven days of being tossed about on his rude seat at the bow of the vessel. And he was irritated to find the tide was out and that the ship could not approach the jetty of boulders that served as the pier at the end of the world. So he had to jump into the water and wade, cursing into his cloak with words that he never permitted to appear in his writings. He was almost to the shore when he realized that he had nearly committed a sin-of-omission. He stopped, turned to face the waters that had brought him so close to the border of God's creation, removed a worn sandal, ceremoniously filled it with water and made the sign of the cross. It was a gesture that later Believers were to adapt to the baptism of infants.

In the preceding five years, Paul had become smaller. His thorn-in-the-flesh no longer hindered his walking. In the rare moments when he saw himself naked (he was still a good Jew, he proclaimed, and he understood the necessity of the Mikveh), he noted his once proud belly's sad retreat. Now its layer upon layer of empty folds reminded him of a tent that was collapsed and packed for travel. He longed to travel; the journey he wanted most was to be with his Lord.

Paul had his own geography of the visible and the invisible world and his entire missionary life was a set of coordinates, plotted on a grid that he shared with no one. To his colleagues, his fellow-Believers, his enemies, to anyone who later observed him in his epistles, his patterns of movement seem haphazard, impulsive, almost random. They were not. He charted the pattern of his life upon a vertical axis and upon a horizontal one, and very carefully.

His horizontal coordinates were measured against the life of Alexander of Macedon. That self-defined semi-god had marched from one end of the world to the other, cutting with his sword a swath that Paul was driven to duplicate with his preaching. What Alexander had done with visible force, Paul was called to do with invisible. Having been to northern Galatia earlier, Paul, in Spain, was completing his mission: to preach Jesus-the-Christ to the ends of the earth. Paul sometimes reflected that Alexander the Great had it easier: after all, he knew he was Son of God, a piece of information that was vouchsafed to him by an Egyptian oracle.

Alexander's being Son of God did not clash with Paul's belief that Jesus-the-Christ also was Son of God, for Alexander's title was limited to earth's flat surface, while that of Jesus extended upwards, to the heavens and thus to the very Godhead. This second set of coordinates, from the earth, to the heavens, with Jesus-the-Christ as the celestial ladder, was the measuring stick that Paul used to assess his own life. Given these two sets of coordinates, Paul knew at every moment where he was in physical and spiritual space and if his colleagues often missed the pattern in his movements, that was their weakness, not his.

Yet, his own weakness galled. Why had he achieved so little here at the westernmost shore of the world? Like a crone hoping to find warmth by raddling the embers of a cold fire, Paul ran over and over again his present failure. Nothing of comfort glowed. All he could remember was numbing weeks, stretching into months, trying to speak proper Latin to the prig-eared administrative class. No hope there. And nobody, save the occasional sea-trader spoke any form of Greek, even the bog-Koine of the Mediterranean seaports. Instead, Paul had laboured in mounting frustration to decipher a tongue he thought he knew somewhat, from his time in Galatia. The similarity to what he knew made his own incomprehension of the dozen or more Iberian Celtic dialects he encountered all the more irritating.

He would head back.

But first, he purged his shame and rage at having failed to create a city of God at the western edge of the earth. He did so the way he always did: by writing a letter. This time he crushed the head of the serpent by using the tongues that had been the witnesses of his defeat. Paul wrote the same letter three times, the first time in surging Koine, the second in halting Latin. And the third copy he had translated into the Iberian dialect that he judged to be the most common in the region.

Then he had the three bound together, placed in a waterproof goat-skin poke and sent for safekeeping to Yacov, brother of Yeshua of Nazareth (who Paul knew as Jesus-the-Christ). Yacov, a silent and ascetic man, preserved memorabilia of the early Christian church, including, it was whispered, several pieces of the True Cross. Paul's letter, which was an epistle to himself, would be safe in Yacov's hands, until the Lord told Paul what to do with it. In later years, such an epistle would have been called a personal memoir, but that is a calm and veneer-like form; and this letter writhed with the torsion of a soul in despair.

It began: "I am Paul. A sinner and the lowest of churls ..."

THE TRANSJORDAN WASTES. 70CE

Jerusalem the Olden

They brought with them only the clothes on their backs, victuals, and some relics precious enough to be worth the risk of life. Of Jerusalem, they had only the dust and smoke. And the memory of one of the most discouraging swatches of time – they reckoned it to be the close of the seventh decade since the birth of their Moshiah – the Holy City had ever witnessed.

How long the covenant framed by Paul and Yacov would have lasted can never be known, but it was already near its stale-date when Yahweh permitted the Great Destruction of Jerusalem to occur. Of Paul, the trudging pilgrims remembered his hectoring manner, his immense girth and his even greater faith in the imminent Second Coming of Jesus-the-Christ. Paul himself had returned to Jerusalem with his collection for The Family. Exhausted by the effort and worry of raising money while shepherding congregations that increasingly bolted from their pens like gormless, legstrong lambs, he had sought spiritual refreshment in the Temple, the centrepoint of all who were faithful to Yahweh. Paul had fallen in readily with Yacov's suggestion that he and some of his fellow disciples should take a very serious vow – a Nazarite vow that involved having their heads completely shaved and their making an oath-bound commitment to a highly as-cetic way of life. This they were to do in the Temple. Unfortunately for Paul, some of his keen-Pharisee former colleagues pointed him out. He was lucky not to be torn limb from limb: only the Roman le-gionnaires saved him. Thereafter, his path to martyrdom in Rome was slow but inexorable. Sometime in the early sixties he was trans-lated into a pious memory.

Yacov fared no better.

His ascetic rigour in studying and observing Torah made him a constant reproach to many of the spiritual princelings who ran tiny religious satrapies in Jerusalem, each dependent upon the Temple, each man making alliances with political leaders of the day. Yacov's sharp tongue did him no good, at least not in this world. One of the pyrotechnic princelings who managed to become High Priest for three months could not take Yacov's criticisms and had him stoned to death. Or so the best sources suggest: other traditions have him being thrown from the top of the Temple and then thumped into eternity with a club of the sort that fullers employ to turn raw textiles into wearable goods.

Wrenching as the two martyrdoms were, they were not the reason that the remnants of The Family, spiritual descendants of Yeshua of Nazareth, now were on their own, a holy people without a holy land.

That came about for another reason: their world had been hit by a meteor, one that blasted a crater that has not been filled to the present day. In what is one of the least necessary conflicts in a world of unnecessary wars, the twenty or thirty (maybe more) forms of Judaism that fought with each other in Jerusalem in the middle of what we now call the first century, managed to push the Imperial authorities away from their general policy of benign neglect. The Romans could take any amount of local religion: two lambs and a bull were donated daily as a Temple sacrifice in Jerusalem for (not to, for) the emperor. And the imperial authorities had nothing against prosperity in the provinces, for taxes followed profits, as well as prophets. What the Romans could not abide was disorder. No order, then no empire. So when a truly wretched procurator, Gessius Florus, tried to loot the Temple treasury, he sparked off a mixture of an anti-imperial revolt in Eretz Israel and, simultaneously, a fight for primacy between several of the Jewish factions. Rome hated becoming involved in such local fracas, but had no choice.

Members of The Family could remember a half-decade of terror, but the details were confused, impossible of order: it was a time when there was no true star sign, no way of metering progress, no way of sorting friend from foe. Certainly, if the moment that Paul and Yacov had so confidently predicted, the return from heaven of Jesus-the-Christ as Messiah ever were to occur, it should be now and the faithful prayed for the moment. Now, when Roman garrisons fought bands of revolutionaries in the Galilee. Now, when Idumaeans and Zealots knifed each other on the very slopes of the Temple Mount. Now, when the High Priest Ananus was put to death by his own people. Now, when Vespasian was slowly marching towards Jerusalem. Now, when at Passover the Holy City was besieged. Now, as the defenders split their time between fighting Romans and killing each other. Now, as a few among the faithful tunnelled out and escaped only to encounter a scorched land. Now, as the Tenth Legion mopped up the remnants of resistance, herding the Zealots into the sewers and killing them there in human abattoirs. Now, as the Romans burned and cast asunder Temple and town, leaving only three towers standing and these as shelter for the occupying forces. Now – even now! – come Lord Jesus!

Nothing. The survivors of the siege of Jerusalem march as if they have been taken prisoner. They shuffle in step, joined by shackles that are as real as they are invisible. They plan to join others of The Family who had escaped earlier. But what will they be joining? Their faith still is in Yahweh, but where will the covenant with him be daily affirmed? Is there no more God because the Temple is no more?

This tiny march, this bedraggled retreat, was one of Time's turning points, and like most really big things, it cannot be observed directly, but seen only in a mirror, one held at a distance. The shuffling remnant of The Family had an opposite number, marching in the opposite direction. Literally: the survivors of one set of Pharisees made their way towards Yavneh, a small town southwest of Jerusalem. Their leader, Rabban Yohanen ben Zakkai, a student of the school of Hillel, had been smuggled out of the Holy City during the early days of the siege: the Romans had granted a cease-fire for the burial of the dead and he had been taken out, lodged beneath a corpse, in a crude coffin. Now the survivors of his lodge of Pharisees hirpled towards Yavneh, replicating in almost perfect mirror behaviour what the remnant of Yeshua-followers were doing: surviving and setting up a new world.

In Yavneh and in Antioch and in the other locations where the two remnants settled, they faced the hideous and unavoidable fact: their religion was dead. Unless ... unless they could find a way to replace the Temple, the one place where God and man touched, in daily ritual.

And these two fragments of the old Yahweh-faith, these two out of the twenty or thirty variants that had scrapped in the days before the Roman-Jewish war, survived and succeeded in creating a redefinition of Yahweh and of his service. The one group, centred in Yavneh, replaced the priesthood of the Temple with the priesthood of scholarship, of Torah learning. A faith in which studying the nature of Temple service replaced the actual service in the Temple. From them came the faith we know as Rabbinic or Talmudic Judaism or, simply, the modern Jewish faith.

And the pilgrims heading north towards Gentile lands soon created a faith in which the daily sacrifice in the Temple was replaced by the once-for-all sacrifice of Jesus-the Christ. They started writing their own scriptures and, within thirty years, had their own New Testament.

Thus, from the ashes of Jerusalem arose two world religions, the modern Jewish faith and what, in the second century, came to be called in most of the Imperial realm, the Christian faith.

All that was in the future. What the pilgrims saw as they headed north was a louring sky and, on the horizon, only an occasional distant flash, like heat lightning, sparks of hope on a darkling plain.

THE ROPE BRAIDERS
150–400 CE

God's Hollow Core

All along the Mediterranean coast and its main tributaries, set back from the water in small towns, were ropeworks. Rope was to the maritime world what the wheel was to the terrestrial: without it travel was difficult, trade nearly impossible. Ropes served as sheets on boats, held sails, lashed cargoes, acted as anchor cables and as mooring lines. Without ropes, a vessel was just an arrangement of large splinters. Rope-making was a trade of many levels and at the top were the braiders, master craftsmen who made the fist-thick cables that firmly moored even the largest vessels. No cheap products of the rope-twister for them. Their cables were made of a series of interlocking knots so that even if a cable were cut, it did not unravel, but held its form and strength right up to the point where it was severed.

One of the tricks of the master braider was to form the interlocking knots around a guide-core. This could be anything reasonably strong and pliable – a long thin piece of tanned leather was best – and eventually it dissolved with everyday use. But only after it had given the braider something to construct things around. Paradox: strength required a hollow core.

The hollow core of Christianity as it attacked the pagan world was trust and understanding. The Christians did not trust anyone and no one understood them. One of the seemingly strangest things about the Believers and their persecutors in, say, the years 150–250 is that neither side had any idea what the persecutions were all about. In none of the martyr histories is it clear that the Christians possessed any practical definition of why they had been arrested. Oh, yes, the world was evil and they were holy. Fair enough, but even to them it must have been hard to explain why some of the faithful were arrested and others not. The idea that the arrogance of the Christian faith might have got up the noses of peoples of other religions never seems to have occurred to the righteous. Keep calling someone a devil long enough and he will act like one, and call everyone in the world except oneself evil and pretty soon the world will be a hell: not a caution that was taken on board. Equally curious was the legal position of the persecutors. Until the first general persecution under Decius in the middle of the third century (when Christians were defined, essentially, as security risks), it wasn't clear on what legal basis Christians could be brought to book. Imperial policy was to tolerate local religions, indeed to help them along a bit if they would keep the peace, so going after the Believers on religious grounds would not do. Hence, one sees governor after governor trying to sidestep prosecuting the Christians, while his local populace wanted them dismembered. The Believers despised the world in which they lived, and it rejected them. In the end, the only charge against the Christians that stands up is that they stood out.

SMYRNA, ASIA MINOR. 156/157

The Black Rainbow

An old man is praying in his home. He prays for two hours. That is not unusual. Nor is his facing the east, for that is the custom of serious Christians. What is unusual is his being gawped at by a phalanx of police and cavalry officers.

This is Polycarp, Bishop of Smyrna, and he is the last person in the Faith to have actually encountered some of the original Apostles. He has been a Christian for eighty-six years and has seen enough of this world to know that it is not really his home. His earthly home is a substantial two-storey dwelling, and when his slave answers the door to admit the police captain (a man appropriately named Herod) Polycarp knows that his life's journey is soon to be over. With the unfailing courtesy that has distinguished his entire life, he invites the police and military inside and orders his slave to prepare food and drink for them, whatever sort and quantity they wish. His only request is that he be allowed to pray for an hour.

So full is he of God's grace that he cannot stop for twice that time and the men who have come to arrest him are dumbstruck by the obvious godliness of the old man.

They really do not want much of him; merely that he say "Caesar is lord," perform a little sacrifice and then he can continue to worship his own god anyway he wishes.

Heaven knows, the captain remarks, we aren't unreasonable.

Polycarp, though, is. He will not bend and ultimately he is brought into an amphitheatre, where, obdurate, he is to be burned. As a sign of respect for Polycarp's self-control, he is bound to the stake that is the centre of his soon-to-be funeral pyre. Otherwise, he would have been nailed to it.

He burns, the twelfth recorded martyr in Christian tradition. He dies blessing the Almighty and a black rainbow appears, an admixture of God's covenant first made with Noah, and the skyborne remnants of the sainted bishop of Smyrna.

Polycarp's holy passing is soon chronicled and he becomes the first person in all the histories of the Faith whose actions (martyrdom) and holy status (martyr) are one-and-the-same. Word spreads; imitation follows.

LUGDUNUM (LYONS), SOUTHERN GAUL. MID-SUMMER 177

Holy Contagion

To Roman authorities, martyrdom is an inexplicable disease. Like so many infections, this one has begun mysteriously in Asia Minor and spread westward. It breaks out, like the pox on the human countenance, at inexplicable intervals and in embarrassing places. The disease disfigures the body politic, and most governors do everything they can to avoid having a bout of martyrdom occur during their watch.

The Faith in southern Gaul owes its start to the Apostle Paul's mission to Spain but, mostly, to later missionaries from Asia Minor who went from port-to-port along the Mediterranean and then up the main river valleys into the interior. Lugdunum was one of their most successful inland forays. There, among believers, the name of Polycarp is revered.

The Lugdunum Christians are a rum lot, at least from the perspective of the local population. Half, or more, of them are "Asiatics," that is immigrants from the sector of the Empire where Greek is the language-in-common. They correspond with the mother churches in Asia Minor in Koine and when they meet in their house-churches they pray in Greek and preach in Latin. Outside, in "the world," as they call it, they set themselves apart from the local Celtic population. They are reluctant to learn the everyday demotic tongue and converts who join them have to employ a form of halting Latin to communicate. Although they do try occasionally to convert the locals, it is an effort conducted from a great height. In their correspondence with their colleagues in Asia Minor, they refer to the Celts as wild and barbarous tribes and they pass on stories of frontier life among the savages.

Hence, when the overwhelming majority of the local population turns on them, the Christians should not be surprised, and they are not. Their interpretation is remarkably brittle, however: they do not see the seething locals as perhaps just-a-bit justified in resenting having their gods bad-mouthed by uppity strangers. Far from it; instead, the Christians expect the Celtic barbarians to resent them, because the degenerate always hates the regenerate. That's the nature of the universe.

During the summer of 177, the Celts finally have had enough of the Believers. The local council bans the Christians from the market square and from the public baths. Yet to the faithful this is only a confirmation of their holiness. Then, more than 100 are rounded up by local authorities and held in custody. This is a genuine expression of popular sentiment, not of Imperial policy: the governor is away at the time.

The governor is no idiot: upon his return he realizes immediately that he has a choice between the citizens running amok and a show trial. He decides to preserve his career. Exactly what the charges should be he never bothers to decide; instead he permits everything from cannibalism to incest to treason to be heaped on the Christians' heads, all of which is a way of saying that they had broken the one immutable rule of Imperial rule: thou shalt not upset the public peace. Although the Celts will be most pleased if the Christians are painfully removed from life, they will have to be satisfied, the governor decides, if the Believers renounce their faith. That, at least, will leave the old Celtic gods with their honour unstained.

What the governor does not count on is the lust of the Believers. It is a mad, debased, sensual longing to undergo the most searing of human experiences and thus to become united with those previous martyrs who have already plunged into spumescent, arcing narcosis. They want to merge, in a unity that is obscene beyond description, with their demigods, Polycarp, Paul, Yacov, and Jesus-the-Christ. At least that is the way the governor understands what the Believers babble out under the truth-inducing benefit of torture. They *want* to die.

Take Sanctus. That, he claims is his name. What can I do?, the governor wants to say aloud, but dares not, what can I do with a man who responds to every question – even the simplest one, such as "are you bond or free?" – with "I am a Christian." He's asked what city he is from, what nation he comes from, and all we get from his lips is: "I am a Christian." What am I to do? He has red-hot amulets of steel placed on Sanctus's belly, his buttocks, his scrotum, and what does he say? He says "I am a Christian!" and in Latin at that, making the Celts all the more livid. What am I to do but have him corrected until he falls obediently silent? What, indeed, is a prudent governor to do?

Eventually, the governor decides to join the maintenance of public order with a celebration of both Imperial and Celtic religions. The great Celtic festival of Lughnasa, a celebration of the sun god, is approaching. Ever since the year 12BCE when a huge altar to Augustus was built on Imperial land directly across the river from Lugdunum, it has been the annual practice to have a tribal congress, where with military exhibitions and gladiatorial games, the Celtic and Roman gods are simultaneously honoured.

On the first day of this circus, the Believers, who already have been severely tortured but still have not fallen from faith, are herded before the baying crowd and made to run a gantlet composed of gladiators with leather scourges. Being beaten by these brutes was a standard punishment for malfeasant soldiers, and it alone would have killed many civilians. By now some of the Christians had recanted, but more than eighty remained obdurate. Over six days, they were despatched, being asked to deny their beliefs, even while being imaginatively put to death. Thus, one Attalus was not only given to bears to be mortally wounded, but then was placed on a specially built iron chair, beneath which an intense fire was built. The crowd loved it. They were livid, however, when Attalus wrenched sound from his pierced lungs, forming words in Latin they could not understand; with his last words he answered the sneering question "what is the name of God?" with the assertion "God has not a name as man has." And then he died.

The prurience that ran as a vein in the hematite of Celtic hatred was nowhere clearer than on the final day, when Blandina, a small, attractive matron in her early thirties, was brought into the arena with a boy of fifteen and a girl a year younger. The young people were tortured and sexually abused before finally expiring. Then Blandina was placed in a basket and presented to a bull.

Thus was Roman civic probity and Celtic religious devotion satisfied. In all, eighty-four Believers died.

The governor had not at all enjoyed these proceedings. But, he reflected, it would be a long time indeed before anybody again tried to shake the devotion of the Celts to their tribal gods.

LUGDUNUM. 180

More Knots

Durable complex knots, the sort the master braiders tied, require more than one strand of assertion and negation. Multiple tensioners are needed. That is why, after the martyrdoms of 177–8, the new Bishop of Lugdunum, Irenaeus, spent so much time writing against heretics, which is to say, against other Christians. He was not a natural writer and his prose stumbles along like a blind pedestrian on a cobbled road. But it was necessary. Irenaeus, whenever we get a glimpse of him, is hunched over a sheet of parchment, trying to put together a codex of warning. He writes something, rubs it out, tries again. He is writing *Adversus Haereses* which today we might entitle with a bit more élan *To Hell with Heretics*, for that certainly is what he meant.

Irenaeus is another "Asiatic." The church has not yet become shrewd enough to appoint a Celt to deal with the Celts. Later Church Fathers are to describe him as "the admirable Irenaeus who brought learning, culture and religion to the tribes of Gaul." At least he speaks the native dialect. Previously, he had studied with Polycarp, then been sent as a missioner to Lugdunum, where he was effectively the number two man. He had the good fortune to be away from Lugdunum during the Celtic upwelling of 178 and now he is back.

Though he is no coward, Irenaeus keeps to the backstreets. In part, that is because he pulls the Believers together quietly, as if he were coaxing out children who were behind a hedge hiding from a bully. He has been appointed bishop. His flock keeps their heads down, scuttle to meet each other quickly, and try not to make too much noise. Irenaeus, though, has another reason for keeping quiet. His real mission is to help his masters in Asia Minor to stamp out heresy and to do that he needs to write a compelling treatise. He complains in his early pages that he is not accustomed to writing and that is no pose; yet his awkwardness carries a force and an obvious sincerity that a more fluid prose would not. This is an ordinary Christian wrestling with other ordinary Christians.

And here, in his splotched, crossed-out, tumbledown sentences, we find a crucial characteristic of the worship of Jesus-the-Christ: it cannot have both diversity and comity. At this moment, Irenaeus is writing about one heresy but thinking about another. He is writing against Gnosticism, which is a fairly fat target and he can go on about its vices without much difficulty. But at various places in his text he slips in references to the heresy that really bothers him – "Montanism" – and these references are like twitches in the eye of an unconvincing prevaricator. They flag his problem and preclude a close observer from being convinced by anything he says.

Montanism is on his mind because Irenaeus had been called to a synod of church leaders to deal with this heresy, just before the trouble in Lugdunum. In a way, the heresy had saved his life. But why should the church need to tie a ligature around this belief? For the simple reason that Montanism, like many of the heresies that the young church asphyxiates, is too much like earliest Christianity to be allowed survival. Montanism comes out of Phrygia, the part of Asia Minor where many Believers from Eretz Israel had settled after the Great Destruction of Jerusalem and its Temple. Sometime in the middle of the second century, one Montanus began taking the example of the Apostle Paul and of the ancient prophets a bit too seriously. He started prophesying, talking directly with the Holy Spirit and soon he had a large following, and it grew as he soaked himself in St. Paul's own belief, that Jesus-the-Christ would come again soon to earth, to end all time. As it later was to do with each developing heresy, the church's authorities first noted that it had to be evil as it appealed to silly women – two of the leading prophets of the movement were female – and, besides, it attracted the wrong sort of males: North Africans and Celts especially.

Irenaeus swithers for he knows that in one way the Montanists are more rigorous Christians than he and his lot in Lugdunum are: unlike his own people, the Montanists do not forgive anyone who funks martyrdom. Anyone who recants even under the most brutal persecution is forever closed out of the flock. Irenaeus has enough self-knowledge to wonder if he would himself have failed the test.

So, he rattles on about Gnosticism, all the while worrying about Montanism and about the depth of his own faith. Others among the circle of bishops are less reflective, and they tie off Montanism, excommunicating its members and seeking out and burning its manuscripts with such efficiency that no texts remain.

Then, they adopt the Montanists' view of the active, animating Holy Spirit and invent the doctrine of the Trinity.

ROME, CARTHAGE, ANTIOCH, LUGDUNUM. 250–251

The Three-Cornered Buckler

Once they are apprised of the doctrine of the Holy Trinity, the faithful embrace it as a shield against evil. Going to their death in the empire-wide persecution of 250–251, many of the martyrs chant a version of this hymn:

> O saving Victim, opening wide
> the gates of heaven to us below,
> Our foes press on from every side,
> thine aid supply, thy strength bestow.

> All praise and thanks to thee ascend
> for evermore, blest One in Three.
> O grant us life that shall not end
> in our true native land with thee.

Though they would not have been comforted by the point, there was nothing specifically anti-Christian in the effort of the Emperor, Messius Quintus Traianus Decius, to revive traditional Roman values, including social discipline and civic worship. The requirement for public sacrifice (and for a certificate that this had been done) applied to everybody.

Most of the ordinary laity among the Believers conform to the Imperial requirements, but many of the bishops do not. For many years afterwards, the church's elders argue about what should be required for readmission to the church for those who had chosen to stay alive.

Decius himself was of no doubt about the necessity of his own policy. Shortly before his own life was ended, in 251 by the Goths, he reflected on his execution of Pope Fabian: "I would far rather receive news of a rival to the throne, than another bishop in Rome."

ANTIOCH. 268

Real Old-Time Preaching

A young secretary, a lad from Galatia who has had the good fortune to attend a gymnasium and then apprentice to a lawyer's clerk, reads aloud to two dozen older men, most with flowing beards and all with countenances etched with wisdom. He has been in the employ of one Malchion, head of a Christian school of rhetoric in Antioch. The young man is a Christian, but he has not quite the fervour that distinguishes his patron and, in fact, he is performing his present task for pay. He is reading a transcript of notes he took at Malchion's direction. The notes are of a religious dispute Malchion had engaged in with the man known locally as "Paul of Samosata."

Despite the young man's reading slowly and very loudly, he is asked often to repeat what he has just said. A couple of the listeners have trouble with his Greek and others are hard of hearing. These are the leading bishops of the Christian church and they are coming to the end of a chase that has taken them four years: to find enough evidence to convict Paul of Samosata of heresy. This synod is mostly the fruit of Malchion's obsession with breaking Paul, but it is not uncongenial to the bishops.

Significantly, the theological deviations that the young stenographer recorded are not very compelling and the bishops do not even bother to keep the transcript the young man made. However, the synod is rivetted and repelled by the stenographer's additional material: on his own initiative he had followed Paul of Samosota on his weekly course of preaching and teaching and the glimpses he obtained of the charismatic gospeller leave no doubt that he is a danger:

" – he demands to be called ducenarius, rather than bishop ... and he courts popularity, especially among the simple folk ... he was observed to preach in a most energetic fashion, smiting his thigh with his hand when he made a strong point ... moreover, he was observed to stamp on the podium, making a crash like a large drum ... he trains women to sing psalms and to do so in worship service ... his followers listen to his preaching and they shout and wave their handkerchiefs and jump about as if they were in a theatre ... the women are especially disorderly and an invitation in their swooning to lewdness of the mind ... the bishops of many of the neighbouring towns fawn upon him ... he implies that a godly teacher is helped by the voice of an angel and he asserts that praising the Almighty with psalms and with a joyful noise is the true communion of holy spirits ..."

The bishops, recognizing that the trajectory of such a rival has to be aborted, take the stenographer's observations as compelling evidence.

Paul of Samosata is excommunicated.

Eventually, he settles in Alexandria and conducts his ministry from his new lodgings, the home of a rich Christian widow.

Before that, however, the bishops have the humiliating task of trying to gain control of Paul's church building in Antioch.

Neither Paul nor his followers will budge. After being baulked for three years the bishops petition the emperor, Aurelian, and he grants them title to the church. Eventually, bailiffs, aided by legionnaires, evict Paul of Samosata and his congregation and the church in Antioch returns to the path of order.

A minority of the bishops believe that employing malicious delation as a way of unseating spiritual rivals is a compromise with the forces of darkness. Most, however, look forward to the day promised in the Revelation of St John when the church will have a civic state to enforce its celestial will.

NAISSUS, THE DANUBIAN PROVINCES. FEBRUARY 272

The Miracle of Birth

At almost the same moment the Emperor's secretary was drawing up the evict-and-seize order for the church at Antioch, a Danubian woman, in her early twenties, was coming to full term. She was the daughter of an innkeeper and, depending on the needs of the establishment, acted as serving woman, locums-manager, and as a hospitality girl. Fat and dimpled like a dumpling, she was a great favourite with the officers on their missions to defend the Balkan frontiers: Helena.

The father of her child was not her husband and indeed she never married. Nevertheless the child did not suffer for his illegitimacy, for his father looked after the lad's interests and had him schooled at the Imperial court. That was typical. The father was one of those commanders whom the troops revere. He led, rather than followed, and he never abandoned any of his soldiers: Constantius I Chlorus.

The birth was routine, if anything that has a fifty-fifty chance of killing a woman can be said to be that. Helena played her part consistently well, taking good care of the infant and then releasing him to be trained for future glory. Eventually Helena had a vertiginous late-life ascent as dowager dam of the man who was, for a time, the most powerful person in the world: Flavius Valerius Constantinus I ("The Great.")

Helena thus followed a pattern well known to the founders and apostles of the earliest Christian faith, but one that their successors now were keen to obscure.

ROME. 293

A Catered Affair

The only thing Constantius I Chlorus did not like about his wedding was the roses. Everything else was fine. His new father-in-law, Galerius Valerius Maximianus, the number two, three or four man in the Empire and himself a son-in-law of the Emperor Diocletian, promised to be generous. Constantius's impending wife, Theodora, possessed a reasonable disposition, as evidenced by her clearly expecting only to be left alone. And the marriage ceremony itself raised him in the eyes of the court.

That, though, was the problem: eyes. The nearly ten bushels of rose petals that were strewn on the couple's path as they left the temple produced a violent reaction in Constantius's outlook. He swelled up quickly, his eyes ran with burning tears and then his face, now round as a pumpkin, completely blocked out his vision. He went into his nuptial bed blind as a rock and immediately passed unconscious.

Still, everything else went well. His father-in-law arranged for him the prefecture of Gaul and that held great potential, for he could control not only the Roman portions of Britain, but could expand, who knows, into the virgin territory of Scotland and perhaps even Ireland. If he did that, his son Constantine, now securely placed in the court of Diocletian, would have a fine patrimony indeed.

THE FOUR-FOLD ROMAN EMPIRE: GAUL, ITALY, ILLYRICUM, AND THE EAST. 303–312

The Great Persecution

The entire empire was poxy. That was the firm opinion of Constantius I Chlorus from 297 onwards. In that year he had to cross from Gaul to Britain and put down a breakaway movement that bid fair to create an independent soldier-state that would have stood, poised like a drawn dagger in the back of Constantius's prefecture. Not that he received a lot of encouragement from the emperor. Diocletian since the mid-280s had quiveringly moved from harm's way: his capital was in Nicomedia (which we call Izmit, in Turkey). And the western portion of the Empire was run from Milan. All that was good news for the Christians, since it left the Bishop of Rome as the leading figure in the city, but it did precious little to bulk up the defences of the western empire.

Antioch. 303. An exorcist, a deacon in the church at Caesarea is visiting Antioch. He sees the city's churches have been gutted and that men and women he knows are Christians are crowding into the pagan temples and sacrificing. He cannot keep his tongue in his head and starts denouncing the proceedings. Soon he is up before a judge and this at a time when the Emperor is on a visit. The exorcist is sentenced to burn. But before that sentence can be carried out, the Emperor Diocletian himself intervenes and has the man's tongue removed and then the exorcist is tortured to death. At least that is the tradition. The man's name was Romanus.

What made Constantius's job in Gaul and Britain even harder was the havering old Emperor's having listened to the lunatic Galerius (a hard military man, Constantius admitted with admiration, but crazy) and having begun a general persecution of the Christians. Jove only knows why, Constantius frequently said, making a bitter pun on the Emperor's alleged origins. Yet, it wasn't because Diocletian was a religious man, although he took seriously his self-minted title of "Jovius" and did believe he was the son of a god; that kind of claim was so common among Roman rulers as to not be worth remarking, any more than a new civic monument would be. It's something emperors just did. No, the issue was something else, entirely.

304. Nicomedia. An Imperial civil servant, one of many Christians in the central administration of the Empire, is ordered to sacrifice to the old gods. He refuses. He is stripped naked and his body is cut into little patches of blood and skin by scourges. Then, as he still does not break, he is rinsed with a mixture of salt and vinegar, the sort of mixture used for marinating animal flesh before cooking. With hideous appropriateness, he is put on a pyre and roasted until, still faithful, he meets his Saviour. The man's name was Peter.

Galerius's own hatred of Christianity was pathological, but how he was able to convince Diocletian to put a policy of general persecution into effect was beyond Constantius's comprehension. Indeed, no one subsequently has ever convincingly explained how he did it. The best guess is that Galerius played a combination of revival-of-traditional-values (a virtual mantra for Diocletian and if he stood for anything this was it) and claims that Christians in the Imperial service were unreliable at best and seditious at worst. The result was that, against his own strong initial disposition, the Emperor Diocletian in February 303 issued the First Edict against Christians. Three more were signed by him in less than two years. Unlike anything the Empire had done previously to religions, the practice of Christianity was virtually banned and worship of the traditional gods was required.

304. Catania. A very assertive man enters the council chamber of the prefect and shouts through the veil that separates the council from the hoi polloi, "I want to die; I am a Christian!" He carries the Gospels with him, a calculated insult to the council. The governor tries to talk him out of his death wish, but the Christian reads the Gospels at him, with the calculated disdain of a matador facing a bull. Therefore, inevitably, he gets the horn: the governor has him beheaded, which at least is quick. The man's name was Euplus.

Constantius had an easier time than other administrators. The strength of Christianity was greatest in Asia Minor and in the curve that runs through the Holy land and into North Africa. In many towns in Asia Minor, the Christians dominated the commercial class and they were moving swiftly into the army and the Imperial civil service. In Gaul, on the other hand, the Christians still were a small minority. And in the portions of southern Britain where Roman writ ran, they were scarce. Beyond the walls, in Ireland and Scotland, they were non-existent. So, Constantius contented himself with destroying all the church buildings in Gaul. He did not find it necessary to shed blood.

304–305. The entire empire has pustules of persecution that crop out in unpredictable places and at irregular intervals: more in the east than the west, but no region is immune. In several legions, the corps are inspected, man by man, and each soldier is required to obey the order to make pagan sacrifice. Many of the Christians who have enough time in rank, buy themselves out of the service. Others face loss of rank and receive hard duty. Only a few are executed, however. Less moderate are the score or so of salt and copper mines that are used as forced-labour camps for civilians. Frequently, the prisoners are tortured first, and slave labour is simply a slow death sentence. Most repugnant to the church at large is the sentencing of several hundreds of Christian women to brothels, some attached to pagan temples, most not. This practice is so rebarbarative that the later chroniclers of the Christian martyrs are unable to discuss it fully: unlike the other martyr-stories, in which the final ugly result of torture is spelled out in the sublimation of holy death, the church can make itself remember only those who escape by some miracle, their virtue intact. In reality most did not. Of these women, of the men in the mines, of the broken soldiers, we know not their names.

When, in the spring of 305, Diocletian shocked the world by announcing that he was retiring as emperor and that Maximianus his co-emperor (technically his equal, but in practice his deputy) was doing so as well, it was good news for both Constantius I Chlorus and the Christians. But not as much as either would have liked.

The new co-emperors are Constantius, who is given the west and Galerius, the east. Effectively the persecution of Christians stops in the west but, if anything, becomes worse in the east.

And Constantius has a lot to worry him. His own first deputy is anything but compliant, and his son Constantine is serving in the east under the lunatic Galerius. Constantius, not even a month into his emperorship, begins to understand why Diocletian had packed it in.

NICOMEDIA. 306; LUGDUMUM. 311; ROME. 312

The Figure

The fleeing figure moves so deftly that it is a zephyr. This is Constantine in adroit withdrawal from the capital of the eastern empire. His father had several times requested of Galerius that Constantine be allowed to join him in the west, but the emperor of the east was long experienced in hostage taking. He had appointed Constantine, now in his mid-thirties and in his prime as a soldier and an administrator, to his own court. The post was one of honour, apparently, but in fact it was a gyve. Keeping Constantine within a sword's length was to limit any untoward plans Constantius might have. Letter after letter from Constantius asked for his son's help in administering Gaul and Britain, and when it became well-known that the older man's health was failing, Galerius was shamed into making a magnanimous gesture. He wrote out a passport for Constantine and told him to be away the next morning. Constantine, calculating, foresighted, and suspicious as a life at court will make a man of mind, waits only until the palace is asleep, and then with the skill of an experienced night-fighter, he is past the guard and away.

The flying figure moves so fast that it nearly leaves its shadow behind.

Constantine rides brilliantly and plans even better. His passport from Galerius allows him to use the Imperial posting system, so he uses the pick of the Imperial post-horses to fly. And just as well, for in the morning Galerius repented of his lapse into generosity and cancelled the letters of permission. Constantine flies from the capital of the eastern empire into Europe, across Thrace and Illyricum and across Italia, into Gaul. Even as he flies before the wrath of Galerius, he shows the ruthlessness of a great general: having chosen at each post-station the horse he wants, he takes out his short sword and slashes the hamstrings of the others. He will not be caught.

Eventually the faithful figure of Constantine stands beside his father, the pair forming a tableau of loyalty and stability. Constantine had caught his father just as he was about to sail from Boulogne. This was not luck, for Constantine willed it to happen. Constantius I Chlorus was beginning the campaign that turned out to be his last. The people he called the Picts were infiltrating the Wall in the north of Britain and playing all hell with the villas and their outfarms. Who these people were Constantius really had no idea, save that no soldier spoke of them without fear: wild, barbaric, uncontrolled were words that were attached to them like remoras to a feeding shark. Constantine stands strong beside his father. The Imperial troops hold firm and for a time the north is free of these fierce creatures whom the Empire has never been able to conquer.

The mounted figure who stands before Constantius's troops at Eburacum (we call it York) is of course his son. Constantine announces in a firm voice that his father, the senior Emperor of all the world, has died of a fistula that stemmed from an old war wound. It is a tragedy, Constantine tells the men, that the Emperor held his high title for only fourteen months, but he died a soldier's death. And his every moment as Emperor was a moment of pure service and honour, he tells the corps, because he had served with you. Those are the late Emperor's actual words as told them to me on his last night before joining the gods. Constantine rolls on. It is a finely calculated piece of oratory and when he concludes, exactly what he wishes to happen indeed does: the troops erupt into cries of "long live the Emperor!" and after modestly retiring to his quarters to consider matters, Constantine agrees to be their new general. Of course it is mutiny and no less so for being directed by Constantine, but such coups were nearly a tradition in the later Empire. Galerius grants him the title of "Caesar," which is not as good as "Augustus," which he desires. Still, from his father's death in July 306 onwards, Constantine is one of the main contenders in a contest for full control of the western empire. It is a contest beyond rational analysis: a many-sided all-in wrestling match conducted in a viper pit and the only rule is that the last competitor alive is the winner.

The figure of Constantine, in full mourning gear, entering the temple of Jove in Lugdunum, was the man at his most haughty. It was May 311, and he had heard the glad news that Galerius, emperor of the east, had finally died. Good form required that he mourn, but Constantine's choosing of the temple in his own jurisdiction most closely associated with the late Diocletian was an obvious way of saying Galerius-was-no-real-emperor. As he strode up the steps, Constantine actually smiled. He was recalling the material that his intelligence collectors had told him over the past few months: how for more than a year Galerius had grown larger and larger, the effect of his always prodigal appetite and of something else, a growth that continued on independently of his gluttony and burst through the skin as an obscene cancer. Maggots and vermin usually seen only on corpses left in the heat and sun came to infest the bloated form. Galerius, in his months-long death agony, issued an Edict of Toleration, a half-way cancellation of the persecution in the east. This was an act of superstition, part of a policy of getting square with all the possible gods, a bribe for a possible analgesic: the Christians would be left alone so long as they included in their worship a prayer or two on behalf of the emperors and the state. Constantine found it satisfactory to learn that none of this had sufficed and that Galerius had died as he had lived, a dung heap covered with flies.

The fierce figure of Constantine in full battle dress was usually enough to command loyalty among his own soldiers and fear in his enemies. This time, as he rides back and forth before his men, something else is in play: his face is irradiated. The effect is as startling as its source is mysterious. It is a darkly cloudy day, 28 October 312, so the radiance is not a reflection.

All the more reason for Constantine's men to take this as a favourable omen. They are preparing for a battle at the Red Rocks, eight miles north-east of Rome. Their opponents are the army of Maxentius, Constantine's rival for the complete control of the western empire. Constantine's men have good reason to be heartened by his glowing countenance, for they know that their Caesar has a special relationship with the sun god: does not his most recently minted coinage show Constantine in profile with that very god? And is it not well-known that the god Apollo, the very symbol of light, has a special relationship with our Constantine? Indeed has not our Augustus actually seen his own features on the face of Apollo? All that is true and gives the soldiers much-needed courage, for the veterans among them can easily see that unless they have the gods on their side, they will never be able to break through the defenses that protect Rome. Heartened as they were by Constantine's being enhulled by the power of divinity, they might well have thought twice if they had known that their Augustus had added yet another god to the panoply that he embraced.

The fiery figure that Constantine had seen on the previous days was not one of his acquaintance and, as a Roman governor, he knew scores of gods. This one appeared at noontime, on a day as bright and sunny as the day of battle was cloudy and dark. The figure held a short sword in each hand and with his arms fully extended, he whirled and torqued through all the variations of the compass, a human "X" tumbling down the corridors of time and space. Constantine knew a divine sign when he saw one. He pondered its meaning and that evening in his tent, his commanders dismissed to spend the night with their troops, he decided that this was the first letter of the word the Believers used for their deity, Christ. He sent messengers to his commanders to reassemble, and early in the morning hours each soldier took a faggot from the cooking fire and charred an "X" onto his shield. They had no idea why, but if the great Constantine ordered it, well, it certainly couldn't hurt.

The victory which followed – usually referred to as the Battle of the Milvian Bridge –converted Constantine into the unrivalled emperor of the west and his opponent Maxentius into a large head on a slender pike.

The two rival figures entered Rome together.

THE EMPIRE. 312–27

Sounds

Iron chisel. Hardwood mallet. Open crack. Insert prybar. Hammer and wedge. Lever and fulcrum. Tamp, grind, overturn and crash. Lift and replace. Constantly. Throughout the empire.

The outward motif of Constantine's empire was noise, not policy. Demolition noise. Construction noise. Quarrying stone. Ripping timbers. Labour gangs grunting work chants as they raise massive stones. Winches squealing. Grinding wheels shrilling. Masons cursing flawed materials. Joiners persuading lumber with main force.

Constantine's triumphal arch. Pagan temples despoiled. Ancient columns removed from temples. Private residences constructed of materials that once housed the gods. St Peter's Basilica. Constantinople, the new capital of the Roman world. The rebuilding of the vandalized Christian churches. Continual noise of demolition and construction.

All was part of Constantine's réclame, and it worked. Noise was the leitmotif for the Emperor's appearance before his public, the signature theme for the operatic persona that he created for himself.

Hear the noise and see him backstage, preparing to conduct one of his frequent public perambulations. He is worried about what headpiece to wear. First he puts on a high-crested helmet that makes him into a more-than-life-size warrior. But is it quite right? He tries on a diadem made of a rope of pearls, probably the longest such string in the world. Oh, that's better and it does not matt his hair. Constantine is very proud of his hair, shoulder-length and golden: in fact, so proud is he that he has it bleached to just the right shade, one that befits an emperor who has always had a close affinity was the sun god, whatever else he may also believe. Brushed, oiled, arranged by hot irons into lissome waves, Constantine's hair still is a bit lacking, so he has interwoven plaits of blonde hair obtained discreetly by his eunuch; they come from one of the savage tribes to the north.

Then, he choses his jewelry. He covers his arms, still muscular from years of soldiering, with bracelets and he puts a precious stone ring on each hand. Next he chooses a robe. No nonsense about white. His collection resembles the robing room for the prelates of some exotic sect: row upon row of jewelled robes, hundreds of patterns, each articulated in precious stone. The emperor likes the floral motifs best.

His decision made, he enters whatever din he is to inspect on this day. The workers stop, for a moment all is silence and, as he passes, everyone bows, as if reverencing a deity.

Constantine's advisors from among the Christian church are made slightly uneasy by the liturgical nature of these appearances, but they are canny enough to keep silent. Some of them can see that this style might be worth imitating.

THE EMPIRE. 312–37

Silence

Yet, the noise Constantine really loved was the absence of noise. Physical noise, the rumble of demolition and construction, that was

the outward sign of inward silence. The streets and churches, municipal buildings and basilicas, could flower properly only if they
stemmed from order. And order was always quiet, Constantine knew.
True order was the rebellion that did not happen, the riot that did not
occur, the treason that did not succeed. Constantine craved order.

That is why he reunited the two halves of the empire, the execution of
his eastern rival being another silence achieved. And it is the reason his
contumacious eldest son, Crispus, had to be suffocated. And his gossip-
mongering second-wife Fausta (or was she the first? Constantine never
bothered to record his previous marriage, if such it was), had to be
stopped from her trouble-stirring forever. Order, order, order. That is the
reason he began to close down the clanging liberties of the Jews. Nothing especially heavy at first – just the odd regulation forbidding Jews to
hold Christian slaves and the prohibition of Jews making any difficulties for converts from Judaism to Christianity – but it was a clear signal:
be quiet, children of Israel, for I the emperor loath your dissonance in
my dominion. Order is the reason Constantine pulled ever-tighter the
laws concerning slaves: slave-owners who killed their chattels by flogging or confinement in chains were no longer liable to any charge;
women who slept with slaves, even their emancipated slaves, were executed, the slave being burned alive; once-free agricultural workers who
had fallen to the status of serfs were, if they seemed to be planning an
escape, now to be confined in chains. Order.

And this lust for order made Constantine, if not a good Christian, at
least a great Christianizer. This he accomplished not by persecuting the
old pagan groups (though he did tilt the state against them) but, rather,
by pressing the church to become more like his vision of the Imperial
state: standardized in behaviour, hierarchical in authority, uniform in
utterance. The logic is simple: the Emperor and the Supreme Deity
have the same need, namely unity among their chosen servants. Thus,
in 314 Constantine has the bishops meet at Arles and they agree that
Easter shall be celebrated everywhere on the same day and that day
shall be set by the bishop of Rome. Also, priests are to stay in whatever
city they have been ordained in, unless their bishop gives them leave to
go elsewhere. Then, in 325, the Emperor forces a council at Nicaea to
deal with the mess the church had twisted itself into once it had invented the idea of the Trinity: fierce views split the Believers, and especially the bishops, about how the three elements relate to each other. In
the actual course of events, Constantine never quite achieves church
unity, never sees enough uniformity to make him happy, never encour-

ages enough of a hierarchy of power to suit his sense of order. But within a century-and-a-quarter of his life, the main branch of the Christian church evolves into the system he desires.

The key is: he inveigles the bishops, considered collectively, along a line most of them wish to go. Like the serpent in the Garden of Eden, or like the Archangel giving Enoch entry into the heavens – take your pick, depending on your own beliefs – Constantine lets them taste a fruit they have not yet savoured; and he shows them a land that could be theirs.

View Nicaea. Of course it possesses an Imperial palace: all provincial centres do. Most of the 300-plus bishops who assemble in Nicaea have never been inside a palace. Some who still survive from the Diocletian persecution have seen such a place but, as one of the oldest prelates noted, in those days they had not been invited to the better apartments. And a few others, court bishops such as Eusebius of Caesarea, have begun to learn to navigate the physical and political labyrinths that each such palace contains. Most of the bishops are very uneasy about being this close to the teeth of the dragon.

Constantine understands this. He wants to convey to them the grandeur of the state but, somehow to make the prelates feel comfortable with it, and thus to become complicitous. He enters the council chamber with the same carefully choreographed style that he employs to open the senate. Like senators, the bishops sit on long marble benches that run the length of the fifty-metre room. They wear various garb, from simple albs to ornate chasubles, with a dotting of fustian provided by representatives of the distant and more primitive dioceses. The acoustics in the palace are excellent – this is, after all, a basilica for provincial affairs and it needs a good debating chamber – and that excellence is unsettling to the waiting bishops. Every cough, every scraping of the feet, can be heard. At last, outside the chamber, the step of civilian feet can be heard: not military marching, but an orderly sort of shuffle and when the door opens the entrants are not the emperor's bodyguard but members of his immediate family. Then, with heads bowed, follow a dozen men known to many of the bishops present: Christians of stature. All this releases the tension that Constantine had orchestrated. Before the council even convenes, the bishops have, in a tiny way, been treated as special and they understand the gesture and are grateful.

Not that Constantine stops being emperor. Twenty paces behind the last of the worthy Christians he enters, not striding, but not in the holy shuffle of the Believers who precede him. He has the gait of a man who knows that when he walks he is not propelling himself as other do across the face of the earth, but rather that the ground moves, at his direction, under his feet. From his collection of jewelled robes, Constantine has chosen a purple garment, one that has so much gold and so many precious stones worked into its intricate pattern, that later the bishops will recall that he was "radiant with light." He advances to the front, looking with what he hopes is paternal good-feeling into the faces of the bishops, who are standing to honour him. A small gold throne is brought and he sits and indicates to the bishops that they may now be seated. Then he rises and lectures them on the need for uniformity and order in the Christian church.

At subsequent sessions, Constantine mixes Imperial power and ritual humility. Before the debates begin, the bishops and their outriders take holy communion. Constantine joins them, but he does so in the white robe of the humble Christian initiate, and this is his attire for the remainder of the council. It is a wonderfully seductive statement, for it involves a sneaky converse: if the emperor is really one of us, the bishops are led to think, then are we not emperors? And if emperors, then do we not need the spiritual equivalent of good, sound Imperial order?

Thereafter, Constantine is the moderator of the debates, a position that involves, in the tradition of the Roman senate and town councils, the right to intervene actively. It is a model the churchmen adopt later, when the western bishops decide to make the bishop of Rome their permanent moderator.

Ignore the theological badminton that is played at Nicaea – it only half-solved the conundrum of the Holy Trinity – and observe instead Constantine's masterful move at the end of the council. Instead of dismissing the bishops to return to their homes, he issues an invitation: would they do him the honour of remaining a month in Nicaea? The beginning of his twentieth year as emperor was to be celebrated and Constantine has decided not to have the event in Rome but here in Nicaea. It would honour the Empire if the Christian prelates graced the spectacle.

Not a single one declined.

The Vicennalia, like all similar anniversaries in the Empire, had been a pagan ceremony and a celebration of the Imperial religious cult; it now gained the patina of Christianity. Not that its character changed much. The bishops had to spend a good deal of will power looking-the-other-way as men, women, young boys, and animals did in public things the bishops thought they should not do even in private.

Constantine put on a special state banquet for the bishops. Thus men, many of whom had had to hide from Imperial troops and all of whom were aware of the recency of state persecution, walked towards the palace in Nicaea, now surrounded by Constantine's personal guards with swords drawn. It was a test of faith and the ranks of the bodyguards opened and the men of faith passed through. They were led to the inner Imperial apartments, rooms rarely seen by any commoners and there, in a massive private banqueting chamber, the heirs of Jesus of Nazareth feasted. Most reclined on couches set in a circle around a central table. There a select band of prelates ate and drank with the Emperor.

One of the most favoured of the bishops later spiritualized this most worldly of experiences. "It felt as if we were imagining a picture of the kingdom of Christ, and that what was happening was no reality, but a dream."

JERUSALEM. 326–328

Finding Jesus

The old lady, almost as wide as she was tall, would have been a figure of fun, except she was far too rich for that. Anyone with a retinue as large as hers, one that included twenty Imperial legionnaires, a purser, a seneschal, a dragoman, two cooks and so much baggage that a full-time wagon-master was required, deserved respect. She was an opportunity on wheels.

"Here is the spot," she announced to her officials. "Mark it well, and we shall have a house of worship constructed."

Her officials bowed respectfully, but when her back was turned they rolled their eyes as if to say, oh-dear-not-again. She had done this several times in the preceding months, as her caravan inched its way from Nicomedia towards Jerusalem or, as the keenest functionaries of the Empire now called it, "Aelia Capitolina."

The long train of baggage and officials would be passing some pathetic little village and the old lady would command a halt and would descend and, leaning heavily on a cane carved from the tusk of a massive elephant, would enter a shop and interview its inhabitants. Several times now she had become animated and had been led through winding streets to interview still more obscure shopkeepers and when they led her to an unremarkable spot, she commanded that this should be the place for a church. To her purser, who was charged with contracting for the building, she would explain what important saint had been martyred here and would prescribe the appropriate nature of the memorial.

This was Helena, mother of Constantine and Empress Dowager of the Empire. She had moved to Rome soon after her son's epochal victory at the Milvian Bridge, and had come under the influence of the strong Christian community there. She had been baptized by no less an ecclesiastic than the bishop of Rome, whom she call "papas" or "papa," depending on the language she was speaking.

Helena was on a mission. Having been named "Augusta" by her son in 324, she had virtually the entire Imperial treasury at her beck. A little less than three years later she began a pilgrimage. She was determined to find Jesus. This would preserve her own immortal soul beyond any doubt and would purify her own family from the stain of Constantine's recent violence: the execution of his eldest son and his wife.

"Are you absolutely sure this is the spot, Excellency?" The purser had never previously questioned the Empress Dowager, but this time he really had to: there was nothing here, just an empty crossroad outside the place the old lady insisted on calling "The Holy City."

"Yes. And if I were you, I should shake my head a little."

"Ma'am?"

"So it remembers how it feels to be attached to a body."

The point was not lost on the purser.

Still, it surpassed mortal understanding how the old baggage had managed to find the exact spot where John the Baptist, still in the womb of his mother Elisabeth, had given that vigorous interuterine salute to his cousin Jesus, who was still resident in the Blessed Virgin. The Gospel of Luke was strong on story, the purser reflected, but weak on geographical details. How had Her Excellency known?

Actually, as she later explained to her son, most of Helena's big discoveries came from visions. Or heaven-messages as she called them. She usually received them in the afternoon. Her custom was to avoid the heat of the day, either by setting up a marquee that kept the sun away and let the breezes flow or, if in a large town, by having the residents of the best inn tossed out so that she could commandeer some peace and quiet. From her days serving in her father's provincial inn, she retained a liking for rough red wines. She could have anything she wished, but harsh, young wines of the sort soldiers preferred, were her favourite. After slowly consuming some fruit and a litre or so of the wine, the Empress Helena slept.

That is when she had her visions. Often they told her exactly where she would find a holy site.

And that, for example, is the mode of divination that led Helena to locate precisely the point on the Mount of Olives where the resurrected Jesus stood just before he was taken up into heaven. There she had the Church of the Ascension built. Among the Empress Dowager's more compelling finds was a cave in Bethlehem where she declared Jesus had been born, and of course she had a Church of the Nativity built. This was an example of the strength of her convictions for, as her seneschal tiredly observed to the purser, the scriptures seem to have Our Lord being born in an inn. Or was it a stable? "Well, certainly not in a cave."

"I fear there is more to come," the purser had replied. "Sooner or later, she'll go for the big one."

He was right. Helena awoke late one afternoon and spoke with an energetic clarity quite unlike the muzziness that usually characterized her when she was working her way back to full consciousness. With a mixture of imperiousness and shrewd practicality, she told her staff exactly what they were to do before sunrise the next day. Very precise directions for major diggings were given. "Tomorrow we will begin our search for the True Cross." "And," she added unnecessarily, "it will, we assure you, be a successful endeavour."

This was heroic. To find anything in Jerusalem from three centuries earlier was difficult; to identity organic matter immensely harder. Since Jesus' day, Jerusalem had been destroyed twice, the second time being nothing less than a levelling of the place. Moreover, a Roman city had been built over the ruins. After 135, Jews were banned from the city and, though a few managed to remain, most of the local knowledge had been lost by Helena's time. No matter. Helena knew where to dig. Having already identified to her own certainty Jesus' tomb and the hill of Golgotha – it had been a wonderfully rewarding pilgrimage, she reflected – she had a line surveyed connecting the two. Then, beginning in the middle and working towards the two ends of the line, she engaged a small army of labourers to strip the earth to a depth of a metre in a swath that was twenty metres wide. Because this land had been levelled by Roman engineers in their creation of the boringly regular grid for Aelia Capitolina, the Emperor Dowager calculated that at some point her corps of sappers would be uncovering earth that in Jesus' time had been far beneath the surface. She was looking for an old well or a cistern or a store-room: any place the followers of Jesus might have hidden the Cross, hoping to return and take it with them someday. Even the purser was impressed by Helena's logic.

What she found lodged inside an ancient well, now plugged solid with earth, was a single timber. It was oak of the sort that the Romans traded with the Germanic tribes: they were perfect for maritime spars or as rafters for large buildings. Helena knew it was the True Cross, not some building material that had been put down the well to keep it safe for future use. No, it was the True Cross all right: if not, then how was one to explain the four large spikes that the labourers found stuck in the crevices in the well's cribbing?

This find truly was a miracle, said the purser, said the seneschal, and said Helena: over and over and over.

A year later, the Empress Dowager died, happy, having followed, she believed, the footsteps of her Lord.

NICOMEDIA. 337

Behold, a New Covenant I Give Unto You

"Timing is the essence of all strategy, military and political." Thus Constantius I Chlorus, on his death-bed in the north of Roman Britain, had advised his son. "And in personal matters too," he added.

Now, on his own death bed – a pure white divan – Constantine reflected with satisfaction that he had always timed things well. His father would be proud: and no more so than in the matter of Constantine's last-moment baptism. Ah, the triumph of it all.

To the bishops of the Christian church (and especially to the court-bishops) it long had been a worry that their Emperor had repeatedly refused to be baptized. Not that they were terribly worried about his immortal soul, for the Almighty could deal with that.

What concerned them was that until Constantine submitted to baptism, it was possible that he might suddenly flip his religious allegiance and start favouring some paganism or other: probably the old Imperial cult, with Emperors as gods. "Quite a temptation, that," Bishop Eusebius of Nicomedia observed to Bishop Eusebius of Caesarea.

These, Constantine's two house-prelates, as he termed them, were the most concerned about his baptism. They knew the Emperor well enough to be aware of his ability to make a lightening-swift reversal of policy. And they understood that if the Emperor died without fully embracing Christianity, the chances of his successors turning the calendar back were considerable.

So both Eusebiuses were terrified when the Emperor fell ill in Constantinople, soon after Easter. He ordered his steward "get me Bishop Eusebius" and the steward had no choice but to fetch both of them. The two collided outside the Imperial apartment and sighed resignedly: this was an old trick of Constantine's, ordering the appearance of one of them with intentional ambiguity and then laughing when both appeared. This time, however, he desired to see both. "We shall be baptized," he told them between bronchial explosions. "Assemble the bishops."

Constantine, it turned out, believed in Christian baptism, but in a slightly unusual way. He believed it was efficacious for the forgiveness of sins, and heaven knows he had enough of them. But he wasn't so sure of how one's sins were forgiven after one was baptized. So, he calculated that he should be baptized just before his death, when he was beyond any significant transgression. When the two Eusebiuses, in the course of providing pastoral counsel, learned this, they visibly relaxed: the Empire as a Christian state was all right, at least for the immediate future. They accepted with no hesitation the plans for Constantine's burial place: he would, he told them, be placed in the Church of the Holy Apostles in Constantinople, the construction of which he had begun in 330. The church was cruciform and his own sarcophagus would lie in the exact centre of the cross, and on each arm would be sarcophagi set up like pillars, one for each of the twelve apostles: six on one side of the Emperor, six on the other. Constantine saw nothing immodest in this.

Failing steadily, the Emperor had himself conveyed to Nicomedia. He stopped at several churches on the way and prayed and confessed and beat his breast. In Nicomedia, more than 100 bishops assembled, a goodly number considering the short notice, and the prudential calculation that being around a dying Emperor could be a dangerous business.

Even in his last days, Constantine manages the bishops brilliantly. He enters for his baptism in full state robes. He takes the Eucharist. Then, dramatically, he removes his state robes and in the pure white of the new initiate, he indicates he is ready to be baptized. Both of the bishops Eusebius notice that his white habiliment is carefully tailored, in the same cut and pattern as the Imperial robes.

Having had his sins, both personal and those the church calls "original," wiped away, Constantine commands that he be carried to his villa at Achyrion, outside of Nicomedia. There, still in his white raiment, he takes to his pure white divan, and, although not happy to die, dies happily.

The direct consequences of Constantine's life and death were not played out for almost a century-and-a-half. The swirl of belief, of costume drama, of councils, civic celebrations and, above all, the seduction by Constantine of the Christian bishops, meant that by the time the Germanic tribes overran the western empire the church in the west had the hierarchy, order and uniformity the Emperor had sought: the blessed silence that was the grail of his strange and perhaps Christian soul.

A new covenant had been cut: the Roman empire had taken as its deity, its Augustus, the Semitic god Yahweh – and, as its Caesar, the divine son of Yahweh, the Jewish prophet Jesus of Nazareth. In turn, the Christian church adopted as its pattern for the body of Christ, the Roman empire.

Thus, at the end of the immensely strong and tight rope that was braided by early generations of Believers, blind knots were tied. These are knots with no loose ends; all the straggly bits are buried inside the rope and the cable is virtually impossible to unpick.

A new covenant, indeed.

THE BOOK OF THE CONQUESTS OF IRELAND 3000 BCE–493 CE

The Beginning

In their end was our beginning: the Pharaohs of pre-time. They prepared their transit to the next world with such exquisite thoroughness that they outlived human memory.

The construction of Dowth, in a bend in the Boyne Valley, is starting. A god-king is providing for his immortality. A hill sixty metres in diameter is being constructed. Drones move to Dowth hewed stones of four tonnes and more from quarries and rock falls, distances of ten to forty kilometres. These are a stone-age people, but they are as far from being primitive as we are from being civilized. Only a very disciplined, hierarchical, rich, calculating society can produce monuments such as this. Dowth is not completed for a millennium, but when it is done, it contains two royal tombs, oriented so as to catch the beginning of the sowing season and the time of harvest – 21 March and 23 September. All this packaged round by several million tons of earth, forming a giant eye looking towards the heavens.

Two other Pharonic masterpieces are soon in process, nearby at Knowth and at New Grange. Those are our names and if we use the old Irish terms for the three creations – *Dubadh, Cnodhba,* and *An Uamh Greine* – we are not any closer to them: for their real names were lost before western memory began, before Homer, before Solomon's temple: previous, previous, previous.

Eventually these calculating machines – each is orientated towards a specific pivotal day of the year – are dressed with stone mantels. The most dazzling is Knowth, covered with white quartz. On a clear day, the sun catches its slopes and light radiates from it so that it forms a sun, one that momentarily has been captured by the earth: god dwelling among us.

The architects of these wonders adore circles. Circles are the shape of god, and the votaries cannot stop making them. Circle-making is their vocation, their addiction, their worship. Within the great circular mounds, they decorate the royal graves with huge stones, patterned with row upon row of circles. Circles encompass other circles, god's image refracting upon itself.

Like most true worshippers, whatever the faith, the devotes become drunk with the spirit of their god; as generations pass, their incised circles begin to loop into spirals and then the spirals start to interweave into each other, so that even a grey stone slab comes alive with the writhing images of their living god. Long after the collective name of these worshippers has disappeared from human conscious-ness, their influence remains in the carpet pages of Christian manu-scripts and in our unconscious and universal knowledge that, ultimately, every snake seeks to devour its own tail.

These people are the victors in the first known Irish conquest. It is false comfort to say that they came from what is now Spain, or from Portugal, or from Brittany. And acknowledging that they had cousins in Iberia and in Wales tells us nothing real about them. No one knows a word they spoke, a king they feared, an ancestor they revered.

Today, even their god has forgotten its names.

HIBERNIA. 1500BCE - 1700CE

The Land

Accept this: you've never been there, even if you've lived there all your life. No offence meant. But going back to 1600 or even 1700 the country would be unrecognizable to you or me, even though we might pick out the odd local spot. The big picture is the problem. Much of central Ireland, now cut up by fields, must have looked like a prairie. The best remaining example is the Currah of Kildare, a handsome plain that would have run, as grassland, bogland, little woods, right across Ireland without a fence and, before the late mid-dle ages, without a road to interrupt it. Thousands of small lakes, now drained out, dotted the landscape, and the larger lakes were big-ger than now, centuries of settled agriculture having lowered them, water being the Irish farmer's primeval and perpetual enemy.

Elsewhere, away from the champaign central plains, woods and bogs prevailed. The cutting of the woodlands began with the neolithic invaders and yet denuding the forests was not completed until the middle of the seventeenth century. Lots of the bogs are gone, partly because they have been drained, partially because, century af-ter century, they were cut for fuel.

So all the events that happen before, say, 1600, happen in a theatre that we have never visited, and are outlined against backdrops we can only intuit. When heroic chariot battles occur in the central plains, they are on a topographical scale now impossible to duplicate; when journeys in the northern drumlins and woodlands are mentioned, they take place in a claustrophobic tangle of scree and tree that is no longer tangible; and when an adventurer crosses parts of the far south or far north, he is frequently traveling and travailing across a desert waste where there is no fodder for horses, no grass, all is heather or bog and there are only tiny settlements, most of which the traveler can pass within a mile of and never know are there.

EMAIN MACHA (NAVAN FORT, COUNTY ARMAGH).
700BCE

The Chariot

"Mount the chariot, boy."
"I shall if I choose."
"Test it."
"I will indeed."

To unclean eyes, the chariot is a paltry thing: wooden wheels, protected by rims of leather over copper. (The culture is not yet acquainted with iron.) The axles are oak, fitted onto beech shafts, their journals lubricated with heavy tallow, the final rendering of boar kills. Two small horses, so compact that they resemble ponies, are hitched to a centre shaft. There are no whippletrees, so controlling the beasts is difficult. That is why a fearsome bit, braided leather studded with pointed shards of shale, is necessary. Chariot driving is only for heroes, and even for them, sometimes fatal.

The young lad, scarcely into adolescence, yet already as strong as anyone in his clan, has no hesitation. He mounts, stands bent-legged, takes the reins in his left hand and an ash stick in his right, and with a violent yell startles his team into flight. Soon he is out of sight.

This not just a boy and some horses. It is the icon of Ireland's second conquest. This time it has been by Celts. They have subsumed the previous peoples. They have done this so completely that they have obliterated all traces of explanation for their victory: no charred habitations, no burial pit, no signs at all of physical victory: they won by cultural superiority and then invented legends of military conquest: though physically aggressive these Celts certainly are. Their habitation at Emain Macha will someday be an impressive royal site of the Uliad and will be reserved for ceremonial uses. At present it is a large circle surrounded by a shallow moat and sharpened pickets stuck into the ground.

"You're back, boy."

"Indeed, so I am."

"Did you not think to bring the chariot with you?"

"No, it was a weak thing. I brought the horses only."

"Then we must hitch them again to another chariot of mine."

"And test it I will."

The chariot was to the Celts what it was to Enoch of the Book of Genesis: a god-created instrument. And the Sages of Blessed Memory tell us that Enoch, having completed the ultimate solar cycle (he lived 365 years) drove his chariot into the heavens; so, too, the Celts' chariot was divine; it encircled their enemies, it unhulled their habitations, it girdled the great circular plate of the earth. The Celts, migrants from the eastern Mediterranean, completely superceded their predecessors.

"Again, I have returned."

"And this time with horses and a few fragments only."

"Surely you can find me better."

"Indeed, I can. My own royal chariot. And should this not withstand your testing ..."

The Celts' weapon of victory was culture, for proud as they were of their physical skills, they could not have taken Ireland by force. Yet, they installed themselves as sovereign curators of an aristocratic world. And the locals, the indigenous pharoahs and their subjects, bought into the new world of the Celts. Perhaps fear was the persuader. But even so, it takes wisdom to do what the Celts did: permit a potential enemy to shelter under one's tent. And it requires great force of character to make him want to do so.

"I am back, King Connor."

"And with my chariot intact, I note."

"And the horses."

"Foaming, I see."

"Yes," Cu Chulainn affirms. "They and your chariots work well under the reins of my will."

EMAIN MACHA. 200 BCE

Ancestors

"And his father was ..."

Professional rememberers counted a lot. One cannot have a world run by aristocrats unless someone remembers who is a ruler and who a commoner or a slave. Emain Macha now was a full royal site, primary palace of the chief kings of the north. Later it would become the equivalent of a cathedral, used only on ceremonial occasions. At present, however, a guild of full-time rememberers and their apprentices – they would be called a college of heralds if this were medieval Europe – resides at the palace.

"His father, sir, was Cu Chulain, warrior supreme to Connor, King of the Uliad, ruler of all the north and ..."

The palace was really an earthen works fort, with wooden palisades and a limited amount of stone work, mostly defensive bollards. Its aristocratic holders made up in fierceness what they lacked in architectural panache. They now knew how to use iron and with short sword or with iron-tipped spear they and their troops were a terror. The arts that they valued were intricate metalworked ornaments and words: epic poetry, poems of praise to themselves, and genealogies of their own lineage, always accurate, as is the nature of the form, right up to the point that the genealogy became fictitious.

"... and the father of Cu Chulainn was the god Lug of the Long Arm, Lug of the sun."

All around Ireland, in the palaces of the several regional kings, the same thing was happening. Keepers of the official memory were blending the real ancestry of their monarch into a genealogical chain that erased the upstarts and by-blows in the chain (for no aristocratic lineage is ever without its jump-ups) and then linked the whole skein into the great mythological warriors and, finally, to divine origin. And thus, each genealogy said, our king comes to us from god.

The ancient Celts had many gods, but no organized pantheon: just a clutch of vigorous deities who use the same clubhouse, but never show up at the same time, fortunately. Of these, Lug was the most important and the Celts of Ireland shared him with their cousins elsewhere. Lugdunum in Gaul was his capital city. And the festival of the sun, 1 August, was his: *Lughnasa*.

TARA (COUNTY MEATH). 100BCE

Spirits

When stories of Cu Chulainn and the warriors of Ulster run thin – and to the King of Tara stories of northern heroes turn stale pretty quickly – the monarch asks for diverting tales. The King of Tara traces his own genealogy to Lug, of course, but merely because he shares divine ancestry with the other monarchs of Ireland does not mean he has to listen to the same epics as they do.

He commands a story concerning Fionn Mac Cumhail, who's a good deal smarter than Cu Chulainn, and a lot more fun. There's usually laughter, or at least satire, buried in each Fionn tale.

The King of Tara fiddles impatiently with his torc, the gold neck ring aristocrats wear. Tonight's reciter is not one of his favourites, for he is the sort who is more priest than poet. The reciter rises, and slowly, almost arrogantly, smooths out the wool cloak that he wears over his linen tunic. Am I, a king, supposed to watch a voice-on-two-legs dress himself?

The king's irritation subsides as the reciter goes into a rich description of Fionn the cattle stealer, how he dressed, what his hair was like, what his companions were like. Ah, the king loves a good description of a warrior. He loves to hear of Fionn coming toward the court and the girls looking over the walls at him, and the details of his accompanying band. The king enjoys himself. Satire, laughter, is on its way.

The reciter proves perfidious. He weaves into his performance a tale of Fionn's being attacked by Strange Adversaries. They attack Fionn and he cannot see them. He cries out to all the gods, "Lift from me those who are invisible to me." The reciter looks the king straight in the eye while telling this tale, a gross breach of etiquette, a virtual challenge. Why, he might as well point a finger at me and tell me that the invisible world will bring me down!

The King of Tara rises and swiftly, before the reciter can utter a curse or taboo, he uses his finely engraved short sword to remove the talking head.

There now, he tells his court, that is how heroes are made.

EMAIN MACHA. 30CE

Seed Time and Harvest

A special set of palings, stakes five metres high arranged in a circle, surround a special visitor. Even the Uliad's nobles gather close and, like children, peek into the enclosure.

The King of the North has been sent a present by his trading partners, Celts from Spain. It is a token of highest respect.

A Barbary ape huddles inside the pen, hugging itself to preserve its body heat.

Despite offerings of honey and meat, it refuses to eat and eventually wastes to a dry carcass, a thin purse of skin over a skeleton of human proportions.

The creature is buried carefully, as if a precious seed is being folded into the earth. The grave is marked and for generations it is watched.

Eventually, when nothing happens, its location is lost and is not found again for nearly twenty centuries.

TARA. 300CE

Promised Land

The father of Conn of the Hundred Battles, King of Tara, only had intercourse with his wife once. And Conn became the father of Connel and of Art. He only had relations with his wife twice. Such was the potency of the rulers of Ireland.

Art, King of Tara, begat Cormac, the wise warrior. Cormac revered truth and prized peace. He possessed a gold cup that was marvelously beautiful and, better still, had a wondrous quality: when three lies were told over it, the cup broke into pieces, and when three truths were told over those pieces, the cup immediately became whole again. It was a sovereign device for distinguishing friend from foe, truth from lies, and the pity for Ireland is that it was lost when Cormac died.

One day, while on his travels, Cormac MacArt came upon a palace. It stood on a wide plain, surrounded by mist. Cormac entered the palace and was met by a handsome warrior who welcomed him. In the evening a man arrived with a pig that could be roasted only if a truth were told for each quarter of the beast that was to be roasted. Over the course of the evening, four truthful tales were told and in the morning the pig was found whole again. It was a glorious animal for feeding the people of Ireland by way of truth and it is a grievous loss that the beast ran away when Cormac died and has never again been found.

Cormac, not knowing where he himself was, asked the warrior, "What land is this? I know it not."

"It is a land where there is no old age. No sadness. No jealously or hatred or arrogance."

"It is not that way in my land," Cormac admitted.

"There is here only truth," the warrior noted.

"Shall we join as friends, then?" Cormac asked. He longed for truth and peace.

They joined friendship and their pact guarantees the truth of the promised land. It will be found again in the future: Cormac died without revealing exactly where that land lies.

THE BOYNE VALLEY. 360CE

The Tip of the Wedge

The first Irish invader of Europe was not a conqueror, but a heresiarch.

Born about 310, of a lower-rung aristorcratic family, he wandered to the southwest of England ("Britannia" as it then was) and converted to Christianity. He had enough brains to learn quickly the different form of Celtic spoken there and sufficient money to gain a good education. And he really believed. He grabbed his new faith like his warrior-cousins at home seized their swords. Like them, he was dangerous.

His requirement for individual heroism did not square with the asiatic passivity of Christianity. He could not accept the idea that only by God's will could one please God. His argument was simple: that everyone has some responsiblity for his good and bad deeds and that a man has to take the first steps towards his salvation himself. Only then does Divine Grace help.

This is the Celtic warrior in Christian armour. No wonder that St. Augustine spent sleepless months writing refutations. And St. Jerome, not the gentlest of Christians himself, denounced the Celt as "an Irish dog."

This warrior – "Pelagius" is his Latin name – presented his arguments in Rome and in Africa. The African church forced his excommunication.

Pelagius died in the Holy Land in 428, a missionary from the Pagans to the Christians, and thus, in the eyes of the righteous, a doomed heretic.

THE CELTIC SEA. 360–475

Little Skin Boats

The nightmares of the inhabitants of Roman Britain frequently feature little skin boats, each filled with very hard men. They come in fleets, twenty to a thousand at a time. The boats are nothing, little eggcups on the pulsing swells that separate Hibernia from Britain. Almost always they land on sea shores south of Hadrian's wall, and once on land, the vulnerability of the tiny boats is forgotten, for their crews are really water-borne wolf packs.

Jewellery is their first choice of plunder, coinage the second. After that, they prefer to take back to Ireland young persons, male or female. In an aristocratic society, slaves are very useful items.

THE LOIRE RIVER VALLEY. 405

Ambition

The wind blows cold off the Alps. Niall Noigiallach, who had raised the Uí Neill to power in the northwest of Ireland now is trying to extend his power to the Continent. His ambition is to win a kingship that extends through Gaul and into Italy. He is camped with his soldiers on the Loire's banks.

"Are you Niall of the Nine Hostages?" The voice is that of a single warrior, a splendid, indeed champion, representative of his profession.

He refers to the nine hostages Niall carries in his train, almost as amulets: five from Ireland, one from the Saxons, one from the Britons, one from the Picts, and one from the Franks.

"I will act as a further hostage for you," the warrior announces. "The Romans wish to parley with you, and I serve as an earnest of their faith." Niall agrees, for this is a hostage worthy of his fame: the new hostage has a shield with a gold rim. He carries an ivory-hilted sword and he shoulders two spears, massive implements with five sharp prongs on each. Niall concludes that the Romans are taking him and his invasion with the seriousness he knows is deserved.

Niall agrees to parley. He walks with squared shoulders across a glen. He feels a cold blast of wind and he understands that a spear has entered his back and in five places has pierced his heart.

ROMAN BRITAIN. 407

Recessional

The records are muzzy, and that tells a story in itself. Yet another Constantine is proclaimed emperor by the troops in Britain. He crosses to Gaul with his soldiers. This time, all the troops follow their Constantine and the locals are left behind with a bit of civil administration and fierce faces, Saxon, Irish, Pictish, flickering in the fires of the night.

ROME. 410

Salons

As the smoke rises from the better parts of Rome, Pelagius looks back, shakes his head, as if to say well-we-had-it-coming, and moves on. He is destined for Jerusalem, as is the cream of the Christian community. There they settle as an alien intelligentsia, a bunch of Czarists in the Parisian salons of their time.

Pelagius, however, never gets along with them, much less with the rattled and querulous Christian hierarchy in Jerusalem. He is too tall, too broad of shoulder, and his refusal to cut his drooping Celtic mustache makes him one of the few unifying points in a Holy Land suddenly full of refugees from the Pagans.

Not-yet-Saint Augustine cannot stand the handsome Celt and he rains upon him his doctrines of predestination, Original Sin, and the Fall in the Garden of Eden.

Perhaps, as most observers believe, the twenty-two books of the "City of God" arose out of the fall of Rome to Alaric. Or perhaps they arose from the recognition that Pelagius, large man, big warrior, had in his lifetime had a lot more of what Augustine, ageing, finally decided he could not himself enjoy.

ROMAN BRITAIN, THE WEST COAST. 416

Birth

A Christian priest, Potitus by name, stands outside a wattle habitation and tries to say divine office in aid of the endangered. His concentration is broken by the wrenching sounds from inside the house. A woman is in child-birth. It is her first child and Potitus is too experienced in the ways of the world to ignore the risks. He has buried dozens of women who died in childbirth. It was always most dangerous for the young ones.

O Heavenly Father, watch we pray thee over these, thy children. His prayers were in Latin, the tongue of church and civic business, but he and his family were more comfortable in domestic speech using the local form of Celtic.

God of all grace and power; Behold, visit and relieve this thy servant. Here he was joined by his own son, Calpurnius. They both prayed fervently, louder now as the screams from inside increased. Calpurnius was a minor functionary of the central Roman administration. Even now, in the backwaters of Britain, that made him a person of stature.

O Saviour of the world, who by thy Cross and precious Blood hast redeemed us, Potitus intoned.

Save us and help us, Calpurnius responded.

From inside, seemingly as part of the liturgy a baby's first startled cry was heard. *And let our cry come unto thee!* the two men, father and son, exclaimed in unison.

The wee child was brought to the door by the midwife who held it up like a hunter holds a trophy. It was a boy, and was immediately returned to its now-exhausted mother.

Potitus was the lad's grandfather, and no scandal that: this was the era before celibacy became the penis ring of the clergy. The boy, destined to be an only child and to be spoiled rotten, was given three names as befitted one of the ruling class: Patricius Magonus Sacutus. Later, in official correspondence he was referred to simply as Patricius and, in the British form of Celtic, as Padraig.

JERUSALEM AND SOUTHWEST BRITAIN. 428

Last Post

Pelagius, the first Irish invader of the outside world, dies in the Holy land in 428. In the eyes of the righteous, he was a heretic.

On the same day that Pelagius dies in Jerusalem, the last official record of the military and civil administration in Britain-of-the-Romans is signed. It is sent to the Imperial centre where it is read, filed, forgotten.

GLOUCESTER. 429

Tidying Up

As the secular version of the Roman empire receded, its religious counterpart expanded. A virtuous example of this transformation is the career of Germanus (eventually St. Germanus), bishop of Auxerre in Gaul. He had trained as a Roman lawyer and had become the effective ruler of a small satrapy before he saw the heavenly light: in his case that the invisible world had a lot better future than did the visible. Hence, his translation to the bishopric of Auxerre. To his new profession, he brought the same dislike of messiness and insubordination that had made him a good civil functionary.

In 429 he is in Britain, on a special, if brief mission: to keep the Christian church in order, even as the Roman empire splays into disorder. He has two things on his mind. The first is the continuing and damnable optimism of Pelagianism. It has to go, for it implies an heretical freedom of the will: that belief must be broken.

And he is horrified by the continuation in Christian circles of the Celtic practice of fosterage. It has been broken elsewhere and must be suffocated here. Among the educated and the aristocratic orders, the Celts still send their children, both boys and girls, to be raised by others; and those same families who send their children away take in other children. This produces a web of feelings, a set of bonds that are unnatural – they are not the family as God intended. And they are hard to control.

Germanus engages frequently in ritual ablutions: only his hands. He washes them frequently, sometimes several times an hour, and he dries them carefully on a white linen cloth provided by an everpresent acolyte. Although he is confident that he can rid Britain of the twin evils of Pelagianism and fosterage, when he considers Ireland he becomes highly agitated. There, he is told, the followers of Pelagius have introduced in the south of the country an heretical form of Christianity. And all the aristocracy and nobility practise fosterage.

He washes his hands time and time again, until his whitened fingers resemble talons.

HIPPO REGIUS (MODERN ALGERIA). 30 AUGUST 430

Litany

In one of the last cities in North Africa to be besieged by the Vandals, the bishop of Hippo is chanting out his own litany. Augustine, in failing health, is ready for death. During the siege he has kept himself in a state of perfect penitence. The only luxury he allows himself is to chant, between prayers, the names of the important people in his own life.

He strings them on a staccato line, familial prayer beads that run from the near- to the far-past: his closest friend, Alypius; Adeolatus his illegitimate son; Bishop Ambrose; Lucilla his mistress; Monica his Christian mother. And, time and time again, he repeats the name of his pagan father, Patricius.

ROMAN BRITAIN. 431

A Special Guest

Another Patricius, a young Briton, lies in the tall grass of a summer meadow. Beside him is someone the family refers to as "our special guest": being good Christians they no longer admit to fosterage, although in effect this is Patricius's foster brother, a lovely lad of eleven. The younger boy is from a chiefly family in the north. He has been sent to the family of Calpurnius to have his rough ways polished. Roman culture still has éclat. The young visitor learns well and in grammar, writing, and declamation soon equals the skills of Patricius.

In truth, that is not difficult, for Patricius is not terribly intelligent and he is rebellious in a lazy sort of way. He does not openly defy his family; rather, he slips away, in mind or body, whenever he can.

The only matter of study Patricius excels at is mathematics.

"How many times does one go into one?" he asks his fragile companion.

SOUTH LEINSTER. 431

God's Rabbit

Rarely has anyone been so flummoxed by Ireland, so right through-othered. No, not Pope Celestine, who had heard that several gaggle of Christians of the heretical Pelagian persuasion were prospering in Ireland. He's an old hand at handling heresy. The confused pilgarlic is one Palladius whom the Pope sends as the first bishop to the Irish Christians. His instruction are clear: forget converting the Pagan Irish to the True Faith. Just get into the paddock those who already follow Jesus. Sterilize heresy and let the next generation take care of converting the Hibernians.

So Palladius spends three decades successfully in that way, but in no other. He slowly visits the various Christians that have popped up in mid-Ireland – some who had known the heretical Pelagius, others who were converted while trading in Gaul, still others who were products of contact culture. Palladius limits his mission to Leinster and all he does is upbraid Christians, making sure that they know they suffer from Original Sin.

He finds the locals rebarbarative, so it is just as well that he makes no effort to convert them. He can tolerate their warlike mentality and their blood sports – he is from Gaul, after all – but he finds their culture primitive. Especially their visual arts. I mean, really, he tells his secretary, a raven-haired deacon, can one have a world where the wee kingies are oxter-deep in tchatchkes? Not likely. And really, what is one to make of their insistence on having shiny ornaments all over themselves and their houses? I mean, darling, a set of obsidian door posts as an entry to a rath made of mud? And they can't write. Really, did you know that before we came here they had just straight lines on a stick? Is it a civilization if it can't even make a curled letter? Oh, how our Lord must suffer looking down upon this place! Oh, don't stop me now: what about the clutter they live in? Churl and king and everyone in between has so much rubbish and food on the floor of their abodes that they just add a layer of clay, rather than clear it out. Every house one sits in is full of smoke and why they cannot put a hearth any place but in the centre of a room is just too, too beyond my explanation!

In later years, three continental helpers come to aid Bishop Palladius. All the holy men live together for they agree with their leader that this country is just too primitive for them.

When he dies in 461, Palladius is taken to the Continent, where he is given a refined burial service of which he would have approved.

WESTERN BRITAIN. SUMMER 432

The Small Boats

The small boats come again: half empty, so as to leave plenty of room for booty. Patricius, slothful lad, lazing at his family's summer villa, is easy prey, a fat stoat to the Irish hawks. More than 100 leather-covered boats descend in this raid, and everyone returns to the homeland with something worth boasting. Slaves are a worthwhile prize.

Patricius has seen the outline of Ireland many times before. When conditions are right, so that the sea mist serves as a huge sea-borne lens, the hills and beach lines of Ireland are visible from Britain. Patrick has never had any ambition to visit there, but now he is being rowed, his hands bound together with tight cords, into a north-flowing tide. His captors, an under-tribe of the Uí Neill of the north, know the Celtic Sea well and they navigate on an unmarked path that eventually leads them home.

One of his captors taps Patricius and points. "Rinn Semhne" is all he says. It is the first part of Ireland that Patricius views close-up. The form of Celtic his captors speak is strange, but it has enough similiarity to his own that Patricius knows that a point or peninsula is being referred to and also that it must belong to someone named Semhne. The land – modern-day Islandmagee – is forbidding: harsh cliffs with oak forest barely visible, like the thin fringe on an old monk's head. As they continue along the length of the peninsula, it becomes clear why the pirates headed for this landmark: around a corner, protected like a child crooked in its mother's arm, is a quiet harbour. The skin boats are unloaded and safely beached. Asked his name, Patricius becomes Padraig.

In his own view (and that certainly has to count a fair bit), this capture and enslavement was the most important moment in the life of St. Padraig. He memorialized it in writing (which he hated to do, so self-conscious was he of his modest education); and in his preaching he commemorated this year – 432 – as the one when his mission started: now, when captured and forced to begin his soul-journey.

The year 432 was a magic year. That was obvious to Padraig, for mathematics was his one field of intellectual distinction. He played with the number 432 all the rest of his life and tried to decipher its magic.

Magic? Just look at the number: 4–3–2. It leads only to a single truth, the One. And, in the long hours that Padraig spends alone, he twists 432 around continually, harrying it for meaning. He discovers that all of its divisors are themselves divisible by two – except the divisor three, the number of the Trinity. Padraig loves this number, 432.

And he is not alone. At the other end of the Indo-European world – the only culture other than Ireland not to be ground down by Roman civilization – a cosmology survives that uses 4–3–2 as its foundation. A period of 4,320,000 years forms a Manvantara or Maha Yuga and is closed by the apparent destruction of the world and by the "night of Brahma."

The magic of 4–3–2 is readily understandable to Padraig's later converts in Ireland. That this number has force is not hard for them to grasp. Only later chroniclers have trouble with it: they mistakenly try to force it into an episcopal succession list, one of those administrative categories the church's civil servants picked up from their Imperial predecessors.

THE ANTRIM UPLANDS. 432–438

A Master's Lot

Being a king is all in the details, especially if you – like I – happen to be a small king. Not a petty king, O, not that slur. All kings must be kingly, ne'er petty, but it is a distance harder to be monarch of a *tuath* if it has only two score hundred common subjects and scarcely twice that number cattle. Mind you, another half-hundred aristocrats, all waiting to inherit my throne don't help. I am Miliuc and if I double as monarch and priest and oft-times have to be my own bard, it is only in part that I possess great talent. In truth, it's hard to find qualified help these days.

And, since we're dipping our toes into truth, I should say, forget my talk of cattle. Yes, I've a few, and, yes, that is the coin of our world, but here in the Antrim uplands we're stuck with sheep. On these raised bogs and sour, ill-drained hills, a bullock won't come to full weight in five years and a regal bull would end up turning grey with age before its testicles began to be scratched by the cursed gorse. It is not a fair land. Nor is it fair that I have the Uliad pressing me on one side and the Uí Neill on the other.

Indeed, it is an offence to a man of talents, a person like you or, to be fully candid, a Rí such as I. For what fills my days are petty details, inharmonius sounds, vexing sights. The worst of these are sheep and slaves. They are tied to me by the weakness of our land. Weak land: thence sheep. Sheep, thence slaves, because no male with even one tiny hair on his private parts will serve as a shepherd. It is a slave's task, not a man's. The sheep make constant noise, march whenever possible into the mouths of wolves, or become the hosts for phalanxes of purulent sores, and die without giving decent warning. The slaves whimper all the time, wipe their phlegm-filled noses on their cloaks, and encourage each other in anile superstitions.

Take Padraig. The Briton. Cost me a copper brooch of my old uncle's. Fine shepherd. Keeps saying something about, suffer the sheep to come unto me, and doesn't lose very many. See him. He always plants himself so that he can observe his flock, true enough, but also so that he can see towards his old home. On a clear day, he will look from Slemish across the sea and then will drop to his knees. Mind you, our Briton doesn't require a clear day for that. I've seen him do the kneeling thing two-score times within a morning. He chants his own druid-words when he does that. Nothing wrong there, as long as he does not lose any sheep. Yet, when questioned about this, he is very confused. He really only partly speaks our language. All his "p"s and "q"s are confused and half the words we use he doesn't know and most of the words he uses we haven't heard and it's all very tiresome.

My brother, they say, would be a better monarch than am I. He covets sheep and finds slaves amusing.

THE SUMMER VILLA. 440

Not an Escaped Slave

I did not run away. I ran from nothing. I ran towards God. As Padraig tells this, a soft breeze, sweet with the curing of meadow-cut hay, is seducing his family. They listen to him, intently at first, but they wander. His mother falls asleep, her will sapped by the pagan god who is the setting summer sun. His father, a deacon in the church and an official of the once-Roman, once-empire, knows the need for discipline, but he too drifts away, mesmerized by the summer insects who plight their lives in a single summer's eve. And there is no priestly grandfather to keep the flock awake: he has been buried for seven years and this, the sabbatical year of his passing, leaves him as only a restful memory.

Like the Apostle Paul, I sought our Lord in the wrong places; and then, praise His Name, He found me. Padraig recites the events of his six years as a chattel slave of the Magus-King Miliuc, a conjuror, a singer of songs, a petty tyrant, a devil in the form of human kind. The story is dramatic, but the way Padraig tells it, there is little narrative. Even Padraig's friends from youth cannot keep their eyes open. Padraig's tales of his daily search of the horizon for just a glimpse of his old home land, his reciting of 100 prayers to Christ our Lord each day, and almost as many more at night, they are so very repetitive.

And then, one day, on Mount Scirte, the angel of the Lord came to me. Go, he said, and look not back over your shoulder. Padraig interrupts his story because no one is listening. Bees hum in the nearby arbour and one of the last larks to have been born while Britain was still an armature of the Roman Empire, sings its reedy song on its way to the empyrean heaven. A coverlet of narcosis is slipping over Padraig's old world.

When Padraig dreams, it is not the gentle Morphean walks into lotus fields that his family and friends ease into as Roman Britain evaporates. His dreams are work: reviews of past encounters, agendas for future action. Yet, his unconscious moments share, with the sloping Unconscious of Roman Britain, long periods of indeterminancy, of gauze moving across an otherwise familiar tableau.

The journey from bondage in the kingdom of Miliuc was an Exodus worthy of a hero, but Padraig feels no pride. To many it would be a miracle for an ill-clothed shepherd to find his way from the far north of Ireland all the way to the south, and there to take sail to the Continent: the more so because he spoke the local language only haltingly (and in later life, used a translator to broadcast any really important pronouncement he had to make.) Yet, for Padraig it was a simple case of putting one foot ahead of the other, as the angel of the Lord had told him. Walk, son, like a true Apostle.

Temptation comes on true pilgrimages, and Padraig's came in the shape of a mixed crew of Irish and Continental sailors who at first refused to give him berth and then agreed and then, oh horror, demanded that he perform the customary Irish peace-gesture of sucking their nipples. This was no prurient requirement, but an invitation to something worse: heresy. Slothful though he had been as a boy, Padraig, coming from an ecclesiastical family, knew of the reason that Bishop Germanus of Auxerre had visited Britain: to stamp out the sins of Pelagianism and of fosterage. The first produced unholy optimism and the second was the creation of an artificial family that was in opposition to the family that God defined, a man and woman and their own offspring. The licking of nipples among men had at first been a way of affirming that we foster brothers are bound as tightly as if we had been suckled by the same mother. And, later, the ritual became an analogy: we men, who suck each other's nipples, will be at peace with each other in the same way as if we were foster-brothers. Padraig understood all this, even if he could not have expressed it with any precision. But the practice was wrong, he knew that, or why would Bishop Germanus be so strongly against pagan fosterage?

So he refused and expected to be beaten, perhaps killed. It was a test from God. The pagans relented and he and his benefactors made landfall safely on the Continent. In his dreams, Padraig always knows precisely where the trading-vessel he sailed on came to shore and he could trace his subsequent two years of wandering with precision. But, when awake, the details become mist and his attempts at description left him sounding silly and, perhaps, brain damaged. All that he can say is that he wandered for two years, had some adventures, met some holy men, and came home to Britain.

And now, as the early evening dew falls and Padraig and his parents emerge gradually from the narcotic charm of late summer, he tells them of one last dream. *An Irishman by name of Victorious came to me. Letters, he carried several. I read them aloud and they had the voice of the sea and the roar of the forest behind them.*

And they said to me:
Young boy.
Holy boy.
Walk among us once more.

THE SEMINARY OF BISHOP GERMANUS, AUXERRE, GAUL.
441

Hard Lines

A sharp crack; a hardwood ruler breaks the silence of the academy. It raps the knuckles of a student so lost in concentration that he gives no indication of having felt its cut.

"Show me, Patricius, what you have done." The master of novices has been peering over the Briton's shoulder for several minutes and he is mystified by Padraig's attack on a very simple exercise: to copy out a Latin translation of a small portion of one of Paul's epistles. The master holds up the work sheet, turns it upside down, then sideways. He is still unsure of what he is reading. It says:

When I became a man,
I put away childish things.

"Well, continue," the master directs and goes away to ponder. Bastard-Latin is all our young Briton is capable of, he reflects, but then feels guilty: if God has laid his hand on the shoulder of the lad, who am I to shove it aside? ... Still, why does the Almighty choose such an unlikely bast ... Ah! the light dawns ... not bastard, but boustrophedon!

Having been set a difficult task by Providence the master endeavours worthily to meet the challenge. He devises special exercises for the lad, and is gratified when Padraig is able to quickly copy out a text as follows:

For now we see through a glass darkly,
.face to face then but

Ah that's wonderful, and it's joy for the master when, after several weeks' hard concentration, Padraig can pen:

Now I know in part; but then shall
,known am I also as even know I

No one ever accused the novice master of being mawkish, but he privately shed a tear of joy when Padraig the Briton finally was able to reproduce accurately St. Paul's great apophthegm:

And now abideth faith, hope, charity, these three; but the greatest of these
is charity.

THE SEMINARY, AUXERRE. 445

Grace Notes

Bishop Germanus had a pet castrato. He was in perpetual subdeacon's orders, so technically he was part of the academy. In fact, he was the bishop's canary. On the Sabbath, in days of clement weather, the great Germanus would share his prize possession with the seminarians. They were told to repair to their cells and each was to meditate upon the life of a saint. Then, from the bishop's enclosed garden, they could hear the angelic contra-tenor notes of the canary. For a brief time the virtues of each saint would blend with the celestial praises of the Almighty and each seminarian would recognize the basic truth, that God is always more than the sum of his details.

Invariably, Padraig meditates upon the life of the Apostle Paul. He completely identifies himself with Paul and yet there is no arrogance in this: no more than a casting of a statue could mistake itself for the original. Whenever he hears the bishop's canary, Padraig replays two sublime visions, ones that had taken hold of him while still in his parents' home after his return from slavery. Of these he had not told his parents. In the first, he hears words of divine wisdom, and these come to him in the same confounding circumstances as Paul's trip to the third heaven – "whether in the body or out of it, I know not." And in the second, a wraith, praying within Padraig, turns out to be nothing less than the Holy Spirit. And Padraig, afrighted, hears Paul's words of comfort, "the Spirit helps our infirmities ... and makes intercession for us with groanings that cannot be uttered."

Auditory hallucinations, perhaps. Yet they are real enough to determine a life. And, when combined with the unmanned and, therefore, otherworldly voice of the bishop's canary, they yield a wave of spiritual harmonics that bears Padraig aloft. From that height, he is able to see the land that, like Joshua, he has been chosen to conquer.

THE SEMINARY, AUXERRE. 446

Pack Drill

"You will be a bishop some day. I promise you."

"Bishop? I am still a sub-deacon and the least accomplished in our form. And, in case you haven't noticed, I'm also the least practised speaker in the entire abbey, save for the mutes, and even they communicate with greater ease than I do."

"Remember your shining saint, the missionary to the Gentiles: Paul complained of being tongue-tied and yet he preached the Gospel almost to the ends of the earth!"

"True ... But I am a long way from being a bishop."

"And that is what I have to tell you. The news comes from the Most Reverend Germanus himself. You are to take deacon's orders in a fortnight, be priested in six months time, and begin a mission in Ireland within a twelve-month! Of course you will not be a prelate, but I know that honour has to come eventually."

All this was news to Padraig and he should have been delighted. Yet a smarmy quality in the messenger besmirched the message. His companion was what the authorities of the seminary called a "soul-friend." Each novice was assigned to an older student and the two were expected to share spiritual counsel. The authorities took care to avoid the possibility of "particular friendships" arising, by which they meant sensual acts. Padraig's soul-friend was a corpulent man whose pale watery eyes were always on the verge of tears. He was reckoned by the authorities to be among the most clever of the scholars and to have promise as a theologian. "So, you must prepare yourself and make your spiritual purge. Then you can be raised to the diaconate."

Padraig had dreaded this moment. The practice in the teaching monasteries of Gaul (and, later, in Ireland) was for a full and final confession of the sins of one's whole life to be made to one's soul-friend before becoming a deacon. Though later supplanted by the practice of confession-to-priests only, this earlier ritual had the advantage of binding the pioneering members of the church in Gaul and the frightening westward islands into a tight little knot of lifetime trust and spiritual intimacy. It worked: when it worked.

Padraig prepared himself for this confession-of-his-life, but he was not at peace, though he prayed long and hard to be granted the grace to trust his soul-friend. He had serious things to confess, did Padraig; equally unsettling was the way his soul-friend kept badgering him to pick a time for the confession. When he did so, the man twisted his hands as if in anticipation of a really good meal, and his eyes watered freely, like salivary glands.

Finally, Padraig made his full confession. The site was Bishop Germanus's private garden where, for such special occasions, a pair of seminarians was permitted to move in slow rogation, hands behind their backs, save when making the sign of the Cross. Three hours of minor sins and long silence elapsed before Padraig told his soul-friend of his one mortal sin: his one delicious hour, spent in the summer meadows of his parental villa, discovering with his family's "special guest" (he still refused to call him foster brother), the permutations of how one could go into one.

Padraig shuddered when he told this. His soul-friend forced him to recount the event in details several times, before finally touching him lightly on the shoulder, a degree of contact unthinkable in other circumstances. "You have made a good confession. All is now sealed, a holy secret between the Almighty, you, and me."

Padraig was comforted, especially when his soul-friend reminded him that Saint Paul had possessed a "thorn in the flesh," and perhaps it was the same secret sin. The soul-friend added, lightly touching Padraig once more, "I certainly hope so."

AUXERRE. 447

Not a Contemplative Order

"Alleluia!" Thus the battle cry of the old spiritual warrior Bishop Germanus. He frequently thought in military terms. He had big plans in mind and Padraig was to be in charge of a flanking movement. Now that the young Briton had been priested, he could be trained as part of Germanus's invasion of the British Isles. The stink of Pelagianism may have been reduced, Germanus recognized, but now the Christians in Britain needed protection. And it was high time to turn Ireland into something useful for the church. It was all very well for that sybarite Palladius to control the few Hibernian Christians, but a bit of missionary zeal might turn the Irish into useful soldiers for Christ. That's where the sturdy Padraig came in. No need for a great mind; mere competence backed by courage would suffice.

First, however, Padraig has to learn to read and write a language in which there is nothing to read, save a few incised sticks. Here, the abbey at Auxerre possessed a treasure of incalculable value: the trilingual letter that Saint Paul had written at the end of his Spanish mission. This is a sacred relic demanding of immense veneration, for it had been preserved by Yacov, brother of Jesus-the-Christ, and subsequently saved from the destruction of Jerusalem. Unlike most other relics, however, it is also a useful implement, for, whatever his own reasons, St. Paul had turned it into a rosetta stone, of Koine, Latin, and Iberian Celtic. The last of these was close enough to the form of Celtic spoken in Ireland that someone with good Latin and Greek could come up with a phonetic version of how the Irish language might be written. That is Bishop Germanus's hope, and since Padraig already spoke a modest bit of Q-Celt, he should be able to teach reading and writing to his Hibernian converts, or so Germanus thought. The only problem, Germanus realized, was that Padraig was thick as

a wall when it came to reading and writing in any language – at au-
rally memorizing scripture texts he was brilliant, but reading, oh
dear, what a mess the man made of any sentence that he had not
heard or seen previously: reversing letters and sometimes whole
words. Ah, God must be trusted.

Thus, Padraig slaved day after day to sound-out the words in
the Pauline epistle and to try to marry them with the sounds that
he could only faintly recall from the years of his own slavery.
Some mornings he was found with his head pressed against the
precious artifact, having fallen asleep trying to master the contents. Not unkindly, the old priest who wakened him wondered if
Padraig was trying to master the Irish tongue by pressing it into
his forehead.

Bishop Germanus finally had to forbid Padraig from studying after
Compline, because of danger to the holy relic: Padraig one morning
was found to have a smudge on his forehead in the shape of the
Cross, where his weary body had intersected Saint Paul's sad and tormented words.

SOUTH BRITAIN; IRELAND. 447–450

Historical Law

History has only one law, and it is very easy to memorize. It is this:
the more that happened, the less historians will know about it. That
was laid down before the universe was built and questioning it is like
questioning the law of gravity: it's just the way things are.

So let Bishop Germanus shout "Alleluia." He is an old man now
and has more rage than breath in him. He is in Britain – by which he
means the confines of what was once the Roman colony – and he has
an army that he intends to use to protect the Christians. Against
whom? Against everybody. Certainly against the raiding Irish and
the infiltrating Picts. Germanus's soldiers are not as well trained as
were the Roman legionnaires, but they are reasonably able and they
are immensely keen Christians. The bishop has taught them his own
battle-cry – "Alleluia" – and it has a chilling effect on the usually
manic and frequently maniac Irish and Picts. The bishop's forces are
also successful against the Saxons. "Alleluia!" But they cannot stay

forever and when Germanus leaves, the periphery crushes its way inward, finally throttling Roman Britain. Now, for the first time in five centuries, south Britain is out of touch with the Continent and, as one Sage of Blessed Memory writes, "with the departure of Germanus, Britain definitely passes outside the range of recorded history."

And Padraig the Briton, the flank-rider of Germanus's last crusade, marches into Ireland. He comes, as his bishop had advised him, with considerable pomp, a chieftain of Christ, someone to be respected. Four hundred years after the event, a vernacular life of Padraig claimed that he came to Ireland with a retinue of twenty-four men in holy orders (including his hewer of firewood and his cowherd). Maybe: that's another magic number – twenty-four is twice the number of the tribes of the Chosen People and twice the number of the original Disciples of Jesus. He and his phalanx land in the south and slowly work northwards, searching for something Padraig cannot as yet define. Some of the local kings are unimpressed with him and he has to ransom his way out of captivity. Still, he keeps marching, looking for a sign. Walking is not a very efficient way to move across a roadless veld, so Padraig purchases several of the little leather boats that had so terrorized his homeland and had robbed him of much of his own youth. A pirate for God, he sails north.

DOWNPATRICK. 450

The Camberwell Beauty

In Java and Sumatra, still a single piece of land at that time, a volcano vents and throws off a pyroplastic flow that for a month boils the sea water at its base. On the scale of the earth's geological effulgences, it is noteworthy, but not earth-shaping. For months after the primary venting, much of the ash that spews forth ascends into the jet stream and circles the earth in the form of millions of tiny particulate satellites. Some of them orbit the world a dozen times before settling to become anonymous additions to the soil and water of the planet.

By the chaotic physics of such events, one band of these tiny satellites chances to group together and to descend upon the west coast of Britain. The dark particulate cloud, a veil before the sun at midday, puts fright to a flock of butterflies who fly above the Celtic Sea to escape. Once airborne above the waves, they have no choice but to keep going and most of them survive to land on a sheltered piece of the Irish coast, a place where water and meadows intertwine as if trying to protect each other from the dark mass of the sea.

Padraig and his retinue are moving slowly into Strangford Lough. They are not very good at sea-faring and, as men of considerable dignity, are acutely aware that they appear slightly ridiculous to anyone who knows anything about boats. They have been careful to hug the coastline as they move northward and are greatly relieved to enter the protected confines of the lough, where two massive arms, formed by ancient drumlins, come down to protect them, and to form a tidal lake that is much less turbulent than is the open sea. The southern portion, where several freshwater streams meet the brackish basin of the lough, appears to have been designed by a maker of aquatic mazes. Islands, rivulets, tidal backflows, form complex arabesques, none unpleasant or dangerous, but none of them obviously leading anywhere.

Padraig notes a fluttery cloud on the horizon. He assumes that it is a flock of blackbirds, but the distance and the colouring of the objects are an optical illusion. Within a matter of seconds, the flight of Camberwell Beauties is over his head and moving further landward.

"Row!" Padraig commands.

The flock leads the procession of little boats in a meandering course and when the Beauties cross the sod-lined shore, Padraig and his men quickly beach their boats and follow. The entire flight of Camberwell Beauties alights on the roof of a wattle-and-daub barn. The sun hits their wings and reflects off them as though they are a hundred thousand pieces of mother-of-pearl.

Padraig recognizes this is a sign, but he knows not what variety: he puts one hand on his scapular cross and the other on a small dagger that lies concealed within his robes. Which will it be Lord?

"Sa'ul." The voice is that of a lad of fourteen or fifteen who has been working in the barn. He has observed the puzzlement on the face of the oddly-garbed stranger and has decided to take his chances with showing himself: one doesn't meet packs of alien druids very often. "Sa'ul," he repeats.

"Yes, I know it is a barn," Padraig replies testily. Padraig's Irish is not wonderful, but he knows the basic domestic vocabulary. "Go and find your master."

As Padraig waits, he watches the Camberwell Beauties and he reflects on God's ambiguous ways. Padraig may not be a great reader, but he has memorized large chunks of both Testaments, and he has observed that the Almighty really likes a good pun, starting with the word "Adam" and carrying on from there. So, this is a blessed place, for the pun – "Sa'ul" is Irish for barn and "Saul," the given-name of the most glorious missionary the Faith has ever had, Saint Paul – is a code from the Almighty.

The butterflies on the barn take flight, not all in a frighted bunch, but as if doing a ceremonial fly-off.

Simultaneously a large man approaches. He comes straight up to Padraig and demands who he is and what is his business. The man's name is Dichu. He is the local king and he has few teeth, a tallow-stained mustache, and as foul a breath as one can encounter short of an omnivore. Face-to face, nose-to-nose, the two men converse, Dichu barking at Padraig, the ecclesiastic replying in halting Irish. Sometimes he has to stop for a time to think of the right word. Gradually, Dichu steps backwards and drops his hectoring tone. The two men walk, alone in a meadow, and then they return and, to the amazement of Padraig's retinue, walk three times around Dichu's barn. Then Dichu bares his chest and Padraig does not hesitate: his followers look on with horror as, for the cause of Christ, Padraig licks the nipples of King Dichu.

The barn becomes Padraig's first church. Two others, also of cruck-truss construction with daub-and-wattle sides, are eventually built nearby. Dichu's barn, though, is the Mother Church of Christianity in Ireland. Arguably, by the heavy irony of imperialism, it is also the Mother Church of the Catholic church throughout the English-speaking world.

That, though, is secret knowledge.

THE BRAID VALLEY. 450

On Fire for God

When Padraig the Briton pulled away from Strangford Lough, it was not in the chaotic form of his arrival, but in stately order. The world now was organized: it had a centre, and once that point had been located, everything could be done decently, and in order, as Saint Paul had commanded. Now Padraig was assisted by King Dichu and two dozen soldier-oarsmen detailed to his protection. And Padraig's small flotilla, which had straggled into the Lough as a refugee fleet, left as a tiny and orderly naval detachment.

As much as the waves and his own land-legs would let him, Padraig stood upright in the leading boat, much to the worry of Dichu's men who feared his being pitched into the sea. They had been told that he was an arch-druid, but that was while he was on land. Some druids don't float.

As the skin boats moved northward, Padraig scouted the land carefully. He was planning for future churches and, at the same time, he was trying to find the route he had been coerced along as a sixteen-year old bound for slavery. He easily recognized Islandmagee and there disembarked. A small-time local leader, reading quickly what King Dichu and a phalanx of his men implied, gave him honour. This was Colman, a grandson of the petty king Miliuc, Padraig's former master. With simple vengeful pleasure, Padraig demanded that a church be constructed at Colman's expense and this was immediately agreed. There in Kilkenan (now the townland of Kilcoan-More), the second church in Ireland was constructed.

King Miliuc was next on Padraig's list, and the meeting between the two would have been one for the ages. Miliuc, however, was bound by the honour code of an Irish king. Learning from his grandson Colman that his own former slave now was an arch-druid, with powers from a strange land and a retinue of acolytes and with the express backing of one of the kings of the Uliad, Miliuc had only two alternatives. One was to walk respectfully towards Padraig and thus unthrone himself: a king who could be looked in the eye by a former slave was no king. Meeting Padraig eye-to-eye, therefore, was a terminal humiliation, nothing less.

Miliuc took his other alternative. He assembled his slaves and servants in his mud-walled palace. He commanded them to collect all his moveable belongings and to bring them into the building. His cattle and sheep, so many as could be corralled quickly, were to be driven into the rath that surrounded Miliuc's palace. While this was going on, Miliuc took formal leave of his family, but gave none of them a gift to remember him by: one cannot remember a nobody and that was what he was planning to become. Finally, he ordered his slaves to stand rigidly at the inside walls of the palace and Miliuc mounted the pyre. The slaves bolted out of the rath like ants from a flooded ant hill. Miliuc's steward was obedient to the end, however, and tossed a burning brand onto the pile of Miliuc's worldly treasures.

By the time Padraig arrives, the palace is down to embers and there is a smell of burned fat, as when the scraps being rendered down for soap-making spill over into the fire. Dumbfounded, Padraig does not speak for almost three hours and then he declaims in the half-priestly, half-warrior mode that he will use so effectively in his conquest of Ireland. "God and only God can know why a man would destroy himself and his eternal life rather than believe." Padraig slowly makes a full circle of the rath. "And God knows that none of his sons shall ever sit on the throne he has left."

Chillingly, and with satisfaction, he adds. "His descendants shall be slaves forever and ever."

DOWNPATRICK AND ARMAGH. 451

Double Vision

"You can't be in two places at once." So pronounced King Dichu, and Padraig, who was in the habit of spending long hours in conversation with this, his first Irish convert, nodded to indicate that he had heard. The talks between the two men had begun as opportunities for Padraig to teach the doctrines of the Faith to the King, but had gradually become sessions where the King explained to Padraig the way the upper level – the kingly strata – of Irish life operated. If Ireland had been Europe, one could say that Dichu was teaching Padraig the rules of geopolitics.

"You can't be in two places at once except you're a bird," Padraig corrected Dichu.

"And that is what you will be?"

"If God wills."

Padraig had a swift intelligence where power was concerned, and one of the power problems in his mission field had only recently become clear. Emain Macha had been overrun. For centuries now it had not been an occupied habitation, but rather a holy site for the Uliad who used it four or five times a year for religious celebrations. Dichu, as a sub-king of the Uliad, had described in detail these ceremonies to

Padraig. And he had explained to him about the slow, but seemingly irresistible eastward shift of the Uí Neill, who came from some awful place in the under-world that was Connaught and had been inching their way, since time-out-of mind, across the west of Ulster. They had bagged a set of tribes near the Bann who now were known to everyone in Ireland (even themselves) as "the hostage-givers." That says all one needs to know about the Uí Neill: they took, others gave. Now that they had desolated Emain Macha, they were equal to the Uliad in control of Ulster: the Uliad were pushed east of the Bann and the Uí Neill ruled on the west. For Padraig all this had an obvious meaning: if he was to be more than a local preacher, he had to work out ways to be in two places at once.

That explains his search for a piece of high ground in the territory now firmly controlled by the Uí Neill. He found exactly the spot he wanted, not far from the desolated royal palace at Emain Macha: a hilltop near enough to the pagan site to be the perfect place to set a church and thereby to declare that a new and true god ruled the neighbourhood. Conversion of the Uí Neills to that god was Padraig's ultimate goal.

A man named Daire stood in his way. Rich, a chief of one of the larger clans of "hostage givers," he was adept at buying peace, and always at the lowest price possible. When Padraig asked for the hilltop, he offered a sunken meadow; when Padraig took the meadow, Daire sent his own horse to pasture upon it; when Padraig cured Daire of a fatal illness, he sent as repayment a bronze pot that held twelve litres, no small object, but hardly a fair trade for an aristocrat's life.

When Padraig took the bronze pot from Daire's retainers, he said "Gratias Agamus," meaning, "let us give thanks."

They thought he had said a druidical nonsense word, or worse, a curse – "Grazacham" is what they made out – and this was an insult. So Daire sent them back to demand return of the bronze pot. Padraig gave it up readily. All he said was "Gratias Agamus."

The coolness of Padraig unsettled the chieftain. He returned with the bowl, bearing it in his own hands. "Keep the bowl, for you are a most unnerving and steadfast man. But keep your 'Grazacham' too, if you will please."

Padraig bowed assent and smiled to himself.

Daire continued. "And the hill top, it is yours."

Thus began Armagh – the high field. Grazacham!

ULSTER. 452–460

Not a Hard Sell

Converting the Irish was not a difficult business, Padraig soon realized, as long as one made it through the first three minutes, and he always did, God be praised. Padraig, steadfast soldier that he was, nevertheless swithered through the first sixty breaths in the presence of any king or aristocrat whom he had not previously encountered. Those were the moments when the Celtic warrior aspect of the Irish personality was dominant and that is a very binary sort of mind. Either the eminence in question practises his backhand and sends one's head rolling, to the great amusement of his retainers, or he turns into an overbearing host, laying on the crackling pig and homebrew in military quantities and spends the next seventy-two hours exchanging stories of heroes and gods. That's when you hook him.

All right: Saint Padraig did not express it that way, but don't think that because Padraig was dyslexic and had a hard time remembering left from right (that made his blessings of his flock at times a bit dicey, if not downright heretical), don't, don't infer that he was soft in mind. Or in tactics. That he was able to make Christianity the leading religion in Ulster in less than a decade was no miracle; it wasn't even a hard sell. It all followed from Padraig's understanding of when and to whom to preach. Have you ever heard any tales – even in the most outlandish and credulous sources, the ones where Padraig is making snow on the plains of Meath – of Padraig actually preaching to a mass of the unwashed? No, Padraig had been a slave and he understood that in an aristocratic society influencing slaves and bondmen and even the average run of freemen was a total waste of time. Might as well preach to the nits and fleas.

Padraig, from Day One in Ireland went for the big fish: kings, usually, and the occasional big-time aristocrat or filthy rich looter-cum-warrior. The conversion of Ireland came from the top down and that's how Big Pat planned it. Catch one king today and you have a thousand converts tomorrow.

And Our Man had a gloveful of tactical ploys, all well thought out, all showing that he really did know who the Irish were. One of these was the commination. This was a rhetorical act he had memorized so that there was no need to have a translator help him. Padraig, as a young man on those god-forsaken, wind-swept hills of Antrim, had paid attention to how his captor kept his duddy we'en of a tribe in line: with a mixture of physical fear and potential shame. The big social control agent among the warriors and aristocrats was fear of being made a fool of, or being memorably ridiculed, and therefore being made permanently to bear shame. So, having figured that shame was the addiction that held the Irish aristocracy in thrall, Our Man gave them what they wanted: a great dose of shame and then release from it. Worked every time. Once a king had been converted, Padraig asked for permission to address the king's court and warriors. Permission gained, he laid into the assembly with the full 100 verbal lashes. He used the twenty-seventh chapter of Deuteronomy as his text (the man must have known most of the Bible by heart). He'd worked out a chant, where he'd go through a skein of shame-producing items:

– cursed is he that smiteth his neighbour secretly ...
– cursed is he that lieth with his neighbour's wife ...
– cursed is he that taketh reward to slay the innocent ...

About twenty of these he had and as he went through them, the assembled nobles and warriors would nod in agreement. After two or three times down the list in full froth, Our Man would make it clear that this was an antiphon, and he'd do both parts at first:

– cursed is he that curseth his father or mother ...
– Amen

And soon the local nobles were with him and were shouting "Amen" with blood-curdling force and some of the keener ones would wave their short swords in the air. It was a wonder. And then Big Pat would lead his mob round the corner, giving them a glorious rolling curse: "It is a fearful thing to fall into the hands of the living God, for he shall pour down rain upon sinners, snares, fire and brimstone, storm and tempest." He'd pause and actually smile. "This shall be their portion to drink."

There's nothing those ill-smelling heroes, princelings and petty nobles respected so much as a good curse and they were transfixed, like an audience at a really great drama. How would the shame of

God's thundering curse be ablated? Here Padraig would go all *sotto voce*. He'd tell them the story of King David and how even that great king and prophet was brought to his knees in his shame. How to avoid this humiliating end? Padraig here would quote large chunks of St. Paul – no, he would *become* St. Paul – and explain how shame was taken out of the world once-and-for all in the humiliation of Jesus-the-Christ. Paul's assertion – as big a theological mirror trick as ever anyone achieved – that the Cross was not a defeat but a victory – was tailor-made for a band of savage nobles who aspired to be noble savages. Physical suffering, humiliation, victory over death; now there was a god! A demanding one, no denying that, but one that could make shame go away.

Heaven only knows what they thought they were doing, becoming Christians, but that's always been the case, whatever the place, time, or religion. What counted is that Our Man – no, Our Great Man – could enter a dun filled with sceptical sword-wielders and leave it as a fortress of Believers. God love him, wasn't he a great wind-blown argosy of a man?

ROME. 455

Home Truths

Vandal hordes sack Rome.

Pope Leo I warns them that if this is repeated, they will acquire a bad name.

BANGOR. 460

St. Padraig Explains the Eucharist

"One of the wonders of the Almighty is that he can place his big ideas in the little heads of man." Padraig is explaining some very complex theology to a band of local aristocrats who already are Christian, but want to know what that means beyond issues of loyalty, something they understand very well indeed. This is not a memorized oration. Padraig is not using a translator, so he is being careful and is speaking slowly.

Padraig's Irish vocabulary is small, and he uses simple language: "bad," "good," "heavy," "light," "small, "big," "very much." To men whose culture honours verbal pyrotechnics – the Irish tribal priests and poets are able to create a rainbow of words and an arabesque of multiple meanings at a moment's notice – the plodding sincerity of the big British missionary is confirmation that he is not one of the usual run of word merchants.

"How does God come to be in the Mass?" Padraig asks rhetorically. "How can something so ... so ..." Padraig searches for the world "divine," and fails ..."so very very very good be found in the ordinary substance of everyday bread?" He looks around, relieved at getting that sentence behind him. "And how can such great goodness be passed on to little human beings?"

While studying at Auxerre, Padraig's mind had been swirled like a blowing leaf by the complexity of the theology of the Eucharist. He was pronounced orthodox and fit for ordination in large part because he had no notion of how to commit heterodoxy. Whatever the Church Fathers said was wisdom was such, but, oh, such complicated wisdom!

His respect for the fathomless working of the Almighty and his own humility before it save him now. Padraig reckons silently to himself that, dear-God-these-people-understand-you-as-well-as-I-do, and that immediately turns into a victorious formula. "I will tell you a tale you already know, but whose meaning was hidden from you."

His audience is surprised to hear him launch into a non-metrical, non-poetic, non-histrionic version of a tale they know by heart: How Fionn Mac Cumhail Acquired His Wisdom. In fact, everyone in the room knows half a dozen ways this story is told. But in all the mixes, one point is constant: Fionn acquires supernatural wisdom by biting on one of his fingers: ordinary item, extraordinary gift. "And that is the way the Mass works," Padraig concludes, "only better. And it works for every one. And every time."

Later, one of his retinue asks Padraig if it really was such a great idea to adapt pagan beliefs, rather than snuff them out?

Padraig sighs and allows himself the trace of a smile. "I imagine that God met these people before I did."

BATH. AUTUMN 461

The Cure and Removal of Internal Disorders

"It is not well."

"No."

"It is not well."

The judgement became a pass-phrase between the dispirited collection of abbots, bishops, and major clergy who styled themselves the bishops of Britain, by which they meant ever-smaller England. Assembling in Bath, most now agreed, was an error: too many reminders survived of the old Imperial days. They were meeting in synod to administer church discipline and to recommend to the Pope a new "bishop to Ireland." Trouble abounded and Grace seemed to have levanted.

"It is not well," a wrinkled abbot asserted.

"No."

"This death of Palladius." The reference was to Pope Celestine's appointee as the first "bishop to Ireland." Palladius had done what was required, but no more: in three decades, mostly spent in south Leinster, Palladius had wiped out all traces of Pelagianism among those few Christians who had picked up that dread disease. "As far as I know, he converted not a single Irishman."

"No." His companion, an Anchorite, was wondering if he would have to sentence himself to do penance for being so talkative.

"That's all right; he followed his instructions," the abbot proclaimed decisively. "But why did he have to be found with his catamite?"

"Yes?" The sin of coarse curiosity now definitely was on the Anchorite's list for self-flagellation.

"And the two of them dead there. Stacked together like two clay bowls. Most unseemly. Bad thing if the Irish savages hear of it."

"Will they?"

"No. The boy was from an Iberian port, a runaway. And, God be praised, immediately the verger wrapped the bodies in a single shroud and put them on board a vessel for the Continent. Palladius, stuffed with cloves and anointed with aromatics, will be given a burial worthy of a saint."

"And the young lad?"

"Been stuffed enough already, I should think. Wouldn't be surprised if he is buried at sea."

"It is not well," chanted the Anchorite.

The abbot made his fingertips into a row of church steeples and considered them for a time. "All would be better, had we a Holy Father." He referred to the recent death of Leo I, known deservedly by his memorialists as Leo the Great. He had indeed possessed leonine strength. In the face of a secular world going to fragments, Leo had strengthened the central church government and made it clear that, in the western church at least, Rome was supreme in matters of faith, doctrine, discipline. "He will, of course, be replaced. That we have no Father right now ... it is ..."

"... not well ..." concluded the Anchorite, who was almost breathless, not having done this much talking in years.

The abbot regarded his wheezing companion with distaste. "Our most pressing problem is Patricius the Briton. Either we call him home and punish him sharply, or we lose any respect with which we still may be regarded in Rome. Och, what trouble!"

With a voice that now was a weak wind in a narrow cave, the Anchorite started to utter his "It is not ..." but was interrupted. "Oh do be still," commanded the abbot, who turned and peremptorily marched away. "Never heard such a gibbering hermit in my life. Man could hardly keep quiet."

Padraig was not a passing vexation to the synod, but a deep difficulty. The consembled "bishops of Britain," as they liked to be known, saw Ireland as their own spiritual satrapy. They had been predisposed to recommend to His Holiness that Padraig be appointed "bishop to the Irish," and would have felt secure in their decision. Except, now there was no Holy Father and, worse, all those rumours about Padraig ...

They stemmed from Padraig's soul-friend, the budding theologian to whom Padraig had confessed his terrible secret, his time spent making clay bowls in the summer meadow of his youth. Just once. Just for an hour. Now, just when Padraig was about to be named as bishop, the soul-friend had felt his conscience force him to reveal Padraig's terrible sin. Curious, really, how a righteous man just has to denounce unrighteousness in others, but there it is. Nothing for it, certainly not silence and forgiveness. And to show his own worthiness, the soul-friend had offered to be Padraig's defender to the bishops. Truly: after having set him on fire, he volunteered to go and fetch a bit of water, to indicate that there were no hard feelings.

All this comes to Padraig in Ireland through solemn men bearing parchment communications secured in goatskin pouches, men who march in their short columns up and down hills like harvester ants on the way to a ripening carcass. He learns that he is both the prime candidate for Irish bishop and the subject of a not-yet-invented Inquisition. Padraig responds with a holy venting that makes the steam jets on Java-Sumatra seem mere vapours. Padraig writes a document, his *Confession* (anyone else would have called it "My Ferocious Defence"). It is one of the few items penned since, say, the year 100, that should be added to the Christian scriptures. The tone is that of St. Paul writing to the Galatians. ("Oh, foolish Galatians ..."), the bewilderment is that of Yeshua of Nazareth ("why have you forsaken me? ...") and the humility, genuine and unfeigned beneath the anger, is that of Padraig the Briton. He begins *I, Patrick, am a sinner. Yes, and the simplest of men; so lacking quality that I am despised by most humankind.* Never mind that he had read and memorized those sentiments earlier in his life. They are his and, equally, so is his holy rage. He has had a sacred trust betrayed by his soul-friend; he has spent his life ministering to people who, among other things, have, first, made him a slave, and later, on his return, taken him captive and forced him to ransom himself and his confreres; he has risked death convincing the children of the aristocracy – especially the virgin daughters of royalty – to take up vows of virginity for the sake of Christ; he has spent his life, like that of the great Paul, carrying the Gospel to the ends of the earth, here to the "Irish Gentiles," a people God loves in direct proportion to their fearsomeness. And Padraig will not, will not even contemplate abandoning the mission he has been given directly by the Holy Spirit. God will shield me in my mission from every evil, and if those evils include you, the bishops of Britain, may the Almighty have mercy on your souls.

There it is. The challenge of the god-roaring warrior to the men with waxen skin and pale pinched faces.

They consider gravely and, in the heel of the year 461, confirm Padraig's succession as the bishop to the Irish.

TARA. 462

No Cheap Tricks

Padraig was uncomfortable with cheap tricks, though he could do them when necessary. He had just made a rope burst into flame,

without being near it, and his audience was murmuring apprecia-
tively.

Cheap tricks demeaned the Almighty. Oh, surely, they were given
to Christ's missionaries to help them to bring the pagans to the light.
But there was something just a bit off about them; a little too much
like cheating.

Padraig's opposition in this confrontation being staged by Leary,
King of Tara, Meath, and environs, was a cadre of pagan priests. They
were good, but who cared? Padraig knew dozens of flashy tricks. So,
when the opposition was done with their counter-trick, Padraig took
a little of a water-looking liquid and made it change colour, three
times. Great intakes of breath for that one.

Padraig was accompanied by only five of his retainers – call them
presbyters, deacons, even bishops, the church had yet to work out its
full system of ranks – and it required considerable courage to march
into the heartland of the enemy and preach the Gospel. The north of
Ireland was now fairly well Christianized at the aristocratic level, but
the rich heartland of Ireland was thoroughly pagan.

Tara, as a sacred and a royal site was used only a few times a year. It
was dominated by an upright stone, called the Stone of Fál, mounted
on a plinth within the great enclosed mount that was Tara proper. King
Leary had arranged the competition between the champions of the old
gods and of the new as the centrepiece of Tara's main festival, Sam-
hain. This marked the beginning of winter, a big moment for any sun-
worshipping culture. Leary was not all that interested in religion, but
now that the kings of the Uí Neill and the Uliad were Christian, the religious question became a matter of honour: the gods of the Ulstermen
versus the gods of the Leinstermen. The fílí, the poets of Leinster, had
made a war-insult about Padraig and his small battalion:

Hatchet-head will come
From across the dumn-mouthed sea;
Dumn brain his coat,
Mulled wine his spine.
His altar faces east,
His people, dumn at feast,
Chant:
Amen, Amen, Amen.

Padraig hardly paid attention to his opponents' next ploy – making
it rain inside a copper bowl, or some such trivia – and tossed off his

own with unfeigned nonchalance; he made his shepherd's staff (he did not allow himself the pomposity of a bishop's crozier), rise from the ground and transport itself into his hand. He was niggled by the question, which never had hit him so hard previously: why is it right to use word-tricks, like retelling pagan stories and giving them Christlike meanings? and why does it feel wrong to do these bits of conjuring?

The answer came to him in a word, and indeed, one of the few Greek words he knew: *Logos*. In the beginning was the Word. Not the hand, not the eye, the Word. God was the Word and therefore all words were God's. So, aren't the scriptures telling me, Padraig, to use words. And only words? That conclusion, whatever its failings in logic, transformed Padraig's mission. For the remainder of his life he did no more conjuring.

Now, at Tara, he walked to the Stone of Fál and to the horror of his audience, whacked it hard, three times. A few of his audience drew their short swords and had to be restrained. "Enough of these baby games," Padraig announced. He did not know the Irish word for "childish."

His translator rose to help him. "We will show you that our god is the only voice you should listen to. We will show you that he can speak silently, through walls. His Word conquers all." Those were Padraig's words. His translator frowned. What was the master up to? Ah, it was gloriously simple! Padraig proposed that King Leary and his bodyguards should go outside and there the king would utter any two or three commands of his own choice. No rhymes, no formulae, just random commands. He would say these aloud to one wise man of the religion of Tara and to one of Patrick's men. The contest was this: each would record the royal words any way he wished and would bring them into the sacred enclosure silently and as quickly as he could. There either Padraig or his chief opponent would read out the royal words. A decisive test.

And no real contest, for the Almighty had given the Christians the alphabet and scraps of parchment and the pagans had only their straight lines carved on tiny sticks.

"Standfast," "Present Arms," "Stand Easy," were King Leary's three commands: he had never been much for imagination. But, when Padraig translated the writing from Latin to Irish (with more authority in his voice than he felt in his heart), Leary granted the

Christians' victory. Any king could see how useful it would be to have a method of quickly and silently sending words through bulwarks and walls. There was a weapon from the gods. Or God: Leary was not worried about the details.

Leary, king of Tara, died a year later, not having had time to employ this new weapon. Like Constantine the Great, Leary was baptized shortly before his death. Padraig performed the rite. It was convenient for him, since he now was engaged in the conversion of the midlands and the south of Ireland.

LOUGH DERG, COUNTY DONEGAL. EVE OF 1 AUGUST 483

St. Padraig's Purgatory

"*No*," said Padraig. "Walk on your knees."

He was correcting several pilgrims, part of a large contingent that circumambulated the shores of Station Island in Lough Derg. This was in preparation for a night-long prayer vigil in a depression in the middle of the island. Padraig had to call on his inner reserves to speak sternly to these pilgrims. They expected him to be as abrupt and arbitrary as any prince with a churl, so that was how he acted. In his heart, however, age had made him into a gentle old man, and he would have liked to have given the occasional word of sweet encouragement or even a comforting touch on the shoulder. But, he resisted: his mission required.

Padraig had initiated these annual pilgrimages a year or two after he had given up doing conjuring tricks. Once he had decided to use only the Word, he was committed to overcoming the enemy by turning the words of the pagans into the Word of Padraig's own god.

"The pagan priests were right to celebrate Lughnasa" Padraig had announced at the start of his homily to the pilgrims. "Only they knew not the right manner nor the real miracle of the day." Padraig knew full well the dangers that the Celtic mid-summer feast presented – what priest of his era did not know the horrors that had been inflicted at Ludgdunum on the feast of Lughnasa? Padraig was adopting the tactic developed independently by scores of Christian missionaries throughout Europe, one each refused to admit to any other: that it was easier to plaster over a big ugly wall than it was to tear it down.

In other words, repaint, rename, capture the tribal practices of the Huns, Burgundians, Vandals, Celts and eventually the barbarians would forget that there had ever been anything other than a Christian meaning to these things.

Here Padraig was coopting for Christian purposes one of the great Celtic festivals, a homage to the sun god: one of Lug's holy days. Each year, Padraig preached a homily to his pilgrims and it was passed on by word of mouth throughout the country. Now, in his twilight years, he told the story softly. Only those near him could actually hear his words, but they turned and mouthed them, as in a deaf-and-dumb show, so that the others could cue their own memory of words they had heard often before. Padraig's Irish, slow as always, was perfect for this silent amplification.

"... Yes, I say Lughnasa should always have been celebrated. It is a day that points us to wisdom." His gesture, pointing due-east, was not lost on the audience: the source of Lug's birth and the source of Christianity's birth were on the same line of origin. "The wisdom is that, like the sun, everything dies." Lughnasa was the first point in the year that the approaching death of the sun was easily conceivable; everyone nodded. "Thus, dear children, instead of celebrating wildly, we ought to already be in mourning. For we can never know for certain that the sun will rise again after it enters its winter's grave." At this point, Padraig was hitting the single greatest fear that ran through all the peoples of northern Europe – Celtic, Germanic, all of them. Their one exposed nerve, the one fear that made them all craven before any god that would serve as protector was this: that the sun would die. That it would not return, ever. The resurrection of the sun was the focus of myriad mid-winter rituals, and so far these had worked; yet, they could fail. Padraig, shrewdly, transported into high summer a set of anxieties that usually were kept at bay until late autumn.

"Dear children: the sun is bound to die each year. Dear children ..." – now he began a ritardando that continued, ever slower, ever more portentous until the end of the homily – "Dear children, some year *the sun will not rise again."*

A very long pause.

"Only our God knows when: but ..." His entire audience knew what came next; nevertheless, he went slower than ever ..." but that day shall come. And in that day, there shall be only one thing that shall rise from the dark, frozen, death-stalked earth." Padraig concluded the homily by himself mouthing the words silently, and these were passed along, a great silent communion service from one rank of pilgrim to another, a pebble in a flat-calm pond. His lips formed the mini-creed: "The only true resurrection is that of our saviour, God's only true son, Jesus Christ, without whom there is no shadow of life."

Silence, then satisfied that his words had been transported to the last reaches of his congregation, Padriag blessed himself and everyone followed his example.

The Lough Derg pilgrimage hangs suspended in time, a metonymn of the way Christianity invaded the Celtic culture of Ireland. It is not an unkind occurrence, merely revealing. By the thirteenth century, the pilgrimage season had extended in time from early June to mid August, blanketing and blurring Lughnasa. Three days were now required for the full ritual. The resurrection message was slowly transformed into a matter of personal post-death benefit: most pilgrims now believed that if one spent twenty-four hours in prayer in the declivity in the island, they would be spared having to spend any time in purgatory after their death.

DOWNPATRICK. MID-MARCH 493

The Three-Ox Team

Had it been a stage-play, the performance would have been difficult: the oxen would have had to take centre stage and heaven knows where that might have led. Three of them, spanned together not in the customary yoke, but rather joined by the tails with a straw rope that ran back to a stone boat, the long flat sections of wood that were used to drag large stones from meadows. This was a divining device.

In the season of Advent in the previous year, Padraig the Briton had retired to Sa'ul, where King Dichu had first permitted him to consecrate a church: a barn, really, and a small one at that. This was sweet country, one of the few places in this foreign land where Padraig felt at home. Padraig divided his hours between preparing his soul for the life-to-come and walking the serpentine shoreline of this, his first Irish parish. The tapping of the waves on the protected shores was the heartbeat of God, Padraig often thought, and he composed brief lines, in Latin or in the languge of the Britain of his childhood. Their rhythms and metrics were determined by God's heartbeat.

Now, pale-blue dead, body cleansed, white surplice covered by full episcopal canonicals, he was to make his last missionary journey. He lay on the stone boat and looked unblinkingly into the face of his God.

No one made a sound. Nor touched the oxen, nor flicked them with a twitch. The beasts stood docilely for several minutes, as if they were old soldiers respecting a dead comrade, and then they were off. The troika arrangement meant there was no common mind; two spanned oxen walk in a straight line or, at worse, a gentle curve; but three, joined aft, circle and haver, lurch foward and waver, a giant defective gyro, a lodestone spinnng on a string. And that was the intention.

St. Patrick (for such he became the moment he died), was a valuable property. Both the warriors of the east – the Uliad – and their relentlessly imperialist neighbours of middle Ulster – the Uí Neill – wanted St. Patrick's mortal remains to be buried within the bounds of their own territory. This was not Christian piety: they would have competed as hard for the remains of any magical figure. The two kingdoms had almost come to combat on this issue and were only diverted by an ingenious compromise. The body of St. Patrick would decide where it was to be buried to await the final resurrection of the dead.

If the whole business was loaded against those who wanted St. Patrick to be buried in Armagh, at least it gave them a slight chance of overcoming the argument that he should be buried where he had died, and also provided for surrender-with-honour if the divination device went against them.

Which it did. The beasts wandered in irregular patterns for several hours and eventually, tired and footsore, came to rest on a modest hill. There the saint was buried.

He had completed a very long journey.

WHO SPREADEST OUT THE HEAVENS, 493–1493

Immortality Has Many Guises

Padraig the Briton's bones are not yet bare but already he has become a demigod, and so he converts more Irishmen to the Gospel of Christ than when he was alive.

The spiritual feats ascribed to him are very close to those attributed to the pre-Christian Celtic heroes: discipline, strength, unusual powers, self-denial, loyalty.

At Armagh, still bidding to become the spiritual capital of Ireland, a web of rich stories is spun around him, making him the Christian version of Cu Chulainn. And some of the tales have a hard reality about them, originating, if not in the life of Padraig, in the lives of his time.

As when: Padraig's sister (ah, did he really have one?) became pregnant. It was from an illicit relationship, we are told by our Armagh story-spinners. Padraig learns of this as he drives his chariot (a Celtic warrior, obviously), towards a church. His sister comes out to confess her sins and kneels at a crossroads before him, trusting to his mercy and to the protection that kneeling on a cross will give her.

Padraig assesses the situation as only a saint, one of Christ's champions, could do.

"The chariot over her!" he cries and three times she is trampled by horses and tramlined by chariot wheels.

Like any true warrior, Padraig had understood the necessity of keeping his family in order.

As the web of tales becomes richer, they are spun into a saint's-life. Patrick the Saint becomes "*papa noster*," the spiritual father of the Irish people; his chroniclers, writing with the interest of Armagh in mind, transport him to that primatial see; and because the Irish Christians, even the pious, do not know their Bible very well, St. Patrick is converted into the Irish version of Moses (he lives 120 years and does tricks with serpents.) Padraig the Briton, who knew his Bible very well indeed, thought of himself as Saint Paul; he wasn't leading a Chosen People into a Promised Land, he was taking the Gospel to the Ends of the Earth where, as he said clearly in his own writings, there dwelled barbarians.

But what a gloriously strong-willed tribe they are! Many are converted by learning that while reaping one of his farms of land (ranking clerics, like aristocrats, were stewards of the earth), Padraig was taken by a strong thirst. And so too were the men who were working with him. Despite having a pitcher of thin buttermilk with him, Padraig decreed that everyone should keep working and not drink until the hour of vespers. "Thirst of the flesh amounts to a mere fico," he decrees.

One of the work gang, Colman by name, dies and enters history as Colman the Thirsty.

No one who hears this account in the sixth century faults Padraig, for he had disciplined himself and others, just as earlier he had kept discipline in his family. "There will be plenty of ale and food in the parish to which we are going someday," he tells his followers.

No professional rememberer – the class who spend days and nights lying on stones in windowless huts, rehearsing the genealogies, tales, and poetry they are delegated to preserve – nor any warrior, can fail to be impressed by Padraig who, as his cult widens, is rechiselled as a combination of druid and champion in preparation for battle. Here is what was being told daily in secular banquet hall and in priory refectory about Padraig's life: St. Patrick, our father, repeated by memory all 150 psalms each day and said another 200 formal prayers as well. He said mass, did baptisms, and said a short divine service to mark each of the seven major canonical hours. Between one canonical hour and another, St. Patrick made the sign of the cross on his face 100 times. At night, he stayed awake until well after the fourth watch. In the first watch, he genuflected 200 times and sang 100 psalms. He spent the second watch kneeling in cold water and the third in silent contemplation. In the fourth, he lay on the bare clay floor and rested with a stone for a pillow and a wet cloak over him, thus mortifying the flesh.

All this and he cured the sick and sometimes raised the dead.

That is the life of a saint.

TARA. 500

Genealogies

"And his father was ...?"

The prism rotates: memory both individual and collective, changes.

In increasingly-Christian Ireland, the professional rememberers are as important as ever, and the ones who do genealogies are extremely busy: the blood lines of all the royalty and aristocracy of Ireland have to be recalibrated.

"His father was Cu Chulainn, the champion warrior of the Uliad ..."

"Who was his father?"

"Lug of the Long Arm, the king of Tara, the supreme spear-thrower of all the men of war who ever lived."

"And his sire?"

"Gomer."

"His?" The pace of interrogation increases: the top of the chain is now in view.

"Japheth ... Noah, who walked with God ..." Back the recitation shoots, back for ten more generations until the apex is reached ... "Adam, whom God made."

"Yes: that is our royal line."

CENTRAL CHINA. 517

Another God, Another Mountain

The emperor Wu-Ti becomes a Buddhist. And, four decades later, the Japanese emperor Shotoko Taishi follows suit. Thus, in two skips of a stone, all the expansion of Christianity, from Paul through Patrick, is made to seem but a small bird, nesting in a tiny paper house.

DULEEK, COUNTY MEATH. 525

God's Viscous Humour

Do not look too closely over their shoulders: the men in dun and brown robes who stand at high desks and copy manuscripts. Do not read what they are copying. They are working in a makeshift scriptorium attached to a stone church (rare for its time) built by St. Kiernan, a disciple of St. Patrick.

It's better to squint, not to see the details, because they are actually copying detailed, petty, vengeful secular texts – law texts, to be precise.

These are the pioneers, the converts to Christianity, who take the alphabet – that faith's greatest gift to the Irish – and these pioneers drag the alphabet back to the Celtic world, where it preserves a mass of law and of story that Christianity, in its pure and imperial continental form, wishes to wipe out. Cultural resistance: the alphabet.

In a land that had almost as many social grades as it had large rivers, the social law was a grid, a legal morphology of dimensions that would have made Linnaeus blanch. Just remembering what the honour-price was for each level of person and each degree of personal injury was a full-time occupation for a professional rememberer, and there was scarcely a synapse left free to ferret out the principles of justice, equity, and power that underlay the code. Now, with the possibility of putting everything on vellum or parchment, so that it does not have to be remembered, everything changes. Legal arguments are no longer about who has the better memory of the pettifogging little precedent, but rather about recorded cases and, often, principles.

Once commentary becomes possible, law can make sense and can be about justice, not merely about power.

These, then, are the revolutionaries, bent close to their desks, converting tiny *aides memoire* and their own memorizings into permanent form. Their successors, often clerically trained, push a bit of scripture into the interstices of the law texts but, basically, they save, in Latin, Ireland's pre-Christian modes of adjudication, gentled now by comment, citation, precedent, principle.

This is the first step towards replacing beheading with begrudgery as the nation's preferred form of social control.

JAVA-SUMATRA, IRELAND. 535–536

Volcanoes

"How could God have been so drunk?" a Chinese official asked. This was years after a long, muffled explosion had been heard and, more ominously, felt on coastal China. Dutifully, civil servants had recorded the phenomenon and the consequences. Several decades were gone before the full effects of the divine emptying spread themselves over the earth and slowly dissipated.

The volcanoes in Java-Sumatra that had been teasing the earth for centuries, finally were prodded into peristalsis and then complete cloachal evacuation. Java and Sumatra were blown into two separate islands; the entire earth was ringed with ash; summer days became pale evenings, and harvests failed. Europe, Asia, the world, everywhere, the world was going wrong. In Europe the small islands of advanced agriculture – places that grew grains rather than pastured cattle or hunted game – were hurt most. As grain crops in the field failed, rodents sought out storage barns, and soon fecal rodent matter was a primary constituent of Europe's bread. Ireland, being mostly a land of cattle, did not at first suffer but then the plagues, bred of rodents, moved in and, eventually, even the grass stopped growing and famine followed.

In such troubled times, the embrace of Christianity by the Irish was accelerated. The old gods did not work, the new ones promised better. The spread of the cult of St. Patrick was an accurate litmus item, a marker of how fast the new religion was conquering the old. Scores of Christian missionaries now fanned out across the country, Irish in origin, but Semitic in message (Yahweh, after all, is not a Celtic god), and they and the volcano had one tangential point in common.

That is: Christianity within Irish society, like the primal eruption in the Indian ocean, released untold amounts of energy and with unpredictable effects.

As Ireland turned Christian, the social equivalent of tectonic plates – centuries and centuries of heavy restraints, codes of behaviour for each rank of society, inhibitions on social mobility, privileges defined by the threat of force, and all this relieved only by occasional outbursts of berserker violence – suddenly all this shifted. A vertical fissure was opened in this society, one equivalent to the venting of the earth's magma through a volcanic chimney. Ireland was not destroyed, but it was energized: immeasurably.

Now a man who in the pre-Christian world was not deemed worthy to hold the bridle of a warrior's horse could become a Christian, acquire knowledge of a superior god. And, if he is a person of real ability, he can enter a band of professional religious warriors, the priesthood that embraces not just a single slice of Ireland, but the entire known world; he can learn a secret language – church Latin – and he can become one of the group of the world's greatest sorcerers, for he can turn ordinary bread and wine into the physical body of the deity.

And beneath the new priestly class are all sorts of outriders: new posts for scribes and deacons and lay-brothers.

Irish society is not destroyed by this volcano, merely rearranged a bit and energized a lot. Goldsmiths acquire new and intriguing tasks: chalices and monstrances; scribes, learning the new trick of the alphabet turn quickly into artists; the spirals and interweavings first developed to worship the sun god now become ornaments on Bibles and books of religious discipline; some, who once would have become warriors, become ascetics and live their lives in constant battle with their own humanity; others become travellers-for-Christ, preaching their own new-found faith to distant tribes even they find fearsome.

God may have been drunk when he set these two volcanos atremble, or merely curious.

IONA, THE WESTERN COAST OF SCOTLAND. 563

Fellow Travellers

Two old friends are about to meet.

One of them, called Columba or sometimes Columb Cille, is a broad-backed, bull-necked man. He has none of the eyes-on-the-ground stoop of the contemplative ecclesiastic. Close kin to the king of the northern Uí Neill and a distant relative of the king of Dál Riada, a kingdom that includes bits of both Ulster and of Scotland, he has a manner that makes people move out of his way. Had he not become a Christian and entered the church, he probably would have been stealing herds of cattle from neighbouring tribes and covering himself in martial glory. Already he has founded monasteries at Kells, Swords, Durrow, and Derry. His great love is the art of manuscript illumination and, acting the role of patron as well as abbot, he fosters an art form that becomes the Irish equivalent of the Gothic cathedral.

Labouring up the hill to meet him (Columba always grabs the high ground; it's an instinct of the nobly-born) is a cleric, also of middle years, sage, but thin and weather-hardened like a strand of pemican. This is Brendan, abbot of Clonfert, and an explorer. Already he has founded monasteries in Wales and he has navigated around most of Scotland, including the isles. He walks with difficulty, not because he is halt or lame, but he simply does not like land. His legs are sea-legs.

The two abbots embrace and as they do so their respective entourages mingle. Columba has chosen to travel with twelve followers, out of respect for the original twelve tribes of Israel and the orignal number of Our Lord's disciples. Brendan has fourteen. He, being both accurate and prudent in all matters of calculation, chooses the full number of original Apostles, plus Paul and Barnabas, giving him fourteen. His long experience at sea has taught him always to bring spares.

For a fortnight the two men revel in each other's company: the release from the loneliness of leadership is a balm to each of them.

Finally, they must part. Columba takes Brendan once more to the spot where he will construct his first monastery on Iona. "My brother, do you really mean to tell me that you will build it on such a soft and gentle spot?" Brendan asks with mock credulity.

Columba permits himself a smile and gestures broadly in the direction of the distant shoreline. "And do you really mean to tell me that you will sail on such calm and restful seas?"

They embrace and do not meet again.

IONA. 565

Be Thou My Vision

"Blessed father, I require help."

Columba looks up from his meditation.

"I am done with the psalter," the monk explains. "It is but a paltry offering to our Lord. But it must be perfect of its kind."

Columba nods in agreement.

"And so, Blessed Father, I require another hand, another set of eyes, to go over it. There must be no errors in the Word."

Columba rises and moves to an arm's length of the brother and stares hard at him. The monk looks down. He would no more look his abbot directly in the eye than a foot-soldier would stare brazenly at a field marshal.

"Why do you bother our community unnecessarily?" the abbot demands. And then, gently, he adds: "Your copy, little brother, is perfect, save for one defect. In one place the letter 'i' is missing. That is your only error."

It was so; and Columba had not himself yet read the manuscript.

IONA. 567

Condign Punishment

Hard but fair.

A man from Ireland, a great and secret sinner, tries to land on Iona to do penance.

His sins are too heinous for that. Columba meets him on the shore. The sinner kneels, riven with remorse and miserable, on the shingle beach. He promises to accept whatever penance the abbot decrees.

"You must never return to Ireland," Columba states and then falls silent. He is considering which of the other laws of divine penance is here relevant.

The man is gulty of having killed his brother and of having had sexual relations with his own mother.

After reflection, Columba decides: "And you must spend twelve years among the British."

THE NORTH ATLANTIC, THE FAROE ISLANDS AND
WESTWARD. 568–570

Those in Peril On the Deep

Considering that Columba had the gift of prophecy, it would have been decent of him to tell Brendan about the whale. It's not that the Sage of Iona had no experience with these beasts. One of his most famous prophecies in fact concerned a whale.

In that instance, one of the *peregrini* – the self-exiled Irish holy men who spent their entire lives moving from one harsh and alien world to another, collecting pain for the glory of their God – told Columba that he would be going from Iona to the island of Tiree, there to increase the mortification of his body and soul. "Little brother, be careful today," Columba counselled. "Do not take the direct route by open sea; skip from island to island, the long way."

"Why so, Reverend Father?"

"On the open sea you will meet a monster of the deep and you may lose your life."

"As you say, Reverend Father." The younger man had no fear of the deep, so he took the direct path. And as Columba had said, when he was in the open water between Iona and Tiree a mountain of a whale came toward him and the wave the beast made almost swamped the boat.

St. Brendan's whale was bigger. It lifted his boat, an ox-hide covered vessel of a dozen metres in length and three in width, slowly out of the water. Brendan and the fourteen men with him prayed fervently. At first they thought that the sea floor was rising beneath them, but then they realized they were on the back of Leviathan. The mammoth beast could have flipped them into the air with one twist of its tree-thick backbone, but it did not. Instead, it was satisfied to take them for a gentle ride before submerging and disappearing without a ripple.

Brendan's boat, built without a metal pin or nail, was less a machine than an organic entity. Bents for the main frame were lashed together by horsehide thongs and to them was lashed a longitudinal lattice of white ash. The vessel smelled like the inside of an abattoir, because it was covered entirely in ox-hides that had been tanned in oak bark and then saturated in grease. A big boat for its time, but wonderfully flexible; it changed shape over time as the sea moulded it through constantly-changing torsion. Brendan and his devout crew kept good records and as they skittered downwind from the Faroes to Iceland to Greenland to Newfoundland, and then back home on the Gulf current, they give us wholly innocent descriptions of phenomena we now assess with less wonder and fear: giant crystals, icebergs in sparkling pack-ice; pods of killer-whales hunting in lethal packs; undersea volcanic eruptions. Their eyes saw new parts of this earth with the same naiveté that some men and women will eventually experience new solar systems.

Brendan returns to his home abbey in Clonfert. The year is 570 and he is content to die, for he knows that further and greater wonders await him in his next life. The world has not changed in the time that he has been on his travels, though shortly before his death, Muhammed, the Prophet, is born.

SKELLIG MICHAEL. 588

Monastic Foundation

Finian's heart held the giddiness that the mad and the righteous know well. He and two oarsmen approached the impossible island at a pace that promised an unpleasant death. This is not really an island, he thought, it is a spike on the spine of the largest beast God has ever placed in the deep. The spike rose to a height of six-score human beings and not a flat spot nor patch of soil could be seen. The foam erupting from the waves that were compressed into the island's narrow and angular bays was the steam from the great beast's lungs. Finian urged his men to pull harder.

The courage of Finian should surprise no one. The massive eruption of energy caused within Ireland by Christianity meant that many a hero went on a seemingly impossible quest. Some of these saintly warriors maintained a blithe spirit founded on a limitless faith in their god. Others, dour sorts, put all their energies into their own immiseration, while worrying constantly about eternity.

Consider the first. Most of the truly blithe spirits, the *peregrini* – so-called because they engaged in *peregrinatio pro Dei amore*, that is, "wandering for the love of God" – left no record. They abandoned home and went some place to live and pray on their own. Sometimes two or three travelled together. A common practice was to get into a coracle, take a week's food, and start rowing. When out of sight of land, the pilgrims just drifted, trusting to the Almighty's guiding hand. If they struck land, they wandered until something told them to bide a while. These were the truly blithe of soul and they almost never returned to Ireland; their ghostlike existence comes to us in passing references by European annalists.

Others engaged in longer and purposive voyages – the Faroes and Iceland were common stops; but even these cordially navigated voyages human ability to control circumstances exceeded. Each required faith that the vessel was being held in the palm of the almighty God. For every voyage that is recorded, hundreds of unmarked journeys were made.

Finian's first landing on Skellig Michael was entirely in the hands of God. His coracle was driven by the sea to the sole spot on the island where landing is possible. Finian never had any doubts that he would be safe. With the tiny boat dragged above the wave-line, he thanked God for the brutal steepness of the climb to the summit that awaited him. He was grateful to have travelled barefoot.

What is sublimely easy for some becomes a lifelong challenge to others, one that in honour cannot be declined. How else does one understand the daily toleration of cold, sleep deprivation, physical labour and strict punishments that characterize the early Irish monasteries? Why would any band of heroes hang on by their fingernails to Skellig Michael, subsisting on birds' eggs, the occasional fish, a few vegetables grown in the artificial soil the holy men build from seaweed, and all the time pounded by waves that have run for 5,000 miles and by winds that scream every moment of day and night?

Finian was right: at the base of every early Irish monastery was a great monster that must daily be conquered.

IONA. SUMMER 597

Final Rights

He is no longer a prepossessing figure. His once-broad body is now a husk and his eyes, which had discerned secret sins in the mere posture of a penitent, are now watery and he views the world through a constantly shifting astigmatic glaze. Yet, Columba is still the abbot and he can still see the future with remarkable clarity.

No great foresight is required for him to know that he soon will die: his body tells him that. Nor is any great discipline required for him to make a thorough inventory of his faults and retail them to the soul-friend who, effectively, is his confessor. Such discipline he has maintained all his adult life.

His monks, who know that he is dying, maintain a tactful distance as Columba performs on quaking legs his final peregrination. They see his actions, but have no idea what act he is performing in his heart. First, Columba circles as large a portion of Iona as he can muster in the long summer evening. He moves entirely in a rightward circle. He is prophesying, but only to himself. He sees in sharp-coloured detail a manuscript that has not yet been begun. It will be his greatest legacy for the glory of God. And he is given a glimpse of immensely rich chalices, reliquaria, monstrances, that other devotes will produce for the church. His vision resembles St. Brendan's when he encountered the sea of ice crystals. So much glory.

The succeeding day Columba makes the same circle, this time moving only to his left. Smell, as much as vision, informs him and he recognizes the sour odour of meadow grass that has been cut but not properly saved. This is not the putrefaction of corruption, but the sourness of sloth. Columba is proud that his Irish church is run by abbots, not by bishops, and that royal families frequently support monasteries as their own. That is as it should be. And the Irish monks' mode of tonsure, shaving the front half of the head, not some silly circle as on the Continent, is good; as is the Irish maintaining the ancient date of Easter, not the new one sent from Rome. All that is fine, manly, and noble. The sour odour that unsettles him as he makes his ever-leftward rogation emanates from the south. It arises from a steaming font in Canterbury where, at the order of Pope Gregory the Great, a legate has recently arrived. He will begin an effort to tame the Irish church. Columba can sense all too well that ultimately the mission of Augustine of Canterbury will be successful.

That evening Columba tells his soul-friend that he has decided to take one more day's journey and then he will rest on God's bosom.

The next morning, the soul-friend watches from a respectful distance as Columba begins his final walk. The abbot's face becomes radiant, a prism reflecting an unshadowed sunrise.

He turns right and views that future once more.

THE IRISH MONASTIC NETWORK. 600–764

The Invention of Intellectual Property

A man with an amiable face and an unlit cigar looks at the Irish economy of the seventh and eighth centuries. He does so from a distance of roughly thirteen centuries and at a high level of abstraction. Although the titles of his major works (for instance his world-changing, *A Theory of the Consumption Function*) make one expect a drudge of soul-deadening quality, in fact he is a connoisseur of the unusual, the ironic, and of the quirks that put real tests to good theories. He leans back in his big swivel chair and laughs delightedly. Observing human behaviour, past or present, is a joy. Scant wonder he is on his way to the Nobel Prize.

What he loves about Christian Ireland in the seventh and eighth centuries is its massive self-deception and its tough economic reality. The social (and especially) the religious leaders of the time talked and wrote of an Irish missionary movement and they probably believed that they were acting selflessly, coherently, and pure. And centuries of Irish ecclesistical historians have concurred. But personal motives and collective effect are two different things.

The economist stands up and hooks his thumbs in his waistcoat as he reflects on a reality far different from a "missionary movement" (any ad exec would be proud of that label, he says) and instead he looks at the pattern of products. The monastery of Clonmacnoise declares itself a refugee centre for intellectuals from fratricidal Gaul and, like Princeton University in the 1940s, obtains front-edge scholarship in turn for providing not much more than room and board. And it gives the Irish church insider-status in Gaul: one of the refugees that Clonmacnoise feeds goes back to be King Dagobert, the Merovingian monarch. The economist loves this: it prefigures the mid-twentieth-century admissions policy of the London School of Economics with African tribal leaders.

From the far south of Ireland a "Celtic thalassocracy" links Ireland to Brittany, to parts of the island we now call "England," and to Visigoth Spain. Secular trade goods are important – pottery, wine and the like are imported, but more importantly, the Irish trade for tricks: for technology, some of it secular, some of it religious. They learn tricks from the Visigoths of ceramic manufacture that soon turn up in the brooches of petty kings and on the surface of holy vessels. From the oppressed Coptic Christans, now under Persian rule and later under Arab domination, they pick up tricks of marking cadencings in everyday psalters, and new patterns and inks for the illumination of major manuscripts.

What the Irish are engaged in is the first documented case outside the Classical World of a trade in intellectual property. How can an economist not love it? In return for intellectual property and, of course, luxury goods like wine, the Irish pay in used ideas and in manpower. That's the great thing about ideas: used ones frequently aren't worth any less than unused, so the Irish, having collected a fair body of Latin literature, both Christian and pagan, flog it back to the Europeans, the Gepids, the Franks, and even the Vandals (now African) who treat it like tomorrow's news.

And the part of the system that the economist likes best – in his graduate seminar he compares the situation to modern oil company executives, trading their knowledge for land and resources – are the missionaries. It's amazing: Irish monasteries from this period run from the coast of Scotland all the way into Ukraine. "Monasteries ...? Sure, call them that, but we're really seeing the first branch plants of an intellectual economy! Abbots? ... Call them regional managers ... Missionaries? ... call them contact-men, rain-makers, sales managers." All this makes the economist very happy. "These guys are so good that a total screwup can just keep on moving, getting fired from one job and bribed in large bundles to take another. All they have to do is convince the locals that they need the intellectual property the missionaries bring with them in their suitcase. The best of the lot is St. Columbanus who never got on with anybody for a day in his life. He was run out of at least four jobs – meaning got kicked out of four countries – for badmouthing the local managers. And yet he ends up with one of northern Italy's best-stocked monasteries, and one of Europe's great libraries being purpose-built for him!"

When explaining this to his students, the economist likes to summarize with a practical lesson: "what the Irish were doing in the seventh century is what we'll all be doing someday. Mark my words."

Then, in deference to a newly-introduced ruling at the University of Chicago, he steps outside before lighting a Cohiba.

RATHLIN ISLAND, COUNTY ANTRIM. 795

Howls in the Night

The ram stood alertly on the crest of a ridge. He was not the sort of beast present-day farmers value. Rangey, with long ropey wool, he could move very quickly. A stranger to the species might have taken him for an off-sort of a deer, save that his rack curved backwards rather than forwards as do antlers. Despite his angular body, he was a prize of his sort, for the Irish, like all Europeans of the time, valued fat-tailed sheep, animals that concentrated all their stored energy in their haunches and especially in their tails: sweet fat.

To stand proudly outlined on a ridge was not the action of a cunning animal. Although he could see most of the dells around him and catch part of the slopes to the beach, he was presenting himself as the most obvious target on the island. Having surveyed his kingdom, he walked along a ridge and he was followed by a train of ewes and lambs that had been grazing beneath the brow of the hill. He and his flock moved, figures of prosperity, secure in habit, for they had never been attacked by wolves or feral dogs.

The Vikings, hunters in packs, sacked Rathlin Island in 795, the first venture in a spasmodic, thirty-year feeding-frenzy. The Irish monasteries, visible and tempting, sat on the skyline like fat rams, and once the Vikings had sacked the softest targets, monasteries and churches, they turned to the secular world. The Irish aristocracy were tough targets, but they had not the same hard edge the Vikings possessed. Aside from their personal treasure, the Irish aristocrats, and especially their children, were valuable as slaves, and the Vikings sent them all over Europe. They made fine house-slaves.

For safety, the monumental illuminated work from Iona that St. Columba had seen only in his mind's eye, was brought back from Iona to the monastery at Kells and it escaped the wolves.

Ireland never recovered the blend of secular and religious force it manifested in the sixth through eighth centuries, but at least when the second wave of wolf packs started to hunt – call the year 913, 914, it matters not – the Irish were no longer fatted sheep. Much more resistance was exhibited though, in the way of a tribal society, some Irish septs joined the Vikings in order to settle old scores with their local rivals. Still, the Vikings were forced to settle down and to defend specific pieces of territory, rather than to run and bay at will any place in the land. The symbolic date for their defeat is 1014, the victory by Brian Boru, and though the victory was real enough, the entire encounter with the Viking empire was chaotic and destructive beyond obvious pattern.

Any killing field possesses its strange artifacts and its own caustic comments on the violence that litters it. Two here. While it is no great irony that the Vikings taught the Irish how to construct towns – Dublin, Wexford, Waterford, Cork, Limerick – the key loan-word from early Scandinavian that the Irish take directly into their vocabulary is one for something they previously did not have and well could have used: the word is "window."

And, indirectly, the Irish Annals reveal the first lineaments of a forever-pattern in the national history: a perplexing and abiding ambiguity about the Irish and empires.

During the period of the Viking invasions, the Irish Annals of course continue to record the results of the on-going local wars between one Irish tribe and another, the wallpaper of Irish social life of the time. Curiously, before the Vikings arrive, local battles are won and lost, but there is little emphasis on the number of the enemy captured: cattle-capturing is what counts. Then, human captives become a matter of considerable importance. This lasts until the Vikings are finally out of the main frame of the picture in the eleventh century, and reports of captives virtually cease.

Why is this so telling? Most probably because the Irish victors were taking the Irish losers and selling them as slaves. Through the trading network of the Scandinavian wolf pack, with whom several Irish kings happily do business, many an Irish youth found himself spending his life in servitude to strangers, sometimes as far east as the Russias.

TARA. 1000

Millennium Fever

The end of the first millennium draws near and to the Irish it's worth a big shrug. The Irish Annals are absolutely clear about this: no general excitement, no worries about the earth's imminent end, no apocalyptic visions of plague and endtime wars. And why should there be? The Irish priesthood is not attracted to the more lurid parts of the Bible – the Apocalypse of Saint John and the Book of Daniel – and consequently the laity do not think in psychotic vocabulary of apocalypse. Besides, the "Anno Domini" calendar is a mystery to most people and even those who know about it aren't sure where the starting date is supposed to be: the virginal conception of Jesus-the-Christ, his birth, or his return from Egypt in the Christian Gospels' version of the Return from the Exodus by the Chosen People. In fact, no one is sure where in the circling calendar, an old year ends and a new one begins. Most of the clergy favour mid-March, but that moves around century by century, like any other fashion. Some Irish prelates prefer 1 February for that is the holy day of St. Brigid, patroness of Ireland: she who died in 524 and was placed in the same grave as St. Patrick. That's an attractive day, for a combination of the New Year and a major saint's celebration blankets its being the day on which the pre-Christan Irish celebrated the start of spring.

If anybody in Ireland should be celebrating the dawn of a new world, it is the Vikings, but they have no way of knowing that, from their colony in Greenland, Leif Ericsson and Thorfinn Karlsefni are now engaged in exploring Newfoundland.

What the Irish are concerned about is a long way ahead: the year our present Christian calendar calls 1096. Generations away, that year is one they dread, for they believe it may be the end of Time.

TIPPERARY, NEAR THE ROCK OF CASHEL. 1096

Real Worries

Already it is mid-year and lots bad has happened. Men of learning worry, kings swither, queens turn melancholy. They are all Christians now in their positive assertions (creeds are carefully memorized and regularly intoned); yet in their worries, their deepest fears, these people live in fear of a pit that was built long before Jesus was a twinkle in the eye of the Holy Spirit. At moments of these primordial fears, Holy Mother Church becomes invisible and all they can see is the blackness that was dug for them when Emain Macha and Tara, Cashel and Knowth were shrines to the sun god and were his apanage.

The year on the Christian calendar is 1096, but it might as well have no number at all. What makes this the year of potential disaster is that the two cycles that count most to peoples whose god is the sun are in unison. Every 532 years the solar cycle and its handmaiden, the lunar cycle, complete their circular dance in the sky. The church, at the behest of Rome-based astronomers, now uses a 532-year cycle to calculate Easter, and two such dances – a total of 1,064 years – have been completed in the years since the birth of the blessed Christ child. Unwittingly, the church authorities have married the new faith to ancient Celtic fears.

The earth has spoken of late. Two years previously, extreme weather killed thousands. One year later, a great plague struck and it still seeps forth, sucking down to the underworld whomever it will. These are not accidents; they are portents.

Of course any system of reckoning, especially prophecies of disaster, needs a starting point and here the Christian veneer on the ancient Celtic sun-worship is thin indeed. For a starting point, the Irish sages (who are these melders of pagan and Christian myths?) take the death of John-the-Baptizer. That occurred, they calculate, in what we could call the year 32, so the clock has now ticked down almost to zero.

Why start there? Because the Bible is really incomplete, the sages tell us and, in fact, John-the-Baptizer was beheaded by an Irishman, thus joining a crime against embryonic Christianity (John after all was Jesus's cousin as well as his fore-teller), with the immutable calibrations of sun worship. That the Irishman was named MugRoth and that he had been trained by Simon Magus (of the biblical Book of Acts), are neither decorators' details nor graffito: Irenaeus of Lugdunum, who knew equally the perfidiousness of Christian heresy and of Celtic prodigality, named Simon Magus as the source of all Christian heresy. So an apocalypse dictated by the sun god's complex cycle is wedded to something very close to a collective original sin, killing the chief forerunner of Our Lord.

There the Christian veneer ends, and one hears instead of psalms and scripture, prophecies such as:

"Two forces shall meet."

"Armies?"

"No, forces bigger than everyday nature. The one will be a rolling wheel that comes from the southeast and crushes everything in its way."

"Will it not stop?"

"Only when it comes up against the Great Standing Stone."

"And the other force?"

"It is the Broom of the North, and it will be invisible, yet sweep destruction a league wide, until ..."

"Until ..."

"It comes to rest against the Great Standing Stone."

There is nothing here of the Christian nightmare, the Four Horsemen of the Apocalypse; this is indigenous. The Great Standing Stone is the traditional place of the annual confirmation of the kings of Munster. The very well-founded fears of the Munster tribes of being ravaged by their enemies from Leinster and from Ulster have been projected into a nation-wide nightmare.

Even here, the details count. One persuasive characteristic of the otherwise-invisible Broom of the North is that it can be seen only by a limited few: drunkards who observe it from the backdoors of ale houses.

And, within the boundaries of this solar-lunar year of terror is born one of destiny's children. To the best of his considerable abilities he will cleanse the Celtic from the soul of Irish Christianity; he will burn more churches than the Vikings; he will be declared a Saint.

RAROTONGA, THE "COOK ISLANDS." C.1100

Serious Travellers

European travellers are beginning to understand how to get in and out of the maritime boundaries of their continent with some predictability and safety. They are at the start of the European era of serious travel.

On the other side of the globe – a concept that is still beyond even the best European navigators – a group of much more accomplished travellers is about to complete their culture's four millennia of intermittent journeying. This has been a reticulation of myriad voyages that has seen the Polynesians course roughly one-eighth of the earth's surface, much of it uncharted maritime regions broken by small islands that barely peek above the horizon.

Now they are setting off from Rarotonga in the central South Pacific, sailing towards the southwest, where they know a large empty island is situated. Finding New Zealand is a major feat, but one that such voyagers take for granted. In fact, like most good things, New Zealand is discovered more than once, so later generations argue endlessly about whose ancestors arrived first.

In their optimism and in their practicality the Maori (for such they become) are markedly different from Europeans of the same era. This is made clear by the fact that they bring along women.

They name the new territory, "the land of the long white cloud," although one particularly clairvoyant tohunga suggests that it should be called "the land of the single vowel."

THE BARONY OF ELIOGARTY, COUNTY TIPPERARY. 1111

The Long Fingernails of the Empress Helena

"Is it real?"

"As real as God himself."

So the Papal legate assures Murtagh O'Brien, king of Limerick and one of the more credible pretenders to the role of High King of Ireland. O'Brien is happy to accept any leverage available in his struggle with other claimants. Prestige as much as military power is the currency that buys the high kingship.

"And you leave it in my trust?"

"Fully. Without reservation. For His Holiness knows of your unfeigned loyalty to him."

The Legate is completing a deal with O'Brien. The Holy Father is in trouble and needs allies. The Salian emperors of the Germanies and beyond are forcing His Holiness to drop the Vatican's claims to most of the papal fiefs and secular revenues. Meanwhile, the Holy Father is trying to get rid of the right of the Holy Roman Emperor and other kings to invest with the staff of office and ring of fealty those bishops and abbots who reside in the jurisdiction of the secular rulers. The Pope does not have much going for him. In 1111, Henry V takes Paschal II and his cardinals captive and forces a deeply humiliating surrender.

Paschal now is planning to repudiate his concessions to the Emperor and he has sent a gift to the leading Irish king of the day, a piece of wood roughly one inch long and half an inch wide. It is presented to Murtagh O'Brien in a case carved of cedar from Lebanon.

"This come from the True Cross as discovered by St. Helena herself."

Thus reassured, O'Brien kneels and accepts it.

He and his family turn it into the currency of prestige. Two generations later, Donogh Carbragh O'Brien endows a Cistercian monastery with lands equal to those of an English earldom. Successive abbots are given the title of Earls of the Holy Cross and later they sit in the Irish parliament as barons of the realm. The abbey that the Cistercians and the O'Briens build for the Holy Cross is situated near a lough and on summer evenings its massive bell tower stretches in reflection across the lake, a cobbled road to glory.

Pilgrims from all over Ireland come to revere the piece of the True Cross and part of their ritual is to run their hands along the Holy Parge that covers the inside walls of the abbey. The O'Briens had added granules of gold ore to the blue clay and cow dung with which the interior walls were plastered and, if occasionally the walls sparkled, the O'Briens' reputation sparkled even more.

The Future Lies Over the Mountains

Saint-to-be Bernard presides over the funeral mass for Malachy of Armagh. His fellow Cistercians are somewhat surprised to hear Bernard assert in his homily: *Malachy outshines even St. Patrick.*

Comparing the recently-dead to a major saint borders on bad form. But what really surprises the mourners is that when the Eucharist is celebrated Bernard does not chant the appropriate post-communion prayer for a dead bishop. Instead, he moves confidently into the prayer for a living one.

Bernard is not a fool. He may be cockle-eyed and stooped, yet he knows exactly what he is doing. This is the first step to the canonisation of Malachy.

Later, Bernard explains, "Our Malachy was born in Ireland of a barbarous tribe; there he was brought up and educated. Yet he betrayed not a mite of his rude origin, any more than a fish of the sea preserves a salty savour." To the obvious approval of his audience, he continues: "How delightful it is that crude barbarism should have given us so worthy a man ..."

Malachy won Bernard of Clairvaux's kudos, *Malachy outshines even St. Patrick*, by having a vision of the mountains and, crucially, of the power that ultimately lay beyond them. Born in Armagh in the star-crossed year 1096, he somehow understood from youth that the church of St. Patrick had to be tamed. By twenty-five – five years before the usual age – he is ordained, and he soon is abbot of Bangor, and then bishop of Connor. Like any Irish prelate, he plays his part in the gang-land politics of secular Ireland, but his soul and his ambition burn with a single recognition: that the Irish church – at least if it was to be *his* Irish church – must have a Trinity of Cleansing. The remaining Celtic liturgies must be replaced by Roman ones; the Irish church, organized around monasteries, had to be recast on Roman lines, in territorial dioceses; and church offices should no longer be tied to individual Irish families.

Where this Trinity was revealed to Malachy is unknown, but he arouses local opposition and has to flee south, to the monastery of Lismore. There he makes an ally of the king of Desmond and using secular forces – soldiers, fire, sword – he convinces many of the southern clergy to adopt Roman practice. And when the archbishop of Armagh dies, that man's wife passes on to Malachy the staff of office. Staff fine: but it takes several years and a good deal of bloodshed before Malachy is able to securely hold Armagh, the primatial see.

The course of Malachy's reforms will never be traced, for the Irish Annals have big missing sections in this period. People alive at the time would have said, just chart the burned churches.

Malachy's sense of self, his divine mission, his supersession of all who had come before him, is shown most clearly in the ostentatious humility of his middle years: he is retiring, he says, to become bishop of Down and to pray. He sets the boundaries of the diocese as they had been in St. Patrick's time. There, at Sa'ul, he founds a monastery, not of daub and wattle as St. Patrick had done, but of stone.

This process is a conquest of the Irish church by a foreign imperium and, as in most cases of successful imperialism, it is effected
less by force from without than by collaboration from within. *Malachy outshines* ...

Malachy in 1190 becomes the first Irish saint to be proclaimed by
the Pope: all the previous ones have been venerated for their holiness,
beatified by generations of mourners, and ratified as saints by the af-
firmation of the faithful.

Malachy outshines even St. Patrick.

ROME. 1156

Merely a Footnote

Nicholas Breakspear, an Anglo-Norman cleric of ability, has become
Pope and he remembers his debts.

John of Salisbury, as secretary to the Archbishop of Canterbury, remembers what his branch of the church is owed.

Ireland.

So, as Adrian IV, Breakspear pays his debts and issues a bull giving
Ireland to the Anglo-Norman king, Henry II. The ostensible reason is
that the Irish church is not reforming itself quickly enough and must
therefore be brought under Norman secular control.

But why involve the whole country? Privately, Breakspear understands that breaking Irish society is the only way to bring the church
into line; it's one thing to sort out the clergy, but the laity needed
breaking if they are to do God's will.

In public, the Pope suggests that, actually, he found Henry II a
most trustworthy sort of fellow.

WEXFORD HARBOUR. APRIL 1172

A Matter of Perspective

Irish kings, such as Diarmaid Mac Carthy and Domnall Mor Ua
Brian, may have hated each other, but they agreed on one thing: that,
though the Normans had the most enormous arses anyone had ever

seen, even these gluttonous mountains became mere specks on a distant horizon. It's all a matter of perspective.

As two score Irish petty kings and a greater number of Norman marcher-lords watch Henry II's ship sail away, they don't talk to each other, for they have mutually incompatible views of what is happening in their uncomfortably shared world.

And King Henry, what did he think was going on? ... Ah, the poor man. The niggling matter of the murder of Thomas, Archbishop of Canterbury, had kept him busy for almost a year with various spiritual purges and he still wasn't quite off the hook when he sailed for home in the autumn of 1171. And he had a lot more on his mind: several of the ham-fisted lords he'd sent to deal with the Irish were threatening to set up independent kingdoms of their own; the blessed Vatican wanted him to be sure the Irish bishops and clergy really were embracing reforms Malachy had terrified them into accepting; and the Irish kings themselves needed a lesson in feudal manners. Henry was not happy.

To Henry's great surprise everything in Ireland had gone well: although he'd have known it was too well if he had a reflective cell in his head. The Irish bishops hold a synod and affirm everything Rome wants; the Irish kings fall over themselves bending the knee to the Norman king and in taking all sorts of oaths of fealty; and the Norman lords give their word as big-time thugs that they won't colour the map outside the prescribed lines.

So Henry sails away victorious and almost virtuous: the virtue comes upon his arrival back in France, where the papal legate, happy with the royal progress, gives Henry absolution for the unfortunate disposal of Thomas À Becket.

After the Irish kings and chiefs watch the wide royal arse disappear, they walk away together, careful to keep their eyes on the remaining Normans. Their collective air is well-that's-done-with-now, so let's-get-on-with-it. The Irish had sung the feudal choruses for Henry II, but they have no sense that their oaths are binding once he leaves their shores, much less that they hold for his successors as well.

For their part, the Anglo-Norman lords are relieved that they can get on with grabbing as much of the country as possible. They too watch the royal vessel disappear with pleasure.

And thus, for two-and-a-half centuries, the Norman (later English) empire in Ireland will spin, a big, slightly off-centre wheel in a gerbil cage. The Norman aggressors will have a good 100 years or so, but the Irish will recover and hack away at their *soi-disant* conquerors, with sword and, increasingly, culture. The Crown will concern itself with Ireland for a bit, but with the Bruce Invasion of 1315–18 and the Black Death and the ensuing War of One Hundred Years, Ireland offers little benefit and great costs.

The only reason that Ireland and the English empire would engage each other closely would be if the shape of the world changed.

A predictor of that potential change occurs as early as 1207 when the tiny seaside hamlet of Liverpool in England is granted a royal charter. In the distant future, Liverpool will at times contain more persons of Irish birth than are found in most Irish cities and counties.

GENOA. WINTER 1299

Sermons from the Far Horizon

The Genoese winter is mild, especially for someone who has travelled through howling winds that pile banks of snow as high as a man's waist. Still, comfortable as he is, the prisoner orders more wood and piles it into the open hearth. He is dictating his memoirs and he finds that although disremembering is easily done when he is chilled, remembering requires a touch of warming. In his mid-forties, the prisoner is hard as a walnut and almost as dark. His warders, though not men of sensibility, notice that he "has the smell of a Tartar" about him. They wonder why a Venetian sea captain is being given such privilege. After all, he had captained a ship, part of a fleet that lost a big battle between Genoa and Venice.

The governor of the gaol understands, however; his orders are clear. Marco Polo is to be treated as if he is royalty: captive royalty, but royalty nonetheless. So, Marco is permitted his unusual clothing – a headress from the court of Kublai Khan and a robe from Shangdu – and he is given a suite of rooms usually occupied by the governor himself. Marco sips a hot drink that the warders are unacquainted with and, with long cogitative pauses, dictates his rememberings to a fellow prisoner: a scribe who had grown not-quite-sufficiently-skillful at duplicating the signatures of men of substance.

The result is the most-read book of travel ever written and one that literally changed the shape of the world. China, Persia, Sumatra (ah, that fateful volcano), south India, Uzbekistan, all become geometric shapes that have relationships to each other. And the idea inevitably arises: if Asia can be reached by travelling to the east, perhaps it can be found by going west. It's an uncomfortable idea to religious authorities and to many secular rulers (who don't want their world rearranged) but ambitious and imaginative merchants, sea captains, venturers, consider it obsessively and yearn for the freedom to try for this main chance.

Only by discerning the right tone and register for each audience had Marco Polo survived twenty-five years in alien lands. His long years in the service of Kublai Khan, as agent and diplomat, and his time as governor of the Chinese city of Yangchow, had left him one of the shrewdest men on the face of the earth. And that is why, though he remembered facts accurately and reported them clearly, he adopted in his memoirs a disingenous simplicity that is misleading. He pretends to be slightly disorganized, he uses the fairy-tale language of one with a naive vision when, in fact, he is gimlet-eyed.

So a story that he slips into his memoir is a parable told so amiably that the reader embraces it before realizing that he is holding a knife: a threat. Here, in compressed form is what Marco dictates to his forger-amanuensis.

"One of the four great Tartar brothers, Alau by name, took, in the year of our Lord 1255 the Muslim city of Baudic. Though the Caliph of the city had one hundred thousand infantry and cavalry, Alau won an easy victory, mostly by cunning, but also by courage. When he inspected the city, Alau found a treasure tower, filled with more gold, gems and silver than he had ever seen before.

"Naturally Alau asks the Caliph why he has gathered such treasure, but yet had not used it ... 'why did you not use it to incite your men? Did you not know that I, a great lord, was coming against you? Why didst you not give it to your knights and soldiers to defend you and your city?'"

"The Caliph said nothing in reply and Alau concluded, 'Ah, Caliph, you truly love your treasures with great greed, so I will give you them to eat.'" Then he had the Caliph taken to his treasure tower and left there without food or drink. He died four days later."

Marco Polo added his own gloss to this tale: "And certainly it would have been better for the Caliph to have given his treasure to his soldiers and loyal subjects for the defense of his dominion than to be put to death with all his people and forever dispossessed."

Or: Christian kings, Holy Roman Emperors, Popes and Cardinals ... let us, the explorers, the merchants, the mercenaries share in the treasure. Or become, as did the Caliph, the desiccated ruler of a misplaced realm.

DUBLIN. 1359

Class Work

Pay attention!

Forget about the Protestants and all that.

Even in the seventeenth and eighteenth centuries they did not chance their hand at anything that hadn't been tried by the Anglo-Normans well before the Reformation.

It's all a matter of class.

Otherwise, why, in 1359 in the areas still held by the the Dublin authorities (read: running-dog lackeys of London) were Irishmen excluded from all secular and religious offices? That's a settler class protecting its privilege. And why, in 1341 had Irishmen in most areas outside the Pale been excluded from church offices? And how did it come about that the Irish were excluded from apprenticeships in the towns of Ireland? (And you thought the Protestants were nasty in keeping eighteenth-century Catholics from becoming lawyers.) So how does it come to be that a popular Anglo-Norman preacher of Holy Mother church is able to counsel his flock that killing an Irishman is no more a sin than killing a dog? Do you really have trouble understanding how the Cistercians (introduced into Ireland by the Saintly Malachy) considered the Irish as sub-human?: bestial was their word. And why were all save a few sycophantic Irishmen excluded from the Common Law, much to their disadvantage?: it's hard to sue someone in a court that says you don't exist.

Right. Go to it. Highest marx for the best class work.

And neatness counts.

PORTUGAL. 1483

Signs

When the rheumatic former-weaver bowed himself out of the court of King John II of Portugal, no one in Ireland should have noticed. Just another dreamer at another royal court. And no one in Ireland can reasonably have been expected to have read the other signs – the ones that revealed that the shapes of the heavens and the earth, the visible and the invisible world, were slowly changing. Ireland was moving, imperceptibly but ineluctably, away from the edge of the world and into the transport lanes, where the heavy goods vessels of empires ran.

At approximately the same time John of Portugal was refusing the proposal put foward by the Genoese weaver Cristoforo Colombo to find Asia by sailing westward, in the nasty little town of Eisleben in the Germanies, a copper-miner had his son christened "Martin," and promised him to the church, if such was God's will.

Meanwhile, one of the church's most devoted servants, a hollow-cheeked ascetic Spanish monk, was taking charge of a particularly difficult local problem. Tomas de Torquemada had just been appointed by Pope Sixtus IV as inquisitor-general for Castile.

ROME. 4 MAY 1493

A New World Revealed

Pope Alexander VI does something even the pagan gods had never sucessfully attempted: he divides a world in half. His bull "Inter Cetera Divina" splits the New World between Spain and Portugal. Alexander has had to act quickly. He has not been on the papal throne for a full year, and he has been caught unprepared by the tidal wave issuing from the bow of Cristoforo Colombo's flagship.

Colombo made it back to his home port on 15 March 1493, and the news of his slightly-mistaken discovery of India (or, the Indies, as he called them) rolled through the ports and courts of Europe faster than the phases of the moon. It was hard to be skeptical of someone who has found "Cuba," which he announced is the home of Kublai Khan, a major character in Marco Polo's travel book.

At this point, the Irish aristocracy, Celtic and Anglo-Norman alike, should have shuddered. The long-distance sailing-ship, whose slow evolution has made possible Colombo's epic journey, may have developed in tiny, unremarkable stages but its effect is clear. The papal decree confirms that Ireland is near the matrix, not the edge, of a world of competing empires. Perhaps it is true that in preparation for his venture, Colombo visited Ireland and picked up as much navigational lore as possible: this makes sense, given the long Irish experience of world-edge navigation. And perhaps, as tradition also holds, a gentleman-navigator named Patrick Maguire was especially helpful, and in fact accompanied Colombo on the first voyage. Perhaps, but the hard gavel of history hits the judge's bench with a sharp rap: whatever the traditions concerning the relations of the Irish and the discovery of the New World, the immediate result is to move Ireland close, much too close, to England. No longer can the London authorities let Hibernia moulder, a back alley reserved for the fighting of feral cats. Now any continental power can easily reach Ireland and thus the country, in London's view, is no longer a back alley – rather, it is a conduit for those who wish to push a knife into England's back. Ireland becomes part of a syllogism, the conclusion of which is obvious: it will indeed have to be regulated and, soon, conquered.

Ireland's new world a-borning, will have harder rules than previously; not that the Normans' were mawkish. The world of secular empires will be intersected ever-more frequently by the empires of the righteous. The signing of Colombo's letters patent by Isabella and Ferdinand of Spain on 17 April 1492 was a world-shaping bill-of-exchange, one that came due in 1493.

And another bill-of-exchange, this one of 31 March 1492, came due at the same time: Isabella and Ferdinand tapered down the Spanish Inquisition. Probably about 2,000 Jews and Jewish Christians had been burned alive and several times that number tortured, pillaged bankrupted, all with the highest legality. Now, from the council chamber of the Alhambra Palace, the Spanish monarchs gave the remaining Jews, 200,000 perhaps, four months to leave the country. (Columbus's log records that his ship had trouble gaining sailing space, so congested was the harbour with ships taking Jews to destinations of safety.) Then, for those who chose to remain, the Inquisitors played out their cruel end game, the one that, in other cultural terms, the Irish would themselves experience. The final move was this: either a Jew stayed and was executed, or the person declared himself to be a Christian, for which he would be tortured, because the Inquisition believed that a sincere Jewish conversion was a contradiction-in-terms.

From this prelude to serious empire-building, the small peoples on the world's sidelines could take a simple lesson: in the broad new world, we will be damned, either way.

NEW WORLDS SEDUCE THE OLD
1488–1610

It Pays to Advertize

The few remaining teeth of Bartholomeu Dias de Novaes hurt. Most of them had been pulled on his long voyage back from the Indian Ocean. Bad diet, bad teeth, the hazards of being an adventuring navigator. Dias rehearsed the words he would use at the royal court to detail his discoveries. The trick was to find words that did not make saliva shoot between the gaps in his front teeth like the emissions of one of the ornamental fountains of which Juan II was so fond. After much reflection, Dias chose the words he would employ to describe the stone pillar – he called it a royal monument – at the point where he had sought land after first encountering what he believed was the Indian Ocean. The miles of rolling sand dunes, tan the colour of a new saddle, green fringe of forest in the background, blue, almost indigo sea rolling in, white foam bubbling – that was the monument, but the words to tell of that glory could not be expressed in Dias's cruelly limited vocabulary. He could, however, tell of casting anchor, leaving the Point, and of being blown far south, farther than any European had been. And when he had worked his way back, he found that he had run east and had cleared the tip of Africa. Satisfied, but a little unsettled by the fright of his crew, he returned home. He told the king that he proposed to name the far spike of Africa "Cape Tempestuous." The monarch congratulated him on finding the road to India, and added firmly, "We shall call that point, the Cape of Good Hope."

Mystery Cruise

As a final reference point before sailing into the north Atlantic, John Cabot used certain constant landmarks of Ireland. Such practice was one of the cabalistic secrets passed by word of mouth from explorer to navigator to explorer in the same way the secrets of alchemy were handed around. Occasionally scraps of map passed from hand to hand. This was Cabot's second voyage westward, and he was well financed and highly optimistic: the English king himself paid for fitting and manning one of the five boats. Cabot claimed he would now find the short, clear path to the riches of Asia.

He believed: at least some of the time. Less than a year earlier he had returned from his first trip and announced to the Bristol merchants who had financed him that he had discovered the island of Brazil and the kingdom of the Grand Khan. This he did in his highly formal, book-learned vocabulary and strong Venetian-Genoese accent. He received a lifetime pension from Henry VII and went about in silk clothing, affecting the airs he believed to be the meed of his titular rank of admiral.

Actually, Cabot had only seen some of the most barren portions of North America: Cape Breton and Newfoundland-Labrador: rocky shores, unpredictable tidal conditions, thin, malnourished trees colonizing barren rock for a tenuous survival and icebergs, blue, present even in high summer. Nobody could prosper in this land, Cabot concluded. But he saw the fish, enough cod to feed Europe decade after decade. And he thought he saw a clear route to Asia.

Four of his five ships returned from Cabot's royal venture, one being broken by a great storm that forced it to find shelter in Ireland. Cabot returned and died soon thereafter. Neither he nor his crew wrote anything down or talked for the record. Maps of the world, though, changed their character and we can guess he made it as far south as the Carolinas, still a long way from Asia.

CALICUT, INDIA. MAY 1498

Tough School: Quick Learning

Degrado: that was the term for men such as Joao Nunes, a convicted felon sentenced to serve on the Portugese exploration vessels. The necessity of forced service by the refuse of Portugese society says a good deal about how most experienced seafarers viewed these voyages. Themselves: they'd go only at sword point.

Intriguing, however, and much less obvious is Nunes's behaviour. He has been deputized by his captain, Vasco da Gama, to go ashore as head of a small contingent who are the first Europeans to set foot on the continent of India by way of the sea route around the tip of Africa. Nunes is taken to two leading local merchants who interrogate him sharply. When asked who his master is, he replies, "The King of Portugal." And what did the vessels of the Portugese king seek? "Christians and spices," Nunes asserts.

This employment of an expendable intermediary indicates Vasco da Gama's having learned a good deal since leaving Portugal, and much of it tactical as well as geographical. He discovered, as he popped along the east coast of Africa – moving like a skipped stone from Mozambique to Mombasa to Malini to Mogadishu – that cocksure Europeans in heavy armour were not the only explorers on the planet. Muslim traders had centuries of experience and were well established in Africa and India already.

A lesson in humility, one made sharper by discovering that the Muslims fought among themselves and that getting caught in any of their local battles was perilous: these weren't naked savages, devoid of military sting. Thus, at every port of call, da Gamma's captains moor their ships at the farthest possible point from shore and they wait for the local Muslim merchants to come out to meet them. The captains rarely go on shore. They do not seek out the Africans, with whom the Muslims are trading. The European innocents who had left Portugal had become hardened, suspicious, and aware of their own fragility.

Only at Calicut does da Gama himself make a determined effort to get past the screen of Muslim merchants. Several times he meets the King of Calicut who tells him that there are Christians in his domain. Though da Gama had been told to look for degenerate Christians by his royal superiors, he was not heartened, for he had already learned too much on this voyage.

When the local king asks da Gama if he and his men would prefer to sleep among Christians or among the followers of Islam, he states in a voice made loud by fear, "We will sleep apart, in a resting place of our own."

COUNTY WATERFORD. 1517–1519

Making the Best of It

It rains; the man is happy.
It shines; the man is happy.
It is daytime; the man is happy.
It is night; he smiles while he dreams.
Strange, and all the more so because he has been marooned, or so most Englishmen would call it.

John Rastell, a pioneer publisher and a courageous one, is a hero of the opening of the human mind. So wide is his view, so optimistic his outlook, that he does not mind two years of virtually forced residence in Ireland.

Like many less amiable optimists, he had intended to trade with one of the New Worlds; he would have liked to establish a Utopia, to use a word not yet quite fashionable. However the small flotilla of three ships that he participates in doesn't head for any New World. One of the boats, under the leadership of the purser, takes up piracy and the others try to limit the damage and bring the feral beast back to reality, if not legality. The flotilla goes ashore in the south of Ireland and at the residence of Thomas Dryvam, gentleman, John Rastell and the purser have a furious argument. The purser damns Rastell to hell and leaves him to the benevolence of the Irish gentry.

The English publisher finds the Irish an admirable race and accepts their hospitality with pleasure. Happy as a lark, he spends his time thinking about perfect societies, rewriting English legal codes, and pondering the nature of Purgatory. After spending two full years in Ireland, Rastell returns to England full of energy. Instead of engaging in mere Good Works, he publishes good works, which last longer.

Among his best items are those of his dear friend and brother-in-law, Sir Thomas More.

Only an event so unjust as the martyrdom of More in 1535 could dent the heaven-sent carapace of optimism that protected Rastell for most of his years. Cruelly, he was not permitted to recover from More's death. His spirit was broken by the Crown, which took exception both to Rastell's being a Royal debtor and to his being an excessive freethinker on matters affecting Crown revenues (particularly tithes). Consigned to prison, he spends his final year receiving miserable dollops of public charity and learning the nature of misery. He dies in 1536, remembering Waterford.

THE EAST COAST OF SOUTH AMERICA. JUNE 1520

And There Were Giants in the Earth

The Bible was right! Yes, yes! The young Venetian nobleman Ser Antonio Francesco Pagafetta was delighted and he made careful notes.

That was his stock in trade: though he passed as a dandy of the Spanish court who only happened to have taken berth on a voyage that, if successful, would be the first circumnavigation of the globe, he was in fact a spy. The Doge of Venice wanted his notes so that Venetian traders could stay abreast of Spain's trade in the eastern islands, the source of the world's spice trade.

So Pagafetta started writing almost the moment he saw the giant. He was naked, about seven feet, six inches tall, and he came along the beach like a capering ship's mast. He laughed, danced, threw sand all over himself. He was friendly enough, for when the Spanish crewmen danced and pirouetted in response to his cavorting, he smiled and was willing to accept food and drink. This was a specimen, Pagafetta realized, of the giants referred to in the book of Genesis (6:4), the descendants of the matings of angels and the children of man.

This first New World creature was frightened when one of the crewmen gave him a mirror; his own visage terrified him. Later, the voyagers encountered extended families of these massive people, and for a while they got along with them well enough. Then the captain ordered that two of the males be grabbed and put on board ship so they could be taken to the Spanish court. Both escaped and from then onwards the Europeans were harassed by a people who could throw stones the size of cannonballs.

Pagafetta was no romancer. About six decades later, Francis Drake encountered the same people and he set their height at seven feet four inches. One of this first lot finally was taken on board ship and he spent the remainder of his life aching with scurvy, his joints swollen, his body covered with sores.

What the Old World actually did to these rare specimens of the New, is a mystery only in detail: the giants were driven extinct and all that was left is a memorial to them in a language that is not theirs: Patagonia, "land of the Big Feet."

MACTAN, THE PHILIPPINES. 27 APRIL 1521

Success

The man with the short sword knows why he is fighting: to save his life, of course. It's what he's been doing in one form or another for the past fifteen years and he is good at it.

But why here? – where the sand turns each step into a torment; where the sun converts the demi-armour into a metal oven; and why are he and a handful of loyal sailors covering the flight of the rest of his crew as they race for the water's edge?

When Ferdinand Magellan took sixty crew men, few with any military training, to deal with 3,000 Filipino warriors, undeniably he was foolish, but he was a European after all, and the enemy weren't. His opponents were headed by a chief, Cilapulapu, who had the temerity to refuse to turn Christian.

Magellan is no zealot for Holy Mother Church, but only recently he has had a religious experience: the intoxicating power that comes of being a successful missionary. On a neighbouring island, most of the leading Filipino chiefs knelt before Magellan and his priests. The Europeans sat on a dais, Magellan on a throne, an altar in front of him. Not only do the paramount chiefs accept baptism, but thousands, perhaps tens of thousands, of ordinary folk flood in to be converted. In the course of fourteen days, so many are baptized that the priests' arms become rubbery, and eventually the holy men are too exhausted to baptize any more. Magellan calculates that he has made more Christians than has the entire Inquisition.

Why then is he fighting on a beach, parrying spear with sword? Ultimately, because most of Europe lacks sufficient fodder to feed its cattle over winter. Each autumn, huge herds of cattle have to be killed in central and northern Europe. Salt and its rare cousin, pepper, are the meat's preservative. Pepper mostly comes from the Spice Islands (part of present day Indonesia). Wondrous other products come from these islands as well: quinine, dyes, cloves, nutmeg, cinnamon, and aromatic spices that are used in foods, medicines, perfumes. But it is pepper that counts.

Magellan has already wandered more than 20,000 miles in his attempt to reach the Spice Islands by sailing westward. He had been to the Philippines previously, in an eastward journey so, technically, he has sailed around the world.

A success.

But he is about to die at water's edge where his men have left him stranded in their own flight. One sword, no boat; one death, no escape. And he dies because no successful European could suffer the insolence of an alien people denying Europe's own God.

WARTBURG CASTLE, SAXONY. 1521

New Geographies. Martin Luther Prepares to Translate the Scriptures

I wouldst not have a Jew in sight:
　They, the stiff-necked, hard and
　proud, who cannot hear how we their
　Scriptures parse; nor see their Holy Land
　as nought but shroud.

I wouldst not Rome were atop the globe,
　Directing the world as if she rode,
　by right above the princes: for from
　Cardinals, rises a Pope. No grace,
　no wisdom, dear God, no hope.

I wouldst have God upon my knee, a
　Bible opened Lord by thee. And
　princes jewelled, kneeling 'round, when
　Thy Thunder: thou makest without a
　sound.

THE AVALON PENINSULA, NEWFOUNDLAND. 1525

Firefly Colonies

John Rastell, bubbling optimist that he was, published in 1525 a volume, the *Interlude of the Four Elements*, that suggests the settlement of Newfoundland. Rastell was an original thinker, surely, but here he was just reading the news. Ireland and Newfoundland long had been linked. Ever since Saint Brendan, the Irish navigators knew of it as a half-remembered, half-imagined place. Irish boats were fishing off of Newfoundland well before Cabot's voyages. They reaped the profits, he got the glory. It was no accident that Rastell's volume appeared after his two-year stay in Waterford, where knowledge of the Newfoundland passage and of the Grand Banks fishing grounds were passed by word of mouth from one mariner to another.

Rastell was a buoyant romantic, but the basis for settling Newfoundland was prosaic, indeed industrial.

Cod.

Miles and miles of seemingly inexhaustible Cod. Europe of the period required protein the way Europe of today requires petroleum: in large, dependable gulps. Well before Cabot's time, mariners from Waterford and Wexford were fishing the Newfoundland grounds. It was something they could do in small boats. They needed one larger vessel to carry them across the sea in, say, February or March, and then they fished from shore in dinghies. They gutted and dried their catch on shore and at the end of summer they loaded the ships, left their huts and windbreaks behind, and were freighted home.

Their fires flickered out, then were relit the next year.

DUBLIN. 1535

Boil's Law

As the world becomes bigger, Ireland becomes more cramped.

Two clauses. Not logically related. But humanly.

As the earth changes from flat to round and its fastnesses from void and formless to rich and habitable, the Irish, as much as anyone else, grab their chances and explore, strip-mine, colonize.

As the English more and more move into Ireland, the Irish have more and more reason to make off for less painful lands.

The boil that cannot be lanced, the seepage of Ireland's able and aggressive souls into new worlds, lasts for more than four centuries. Diaspora, slow at first, gathering momentum decade by decade. So debilitating does the diaspora appear that four centuries later, frightened observers will ask, are the homeland-Irish destined to vanish from the face of the earth?

1535 is the date of enactment for this Boil's Law. The earls of Kildare, uncrowned kings of Dublin and the Pale, crash. Silken Thomas, Lord Offally, the son of the ninth earl of Kildare mistakenly concludes that his father, who is in London, has been executed. Silken Thomas leads a revolt that effectively ends in March 1535, when at Maynooth Castle, his soldiers, having surrendered, are given the pardon-of-Maynooth, by a hard English general; they are slaughtered. Thereafter, Dublin and its outlying regions are run directly from London. Henry VIII sees to that. Silken Thomas and five of the Fitzgerald uncles are executed in London in 1537, the sort of thorough administration King Henry finds satisfactory.

The first true conquest of Ireland by England is in train. And if it takes somewhat more than a century-and-a-half to complete, its duration is remarkable.

The direct rule of Ireland that is introduced in 1535 lasts until 1921 in most of Ireland and, apparently, forever in portions of Ulster.

And, the small fissure between Protestant and Catholic that is introduced at the same moment, widens, and will last longer than forever, God knows.

LONDON. 4 DECEMBER 1536

The Start of an English Family

Antonio Bruschetto, wealthy Italian merchant, receives his letters of denization. He is now English. He has bet his life and that of his family and his future heirs on the revolution that is occurring in damp and backward England under Henry VIII. Few continentals would have agreed with him, but Bruschetto sees the future.

Bruschetto is no Marco Polo. He is in plump middle age, and has no wish for adventure: he's betting on a winner. For several years, Bruschetto has been a conduit for business conducted in Italy by English aristocrats and large merchants. He is trustworthy, gives value for money, and keeps his mouth shut, so each year his reputation grows. His clients include Sir Thomas Gresham, founder of the Royal Exchange, and William Cecil who, as Lord Burghley, eventually becomes Elizabeth I's chief minister and, not incidentally, the man who makes sure that Mary, Queen of Scots, says goodbye to her head.

So Bruschetto moves to London, takes both a town and a country house and controls his continental web from England. He has agents in the major European capitals and, on really important matters, still travels himself to negotiate important contracts for his principals.

Bruschetto's great strength is that he is as unremarkable, indeed, as boring, as he is percipient: the perfect configuration for a life as a confidential agent.

He has five sons and three daughters, and he makes sure that they become properly English. He says he has no higher ambition than that.

ST. MALO, FRANCE. APRIL 1540

Translators Wanted

Acquiring a proper noble savage is crucial to any empire builder. They come in all sizes and social grades: this Jacques Cartier knew and he was always on the look-out for useful examples.

He had obtained one of his best in Brazil in the 1520s when he was a freelance master pilot, working for French merchants. She was a lovely brown thing and taught him how New World agriculture worked, and useful words, such as "maize." In turn, Cartier taught her submission and serviceable French. It speaks well for his power of command that his wife not only accepted this mistress into her society, but stood godmother to her as well.

Much later, after two voyages deep into North America, searching for the Northwest Passage to Asia on behalf of his royal master, Cartier considers that perhaps the path to riches may be shorter, if only he can find the right sort of guide. Thus, despite its being Lent, he feasts a tall, smooth-faced Irishman, Garret Fitzgerald. He is a younger son of the ninth earl of Kildare and the brother of the ill-fated rebel, Silken Thomas.

As they perambulate the town, the short, intense Cartier and the languid Irishman make a strange pair. Cartier wears a white lace stock, velvet flop and of course his sword. Fitzgerald has on a "saffronyd shurtt" (according to an English spy who watches them closely), and is bare-headed, "lyke one of the wylld Irish." The two men are accompanied, as if by chaperones, by a Fitzgerald family priest and by another Fitzgerald kinsman, even taller than Garret.

Cartier assiduously courts his Irish visitor, even though he discounts the young man's claim to have a right to be king of Ireland.

Nevertheless, Fitzgerald's Irish patrimony is large enough to envy, royal pretenses or not. And, while Fitzgerald wants his family's Irish lands back, Cartier can see the attraction of gaining an Irish seigneurie a few day's sailing from France. Cartier hopes that the Irishman will be as useful to him as were the two Amerindian men he kidnapped on his first voyage to "Kanata." That was one of the words they taught him, and if it meant "settlement" in Iroquois, who was to say that a broader usage might not someday be justified?

Fitzgerald, however, departs from St. Malo with the intention of asking the French court for aid; but then he changes his mind and goes to Rome to try to unsettle diplomatic relations between England and France.

Less than a year later, Cartier is sent by his royal master to create a colony far up the St. Lawrence River. His colonists are mostly felons who have to be chained together and escorted onto Cartier's vessels. Cartier spends the worst winter of his life, freezing among criminals: failing, truly miserably.

MOUNT ST. MICHAEL PRISON, FRANCE. 1547

Cutting a Covenant

"Should we escape?"

The other prisoners consult the wise man. He is only in his mid-thirties, but his full beard and deep-set eyes give him an air that, in other contexts, would be rabbinic.

"Is it right for us to escape?" The prisoners press in on the sage. They are natives of St. Andrews, Scotland. They have been captured by French raiders and are being kept as galley-prisoners of the French navy.

"Will not our escape subject our remaining brethren to more severe treatment?" they ask the wise man.

Surprisingly, the rabbinic figure asks no questions of them. He silently considers and then, as if coming down from a mountain, gives judgement. Yes, they are permitted to escape. It is a moral act, so long as it is done "without the blood of any being shed or spilt." He continues. "It is well to seek our own freedom, but to shed any man's blood for freedom, to that I will never consent."

John Knox remains behind and spends a painful year-and-half in the French galleys. During that time, he turns inward, and his rabbinic inclinations deepen. He comes to slice moral principles very supplely and very thin. Everything that he considers he frames in the terms that Jehovah (so he calls him) gave to the Chosen People: *if* one does such-and-such, *then* this or that will happen. This is not aberrant. Originally a Catholic priest, Knox is now Protestant, of the sort who talks of Jesus but who models his behaviour and practices on the Patriarchs of the Old Testament. He knows Hebrew well and understands that the if-then thinking of Patriarchal morality is one of the forms of the human covenant with God. In Hebrew, one "cuts a covenant" with the Almighty.

Eventually, John Knox so saturates Scottish religious and political thought with the covenantal outlook that for centuries after his death Scots and Ulster-Scots think of themselves as peoples of the Covenant: and that they have cut a special deal with God and thus with each other.

ST. MALO, FRANCE. JANUARY 1551

Any Master Will Do

The hunched, phlegm-ejecting old man never stopped selling. Sebastian Cabot, son of the great John Cabot, has spent his life trying to be half as courageous and twice as successful as his father. He has captained some voyages to new worlds and has claimed to have made several more. Now he is trying to interest Jacques Cartier, still alert, intense, and aggressive at age sixty, in a project in the Amazon. Cartier has credibility with the French government, so Cabot sells hard.

The Amazon, Cabot says, could become a beneficial land, a verdant breadbasket for all of Europe. That is the kind of thing any royal patron had to hear eventually, since all Christian monarchs had a duty to act as stewards of the earth. The real point, Cabot explains in a confidential tone, is that somewhere in the Amazon lies Eldorado. This is not a loose term. It means "the gilded one," and originated in the 1530s when the Spanish seized an Amerindian who was covered in gold dust. "El Dorado" grows and now explorers believe that there is a chief who dresses entirely in gold. Quickly "Eldorado" comes to mean land of the gilded-one, the Golden Kingdom. What Cabot wants to find is a civilization like that of the Incas, one that can be plundered and, if necessary, enslaved.

Cartier is sceptical: Cabot's reputation as a romancer is too well known.

Cabot returns to his home in England and writes to Charles V of Spain, for whom he has laboured, off and on, for three-and-a-half decades. He tells the Spanish king that the French are about to send 4,000 soldiers to the Amazon.

Too obvious: Charles V resists the temptation.

Cabot goes about Bristol and London, flogging his mucus-coated dream. No takers.

Finally the dream breaks free of the old stager and melds with others of an equally fanciful nature. Thus, when Sir Walter Raleigh, near century's end, reports on a cruise he made off Guiana, Raleigh marries Cristoforo Colombo's report that a legion of warlike women existed somewhere in the Caribbean with the assertion that the peoples of the Amazon stored their wealth in plates of gold.

COUNTY FERMANAGH. 1566

Value Given

The Maguire, chief of Fermanagh, is explaining to his Dublin visitor the rules of life.

Everything, he says, has its just price – its *eric*, the fine a person is liable for, if he destroys the item. For instance, the killing of a very prestigious chief might require an *eric* from the murderer of twenty-one head of cattle, perhaps more.

The Maguire is fishing for information, even as he gives it. The Dublin visitor is from the Castle and he will be sending a sheriff to the county, to keep order and enforce law in what previously has been known by the name of Maguire's Country.

"Your sheriff will be welcome to me," Maguire affirms. "But let me know his *eric* so that if any of my people put him to death, I will know what fine to levy."

CUSHENDUN, COUNTY ANTRIM. 2 JUNE 1567

Calculation

Banqueting with the MacDonnells of Antrim was always dangerous, Shane O'Neill knew. Poisoning, beheading, and heart-ripping were among their traditional ways of treating guests. Even their close allies left a feast with the MacDonnells delighted if they had merely been the butt of a coruscating satire and been urinated on by a drunken swordsman or two. Those dangers Shane understood, but he was in deep trouble and calculated that the MacDonnells were his last hope.

Calculation was Shane O'Neill's weakness. A warrior of ferocious ability, his brain was run by adrenaline, alcohol, vanity and, mostly, habit. His habits until recently had been remarkably successful, if unreflective. He had worked over the tribes of Ulster, O'Donells, MacDonnells, and half-a-dozen smaller septs, and, as ruler of Ulster, had kept up a maddening series of raids on the Pale. The lord deputy of Ireland was unable to do much except chase Shane and his raiders, like a lone shepherd after a pack of wilderness-wise wolves.

Pride. The pride of the man was as vexing as was his unstoppable vandalism. He ridiculed the English attempt to set up the eleventh earl of Kildare as a puppet colonizer of Leix and Offaly. "Housebroken cur of the foreign churl," he called Fitzgerald who, understandably, was doing whatever he could to undo his family's fall after the disaster of Silken Thomas's rebellion. From Ulster, Shane attacked the colonists, almost all of whom were Irish in some sense, rather than new English invaders. Shane, as equitable a marauder as Ireland ever produced, sacked estates, stole cattle, burned outbuildings of Gaelic chiefs, Anglo-Norman lords, Catholics, Protestants, Palesmen, retainers of Dublin officials, with complete indifference to complexities of ideology, ethnicity, religion.

Shane O'Neill had appeared before Queen Elizabeth in 1561–62 and, though he was completely within her power while in London, he scared her. Shane returned to Ireland convinced that, with Elizabeth's concurrence, he was the prince of Ulster; Elizabeth kept her own counsel. Shane had to go.

Now Shane lay still, his head on the MacDonnell's banquet table. With one dangling eye he seems to look himself in the face.

He had not calculated that Elizabeth would commit her resources to a serious attack on his self-declared kingdom or that instead of chasing him through Ulster's forests and defiles, her lord deputy, Sir Henry Sidney, would patiently burn the countryside and would use

Shane's tribal enemies as surrogates, the O'Donells in particular. The new approach worked.

Shane, reduced to alternating periods of raving lunacy and impossibly optimistic plans for violence on an apocalyptic scale, can never have calculated less well than when he threw himself on the mercy of the MacDonnells, whom he had long tried to crush. And then, at table, he had responded with ill-thought pride to taunts that came to his ear from below the salt.

Now a MacDonnell, a one-armed fighter who had lost a limb in the endless battles with O'Neill, severs Shane's dangling eye from its stalk and tosses it to a favourite dog.

Shane O'Neill's head is pickled in a pipkin and forwarded to Dublin. It is placed over the central gate of Dublin Castle, where Shane can keep one-eyed watch on things.

MUNSTER. 1569

The Big Picture

Colonel Humphrey Gilbert arrives as military governor of Munster. He has virtually unlimited judicial and political powers under martial law, but not enough of an army to clean up the province. Therefore, he introduces new tactics, designed to magnify through terror the fear his military force engenders. For one thing, he begins executing Irish non-combatants as well as soldiers. And, realizing that fear is most effective if made memorable, he engages in some very bold artistic arrangement. He orders

that the heddes of those (of wha sort soever they were) which were killed in the daie, should be cutte off from their bodies and brought to the place where he incamped at night ...

Gilbert intends to pardon some of his Irish enemies, but only after they have walked down an avenue of the dead.

... incamped at night, and should here bee laid on the ground by eche side of the waie ledyng into his owne tente so that none could come into his tente for any cause but commonly he must pass through a lane of heddes which he used ad terrorem ...

Gilbert, in common with the ruck of English adventurers who swarm into Ireland, has not the forces to subdue the Irish. Indeed, the entire Elizabethan attempt to conquer Ireland fails, but it is a practice-round for three techniques that, when applied in the Americas, are notably successful: using private adventurers, backed by joint-stock financing whenever possible; mounting a concerted propaganda campaign in England, particularly London. And knowing in one's mind and heart, even before encountering a single representative of the indigène, that they are brutal savages and must be treated as such.

... and yet did it bring great terrour to the people when thei sawe the heddes of their dedde fathers, brothers, children, kinsfolke and friendes, lying on the grounde before their faces, as thei came to speak with the Colonel.

RATHLIN ISLAND, COUNTY ANTRIM. APRIL-SEPT 1575

Civic Debts

All that Francis Drake received from the venture was his share of the nearly 3,000 sheep, and 600 horses and cattle seized on Rathlin. His men picked a few items off the bodies of the roughly 500 men, women and children whom they had helped to hunt out of the caves of Rathlin. Mostly, the booty, such as it was, went to the tiny army of Robert Devereux, earl of Essex.

Drake had placed his small flotilla (three frigates), men, and ammunition at Essex's disposal, forming in effect a navy. And that was what Essex needed, for he had been engaged since 1573 in an effort to pacify Ulster, especially the far north. The arrangement he had with the Crown was simple: spend your own money and if you win, you can keep most of your spoils. Trouble was, the O'Neills were impossible to break, and their sometime ally, Sorley Boy MacDonnell was less fierce, but more elusive. He had holed up in a fortress on Rathlin Island.

Francis Drake, rich with the rewards of slave trading, piracy, privateering, and, one must add, part-time English patriotism, knew that he owed something to his country. After all, his previous eight years of rich association with his older cousin John Hawkins, was only possible by Crown permission. The trade he had learned was to slip down the coast of Africa, avoiding Spanish vessels, and to take slaves to any place that wanted them: the Spanish colonies in Mexico, tiny settlements of all nations in the West Indies, any place. Then, a bit of privateering, or trading in exotic oils, dyes, herbs, and a quick run home. It was a great world and, yes, he owed his country something.

Had Essex ever won anything worth having, Drake would have turned a fine profit. The massacre on Rathlin was Essex's greatest victory, however, and it was tainted by Sorley Boy's having slipped away. By 1576, Essex was back in England, dying of dysentery.

Drake, having lost much of his fortune on this bit of naval patriotism, returned to his previous pursuits, including circumnavigating the world.

DUBLIN. JANUARY 1576

A Young Man of Affairs

The most talented of the five sons of Antonio Bruschetto and his Italian wife goes by the name of Ludowick Bryskett, or, sometimes, "Brisket." It's a good mix, his Christian name indicating a worldliness that is confirmed by his fluency in Italian, French, and modest ability in German, while brisket is nothing less than part of the roast beef of Old England.

His father, Antonio, has stayed close with William Cecil, doing pieces of continental business that were too important to commit to paper and, in his early twenties Ludowick had himself been sent on confidential business to Italy. Cecil ran a tight network (including his own secret police force) and when his client, Sir Henry Sidney, was ordered to Ireland for his second tour as lord deputy in 1565, Ludowick Bryskett was dispatched along as a messenger-courtier-factotum.

Bryskett made his father proud: he ingratiated himself brilliantly with both Sidney and Cecil: very big players. So when young Philip Sidney (who, incidentally, already was a great favourite of Cecil) at age eighteen in 1572, was sent on the grand tour of Europe, Ludowick was one of the two companions sent with him. Twenty-seven years of age and polished in continental manners, his task was to be agreeable company, to carry home the dead-drunk youth, to check for cleanliness the prostitutes the young man slept with, to polish his manners and, most importantly, to be ready to die, if necessary, defending his charge's life.

Perfect: a polished young gentleman, trained from his earliest days to be discreet and loyal.

Now, in 1576, when Sir Henry Sidney begins his third tour as lord deputy of Ireland, Ludowick Bryskett comes with him as clerk of the Irish privy council. He picks up other pieces of patronage, the controllership of customs duties on wines imported into Dublin, Waterford, Limerick and Cork, and later the clerkship of Munster. He has no scruples about what the English of his generation are doing to the Irish and in 1582 acquires an estate at Macmine, near Enniscorthy, County Wexford. It is not vast, only 120 acres, but as former church lands it had been well tended and is a prize.

Bryskett, charmed by life on the borders of adventure, decides to become a part-time paragon among the barbarians. He has a protégé, and later friend, in Edmund Spenser; Bryskett visits Philip Sidney in London: and he becomes part of Raleigh's Irish circle. All the time, he thinks of himself as living a noble experiment: to find out "whether the life of a borderer be alike perilous until all men?" Or, was he special: "to see if a just and honest simple life, may not even amoung the most barbarous people of the world breed security to him that shall live near them or among them?"

LONDON. 9 MAY 1576

Fairish Rewards

The great seal is placed on the parchment and sent to the earl of Essex, who now spends most of his time in Dublin in a bedroom, sitting on a chair fitted with a chamberpot. Essex has returned from Ireland, ultimately unsuccessful, but still demanding of rewards. When he receives the parchment he is deeply puzzled and spends most of the day on his commode, reflecting with all the intensity of a medieval monarch who has just received a report from one of his court spies.

Part of the message he takes in with mild gratitude. He has been granted the Barony of Farney in County Monaghan. This was a locale he had particularly fancied when first he saw it, marching with his small army northward into O'Neill country. But the second grant? It's a place he has soldiered past, but never desired. It's just a hook of land, a deformed finger crooked into the Irish Sea. What Essex wants is the harbour, Larne, that this wee peninsula protects.

Still, he briefly becomes the possessor of Islandmagee, the first bit of Ireland that St. Patrick had viewed at close hand, after he had been taken slave. Essex dies of colon cancer not long after receiving his fairish rewards. He had spent even less time on Islandmagee than had St. Patrick, and the land is out of his family a generation later.

PORT SAN JULIAN, SOUTH AMERICA. 2 JULY 1578

Irish Resolve

I shall die as a Gentleman. Thomas Dougherty is determined to carry off his last hours with élan. *The captain is a madman, but I must not ...* Dougherty stops, refusing even to visualize himself losing control.

He's right. Drake is a crazed zealot, with delusions of persecution. He had convened a jury of twelve crew members and terrified them into finding Dougherty guilty of mutiny. The evidence was slim to non-existent. Thomas Dougherty and his brother James had sailed with Drake on the voyage that eventually circumnavigated the globe. That was sensible, as there were big prizes to be won. But neither of the Doughertys had picked up the suspicion – no, the conviction – Drake had of their being treacherous. This trial for mutiny had been determined even before Drake and his five ships sailed from Plymouth in December 1577.

And yet, we were such close friends. That was the problem. Thomas Dougherty and Francis Drake had become close companions during Essex's short war on the O'Neills and the MacDonnells. Each had thought to do well; neither had. And when Essex's campaign faltered, Drake and Dougherty started scheming, undercutting Essex in Dublin and in London. What Drake feared was that Dougherty would do to himself, what both he and Drake had done to Essex. So, Thomas Dougherty is sentenced to death as a preventative measure: perhaps Drake is not crazy after all, merely prudential in the manner of any successful tyrant.

Here comes the tyrant now. Dougherty rises. "Yes, Captain, I shall be content to take Holy Communion with you." They do so, using the rite of the English Church.

Then: "Yes, Francis, for old days' sake, you must call me Thomas." And: "Yes, Francis, I shall breakfast with you." And: "Yes, Francis, I shall drink a toast of wine with you." Finally. "It is indeed time: yes, Captain."

Drake then proceeds Dougherty onto the foredeck where the Irishman positions himself on the executioner's block. Dougherty permits himself the smallest of smiles, for he knows that he has kept faith with the last of his ambitions.

CORK CITY. AUGUST 1580

Royal Favour

Walter Raleigh, just twenty-six, but already a veteran of the brutal Huguenot wars in France, has sussed out the only trustworthy means of promotion: to gain the favour of Elizabeth, the Virgin Queen.

His big chance comes when he is sent to Ireland. Elizabeth has little interest in the place except as a potential for profit or, she shudders, as a sinkhole of expense. She knows that Philip of Spain, with the Pope's blessing, is preparing an invasion of Ireland. And the Fitzgerald family – the earls of Desmond, proud Old English Catholics who are now more Gaelic than English – are willing to fight a Catholic holy war.

In August 1580, Raleigh makes his first impression upon his superiors in Ireland and ultimately upon the Queen. Sir James Fitzgerald, brother of the earl of Desmond was captured and brought to trial. Raleigh, who held the rank of captain and a second man of equal rank, Captain Sentleger, were constituted a legal commission to deal with him.

Upon the recommendation of this drumhead jury, Sir James was hanged, drawn and quartered. His body was spread above the city gate of Cork, there to dessicate for weeks and to communicate a moral lesson to all who passed beneath.

The other brother of the earl of Desmond, Sir John Fitzgerald, was killed in a skirmish during the following year. At that time Raleigh

was acting governor of Cork. He commanded that the corpse be beheaded and the body suspended, hanging upside down by its heels,
over the River Lee. There it hung for three years until it was a skeleton.

The head of Sir John, however, was not used so prodigally.

Raleigh sent it to the Virgin Queen, describing it as "a goodly gift to
Her Hignesse."

SMERWICK, COUNTY KERRY. 10 NOVEMBER 1580

Moral Dimensions

About 400 Spaniards and a few Italians and 200 Irish soldiers, women
and children, are surrounded in a seaside fort they optimistically call
"Del Oro." Lord Grey de Wilton, newly arrived chief deputy from
Dublin, is in charge. He is a hard man and easily vexed. Three days of
fighting in unrelenting autumn rain do not improve his disposition. Nor
does the garrison's refusal not once, but twice, to surrender and this despite heavy land and sea bombardment. Finally a white flag is sent out
by the defenders and the cry of "Misericordia!" "Misericordia."

Lord Deputy Grey treats briefly with the Italians and Spaniards,
the leaders of whom declare they have been sent by the Pope to defend the Catholic faith. His statement to them and to their Irish allies
is simplicity itself: surrender to me and yield yourselves to my decision as to your life or death.

They do.

And he did them.

A few of the ranking officers were parcelled out by Grey to his own
favourite officers, so that they could make profit by holding the foreigners for ransom. The majority (and all the Irish) are ordered killed.
The orders are given to a Captain Macworth and to Captain Raleigh
to perform the mass killing.

Raleigh, had he any reservations, did not show them. Six hundred
or more disarmed persons were put to death by the sword. His own
weapon must have been inches deep in human tallow by the time the
slaughter was over.

In December 1581, Raleigh was sent back to London with despatches. He was now a man of achievement, and soon became a

Royal favourite. He was admitted to the small circle of Elizabeth's friends whom she permitted informal conversation and amusing sallies about the lesser breeds of the human race.

OFF THE AZORES. 9 SEPTEMBER 1583

Missing the Boat

On 13 June 1583, on a large barque, modestly named "Raleigh," Walter Raleigh missed the boat. He was part of an expedition sailing from Plymouth headed by his half-brother, fifteen years older than he. That expedition, it turned out, planted the first colony in the Americas that can be labelled "English," although in the manner of the time, being an English colony only meant the English Crown was in charge: its inhabitants were, as usual, a mixed lot of English, Scots and Irish. On Raleigh's vessel, fever broke out among the crew and he returned to port, abandoning the expedition. Thus, a big historical moment was missed.

Despite their aggressiveness and predilection for violence, missing the boat was a habit of Walter Raleigh and his half-brother Humphrey Gilbert, and nowhere was it clearer than on Gilbert's 1583 expedition to Newfoundland. No, actually it was not a habit; it was the family's disease.

Gilbert followed a pattern common to many founders of empire from the mid-sixteenth through the late-seventeenth centuries: he had done his apprenticeship as a colonizer in Ireland, where he was governor of Munster from 1569 to 1571 and was knighted. Sir Humphrey stole as much as he could from the Irish, but it was not enough for him, just as subsequent ventures were not enough for his successors. They all wanted more, and the way to get it was to find a New World where the natives weren't quite so truculent. Sir Humphrey spent fifteen years badgering the Crown for money for a New World expedition, and writing effective propaganda pieces about places he had never been. He and Raleigh had taken one voyage under royal charter in 1578, but were forced to scamper home when Spanish ships attacked.

Now, Gilbert succeeds, momentarily. His second expedition, the one Raleigh missed, lands near what is now St. John's, Newfoundland.

There Gilbert assembles the local fishermen, mostly men from the British Isles, and goes through a ritual that turns them into England's first New World colony.

A brick of turf is cut.

A hazel wand is waved over the turf and the land is declared Her Majesty's.

The now-sacred turf is stored in the commander's locker.

Thereafter Gilbert explores for a time and discovers a silver mine.

He gives portions of this New Land to some of his officers and he prepares to return to Plymouth, wreathed in glory.

But here the family disease strikes. He, as commander of an expedition that is bringing to Elizabeth I her first real colony in the New World, should travel carefully. However, a rumour runs through his crew that he is a coward and, to disprove it, Gilbert refuses to go home on the *Golden Hinde*, but stays on the *Squirell*, a tiny frigate of nine tonnes at best. In one of the nastiest seas any of the mariners have ever seen – "breaking high and pyramid wise," the survivors described them –the *Squirell* is a leaf in a foaming cataract. The last the mariners on the *Golden Hinde* see of Sir Humphrey is his sitting on the mainmast, with a book in his hand.

His last observation is as much that of a theologian as an explorer. "We are as near heaven by water as by land."

THE LONDON ROAD, NEAR BRISTOL. SUMMER 1587

Lost Worlds

A woman of mature years walks out from Bristol. No, not a gentlewoman in the English sense, nor a country woman. A lady: her demeanour makes that clear. And she has two attendants with her. She is dressed strangely, however, and, indeed, she is walking. This puzzling creature is Eleanor, widow of the executed sixteenth Earl of Desmond. Whether or not she is, in law, the dowager countess of Desmond is a nice point, as her husband was attainted.

This Irish lady knew the state of accounts, but her head was unbowed. The Desmonds had everything they owned escheated to the Crown, a half million acres in Munster, or so they claimed. Their ownership had been shared in various Celtic joint tenancies with their tenants, but now that was null. The lands were held by the Crown and the Munster tenantry had been driven by the war of 1579–83 into eating the carrion of the land, as if they were themselves crows or vultures. The wretches went someplace, God knows, but where? The rich southland of Ireland was a desert.

The Countess made her march to London and was successful. The Virgin Queen consented to see her and, satisfied that the Desmonds were indeed broken completely and that the south of Ireland now was safely in English hands, she granted the Countess £1,100 annually, a generous amount. The Queen permitted the Countess to remain in a tumbledown castle five miles from Youghal.

This was a long way down, for the Countess and for Ireland: in 1579, she had been the wife of Elizabeth's wealthiest Irish subject.

KILCOLMAN CASTLE, COUNTY CORK. 1589

Truly Gifted

"*Traitors, murderers, thieves, coseners, cony catchers, shifting mates* ... The London government collected intelligence on the sort of person who had flooded into Munster after the end of the Desmond Wars in the early 1580s ... *runners away with other men's wives, some having two or three wives, persons divorced living loosely, bankrupts, carnal gospellers, Papists, Puritans, and Brownists.*" That is hardly surprising, for water runs to its lowest point, and Ireland in the late sixteenth and seventeenth centuries was the pooling point for thousands who had been in trouble – criminal, financial, matrimonial – elsewhere in the British Isles: Munster in the late sixteenth, and Ulster and Munster in the first forty years of the seventeenth century, and the entire country from 1641 onwards. Upwards of 100,000 "colonists" came into Ireland between 1580 and 1680, a fairish number in a population that ran between 1.4 million in 1600 and 2.1 in 1641 and 1.7 in 1692. Some colonists were virtuous and pious, some insensate and immoral, still others, cultivated and aspiring to aristocracy. All were aggressive, brutal, morally one-eyed. They had to be: this was a frontier, the place one gained only if the natives lost.

Walter Raleigh, as one of the aspiring and aristocratic, did not much enjoy his visits to Ireland, but when there he dealt with people he considered civilized and useful. "Say on, dear Edmund, say on," he now repeated at intervals as his host, Edmund Spenser, read to him long swirls of intricate verse.

Spenser, like Raleigh, was a man whose hard and instinctive brutality was constantly being overlimed with a wash of chivalry; and that wash then was enhued into a mural, one so graceful that the viewer forgot that the artist had used a pigment whose fixative was blood.

"I shall arrange you an audience with the Queen. You shall read those words to her and she shall fall before you as a swan before a golden arrow."

Spenser and Raleigh had first met at Smerwick, County Kerry in November 1580. Raleigh was one of the officers whom Lord Grey de Wilton, lord deputy of Ireland, had commanded to massacre the Spanish, Italian and Irish garrison after it had surrendered. Spenser, newly-arrived from England, was secretary to the lord deputy. He watched the slaughter with the eye for detail that was to be so useful to his poetry. On his path to Smerwick, Spenser had observed a harvesting of seals by a crew from a coasting barge and he was struck by the similar techniques employed in each massacre.

Edmund Spenser did well in Ireland, but certainly not by doing good. He became in time one of the commissioners for militia musters and clerk of the Council of Munster. Whatever his title, the job was the same: shove aside, kill, if necessary, the native Irish and thus civilize the land. Spenser acquired a succession of estates, the most important being the long-lease of Kilcolman Castle and its more than 3,000 acres.

Raleigh, who loved to do well by individuals who could do well by him, arranged for Spenser to read to Elizabeth I some of the material that eventually became The Faerie Queene. She responded by granting Spenser a pension of £50 a year and the poet thereafter dropped Raleigh as a noble icon into his verses like a cook inserting candied cherries into a particularly rich Christmas cake.

Among the army of 100,000 thousand colonizers of Ireland between 1580 and 1680, Edmund Spenser is not unique in his strategic values – he has no trouble with the Smerwick massacre or with inducing famine in Munster or with the judicial murder of Irish landholders who stand in the way of the new men. He is unusual (but not unique) in having the moral sensibility to loath himself unconsciously, even while justifying hard policy publicly.

Thus there he stood, whylest high over his head,
  There written was the purport of his sin,
In cyphers strange, that few could rightly read,
*BON FONT: but **bon** that once had written bin,*
*Was raced out, and **Mal** was now put in,*
*So now **Malfont** was plainly to be red.*

LONDON. 1590

Body Count

Exactly when tobacco first came to the Old World is not known, but certainly a good deal of it arrived back with Sir Francis Drake. One of Drake's officers, the experienced colonizer, Captain Ralph Lane, taught Sir Walter Raleigh how to drink tobacco properly. Raleigh mastered the elegant use of the pipe and, more than any person of his time, made smoking tobacco a fashion. As a leader of fashion, and a Queen's favourite (albeit a sliding one), he was well worth imitating. Raleigh was tall, slim and had a high forehead. He had a habit of holding his head acock, so that he was always looking down his nose at whomever he was addressing. A pipe went well with that pose. And his ability to use a long pipe as a graceful extension of his arm while making a point about geopolitics gave him a serious air. Mind you, his propensity to wear bejewelled shoes, coats with gold and silver decorations and, on occasion, a starched cambric stock of up to a yard in diameter around his neck, made him sometimes appear to be a very large and expensive marionette.

Raleigh gave smoking parties at his house and for a time they were one of London's most desired invitations. No food was served, just mugs of ale. These were male gatherings, and those who participated liked to think that they represented the best minds, the sharpest writers, the most worldly statesmen of England.

On his Youghal estate, Raleigh introduced tobacco, but in Ireland it remained a mere curiosity crop. It was commercially cultivated in Trinidad at least as early as 1593 and in Virginia in 1616 and there it soon became an economic staple because demand from the Old World grew so quickly.

It would have been beyond the understanding of the vainglorious Raleigh to comprehend that the single greatest influence he was to have upon history was his leading role in making tobacco-drinking humanity's most fatal addiction.

TULLAGHOGE, COUNTY TYRONE. SEPTEMBER 1595

White Magic

Hugh O'Neill, earl of Tyrone, is enthroned as The O'Neill. Perhaps he has no choice. If he does not take the title, vacated at the death of Turlough Luineach O'Neill, someone else will. Yet, he is pleased with the force of circumstances, for he is asserting that he is more than the earl of Tyrone by leave of the English queen.

Tullaghoge is a sacred site, the place of enthronement of successive O'Neills since time-out-of-mind and, more practically, almost the geographic centre of their kingdom. Like many such sites, its modest physical appearance belies its spiritual power. A simple rath, with a few mud-and-stone dwellings inside, it contains the sacred stone chair of the O'Neills.

The ceremony is ancient. Hugh O'Neill enters, dressed in the Irish fashion, in a long mantle. He already has been immersed in a bath, a ritual cleansing that goes back to the mikvah of the Chosen People. He is barefoot. A white rod, emblematic of the purity of his election and of the character of his future rule, is waved over his head. Then he sits on the throne and is given the white rod. One of his chief subjects kneels before him and places a shoe on his right foot. Another does so on his left. Simple, unambiguous symbols.

Once invested, the O'Neill becomes not quite a king, but close. Thereafter he is a man with the powers of royalty. That is why not only the under-chiefs and representatives of subordinate clans attend, but three of the Catholic bishops of the northern and western dioceses are also present.

A year later, O'Neill begins a war with the English queen which he comes within an ace of winning. Unlike the Gaelic and Old English leaders of Munster, who are no match for Queen Elizabeth's forces, O'Neill's Ulster army is larger than hers, better disciplined, and O'Neill is a military genius in the field of hit-and-run warfare.

And in his favour is the alliance he skilfully negotiates with the Spanish.

His throne may have appeared uncomfortable, but it suited him perfectly.

LONDON. 1596

Names

Walter Raleigh changes the title page for the fifth time. His printer is in the final stages of preparing Raleigh's book *The Discoverie of the Large, Rich, and Bewtiful Empyre of Guina* on his expedition of 1595, and Raleigh wants some of the book to be accurate.

He rubs out his previous choice, R-a-l-e-i-g-h, and substitutes the spelling that the rector had inscribed on the parish register at his birth: R-a-l-e-g-h.

There. He feels better. Accuracy is often pleasant and, besides, "Raleigh" sounds like something that has not yet been invented.

CORK CITY. NOVEMBER 1598

Reparations

The food tasted terrible, but he was accustomed to that. Plenty of it, at least. Edmund Spenser, who had enjoined starvation as public policy, as a means of bringing the brutal Irish to heel, could no longer sit to table as he wished. The native Irish across Munster fought their own corner, and from the mid 1590s, no place was safe from their aggressions. Spenser, at Kilcolman Castle, was "boycotted" before the word was created. (Had history any real justice, Captain Hugh Boycott, in County Mayo in the 1880s would have been "Spensered.") His servants left. Although he was sheriff of County Cork, the local victuallers and tradesmen rudely refused to sell to him; all his foodstuffs had to be brought from Cork City. He was reduced to having his provisions boiled in a continuously-cooking stockpot that became so thick with oleaginous flotsam that only with difficulty could he push a tin cup through its surface. Then, in October 1598, as part of an indigenous resurgence, Spenser's Kilcolman Castle, the hallmark of his gentility, was burned. Now he rents a room in Cork City, eats meals cooked by a slattern, and waits for a berth on a boat to England.

Edmund Spenser dies in London, January 1599. Some contemporaries say that he starved to death but that is unlikely, for the Irish had taught him that one can eat just about anything, as long as one does not look at it too closely.

The Munster Plantation, to which Spenser had given most of his life's energies, does not so much stop as stumble into unregulated chaos. For the next forty years, Old Irish, Old English, New English, Dublin authorities and the London government snatch, snarl, and tear away for themselves whatever bits they can clamp in their jaws.

In 1598, while still at Kilcolman Castle, Spenser had written concerning the Irish who surrounded him: *They are all Papists by their profession, but in the same so blindly and brutishly informed for the most part as that you would rather think them atheists or infidels.*

The Spenser family manages to hold on to Kilcolman. In 1641, on the eve of the Irish civil war, the Spensers are Roman Catholics.

KINSALE, COUNTY CORK. 24 AND 25 DECEMBER 1601

Christmas Gifts

Early-modern Irish embraced thirty-two separate words that mean fool, idiot, moron, imbecile.

The O'Neill – Hugh O'Neill, earl of Tyrone – used thirty-three to denominate Don Juan del Aguilla, the commander of the Spanish force that he now had to rescue. O'Neill's dream of aid from the Spanish had come true: a chance of real victory should have arrived with Aguilla's 4,000 men.

Instead this baboon's dropping, this misbegotten son of a tree stump, this fool's fool, this ... this *person* had landed at the farthest point in Ireland from O'Neill's northern base and then had been surrounded by Charles Blount, Lord Mountjoy, the new lord deputy of Ireland and a very skilled tactician.

Honour made O'Neill go the length of Ireland to the rescue of the Spanish, allies and fellow Catholics, and he encircled the Crown forces who were, in their turn, encircling the Spanish. Coordinated planning between O'Neill and the Spanish was impossible and Mountjoy kept the Spanish immobile and then turned his superior cavalry on the Irish. O'Neill never would have risked a set battle save for *those ... those ...*

The defeat at Kinsale sounded the death knell of Gaelic Ireland, though battles continued for another two years.

O'Neill, retreating northwards into the maze of lakes and forests that protected Ulster, reviewed all the words he knew for persons of Aguilla's small mental capacity. All thirty-two words and, finally, that, that, that *Spaniard.*

YOUGHAL, COUNTY CORK. 1602

More Missed Ships

Sir Walter Raleigh is about to admit that he has once again misread the signs and has missed his ship, the one that was to take him to El Dorado.

His first failure was to abandon Sir Humphrey Gilbert in the 1583 voyage that gave the Crown claim to Newfoundland. Then, after having convinced the Virgin Queen to give him speculative title to all the land from what is today Maine to Florida, Raleigh sponsors two ventures to this new land, which the Queen permits him to name "Virginia." His organization of the Roanoke Island colony in 1585–6 was notable for the dictatorial figure of Sir Ralph Lane, who had been military governor of Kerry and who brought a number of Kerrymen with him. This venture under Raleigh's patronage failed, as did another attempt of 1587. Considering that he had had most of North America as his fruitbowl, he had managed to pick out very few cherries.

Then, in 1587, he had returned to Ireland. In Munster, the attainder of the earl of Desmond had opened huge tracts of land. Systematic burning of crops and habitations did to the everyday Irish – both "mere Irish," and "Old English" – what military conquest had done to their native aristocracy. Into this Balkan desert came English land-seizers, younger sons on the make, middling men wanting to be gentry.

Sir Walter Raleigh (he had been knighted before his first Virginia fiasco) and his compatriots were permitted to seize and divide most of Counties Cork, Kerry, Waterford, Limerick and a bit of Tipperary. Sir Walter picked up 12,000 acres, more or less, in Cork and Wexford, including the house "Imohilly" that previously belonged to the preaching friars of Ireland (and he acquired varying, rather shaky titles to another 30,000 acres of less desirable land).

The massive Munster plantation would come apart in the Irish rebellion of 1598, but some estates, such as Raleigh's, were still secure and potentially profitable.

At "Imohilly," Raleigh meets Sir Richard Boyle, secretary of the Munster colony (or "Munster presidency" as it was then known). Boyle is well on his way to being the earl of Cork and the real power-broker in Munster. What Boyle understands is that Raleigh is not managing his estate with any rigour. He plays about planting potatoes, tobacco and tomatoes, brought from the New World, and writes proposals for grand voyages of exploration: what Raleigh should be doing, Boyle knows, is screwing down the remaining local peasantry and being sure that the impoverished Irish gentry do not ever rise again.

Raleigh sells the massive estate to Boyle for £1,500. He says that the place is not worth the bother of his head.

TULLAGHOGE, COUNTY TYRONE. 1602

Pounding Salt

Lord Mountjoy understands his enemy.

Two of his sergeants are wielding long steel bars, inserting them into cracks in the base of the regnal chair of the O'Neills. The chair appeared to be made from a single piece of stone. It was asymmetrical and smooth, as if formed by brute geological force and sanded by aeons of time. In reality, it was cunningly constructed of four large blocks of stone, a minor masterpiece of stone carving.

The arms of the throne come away easily, but the base is adamantine, refusing to surrender its authority.

Participating in this destruction is an honour, and only when the sergeants are too arm-weary to ram the prybars into the rocks, do they pass their tools on to private soldiers. The throne finally surrenders, and when it is reduced to chunks of a portable size, they are distributed to the soldiers to be pulverized with mason's hammers. "Dust only shall remain," Mountjoy decrees.

In silence and immobile, as if they have themselves been stunned by blows from the hammers, the old people of the rath see their patrimony becoming dust, save for one shard, the size of a pullet's egg, that Mountjoy places in his pocket.

MACMINE, ENNISCORTHY, COUNTY WEXFORD. JANUARY 1605

Whence

Sixty years old, cataracts forming on both eyes, Ludowick Bryskett stares into a flickering fire. He has lost all the notions his Italian father had taught to him – that a true Englishman is both worldly and loyal to his patron, is a poet among friends and a swordsman among barbarians, and that knightly service inevitably produces ample rewards.

Macmine is now only partly habitable and portions of the greathall where Bryskett now sits have no roof. No matter. Ludowick Bryskett is numb.

He asks the flames how could the barbarous Irish so easily defeat him and his kind? He and his friend Edmund Spenser were both burned out in the uprising of the autumn of 1598, Spenser scurrying to Cork and to an impoverished death in London, Bryskett haring with his family to Wexford and a humiliating round of begging for jobs from his one-time friends in London.

How, he wonders, could a confidential courier's assignment result in 1601 in his being captured in Flanders and then ransomed – no, worse, exchanged – for a Jesuit! a Portuguese colporteur who had been on his way to convert the Brazilians when his ship encountered two English vessels. Not being held for ransom was the equivalent of being labelled obviously-not-needed-on-voyage.

Why, he asks the fire, does his majesty, the new king, whose hand I only recently kissed at Hampton Court, take away from me the only state post I still have, the clerk of casualties in Ireland, and a paltry thing even that is?

Yet, Bryskett is not so much bitter as puzzled. The English knightly code does not seem to work, and he cannot put his finger on exactly why. His biggest puzzlement about the code revolves around one observation.

He has spent much of his adult life with the men that contemporaries consider the great masters of poetry of their age, Philip Sidney and Edmund Spenser, and with Walter Raleigh, already well thought-of and destined by most seventeenth-century authorities to be deemed the finest prose writer of his time. And each was magnificently ruthless in dealing with native barbarians. What Ludowick Bryskett wants to know before he sleeps is this: does absolute mastery of the English language make one more effective at killing Irishmen?

Or, possibly, is it the other way round?

TOWER OF LONDON. LADY DAY 1605

Bill of Fare

Sir George Harry was obsessive about collecting his dues. He had to be, for as lieutenant in charge of providing the food and sundries for prisoners in the Tower, he had to pay for victualling out of his own pocket and then wait until his statement of account was met by the prisoner or by the exchequer, depending on the individual case. So, the Day of Our Lady having arrived, he immediately made up his account.

Sir Walter Raleigh, who had plotted against the king, had been fed for a quarter of a year, from the feast of the Nativity until the feast of the Annunciation of Our Lady, thirteen weeks, for forty-five pounds, an amount that included the housing and feeding of three servants.

James McThomas Fitzgerald was holder of the title of eighteenth earl of Desmond in Irish practice, if not in English law. The sixteenth earl had been captured and killed in 1583, his lands escheated. The seventeenth earl had died in London in 1601, having spent the years 1579–1601 in the Tower. Now the eighteenth earl was imprisoned in the Tower. He was without servants, so his quarterly dues came only to thirty-nine pounds.

The Desmond line ended with the eighteenth earl's becoming ravingly insane and expiring. He was buried in the chapel in the Tower in 1608.

Raleigh, fellow prisoner of the eighteenth earl, briefly escapes his posthumous company in March 1616, when he is for a time set free.

ST. PATRICK'S CATHEDRAL, DUBLIN. 1607

Capturing the Numbers

In the small, narrow-windowed room to which his recent appointment as chancellor of the cathedral entitles him, James Ussher scratches marginal notes alongside long columns of figures. So much to do, so much time to capture.

Ussher is also Regius Professor of Divinity at the raw young Protestant institution, Trinity College, Dublin and though only twenty-six years of age, he is already marked out to become one of Ireland's finest scholars in his era: Syriac, Hebrew, classical languages, continental European theology, he is mastering the lot.

His deepest interest in life is: time. When did it start and where is it going? He works on a manuscript that he began at age fifteen. He wants to know when God created the earth and from that all manner of inferences, even predictions, are possible. As a young undergraduate at Trinity (he had entered at age twelve) Ussher had brought his world chronology from the Creation down as far as the Book of Kings, and this stayed solid in his *Annales* published in the 1650s and in his posthumous *Chronology* (1660).

Laugh not. If he concludes that the world was created in 4004 BCE, that is not lunatic: the best contemporary rabbinical scholars, of whom Ussher has no knowledge, calculate that it began in the equivalent of 3764 BCE, give or take a few moons. The problem, of course, is not with the calculation, but with its assumptions. And even then, I ask you, how many years does human history, real human history, not geological or archaeological history, need? There's no human story that we know well enough to be accepted as real history – as history with any individual's face limned finely enough to be recognized – that occurs before Ussher's, or the Rabbis' date for Creation.

OFF THE SPANISH COAST. 29 SEPTEMBER 1607

Leverage

When St. Helena had discovered in the Holy Land the remnants of the True Cross, she had known that it would work miracles. Hugh O'Neill, second earl of Tyrone, was fortunate in having one sliver of the Cross encased in a gold crucifix. He needed a miracle now.

Planning for his present sea adventure had been uneven. Conor Maguire, a northern aristocrat and ally of O'Neill, has passed from Ireland to Brussels and then to Brittany. Disguised as a merchant in wines and salt, he hired a French ship, decked it out with fishing nets to give it authenticity, and landed it secretly in Lough Swilly, County Donegal. The vessel was ill-provisioned, however, and its passengers had to buy beeves in Ulster markets and slaughter them. Only five water barrels were on board and most of these were full of small beer.

Nevertheless O'Neill, the largest figure in Gaelic Ireland, his O'Donnell allies (titularly now the earls of Tyrconnell), the Maguires, and the bulk of the native aristocracy of the north of Ireland, covertly make their way towards the French vessel. O'Neill himself spends an evening at Slane on the River Boyne with Sir Arthur Chichester, Lord Justice of Ireland, and the hand that soon will reshape the topography of Ulster. Then O'Neill slips off, and he and ninety-eight of the leading men, women, and child-heirs of Ulster sail for the Continent. The day is the fourteenth of September, 1607, the feast of the Exaltation of the Holy Cross.

Why the marrow and sinew of the Gaelic aristocracy of Ulster collectively levant is something they never tell themselves. Few of them ever see Ireland again and none of the central figures do. Instead, they spend their lives in the courts and wars of Continental Europe, forever proud, forever out of place. Their absence transforms Ulster from the prickliest thorn hedge in Ireland to the most accessible frontier. It will be much easier for ambitious speculators to conquer than was Munster.

Hugh O'Neill holds tightly to the stern rail of the French vessel as it plunges up and down in brutal seas. They have been thirteen days in a continuous gale and he worries that the ship will break apart or that they will come upon an unmarked rock or an unforgiving coast. O'Neill has a long coil of rope tied to his most precious possession, the golden crucifix with the piece of the True Cross inside. This is no scapular crucifix to be worn about the neck, close to the heart. It is nearly as big as a bishop's crosier.

O'Neill throws the crucifix overboard. It does not sink, but lies flat in the water, Jesus' arms outstretched, embracing heaven even as his back smooths the waters. Perhaps it is the shape of the object and its relationship to the speed of the by-rushing seas; O'Neill is able to pay out thirty yards of rope and still Our Lord floats. It is a miracle, O'Neill believes. And in confirmation, the seas begin to calm.

SILENEN, SWITZERLAND. 17 MARCH 1608

Holy Days of Obligation

The passage of the aristocracy of Ulster from France through the Swiss Alps and finally to Rome is dignified and, in several cities, celebrated. Hugh O'Neill, however, is in a hurry to reach the capital city of Christendom, for only there can their purity of purpose be validated: and, perhaps, their mission in abandoning Ulster be revealed to them. In their desire to make time, they ignore the feast day of Patrick, the saint to whom they owe their own Christianization.

The party moves into the Alps and encounters mountains full of snow, trails packed with ice. On a narrow arch called the Devil's Bridge, one of the pack horses loses its footing and crashes several hundred feet to the river below. It was carrying £120 in coinage and, more important, the sliver of the True Cross. O'Neill stops the progress and spends a day-and-a-half trying to rescue the treasure: the dead horse finally is dragged up the icy river bank, but the money is lodged on an ice-choked riverbed and cannot be retrieved. Worse, there is no trace of the Cross.

Is fortune turning against us? his followers ask O'Neill. No, he tells them, we still have our human icon with us: the infant Hugh O'Donnell. He is second in the line of O'Donnells who are heirs to Tyrconnell and who have the English earldom of that name. The child, between two and three years of age, is widely believed in the north of Ireland to be the fulfilment of a messianic prophesy. One of the saints of Tyrconnell had prophesied that when an O'Donnell child with six toes on one foot (and only one) was born, deliverance was at hand: the Irish of the north would rise up and drive the English out of all Ireland. O'Neill is comfortable with this prophesy, for the O'Neills and the O'Donnells are widely intermarried.

The blessed eleven-toed infant keeps the party from further harm. That was as far as his divine mission extended. He died childless in Portugal in 1642 and was buried alongside his mother in a Franciscan convent in Louvain.

ROME. 5 JUNE 1608

Justification by Faith

Finally: moral certainty. Abandoning Ulster was a holy act.

Eight Irish aristocrats, the cream of the Gaelic world, are selected to carry the canopy over the Blessed Sacrament from St. Peter's to St. James's (a lesser Roman church) and back to St. Peter's. This is a singular honour, usually reserved for royalty or for the ambassadors to the Vatican of the several Catholic countries. The honour is all the greater because the Pope himself carries the Sacrament, so the participants are in the presence both of Christ's Body and of Christ's Vicar on Earth.

Yes, God is saying to us, yes, you did right to leave Ireland. You are on a holy path.

Exactly a week earlier, O'Neill, O'Donnell, Maguire, and a handful of other Irish chiefs had been specially invited to be present at mass in St. Peter's on the occasion of the canonization of Saint Francesca Romana. The Irish, at the Pope's instructions, were given places of honour.

On the following Sunday, His Holiness receives the wives and sisters of the Irish nobility and, after allowing each one to kiss his foot, gives them his blessing.

Surely those are signs.

If so, then so are the quick contradictory counterpoints.

A fortnight later, bored with the confines of Rome, O'Donnell and his chief heir and the sole heir of O'Neill, go off to Ostia. They pick up a virulent fever and all three are dead within two-and-a-half months.

Thus perishes the adult leadership of the O'Donnell sept.

Even more crippling is the death of young Hugh O'Neill, heir to the titles of O'Neill and of the earldom of Tyrone, the young man who was intended to take the place of his father and to lead the re-conquest of Ulster.

ULSTER. SUMMER, 1608

Architecture

The abused shard of stone that Lord Mountjoy had taken from Tullaghoge becomes the head-of-the-corner, the foundation quorn for a new order.

In summer 1608, assizes are held throughout Ulster. Surveys are set down. Boundaries defined, so that Ulster can be eviscerated. Virtually all of six counties are escheated, though by what legal principle is never disclosed.

The peasantry are not immediately affected. Some of them say, with more cynicism than wisdom, that one set of overlords is the same as any other. As the Plantation of Ulster progresses, they change their mind.

MISPLACED FILES
1610–1660

All Theft Is Property

Ten Englishman in shackles are loaded onto a Royal navy vessel and taken to London where they are tried for piracy. Five had started their pirate careers while they were unengaged seaman in Munster ports.

As the world keeps changing shape, Ireland becomes for three decades the outer rim of the pirate circuit. From February to May the buccaneers work the coast of Spain and Portugal. After that they base themselves for four or five months in Ireland and prey on the Newfoundland and North American trade, and after that they go off-shore and focus on plundering the Spanish in the West Indies. The Royal navy is so stave-broken that it can do little about them, even as they roost ashore in Munster and buy and sell there.

As in all the world, yesterday's heroes are today's criminals and many of these pirates had been lauded by King James for attacking the Spanish – until, that is, 1604, when the Anglo-Spanish war ended and privateering suddenly became piracy.

As many as 1,000 pirates visit Munster in a year, and they get on well with the New English, for piracy on sea and wholesale theft on land are similar activities. Intermarriage is frequent and the adventurer class in the far south of Ireland adds rough men to its ranks. That and protection money bind the two communities.

The ten Youghal pirates are small time. They either die in prison awaiting trial or are sentenced to forced service in naval vessels. They are, however, part of the explanation of why, in the 1630s, as the West Indies opens up, men, merchants, ships from Munster are so quick to grab opportunities and to start tiny Irish empires in the then-richest part of the New World.

There's nothing like experience.

Writer's Block

For almost a decade Sir Walter Raleigh's friends have been bringing him books and manuscripts. His gaolers joke that he must be heating his apartments with them. Actually, Raleigh has been engaged in *The History of the World* and it has grown to five volumes with scarcely any effort. Read and scribble, read and scribble, it passes the days and fills the mind.

Early in 1614, Raleigh encounters writer's block, something new to him and, in his bland world, slightly intriguing. Having always schemed freely and acted unhesitatingly, this business of historical reflection is alien to him. Yet, he has done very well, bringing the story of humankind all the way from Creation to 168 BCE. And a very nicely told story it is: linear in tale and unified in theme: the unfolding of God's will in human time. John Milton will imitate it, doing a poetic version of Raleigh's elevated narrative. Raleigh, who rarely suffers from modesty, knows he has written wisely and well, and wonders why can I not continue?

Not ... not for long, however: he tacks on a few hundred words covering the Roman empire, and sends the entire bundle off to be printed. It appears anonymously, but the king knows who wrote it and tries to suppress the *History*.

Raleigh hit the wall at exactly the point where his reflections stopped being a game played with the past and became a predictor of a real and disordered future. In the five volumes he was able to complete, the international navigator laid out a straight line. The Creation of the world was its anchor point and in a clear sequence, the story of the children of Israel was followed by the history of the children of Helas. But now, approaching the high Roman age, he is blown by a strong wind onto a lee shore. He has to tell the story of Jesus-the-Christ and he must chronicle the apogee of the Roman empire and these two things are not linear, but intermix, and Semitic and Roman histories entwine in patterns chaotic and random. Sir Walter is not above cheating, but this is fortune-casting for himself. If, as he is beginning to realize, human history is not linear, and does not progress but merely happens, then his own future is not necessarily in front of him. He may be merely the flotsam of his own chaotic past.

Indeed: Raleigh is freed from prison in March 1616 so that he can return to a place that never existed, the Eldorado situated on the Orinoco. He returns to London having failed to turn even one of his lies into reality, and in October 1618 the writer's head is placed on the block.

Raleigh's *History* lived, however. Reprinted nine times (with his name now affixed to it) in the seventeenth century, it is one of the era's most popular works. And, despite Sir Walter's having been an instinctive sycophant before royalty and an unremitting opponent of the natural rights of any people but the English of his own class and above, he becomes a republican and radical icon, an heroic martyr. According to mid-seventeenth-century radicals, he died a victim of arbitrary monarchy, a fallen tribune of the people.

Not linear. Sir Walter was right to stop the *History* where he did: for there is no room in it for people like him.

COUNTY WEXFORD. 1620

Menace

He's seen enough: Anthony Briskett makes up his mind. He's getting out. He is by birth what his grandfather Antonio Bruschetto had admired and his own father Ludowick Bryskett had become by dint of striving and polishing: an English Protestant gentleman. And it's not worth the trouble, not here. Oh, he is hard enough to take being surrounded by hostile Catholic families of Gaelic origin and by those of English stock and he carries more than one weapon with him wherever he goes and his doors are barred at night and his windows have metal gratings over them and he keeps a loaded pistol always to hand. What he cannot weather is the government of Ireland, more changeable than a weathercock, less trustworthy than the heart of a whore, a government that is as much a menace to its loyal servants as to its sworn enemies.

When Anthony Briskett was twenty years of age, in 1612, his father died. Anthony came into his majority and into the Macmine estate a year later, only to find that the lord deputy of Ireland, Arthur Chichester (Baron Chichester, 1613) had decided to rearrange almost all of the land titles of north Wexford, never mind if they were held by persons pro- or anti-government, Catholic or Protestant. The land titles were all surrendered to the Crown. Anyone with less than 100 freehold acres simply lost the land; a very few persons had their estates confirmed, but three-quarters of the remaining estate holders lost their lands entirely, while the rest received supposedly-equivalent grants elsewhere in Wexford. Anthony Briskett was slapped away from Macmine as if he were an insect on the wall. He was given an inferior 120 acres elsewhere and told to be happy with it. Briskett kept quiet, and just as well. When, in 1620, a group of 200 former gentry, still protesting, waited on the new lord deputy, Sir Oliver St. John, they were clapped in gaol and a score of the noisiest protestors were shipped to Virginia.

Anthony Briskett knows that there's an entire New World where the government's hand is weak and the natives no tougher than those he has to deal with every day. He devotes himself to arriving there, as an estate master at minimum, as a feudal lord if possible: Protestant gentleman bedamned.

RIVER GAMBIA, SENAGAMBIA, WESTERN AFRICA. 1621

Frame of Reference

Richard Jobson has seen enough of the world not to be surprised at any native custom, but this celebration is new to him. He is 300 miles up the River Gambia. Unlike later English explorers of Africa, he is interested not in slaves, but in gold. All around him a great fair is taking place. Every large tree is an umbrella for a campfire. Dancing is continuous and music is made with an instrument keyed like a virginal and played with two leather-tipped sticks. It produces a music in a tonal scale unlike anything Jobson has ever heard. All around, women dance in a strange posture: bending their knees wide apart and tipping their bodies forward, as if in pain. The men, like the women, dance naked. Each of the men dances alone, a sword or short knife in his hand.

Like many members of the Guinea Company, Jobson has spent his apprenticeship in the colonization of Ireland, or at least in trying to make a quick fortune from the place. His frame of reference is Ireland, and whenever he needs to compare an unfamiliar African practice to something he knows, it is to Irish native customs.

So, when he observes a court bard-musician among the Mandinka, he likens him to the "Irish Rimers" who attend the Gaelic chiefs. A Mandinka burial ceremony, with its fulsome praise of the deceased and its atonal, otherworldly mourning is compared to mourners keening the Irish dead.

The Fulby, a subordinate tribe, part west- and part north-African, reminds him of gypsies. In their moving herds of cattle from one temporary spot to another, he sees the transhumance of Irish upland herdsmen; their male warriors are forever on the move, like Irish kernes. And the women. The Fulby women, despite their mud-and-cattle way of life, are hygienic paragons compared to the Irish. "With cleanliness your Irish women hath no acquaintance."

Yet, Irish adventuring has not prepared Richard Jobson for the ritual circumcisions he now witnesses. Several sixteen-year-old boys are cut amid the noise of drumbeats that, intermingled with shouts of pain, rises to a crescendo so loud that Jobson can only describe it as "a great roaring noyse." It takes three cuts to remove the prepuce of one lad, and Jobson reflects that most peoples willingly do to themselves things they would not accept from even the most tyrannical of conquerors.

DROGHEDA, COUNTY LOUTH. 1626

Gifts of the Spirit

James Ussher, now Lord Primate of All Ireland, settles into the archepiscopal palace. By Protestant reckoning he is the one-hundredth incumbent of that see and the direct heir of St. Patrick. Ussher resides in Drogheda, mostly, or in Dublin: for Shane O'Neill had torched the Armagh cathedral and the archbishop's palace in 1566. Ussher lives comfortably in Drogheda. He, like most English-speakers who have no Irish, call it "Tredagh."

Ussher takes pride in being St. Patrick's heir and writes learned explanations of why Irish Protestants, rather than Irish Catholics, are followers of the True Faith. Everything he puts into print is very rational. Later Irish Anglicans point to him as the most outstanding Irish churchman ever, save of course St. Patrick.

In his own ground, in his own time, James Ussher is similar to the scientists of his era, who are one-half chemist, one-half alchemist, or the mathematicians who are also astrologers. Since his youth, he has been deeply entranced not just with chronology but with numerology; not just with the delineation of the past but with predicting the future. His clergy love him for it. In public he provides them with burning, albeit ambiguous prophecies. In private he tells his trusted circle, the nature of things-to-come.

The architecture of the episcopal palace in Drogheda was rationality outside, necromancy inside. Its form was four-square, wood covered with stucco, plain; inside were two dining rooms, one for formal occasions, the other for deep discussions with his acolytes, and a chapel, approached by a gallery. After prayers in the chapel, Ussher's practice was to talk far into the night. To his favourites, he showed pages of calculations that revealed, among other things, that the earth would endure, from Creation to Final Destruction, exactly 6,000 years. And he explained to his intimates the sermons and homilies he had preached which contained encoded prophecies that he now made explicit: in strictest secrecy.

One of these prophecies was preached in 1601 and in it Ussher reckoned that forty "days," meaning years, would pass before a great disaster would fall on "Judah," the Chosen People of the Almighty, in this case meaning the Protestants of Ireland. Another, preached in St. Mary's Church, Cambridge in 1625 repeated Samuel's ancient prophecy that "if you do wickedly, you shall be consumed, both you and your king." That would happen again, within their lifetimes, Ussher darkly noted. And he showed his earnest disciples that, in 1624, he had given a public speech, indicating that the greatest stroke against the Reformation in Ireland was yet to come, but that the utter ruin of the Roman church in Ireland would follow.

As candles burned down, these prophecies were marked and inwardly digested.

Ussher uttered many more.

After his death in 1656, his disciples consented that these predictions, privately made specific and told to them by the archbishop, had all come true, largely.

DUBLIN CASTLE. 1629

Learning Curve

In the long skein of Crown representatives in Ireland, Henry Cary, Viscount Falkland, Lord Deputy 1622–29, was the only one with a backwards-bending learning curve. Everyone else, even the thickest, left Ireland knowing more than when he had arrived. Not Falkland.

The training ground for the Viscount was Newfoundland, not a spot that one would immediately associate with efficient government, even in the seventeenth century. Cary (who was given a Scottish peerage in 1620), received in 1610 a strip of the Avalon Peninsula, Newfoundland. His idea was to fill it with Irish as well as English settlers – so long as the Irish were not Gaelic speaking: in other words, Old Catholics, not Native Irish.

Falkland was the first Crown representative in Ireland to try to convert lessons learned in empire into a how-to manual for Ireland. Every other chief governor to that point had done the opposite: hammered the Irish and when they had their practising done, had gone and played the game for bigger stakes in some New World.

If, when Falkland left Dublin in 1629 he was not kicking and screaming, that was only because he did not understand the trouble he was in. Dismissed from office, he was in for three years of public trials and a stress-induced death in 1633.

Falkland's problem had begun when he cheated the O'Brynes out of some lands in County Wicklow and took much of it for himself. They were not a petty clan: they raised hell. Still, Falkland's real problem was that he was not very good at his job, which involved very delicate negotiations if the Crown's interests were to be protected without civil strife ensuing.

But his tiny Newfoundland colony, had taught Viscount Falkland all the wrong lessons. That far colony worked for a time because he was able to impose three grand simplicities: keep the local indigenous population away from the colonists; maintain a single language, English; and allow only a single religion. Falkland did not much care which one, though he was Protestant himself. He could have lived with Catholicism, but not with a sectarian divide.

Sensible ideas for a colony, maybe; but try to run Ireland that way.

SOUTH MUNSTER, IRELAND. 1631

Brisk Trade

"Pray for their souls."

That advice, in Irish, English, Latin, was the best the soul-keeper and elders of the tribe could tell the keening women, the hysterical children, the dumb-struck and stone-faced men. "Some day, God willing, they will be taken to a better land."

South Munster was a harsh enough place to live with the New English and Old Irish and Old English all scrambling for land; and the seducers from the West Indies drawing away robust young men and women for indentured servants. And Munster was still a pirate-zone, infested annually by European cut-throats who traded their booty, intermarried, stole, occasionally kidnapped.

Yet the people somehow adapted.

They forgot, however, that in a pirate zone trade not only was brisk, but that it ran two ways: it was all very well to act as receivers for Spanish and French booty, but the native Irish forgot just how open their own coastline was.

Suddenly in 1631, a fleet of North African corsairs swept down upon them. Their attack focussed on Baltimore, Co. Cork. The North Africans seized more than 200 Irish for slaves. Heathens enslaving Christians! what could be worse?

"Pray for their souls. And for the servants of King Charles," the elders advised. And eventually Charles I, sick of gnat-bite land invasions and of African piracy on English merchant ships, put together a fleet and in 1637 attacked the African pirate port of Sallee. Eight ships and nearly 1,000 sailors and marines finally stormed this, one of the several corsair strongholds on the North African coast. They freed 339 Christians – that's how one counted people in these matters. Among the Christians were fifty-six Irish people.

What happened to the 150-plus Irish still unaccounted for? They, and several hundred others who had been enslaved over the years by the Islamic pirates, were forever lost in the brisk Arab trade in people. They tumbled down the African continent, at first being the prized possessions of caliphs and then, as they grew older and less useful, became the domestic kick-dogs of merchants and the swill-carriers of desert ostlers.

"Pray for their souls."

SPAIN. 1636

For the Love of God

Captain Bernard O'Brien, who viewed himself as a great colonizer, suffered the indignity of captivity in a Portuguese gaol in an Amazon frontier town and then of being relieved from irons by way of trade: he was dealt to the Cururi indians, who were cannibals. He picked up enough of their language and comported himself wisely enough to avoid becoming nutrition. Captain O'Brien's tortuous trip back to Europe does not bear recording (although, as was the case with so many early colonizers, that did not preclude his recording it), save for its conclusion.

In Europe he showed how consumingly addictive the process of colonizing could become.

He repeatedly petitioned the king of Spain for support for yet another Amazon colony and, when he ran out of economic arguments, he pointed out to his Spanish Majesty that the English and Dutch had settlements in the region: they were making the natives into heretics.

DUBLIN. APRIL 1640

God's Special Providence

By God's special providence Archbishop James Ussher, his wife and daughter board a ship for England. He never sees Ireland again and, though his own life in England is not easy, he avoids the troubles that he has prophesied for Ireland.

Before leaving Drogheda, he instructs his domestic chaplain in the intricacies of misery that will befall the Protestants of Ireland.

In October 1641, a Catholic conspiracy of compact dimensions gained spontaneous adherents, reached a critical-mass, and became a self-sustaining, and uncontrollable *jacquerie*. Local scores were settled. The bodies of Protestant families clogged the watercourses of several Ulster baronies. The smell of burning humans, congregations incinerated inside their heretic churches, drove the dogs of the Irish chieftains berserk: they knew that when meat was cooked they could count on a feeding, yet where was the hearth, and where the fat-dripping beasts who should be roasting there?

Perhaps, in a conservative estimate, 4,000 Protestants (mostly, but not entirely of English or Scottish origin) are killed immediately and another 8,000 die as refugees through starvation and disease. The numbers are immediately exaggerated in the propaganda war that follows, but the real numbers are impressive enough.

Archbishop Ussher has all his private property in Ireland seized or destroyed by the Catholics and he makes a wobbly livelihood by serving as preacher to Lincoln's Inn. For a time he is given the income of the bishopric of Carlisle, but parliament stops that. Had he not later been voted £400 a year (confirmed still later by Oliver Cromwell), this heir to the throne of St. Patrick would have been reduced to the standard of life of an English curate.

Ussher is remarkably patient. He does not complain.

He has seen his first prophecy made true.

EUROPE. 1641FF

Mild Geese, Wild Geese

Irish theology students and Irish soldiers had criss-crossed the continent for a millennium, but it is the Rebellion of 1641 and the subsequent Civil War and the decisive Protestant settlements of the Irish issue that produce the flight of the mild and the wild geese. It continues in full flow for a century-and-a-half and then tapers downward. But it never totally stops.

From the mid-seventeenth century, it became common to ordain promising young Irish men as priests and then send them to a Continental seminary for training. These youths were literate, knew some Latin, and were devout; but they were desperately in need of special, indeed rehabilitative training. Hence, the Irish colleges that emerge in several Catholic universities. The young seminarians often are impoverished as well as untrained, so some colleges give the Irish students the right to perform funerary rites and thus to cadge enough for their bed and board. They are, technically, priests. Probably 400 Irish priests were trained at Louvain in the seventeenth century and 3–4,000 in Paris in the seventeenth and eighteenth centuries. Usually they did six years' study and then returned to Ireland as fully competent priests. There, though, is the rub: many of them find careers as priests in France or Spain or in the Catholic portions of the Germanies and Ireland loses many of the brightest minds of the country, generation after generation.

The wild geese had been migrating to Spain in numbers since the Desmond Wars in late sixteenth-century Munster and, in the 1630s,

Irish regiments were added to the French army. Still, it was after 1641 and the subsequent Irish Civil War that the Irish come to form a continuous stream of military mercenaries.

Wild geese: as romantic an image as Ireland produced since the legend of the children of Lir and the Swans: carrying with it aristocratic overtones, the plangencies of exile, the sound of collective responsibility, the loyalty of nation away from the national home. Most of the wild geese, however, are ordinary foot soldiers who follow their officers and clan leaders (often the same thing), as those officers negotiate the best deal they can for themselves. Most are hard peasants, with the sense of self that a sword and training in killing will drape on a man's shoulders. Many of them travel to the Continent with wives and children in tow, or acquire women abroad, so that little colonies of Irish mercenary families dot the Continent. Death, or just going native – they desert and blend into the European peasantry – deplete their numbers, but clandestine recruiting in Ireland during the seventeenth and eighteenth centuries fills the vacancies.

Fine mercenaries, mind you. Probably 12,000 died heartily fighting for Spain in the late 1640s, and 30,000 or more joined the Spanish or French armies in the later days of Oliver Cromwell's harrowing of Ireland. Being mercenaries, and given that France and Spain were at war, they sometimes fought each other with professional zeal. And, on several occasions over the next century, they follow their officers in switching employers when the price is right, sometimes in the middle of a conflict.

And why not?

LONDON. 31 JANUARY 1649

Vertigo

The vertiginous drop turns Archbishop Ussher, now in his mid-sixties, queasy. He has always hated heights, yet he and several ecclesiastics and temporal lords are perched on the roof of the Countess of Peterborough's house, near Charing Cross. They are waiting for the tragedy's last act.

Ussher is not delicate. In 1645, he had walked alongside his long-time friend, Thomas Wentworth, earl of Strafford, formerly lord deputy of Ireland, as he approached the executioner's block. He knelt beside the block and prayed with Strafford and watched the execution without flinching. It was an unjust act, Ussher believed. "Never has so white a soul returned to his Maker," he pointedly told King Charles. But not an event that spun the archbishop into despond.

Today's does. *If you do wickedly, you shall be consumed, both you and your king.* His prophecy, the ancient prophecy of Samuel, his own indelicate vertigo, all come together and Ussher fears that he will spiral off the countess's rooftop just as the kingdom spirals into the prophesied conflagration.

Charles, monarch of Ireland, England, Scotland, comes into view, and while being led, he talks. From this distance, it is unclear if he is making a formal speech. Ussher points his fingers heavenwards in prayer and cries unashamedly. As the king is stripped of his cloak, doublet, waistcoat and has his hair pulled back for the convenience of the executioner, Ussher stares downward and sees in swirl the end of his known world. He faints and, had his servant not caught him, he would have slid to the pavement below, reaching eternity a minute before his monarch. As it was, his swoon prevented his seeing the actual beheading.

He took to his bed and prayed continuously for the soul of the departed.

At such moments, the life of a prophet is not easy.

DROGHEDA, COUNTY LOUTH. 11 SEPTEMBER 1649

Archbishop Ussher's Third Prophecy

The archbishop with the long face has met the man with the bad haircut only once. Soon after the execution of King Charles, Oliver Cromwell had sent for Archbishop Ussher. For several weeks, Ussher refused to appear. Then, in a curt interview, he obtained a promise from Cromwell that a few emoluments would be tossed the way of the Irish Anglican clergy, who, though tainted by episcopacy, at least were Protestant. Or semi-Protestant: Cromwell wasn't too sure.

Oliver Cromwell simplified Irish politics considerably. For nearly a decade a civil war had raged in Ireland, with five or six sides active at any moment. A confusing kaleidoscope of alliances dominated the scene. In London, Archbishop Ussher kept in touch with this mess and waited for his third prophecy to come true: whatever his many vices, Oliver Cromwell might be the swordhand that fulfilled Ussher's third prophecy, the utter ruination of the Roman Church in Ireland.

Alas, poor dear Drogheda! Ussher feared for it. For most of a decade Drogheda had been in the hands of various rebels. They treated the palace of the Protestant archbishop with superstitious respect for, being a religious building, it was best to deliver it as booty to some religious purpose. For a time, Ussher's domestic chaplain remained inside, under house arrest, and became increasingly dejected by the daily news of the rialto. The archbishop's residence contained one of the finest private collections of antiquarian manuscripts and books in the British Isles. What should be done with them, instruments of the Protestant demons as they perhaps were?

The populace were for burning the Protestant chaplain and using the manuscripts and books instead of faggots. The Catholic clergy, however, knew that the texts could be cleansed of their heresy and they spoke of James Ussher's library as a momentous prize of conquest. To Ussher's relief, most of the material was smuggled to Chester, England, early in the conflict.

Drogheda was relieved in an entirely different way. Oliver Cromwell and his New Model Army of roughly 10,000 men surrounded Drogheda, held by a mixed force of Irish and English of perhaps 2,600, under a royalist commander. As a stoutly-walled seaport town, it was not easy to assault, so the Irish and royalist English forces gave a haughty dismissal to the demand that they surrender. Cromwell, under the then-prevailing rules of war, was justified in declaring that no quarter would be given in the battle that followed.

But, dear Lord, how did he justify the murder of several hundred civilians? Beheading the royalist commander and hacking him to pieces was biblical: having lived by the sword, the man died by the sword. But where did the women hidden in the vaults of a Catholic church enter the equation? Did the five days of massacre, in which at least 1,000 civilians were mutilated or, if lucky, killed, fit any known template? Killing two-and-a-half thousand soldiers, perhaps that was war, but this was the beginning of the mini-apocalypse Ussher had prophesied, surely: it assumed the form of slaughter, by Jehovah's swift sword, of the Roman beast.

And, if much the same thing occurred in Wexford City a little more than a month later, who was Archbishop Ussher to criticize the Almighty for using such an imperfect person as Cromwell to exercise His will?

The Heart of the Matter

"The man, false as a harlot, refuses his promises to me."
"Indeed?"
"He has broke his word with me, to aid my clergy. And when I remind him of it, he refuses to perform what he in honour promised."
"Not a man of integrity is he, Archbishop?"
"He is a species of man who has all guts and no bowels." James Ussher has just returned from his second, and final interview of substance with Oliver Cromwell. Though in his early seventies and in fading health, Ussher's discussion with the Protector had been carried on with the energy of a crusader on a mission while, in contrast, Cromwell was withdrawn, tired and abrupt.

An ulcer grew on Cromwell's neck and the Protector was more interested in speaking of his surgeon's diagnosis than he was in considering the details of Irish religious affairs. Near the end of their fruitless conversation, Cromwell pointed to the tumour on his neck. "If this core were cut out, I should soon be well."

"I believe that the core lies deeper," Ussher replied. Less frank talk than this had cost men their lives. "There is a core that must be taken out or else it will not be well."

"Yes."

With cunning ambiguity, the archbishop added, "The core is in the heart."

"So it is," Cromwell agreed with a sigh.

Discrete Judgements

Speaking to his friend, the Rev. Dr. Gauden, destined to become bishop of Exeter, James Ussher utters one final prophecy on matters of state. He admits that Oliver Cromwell could well be the hand on the Almighty's sword: but he also knows that the hand could be leprous, for the Scriptures teach that the Lord is not too fussy about how clean his tools are. Pacing his private apartments, reviewing for Dr. Gauden the conversation he has just conducted with the ulcerous Cromwell, Ussher stops in mid-sentence and in mid-room. In a voice summoned from his youthful fame as a pulpit orator, he pronounces: "That false man will have little cause to glory in his wickedness. *He shall not continue long.* And the King shall return."

This prophecy never comes to Cromwell's notice, but it would not have changed his angle on Ussher if it had. Cromwell distrusts Ussher as an advocate of episcopacy and, who knows? as a crypto-Romanist; yet Cromwell, for all his denunciations of Romish magic, is a superstitious man and he knows that Ussher, at minimum, is a seer.

That is why, when James Ussher, now purblind as Tiresias, dies in 1656, the Protector directs that he shall be buried, with full honour, in Westminster Abbey.

Cromwell knows his Scriptures well, and accepts that prophets, though they chafe like the horsehair cloak of some ignorant Romish ascetic, are frequently the Lord's anointed; and Cromwell has noted that the Lord has a very bad temper, not unlike his own.

IRELAND. 1652–1660

The Harrowing of Ireland

Molly Hore, lady of Kilsallaghan Castle, seven miles north of Dublin, walks alone and slowly. She tries not to appear watchful, but she needs to avoid attracting attention. Warily, she enters the stables. Empty of humans. The smell and sound of horses is comforting as she climbs on a stile, throws a rope over a rafter and ties a noose. The horses pay no attention as her life expires. She, her husband, and family had been served with a legal summons demanding that they leave their sweet Dublin lands and relocate somewhere amidst the harsh rocks and bogs of Connaught.

Even before their victory in Ireland was complete, the Cromwellian leaders knew what they wanted of Ireland: an empty space. And, so, effectively, the entire country was confiscated. The exceptions were the properties of those few individuals who somehow had kept their hands clean during the decade of civil war and also had not fought against Cromwell. Put simply, the Puritans envisaged abrogating all Catholic land titles and drawing a new world on the blank piece of paper that Ireland would become.

Christopher Eustace, Esq., of County Kildare, had his estate taken, but recovered it when a king sat again on the vacant throne. The price Eustace paid for his years of displacement was that he went mad and what had been an estate of a gentleman became the asylum of a lunatick.

The scale is wrong. Ireland contains roughly two million persons, of whom 20 percent in 1652 are Protestants. (The enormity of the Irish civil war and then Cromwell's intervention can be judged by the best estimates being that approximately 400,000 persons had vanished since 1641.) Still, there are too many people to be pushed around as if they were water, so the Irish tenantry are left alone for the most part: they can be dealt with later and, besides, they are useful helots. The commissioners who deal with land, therefore, are focussing on the Catholic leaders, the gentry and aristocracy, the respectable small freeholders. They are the enemy.

On 30 January 1654 several Catholic gentlemen, their families left behind, face the Commissioners for Ireland at Loughrea and are given certificates that specify the lands they are to occupy in Connaught, replacement for their previous estates. They are required to be on the lands and have their wives and families with them by the first of May. The sign that they have settled in properly, and thus that their new lands are confirmed, is that each gentleman shall have built a hut to house his family.

So many grabbers: Cromwellian soldiers, merchant-adventurers who have financed Puritan schemes. So many debts owed by the government. There is not enough Ireland to go around. And confiscation is devilishly slow work, given the state of Irish records. Even so, nearly 2,000 major Catholic landlords are ordered "transplanted" beyond the Shannon. There they are allocated diminished portions of lands, and these are taken from local landlords. The resulting disputes among new and old Connaught landholders must have resembled feeding time at a disorderly kennel.

Like a large bowl whose meniscus becomes thin and finally ruptures, Ireland loses population on all sides. By arrangement with the

Spanish government, the Puritans allow Irish swordsmen to be recruited for Spanish service. Nobles and their families escape to the Continent. Young men and women, not content to work for the new English landholders, take indentured passage to Montserrat, St. Christopher's, or the Chesapeake colony. And still the loss is not enough for, no matter what the number, there will always be too many Irish for the Puritans to stomach.

How it would have ended, even Archbishop Ussher could not have known. He was right, however: a king again sat on the throne. In 1660 the Restoration stopped the creation of the New Model Ireland in mid-stride.

THE EMPIRE OF THE OBSCURE: THE WEST INDIES, 1620–1667

Tiny Blisters

The Irish had been there eight years, good years really, when the 200 Englishmen of Thomas King came into view. Fourteen Irishmen. No more. They had been living in comfortable and profitable isolation from all but the rarest of European contacts. The newly arrived English were amiable enough and when the English re-shipped upstream to found their own colony, the Irish gave them a formal salute and then began to wager how many would survive a year.

Since 1610, little blisters of colonies had been breaking out in the Amazon and its basin: English, Irish, and joint ventures between English and Irish merchants, as well as English-Dutch projects. And around the corner were the Portuguese, using Brazil as their battlement.

The fourteen Irishmen were happy enough. They had built a stockade. In any case, the local Carib and Arawak, though hostile to each other, were compliant with the few desires the Irish expressed. The Amazon could be either a graveyard or a soft life, depending on how a settler played the place. Shrewdly, this tiny Irish band did not unsettle the local life, but used it for their own ends. Dyes and medicinal plants were acquired without upset to the locals, and in exchange for trinkets the indigène were willing to grow tobacco in quantity. The river was full of food, large turtles and fish for which the Irish had no name.

This tiny colony became its own exotic world. The settlers spoke an amalgam of English, Irish, and at least two Indian languages: their conversation, could we hear it, would be a rosetta stone of early sixteenth-century tongues and would make the reputation of any linguist who mastered them.

These settlers formed Ireland's first new colony in roughly 1,000 years. They were the operatives of one Philip Purcell, a Munsterman who had made trips to the Caribbean in the early years of the century and learned of the Amazon's potential as a meadow rich in exotic crops. What can have been in the heads and hearts of the fourteen men he recruited from the south of Ireland? What made life in an unknown world preferable to remaining at home?

In the same year, 1620, a second Irish colony is established. It, like Purcell's, is a private money-making exercise. This one is led by a Captain Bernard O'Brien, who claims to be closely related to Donat O'Brien, earl of Thomond. His party settles downriver from Purcell's.

For both groups, the early 1620s are prosperous times.

And for O'Brien, the leader, they are good fun. He makes a trip up-river and reports upon his return that he has seduced an Amazon queen. His own private parts, he says, are of the dimensions such a conquest requires.

DUBLIN. 1623

Seminal Flow

Ireland, especially Munster and south Leinster, had too many left-over gentry, both Gaelic and Old English. *Though they have not six-pence to live on, they disdain to follow any trade, but only some turn foot-boys ... They press to other men's houses of their acquaintance or alliance, and there spend their days idle to the excessive charge of house-keepers, who there perpetually be pestered with such guests.*

Thus Sir Arthur Bourchier, afterwards fifth earl of Bath. He did not much like the Irish – his father had been one of the Elizabethan plun-derers of south Munster – but he was a shrewd observer. He had spent months in 1622 touring the south of Ireland as part of a London-created commission that was to report on the continuing cockups of the Dublin regime; things such as the mess in land titles in Wexford. Sir Arthur had a biological explanation of why the number of minor Irish gentry, the loose-ends chieflings the government so feared, had increased greatly since the Irish defeat of 1603. *This kind of rabble, and many others of the mere Irish ... have multiplied to an incredible number far more than here [in England] for two reasons: because they generally (be they ever so poor) af-fect to marry timely or else keep an unmarried [woman] and cohabit with her as their reputed wife; and they take much felicity and content in their procre-ation and issue; and because they devote themselves to idleness and rest and do feed altogether on moist meats, they abound with more children than such are pains to dry their superflous humours.*

ST. CHRISTOPHER [LATER "ST. KITTS"], THE LEEWARD
ISLANDS. 24 JANUARY 1624

The Shape of the World (1)

Each generation of humanity changes the shape of the world. Captain
Thomas Warner, his wife and his son Edward, aged thirteen, and a
party of about fifteen men, take control of the island in the name of
his majesty James I and VI. They encounter three Frenchmen, but
they are docile. Tobacco and provision crops are planted. So strong is
the optimism of Warner and his party that even the hurricane destruction of their crops in mid-September, 1624, barely dampens their
enthusiasm. St. Christopher will be the mother colony of the English
empire in the Caribbean.

To Captain Warner and to his contemporary adventurers, Spanish,
Dutch, Portuguese, the earth was in theory a globe, but they were too
practical to act upon that theory. In fact, for mariners of the fifteenth
through mid-nineteenth centuries, the earth was a deformed, oblong
structure, something like a half-deflated rugby ball being squeezed in
the paws of a giant prop forward. That is: one could not travel around
it as was to occur later in the age of air travel, using Great Circle geometry. Instead, one had to pass down the valleys on the crumpled globe's
surface. Otherwise, it was all uphill work. Thus, when Thomas Warner
brought over subsequent loads of settlers, his vessels sailed from
Kinsale or Plymouth southwards until in the vicinity of the Canary
Islands they picked up trade winds that blew them westward for a
month or so. Good luck and good navigation were needed, and
prayers, for if the ship missed its tiny target, an island in a vast ocean,
weeks were required to work back against the prevailing winds.

Warner had come to know of St. Christopher by an even more ar-
duous path. He had been part of the Guiana Company's 1620 expedition to the Amazon. After two years, he left and sailed with a small
party up the Lesser Antilles, island-hopping, and on St. Christopher
he found the perfect spot for a settler world. Forget finding Eldorado:
grow tobacco and indigo. The local natives, Caribs, were led by a
friendly chief, Tegramond, and seemed peaceful. This was the place
to start an empire of settlement.

Having seen his future, Thomas Warner worked his way north, and
then caught winds that drove him eastward and home: ten weeks of
unremitting toil.

As the son of a Suffolk-farmer, Warner can describe topography and crop lands and water tables and potential crops and their yields convincingly. He has powerful friends, the earl of Warwick and John Winthrop (of Massachusetts fame) and he picks up investors. His talk of deep soils, abundant fresh water, safe anchorage makes the island seem the perfect tobacco garden.

So, in 1623, Warner starts the next leg of his voyage around the crumpled earth. He sails with a few men and his own family to Virginia, where he evangelizes for St. Christopher. He picks up only a handful of recruits, which is why his party, as it finally settles on the island of St. Christopher, has fewer than twenty members.

It's an amazing place, is St. Christopher. Fertile. Friendly natives. Peaceful co-existence with the French. Tiny. Perfect. Too good to be long real.

THE LOWER AMAZON. MAY 1625

Behold, Our Neighbours!

Rarely do they smile, but the opinion held by the Irish of the Carib, Arawak, Wacacoia and others is wrong: the natives do have a sense of humour. They think it very funny when Captain Bernard O'Brien ventures into the rain forest to tell them to stop fighting each other. He wants them to behave like good Christians.

That was his last public act before he set sail for Europe to raise funds for more colonization. In Catholic countries he emphasized that the Irish colonists were good Catholics and, to the Spanish, he added that they had nothing but love for the Spanish king. To every potential backer he approached, O'Brien pleaded the need for protection from the Portuguese.

Scarcely had the natives returned to their avocational butchery of each other than happiness smote them in the face and they actually laughed. For: into the basin comes Captain Pedro Teixeira, fifty European soldiers and 300 Indians. The native observers had no way of knowing in advance that Teixeira was one of the best of all of Portugal's frontier warriors, but they immediately admired his skill. It was a joy to see how, despite the defensive cooperation of the Dutch, English, and Irish settlers, he cut them to pieces, wiping out three of their forts. Philip Purcell of the Irish colony was killed and his brother James taken prisoner. The scale of Teixera's campaign was Lilliputian by the standards of continental European warfare, but he made up for this by maintaining a ruthless intensity.

The savages are fascinated to observe the civilizing force of the European warlord.

Some seventy of the Irish, drawn from all over the basin, surrender to Teixera, trusting in his honour as a fellow Catholic.

The natives smile as fifty-four are put to death, randomly.

LONDON. 13 SEPTEMBER 1625

The Shape of the World (2)

A slight smile, that is all Captain Thomas Warner permits himself, but he is happy in a Suffolk Puritan sort of way. He holds a large piece of parchment, engrossed with the Great Seal, that details letters patent, making him and his commercial associates the king's lieutenants over several islands in the West Indies. This is what he had returned to London for and he garnered this prize even while his second load of colonists was digging in, literally, on St. Christopher. Warner is lucky. The new king, Charles I , was intent on putting a thumb in the eye of the Spanish by expanding his own empire. Warner's letters patent are not quite the same as a grant of ownership – that still was held by the Crown – but they will do very nicely, thank you.

When he closed his eyes, Warner could see a navigational map. And he could see the world as it then existed more clearly than any cartographer or colonizer or chronicler saw it from, roughly, 1700 onwards. The territory placed in Warner's custody – the Leeward Islands of St. Christopher, Nevis, Montserrat and the Windward Island of Barbados – were destined to be "British America." With Antigua soon added and Jamaica captured in 1655, these islands, not the mainland colonies, running from Newfoundland to Virginia, were the substance of the seventeenth century's New World. The mainland colonies scarcely counted, being either empty of profits or full of prophets.

These islands (and a few little isles tucked in among them) were the Empire. They were perfectly located to the windward of the big

Spanish colonies and off the main Spanish sea lanes. The French and Dutch were all around, but easier to deal with. England's commercial empire, an empire of settlement rather than of pillage, as was the Spanish empire in Latin and South America, was here in the islands. Warner saw the present and the immediate future accurately. We resist the clarity of his vision. Mainland America is so important. Not always.

From Warner's day until the close of the Glorious Revolution, William's revolution of 1688–91, 60 percent of emigration from the British Isles was to the Caribbean. Indeed, prior to the completion of the Restoration Settlement in the mid 1660s, three-quarters of the human flow from the British Isles was to the Caribbean. Mainland America counted, but not as much. Even if we take all the migration up to the American revolution, as many English, Scots, Irish went to the West Indies as to Mainland America and if one adds in Africans (strange how they are so easily forgotten, isn't it?) the total trans-Atlantic migration to the West Indies exceeds that to the mainland.

And we resist even more the other fact about this Caribbean empire-of-the-obscure: up to 1660, nearly half of its white population was of Irish background, and even on the eve of the Glorious Revolution the Irish were roughly one-third of the "British." And, for reasons of religion, many of them were quite pleased that this, England's seventeenth-century empire of settlement, was far from transparent to everyone, and most especially not to the London authorities.

ST. CHRISTOPHER, THE LEEWARD ISLANDS. NOVEMBER 1625

Domestic Life

They aren't at all like modern gardeners. Neatness is irrelevant, and they slash and burn as preparation for planting. Aesthetics are never considered. They plant to eat, they harvest to survive. Maize, wheat, plantains, pease, tough little red peppers, apples that are gnarly as walnuts, plants that yield dyes, and indigenous cotton that grows on short stalks and when cut, makes blissfully soft bedding. Everything grows in a great tangle, rows of one species intersecting at obtuse angles those of other species. These people are not conservationists.

When the soil is worn out in one garden they simply abandon it to the jungle and slash and burn new gardens in the bush.

They are a solemn people, rarely given to smiling and they laugh only in moments of intense cruelty, as in battle. Words are hoarded, as if wasting them depletes some linguistic bank account that can never be replenished. Melancholic in appearance, they seldom speak unless spoken to. Personal names are used as sparingly as possible.

These are the Carib, but the same characteristics hold for the rustics of southern England who predominate in Thomas Warner's first two shiploads of settlers sent to St. Christopher.

Warner shows considerable diplomatic skills in making friends with the chief on St. Christopher, Tegramond, for the Carib are not to be taken lightly and do not take easily to strangers. For the past 200 years they have been on a long northward march, beginning on the South American mainland, skipping from island to island, driving out the Arawak and the Ciboney. They are hard people, able to raise marine corps of 2,000–3,000 warriors who move in *pirogues*, 60–80-man war canoes and can sweep down on the coast of any island, slip ashore and attack the inhabitants. They are especially good with poison darts that can be dispatched much faster than sixteenth-century firearms can be fired. Earlier, when Christopher Columbus encountered the Arawak, they told him horror stories of the Carib, including the disinformation that they were human flesh eaters – thus, through the corruption of usage, the word "cannibal."

By the time of the English empire's beginning in the West Indies the Carib are scattered thinly, all the way up to Puerto Rico, which they raid from off-shore islands. The luck of the English, however, is considerable. On most of the islands that form the basis of British America – Barbados, Montserrat, and Nevis, most importantly – the Carib have only temporary gardens that they use in case of war, and no permanent habitations. Antigua and St. Christopher house permanent populations, but they are peaceful, at least that's the way Thomas Warner left things in 1625 when he returned to London to obtain his licence to colonize.

While Warner was gone, a battered French privateer anchored and its officers and crew came ashore on St. Christopher. They had been badly hammered by a Spanish vessel and now wanted to give up buccaneering. They settled on the island and a formal sharing of St. Christopher between the two nations began. The French held the two ends of the island, the English the centre. This arrangement lasted for nearly four decades, broken by occasional fighting interposed on the island from outside. Mostly, they coexisted peaceably and even cooperated, for they created a common enemy.

Witness: when in November 1625, Carib bands from other islands appear on St. Christopher, the English and French both panic. They do not understand that migration up and down the Antilles is standard practice for the Carib and that if they were planning on attacking the Europeans they would not be visible: Carib forays were lethal, usually night-attacks. The Europeans, however, engage the Carib and the natives clear off. They return a month later and a pitched battle ensues. For the moment they are defeated, driven from the island they know as Liamuiga, the Fertile Island.

Domestic life returns to St. Christopher. Solemn, unsmiling men, and a few women, slash and burn and plant maize, wheat, plantains, pease, rough little red peppers, and their newest crop, tobacco. Unlike the Carib, they do so in constant fear of attacks from avenging hordes of naked men who, the settlers believe, eat their enemies.

ST. CHRISTOPHER. SEPTEMBER 1626

Family Formation

It's a challenge every time he enters her.

Captain Thomas Warner has returned to St. Christopher and so too have the Carib. The French, the Carib, the British-Isles lots live uneasily. Warner has brought back a shipload of colonists, including a pack of Irishmen, and now his people are the strongest on the island.

Warner has been copulating with one of the daughters of Chief Tegramond ever since she was given to him, as a welcoming present by the chief. Now, with relations between the Carib and the British so strained, it's more than ever a challenge: as always, she is passive and withdrawn and his challenge is to make her show some emotion. If all else fails, pain makes her show fear.

She knows her duty and neither she nor Warner question it, for she has been allocated a role and that is both fate and duty. Warner never knows her real name, for she keeps her soul-name to herself, but he thinks of her as red-bitch and bites the back of her neck when he takes her from behind. Nightly she finds her way to him, slipping through the bush silently, a prey moving perversely into the visual field of a nighthawk.

As his captive animal, she shows loyalty. It can be no other way. One night she tells him that her people are planning a surprise attack upon the British.

Warner responds.

He and his men massacre the bulk of the Carib population of St. Christopher, a military achievement of some moment. Chief Tegramond, sleeping in his hammock, is pierced through with swords from all directions, and his blood dribbles to the ground in droplets, like whey dripping through cheesecloth.

The locals flee and when they return with help from Antigua, also part of Tegramond's domain, the British defeat them again and then burn out the indigenous population of Antigua.

As trophies, Thomas Warner keeps alive both Tegramond's daughter and one of the chief's infant sons. The daughter is pregnant with Warner's child. Eventually Tegramond's daughter and his son, and Warner's new half-caste son, half-Carib, half European, and named Indian Warner, are housed together, in a small compound. Fifty yards away, in the main house live Warner, his second white wife (the first had died of a tropical illness), his teenage son Edward and his infant child Philip from his new marriage.

Warner's second wife hates the sight of the half-caste infant in the nearby compound. "He should be a slave" she says.

Captain Warner continues to meet red-bitch, but now, when he approaches her she shows no fear and asks contemptuously, "We make more Indian Warner?"

BARBADOS, THE WINDWARD ISLANDS. 20 FEBRUARY 1627

Nasty from the Very Beginning

Seventy-four white settlers are set on shore. Their leader thinks of himself as their owner: Captain Henry Powell, and his brother John Powell, had claimed Barbados for the united Crowns of Great Britain and of Ireland in May 1625. Now he returns after arranging adventure financing and a Crown licence.

From its earliest days, Barbados is the nastiest of the West Indian colonies for anyone below the ownership class.

Seventy-four white men arrive as colonists in 1627. No women. By the time the first census of the island is taken in 1638, all save six of them have left for less harsh societies.

Barbados attracts the least generous, least able planters. Men such as Henry Winthrop, who comes along as a pseudo-gentleman, one of the twelve magistrates on the island. He is the scapegrace son of John Winthrop, soon to distinguish himself as the governor of Massachusetts. Young Winthrop sends home to England samples of the tobacco that the settlers grow: it is, his father adjudges, foul, full of stalks and evil coloured. Young Winthrop lasts less than two years.

The only cadre of early settlers to stay long on the island do so because they cannot leave. After making initial settlement in 1627, Captain John Powell sails to Guiana where he has contacts with Dutch colonists. He buys from them tobacco seeds and indigo plants and food plants, maize and cassava, and he is lent the services of thirty-two Arawak who have voluntarily been working with the Dutch.

Powell promises to return them to their home within two years, for by then they will have taught his white settlers how to nurture the new crops.

British ingenuity, brutish economy. The Arawak are immediately turned into slaves and are not freed until the Cromwellian revolution of 1655.

LONDON. 2 JULY 1627

The Shape of the World (3)

Parties to the right of him
Parties to the left
Thundered and roared.

James Hay was one of the few reasons James VI of Scotland could stand being James I of England and Ireland. God, the king hated London and its short-arsed Puritan parliamentarians and its long-necked high churchmen and its knees-together ladies of the bedchamber of his Danish wife who kept a closer eye than ever on him, now that he had moved south of Watford Gap. Hay, the most splendid party-giver, host, retailer of filthy stories, reconciler of duellists, friend of the randy, procurer of the promiscuous, made life bearable, and King James would no more have moved to London than to Inverness, if it had not been for the continuing comfort of Hay, his confidant, his fool, his analgesic.

James Hay, despised by many, but hated by none, is knighted, becomes a gentleman of the bedchamber, successively Baron Hay, Viscount Doncaster and first earl of Carlisle, and is granted lands, though never enough to pay the cost of his prodigal hospitality. Hay makes the transition to the court of James's successor, Charles I, effortlessly.

To help with the payment of his considerable debts, the now-earl of Carlisle convinces Charles I that royal authority and the baiting of the ever-villainous Spanish can be accomplished in one deft move: the king will assume as a royal fiefdom all the West Indies and then grant them in feudal tenure to a loyal, and of course noble, vassal, who will in turn farm them out in strict feudal terms to several levels of underlings. At each level the duties of the tenantry to the monarchy shall be affirmed and, oh joy! the Spanish will hate every detail.

Thus, 2 July 1627 a royal patent is granted to everything that the English hold, or even hope to hold, in the Lesser Antilles. And, surprise, the feudal tenant in chief, holding all this directly from the monarch is James Hay, earl of Carlisle.

Quick witted, Thomas Warner makes his obeisance to Carlisle and is granted the feudal governorship of St. Christopher, which he intends to populate with his own sub-tenants; and he is given a watching-brief over Nevis, Antigua, and Montserrat.

Slow-witted and stubborn, Henry Powell of Barbados does everything he can to thwart the royal grant to Carlisle and a civil war on his island, populated by roughly 1,800 persons in 1630, is narrowly averted. Even so, the crops are not planted and 1630–31 is the Starving Time. Powell and his allies lose.

British America, then, is a world that looks like a bird, but swims like a fish. Its most important portions are in the West Indies, and they are destined to grow exponentially in the next forty years. From the perspective of the merchants of the city of London, they are a mercantile world. Merchants club together, rent bottoms, trade to and from the West Indies in what seems like a pure capitalist world. Risk, reward, it's all calculated actuarially.

Yet, in the West Indies, the control of everyday life, justice, land allocation, regulation of imports and grading and transport of exports, are affected hugely by personal caprice. Each profitable jewel of an island is held by a feudal proprietor whose power is limited slightly by the laws of England: but mostly by what he can get away with.

KINSALE, COUNTY CORK. AUGUST 1627

Cargo

The first full shipload of Irish settlers for the West Indies is being loaded. It's easy work, for sturdy young men and quite a few young women want out of Ireland. And a bit of adventure would not hurt. The vessel's captain and part-owner is Anthony Hilton, a Durham man who has been employed by the merchants of Barnstaple, England to voyage to Virginia. On the way he had called at St. Christopher and made friends with Thomas Warner who gave him permission to start his own wee plantation on the windward side of St. Christopher.

The easiest place in the British Isles to find able bodies for colonies was Ireland, and Hilton shrewdly ties himself in with some Irish gentry who know a good thing when they see it; shipping out Irish youth is a good deal more profitable than selling cattle.

The young migrants are dressed in Irish rural garb of their time, a long shirt that drops well past the crotch, a tunic over that, and then a long coat and a primitive pair of shoes. They are uncovered from mid-shin level downwards and their shins and calves are crisscrossed with scars and so hardened that they scarcely possess feeling.

This gear serves them well on St. Christopher. With the tunic and coat thrown aside, and a woven hat to cover them, they are much more comfortable than workers on the English side of the island, who wear "proper" clothes. The Irish cut bush, and build simple houses, using the Y-shaped crutches of trees as frames, just as they had done at home: save the walls, which are woven from palm leaves. House gardens and tobacco rows are planted. They talk to each other in Irish, though they are learning English by dealing with their feudal overlord, Captain Hilton.

Soon they learn much more English and much more about the English. In revenge for Thomas Warner's massacre of the Carib of

St. Christopher and Antigua, a flotilla of Carib sweep down upon St. Christopher and here, as so often, the Irish pay for English sins. The Carib attack their tiny plantation and the survivors among the Irish hie to the leeward side of the island, and there become part of the English-speaking colony.

Captain Anthony Hilton survives, and within a year he fills his ship with tobacco and returns to Ireland to sell it. He's still convinced that this colonial business is the road to riches.

LONDON. JANUARY 1628

Tooraloora

Even the most venial royal courtiers laugh: Sir Pierce Crosby, one of the Gaelic Irish Catholics who is converting himself into an English-speaking Protestant gentleman, has made a proposal to King Charles.

Crosby would like a grant of £5,000 from the Irish revenues and two prize ships. He would then transport ten companies of the Irish Regiment into any "rich and fruitful part of America, not inhabited by any Christians." Crosby notes that a goodly portion of the land will be granted to himself as chief undertaker.

There is less-than-nothing in this for King Charles, for Crosby adds a foot-shooting postscript concerning the character of the Irish Regiment. "The major part of the officers and many of the soldiers are Protestants."

NEVIS, THE LEEWARD ISLANDS. 1628–30

Career Change

Anthony Hilton, believing strongly that colonization was the route to riches, engaged partners and then obtained a feudal grant from the earl of Carlisle to the island of Barbuda and other (undefined) islands in the West Indies that were still unsettled. He loaded ship with English and a few Irish indentured servants and sailed.

Barbuda.

Captain John Smith, who had been around the New World enough to know that one should never believe good news, shook his head in wonder at the way men such as Hilton wagered their lives on the vapourings of misinformation. Barbuda! Someone named the place Dulcina and soon adventurers were convinced of the excellence and pleasantness thereof. And when they land on it, they find the island is a barren rock. (In fact it later is used as a prison island.)

Captain Hilton proceeds southward and reaches an isle more to his liking, Nevis, near St. Christopher. He already has 75 or so settlers on board, and he leaves them at Nevis and proceeds to St. Christopher where he convinces an equal number of his former settlers, Irish, and a few English throw-ins, to join him. This is done with the blessing of Captain Thomas Warner who, from St. Christopher, acts as godfather of the new colony. It's a nice little island and they grow tobacco.

Better for the servants than the masters: when Thomas Warner goes to England to smooth affairs at court, the man he leaves in charge of St. Christopher tries to murder Captain Hilton. The two remain literally at daggers-drawn until Warner returns.

Anthony Hilton reassesses the colonization lark. It's not all he thought it would be. In 1630, he leads a shipload of his colonists to Tortue, an island off Haiti. It is in theory under the Providence Company, but in fact it is a base for privateering. It's a sharp career change for Hilton and a continuing education for the young Irishmen he had taken to St. Christopher and who later chose to follow him to Nevis and now to a life of mayhem.

LONDON. 1630

Sucking Up

How he hated the sycophancy and loathed the waste of money. Bowing deeply to rouge-faced old courtiers and paying compliments to their wives, compliments so extravagant that they would not have been believed by a Chinese emperor or a panjandrum Pharaoh. Treating to elaborate meals the mincing secretaries of great men of the day. Conversing archly in the now-rusty French and Italian that his father had forced down him, when all his real neighbours spoke some kind of growl. Listening raptly to pointless stories by men who had known his father and some few, his grandfather.

Anthony Briskett abhorred every moment and regretted every penny. But now in his late thirties he knew that this was his last chance at escape from the life of the Irish frontiersman. Living on 120 acres of sour land, surrounded by Catholics who hated him, and ignored by a Dublin government that viewed him only as a picket in a long and spiked fence, that was no future.

So, tricked out in new silks that had cost him his best horse, he played the bumboy to everyone who could help put him in the good graces of the earl of Carlisle. However much he devalued the genteel part of his own upbringing, he was fortunate: the tendrils of contacts his grandfather and father had with the Cecils and the Sidneys still were there, and Briskett knew how to carry on a polite conversation. He could talk of the family-friendship with poor dear Edmund Spenser; and in certain court circles it was now safe to speak again of Sir Walter Raleigh as an old family friend and as an exhibit of true English nobility.

When he really had to do so, Anthony Briskett could speak with the I-am-trustworthy mien of Antonio Bruschetto or with the convivial laziness of Ludowick Bryskett. He hid his ambition and his ruthlessness. He was rewarded.

Early in 1630, the earl of Carlisle granted him feudal control of Montserrat in the Leeward Islands, an isle that Columbus had sighted but had not found worth setting foot upon.

No matter. Anthony Briskett knows exactly what he will do: he will create his own fiefdom. He will fill it with Irish churls and middling gentry. And, by Christ, he will control.

MONTSERRAT, THE LEEWARD ISLANDS. 20 JULY 1631

Ecce Homo

"Footprint."
"Definitely. Footprints."
"Man's."
"Definitely man's."

Sir Henry Colt, an English adventurer from St. Christopher, surveys Montserrat. It is rough and mountainous, he records, and full of wood. There are no inhabitants visible, but some people have been on the island within the previous week or so.

"Indians."

"Certainly Indians."

"Carib."

"Carib, probably."

It is diagnostic of the assumptions of the British-Isles settlers that he can deduce even more:

"Naked."

"Yes, without question. Naked."

ANTIGUA. 1632

The Shape of the World (4)

"Beyond the Line." Everyone in the West Indies lives Beyond the Line.

Originally that was a geopolitical statement, but it became a matter of moral typology.

1598: in a secret clause in the treaty of Vervains between Spain and France, they agree that whatever peace they might make in European lands, there was no truce west of the Azores or south of the tropic of Cancer. Other European nations follow suit, so that allies on one side of the Atlantic often are enemies on the other. Every foreign ship is a potential enemy vessel, every commercial trader a potential spy. This ends only in 1713 with the treaty of Utrecht.

Living beyond the line meant more. *It meant a general flouting of European social convention. The sixteenth and seventeenth centuries plainly showed that Spaniards, Englishmen, Frenchmen, and Dutchmen who sojourned in the tropics all tended to behave in a more unbuttoned fashion than at home.* Thus Richard Dunn, historian.

"Unbuttoned fashion": perfect phrase, and well exampled by the Warner family. Having wiped out the Carib on Antigua, Thomas Warner in 1632 appoints his eldest son Edward, now twenty-one, as governor of Antigua and directs him to go about settling this fiefdom. Edward imports indentured labourers from the British Isles, plants tobacco and indigo and starts a family of his own. In 1640 the Carib, now centred on Dominica, sweep down and, besides killing labourers, take Edward Warner's wife and children hostage. He pursues them fearlessly and rescues his family.

A good family man? A little later his wife gets on his nerves and they quarrel. He has her imprisoned.

Try that in Suffolk or any place else on the law-ward side of the Line.

THE LEEWARD ISLANDS. 1632

Progress

Eighteen Irishmen. Survivors of at least a decade in the Amazon. Veterans. They are among a larger group of Irish and English prisoners held in a tiny prison in Caete, a Portuguese frontier town of 300 settlers and eighty solders. They are the sacrificial foot soldiers of empire, the fodder of other men's optimism. Some had escaped the 1625 disaster by hiding in jungle. After a time they regrouped at Tauregue. Others had been captured by the Portuguese, escaped, only to have been captured again in the next Portuguese sweep, that of 1629. Now, after nearly a year of imprisonment on a diet that would not be sufficient for a dog, they are desperate and bitter: hateful of the Portuguese and contemptuous of their fellow prisoners, Irish and Englishmen who had been sent out by the suicidally optimistic Guiana Company. That venture – can it even be given that much dignity? – that lunacy, fronted by nobles, funded by merchants, its ranks filled by fools, had succeeded only in drawing ill fortune back to the lower Amazon. Did they really think that the Portuguese would not return?

Eighteen Irishmen seize one of the Portuguese governor's small boats and begin a three-year odyssey, moving from one parched island to another. Eighteen Irishmen finally sight Trinidad.

Fourteen Irishmen go ashore. They search for water, first, and then for food. Four of the weakest men remain offshore in the boat, a makeshift anchor holding the vessel in place. The tiny boat, no more than a cork in the ocean, is carried away by wind and tide. The four skeletal men fetch up on the Spanish island of Margarita. Three of them are sent to Spain, the fourth is too debilitated to survive. The three sent to Spain are surprised to learn that the Spanish crown will not give them protection if they decide to re-settle in the Amazon. One of them stays in Spain, enlisting in the army and the other two return to Ireland, impoverished, gristled as dried meat, disillusioned.

Fourteen Irishmen on Trinidad, their boat gone. They forage for food. They are good at native languages and they are in a Carib-speaking area, one of the tribes whose tongue they have mastered. With the aid of friendly Indians, they construct canoes by hollowing out massive trees; this for the most part with stone age tools they fashion for themselves. Months later they sail. Fourteen Irishmen cross treacherous seas and land at the mouth of the Surinam River, where a rudimentary English colony recently has been formed. English is the language of one of the tribes whose tongue they have mastered.

Fourteen Irishmen go their separate ways. Some catch berths on barques that trade with the Antilles. Others rely on their self-made canoes. All of them make it to the Leeward Islands in the Lesser Antilles. Six fetch up on St. Christopher's. Five make Montserrat, where a colony that is almost entirely Irish is in the making. And three go on to Barbados.

Five Irishmen, out of the fourteen who made the Antilles, eventually straggle back to England, where they are treated as an alien species, so strange are their manners.

MONTSERRAT. 1632–34

Motley Crude

Anthony Briskett is a quick study as a neo-feudal baron.

His fiefdom is pleasing enough. Three decent harbours, the best of which he names "Kingsale," the most common Englishing of Kinsale. Steep hillsides, covered in harsh bush, but good rich soil beneath the scrub and vines. Water, fresh water, plenty of fresh water on the leeward side of the island. Briskett cannot see the hidden world, the hurricanes, earthquakes, volcanic ventings that make Montserrat the hard-luck island of the West Indies. For the moment, the earth is peaceful.

What Briskett immediately realizes on his first survey of Montserrat is that however rich the island's soil, it's no good without labour, immense amounts. That's where real feudalism and this seventeenth-century play-around differ. Real feudalism works only if there are tons of surplus labour.

More quickly than the magnates of the other Leeward Islands, Briskett understands that the best source of unused labour is Ireland. He imports indentured servants from the milling and underemployed youth of Munster – Ryan, Collins, Barry, Sullivan, Roche, Callaghan, Driscoll, Cormack become standard Montserrat names. He accepts cash and fealty from Old English gentry families in Ireland, Catholics who are being squeezed both by the Dublin government for their religion and by the Gaelic Irish for their attachment to Dublin – Allen, Meade, White, D'Arcy. When some of the few Catholics in Virginia leave because of persecution, he takes them, and he admits as middling gentry the surviving handful of Wexford Catholic landlords who had been transported in 1620 to Virginia for daring to complain about their Irish lands being tossed about in the surrender-and-regrant process. The men from the Guiana Company colony in the Amazon, gnarled little nuts of men, brown, hunched, desiccated, yes, they can stay. Indentured servants who have served their time on St. Christopher or Nevis or Barbados, certainly. Englishmen, of course, whether servants or middling gentry. Mostly, though, Irish of all sorts. By the mid 1630s he has several hundred white men working on his green volcanic outpost, and a lovely commercial loop in place: he fills ships with tobacco and sells it in Ireland; he fills the ships in Ireland with indentured servants and aspiring gentry and they either settle in his island-world, or he auctions off the work-contracts of the young servants to planters on other islands. Feudalism with a modern twist.

KINSALE, COUNTY CORK. MAY 1636

Oh for a Thousand Tongues to Sing

Thomas Anthony, a master mariner who specializes in collecting shiploads of indentured servants and taking them to the New World is successful at his job, the same way some fishermen are lucky for a season or two, but the whole business is a mystery to him.

Why am I always working for Puritans? he wonders. The colonial barons, such as Warner and Briskett, run their own servant collection agencies, but among the specialists in the business it's mostly Puritans who put up the money and gamble on people's lives. Maybe they don't consider servants to have lives.

Why, in the name of all that's holy, did a Dutch bastard have to arrive here a week before I did? The Dutch, who will trade anything with anyone, had loaded up with the best of the youth of south Munster, young men and women whose indentures would fetch good prices on the raw tobacco and, increasingly, indigo plantations.

However did those backward Irish sprats and slatterns come to know so much about conditions on the several plantations in British America? Captain Anthony had intended to load a cargo of servants and haul them to Virginia. They would have none of it. Already a whole network of communication existed among the Irish, and they knew accurately, even at servant level, the varying conditions of the island and mainland. They refused Virginia. Neither would they go to Barbados, where the Irish, they already knew, were treated worse than any place else in the West Indies: longer indentures (six to seven years as against four to five on the other islands) and they were kicked around as Papist dogs, even the Protestants. This lot wanted St. Christopher or nothing, so Hilton surrendered and agreed to take them all to that island. There, and on Nevis, they would be part of a snarling ethnic mix, but at least near-half the population.

Was it really necessary for the mayor of Kinsale to put me in gaol for two days? After all, I only kidnapped two servants and the New World would have done them a shower of good. That Captain Anthony attempted kidnapping stemmed from his experience in England. There grabbing drunken or drugged youthful servants was known as "Barbadosing," for that's where they usually landed. Ireland was different: whatever its problems, the market for Munster labourers was a free one. With one exception: every shipload had two or three felons, whom the local authorities pardoned if they would "volunteer" to be indentured servants in the West Indies, and never return. Better than hanging for them, certainly, but they weren't happy travellers or ideal settlers.

Ah. I wonder how many of this mob will die on the way? They seem healthy enough, but the Irish are terrible ones for the dying. In the actual event he landed safely fifty-three of the sixty-one servants he had loaded, an average rate of survival. He sold each of their contracts for between 450 and 500 pounds of cured, good quality tobacco – worth about £7 sterling – and returned to the British Isles to repeat the circuit.

How long, I wonder, until the islands fill up?

DUBLIN. AUTUMN 1636

Still Good at It

Anthony Briskett may loathe courtiers, but he has the reflexes to be a great one: news of the death of his neo-feudal master, the first earl of Carlisle, in March 1636 reaches Montserrat and two days later Briskett is sailing for the British Isles. He'll bend his knee and touch his forelock and perform unnatural acts as quickly and as often as necessary to keep his own domain.

The second earl of Carlisle proves easy: he is waist-deep in debt and renews the grants his father had made in the West Indies for small bags of ready cash.

Having come all this way, Briskett wants something more. He treats with the Dublin Castle authorities and then, having paid them liberally, he writes to King Charles I, petitioning that in future his tobacco be allowed into Ireland at the same special rate that Captain Warner's and others are permitted.

He is fairly confident that this will be granted, given that Dublin Castle has been bought, but just to be sure, he adds a concluding paragraph to his petition. He points out that he would like to expand his Montserratian satrapy, *where your petitioner is erecting a Church of Stone and Bricke, for the glory of God, and your Majesties honour.*

Briskett choses not to disclose that he has no intention of appointing a rector. And, indeed, on Montserrat, despite the erection of six Anglican churches (actually, two churches, each twice-destroyed by disasters and rebuilt) no clergyman of the Established Church of England and Ireland was appointed until 1678, well after Briskett's own life was over.

Anthony Briskett understood something besides how to truckle to English royalty: that to run an Irish colony successfully, it's best to confine religion to empty buildings and their encircling graveyards.

BARBADOS. 1637

Strange Fruit

Probably good for something. Can't tell what. Those Dutch, always trying to sell us something. Let some one else plant it, I say.

Pieter Brower has brought from Brazil the first canes of sugar. They have great promise, he tells the plantocrats of Barbados and they smile vacantly.

A few of the planters have their servants cultivate the new plant and it has some useful properties. The canes can be mashed so as to produce a sweet syrup that is palatable if taken after a large meal. And cattle love the canes and grow prodigiously when fed on them. A lazy bullock will jump to its feet and try to break tether when the servants approach with the sweet fibrous canes. The left-overs of the plant make sovereign green manure.

It's a useful crop, certainly, suitable for the field edges, the margins left where the real crops, tobacco and indigo, stop.

THE LEEWARD ISLANDS AND BARBADOS. 1630–40

The Great Tombola

"Tobacco is a dirty weed; it satisfies no normal need." Except in the seventeenth century it did. Tobacco, for a brief time was the hand that cranked a high-ratio lottery, a massive tombola for the landless, the exploited, the underfed; it offered a better-than-even chance for the denizens of the bottom class to improve their lives and, if they were persistent, percipient, and lucky, to become substantial, maybe even rich, settlers.

Take a handful of tobacco seed. It is one of nature's marvels. Recognize that even if you don't approve of what humanity does with the final product. Take half an ounce of seed, a weight so small that if it were placed on the toe of your shoe, you could not feel it. From that half-ounce can grow twenty to twenty-five thousand plants. They are ready to be harvested six months after planting and even if one adds curing time and transport from the West Indies to the British Isles, the turn-around is a year-and-a half from seed to shillings.

This is God's gift to the poor, the more so because growing tobacco demands a great deal more human labour and much less land than do conventional food crops.

The poor suddenly become valuable – their labour is absolutely necessary – and, as compared to land, labour becomes more valuable, land less. The early days of tobacco growing are the perfect time to trade labour for land.

Yes, watch the indentured labourers, as they slash bush, break soil to friability, plant each seed individually, hoe weeds and on and on through the whole process. Notice, surely, that they are working ten hours a day, six days a week; that most of them, save the recently-arrived Irish in their long kilts, wear coarse smocks and loose trousers made of Osnabrug, a fabric that when new is coarse as canvas; notice that someone is always pushing the labourers; and often it is baking hot. And then, gain some perspective: in the entire world in this era, most human beings are draught animals; the temperatures of which contemporaries complain are more temperate than the summer temperatures of much of North America; sixty hours of labour would, in mid-nineteenth-century rural American agriculture, have been a short week. Really, these people are not working any harder or under any harder conditions than Latino stoop-workers in the USA in the 1950s.

"Black slaves in white skins." Toss that phrase in the dust bin. It was well meant, the utterance of a good politician, but a weak historian. These workers you observe in the 1630s are not chattel and are not the Marxist kin of the black slaves, for African chattel are a rarity at this time. These whites have *chosen* to be here, to work, to sleep exhausted in palm-sided huts, and to work again the next day because this is the road they have surveyed out of their particular British hell.

For an indentured labourer in the Leewards has usually worked off his indenture in four to five years, and even in Barbados it is less than seven years in the average case: when time is served, the labourer receives freedom-dues, averaging £10–12 or its equivalent in tobacco or indigo. And that amount will buy at least a long lease of a decent plot of land, enough to start one's own small tobacco farm. This in the 1630s on all islands, and on Montserrat and Antigua well into the 1660s.

It's a small window in time, and it closes when all save marginal lands are taken and that's in the mid-1640s on Barbados and earlier on St Christopher and Nevis. But even when land becomes too dear to lease with one's freedom-dues, the formerly indentured labourer still has one fine thing going for him (besides the money in pocket): he is the seller of free and mobile labour, his own, in a world desperately short of labour.

So don't patronize the young men, and a few women, who load themselves onto ships for the West Indies. And, especially, not the Irish. They are not prisoners, nor fools, nor naïfs being seduced by English con-men. The youth of Munster, who make up most of the Irish servants, have solid knowledge of the harshness that lies ahead of them and calculate, correctly, that the odds are in their favour and that they will be better off in five years' time in the West Indies than they are at home.

They flood into the Caribbean. Despite planters' pleas for more English and Scottish indentured servants, it's the Irish who keep coming.

BARBADOS, 1640; DROGHEDA, COUNTY LOUTH, 1649

Good Seed, Bad Seed

Debtors' prison was not a rare event among young gentlemen. Debtors' prison on Barbados was. Thomas Verney, a younger son of a distinguished Bucks royalist family, had tried to restart his disordered life by becoming a big – 100 acre – tobacco farmer. He leased land and then wrote to his father, a confidant of Charles I, asking for twenty indentured servants to be sent to him, including a brace of carpenters and two weavers. His father, Sir Edmund Verney, ignored him. Young Thomas, not chastened, followed up with a request that his father send him 100 convicts. No luck; next step, debtors' prison.

Fortunately for Thomas Verney he came of good family. He was released from debtors' prison and exiled from Barbados. Being banished from Beyond-the-Line was almost an achievement.

His elder brother Edmund stayed true to family tradition and standards. He followed the Irish Protestant royalist, the earl of Ormond, and was killed by Oliver Cromwell's men at Drogheda.

YOUGHALL, COUNTY CORK. 2 AUGUST 1642

Gentlemen Without Horses

At Youghal courthouse, the names of several hundred Munster gentleman are read out. They have been indicted for treason and outlawry is being pronounced. The event is similar to the rehearsal of an extremely long stage play: the monologue runs forever and there is almost no audience to hear it.

The names are of the gentry who in some way or other had taken part in the rebellion of late October 1641, and they are to lose their lands and, if apprehended, to be executed. The definition of treason used in this instance is very wide: many of them are guilty only of being unable to prove that they had been constantly-loyal to the Crown. Three judges of King's Bench take turns reading out portions of the long list. The defendants have the good sense to be nowhere near the courthouse and their names hit the hard plaster walls, but make no echo.

Gallway

Nugent

Nagle

Power

A Christian name, a surname and "gent" after each one. Mostly they are old English families, Catholics of three or four hundred years background in Ireland, instinctively loyal to the Crown, albeit disdainful of the Dublin administration, and now on the wrong side of the system.

Many of the names turn up in the Leeward Islands and a few in Barbados. Most are able to arrive with their gentry status intact, a few gold coins in their frock coats, and a desire to lease land and hold servants. An impoverished few must come as indentured servants, but they are not biddable servants.

Collectively, they help to explain a bit of one of the biggest mysteries of the Irish civil wars – the reduction of the Irish population by approximately 400,000, far more than were killed or starved. A big band, perhaps as many as 10,000 when their families are included, escape to the New World, mostly the Caribbean, and there try to reestablish their social position and to do so quietly.

And, collectively, they cause the West Indies to be in the 1640s a much different place than it was in the 1630s. As they rent plots of land from the neo-feudal barons – Thomas Warner, Anthony Briskett and their like – they bid up the price of land and make it increasingly difficult for the little men, the indentured servants now out-of-time, to find an affordable piece of ground. And, by taking twenty acres, fifty acres, and hiring servants, they become a thick layer of prickly gentry between the original marcher lords and the lower tenantry. Call it sub-infeudation. It limits the powers of the original grandees, for now, though they are themselves waxing rich quickly, they have to put up with aggrieved, disobedient and highly mobile, formerly-indentured men and women, and a gaggle of fallen gentry from the Old Country who are punctilious about status and willing to fight a duel at the slightest imagined insult. And all this at a time when the last thing any island's governor wants is to call the islands to the attention of the home government, for in the home islands a civil war binds the three island nations together into a hydra of confusion and bloodletting.

Anthony Briskett is smart. He bends so that he does not have to break. In November 1642, the poorer planters (mostly former indentured servants) were pinched hard enough that they declared a partial rent strike. They would no longer pay their feudal dues to the earl of Carlisle, but would pay only into Briskett's hands the feudalities that they owed. He goes along with this, while making the larger planters, many of them new arrivals from Ireland, pay feudalities directly to Carlisle. Given the influx of new men, the total paid to Carlisle stayed level and local peace was preserved. Very close, though.

BARBADOS. 1642

That Strange Crop

Dutchmen, who have been growing sugar cane and processing it in Brazil, arrive in Barbados. Wherever they trade, they are sensitive to local politics and they have begun to feel unwelcome on the mainland. They're right: the Portuguese expel them wholesale in 1654.

This early lot brings with them the knowledge the settlers in Barbados have not possessed: how to turn those tough fibrous stalks of sugar cane into something more useful than cattle feed or syrup.

It takes four or five years for the Barbadian settlers to learn how to grow sugar cane so that it can be harvested efficiently – unlike tobacco, an entire field has to be planted and harvested at once and it takes fifteen months for the canes to ripen fully under Barbadian conditions.

Another three or four years are required to perfect the basic technology of sugar manufacture from the canes. By 1650 the island's planters are producing a goodly amount of both white and brown sugar. Although most of the settlers still grow tobacco and indigo as their main crop, they now sit on their verandas, planning when to switch to growing a product that is not so much a crop as a way of life.

ST. CHRISTOPHER. 1642

Time for the Amendment of Life

According to the poet. Before the last capital prisoner in Crumlin Road Jail, Belfast, was topped. An old republican it was. Confided in the chaplain. "This will be a lesson to me, Father."

Captain Thomas Warner, given time for amendment of life, learned two lessons: that he was not an emperor and that the heirs of the English Protestant colonists in Ireland could be as hard to deal with as were the Irish Catholic peasantry: sheer demented hell.

When, in late 1641, a first "revolt" on St. Christopher occurred – really gentry and former servants who complained while holding their hands on the hilts of their swords – Warner, acting as if he had all the power in the world, rudely told them to go away. These men had grievance: Warner's one-man rule and, more importantly, his arbitrarily cutting off exports of tobacco to the British Isles, for, like a modern oil sheikh, he hoped to drive prices up. In fact, he merely impoverished his island.

This raised the avatar Phane Becher, a descendant of a Munster undertaker, and the re-incarnation of everything acquisitive, sociopathic, and ruthless in the earlier generations of English planters in Ireland. Becher had been on St. Christopher only three years and, though starting with little save his letters of introduction – his uncle was Sir William Beecher, clerk of the English privy council – he was now worth a fortune. Known as Lying Becher, he imported everything from needles to playing cards and charged several hundred percent mark-up. He lent money at usury. He watered the wines he imported and challenged to a duel anyone who dared say so. Becher led the battle against trade restrictions in general and Warner in particular. Faced with a protest by nearly 1,500 inhabitants, Warner salved them by providing a twenty-four member elected assembly and freer trade.

Warner was recognizing a fact of life. He might be Beyond the Line, but he was no czar. Neither he nor any of the other colonial governors had an imperial bodyguard, much less a standing army, and if their subjects became individually stroppy that was one thing – flogging or banishment without trial was easy – but feudal prerogatives gave way to mob force or one lost one's head.

Warner learns to isolate, not consolidate, his opponents. In 1643, he rounds up a mob of quarrelsome Irish Catholic small farmers and servants and corrals an equally troublesome bunch of Englishman. He sends the English to Antigua where his son puts them in their place; and the Irish are shipped to Montserrat where Anthony Briskett is willing to domesticate them.

BARBADOS, 1643–44

Legislating Morality

ITEM: A Dutch ship calls in at Barbados in 1643. Its captain offers for sale fifty male slaves. This is nothing new. There are a few slaves on Barbados and the Leewards. Yet, the governor, Captain Philip Bell, has them immediately set free.

Because they are Portuguese, taken prisoner off Brazil. He refuses to countenance white men, Christians no less, being offered for sale.

Something has occurred in the rules of British-dominated life: without ever writing out a convention on the subject, it has been agreed that slaves must either be African or native. No whites.

ITEM: The larger planters of Barbados have been granted a legislative assembly. In August 1644 they enact, with the governor's approval, a statute prohibiting the landing on their island of Irish servants and settlers.

The Irish ignore it.

BARBADOS. 1647

Independent Observation

Although he never phrased the question overtly, Richard Ligon, who arrived in Barbados in 1647, wrote an entire book explaining why, of all the Caribbean islands, Barbados was the limiting case – the worst place for a small man, indentured servant or tenant farmer. Just the men. The women: any white woman who still had a few of her own teeth and was not overtly syphilitic, was all right in the Caribbean. As one observer said of Barbados in the 1650s, "a Bawd brought over puts on a demour comportment; a whore if handsome makes a wife for some rich planter." For men, though, it was different.

Upon the arrival of any ship the planters go aboard: and have bought [the indentures] of such of them as they like, send them with a guide to his plantation … [He] commands them instantly to make their cabins, which they not knowing how to do are to be advised by other of the servants that are their seniors. But, if they be churlish, and will not show them, or if material be wanting to make them cabins, then they are to lie on the ground that night.

It's all the luck of the draw, good master or bad, reasonable, fair or ill-tempered and drunken.

As for the usage of the servants it is much as their master is merciful or cruel. Those that are merciful treat their servants well, both in their meat, drink and lodgings and give them such work as is not unfit for Christians to do. But if the masters be cruel, the servants have wearisome and miserable lives.

That's no different from any other island, but Barbados had a long tradition of harsh masters. For one thing, unlike the Leeward Islands, it did not have an ethnic mix among the landlords. Almost all the planters were English and though they fought among themselves on Royalist-vs-Roundhead issues, they agreed on their need to keep the peasantry in its place and to limit Irish and Scottish intrusions as much as possible. Further, Barbados lacked the major limit on arbitrary behaviour that held in the Leewards. By virtue of its location as the only significant English colony in the Windward Islands, it was isolated, a barrier of French colonies separating it from the rest of the British West Indies. So, while an abused servant on, say, St. Christopher, had a reasonable chance to escape a harsh master and to make it to Nevis or to Montserrat, the indentured servants on Barbados were stuck: that's why the Barbadians could enforce longer indentures than could the planters on the Leewards and could work their servants harder.

I have seen an Overseer beat a Servant with a cane about the head, til the blood has flowed, for a fault that is not worth the speaking of ... Truly. I have seen such cruelty there done to Servants, as I did not think one Christian could have done to another.

Bad as it was, Barbados was about to become much worse. It was the lead-colony in going into sugar production. This begins in the late 1640s and, by 1660, most of the one- and two-man tobacco and indigo farms are squeezed out. Indentured servants and former servants are worth less as labourers in a sugar economy than in an economy of tobacco and indigo. Slaves fit better.

MONTSERRAT. 1647

Caribbean Gothic (1)

The funeral cortege from Waterwork Plantation, the finest house on the island, takes two hours to wind its way down hill. Governor Anthony Briskett has died in his fifty-seventh year and is being taken to the parish church of St. Anthony, in theory a sacred site named after an Egyptian hermit but, in the fashion of a West Indian supremo, named by Anthony Briskett in his own honour.

Even though the road from the plantation to the village of Plymouth is the best on the island, the ox-wagon that draws Briskett's body has to stop several times at treacherous sinkholes. Then the wooden casket is unloaded, the cart goes on past the danger point, and the casket is reloaded. Family members follow on horseback and household servants walk behind, creating a small air stream of dust as they shuffle downhill.

The old order was passing in more ways than one. In 1647 the second earl of Carlisle had leased his feudal grant of the Leeward Islands and of Barbados to Francis Lord Willoughby, a Presbyterian member of Parliament, but hardly a Calvinist: he changes sides several times in the next dozen years. Willoughby could not make his authority over Barbados hold, but the Leewards granted him nominal authority. Thomas Warner kept St. Christopher and Nevis, but he dies in 1649. With Warner and Briskett, the most experienced and successful of the neo-feudal governors gone, the world would have changed in any case, but with the execution of King Charles I, clear lines of communication, much less of authority, between London and each island disappeared. During the 1650s, the West Indies were farther Beyond the Line than ever. On the Leewards, the stronger tyrannized the weaker and throughout society, security of person and property vanished.

At Briskett's graveside the service of the Established Church was read slowly by a man from St. Christopher who claimed to once have held a living in Somerset. His shaking hands and raddled face spoke of a life of much communion with wine.

Staring vacantly into the grave is the late governor's still-too-young wife, Elizabeth, age thirty, and his son and heir Anthony Brisket II. He is much too young, in that he is only eight years of age and will have to be a ward of his mother and of some as-yet-to-be-named male. Women could not on their own be assigned as guardians in chancery.

A few feet back from the graveside are two men who covet the Briskett fortune. And yet-further back are retainers, each of whom has an interest in the way the estate is settled.

It's a tiny solar system, arranged around a black hole.

BARBADOS. 1649

The Road to the Finland Station

Rats skulk out at night. Individually, noses twitching for the scent of advantage. During the day they often den up together, as if they are family.

One servant. One. Scuttles under cover of night to his master. He blubbers, he cries, he falls on his knees and asks forgiveness, while in his heart he hopes for the reward of a linen shirt and perhaps even a pair of boots.

He reveals that the servants were resolved to fall on their masters at daybreak, kill them, and take over the island. The plan is realistic: the planters' timber houses are easily accessible and, in any case, the servants are familiar figures, not apt to raise suspicions: the planters worried about Carib, not about Britons.

Forewarned, the planters load their muskets, shutter the windows, and, later, stage circus-like executions.

Thus fails the closest attempt at true social-class revolution ever to occur in the English-speaking world. Not a change-of-management, a revolution; not a nationalist or religious uprising: a tidal upsurge of the oppressed class against the oppressors. Pure. Simple. Scuppered by a single rat on a dark night.

ANGUILLA, THE LEEWARD ISLANDS. 1650

Short March

Francis Lord Willoughby leaves two marks upon the map. Anguilla, an eel-shaped isle, just six to ten feet above sea level, resting north of St. Christopher, is settled. Short of water, it is suitable for grazing cattle and sheep, but not for crops. Two-and-a-half decades later, it has a population of 250 and, an indication of its unique pastoral nature, no slaves.

Willoughby's second mark was the navigational "x" placed on marine maps at the spot where he was drowned in August 1665 on his way to fight the Dutch. The coordinates were marked because Willoughby had with him the Great Seal of the Leeward Islands which he carried about with him as if it were a piece of the True Cross. Without it no significant legal document executed in the islands was valid.

After several futile searches, a new seal was ordered from London.

ST. CHRISTOPHER. 1650

Caribbean Gothic (2)

Two men in their thirties. Strong. Ambitious.

Samuel Waad, Jr., thirty-two years old, of Dutch extraction by way of Devonshire. He is one of the largest planters on Montserrat and he has married, at the Established Church in St. Christopher, Elizabeth Briskett, young widow of the late Governor Briskett of Montserrat.

Elizabeth Briskett *née* Elizabeth Osborne.

Roger Osborne, thirty-eight years of age: he has come to St. Christopher not only to witness his sister's marriage, but to act upon his appointment as the governor of Montserrat. He is from an English Protestant family who came to Ireland as frontiersmen in the 1580s.

Osborne, who was briefly the male guardian of the wealthy and fatherless Anthony Briskett II, his nephew, relinquishes that position now that his sister has re-married. Samuel Waad, Jr. becomes the male guardian.

Both Osborne and Waad recognize that they stand in each other's way. Osborne, though governor of Montserrat, has no chance of looting the inheritance of Anthony Briskett II – running to 1,500 acres and several plantations – if Waad stands guardian. And Waad, though he has the inside track in picking over the movable chattels on the Briskett estates, cannot transfer land titles to himself without the cooperation of the chief legal officer of the island of Montserrat, Roger Osborne.

Fortunate it is for young Briskett that they detest, and thus cancel, each other.

MONTSERRAT. 1651

Ghost Dance

For a time they run about in the moonlight, most of them in panic, a few laughing, as a ghostly figure flits among them. They are Carib, looting Montserrat, and they have found their way into the sacristy of St. Anthony's church. There a few yellowing surplices are stored for the convenience of Anglican clergy who visit every year or two. One of the Carib has put a surplice over his head and surprises the new arrivals at the church. When they finally stop running and creep back, they agree that it is a great joke and then go back to their pillaging.

This is the first time Montserrat has been attacked by the Carib, probably because it was not a place of permanent habitation for them, but the planters and their servants have long lived in fear. They know the stories of attacks on St. Christopher, Nevis, Antigua and of the poison darts used so effectively. The Montserratians, like all the whites on the British islands, have built the Carib, who are formidable indeed, into monsters bigger than can be seen even if one closes one's eyes. The Carib do, indeed, appear like silent lightning, two or three thousand of them in *pirogues* that need not heed wind conditions. They attack and kill quickly. They are not, however, cannibals, as is universally believed. Nor are they on a war to extinguish all whites. They have an alliance of sorts with the French and they make their home on French islands. Some Puritans say they are directed by the French priests.

More fortunate in this regard than most of the Leewards, Montserrat is visited every fifteen years or so – 1651, 1667, 1682 – whereas most other islands are hit at least once a decade.

The loss of property and of life is considerable and for months afterwards no one sleeps an entire night without waking for a moment and listening in a cold sweat to the snap of a twig or crackle of leaves as a cat or a feral pig makes its way down the byways of a black night.

Richard Osborne as governor of Montserrat knows that he can do little except drill his ragtag island militia a bit more often. He reflects on the raid, noting that one of the leaders he glimpsed in the moonlight powerfully resembled the late Captain Thomas Warner. And, Osborne wonders, what exactly is it that the Carib use on their poison darts?

LONDON. FEBRUARY 1652

Out of Their Time

The Council of State briefly considers the state of the West Indies, especially Barbados. Too many strong and energetic young men have served their indentures and are now "out of their time." They are a danger to public order and an economic liability. "Barbados cannot last in an height of trade three years longer" unless these people find maintenance and employment.

Of course: start another colony. There are already 150 "lusty, well-armed" British and Irish men in Guiana. Show the young men of Barbados, St. Christopher, Nevis and Montserrat that there is profit to be made and they will flock there.

The experience of Walter Raleigh in Guiana is pointed to as an example, which shows how his stock had risen after his head had fallen.

Nothing is done and men out of their time begin the century-long drift to the American mainland where they are very good at pushing at frontiers.

BARBADOS AND THE LEEWARD ISLANDS. 1652–60

Trussed Like Thieves

Like many a gifted tyrant, Oliver Cromwell understood that to deal with large bodies of enemies, he either had to kill the lot or ship them to some place unpleasant where he could keep an eye on them. The practice-run for his eventual Transportation-to-Connaught scheme in Ireland was his attempt to exile several groups to the West Indies, most often to Barbados. His people needed the practice: of the dozens of orders-in-council to round up and ship one group or another, at most one in four were actually acted upon. And, though Cromwell personally had ordered in 1649 that the Irish military survivors of his conquest of Ireland be Barbadosed, none were sent until 1652. Dictatorships, even of the righteous, are rarely efficient.

The idea of sorting out undesirable groups and dumping them Beyond the Line was enticing to the Cromwellians and between 1652 and 1657 one can uncover scores of cleansing legislations: round up all the vagabonds in England, especially the Irish, and float them away; send 1,000 Irish girls and boys under age fourteen to Jamaica (captured by the British in 1655) where they can learn to work like proper English persons; take away the 1,200 prisoners held at Carrickfergus, Ireland and Portpatrick, Scotland and give them ten-year indentures as servants; and, all those Irish gentry who resist being moved from their ancestral estates to Connaught, well, if they won't go Beyond the Shannon, then they shall go Beyond the Line!

These attempts and a score of others too banal in their evil to be worth recalling would have sent approximately 60,000 persons, mostly Irish, involuntarily to the West Indies. And if the efficiency of the Cromwellians had matched the intensity of their hatred, these would have been martyrdoms.

A realistic number – calculated from the disembarkation ramps rather than from the fantasies of the Righteous – is 10,000 men and a few hundred women transported. Overwhelmingly they were Irish and most of them were sent to the one place that they were least wanted and least-needed: Barbados. They were not martyred. Vagabonds and petty criminals were handed four- to six-year indentures as servants and the soldiers ten-year stints. The only ones who received life sentences were murderers and other very serious felons.

Save the felons, everyone was freed at the Restoration of the monarchy in 1660.

They became part of that ever-larger floating army of Men Out of their Time.

MONTSERRAT. DECEMBER 1653

Caribbean Gothic (3)

Elizabeth Osborne Briskett Waad's leg goes numb and she quickly sits down. Her personal servant, a white woman from Devonshire, looks at her curiously and enquires, "Anyting the trouble, ma'am?"

"No ... Yes ... perhaps it is merely the baby." Elizabeth is seven months pregnant. She and her husband Samuel are keen on having another child, a son preferably, as a back-up heir in case something happens to Anthony Briskett II. That is not cynicism, merely a recognition that life-expectancy in the tropics is short.

The numbness spreads and Elizabeth has trouble speaking. "Fletch the do'or," she commands, her lips scarcely moving.

By the time the doctor arrives from Plymouth, Elizabeth is nearly catatonic. She lies on her back, barely breathing. Her eyes are the only part of her countenance that is mobile and they scream.

"Doubtless it is this late-in-life child-bearing," the physician pronounces authoritatively. "Women are not made to bear beyond age thirty, in my view."

He takes a small funnel, props Elizabeth up, and drains a half-pint of laudanum into her. Then he shuffles through his scuffed black medical bag and finds a small brass instrument. It has a sharp head, about the size of a fingernail, and a small spring-stead band that allows one to make the razor sharp edge of the steel fingernail jump a quarter-of-an-inch, with force and precision. This he places against Elizabeth's lower forearm and he quickly drains away a quart of blood.

"There, that should calm the ill-humour."

He is not a reflective man, nor a very good doctor; none in the West Indies are. But the physician has noticed that Elizabeth's symptoms are remarkably similar to those he has seen in several persons who had been hit with the poison the Carib place on their darts.

No Carib near, so doesn't merit thinking about.
He tells the maid, "She'll sleep well now, I warrant."

THE LEEWARD ISLANDS. 1650–60

God's Short Visits

The Capuchins and the Jesuits fight each other for the rights to the souls of the West Indies. White souls.

Two Irish secular priests from the diocese of Tuam had served for eighteen months on St. Christopher and the nearby islands, but they had died. Life is short for everyone in the Caribees, even those who deal with eternal life.

The Jesuits apply in 1640 for Vatican permission to start a mission on St. Christopher. The Capuchins, a French-language order based in Normandy, say no, and they win. They provide priests for the several French islands and for the French portions of St. Christopher. English-speakers either go without or, on St. Christopher, sneak across the island's boundary line and take the sacrament in the French church.

Only in 1650 are the Jesuits permitted to found a mission for English-speaking Catholics, and it is a one-man operation. Father John Stritch, an Irish Jesuit, builds a small chapel on the French side of St. Christopher and from there provides confession, baptisms, marriages and funerals for English-speakers and for those more comfortable speaking Irish. A Catholic priest was not officially to be tolerated in the days of Cromwell but, in fact, the officials of all the Leeward Islands allowed him to perform his pastoral duties as long as he kept his head low.

On Montserrat, for example, he pretended to be a timber-feller and Catholics came into the bush to hear mass, and to have their children baptized. Baptism and formal naming of the child was the ritual the Irish peasantry most desired. The second was marriage, for none of those who had acquired wives in the West Indies was married according to the forms of the church. The governor of the island knew full well what was going on, but he also knew that closing down the religious services would cause a local civil war. The same on all the Leewards: a quiet compromise was reached. Catholic services were permitted, but no mass houses were to be constructed, no steeples, no bells, no crosses in public places.

It worked, and during the 1650s, the hard years of Cromwellian intermeddling, religious comfort was available to Catholics.

Father Strich returned to Ireland and his place was taken by the wonderfully named Father John Grace, of the diocese of Cashel.

Saints, perhaps, but when the missions of Fathers Strich and Grace were done, Holy Mother church gave the Leeward Islands only the occasional casual glance. Montserrat, for example, the most Irish Catholic of all the West Indies, was served sporadically by French priests from Guadeloupe and Martinique. It received no priest of its own until 1756 and a church building only in 1852.

As for the Established Church, it built churches, since that was a part of the civic order, but only two or three functioning priests were present in the Leewards at any time. In 1671, the governor of the Leewards noted that there were forty parishes in the islands, but only three clergy to serve them – "one drunken orthodox priest, one drunken sectary priest, and one drunken parson who had no holy orders."

Apparently, what God gave least about the Leeward Islands was a damn.

BARBADOS AND THE LEEWARD ISLANDS. 1650–60

The Sweet Narcotic

Burn your lecture notes. They're wrong.

The English Industrial Revolution did not begin in the cities: did not involve major inventions: and did not reach critical velocity in the late eighteenth or early nineteenth centuries.

It began in rural areas. It involved crops, not industrial products. These crops demanded both new technologies and new labour organization. And it occurred in the mid-seventeenth century in the West Indies. The lead-sector was the godawful island of Barbados, made more awful by its planters perfecting new ways to turn labour into a faceless, malleable, wasteable entity, and this just at the moment the Old World was exporting to the New thousands of persons who could not be melded into the new machine.

Consider sugar. It is not a crop, it is an industrial entity. Tobacco, indigo, provisions, those are crops, planted by an individual, cared for, harvested, marketed. In each case, the whole process can be done by one person, or at most by a family, and if large cooperatives are often involved (call them partnerships or businesses if you wish) that is a matter of convenience. The building block of these economic molecules is still the individual atom, the idiosyncratic human being who provides labour and management and five acres will support a household.

But sugar. To work it requires big areas (thirty acres minimum, a six-fold jump in the entry-threshold): areas clear of shrub, hedge, weeds. The soil must be tilled and the young shoots set within a day or two of each other, and then hoed, or hand-weeded evenly for fifteen months – and then harvested in delicate synchrony. That is because crushing, boiling, extracting and crystallizing the sugar requires critical masses of cane. Too much cut and it goes bad: too little and it isn't worth firing up the machinery.

This sugar-making is industrial and labour employed in the process is faceless. It has to be disciplined, able to work at a certain rate, and that is all. No judgement, no independent thought, just large gangs of diligent labourers.

It's the end of the little men, free or indentured. To run one's own sugar-producing equipment requires at least thirty acres of cane and the planters who turn to sugar buy out the small five- and ten-acre little men, the former indentured servants who have made a life for themselves. No tragedy for those who sell up and move to another island or to the American mainland, but it reduces the prospects for all the succeeding indentured servants. When out-of-time, they won't be able to afford a piece of land.

Taking a crop of sugar cane from tilling to crystal involves fifteen months minimum and, given a bit of downtime, a year-and-a-half is a fair go. But indentured servants are around for only three or four cycles, at most, and free labourers demand much too high wages.

It's the final term of an economic syllogism: the sort of labour required by this first Industrial Revolution can be of only one sort: slave.

Barbados, the leader in this revolution, was overwhelmingly given to sugar cane production by 1660; St. Christopher and Nevis roughly half-way by the same date, Antigua less, and Montserrat only about one-quarter.

Beyond irony: that at the exact moment the Cromwellian stirring of the British Isles forces more and more white men and women to the

West Indies, the use for them diminishes sharply. Not a recipe for happiness.

MONTSERRAT. 1 MAY 1654

Caribbean Gothic (4)

As Samuel Waad marches into St. Anthony's churchyard one of his six guards trips over a low memorial stone. The churchyard is perpetually neglected and, save for an occasional visit by a mob of goats, is never trimmed. Damned awkward, these concealed gravestones in knee-high grass.

The minute his sister's body was in the ground, Governor Roger Osborne had turned to dislodging Samuel Waad: from the guardianship of Anthony Briskett II, from Waad's three estates (each of which was better than Osborne's own), and, if necessary, from life itself.

Did one not know better, one would infer that Samuel Waad is in charge of the armed party. He moves confidently, his back straight, while the guards, five Irishmen and an Englishman, draggle their way, like worn-out militiamen following a mustard-keen captain.

Governor Osborne insulted Waad in public, passed untruths behind his back, and did everything he could to provoke Waad into taking a false step: anything done against the governor of the island would be sufficient, since Beyond the Line *lèse-majesté* provided legal cover for most forms of judicial murder. Waad, though, shrewdly stayed quiet.

While his executioners fiddle with their firearms, Samuel Waad walks to the wall of St. Anthony's church. He kneels briefly and then turns around. He is wearing a white blouse, open at the neck, and no coat. The last thing he wants is metal buttons on his breast. They will only deflect the balls and thus prolong his agony.

Finally, in April 1654, Osborne discovers Waad's Achilles' Heel, his sense of honour as a gentleman. When a friend of Waad's is paying him an extended house visit, Osborne has the visiting gentleman arrested on the charge that the man had with a cane attacked a tailor. This was spurious: Osborne could not care a fig for the well-being of a hump-backed, myopic, mendicant tailor, but it was a challenge that Waad had to meet or lose his own standing as a gentleman: staying under a gentleman's roof, one is also under his protection. Samuel Waad had certainly been capable of sharp practice himself and, given the chance, would have skimmed the cream from Briskett-minor's fortune, but he was a gentleman.

"My friends, suffer me a pint of water, if you please." It's more of an order than a request, and after a moment's hesitation the lieutenant in charge of the execution party nods and one of the privates goes to fetch it. Attracted by the stirring in the churchyard, several inhabitants of Plymouth are now leaning on the outside of the church wall, silent, intent.

Samuel Waad had faced down Governor Osborne, forcing him to either show evidence of his own friend's ill-behaviour or release him. That done, Waad overstepped. He put in a letter to Osborne a series of insults that were unforgivable because they were true. Among them: that Governor Osborne kept in his employment an Irish murderer (one Lieutenant Dabram) and a recently pardoned felon (Nathanial Read); that Osborne kept Irish Catholics in arms (true; as a sort of praetorian guard); and that Osborne fornicated with the gentry wives of his fiefdom (true indeed). This letter, and subsequent exchanges, could be interpreted as an attack on the government of the island, and thus treasonable, and in April Osborne was ordered to appear before the general court of Montserrat. The island's population looked forward to the event, for a great deal of dirty linen would be washed: planters actually vied for jury duty.

Samuel Waad ceremoniously raises the pint mug of water. He speaks over the head of his executioners who are forming themselves into a ragged line ten yards away. To the score of observers outside the churchyard he offers a toast. He dies, he says, with good conscience and for having defended his country against tyranny. He wishes for them freedom and prosperity.

Governor Osborne was deft in his malice. When Waad and the jury members and a hundred-odd spectators appeared for the court of general session, he announced that this was not an open trial. It was a court martial and as such would be held in secret. Samuel Waad, like every able-bodied white male over eighteen, was a member of the militia. So, Osborne charged him with insubordination and mutiny. The court martial, held two days later, was presided over by Osborne as chief judge, and among the military jury were Lieutenant Dabram and Nathanial Read. The courthouse was encircled by a platoon of armed Catholics whom Osborne had brought up specially from the Irish-speaking ghetto at the south end of the island. The secret trial took only the morning and by two o'clock in the afternoon Samuel Waad was being marched to the churchyard.

"Ready, now, Mr. Dabram," Waad says to the chief of the execution party. Lieutenant Dabram looks around to see if Governor Osborne is present. He is not. Dabram shrugs and gives the order to fire.

It took Governor Osborne less than a month to grab for himself Waad's three estates. One of these had a stone house, the best on the island; and Waad's 70 cows, 500 sheep, four horse, fifty slaves, thirty indentured servants, 20,000 pounds of refined sugar and 350 rolls of tobacco were taken. Value: approximately £12,000.

Waad's family in England protests his murder and the sacking of his estate to the Lord Protector. Cromwell passes the matter on to the governor of Barbados to investigate and he does nothing.

It was a good year for Governor Roger Osborne, and he had not yet even begun to pillage the estate of the minor Anthony Briskett II.

LONDON. DECEMBER 1654

Western Design

Oliver Cromwell read little, but he read well. He read, marked, and inwardly digested some few texts, one of them a book by Thomas Gage, an English Catholic priest, who had changed sides. The book, published in 1648, said, rightly, that Spain's power in the West Indies was slipping and, less accurately, that taking the string of pearls that was the glory of the Spanish main – Cuba, Hispaniola, Puerto Rico – would be easy.

Thus, from Westminster, Cromwell sends the order for a quiet departure of a fleet to do the work of the Lord and attack the Spanish colonies. He sends only the dregs of his army, 2,500 untrained vagabonds, and officers scarcely better than their men.

The fleet stops in Barbados and the Leeward Islands and picks up more than 4,000 volunteers, men out-of-time who have little to do with themselves and big dreams. Eight hundred of these rough men come from St. Christopher where land is scarcely available for the small farmer. And 3,000 are from Barbados, where the overcrowding is even worse.

Unlike the infantrymen sent from London, these volunteers have had elementary militia training, and actually a few of them are soldiers who had fought against Cromwell and had been banished to the West Indies.

Recruiting on St. Christopher would have been more successful, had not Captain Butler, in charge of the recruiting party, become so drunk that he vomited all over the saddle he was mounted on and then slithered to the ground, desperately clutching at his horse's mane as if he were sinking into quicksand.

CONNACHT. 1 MARCH 1655

Dead Line

The earth trembles as Connacht receives the vanquished: Catholic gentry exiled beyond the Shannon. They shuffle in before the final deadline and the whole province is convulsed, as if the earth has been poisoned. That is what Cromwell wills.

The existing Catholic landlords, many with lands that their families have held for centuries, are tossed about as their titles are called in and they are moved, reduced.

Hatred for the Puritans is deflected. Beyond the Shannon, the Catholic gentry spit on each other.

That is what he wills.

JAMAICA. 10–17 MAY 1655

Behold the Conquerors

They argued later about who had run farthest and fastest. Everyone save the men from St. Christopher agreed that it was the Kittians who had been the first to break and run and very swiftly. The defeat of the

English invasion of Hispaniola was so abject that the only laurels were those awarded in the Cowards' Olympics.

Sailing away, the incompetent and disputatious officers of the Western Design agreed only that they still had to attack something, anything Spanish, and overcome it. They studied their charts and decided, by a toss of a coin, on Jamaica. Jamaica, used as a provisioning island by the Spanish, had thousands of pigs, cattle and only a tiny garrison.

Even so, in capturing Jamaica – and thus increasing by tenfold the land area controlled by the English Empire in the West Indies – Cromwell's forces managed to lose nearly 1,000 men, mostly to the maroons and escaped slaves who lived in the hills and were armed by the Spanish. On the other hand, the conquerors managed to kill more than 20,000 cattle, removing the prime cuts and leaving the rest to rot.

LONDON. 9 JUNE 1655

Not a Moment Too Soon

The Council of State meets with the Lord Protector.

Considering all the known and foreseeable circumstances, they decide to send 2,000 Bibles to the soldiers in the West Indies.

MONTSERRAT. DECEMBER 1655

Caribbean Gothic (5)

As a colonial governor, Roger Osborne is within his prerogatives in presenting a petition to Oliver Cromwell.

He states that he is the legal guardian of Anthony Briskett II, son of the former governor of Montserrat; that the late Samuel Waad had seized the estate of young Briskett; that Waad had been executed for mutiny.

Governor Osborne requests that the orphan, Anthony Briskett II, be continued in his father's estate, and, by unspoken implication, in the care of his excellent guardian.

LONDON AND MONTSERRAT. 1660–68

Restorations

What a lovely piece of planning. James FitzEdmond Cotter of Carrigtwohill, County Cork, puts the final touches on the assassination plan. He feels very very good. It's a deft mixture of strategy, malice and god-granted justice. Cotter, of a royalist and Catholic family, had lost his estate in the Irish civil war and now he could repair his status and enjoy himself at the same time. He was a good mercenary officer and liked his work. When Charles II returned to the throne, one of his first orders was that the killers of his father be hunted down and dealt with. James Cotter and two fellow Irish royalists track John Lisle, who had been one of the stage managers of Charles I's trial. They find him in 1664, in a small, strongly barred house in Lausanne, Switzerland. He rarely comes out. But he does his sabbath duty, for he is a staunch Puritan. Cotter and his men wait and shoot him on the steps of the chapel, before he has had a chance to utter a single prayer.

Anthony Briskett II and King Charles II had three characteristics in common: in 1660 each was restored to his patrimony, Briskett by coming of legal age, Charles age thirty, by the guile that comes of having learned to survive in an illegal age. Each man felt that he had been robbed: Brisket II, though he received from Governor Osborne's guardianship three estates including the prize Waterwork Plantation, found them denuded of stock and short of servants and slaves. Charles II knew that he had been cheated by the regicides and their successors: perhaps of half the world, so he believes. And each man wants revenge. The difference is that Charles knows that revenge is best achieved cold and at a distance; Briskett – too young – wants blood on the end of his own knife.

What a gormless, unthinking, absence of planning. Anthony Briskett II, hot on revenge against Governor Osborne, places himself on the side of the enemies of King Charles II and eventually obliterates himself.

Charles, upon being restored in 1660, had too much to think about to give the West Indies much attention, so he simply revived the Carlisle Patent. Then, when he had more time, between 1663–68, the entire business was converted into a Crown colony. Not much changed immediately in the islands, but anyone who now went against the government was directly engaging the Crown.

During 1666–67 a French *démarché* overran the English portions of St. Christopher, and Montserrat and Antigua were captured and looted. The French occupation of Montserrat lasted from February through July 1666. The substantial planters, composed equally of Irish and English, fought the French and then fled in large numbers: 600 went to Jamaica alone. In contrast, a compact band of Irish Catholic small farmers, living on the southwest of Montserrat, welcomed the French. Surprisingly, at their head was an Irish Protestant gentleman: Anthony Briskett II.

No question: young Briskett is taking his revenge on Governor Osborne by displacing him. Osborne, wisely, hies to Barbados and safety. For six months after the French leave (the so-called Peace of Breda becoming effective in July), the Irish rebels hold on to the island. Probably they represent two-thirds of the island's population, and this may have been Ireland's first successful revolution: led, apparently, by the great-grandson of an Italian immigrant to London.

There is no noble ending, only bathos and vice rewarded. When it becomes clear that soon the Crown forces will mass and recapture Montserrat, the remaining substantial citizens of the island petition the Crown, declare their loyalty, and denounce the rebellious Irish. Prominent on that petition is the signature of Anthony Briskett II, who now claims that he had been forced to become head of the French puppet regime and then of the minuscule Irish republic. And, he adds, playing the red-race card, he had done it only to protect the island against the Carib!

Briskett has all his property seized, but keeps his head. He slips into the swirl of nameless men who are the flotsam of England's obscure empire.

Roger Osborne floats home in substantial style. He settles on his wife's estate in Ballycrenane, County Cork, and, through his agent on Montserrat, gradually sells all of his island properties.

THE MAINLAND COLONIES
1584–1690

All the World

Surely John Locke was correct when he declared *in the beginning all the world was America.*

Then, as now, some preferred to visit rather than abide. That had been the view of St. Brendan.

Irish treasure hunters enlisted with Spanish or Portuguese and made the American shore, but their names are forever lost, as were in most cases, their lives. They were hard men, made brown by the sun and salt, illiterate, courageous, with a threshold of pain so high that they could drive a spike into their hands and not cry out.

Unlike them, Richard Butler, the first Irish person we know by name in modern times, was a polished specimen, albeit durable. He had been a boy-page for Walter Raleigh. Of a once-aristocratic family from Clonmel, he graduated into the confidence of Raleigh, and was included in the party Raleigh sent out in 1584 to spy out the land for a colony.

Now in his mid-twenties, Butler is the ideal mixture of noble manners and ruthless aggressiveness. He says he has a special nose, one that can detect danger and distinguish the direction of its approach.

Roanoke Island looks like Eden and the nearby land – which Walter Raleigh soon names "Virginia" in an attempt to sweeten the Virgin Queen, Elizabeth I – seems to Butler to be paradise extended. He meets natives and they are friendly. Butler, quick as a tree marten, learns bursts of their language. This verdant paradise (oh, how Raleigh will sing of it to the Royal Court, like an ancient bard), this Virgin's Land has a faintly noisome miasma: Richard Butler recognizes it as the smell of treachery. He is glad when his captain decides that they will return to England and report to Raleigh.

Reluctantly Butler goes back to the Americas in 1585 with Sir Richard Grenville (a cousin of Raleigh) and he explores further. But he refuses to stay with the 108 men who are left as a colony. He knows that Eden can be dangerous.

And though the men of 1585 are brought home in 1586, Raleigh tries again in 1587. A mixed company of 117 men, women and youths is sent to Raleigh's Virginia. Richard Butler refuses outright to go with them, telling Raleigh that the land will swallow them.

He is right. The settlers of the Lost Colony are never heard from again. *In the beginning*, said the Talmudists, *all the world was Sheol*.

"VIRGINIA." 1586

Neighbourly Relations

"Well shot, Nugent!"

Sir Ralph Lane (knighted 1593) spent most of his life governing Irishmen when he could and killing them when he couldn't. He had been high sheriff of Kerry at a time when that was like tiger hunting in high grass. And he would spend his later years fighting the Irish all over Munster. Given his winning way with people, he was a natural choice for governor of Raleigh's first Virginia colony, 1585–6. In governing Kerry, Lane had learned that the most trustworthy servants and bodyguards were Irishmen who, for reasons of family grudges, were keen to join the invading English and inflict vengeance on their own local enemies. In Kerry, Lane had been well served by Edward Nugent, his personal servant, and Edward Kelly, his bodyguard. Yes, the original Ned Kelly.

Now, Kelly! Move your legs, you whore's get!

Lane, accompanied by Nugent and Kelly has been fossicking on the mainland, looking for El Dorado. When he encounters the mainland natives, he practises the social skills he had honed so sharply in Ireland. At first relations are amicable, but Lane, in his English manner, makes increasing demands upon the locals. When the indigène say, no, we've done quite enough for you, he returns to his small colony, and leads a raiding party in burning the mainland village.

"*Haha! There Kelly. Nugent has beat you to the prize!*"

The prize is the local chief. Fleeing from his burning village, the man is shot in the arse by Nugent, who had been aiming higher but underestimated the speed of his quarry. Both Nugent and Kelly race after the native. Nugent, surprisingly fast on his feet for an indoor servant, beats Kelly to the hobbling Indian. He therefore has the pleasure of plunging his short sword into the man's back. Then he severs the chief's head and brings it to his master: proud as a retriever bringing back a woodcock to its owner.

MUNSTER, ULSTER, JAMESTOWN. 1607

The Invisible Architect

Study the drawings. Convert the old sketches to modern blueprints. Better yet, use computer graphics. You will find that they were drawn by the same mind, though not the same hand.

Consider the fortified home farms of the English adventurers who are subduing the south of Ireland. Look at the earliest settler domiciles that are appearing on the borders of Ulster. They are not English castles but, instead, working farmsteads. They are in equal part agricultural structures and protections for the farmers and their servants. These are not the medieval castle, designed to be a citadel in long-siege warfare. They are a more practical invention, a large fortified enclosure that protects the inhabitants and their possessions from enemies who do not possess siege engines or artillery, merely fearsome dispositions. Retro. These are the re-invention of the raths of the ancient Celtic world. The English adventurers who are colonizing Ireland use them as their mode of advance. Portions of Ireland are dotted with these eruptions that disfigure the landscape like a necklace of smallpox pustules.

Now look at the plans for Jamestown, the first permanent English-language settlement in the Americas. It is an enclosed, palisade-and-earthwork structure and has the same practical lineaments as the Irish forts. It *is* an Irish fort, and scant surprise that. Ireland is the laboratory, the place where the tricks of settling among a hostile native population are being worked out. And, although there are not more than a handful of Irish in the first settlement, the Virginia Company, which runs the colony until 1624, has two score Irish adventurers in its co-partnership and another score of gentlemen in the company who have had experience in fighting the Irish. They know what the shape of an imperial attack engine has to be.

Practice does not, however, make quite perfect. The Irish architecture of Jamestown resists native attack for fifteen years, but in

1622 the Indians overrun the settlers and kill 347 of them. Some survive.

CORK CITY. 1626

Mixed Farming

When Daniel Gookin tallies his holdings in Munster, he sees not livestock but cargo; and not tenants, but carcasses to be transported.

He is one of the new men: "new" meaning that he understands commerce. He is nominally a Protestant, but can be either Catholic or Protestant when it suits him. (His son becomes a Puritan fanatic, but that's another matter.) Gookin's land comes from the New English earl of Cork, now the richest man in Ireland.

In 1621 Gookin begins a trade with the Virginia colony. He has trouble at first deciding if he should trade cattle or indentured servants with the Virginians. Eventually he decides on his own version of mixed farming, varying his product according to market demands.

And he has started his own branch plant on 1,800 acres that he is granted on the James River. He founds Marie's Mount at what becomes Newport News. Given his direct experience as a settler in Munster, he knows how to make a first rate defensive structure, with palisades and cannons. Thus, Marie's Mount withstands the native assaults of 1622 much better than does Jamestown. Gookin, having presided over the launching of this outpost of his trading world, leaves two of his sons in charge and returns to Ireland.

He needs to take care of business. He has been shipping young Irish men and women, mostly native Irish, but a few new Protestants as well, to the Virginia Company's colony. Lately the Virginia purchasers of Gookin's indentured servants have been complaining about the low work-rate of the Irish peasants.

Gookin decides that in future he will give more space on the ships he sends to America to the cattle he breeds and less to the Irish youths he is trying to clear from his own estates.

Ever the clever optimist, Daniel Gookin in 1626 becomes one of the original patentees of the Guiana Company. Now there, he calculates, should be a real market for my surplus Irishmen.

FERRYLAND, THE AVALON PENINSULA, NEWFOUNDLAND.
19 AUGUST 1629

On to Maryland

George Calvert, first Lord Baltimore, is writing to King Charles I. He does the usual opening two pages of flattery in a perfunctory fashion. His hands ache and he just cannot find in himself the full afflatus that real royal flattery requires. Soon he goes to the heart of the matter, that his success as a colonist has been almost as unpleasant as failure. *I have mett with great difficultyes and encumberances here which ... enforce me presently to quitt my residence and to shift to some other warmer climate of this world ...* Baltimore had indeed suffered, but he had kept it to himself, his external dignity intact. Twenty-two years later, an English fisherman, Robert Alward, who had worked the area, testified that Baltimore had been all business. He had made forts and defence platforms and at considerable cost had provided ordinance and ammunition to protect what was now the English domination of Newfoundland ... *to some warmer climate of this new world, where the wynters be shorter and less rigorous. For here, your Majesty may plese to understand, that I have fownd by too dear-bought experience, which other men for their private interests always concealed from me ...* Baltimore, his wife and children, had spent 1628–29 in rheum-causing dampness, in cold that was never so severe as to be unbearable, but so constant and enduring as to be unescapable. They were the royalty-aristocracy-and-gentry of a community, mostly Irish, that Calvert (he was created a baron in 1625) had founded in 1621, and had first seen, briefly in the summer of 1627. Even with a few English naval and adminstrative officers around, it was a social slum. And the cold and damp! Lord Baltimore required three attempts before he could complete the letter to his monarch without its being splotched with the perpetual droppings of his Chinese clock of a nose ... *always concealed from me that from the middest of October to the middest of May there is a sadd face of wynter upon all this land,...* Whether or not Baltimore had intended Ferryland to be a Roman Catholic colony has never been proven, but it is probable. There were three secular priests with him in his year-long stay in Newfoundland, but that is not absolute proof of anything. Nor is it clear whether or not Baltimore, who publicly turned Catholic in 1625, had been one earlier, some say in 1621 ... *all this land, both sea and land, so frozen for the greatest part of the tyme as they are not penetrable; no plant or vegetable thing appearing out of the earth until it be about the beginning of May nor fish in the sea* ... But Catholic or not, he was no respector of the Irish, except as potential Newfoundland colonists. In 1625, upon giving up his position as a ranking courtier because of his Catholicism, Baltimore went to Ireland, where in 1613 in County Wexford he had previously acquired land. These properties had been wrenched from the control of the Irish during the late Irish wars, and he was required to fill them with English Protestant planters. ... *My howse has beene an hospitall all this wytner, of 100 persons, 50 sick at a tyem, myself bieng one – and nine or ten of them dyed. Hereupon I have had strong temptations to leave all proceding in plantations* ... He had tried earlier to plant with Protestants, Irish lands of 2,000 acres that he was given in County Longford. This failed. Now, at age fifty, he was reduced to coughing and begging for crumbs from the royal table. ... *I am determined to committ this place to fisheman that are able to encounter stormes and hard weather, and to remove myself with some forty persons to your Majesties dominion of Virginia, where, if your Majesty will plese to grant me a precinct of land* ... Which is what Charles I did. He gave Baltimore a portion of the Virginia tract that is now Maryland and a slice of Delaware. Baltimore was more successful posthumously as a colonist than when alive. He never recovered his health from his Newfoundland sojourn, and he died in 1632, before the Maryland charter, which passed to his son, became final. And Ferryland, the brutally exposed Newfoundland port that he left to those who could stand storms and hard weather, continued, filled mostly with fisher families from Ireland.

GROOMSPORT, COUNTY DOWN. SEPTEMBER 1636

An Ocean Too Far

The fugelman for the harbour master of Groomsport waves his flag in a burst of self importance. From the *Eagle Wing* he looks like a preposterous shore bird, one that is trying to fly on only one wing. For several weeks, the *Eagle Wing* has been cleared to exit Belfast Lough and, indeed, all of Ireland, and this last minute confirmation is simply for the public record. These people, 140 men, women and children are pointing towards the Massachusetts colony.

Ye have seen what I did unto the Egyptians and how I bare you on eagles' wings, and brought you unto myself (Exodus 19:4). The emigrants have heard dozens of sermons preached on that text and now they chant the verse over and over as a collective prayer. Most have their eyes shut, their heads inclined downwards in respect to the Almighty. Their chant continues until, voices overlapping, it becomes a mumble lost in the winds that freshen quickly as the Irish Sea hustles them out of their home harbour.

John Winthrop, governor of the Massachusetts colony, sees them as a perfect addition to its holy ranks. He even sent his son, John Winthrop Jr. to assure them of safe haven on the American side. These people are Believers. They all have experienced, either directly, or through some member of their family, the life-changing force of the Six Mile Water Revival of the 1620s. This Ulster paroxysm is the model not only for later Ulster revivals, but for similar American events. Presbyterians, they are no longer welcome in the main Synod, for they will not accept discipline. When the Holy Spirit speaks to them, they obey it, rather than the Moderator or Court of Kirk Sessions.

After John Winthrop Jr. visits, they draw together in Belfast and construct their own sailing ship. Big ocean, small ship: so, sensibly, they think of arid desert and especially of the Exodus of the Chosen People from Egypt. Contemplating the long, lissome sand dunes of the Sinai has kept their minds off the vicious chop, swell, and wind-howl that they observed even while in port.

Past the Copeland Islands, the wind turns wrong and they are driven into Lough Ryan. What a mad time of year to sail the North Atlantic! As they beat out of that Scottish harbour, their two clergymen preach on the text *What manner of man is this, that even the winds and the sea obey Him! (Matthew 8:27).* Soon they discover that their home-built boat leaks badly and they stop for repairs in the Kyles of Bute. And then out again into an ocean that grants no dominion to their Lord.

The hurricane that soon visits them is not sent to try or better them; it is a malevolent spirit that wants to best and destroy them. The *Eagle Wing* barely makes it back to Belfast Lough.

They do not try again. Their ministers are driven out of Ireland by the orthodox Presbyterians and they, and remnants of the flock that tried to reach America, settle in Scotland. There they remain permanently at sea, a people without their own land.

MACROOM CASTLE, COUNTY CORK. 1660

A Son Remembers

Forty years after the event, William Penn the Younger recalls the moment of his first true spiritual revelation. It came through the intervention of his father, Admiral William Penn.

The admiral was loyal to the navy and to his own family and beyond that was willing to work for either Cromwellians or Royalists or both. He had spent nearly a decade patrolling the Irish Sea and then had led active squadrons in the West Indies, with mixed success. He was temporarily retired in 1654 and took his family from near London to Ireland.

Of course Ireland. His wife had inherited two estates in County Clare, seized from the native Irish sometime before the Civil War. These had been taken back by the native Irish in the Rising of 1641 and the Penn family hoped to recover them. More importantly, Ireland was the only place in the British Isles where good land was still there for the grabbing, and Oliver Cromwell granted Macroom Castle, the home of the earl of Clancarty, sometime Catholic general in Ireland, to Admiral Penn. He moved his family, including twelve-year-old William, into the castle and surrounded the place with as many of his relatives as he could bring over. They lived in daily fear of the natives.

None of this is central to the reminiscence of William Penn, the son.

Instead of the half-cleaned, draughty old castle, and in place of the hatred of the Penns and their like by the native Irish, Penn recalls a fireside moment, its warmth preserved in his heart like a warm coal.

That moment, when young William was sixteen or seventeen, was occasioned by the admiral, who had remained an orthodox Anglican all through the Cromwellian period, inviting to Macroom Castle the wall-eyed Oxford tradesman and Quaker evangelist, Thomas Loe. An incandescent moment. As the coals in the grate burned lower, the plain-spoken Friend talked of meeting God directly, without church or presbytery. He talked to the heart and, first, the Penns' black slave broke down in sobs; then tears rolled down the admiral's cheeks; and young William, finding that the thoughts of his own heart were being read aloud, fell into a trance.

He became half a Quaker. His father recanted and for a time threw William out of the family home for his religious enthusiasm. That rustication was, the great William Penn later reflected, part way to heaven and half-way to Pennsylvania.

LONDON. JANUARY 1662

A Father Worries

Samuel Pepys disliked Admiral Penn, but he admired the man's abilities. And feared him a little. Penn had managed the transition from Cromwellian to Royalist so well that he was knighted at the Restoration and named as a commissioner of the navy. For Pepys, it was a matter of getting along with one of his superiors, so he frequently spent evenings at plays or the opera with Sir William and he frequented the family's London home. Mrs. Penn, he observed in the massive diary he was keeping in a unique form of shorthand, was a round-faced Dutchwoman (here he missed; her first husband was Dutch, but she had grown up in Ireland). She was slatternly, let her stockings sag around her ankles and her cooking stank like the devil. Yet he liked her for her wit, and. was willing to put up with her experimental cuisine: he first ate melon and first tasted an infusion of tea at the admiral's table.

With Sir William, Pepys spent endless hours going over navy accounts and preparing logistical plans. And Pepys ever listened. The admiral had family problems. His son William, half-Quaker and complete Non-Conformist, was sent down from Oxford in November 1661 for his religious deviation. At first, the admiral treated this as a joke and he, young William and Pepys, met at Pepys's house after the theatre and became very merry.

Now, two-and-a-half months later, Admiral Sir William calls on Pepys when the diarist is at home, walking in his garden. Agitated, the admiral wants help in taking his son from Oxford and finding a place for him at Cambridge. Does Pepys know a tutor who would take him? The diarist promises to think about it. He knows no suitable tutor, but will write to friends.

Later in a crowded day, Pepys takes his wife to supper at Sir William's. And then, home to bed.

LONDON. 1663

Well Called

The second brand-name in American history (the first was "Virginia"; and "Maryland" was too generic to count) comes into being. Charles II, paying his debts after his Restoration, gives eight of his loyal supporters a bit of land. It begins south of Virginia, covers the territory from 36 degrees north latitude to 31 degrees, and runs from the Atlantic to the Pacific Ocean, or so he thinks.

The recipients are quite willing to latinize the name of His Majesty and "Carolina" comes into being.

Four years later, the Carolina proprietors are also granted the Bahamas.

Given a natural path to the Caribbean, the proprietors recruit for Carolina men and women from the British Isles who have served out their indentures in the West Indies. These are a proven entity as settlers – they have survived, that is their great virtue. As sugar cane cultivation displaces the small tobacco and indigo farmers of the West Indies, there is diminished opportunity for out-of-time servants to become land owners. Thousands of these "West Indians" settle in Carolina. They enter one-by-one and disperse to find their fortunes; they leave few records and their footprints soon are worn away by the wind.

CORK CITY. 1665

The Family Firm Matures

Thomas Gookin, nephew of Daniel Gookin, the pioneer exporter to New Worlds of young Irish men and women, expands the trade. He is known as the "Sovereign of Clonakilty" and is a large landlord. However, he leaves the running of his estates to his agents and mostly directs from Cork City his trade in human labour. He and his harbour staff collect young men and women and fill the holds of transAtlantic vessels. He and his family are now unbendingly Protestant but in business he, like the money he makes, is blind to religion. All he does is offer a chance to men and women who don't like the look of their future in Ireland. The ones with trades travel free and are in great demand all over the West Indies and the American continent. Those without skills sign three-to-five year indentures as labourers. They too are wanted, especially in the West Indies, where the growing African slave population is a threat to white supremacy. Being an indentured servant can be hell for a young Irish woman or man, but once their time is served they are sought after: the men are especially good as slave overseers.

It is all voluntary.

"I force no one," Gookin frequently asserts and he is accurate in a narrow sense. Thousands of Munster's most energetic young people consult their self-interest and decide to become people of the New World.

CORK CITY. 1667

The Second Half

"Is it thee, Mr Penn?" The elderly Quaker draper barely recognizes William Penn. She had known him as a young man and it was she who had been the connection to Thomas Loe and the epiphany at Macroom Castle the better part of a decade earlier. William Penn is no longer a youth. He has been on the grand tour of Europe and has spent terms at Lincoln's Inn. Now he is the representative of his father in cleaning up the post-Restoration mess on the family's Irish lands: in the re-harrowing of Ireland, Admiral Sir William Penn lost his Macroom estate and was given another, eight square miles in extent, "Shanagarry" on the road to Youghal. Trouble was, the previous holder of those lands, a tough ex-Cromwellian soldier, refused to move and it was young William's job to get him out.

As William talks to the Quaker woman, he is heart-scalded by the distance between her simple mode of speech and dress and his own foppishness. Yes, he is doing well in the world: he is known at court in Dublin and locally he is in tight with Thomas Gookin, the Sovereign of Clonakilty, and he has settled Captain Charles Gookin on one of the out-farms of the Shanagarry estate. No, he is not happy in himself.

"I would go far to hear again Thomas Loe."

"There is no need. He is in Cork."

Penn is ready for the completion of his conversion. He attends Meeting and spends long hours in prayer with Loe and soon his present and future is in the Society of Friends.

LONDON. SEPTEMBER, 1670

Not the Quiet Friend

The trial is a circus, but it is a crucial link in the skein of cases that eventually produce the greatest protection of free speech yet devised, the American Constitution and its amendments. William Penn is being tried at the old Bailey for conspiracy to start a riot. The trial runs for four days.

As Penn and his alleged co-conspirator, Captain William Meade, are brought to the bar to testify, the lord mayor of London and the court recorder make it quite clear that this will not be an impartial trial.

Mayor:[to the clerk:] Sirrah. who bid you put off their hats? Put on their hats again!

Action: [An officer of the court places the hat on each defendant]

Recorder: [To the defendant] Do you know where you are?

W. Penn: Yes.

Recorder: Do not you know it is the King's Court?

W. Penn: I know it to be a court, and I suppose it to be the King's court.

Recorder: Do you not know there is a respect due to the court?

W. Penn: Yes.

Recorder: Why do you not pay it then?

W. Penn: I do so.

Recorder: Why do you not pull off your hat then?

W. Penn: Because I do not believe that to be any respect.

Recorder: Well, the court sets forty marks [£5] as a fine for your contempt of court.

Penn and Meade are fined for not removing the hats that were jammed onto their heads at the order of the lord mayor! Manifestly, the table is tilted.

What William Penn and Captain Meade are charged with, conspiracy to incite a riot, was a code: they are Quakers and they had been preaching at – and outside of – the Friends' meeting house in

Gracechurch Street. The char-lines of the Great Fire of London are still visible on that thoroughfare and it was not lost on Penn that he had engaged in re-birthing the soul of London from the ashes of its carnality.

One of the official discoverers of the evidence against Penn and Meade is the proleptically named Lieutenant James Cooke.

Court: What *number do you think might be there [in the street]?*

*Lt . Cook: About t*hree or four hundred people.

Penn's co-defendant, Captain Meade is, like William Penn, a great contradiction. He is a former Cromwellian soldier, who did well at killing Irishmen. Now he has become a successful London linen-draper. Like Penn, he hears no dissonance in demanding Toleration, while at the same time damning Rome to eternal torment and seizing lands from the Popish Irish, whom he, like Penn, openly despises.

When the court asks Penn how he pleads, he refuses to say "guilty" or "not guilty," but instead asserts the rights of religious practice and of free assembly.

W. Penn: We confess ourselves to be so far from recanting, or declining to vindicate the assembling of ourselves to preach, pray, or worship the Eternal, Holy, Just God, that we declare to all the world ... Nor shall all the powers upon earth be able to divert us from reverencing and adoring our God who made it.

Prosecutor: You are not here for worshipping God but for breaking the law: you do yourselves a great deal of wrong in going on in that discourse.

Ineluctably, Penn's argument leads him to question the law itself.

Recorder: Sir, will you plead to your indictment?

W. Penn: Shall I plead to an indictment that hath no foundation in Law ...

Recorder: You are a saucey fellow. Speak to the indictment ... The question is, whether you are guilty of this indictment.

W. Penn: The question is not whether I am guilty of this indictment, but whether this indictment be legal ...

More of this and then the jury goes out. It returns and pronounces Captain Meade to be not guilty of riotous behaviour or of conspiracy to riot. They do not decide on Penn, except to state that he was guilty of street noise. This is very very canny: a conspiracy of one person is impossible, so they do not need to make any decision on the conspiracy charge. And street noise? Who cares.

The lord mayor of London, who was the presiding judge, goes apopleptic. He orders the jury held in the Hole for a couple of hours, but they refuse to change their view. So he confines them overnight without food or water. They still will not change their verdict. Enraged, the court fines the jurymen for breaking their oaths – a preposterous charge: they have taken their oaths very seriously indeed.

The jurymen refuse to pay the fines and are sent to prison along with William Penn and Captain Meade who refuse to pay their own fines for not taking off their hats in court.

Not until November are they all freed on a writ of *habeas corpus*. And four years later, the freedom of the jury to render decisions without interference is confirmed by the lord chief justice.

A fine circus, certainly, but more: the noisy Quakers' views on freedom of religion and assembly are immortalized in *A Compleat Collection of the State Tryals* of 1719 and are quoted directly at the 1735 New York trial of John Peter Zenger, a fundamental freedom of expression case. And this directly influences the constitutional framework of the American Republic.

NORTHUMBERLAND COUNTY, VIRGINIA. OCTOBER 1671

An Ordinary Family

Case. Charles Fallin is in Virginia, buying land, an ordinary act, by an ordinary member of the above-the-tenantry class of Irishmen. This branch of the Fallins hails from Roscommon where they were middling native Irish gentry in the late 1500s and insecure and confused former-gentry in the mid 1600s. Several of the alpha males do what is sensible, and protect their social position by mining British North America. They turn up in the records of the seventeenth-century colonies under a variety of spellings – Fallon, Fallin, Fallamhain, Fallan, Falloom – but always on the make, scratching with their fingernails to hold on to their status: Montserrat from the 1640s onward, Barbados in the 1670s and '80s, Virginia in the same period. They circulate through the Old Empire, keeping in touch with each other, looking always for the main chance. Catholic in the sixteenth century, they are Protestant in the seventeenth.

Context. Kevin Kenny, an amiable historian, estimates that, of the 50–100,000 Irish who left for British "America" in the seventeenth century, three-quarters were Roman Catholic. Sensible guess: it can only be a guess. And he is dead on when he says that these people disappeared from the record, at least as a distinct group.

Why? They turned Protestant and intermarried with the majority in the West Indian and mainland colonies: not always in that order.

And why that? There was little opportunity for them to remain Catholic. The Catholic church in the British Isles was wobbly and did not have resources for an Empire-wide mission, even if the imperial authorities would have permitted it. (Compare this to the French and Spanish portions of the western hemisphere, where priests march along with the conquerors.) And Rome itself cared not a fig for the American colonies. Pleas for missions to the West Indies and the British American mainland went unanswered. So, on the ground, everyday people, when they wanted divine help, went to the same source of solace that their neighbours did and this, almost universally, was some form of Protestantism.

Case. By 1696, Charles Fallin is a substantial land-owner and slave-holder. He is listed as one of the People of Quality. As a trustworthy member of both the established order and the Established Church, he is granted additional free lands.

Context. The man is sane. In all of the colonies of British North America there is a blanket of penal laws, legislated at Westminster. Momentary bubbles exist – Montserrat and early Maryland and Pennsylvania – but they are temporary. There are certain things you cannot obtain if you are not Protestant: such as land grants in Virginia. In the next century, an indigenous American penal code will develop, colony-by-colony, and the pattern of religious conversions, whether of conscience or convenience, will intensify.

LONDON. 1681

The Uncomfortable Chapeau

William Penn always had trouble with hats: a Quaker problem. First there was that awkwardness in the lord mayor's court in 1670 that sent Penn to prison for a spell. And then there was tension every time he was granted a royal audience which, as the son of Admiral Sir William Penn who had been a key to victory in the Anglo-Dutch War, was a frequent occurrence. Penn the Younger would enter the royal presence with his black saucer of a Quaker hat firmly perched on his head and Charles II, who was intrigued by the Quaker blister, would take off his own. And when Penn would protest, the King would say, "Yeoman Penn, only one person may wear a hat in this room." It turned into a ritual, but an uncomfortable one, for it could be re-interpreted as being *lèse majesté* on Penn's part anytime King Charles wished.

The deeper problem with hats for Penn was that his Quaker spiri-tual brothers and sisters continually warned him that his head was growing too large for his hat. They put him in a perpetual bind of conscience. He was expected to argue the case at the royal court for releasing imprisoned Quakers and for tolerating their public worship services and, simultaneously, poor Penn was upbraided for spending too much time in The World. Under the Quaker system, Penn could never do the right thing: so, swithering in conscience, he always did more. Both in his missionary efforts and religious writings and as Quaker emissary to The World.

Improbably, William Penn becomes the largest private landowner on earth. Since it occurred in God's service, it must have been God's will.

Thus it happened: Admiral Sir William Penn had been well-loved by the royal family, both Charles II and the Duke of York (the future James II). He had drawn up the Duke of York's Sailing Instructions, which reformed the fighting style of the Royal Navy (it was a sim-ple thing, but brilliant: he taught the captains to attack in a straight line, rather than higgledy-piggledy), and Penn had borne the title of Captain Commander in the defeat of the Dutch, who, among other things left their mainland territories to the English.

A moral debt was owed to Penn and more than that: Admiral Sir William had provisioned and armed Royal Navy ships out of his own pocket, and now the Crown owed about £16,000 to his heir, William.

In return, Charles II and his brother show their gratitude by dump-ing some nearly valueless land on William (they had been about to sell it for £1,200). Grandly, and with the approval of his brother the Duke, King Charles gives Penn in 1681 land that is titularly held by the Duke of York: it lies between New York and Virginia and the tract is so large it is undefined. And, subsequently, in 1682, the Duke of York makes a personal gesture and adds to the grant what he calls West Jersey: now most of Delaware.

A world. To be owned by one man. The Quakers chaff at Penn, for though he is doing this for them, he must be kept humble. That be-comes harder, as Charles II rules that William Penn's plan of naming the main grant "Sylvania" is daft: people will think it is a swamp. The king insists that, in honour of the late admiral, it be named Pennsylvania, and William has no choice but to agree. As a result he has to spend endless hours in ritual humility before his Quaker brothers and sisters, assuring them time and time again that their refuge in the New World is not named vaingloriously after himself, but his father; that he had no choice in the matter; and, that, really, "Penn" is the Welsh word for mountain or hill or something.

Under such scrutiny he finds that, dear God, his hat is giving him a head-throb as if a nail were being driven into it. He can scarcely wait to sail.

SOMERSET COUNTY, MARYLAND. 1686

Near the Front of the Queue

They are not quite at the front of the long line of Irish immigrants that settle in the mainland American colonies, but they beat the outrush from Ulster that begins in the early 1700s. They are different in attitude and social class from the run of Presbyterian small farmers that follows them.

Captain Robert Bruce Pollock, rigid posture, well-dressed, with a proprietorial air even towards the vessel his family has travelled on, removes to the New World for what he thinks of as dynastic reasons: the land he held in Ireland would not support an estate for his eldest son with enough left over to put his next five male heirs into the church or army; and sufficient dowry money for his daughters was out of the question. Plus: as a shrewd observer of Irish politics, he is not sure that his sort of people will survive with the Catholic monarch James II on the throne.

The Pollocks are a bit unusual: Scottish gentry who settled in Ireland in the mid-1400s and, when Scotland turned Protestant, so did they. They shared Presbyterianism with the later Scottish invaders of Antrim and Down, but looked on them as parvenus. Indeed, Captain Pollock, having married the younger daughter of the lord chancellor of Ireland, becomes an adherent of the Established Church; never mind that most of his cousins are hard-kirk Presbyterians.

In his early days in Maryland, the captain bears the noble air of a gentleman who knows that he is making a virtuous sacrifice. Already he has decided to sacrifice the name that the gentry line of his family has long borne – Pollock: for in the British colonies of North America the demotic form, "Polk," common among his more vulgar cousins in Ireland, will wear better.

This attitude, of being a touch superior to the ordinary run of Ulster migrants, is maintained in the male line among the descendants in America of Robert Polk, and it makes them act slightly differently from the run of Irish-American Ulsterfolk. That holds even after they've been surrounded for several generations by the demos, and even intermarried with women so fiercely Presbyterian that one could use their countenances for cast-iron pans.

Captain Polk settles first in the tidewater belt of Maryland, where many early pioneers from Ireland, both Protestant (mostly from Ulster) and Catholic (mostly from the British West Indies) reside. Later, one of his sons takes the family inland, to the opportunties of the Cumberland Valley in Pennsylvania. Subsequent generations move to North Carolina, where they do well, and finally to Tennessee, where they are out-and-out wealthy: by frontier standards.

But different. With one exception, they refuse to adopt for their children those Old Testament first-names for their male children habitually employed by deep-dish Ulster-Irish: Joash, Solomon, Malachi, Adonijah and the like. Stout English names only, save for Ezekial Polk, who in the American War of Independence manages to show his individuality by being both a captain on the patriots' side and, suddenly, a non-captain, for making a peace pact with the local Loyalists.

This Ezekiel has a son, Samuel (by then an everyday American name, not a biblical flag of recognition), who marries an old line Presbyterian woman, Jane Knox, a great-grandniece of the Presbyterian saint John Knox. They produce their first child, James Knox Polk in 1795. He is destined to become the eleventh president of the United States.

Infant James is brought forward for baptism and all hell, by theological standards, breaks out. His father Sam, who long has thought Presbyterian formularies to be backward, refuses to affirm that he believes in the Full Faith. The baptismal service erupts into a row between Sam and the Presbyterian clergyman. Sam says some very rude words and pulls his wife, infant in arms, out of the church. No baptism for James Knox Polk.

And, although the future president eventually marries a Presbyterian woman even more fiercely dour than his own mother, he refuses for his entire lifetime to accept Presbyterian baptism or to adopt the other formularies expected of Irish Protestants in the back-country.

Only on his death-bed, in June 1849, does James Polk undergo baptism. He chooses that it be done according to the rubrics of the Methodist Episcopal Church, a denomination that sprang from the Church of England and which emphasized the Free Will of all individuals to decide their fate both here on earth and in the world to come.

Contemporaries were mystified by the decision: Captain Robert Pollock would have understood.

NEW YORK. 6 JUNE 1690 (O.S.)

Opinion

Word that James II, Catholic, absolutist, had taken power in Ireland provokes a spontaneous riot in the city. The lieutenant-governor is threatened with an adze and thirty men are arrested for riot and for swearing they would pay no more taxes.

The populace's anti-Catholic opinions are left unslaked, however. New Yorkers will have to wait another fifty years before they are allowed to execute in public an Irish Catholic priest.

THE BOYNE RIVER. 1 JULY 1690 (O.S.)

Scout

Not gentry; not trying to be. Unshaven, big-knuckled, flint-eyed, a hard man. James MacKinlay, trooper. A Scottish scout with the Williamite forces, he has sussed out the weaknesses in the enemy's flank and retreat lines. Now, a respectful distance from his king and officers, he watches with satisfaction as the Jacobite forces are routed.

A natural scout, always aware of niches and anomalies, he finds for himself in Ireland a small farm, whose Catholic owners have fled. There, among Presbyterian small farmers and weavers, he produces more children than the land will hold and, without any sense of cruelty, exports them.

Who knows if his eldest son Davie is Irish or Scottish: the family does not think in those terms. The lad is apprenticed to a weaver at age seven. It's a remunerative skill as rural trades go, and portable. Indoor work, with a fascination in the patterns of linen designed as the shuttles of the loom are thrown back and forth to produce a creation that, when bleached and finished, will be a small work of art. Trooper MacKinlay feels he is being a kindly parent when he sends the young lad at age twelve to York County, Pennsylvania to lodge with old military friends.

David McKinley, as he spells his name in America: David the Weaver, a good sensible name to insert in a presidential genealogy.

THE EMPIRE OF THE
AMBIGUOUS: THE WEST
INDIES, 1668–1690

Gentlemen On Foot

Gentlemen. Catholic. Old Irish and Old English. Transported beyond the Shannon or, having been shoved aside by new grabbers, subsist in the shadow of their former estates.

Gentlemen. They are treated with respect by their former tenants and are given food and shelter. They are men of duddy clothes, save for the silken waistcoats and horsemen's boots, items whose respectability they cling to. Men with carefully wrapped pieces of parchment folded in their small bag of personal treasures: the title deeds to lands they once held.

Gentlemen who in the backwash of the Restoration of monarchy believe they will receive their old lands. Some few do, but the commissioners of inquiry into land titles proceed agonizingly slowly. Most Catholic gentlemen receive only a sharply reduced piece of land, often distant from their original estate. And most receive no compensation. Catholics, who, on the eve of the Civil War owned six-tenths of Irish land, are reduced to well under one-fifth by the Cromwellian harrowing of Ireland and, by 1688, when the Restoration settlement is complete, they have just a bit over one-fifth.

These are gentlemen, make no mistake. They refuse to engage in manual labour or trade. They demand and receive loyalty from their former tenants and they are passed from cabin to cabin like aged relatives, receiving a fortnight's lodging and food here, a week, or a month's elsewhere.

They are the seventeenth-century's forerunners of the puzzled and proud gentlemen of the mid-twentieth century: former landlords among the Anglo-Irish who sit in cracked leather chairs in private clubs and refuse to notice that the windows are streaked and sooty and that the steward can no longer afford to light a coal fire, even on a cold December afternoon.

BARBADOS. 1668

Mailed Fist

Servants and negroes stare open-mouthed as he walks past. That is a gross breach of etiquette and were he a local planter each of them would be whipped. Freeman, artisans and the owners of five-or ten-acre plots, scurry out of his way. Wealthy planters, wearing full London gear, even in this stifling heat, bow to him, although they have not been formally introduced. He is someone to be treated with formal respect, even if one does not see the twin bulges that protrude at hip level beneath his military coat. As he walks, he repeats to himself a poem that he has himself translated and adapted from one of the O'Gnimh poets of the north:

> With love of Clan Fogarty in my heart
> And detestation of Ireland's foreigners,
> As though I loved the English better,
> I go among them.

William Stapleton has just been appointed governor of Montserrat by William Lord Willoughby, who in 1665 replaced his ill-fated (drowned) brother as governor-general of Barbados and the Leeward Islands. As Willoughby explains to his masters in London, Stapleton will be particularly good at dealing with the contumacious Irish peasantry on Montserrat. Willoughby's troops had already hunted the woods of Montserrat and flushed out 400 rebels. They had hanged a few and the rest swore to be loyal. The oaths would be kept, Willoughby reckoned, as long as a hard local governor was present.

That's mine, Stapleton told Willoughby as the two men went over a crude map of Montserrat. He was pointing to the Waterwork Plantation, the one-time jewel in the fortune of Anthony Briskett II and before that his father, the founder of the Montserrat colony. Lord Willoughby did not argue: if that was the price of the man's sorting out the Irish, so be it. Stapleton came by his knowledge of the Irish honestly. His mother was a Fogarty and his father, Redmond Stapleton, an Old English Catholic of Thurlesbeg, County Tipperary. The family had lost its lands in the early days of the Irish civil war, and William became a very adept soldier of fortune, serving in several brigades on the continent and not at all fussy what side of any given conflict he happened to be on.

His temper is fierce, his language frightening, yet both his anger and his words are always precise. He will, in his gentler, sunset years write to his agent in London, *Were I near you I would dash your teeth and words down your throat, forbear at so great a distance else I do not question to have those there that will correct your insolence and ingratitude.* Now, in his mid-forties, his anger and his words are even more violent, but always precisely aimed.

Only two years earlier, Stapleton had been in Newgate Prison, London, because he had directed his anger at a fellow officer, and had killed him. Fortunately for Stapleton, this was treated as a civilian, not a military offence. Even so, Stapleton might well have been hanged but, luckily, William Willoughby was in London to raise a regiment of soldiers under Sir Tobias Bridge to defend the Leewards and Barbados. Officers of Stapleton's experience and resolve were rare and, instead of being tried for murder, he became a lieutenant-colonel in Sir Tobias's regiment.

Stapleton's turn of fortune followed upon the intervention on his behalf of another Irish officer recruited to West Indian service: James Cotter, assassin of the regicide Lisle and another of the brotherhood of Catholic gentry dispossessed during the Irish civil war.

When it came time to fight the French on St. Christopher, Stapleton, Cotter and several other Irish officers refused to listen to the cautious English commanders and they scaled a sharp vertical rift and engaged in seven hours of close-range combat with the French who strongly outnumbered them. Stapleton himself was wounded, but saved the English colours from being taken in battle: exactly the kind of useless heroism that makes a military reputation.

Then, to the immediate dismay of the English officers, Stapleton, Cotter and the other Irish soldiers of fortune chatted away with their French opponents as if they were old acquaintances. And, subsequently, Stapleton was an intermediary in settling matters with the French concerning St. Christopher; none of the English officers was sufficiently fluent.

In the world that William Stapleton surmounted, words and action were close, and hard words could be uttered only by those whose hands were encased in mail.

MONTSERRAT. 1668

Pure Speech

The Leeward Islands are the site of the British Empire and Commonwealth's first Multicultural Language Enforcement Act:

Whereas there are several persons of his Majesty's subjects of his three nations, that is to say, England, Scotland, and Ireland, residing in the Island, and often times as well in Drink as sober ...

A nicely balanced phrase that, ...
certain Words of Distinction do arise between his Majesty's Subjects of the said Three Nations ...
Terms of distinction?
such as English Dog, Scott's Dog, Tory, Irish Dog, and many other opprobrious, scandalous, and disgraceful Terms, and by certain Quarrels that may arise by reason of such ill Language by the several Natives of the said Three nations, to the endangering the Loss of the Lives of many of his Majesty's good subjects of the Three Nations ...
What will happen?
The offending shall be proceeded against as Violaters and Breakers of his Majesty's Peace in this Island ...
Is that all?
But if it shall happen that any Affrays, Murders, Bloodshed, Riots, Routs, or unlawful Assemblies shall be made or stirred up in this Island by reason of any such Word or Words of Distinction ...
Yes?
The Person or Persons ... shall be proceeded against as a Mutineer or Mutineers ...
Fairly strong: considering that within recent memory mutiny was the reason given for execution of a civilian by the island's governor.

BARBADOS. 1668

The Names of Fear

Having survived the recent war with the French much better than had the Leeward Islands, Barbados should have been on the road to modest felicity.

Yet, two words run through white society, each bringing a cold chill. Neither one refers to a chimera.

Creole. It indicates something much different from its several modern linguistic and ethnic meanings. At that time and place, Creole was the word for the second generation of African slaves, those born in British America. They were different from their parents: they had never known Africa, were not mourning a missing world; they were no longer tribally divided from one another; they had learned patter-English and thus had a language in common among themselves, and they knew what their masters were saying, doing.

As William Lord Willoughby explained to his superiors in London, the slave owners on Barbados (most of the white population, save indentured servants and the very poorest, had a slave or two) were worried that the *Creolian generation now growing up and increasing may hereafter "mancipate" their masters.*

Barbados, as the first fully successful sugar colony (Jamaica would not catch up with its production until the 1720s), was the predictor of the Caribbean future. Already its slaves doubled the number of whites, and that proportion was growing. It was to happen all over the British West Indies, only later: with each cane of sugar there grew a germ of white fear.

And **Irish Papist** or simply **Papist**, the other name of fear. The embittered Irish soldiers Barbadosed by Cromwell clear off quickly when they learn of the Restoration Settlement: to Jamaica, the Leewards, the Chesapeake area, or back home to Ireland. Left behind are two sorts of Irish: one of these is the small proprietors who are being slowly squeezed out of business by the growing sugar plantations; they either will sell up and leave soon, or they will become overseers of slaves, the middlemen of oppression; they comprise about half of the Barbados militia and, though not useful soldiers, will be on the side of established order.

The other Irish are impacted Catholics, caught in poverty traps: poor whites, unable to do well even in an economy where white labour is in demand. Already the northwest end of the island has a community of poor Catholics barely eking out a subsistence living. These people, and their counterparts scattered around the island, take the brunt of the anger the Africans would like to direct at their masters – "white slaves" they are called by the men and women who really are slaves.

The deepest Barbadian fear is that Creole slaves and subsistence Papists will combine.

MONTSERRAT. 1668

Not Cowboys: Ranchers

Many lies are really hopes wrapped in shiny paper.

The lie the Irish have most told themselves since, roughly, the end of the Great Famine to the present day is this: that our family has always been Catholic or always been Protestant and we have stayed true to the Faith, whatever anyone else may have done. That lie arose after the

Devotional Revolution of the mid-nineteenth century. Actually, if they knew their seventeenth- and eighteenth-century ancestors, almost every Irish family would have seen that people were back and forth across the religious divide like ferrets in a rabbit warren: whatever turn it took to get the practical job of life done, they took it.

And Beyond the Line, where churches were few and pastors fewer, the Irish were Catholic and Protestant and Catholic and Protestant: the same people. And ofttimes they were both at the same moment.

The Gallway family of Munster is a good example. Longtime Catholics and royalists, they were deprived of their lands after the Catholic rebellion of October 1641: Sir Jeffrey Gallway and his sons William and David. They rebuilt the family fortune by using Empire as their lever. After the Restoration they reacquired enough of the family resources to permit the younger Gallways to prospect for fortune on St. Christopher and Montserrat.

David Gallway is a model of the successful ambiguous imperialist, for he keeps his profile as indistinct as possible, consonant with respectability. Despite his Catholicism, he has no trouble taking the oaths to support the established state and church that are required for his becoming a justice of the peace and for his becoming a major in the militia. He is one of the respectable citizens, the large landowners who in 1668 petition the Leeward Islands government to put down the Irish Catholic rebels on the south portion of Montserrat.

And that is where he makes his own fortune. By ranching in the south of the island. He is no cowboy, but instead an Irish landlord of the mercantile era. He has no tribal loyalties. He slowly builds up the largest estate on the island, 1,400 acres, by purchasing, parcel by parcel, the lands of the small Catholic farmers. His idea of farming is quite brilliant. Knowing that the two biggest imported items to the West Indies are beef carcasses and salt fish – protein provisions – he runs a cattle ranch and sells provisions without the need for long distance sea transport. He does this discreetly, with his head down as much as possible: when he is appointed the census taker for his portion of the island (only gentry were literate enough for this task), he cannily leaves himself off the document altogether.

David Gallway's son and grandson succeed him on the estate. Another family lost to the Faith? No. They observed Anglican forms when necessary and Catholic when possible. Middle-gentry such as the Gallways certainly understood the Catholic-Protestant divide as a political one – often, as in European wars, a mortal one – but they did not see the divide as being an unbridgeable theological chasm. So, having lived as quiet Anglicans, they were not being untrue to themselves when, as quiet Catholics, the grandson of David Gallway of Montserrat leaves in 1734 £20 in his will "under injunction of my mother to some Roman Catholic Church in Ireland." And a year later, another grandson of David Gallway, Nicholas Gallway of St. Christopher, is the co-donor (with Mary Skerret of a County Galway family) of a chalice to a chapel at Castletown Kilpatrick in County Meath. "Pray for them," is the donors' wish, inscribed in Latin.

MONTSERRAT. 1668

House Rules

As governor of Montserrat, William Stapleton convenes the council and assembly of Montserrat. They obediently pass the laws he requires.

One of the most important is "An Act for raising the Maintenance for a preaching Minister." The recent war with the French, the act declares, has left the island destitute of a preaching minister (actually, it never had had one) "to the Dishonour of Almighty God and scandalizing of the Protestant Religion." Therefore, 14,000 pounds of sugar, or its equivalent value in other crops is to be set aside to pay for a cleric for preaching and performing the sacraments "according to the canons of the Church of England *and the known Laws of the said Realm.*"

That last phrase is the key. Stapleton, as a Roman Catholic, was going carefully through the motions of affirming his loyalty to the Crown and to English statute law.

His statute did not include provision for actually appointing a clergyman and he was able to avoid that for another decade.

PORT ROYAL, JAMAICA. 2 JANUARY 1669

Well Met

Just as the man with the huge face begins to tell his favourite story, his ship explodes beneath him.

The story was a good one, the sack and pillage of Puerto Bello in Panama, one of his recent achievements. As he tells the story, the veins in Captain Henry Morgan's bulbous nose expand and seem to become a map of a land not yet discovered.

He has just completed his favourite part of the tale, where he and his buccaneers have scaled the inner city in the face of stiff opposition from a Spanish governor who refused to surrender. Morgan, who had already collected a large body of civilian prisoners, picked out the priests and nuns in the group. With daggers poking at their nethersides, the religious were sent up to the top of the city wall and the Spaniards, never mawkish, shot them one after another. Morgan's men followed, took the city and looted and raped for three drunken days. Morgan himself returned with one-quarter million pieces of eight.

Ever since the 1666–67 war with France, the buccaneers in Jamaica have been co-equal to the official government. Morgan operates under official letter of marque and Port Royal is the hardest town in the New World. Morgan, with his pick of the New World's violent and psychotic males, has a force of eight privateers and his own ship, a former Royal Navy frigate. He plans to set to Maracaibo on the north coast of South America, and then, who knows? Panama again? Cuba? the Spanish colonies on the North American mainland?

He and his eight captains are sitting on one side of the quarter deck, drinking heavily, when an explosion in his frigate's powder magazine rives his vessel. It sinks in minutes, killing more than 200 crew.

All eight captains and Morgan survive.

Overnight Morgan reconsiders his position, decides buggermejesus, and simply sails with eight, rather than nine ships.

GALWAY CITY, BARBADOS, MONTSERRAT. 1670

Cousins

The Blake family network is in place. Thomas, the eldest son and Nicholas, the youngest, stay home in Galway where they are merchants. John and Henry jointly buy a plantation on Montserrat. Henry runs it and John goes to Barbados where he makes trading contacts with the Dutch. Soon the Blakes comprise a family trading network that involves tobacco going to Galway, all manner of provisions moving to the West Indies, and a fair bit of smuggling within the Caribbean, plus sugar production and the buying and selling of slaves.

At home, in Mullaghmore, County Galway, the *paterfamilias*, John Blake, Sr., sits in the twilight and curses his own cousins. That's human nature. The Puritans and Cromwell have shoved down the Blakes, down from their rightful station. Oh, old John Blake knows that, but all he can remember every night is the immediate vexation of having been helped in his time of need by various cousins – cousins that now want their money back and they're all aggressive as a sow at swill, and John Sr. remembers their fathers and mothers, and, och, they always were like that, the lot of them.

When confronted by hostile Protestant land commissioners, this branch of the Blake family could stare them down by tracing accurately and convincingly its descent through eleven generations, from ancient "English" (meaning Anglo-Norman) stock. The Blakes could do so without suffering a single blot, a single provable instance of their having gotten offside, having become rebels, in all that time. At their peak, they had held several minor castles, thousands of acres, and were repeatedly mayors of Galway City.

When, in 1650, Catholics were deprived of the right to own or rent houses within corporate towns, the Blakes were expelled from Galway City, along with many of their cousinhood – Martins, Joyces, Frenches. But they held on to their lands in the countryside. John Blake Sr. had stayed resolutely out of the Civil War and was one of the few people who could qualify as being what the Cromwellians called "an innocent papist." Never mind: in 1655–56, the family lands were grabbed in the Cromwellian remaking of Ireland and given to Catholics from outside of Connacht. John Sr. received 668 acres of nearly useless wasteland at Mullaghmore.

Cousins provided loans – names such as Darcy, Skerrit, Browne Lynch, FitzJames, Kirwan, as well as distant Blakes – and that is the pain. *By the tyrannical usage and uncharitable proceedings of my cousin Martin Blake, I was necessitated to sell my few cows to make him payment ...* John Sr. writes to his son Henry.

The two West Indian sons send remittances to their father, keeping him in tea and diminished dignity, but they too have financial worries. The more disciplined of the two (Henry) by 1676 clears all his debts in Ireland and the West Indies, sells his share of the Montserrat estate to his brother John Jr, and returns to Ireland with enough money in hand to buy two estates, one in Lehinch, County Mayo, and the other near Renvyle, County Galway. He dies in 1704, leaving his own family prosperous, nothing owing to any cousins: the Galway equivalent of a state of grace.

NEVIS. JUNE, 1671

Society Page

On the page of the Leeward Islands social calendar that excludes instances of bloodshed, duels, piracy, and horsewhipping, the unrivalled high point is the marriage of Anne Russel to William Stapleton. She is the niece of Nevis's largest landowner and daughter of Colonel Randal Russel, a major planter, albeit a tenant of his magnate brother. Soirées, formal banquets, even a mock-charivari mark the occasion. It is a good alliance: Stapleton gains access to one of the two or three richest families in the Leewards and the Russels gain the most forceful character in government circles. Besides, Stapleton has an Arthurian side of his character and he has decided that he is in love with Anne: he will spend the rest of his life, he vows, staying on her right side, which is a good idea as she has a terrible cast in her left eye.

The fortnight of celebrations reveals the way that Nevis's white society is spreading apart socially as the sugar-and-slave economy becomes dominant. Twenty years earlier, the celebrations would have included every white on the island who wasn't a servant, and would have been distinguished by barrels of rum punch in the market square in Charlestown, huzzahs for the couple, and gunfire into the air. Now the white poor – defined as anyone who does not own a slave – are permitted to gape at their betters, but not to participate.

Above that, two simple matters place everyone on their precise spot on the planter society's social grid.

First, does a man (and yes, it's a male world), have the money and initiative to have obtained a white woman, preferably a wife? A generation ago, all save the richest planters were men on their own or domiciled with black or native women. That's changed. Now, single males are not ruled out of society, for some of them are rich and others are dangerous, if excluded, so they still have a place; yet everyone knows that the ability to create and support a family like that in Britain, no, actually, London, is the height of civilization. It is an expensive proposition, but a family allows for heirs, the passing on of property and, eventually, for moving back to the British Isles with gentility.

And, second, does a man own a house with windows? A few of the small planters still live in cruck-trussed houses that are no bigger than a cow-byre in England, and have daub and wattle walls and thatched roofs. The modest planters and their wives live in sawn-lumber homes, square in form, hip-roofed, with wooden floors and an outdoor hearth. Instead of windows, these houses have louvres or thatched screens. The furniture is simple: a wooden bench and slab-wood chairs, rather than a divan, sleeping hammocks (or if they are socially on-the-rise, a ticking bed), wall-hooks for clothes storage, and a few pots and pans. But, ah, those families with windows are a class apart. Windows are used only in "English-style" houses. That means any number of styles, but all of them silly for the tropics: low ceilings, two and three storeys, chimneys running through the house, and leaded windows that cut off the breeze and, besides, cost a fortune to import.

With the experienced eye of a veteran soldier of fortune, William Stapleton plots on the social grid all of the well-wishers whom he encounters.

He and Anne Russel are married by a Church of England parson. Stapleton agrees that their children will be raised Protestant, even if they are male.

DOMINICA, THE WINDWARD ISLANDS. JUNE 1671

A Useful Tool?

Sir Thomas Lynch, on his way to become governor of Jamaica, misses the Russel-Stapleton marriage because he has to divert to Dominica. There he was to "caress the chief Indian Warner, that he might continue his friendship to the English." He fails. Warner is some place inland.

Indian Warner is the most ambiguous of figures in a world where confused, secret, and multiple identities are the rule. He does not know who he is. One day he is white-English, the next day Carib. He hates both halves of his identity and hates himself for that. He gains peace by violence and is proficient at killing representatives of both communities. He can use bow-and-poisoned-arrow and sword and musket equally effectively.

The English employ him as a useful tool, and feel smug in doing this. This goes back to 1660 when, in the West Indies, the French, Carib, and English made a peace treaty. The English, wanting to gain suzerainity over Dominica, as yet unsettled, made Indian Warner "governor" of Dominica. His Carib mother now lived there and he settled in as a combination English official and indigenous chief. His connections with the English Empire are helpful to his people, as there are "French Caribs" on the other side of the island who are hostile to his mother's clan. Warner is also useful to the English in helping them to "buy" the island of St. Lucia from the Carib.

An ambiguous life.

Indian Warner does not like to close his eyes. He sleeps in a hammock with his eyes locked on the black sky. He has trained himself to make the stars turn off. Otherwise, if he closes his eyes, he sees his English step-mother and remembers in rolling, unstoppable detail the years when he was her slave. That was immediately after the death of his father, the patriarch of St. Christopher, Thomas Warner, in 1649. She had made him carry water and sticks for the black cooks and had called him Nigger Warner. His escape to Dominica in the 1650s did not bring surcease, but it led to a knowledgeable resolve: if ever he were to become a savage animal, it would be of the kind the English most fear, an animal that defends itself.

NEVIS AND ST. CHRISTOPHER. 1671–72

A Weak Constitution

"She's fair prize and she's mine."
"She's fairly licensed and she is not."
"She's mine and were she the Duke of York's own, she'd be mine."
This at Nevis in June 1671, at just the time the Russel-Stapleton wedding celebrations were occurring. The argument concerns a boat, the *James* of Belfast and Sir Charles Wheler, the governor-general of the Leeward Islands, whose government has just been separated from that of Barbados. Although the vessel, owned by a respectable Belfast syndicate, has been trading with full licence un-

der the Navigation Acts in the Leewards for several voyages, Sir Charles boards her on the grounds that she is Dutch built. When the captain refuses to pay Sir Charles £150 in protection money, he arrests the ship's master, puts him in gaol on short rations, and seizes the vessel.

Hardly heinous by the standards of West Indian government, merely arbitrary. Sir Charles, however, is unfit to be governor-general of St. Christopher, Nevis, Montserrat, Barbuda, Anguilla, Antigua, not because of his high-handedness, but because he does not understand the nature of the constitution, either his own or that of the West Indian colonies. There are only three articles in reality

– *A governor can be arbitrary, even tyrannical, provided he is sufficiently strong.*

– *a governor can be malleable, even timid, provided he is corrupt.*

– *but no governor will be successful if he is both arbitrary and weak.*

Sir Charles Wheler has a weak constitution and that is fatal. He would have been forgiven seizing the *James* and a dozen similar acts; nor would his theft of government stores have been commented on, had he had spine. But in July 1671, he negotiates on behalf of his subjects with the French on St. Christopher and he loses all credit. The French, who were supposed to give back to the English the portions of St. Christopher they had captured in the 1666–67 war, had stalled and the formerly-English parts of the island were depopulated, and going to weed and bush. Wheler agrees to a French proposition to give the owners of the St. Christopher's property only months to reclaim them. This, considering that many of them were back in the British Isles, was impossible.

A weak man is Wheler, and he has to be recalled. (Eventually Charles II of England and his French counterpart settle the St. Christopher matter satisfactorily at regal level.)

Wheler catches word that a recall letter is being directed to him by special messenger.

He flees to the French sector of St. Christopher. Then to Martinique. And then, by French ship, to Europe.

The messenger, William Stapleton, never catches him. But in addition to carrying the recall instructions for Wheler, he has a royal commission naming himself governor-general of the Leeward Islands.

He is not a weak man, nor unaware of who his friends are.

One of his first acts, in May 1672 is to appoint as his lieutenant a new governor of Nevis, his father-in law, Colonel Randal Russel.

THE BRITISH WEST INDIES. 1660–1688

Patterns in the Sand

The ants are frequently on the move. The trails they leave in the sand blow away quickly, but there are only a finite number of directions for them to go. The harder part is to reckon with any accuracy how many there are in any given place. Nobody ever gets a really accurate count of the layers of drones, soldiers, aristocrats and royalty that live in any particular sand hill. Granted, one can observe the columns of workers marching in, and one can see others leave; but they do so very quickly and often under cover of night, so the arithmetic is always blurred.

Between the Restoration and the Glorious Revolution, the number of white people in the British islands in the West Indies increased somewhat. In most years, more servants and more middling gentry and merchants arrived than left.

Heaven knows there were plenty of reasons to leave. Most of the former soldiers transported by Cromwell responded to the news of the Restoration like whippets to a starting bell; the five- and ten-acre small men of St. Christopher, who were sold out to the French by their betters in 1666–67, did not get their lands back until 1672 and by then most of them had permanently abandoned that island; small and medium planters, doing well enough, became ambitious, greedy, and tried their hands elsewhere. Jamaica was very seductive, and lawless as it was, it provided land grants at cheap rates, so that a ten-acre settler on Antigua could become a hundred-acre planter on Jamaica. The reason the whites, first, second and now even third-generation West Indians, left were as various as the people themselves: experience of frequent piracy, of Carib attacks, the annual visitation of some island by a massive hurricane, an earthquake or a volcanic eruption, these left some longtime settlers in poverty, needing to start anew, and others were left simply fed-up and wanting to get someplace else, anyplace.

The Leewards and Barbados were in a trap. The authorities were dead-frightened of the growing African population that came with the ever-increasing sugar production. But that sugar economy reduced the long-term opportunities for whites below the overseer class. So, some islands tried to force people to stay. Indeed, Montserrat in 1676 went so far as to try to prevent by force James Carroll, an Irishman who served briefly as governor of the island, from migrating with his family and twenty-five servants and slaves to Jamaica. More effective were the recruiting drives for indentured servants that the leaders of each island conducted. But, except for Jamaica which was attractive to young men and women of ambition, the colonies had to take mostly dregs. William Stapleton picked up 100 prisoners from the west of England. Christopher Jeaffereson, an aspiring young squire on St. Christopher, made a business of taking criminals from London as indentured servants. His first voyage was marred by his not putting any shoes on board for his charges and in protest their stripping themselves bare upon arrival and walking on shore buck naked.

So many left ... to ... to ... where? They left to move from one island to another; they returned to the British Isles; migrants from Barbados turned up in large number in the Carolinas. Virginia and New England gained from all the islands. Many migrants failed and returned full circle, to their West Indian points of departure.

New England is a dangerous place for Catholics, yet some turn up there. Goody Glover, the Irish-born widow of an Irish-born Catholic could not make a living on Barbados after her husband died. She and her daughter took sail to Boston where they had found posts as washwoman and nurse to a Puritan family. After refusing her employer's attempts to convert her from popery, Goody was accused of witchcraft: some of her employer's family had started to have fits and there could be only one explanation. The case was prosecuted by Cotton Mather and Goody reduced to nil any chance of acquittal she might have had by insisting on speaking only Irish during her trial. She was hanged on a sunny afternoon in 1688 before a large crowd.

The sentence was undoubtedly just, Cotton Mather noted in his journal, as she was not insane: five doctors testified that she was *in no way crazed in her intellectuals.*

ANTIGUA AND MONTSERRAT. 1672

Brotherly Feeling (1)

Like a double-bladed Portuguese fighting knife, Indian Warner was a dangerous tool for the English to use: he could do as much damage to them as to the Carib or the French.

Indian Warner is still nominally governor of Dominica when, in early 1672, his half-brother, Philip, is appointed governor of Antigua; half-brother and wholly white. Of almost identical ages, mid-forties. But the woman who had made Indian Warner a slave and, worse, a servant of slaves, had been the doting English dowager empress who promoted the fortunes of Philip Warner.

Indian starts raiding. He has no conscious sense of why he does this, nor any sense of an alternative. Boats rise and fall on the tide and have no choice. They simply obey. So too Indian Warner.

He leads a raiding party on Antigua and his men kill two planters and leave two crippled for life. Then he attacks Montserrat. The Montserratian planters fight back with surprising effectiveness and, though Indian escapes, two *periagoes* are lost and twenty-eight Carib raiders are captured. When they are passed on to William Stapleton, he masters his own displeasure because of a rumour running wild through the Indies: that there is a fortune in silver to be mined on Dominica. Without Carib support it will be inaccessible.

The Carib are released. William Stapleton is able to wait for his revenge. Indian Warner is unable to cease his raiding.

There is no silver worth mining.

NEVIS. 1672

Job Application

The form is short and that is a good thing as the applicant does not read very well. He is very far-sighted, but refuses to wear glasses.

Question 1. Are you and have you always been a Royalist?
He smiles and check the appropriate box:

☐   ☐   ☒
Yes   No   Absolutely

Question 2. Are you a Papist?
Oh well, might as well be honest; they'll find out anyway:

☒   ☐
Yes   No

Question 3. Have you ever assassinated a regicide?
Easy one, that:

☒   ☐
Yes   No

Question 4. If yes: like to again?

☐   ☐   ☒
Yes   No   Love to

Question 5. Are you related by blood or marriage to William Stapleton:

☐   ☐   ☒
Yes   No   Not yet

In effect that was James Cotter's employment application. The minute his old war comrade, William Stapleton, was named as governor-general of the Leeward Islands, Cotter wrote to King Charles II, who already was in his debt, asking for a post worthy of his talents. This would be, Cotter suggested (and here he had Stapleton to thank for the idea) his appointment to two new offices Stapleton wished to create: the secretaryship and the marshalship of the Leeward Islands. In practice, this would give the appointee control of all legal documents produced in the islands that required any kind of notarization, and also of the prisons. Cotter had no intention of doing any of the work himself – no gentleman would – but it would be a very nice income.

William Stapleton wrote to London favouring the application and it wound its way past the Lords of Trade and Plantations and through the courtiers and to Charles II and in 1676 James Cotter was given the combined posts for twenty-one years.

There was a minor new obligation incurred in Cotter's successful job application: he had to spend the latter part of 1676 skulking about France in disguise, trying to find and kill the extreme republican Edmund Ludlow, one of the signers of the death warrant of Charles I. No success, but Cotter had sincerely tried and now he had his new West Indian posting.

Back in the Leewards, Cotter lived on Montserrat (the 1678 census has him in charge of the local lock-up with ten prisoners) and kept an eye on Stapleton's plantation on that island.

For William Stapleton – he became Sir William in 1679 – finding someone whom he could trust to take care of his spinster sister was a great worry, for she was mentally limited: any number of greedy second, third ... fifth sons of planters could be found who would marry her for the plantation she would receive as dowry, but Stapleton needed someone he could trust, one of the ambiguous men who, like himself, had secrets. James Cotter's becoming Mary's husband and protector was a great relief to Stapleton.

As reward, James Cotter in 1680 becomes governor of Montserrat, a post that he keeps until 1685, despite his spending more than half of his governorship in London and Ireland. Retiring with his wife to Ballinsperrig, County Cork, Cotter resigned the Montserrat governorship in 1685, but kept receiving the fees for his supervision of the legal instruments and the gaols of the Leeward Islands.

A good career, ended as it had begun in royal service: Cotter worked and fought heroically for King James II and was given a Jacobite knighthood. In 1689 the attorney general of England deprived him of his Montserrat posts on the grounds that he had been a royalist rebel and a Papist, information that, in fairness, one must admit he had included on his employment application.

ANTIGUA. 1673

Brotherly Feeling (2)

Philip Warner's pleading for his half-brother's life is not impassioned. He knows William Stapleton too well to proceed with anything but cool dignity, for almost anything can set off the governorgeneral's notorious temper. Appeal to him once, coolly, as a fellow gentleman. Then cease.

Indian Warner has been caught while raiding Antigua and Stapleton wants him hanged, then cut in quarters and displayed publicly where the ravens can pick clean his flesh. He's employed that punishment often for pirates and Carib, and it is quite satisfying. Stapleton is more than usually inclined to dismember Indian Warner, because he has become convinced by an old, possibly true, rumour that years earlier Indian Warner had killed Thomas Russel on Montserrat. The Russels now are part of Warner's extended family. Stapleton goes quietly reflective after Philip Warner, his subordinate governor on Antigua, pleads. He's thinking that maybe it would be better to suspend Indian Warner in chains and let him expire slowly.

During these negotiations, Indian Warner is silent. He has no idea of why his half-brother feels compelled to save him.

Philip Warner, having said his piece, also stands silently. Neither does he know why he is pushed along this salving course.

William Stapleton slowly pulls himself from the pleasure of contemplating Indian Warner's demise.

For all his violent chivalry, he is a political person. He understands the importance of the Warner dynasty on Antigua and the popularity of Philip Warner as governor.

He stares at the brothers who, in the shadows of the late afternoon, resemble bronze figures. During his soldiering years, he had seen similar statues in a nobleman's garden in one of the Italian states.

No oration is necessary. William Stapleton looks into the eyes of Philip Warner and says, "Next time."

Slowly he moves his sword hand across his throat.

He nods contemptuously in the direction of Indian Warner.

"Next time, he is your responsibility."

"Next time," Philip Warner agrees.

NEVIS. 1674

Ink-Clouded Waters

Unusually for a soldier, William Stapleton likes the sea. To most soldiers of fortune the sea is merely a badly paved and bumpy highway between two pieces of land. Stapleton spends hours being rowed about in a lighter. He collects marine specimens.

The sea creature he most admires is the inshore squid. It lives among the coral where it blends perfectly, seizes its prey efficiently and, when attacked directly, confuses its opponents by clouding the water with artfully directed jets of ink.

In 1674, Stapleton is in trouble with London. Not the usual complaining from the Lords of Trade and Plantations concerning his living on Nevis rather than on St. Christopher which is the official headquarters of the Leeward Islands: that carping he can afford to ignore. This time it is real trouble. Sir Charles Wheler, the runaway former governor-general of the Leewards had absconded with the pay for two companies of soldiers, and to pay them the local court had sequestered an estate of Wheler's on St. Christopher. In his turn, Wheler, who had now returned to England from the Continent, noised abroad that Stapleton was "an Irish Papist" and, most dangerously, he called this to the attention of the Lords of Trade and Plantations.

Stapleton of course was an Irish Catholic and, since 1672, this was once again a difficulty for a gentleman. Under pressure from the keener Protestants in the English parliament, Charles II had reluctantly give the royal assent to a Test Act: it required holders of all civil and military offices to take communion annually according to the form of the Church of England and to take an oath renouncing the Papal power to depose temporal monarchs – and, more importantly, to reject the doctrine of transubstantiation. No good Catholic, not even a shirt-tail one, could do that. Whether or not the Test was required in the West Indies was a difficult matter. No one really knew, and the Lords of Trade and Plantations both wanted to keep out of trouble with the witch-hunting Protestants and to maintain good order in the colonies. In the Leewards they had the ablest governor any place in their ambit – William Stapleton – and they needed to keep him in place.

The measure of Stapleton's ability is that he understands their problem, and defends himself in exactly the way that makes them most comfortable.

He creates a piece of rhetorical art that is so carefully constructed that it shows no sign of artifice.

That is why, in mid-July 1674, Stapleton is being rowed slowly by two marines in a flat-bottomed lighter. He has them move as gently as possible across the top of a sheltered coral reef. He sits in the stern and holds a portable scrivener's desk, of the kind most sea captains and colonial officers own, on his knees. Were this Venice, he could be the Doge.

The letter he carefully drafts to send London is transparently spontaneous in tone. Stapleton denies having anything to do with the seizure of Sir Charles Wheler's plantation and then takes on the religion issue; he has been accused of being Romish. *I hope I have enough religion to save my soul.* Good that: avoids entirely what kind of religion it is. *But what little I have has been learned amidst the noises and drums and trumpets of his Majesty's service.* He reworks this several times until in a single phrase he has enclosed an entire syllogism:

Major premise: His Majesty is head of the church and state.

Minor: His Majesty has, through permitting me to serve him, taught me religion.

Therefore: the religion I have is consonant with that of the state and church which his Majesty heads.

Unless of course one wishes to denounce His Majesty as an heretick. And to make sure that his loyalty to the Crown is to be taken as an overriding virtue, *I pray to Almighty God that it would do me no good, if I would not venture one, but one thousand lives – had I them – to defend the Sovereign's right. And I would destroy all manner of persons – emperors, kings, popes or prelates, that invaded any part of His Majesty's territories. One thousand lives, all mine, aye, so I would give.*

It works; no perjury, fervid loyalty and their Lordships are able to protect Stapleton from the Protestant hardliners. He can never relax, though. A petition in the English house of commons in 1678 asks the king to recall all Papists with offices anywhere in the world and the wording is aimed specifically at catching Stapleton.

The king demurred.

Stapleton further skilfully clouds the waters by making a show of great concern for the interests of the Established Church. In 1678 he finally appoints a rector to Montserrat, a benefice that in theory was under the Bishop of London, but in fact was in his own gift as were those of all the Leewards: the islands, not London, paid the clergy's stipends. Stapleton puts in place a tame, amiably corrupt young man who actually, at age twenty-one, is below the canonical age for the post, but no matter.

When, in 1680 James Cotter has to report on religion on Montserrat, Stapleton ghosts his letter. *Our ecclesiastical affairs are to the best of our endeavour agreeable to the canons and constitutions of the church of England*, a declaration that even a Jesuit missionary could have signed: best of our endeavours indeed!

A year later, in a cloud of ink that could have been a parody, were Sir William Stapleton's career not always in jeopardy, he writes to the Lords of Trade and Plantations, telling how well treated the clergy are and asking for more. *I have prayed my Lord Bishop of London to send over four able ministers to these, and not young graduates. There is an absolute necessity, my Lords, of having as a cleric a man of parts in St. Christopher for there are no parish clergy on that island. But is found there French and Dutch Calvinists and Lutherans. And these are as great an adversary to the Church of England as they are to each other.*

What a lovely concern for an Irish Catholic to have, the defence of the Protestant state church against Calvinists and Lutherans: not, notice, against Roman Catholics.

Sir William has a marine pool constructed at Nevis where he keeps and feeds prize specimens, including a large squid so admirable and successful that he never sees it.

PORT ROYAL, JAMAICA. 1675

A Crying Shame

Courageous though he is, Thomas Lynch openly cries tears of gall and bitter almond. He has spent five years as governor of Jamaica, fighting for the future. His enemy was the bandit capitalism of the buccaneers; his prescribed future was the slave capitalism of the sugar world. Leading the island's planters in open opposition to Captain Henry Morgan and his banditti required immense courage.

And Lynch almost had won. Morgan had been taken in chains to London for overstepping the wide bounds of his buccaneering licence. There the king had been charmed by someone so adept at badgering the Spanish and had pardoned him. Then Morgan was knighted.

Morgan returns to Port Royal in the company of a new governor who is to replace Thomas Lynch. Morgan and the new governor disembark at the jetty and are greeted by a festival: guns firing, whores throwing their skirts up, buccaneers being sick upon each other. The news that makes Lynch cry is that Sir Henry has been named the new deputy governor of the Jamaica colony.

LONDON. 1675

Brotherly Feeling (3)

As a good citizen of the Empire and a successful planter, Philip Warner looked forward to his time in London. It was therefore unsettling immediately upon arrival to be arrested and taken to the tower of London. "Think you that I am Sir Walter Raleigh?" he asked.

After eight months in the tower, Warner was on his way back to the West Indies as a prisoner. He was no longer governor of Antigua and he was to be tried in Barbados for murder.

And all for doing his duty as a white man and as a citizen.

When, in November 1674, word had reached Nevis that a mass of Carib on Dominica were preparing a large raiding party, Governor-General Stapleton decided on a pre-emptive action. The Carib were reported not to be "French Carib," but "Indian Warner's."

Stapleton issued a formal commission to Philip Warner to deal with the problem.

No details were necessary. Warner understood what was required.

On Christmas day, 1674, he and a tight little army landed on Dominica. They engaged purchasable native guides and first killed a few French Carib and then attacked and killed several of Indian Warner's band.

The two brothers then agreed a truce. They embraced and they and their lieutenants feasted and drank heavily. Rum in every form: raw, in punch, in fruit skins. Rum. And while Indian Warner and his men became legless, Philip Warner and his men held back until, at a signal, they fell on the Carib. Indian Warner's throat was slashed so deeply that his final breath was issued directly from his lungs into the salt air in a spray of red vapour.

His actions brought Philip Warner no immediate joy, though later he reflected that it greatly simplified family relations.

He could not understand why the London authorities were so angry with him. Granted, the peaceful settlement of Dominica now was impossible, but he had been, in truth, following orders.

BRIDGETOWN, BARBADOS. 1675

Descriptive Terms

Although John Blake did not do as well in trade in Barbados as his brother Henry did on the plantation they jointly owned on Montserrat, he was happy in Bridgetown. It was not Ireland. No priests. Fewer cousins. No wife: she was in Galway.

A good loose life amidst the dignity of Bridgetown's English-style buildings and well-ordered streets, a legacy of the town's having burned to the ground in 1666, and having started afresh. A hundred taverns, a dozen brothels. No priests, fewer cousins.

John's comfortable state ends in 1675 when his wife joins him. Not all is lost, for he arranges that a Galway servant woman whom he remembers with erect fondness will accompany the family. *I am much troubled for that whore (as I am credibly informed) came out along with my brother John's wife.* Thus the righteous report by brother Henry on Montserrat, back to the family's elder brother in Galway City. *I am afraid she may be the occasion of his confusion by her seducement,* Henry said cluelessly and added, *I pray God preserve him.*

John, trying to keep in his elder brother's good book, explains why he needs the "wench." *My wife being, as I find her, of very weak constitution, cannot discharge all herself, for washing, starching, making of drink and keeping the house in good ordere, is no small task to undergo here.* Eventually, he promises, I will get rid of the wench, when a *'neger' wench I have bought* is trained.

A year later, John takes over the Montserrat plantation when Henry goes back to Ireland. The business is conducted using yet-another Blake family relative as the factor. *Dear Brother – I have this day delivered possession unto my cousin Edward Bodkin of the plantation and 'negers' for your account ... your loving brother, H. Blake*

Unlike Henry, John had no intention of ever returning to Ireland. He soon had thirty-eight slaves and eventually became one of Montserrat's largest planters. He died in 1692 and his estate went to his only surviving legitimate child, a daughter, married to Nicholas Lynch, an Irish planter on Antigua. He also left several illegitimate by-blows.

John Blake, like some other Irishmen in the West Indies, preferred a world where one owned negers, and could consort with whores, keep wenches, and encounter few cousins and fewer priests.

BARBADOS. SEPTEMBER 1676

Mistrial

Colonel William Stapleton deeply hates Indians, specifically the Carib. The settlers in his domain are perpetually tempted to leave the islands because of "murders, rapes etc" by the Carib. His settlers are more destroyed by watching and warding against these heathen than by any other cause. Many are taken by "malign distempers," contracted while on guard duty.

He uses the same vocabulary and has the same mixture of incandescent hatred and settler's-fear that was found among the Protestant settlers who took his own family's lands in Ireland. For the rest of his life in the islands, he reports proudly to London on his "Indian hunting": a mixture of sport, vengeance, and colonial management, not unlike rebel hunting and, later, croppie hunting, at home.

Now, though, he has a more immediate problem. As a good commander he is loyal to his subordinates. Philip Warner is brought to Barbados in the frigate *Phoenix* and is to be tried by a commission of oyer and terminer for killing "certain Indians in Dominica." This is outside of Stapleton's jurisdiction and he knows that in Barbados a Leeward Islands planter is apt to be convicted of virtually any charge whatsoever.

Hence, he acts.

Stapleton has the witness who is the cornerstone of the prosecution's case, Captain Peter Hamlyn, who had ferried Warner to Dominica on the hunt-and-kill mission, arrested on charges of privateering. The witness was in irons on his way to Holland when Warner's trial took place, the Dutch governor of Curaçao performing this favour for Stapleton. All the minor witnesses got the message and their testimony became strangely inconclusive.

Philip Warner walks free, and though London will not permit him to recover his post as governor of Antigua, he is more popular than ever and is elected by his fellow planters as speaker of the Antiguan legislative assembly.

Family Arrangements

Only slightly more than a decade after taking up his first official appointment in the Leeward Islands, William Stapleton was able to send his sons to London to be educated properly. He had gone from being an impecunious Irish mercenary officer to being an imperial force. He sends his eldest son, James, to England in 1678 and his second, William in 1679. They are accompanied by trusted negro slaves who, while in

England, are referred to as servants. Anne Russel Stapleton travels to London in 1679–80 to be sure the lads are receiving a decent Protestant education, but mostly to revel in being addressed in London as Lady Stapleton the moment William's knighthood comes through. The lads are boarded and taught in a small preparatory school and, once their mother has returned to Nevis, are under the broody eye of their great-aunt, Lady Marsh. Although their father had intended for them to attend Westminster School, she keeps them out of it as being too brutal an establishment entirely. Thus, when Stapleton finally retires as governor-general of the Leeward Islands in 1685, his sons still are in a cosseting prep school.

Taking care of family was one of Stapleton's great virtues or vices, depending on one's view. He brilliantly ran a small colonial empire and made it look from the outside like a Roman proconsulship; from the inside, it was regulated like an Irish petty kingdom. He took care of his own and expected them to take care of him. Thus, the governorship of Montserrat, which he himself held into 1672, was given to his eldest brother, Edmund Stapleton from 1672–79, to his old swordmate James Cotter from 1680–85 and to Stapleton's younger brother, Redmond, from 1685–87. Nevis, the island Sir William most prized, was administered during his regime almost entirely by various in-laws, the Russels, except for brief periods when he took over the local government himself. St. Christopher, so badly sacked during the French War of 1666–67, was not worth much attention, but Antigua was. Philip Warner, who had a virtually hereditary claim, was put in as governor from 1672 until his family difficulties in 1675. Then, after a brief period when the governorship of Antigua was held by a London appointee, Stapleton had his young brother-in-law, Thomas Russel, put in place.

None of this was corruption by the standards of the time. The salaries of each island's governor came from votes of monies by local assemblies. Putting in local men, individuals who got on well with the big-governor, Sir William, and who were not too fussed about trading with the Dutch or with the occasional pirate, kept the planters happy.

Nor did Stapleton make money directly on his own office. Not directly. The governor-generalship, which was paid by London, was worth £700 a year, but it was always late. The expense of defending the islands was supposed to fall both on local taxes and on London, and both were behind in payment and rarely paid in full. Hence, we find Stapleton in 1676 complaining to one of his London superiors that two companies of soldiers are barefoot and would the Lord Treasurer please hurry and pay their arrears? And there is a sense of comic opera in Stapleton's having to put together – out of his own pocket money – uniforms that will keep the local militia's morale up: blue trousers and white bandoliers and tunics captured from the French, modified by the addition of British flashing.

No, the way Sir William Stapleton became immensely rich in land and slaves was simplicity itself and well within London's policy of having the colonies bear the brunt of the cost of their own governance. Stapleton simply awarded large plantations and chunks of land to his family, to in-laws and, indirectly, to himself. For example, he had been given Anthony Briskett II's Waterwork Plantation in 1666 as the equivalent of a signing fee, for taking on Montserrat's governorship. In May 1678, a vacant piece of land of several hundred acres was granted by the crown (that is by William Stapleton) to his brother-in-law, Col. Sir James Russel, who in 1680 flipped it back to Sir William. On Antigua, he effected a crown grant to his brother Redmond of two plantations, totalling more than 1,000 acres in 1679 and then William purchased them back from him. Purchased? One would be surprised if these were anything but fictional transactions: William Stapleton granted land to William Stapleton. On Nevis, Stapleton in 1678 was so brazen as to make a crown grant of 502 acres to a Major Pim on one day and to buy it for himself on the same day. There, and a dozen similar transactions, are where Stapleton's fortune came from.

Stapleton cannily refused to play the rich West Indian planter, with English estates and aristocratic ambitions. He stayed home. He kept out of the official censuses (which he, as governor-general, conducted) of property and slaves. He took care of family.

JAMAICA. 1684

Almost the Glorious Revolution

The man with the large head now scarcely moves. Captain Sir Henry Morgan, no longer deputy governor of Jamaica, has been losing battles for the last half-dozen years to the slack-jaw sugar planters who think that organizing work gangs and beating slaves is man's work, equal to commanding ships that are crewed by the demented, and skewering Spaniards. The planters are inexorably gaining control of Jamaica. Standards, Morgan laments, are dropping.

Movement is hard for Captain Morgan because of his gout. No amount of blood-letting empties the viscous fluxes and ill-humours from his blood. He spends most days in a cane-wicker chair, one foot raised and placed in ice that is brought at great expense from Newfoundland. He drinks prodigious amounts of rum punch and alternates surveying the harbour with his brass telescope and sleeping fitfully.

Captain Morgan can read well, which is an achievement, considering that he was sold as an indentured servant into the West Indies before his tenth birthday. He enjoys the English papers, mouldy as they are when he receives them, for they list cargoes of ships and a man, even a decrepit man of fifty, can dream, can't he?

A parcel arrives with the latest papers, a book from England and a note from an English admirer. Morgan's fingers are too damaged to permit him to open the carefully-tied parcel himself. He bellows for a house slave, who opens the parcel with Morgan's pen knife. It is in the shape of a crucifix, a delicate prize from a Spanish ship, a present intended perhaps for a lady.

Two days of reading the English version of Alexandre Oliviere Exquemelin's *History of the Buccaneers of America* leaves Morgan in a rage. The book, just released by the London bookseller W. Cooke, had enjoyed previous Dutch, French, German and Spanish incarnations, each of which was tilted by its translators to glorify local feelings. Sir Henry was so enraged by what he read that he forgot his gout and kicked two of his household staff, causing them more pleasure than discomfort as Morgan hopped about in pain.

Then the man who had killed hundreds, perhaps thousands, and had terrified the entire Spanish navy acted. He hired a lawyer: who demanded that the publisher of the English edition remove the parts that made Morgan out to be a ruthless thug. Truth being no defence under English libel law, the publisher surrendered and in settlement *The History of the Buccaneers* included a preface extolling the virtues of Captain Sir Henry Morgan.

On 25 August 1688, Morgan's liver gave up the unequal task to which Sir Henry had assigned it, and soon thereafter he passed into the mephitic cloud of his own legend.

BARBADOS. 1686

Fear

The apocalypse of the Barbadian planters' imagination had only two horsemen: creole slaves and Irish Catholic servants. They would bring about a Meggido of blood, ankle deep, the blood of whites. So the Barbadian planters long had prophesied.

In 1686 Governor Edwyn Stede declares this to be the year of the Apocalypse; he has heard it whispered in the alleys and had read it in the writings of Nostradamus.

He investigates.

He arrests eighteen Irish Catholic servants and twenty African creole slaves.

Following further investigation, he frees all the Irish Catholics, for lack of evidence of their guilt.

The twenty blacks are executed for lack of evidence of their innocence.

LONDON. 1686

Curious Recessional

Deceptive plant, ivy. When the tapestry of its leaves withers, it slowly dies. Then the suckers and tendrils that have held it to a cliff face that seemingly could not be colonized by anything living are revealed. And the secondary growth, separate species that use the ivy colony as footing for their own parasitic advantage, become obvious. Then they, shorn of the protection of the ivy leaves, slowly aetlioate and disappear, leaving only a skeleton of raw relations: the ivy's tendrils, the raw rock face.

William Stapleton in the early 1680s began to prepare for his own demise and in so doing revealed the social adhesive that had worked for him: always remembering that he was a man of talent, bad temper, and raw courage. In 1681, when his fellow soldier (and now son-in-law) James Cotter returned to County Cork, ostensibly for a furlough, Stapleton entrusted him with the sole complete copy of the laws of the several islands under Stapleton's charge: these to be delivered to the Lords of Trade and Plantation. And, in the same year, Stapleton fired his man-of-business in London and gave power of attorney to a Cork lawyer, a commissioner of the Irish excise and hearth tax, who practised in London: Patrick Trant, who was James Cotter's cousin.

A curious inheritance came to Stapleton in 1684, an estate on St. Christopher, where he had held almost no land previously. This was from "Father de Nogle," a Catholic hermit whose Anglo name was Nagle. And, it is hardly unrelated that John Nagle, a Cork man, factoring in Dublin, was used by Patrick Trant to conduct William Stapleton's business in Dublin.

When in full foliage, Stapleton had depended upon two modes of adhering to fortune's slippery wall: his immediate in-laws, the Russels, and a network of contacts that ultimately ran back to the river valleys of County Cork. The first was visible and Stapleton kept his Russel contacts clearly on display. The Irish network, localized in origin and thick-matted by intermarriage, cousinhood, mutual survival in unpredictable wars, he camouflaged brilliantly.

Knitting together in patterns of which we can only see a tithe, were Nagles, Cotters, Trants, and, ultimately Burkes. In the long-scheme, the Presentation Order founded by Nano Nagle owed some of its ability to help the poor of Ireland to family fortunes preserved and remade through the West Indies; and Edmund Burke's freedom of thought and speech was in part based on the slavery of hard-marched platoons of African blacks.

Not all its adherents were symbiotic, as the Stapleton family eventually learned. Sir William, health failing, had requested a furlough in 1683 and was granted one in 1685. He returned to London, bringing his third son Miles to join Lady Stapleton and the other two boys, James and William. Sir William expected his health to improve and to return to his Leeward principality. His health did not improve, however, and in 1685 he and the boys went to Paris where he was to take a cure. The three boys were enrolled in a Catholic school, though this was accepted as a temporary expedient: the family concordat still held, the boys would be raised Protestant.

Sir William died on 3 August 1686 leaving several square miles of choice plantations on four Leeward islands, hundreds of slaves and substantial lands in England.

Immediately upon the death of Sir William, the lawyer Patrick Trant gave orders to the superior of the boys' convent school to lock up the three Stapleton children and not to let Lady Stapleton approach them.

The children were sent to Douai, the favourite continental boarding school of the Irish Catholic gentry. Young Sir James, the eldest, managed to escape, in 1690, an unbroken Protestant, but an unintentional martyr. He died aboard ship. His younger brother William (now Sir William) took firmly to Roman Catholicism and to West Indian planterdom: he returned to Nevis and there married his first cousin, Frances Russel, and thus placed himself in line to far-and-away the largest fortune in the Leewards.

Lady Stapleton, now a widow, accrued her own estate, but it was sadly diminished. Patrick Trant (who became Sir Patrick under a Jacobite knighthood) had been faithful perhaps to the One True Church, but not to his employer. At least £8,000 in cash had clearly been embezzled by Trant, but by the time the widow obtained judgement he had already been declared a Jacobite traitor and there was nothing to seize.

Sometimes parasites leave permanent stains long after their host has vanished. William Stapleton left few monuments. In the Leeward Islands, no Stapleton plantation remained under that name, but "Trants" on Montserrat survived slave Emancipation and then became a topographical landmark lasting into the late twentieth century.

And, just as the Montserrat branch of the Trants prospered, so too did the Irish branch, always suitably adjusting their behaviour to fit the colouration of their protectors. In 1781 Dominick Trant was elected MP for Kilkenny in the Irish parliament: as a Protestant, of course. His brother-in-law, John Fitzgibbon, was Earl of Clare and the Irish Lord chancellor. And his sister-in-law married into the Beresfords, the most powerful Protestant clan in Ireland.

It's all about trust and finding the right protective foliage.

DERRY. 2 JULY 1689

Pas de Deux

The Catholic-Jacobite forces have collected all the Protestant tenants they can find: small-holders, barely making do in a hostile countryside. Children, women, men, all are herded like cattle towards the walled city of Londonderry. There the Protestant-Williamite forces are holed up. They are down to boiling boots and eating rats as nutrition. A thousand more mouths to feed may break them.

At a distance, the defenders of Derry cannot discern who the herd might be, and as it shambles forward the defenders fire into the crowd. Later, they take it as miraculous that not only did they not injure any of their co-religionists, but that three of the Catholic drovers-of-humans have taken bullets and died.

The herding-of-the-Protestants is the iconic moment in the war of 1689–91, the only war when English and Irish forces were evenly matched. The Catholic-Jacobite-Absolutist forces had one disadvantage as compared to the Protestant-Williamite-Parliamentary army. King James II was a poltroon.

The Protestant small-holders are left at Derry's walls to join in the starvation of the garrison. The defenders respond by erecting a gallows. There are a score of prisoners-of-war in their hands. They write to the Jacobite commander promising to hang each soldier unless the Protestant civilians are allowed to return to their homes. He blusters, but two days later, the civilians are permitted to scuttle away to safety.

A perfect moment: a balanced dance.

NR. ST. CHRISTOPHER'S, THE WEST INDIES. 1689

Mixed Drinks

The trouble either started with bad bartending or flawed Human Resources policies: in modern terms.

The crew of the *Prophet Daniel* had taken as prize a small Spanish vessel and was splitting up the booty. There was a formula for this and, in fact, they had all signed articles in English, the captain's language, detailing any share-out. The difficulty was that the crew, besides being half French and half Irish, were also mostly illiterate so they could not have known exactly what they had fixed their "X" on.

Their modest victory over the Spanish in hand, the captain had ordered extra drink to be issued in celebration. The first mate told the cook not only to bang up extra grog, but had the several Madeira casks that were on the Spanish prize broached.

Rum and fortified wines don't mix well: no better than do Irish and French cut-throats.

The two groups fell to arguing about the division of their prize and soon, in the confines of a vessel no more than ninety feet long, a team death-match ensued.

The Irish, some missing appendages, others gored in body, blinded, all dripping with blood from several wounds, were the last men standing.

THE BOYNE RIVER. 12 JULY 1690 (N.S.)

Tipping Point

Straight backs and full stomachs win big battles.

The two kings, James and William, face each other and William's back is straighter. He contributes directly and courageously to an epoch-making victory; James wastes his resources and, the battle lost, races towards safety with the speed of a steeplechase rider. Three days later he sails from Kinsale to France.

The stomach: William understands. His victory was in large part one of logistics, and therein lay an unexpected benison. He brought to the fore, as one of his chief supply officers, a Dublin merchant who hailed from Holland.

Bartholomew von Homrigh: father of Jonathan Swift's "Vanessa."

GLORY IN SOME FASHION
1690–1785

Yes, I Fought With Sarsfield

What is called an alpenstock by ice-climbers in the European mountains is adopted by Hugh Balldearg O'Donnell as his personal symbol. Actually, it's merely a pike turned upside down, but Balldearg (as his men referred to him) carried it the way a conquistador carried the staff of his nation's flag: every place he planted it, every step he took, he made a claim. In Balldearg's case, the claim was that he was himself the centre of the earth and he served himself, not a monarch, not a cause, unless those things served him.

Like many of the O'Donnell aristocrats, he was given refuge and substantial emoluments by the Spanish monarch. Good soldiers, the Irish, is the Spanish calculation. In the late 1680s and early 1690s this is necessary: Spain, England, Sweden, the Netherlands and some of the German states are in an ecumenical alliance against Catholic France which, under Louis XIV, is kicking them severely.

Balldearg, hearing the distant fifes of the Jacobite cause in Ireland, leaves Spain without permission, and raises a horde in Ulster. This is not an army, but an armed mob of 10,000 or more men from Ulster and northern Connacht. For Balldearg, aiding Patrick Sarsfield is not a patriotic act, but a chance to grab vast lands for himself, if the Jacobites win.

The men Balldearg brings are so undisciplined, and Balldearg himself so given to arguing with every other commander, that they do more harm than good to the Jacobite cause. Sarsfield later confides to General Ginkel that he wishes he had thrust that "damned pike" through Balldearg's body.

Balldearg O'Donnell surveys the thousands of Irish being killed at Aughrim and immediately begins his own negotiations with King William's General, Ginkel. He and part of his remaining mob join the Williamite cause and with enough effect that Balldearg is treated with honour and recommended to King William as an officer of great merit. He settles in London, where he pursues the title of earl of Tyrconnel. It does not come quickly enough, and in 1692, he and 700 of his old followers leave England and enter the Spanish service. The Spanish recognize his earldom, and he spends the next five years recruiting deserters from the Catholic army of France to join the Catholic army of Spain, in aid of the alliance with Protestant England and its other European Protestant and anti-Jacobite allies.

The man with the alpenstock would never have seen himself as a traitor to anyone, least of all to his own honour. He was a professional military man in the era before that concept became all sticky with the marmalade of nationalism and patriotism.

LIMERICK CITY. 25 SEPTEMBER 1691

Wild Geese

"What do you think of the Irish now?" asks Patrick Sarsfield, the most courageous of the commanders left to fight the Jacobite cause after King James had fled Ireland.

"What we have always thought," replies one Williamite officer with careless insolence.

"Change kings and we will fight you again," Sarsfield suggests.

With the two kings gone from Ireland, one in full fright, the other full of confidence, the war-of-the-two-kings was fought by surrogates. The outcome was not in doubt, for King William's forces were superior now to King James's and were continually becoming stronger. The real question was: what would peace cost? Could it be bought with less than a river of blood?

Patrick Sarsfield, created earl of Lucan by King James in February, 1691, stalled the inevitable, but eventually had to withdraw to a defensive redoubt: Limerick, an island citadel that was as hard to take by siege as any place in Ireland. Against him was Godard van Reede, baron von Ginkel, one of Europe's best generals, and an economical one. The cheaper peace came, the better all around, he reckoned.

Ginkel's forces managed to form a wobbly causeway on the gunwales of small boats across the Shannon. Then Ginkel attacked a brigade of Irish soldiers who held one of the bridges that led directly to the main Irish redoubt. At the worst possible moment a French officer (ah, the danger of having such good friends) in charge of the gateway, raised the drawbridge, leaving the Irish hopelessly trapped. They died in such numbers that, when the fight was over, their corpses were stacked on the sides of the bridge, like cordage, higher than the ledges of the bridge itself. The river below was said to resemble a stream full of drowned sheep.

Thus Sarsfield treats with Ginkel. And an amicable business it is, for each man wants this affray over and wants to continue his own career. Ginkel invites Sarsfield to dinner, and the Irishman accepts, and sends a dory loaded with claret as a *douceur*. Several dinners ensue, and not only are military officers present, but so too are lawyers and the Catholic archbishop of Armagh (the head of the church in all Ireland) and the archbishop of Cashel.

No treaty emerges, but several articles of agreement are joined, some agreed with more sincerity than others.

Sarsfield cares most about his career. He needs an army if he is to be anything other than another former aristocrat, yesterday's hero. He wants to take his army to France. Ginkel agrees: better they fight for England's enemies in any place but in Ireland. There are details: hostages will have to be left behind as security for the vessels that the Williamites will provide to take Sarsfield's officers and men to France; and each man has to be given a choice of going to France, demobilizing in Ireland or joining the army of King William. Sarsfield agrees, and then has his men cooped up so that it is difficult for them to do anything but go with him. Catholic priests preach to the troops, telling them that for the salvation of their immortal souls, they should follow Sarsfield and fight for a Catholic king in Europe. Eventually, 11–12,000 serve with Sarsfield in France. Two thousand or so decide to fight for King William and the Protestants, and another two thousand take their chances and just go home. The men who sail to France are in the van of a train of tens of thousands of Irishmen who will serve France during the eighteenth century.

"Civil" articles are agreed, purporting to guarantee the property and religious rights of the civilians and soldiers who remain in Ireland, provided they had been under the protection of the Limerick garrison. Everyone else was to receive the privilege of freedom of worship "consistent with the laws of Ireland, or as they did enjoy in the reign of King Charles II," a meaningless phrase as the laws of Ireland were extraordinarily plastic and given to frequent redefinition.

Silly: the hammering out of these details.

For: the moment Sarsfield's army is gone, there is no Catholic force to make inconvenient the breaking of these agreements.

With the narcissism of the true warrior, Patrick Sarsfield leaves as a hero. He becomes a full marshal in the French army. He has not the slightest awareness that he has left the country to the wolves. And, with complete sincerity of spirit and opacity of mind, he is able to affirm in his dying breath, bleeding from a musket ball taken in the chest while commanding a French cavalry unit in Luxembourg in 1693, "would to God this were shed for Ireland."

WARSAW, POLAND. 1694

Mass Observation

To the county Kerry Catholic physician, Dr. Bernard O'Connor, the religious practices of the Polish common people are endlessly fascinating. He is especially taken by their manners at Mass and he attends peasant chapels every chance he has. The worshippers' practice of drawing knives and swords and brandishing them in the air at the reading of the Gospel never fails to delight him, although their readiness to defend the Faith is slightly dangerous. He usually stands in a side aisle out of range of any excessive expression of religious fervour. Then, when the Host is raised, he is even more enthralled. The communicants slap themselves in the face and beat their heads on the bench ahead of them or, if they are kneeling on the bare floor, upon the paving stones. They do so with such force that the thumping of penitential crania can be heard far outside the church.

O'Connor, just twenty-eight years old, is one of the ambitious, brilliant and very worldly gentry Catholics who leave Ireland during the late seventeenth century. Fluent in French and Latin (as well as English and Irish), he receives his medical degree from the University of Rheims in 1693. Through a mixture of charm and outright scientific brilliance, he is within a year made court physician to King Jan III Sobieski, king of Poland.

Even the Polish royal court is a backward place to an ambitious young doctor, and after a year he moves to England, shortens his name to Connor, becomes an adherent of the Church of England and is admitted to the College of Physicians and elected to the Royal Society. He is a very good scientist indeed and soon is guest-lecturing at Oxford.

In his spare moments, Dr. Connor writes the first history of Poland in the English language.

Then, in his thirty-third year, he takes a fever and dies. The last person to talk to him is a Catholic priest from Ireland who speaks to him in Irish and, satisfied with his penitence, gives him extreme unction.

NEW YORK. 1696

A Calm Disposition

Darby Mullins often said that it was a good thing he took to the sea, for the sea certainly took him.

A country lad whose home was eighteen miles south of Derry, he was good with the loy and useful in a faction fight. He was roving a side road one day in 1681, when he encountered three jovial strangers who offered to treat him to some punch if he would show them the way to a tavern. That task Darby could do with his eyes shut, and soon they were there: press gangs were common near the seaports. They weren't looking for naval recruits but for strong farm lads to serve as indentured servants in the West Indies. There the shortage of white servants was acute, the more so because the memory of Cromwell's transporting Irish men, and a few women, to the islands still was sharply remembered.

A strange form of kidnapping, for the victim worked his own ransom: Darby, trussed like a turkey until he was safely aboard ship in Lough Swilly, was forced to sign on for four years of indentured labour with a Jamaican planter. Physically strong, and of a philosophical bent, Darby looked at the tools his first overseer handed him and reasoned that they weren't much different from those he was accustomed to using. And being cursed at by an overseer wasn't all that different from being cursed by his own father.

Four years later, his indenture over, Darby Mullins is one of the men the West Indies prizes: a healthy, experienced white man whose labour is his own to sell. By the time the massive earthquake of 1692 destroys Port Royal, he has enough money in his pocket to buy and stock a tavern in Kingston. He also acquires a white wife, a sure sign of prosperity in the woman-scarce West Indies.

Listening to the bragging of the drunken thugs who fill Jamaica – pirates, privateers, a mixed-nation and, sometimes-mixed-race babble of hard men – gives Darby ideas and he, like so many Irish former-servants from the West Indies, decides to expand his fortune in the American colonies. He works the docks of New York and then sails as a part-owner of a vessel trading to the Madeiras: a hard voyage and on his return he finds that his wife is fatally ill.

What use has a man with a house, furniture, linens, if he has no wife? Darby Mullins sells all that, buys a twenty-ton ship and does a coastal trade delivering wood to New York. Good money, no glory.

Then in 1696 the trumpet sounds. William Kidd – the Captain Kidd of legend – is given a letter of marque, a royal licence to become a privateer, and he issues a call for volunteers. They will, according to the privateer's licence, be suppressing piracy. Hard men, experienced seamen, men who know the West Indies, are Kidd's first choice and Darby Mullins makes another sea change.

And just as the change from being a draft animal in County Londonderry to being one in Jamaica had not much fussed Darby Mullins, neither did it bother him when Captain Kidd changed his vessel from a privateer to a pirate ship. Sailing shoal-filled waters, blind-siding unsuspecting merchant vessels, burning, shooting, hand-to-hand combat, are activities not much different from chasing pirates, except safer: Darby's philosophic disposition serves him well.

When, with Captain Kidd, Mullins is hanged in England for piracy in 1701 his last words are an approving comment on the view from the scaffold.

LONDON. 1696

The Gospel Truth

When the witness at the Old Bailey rose to give his testimony, he spoke French. "Not speak English," he declared.

Lord Chief Justice Holt responded, "If he cannot speak English, there must be an interpreter." This was a major trial, and fairness was crucial: Thomas Vaughan was being tried for High Treason on the High Seas. Five high court judges were sitting on the case.

"The defence must find an interpreter," argued the solicitor-general, who was prosecuting the case. "He is their witness."

Thomas Vaughan's case – and thus his life – depended on linguistics as much as on law. He fully acknowledged having been the captain of at least two French warships that had fought against the Royal navy.

His defence was brilliantly simple: he was not a subject of the Crown – and thus not guilty of treason – but a French-born citizen and thus a prisoner of war. If he were a natural-born subject of the British Isles, he would hang; if French, he would be returned to France with all the punctiliousness one set of officers owed to another.

Captain Vaughan's case depended on three witnesses, each of whom would back up his assertion that he had been born in Martinique and of a father who, if not French-born himself, was a naturalized French citizen. This was possible, given that the West Indies was a whirlpool of constant aggression and ever-changing possession. Beyond the Line lots happened that went unrecorded, including deaths and births. It was not surprising that Vaughan could produce no documentary proof of his birth.

His first two witnesses, who claimed to have known Vaughan as a Frenchman in the West Indies, did well. The third witness, however, was fatal.

"We will send for an interpreter immediately," Vaughan's barrister assured the court. "In the meantime, may I respectfully suggest to your lordships that ..."

"No need. No need, your lordships!" The interruption came from a law clerk in the back of the courtroom. "He speaks English as well as I do."

"Approach the bench."

The clerk's information was devastating. This "French" witness had long been a bailiff's assistant and had served writs over half of London.

"Prithee speak English," the Lord Chief Justice sarcastically directed the French witness. "As well as I can, my lord, I will speak," he replied, trying to keep up the pretence.

Thereafter the trial slid into farce. Without much effort, the prosecution was able to prove that Captain Thomas Vaughan was the Irish-born son of a Protestant military adventurer, who had gone to Ireland during the rebellion of 1641, settled in Galway City, married an Irish woman and prospered. The late Mr. Vaughan had owned a public house, been overseer of the Galway City market, and for a time traded in person with the West Indies: thence the source of Captain Vaughan's big lie. Unfortunately, solid testimony showed that Vaughan's mother had never been out of Ireland in her life.

Thomas Vaughan was Irish born.

That he had turned Catholic as part of his successful career in the French navy had nothing to do with the verdict. He would have been hanged and had his head placed on a pike even if he had been a godson of King William himself.

THE INDIAN OCEAN. OCTOBER 1697

Discipline

"Lousy Dog," hollered Captain Kidd, standing no more than six inches from the face of an Irish deck gunner, William Moore. The Irishman was one of the men in Kidd's crew who had objected when the captain had decided not to attack a well-armed Dutch vessel, *The Loyal Captain*. The moment had been one of near-mutiny and Kidd had barely maintained control.

"Lousy Dog!" he repeated, spit showering Moore's face.

Keeping silent in the face of this tirade was the only wise course. Instead, Moore replied, "If I am a lousy dog, you made me one!"

Kidd turned, grabbed a wooden bucket with heavy iron hoops around it, and smashed Moore on the head. The gunner slumped to the deck. No one dared go near him. He bled heavily, but eventually the wound on his head clotted, so that his hair resembled a garden filled with vermillion tussock-grass.

Even with Captain Kidd drinking himself into oblivion behind the barred door of his cabin, no one dared to help William Moore. Finally, like an expiring worm, he pulled himself into a corner, twisted his body into a knot that no sailor could ever untie, and slowly died.

WATERFORD CITY. 1714

Continental Polish

In mid-autumn, contrails of dust drifted over the hills outside of Dublin, Cork, and Waterford. This was the time of the annual cattle drive. Despite the increasing poverty of the tenantry, the mid-lands of Ireland were not mostly given over to potato raising or to other arable crops. The rich grazing lands were reserved for cattle, the domain of boney beef cows that produced a calf annually. In the autumn the drive began: store cattle, bullocks and cast heifers, destined for the English midlands where they would be fattened; old bulls, past their prime and ready for immediate slaughter; barren cows, now useless, half-starved ambulatory skeletons.

The Irish, like all rural societies, enjoyed occasional cruelty to beasts, especially when it was free – and if an animal was destined for slaughter in any case, why not have a little fun as it stumbles on its way?

The thousands of Irish soldiers who served in continental armies transmitted back home sophisticated European forms of animal cruelty; the best came from Spanish veterans.

Thus, the Corporation of the City of Waterford passes an ordinance in October 1714: "that a bull-rope be provided at the charge of the city revenue." This is a special collar and rope. When the dust cloud that marked a herd of market cattle coming towards Waterford was seen, "a rope, a rope!" would be the cry. And the most aggressive of the drovers' bulls would be driven into the city's bull-ring: not a well-constructed Spanish ring, but nevertheless a special place distinguished by a heavy tether-pole surmounted with a copper statue of a bull. There, in a mixture of Spanish and English pleasures, successive tethered bulls were tormented by heroic young men on foot, and then the bulls, frothing mad, were set upon by purpose-bred Irish bull-dogs. These canines looked like a monkfish, seemingly all head and no body. Their jaws were large enough to surround a bull's snout. When they latched onto a bull, they often would not let go even after the animal was dead.

Frequently the dogs' trainers had to fracture a cur's ribs, or a leg, in order to make it give up its prize. In exceptional cases, a dog would lose its grip only when a leg was amputated, and a few legendary bull-baiting dogs fought on three legs.

Only in 1798 did the Waterford council ban bull-baiting and take down the pole that had held the totem of this ancient sport. By then, Waterford had human blood sports to consider.

OUT OF NANTES, FRANCE. NOVEMBER 1721

Monkeys in the Tree Tops

Philip Roche, an experienced mate, understood the agronomy of piracy. So he and Pierce Cullen and Andrew Cullen had seized a small ship at Cork, with the calculated intention of working their way into the upper canopy of the pirate forest, where the richest pickings were to be found.

They took the vessel to Nantes and there they exchanged it for passage and shares in a somewhat larger coastal trading vessel. As experienced seamen and as men of apparent substance, they were left in charge of the vessel at various times while the master and mate slept. They were a useful addition to the ship's crew, so it seemed, for her complement of seaman was half Irish and English and the vessel required "linguisters" to relay orders to them in Irish or English.

One night as the captain and mate slept, Roche convened the Irishmen in the crew and told them that he and the Cullen brothers were victims of French predation at sea and they could either act like Irish patriots and kill the French members of the crew or be sliced to pieces themselves.

Roche then ordered three Frenchmen and the cabin boy to scamper up the main mast and do some work on the top sails and when two descended, their job done, he and his Irish mutineers beat them to death and tossed them overboard.

Thence followed a *danse macabre* in the tree-tops as the cabin boy and an able-seaman jumped from sail to sail with Roche and his men in pursuit. Roche deftly grabbed the cabin boy and flipped him into the sea as easily as if he had been a monkey in a rain forest.

The fourth French seaman, jabbering for mercy, descended to the deck and had his head bashed to jelly. The remaining French crew and officers were herded into a scrum, and there they pleaded that as Christians, as believers in the same blessed Jesus, as subjects of the same True Church, they should be left alive, to serve alongside their Irish brothers.

The massacre that followed was so messy that the ship had to be washed down. The ship's former master and his first mate were lashed together, and after being permitted to say their prayers, tossed overboard.

Philip (now Captain) Roche had a lively career at the top of the pirate forest, before his inevitable and fatal fall.

The curious aspect of Roche's career is that when the author of the pseudonymous *General History of the Pyrates* wrote of him in 1724, he freely admitted that he had forgotten most of the details of Roche's vertiginous career, but he had no doubt that Roche was an unusually handsome man. *He was a brisk genteel Fellow, of thirty Years of Age at the*

Time of his Death; one whose black and savage Nature did no Ways answer the comeliness of his Person.

For a brief moment, Philip Roche had been the handsomest predator in the forest canopy.

SOUTHERN SWEDEN. 1721

Napalm in the Morning

"My God, I love the smell of a village in the morning."

Since the time of Alexander of Macedon, every truly professional military officer has felt that way. There's something about still-smouldering thatch and black-spiraling shards of flame coming from tight-packed granaries, that gives a man an appetite for his day's work. The morning shafts of sunlight emerging through broken walls and windowless houses makes a shifting pattern on the ground that a real officer loves just as much as a monk loves the interplay on the abbey floor of light from a stained glass window.

"Dearest God, on such a morning it is a wondrous thing to be alive." That, in French, was the half-prayer, half-cry of triumph of Major-General Peter Lacy, one of the most distinguished of the patriots to exile himself from Ireland as a follower of Patrick Sarsfield. He had joined the Athlone Regiment of the Irish Jacobites at age twelve and had served in the Irish Brigade for one of the German princes. So keen was he that when Peter the Great of Russia recruited a cadre of foreign officers, in 1700, young Lacy was among them. He rose quickly in the Russian War against Charles XII of Sweden. Killing came naturally to him, and he understood the need for patterns of termination, not just the last-man-standing brutalities of the primitives. That is why, in 1719, he had burned two Swedish coastal towns and 135 surrounding villages to the ground.

And that is why, now in 1721, he and his 5,000 troops are torching another two towns and more than 100 hamlets and cross-roads villages.

Unlike later professional officers – who benefit from the petroleum-distillate age, when human bodies are made flammable, indeed, incandescently so – Peter Lacy is not able to enjoy the burned-bacon smell of human flesh, or the unmistakable tang of human hair that has been burned to its roots in its owner's skull. He has to content himself with observing the local domestic animals as they rip at their former masters. He sits motionless on his horse and watches a sow, her litter sucking at her teats, as she gnaws on an arm that once was attached to a farmer, large and strong.

General Lacy's only regret is that he must visit his pogrom upon peasants and small merchants. There are no soldiers to engage and thus no medals for valour to be won. His embarrassment at this lack of chivalric challenge is revealed in his diary. *I know of no other way of forcing the Swedes to make peace.*

WESTMINSTER. 1722

Guest of a Nation

Arrest and nearly fifteen years imprisonment in the Tower of London brought out the best in George Kelly. He enjoyed himself.

Kelly (B.A., TCD, 1706) was one of the few Irish Protestant clerics to pledge his fortunes to the Jacobites. Not that he was much of a cleric: he never bothered to take his M.A. or to go beyond deacon's orders, but in 1718 he preached a sermon in Dublin favouring the Old Pretender as the rightful king of Ireland. He moved to Paris quickly thereafter and then returned to London where he was the confidential intermediary of Francis Atterbury, the Jacobite Dean of Westminster and Bishop of Rochester.

Arrested and sent to the tower in 1722, George Kelly began to enjoy himself. He was given an interrogation by a committee of the House of Commons and then the full spotlight before the bar of the House of Lords where he made a brilliant speech. For his pains, he was to be held in the Tower for an indeterminate time.

Then his real fun began. The Crown, still trying to place a capital sentence around his neck, frequently put him in identity parades. He showed up for each dressed outlandishly – in a nightgown and cap, in workman's garb, or other items he bribed the guards to provide.

At first Kelly was held in a small room, but he had friends with money and he claimed to have asthma so, by early 1723, he was in a roomy apartment on the south side of the Tower and allowed to take constitutional walks on the parade ground. Cheerful, liberal with his tips to the guards (legal, within reason), he soon had his own coach within the Tower walls. In 1728 he was given the privilege of attending the coffee house within the Tower and of dining at the Officers' Mess. Five shillings a day were coming to him from Jacobite sources and he spent them well. In 1730 he gained the privilege of going anywhere he wished within ten miles of London, provided he took a guard with him and returned in the evening. If he could have run for Lord Mayor of the Tower, he would have won. The dinners he gave were a highpoint for warders and gentry prisoners alike.

Of course, he had to escape eventually, pleasant as life was: duty was duty. But as a gentleman he had given the governor his solemn word that he would not escape when he was outside the castle. So George Kelly had to arrange to escape from within. This he did in disguise in 1736, and a very self-denying act it was.

Not that the rest of his Jacobite career was unpleasant, just a reduction in his standard of living. He landed in Scotland in 1745 with the Young Pretender and, that disagreeable business complete, spent his declining years on an ample pension at Avignon.

THE BLACKWATER VALLEY, COUNTY CORK. 1724

Marriage Bond

The son and daughter of two middle-gentry Catholic families do what their families desire: form a marriage alliance. This is a practical necessity if families of their sort are to hold on to their lands. It is especially true of holdings in the lush Blackwater Valley, no less desirable, and thus no less vulnerable, than when Edmund Spenser apostrophized it in *The Faerie Queene*.

The couple marries under Church of Ireland forms, for only a marriage validated by the Established Church will guarantee that their offspring will be permitted to inherit family lands.

Two years before the wedding, the groom, Richard Burke, had conformed to the Anglican Establishment: as an aspiring lawyer in the period of the penal laws, he required a certificate of conformity to the Church of Ireland if he was to have full access to the courts.

The bride, Mary Nagle, necessarily affirms Protestantism prior to the marriage ceremony, although after the marriage is solemnized she returns to practising the One True Faith.

Events of this sort, pragmatic evasions of the penal laws against Catholics, are an everyday event and, whatever their transcendental worth, they significantly limit the impact of the anti-Catholic legislation.

This particular union produces in 1729 a son, Edmund Burke: a gift to a nation that desperately needs someone who, born into the complexity of a small local universe, can understand the simpler patterns of the larger outside world.

DUBLIN. 1728

The Peculiar Condition

Whoever would rightly understand the actual State of Ireland, ought principally to inform himself of the peculiar condition of its Catholic Inhabitants. Thus wrote Denys Scully at the beginning of the nineteenth century. He provided the first comprehensive statement of the penalizing-laws – the "penal code" or "penal laws" – the Upas Tree that had frowned over Ireland for most of the eighteenth century and whose toxic tendrils did not completely wither until the mid-nineteenth. That Scully found it necessary to write his legal commentary anonymously says a great deal.

The "peculiar condition" of the Catholics after their defeat at Limerick in 1691 is simply stated: they lived in a state wherein the religious minority had the ability and desire to persecute the religious majority. That was the cruel twist: for, in fact, nothing the Protestants of Ireland did to the Catholics by way of screwdown legislation was not done according to European precedents in the Catholic-Protestant gang fight. The only difference was that in Europe, the majority persecuted the minority, not the other way around.

Neither in the eighteenth century, nor anytime since, has any historian fully catalogued the Irish penal laws and assayed their actual effect. One legal provision really counted, however, and that was a bill introduced into the Irish commons in 1727 and passed in 1728. It excluded Roman Catholics from the franchise. Even though the Irish House of Commons was infamously corrupt, and although the Catholics had already lost the right to sit in both the Commons and the Lords, the franchise was the one lever whereby the Catholic middle- and upper-classes could jam the gears of government. (That the small tenantry, Catholic and Protestant, were excluded from voting goes without saying; property was the basis of voting rights.) Only twenty useful members of parliament would be enough to block the worst anti-Catholic measures, Denys Scully estimated, and they were to be had if the Catholics had the vote: liberal Protestants despised the penal legislation and, in any case, some of the boroughs were so corrupt that, in several of them, two dozen Catholic voters could have purchased their own MP.

So, the 1728 measure taking away Catholic voting rights was the heart of the penal code. When in his full manhood, Edmund Burke surveyed the situation he declared, "*the taking away of a vote is the taking away the shield which the subject has, not only against the oppression of power, but that worst of all oppressions, the persecution of private society and private manners.*"

What neither Edmund Burke nor Denys Scully noticed was that the penal code, like the Upas tree, poisoned all that grew beneath it – and did nearly as much damage to Protestant culture and religion by its institutionalization of false superiority, intolerance, manipulative theology, triumphalist history, systemic discrimination against Catholics of ability and legalized theft of Catholic property – as ever it did to the Catholics.

A simple litmus item makes this clear. Throughout the eighteenth century, Catholics and Protestants left Ireland in their tens of thousands. As far as the incomplete and mouldering records can talk, they say that Protestants left in proportionately higher numbers than did the Catholics.

What approached hell for many Catholics was not, for the run-of-the-mill Protestant, anywhere near paradise.

COUNTIES CORK AND KILDARE. 1735–1744

Mixed Education

In later life, when at the summit of English political eminence, Edmund Burke traces his educational roots, he begins at Trinity

College, Dublin. That is true as far as it goes but it does not go far enough. Burke's characteristic economy of truth begins with his disguising his early education.

At age six, young Master Burke is sent to live at the foot of the Nagle Mountains in County Cork: this is the ancient Irish practice of fosterage, eighteenth-century style. He is placed in the charge of an uncle, Patrick Nagle, and is sent to one of the "hedge schools." Technically, these are illegal Catholic schools, but mostly the authorities turn a blind eye to them. So long as Catholic parents are willing to pay the schoolmaster, they provide a decent primary education.

But no old school ties.

At age twelve, Edmund is sent to a Quaker school at Ballitore in County Kildare. It is a good classical school and prepares him well for Trinity. The head is Abraham Shackleton, a Yorkshire Quaker who, though a pacifist, had no inhibitions about moving to Ireland in the early eighteenth century and profiting by the widespread shucking of the Roman Catholics of much of their property consequent upon the Williamite War. Burke receives a solid education and, equally important, becomes close friends with Richard Shackleton, son of the headmaster. They remain close at Trinity. Young Shackleton is the first real Protestant whom Burke comes to know well.

The Shackletons' school at Ballitore continues for several generations and turns out some very interesting minds: not least, Paul Cullen who enters in 1812 and who becomes the nineteenth century's most powerful Catholic ecclesiastic, excepting of course some of the Popes.

CRIMEA, UKRAINE. 1737

Even the Winds and the Seas Obeyed

As soon as the troops under General (now a full general and field marshal) Peter Lacy reached the far side of the Sea of Azov, they fell on their knees, blessed themselves, and declared that their general had divine power. Regiment after regiment of an entire army did this. Four days were required to complete the crossing.

Russia was once again trying to annex the Crimea from the Khan who held it under Turkish licence. Lacy, lucky as he was bold, decided to cross the Azov Sea at a narrow point. The sea was shallow, from three to fifty feet, and affected by the rate that fresh-water rivers ran into it, by its own tidal pattern and, most especially, by wind. With amazing good fortune everything fell into line and with the aid of a few portable bridges, Lacy took an entire Russian army across.

Lacy's troops, Orthodox Christians, had been read the scriptures often enough to recognize the pattern and they argued amongst themselves whether they should compare their general to Moses at the Sea of Reeds or to Our Lord on the Sea of Galilee.

FONTENOY [BELGIUM]. 30 APRIL 1745 (O.S.)

On Fontenoy!

In their most valorous hour, the Wild Geese wore bright scarlet uniforms and Crown shoulder patches. This was the Irish Brigade, fighting for France against the British and Dutch in the War of the Austrian Succession. The brigade, under Charles O'Brien, sixth Viscount Clare, comprised one cavalry and six infantry units, some with artillery pieces. The battle flag of the unit led by Thomas Lally embodied the *realpolitik* of the situation: a cross, in which the harp of Ireland was surmounted by the Stuart crown. Church, King, Ireland.

The English under the Duke of Cumberland overran the French centre and were about to take the day. They, like the Irish Brigade, were wearing red. Thomas Lally led his men to the apex of the English attack. As the other Irish regiments came forward to hold the English temporarily at bay, Thomas Lally brought his four heavy cannons into close combat, a new tactic. He had his gunners blowing shrapnel, cannon balls, pebbles, musket balls straight into the chest and face of the enemy who raged forward. The artillery men kept their discipline under extreme pressure and the English infantry was not so much stopped as disassembled. Later, some of the victorious Irish made a macabre game of trying to match the limbs of the fallen with the trunks of their bodies.

Thomas Arthur Lally, born in 1702, the French-born son of a Jacobite officer from Tullanadaly, County Galway, went into the French history books as Thomas Count Lally de Tollendal. Voltaire apostrophized him in a memoir of Lally's bravery at Fontenoy, a benediction as ambiguous as the kiss of a wasp.

IRELAND. THE PENAL ERA

Chance's Grand Kingdom

The addiction to gambling, always a way to pass slow time, becomes pandemic during the penal years. For the poorest, it is a form of hope for those who have none. For the parasitic classes, it is a way of turning moral vacuity into entertainment. The Irish will bet anything, their dreams, their lives.

Among the peasantry, the great enemy of the old culture of ancient tales told by wandering story-tellers around a warm hearth, is not the Ascendancy, but the packs of tattered and besmeared playing cards that circulate in town and country alike. Entire days are spent in contests over no more than a sixpence. Or for a salted herring or two. If cards are not available, pitching farthings or stones against a wall will do. Anything to distract the mind with a short-term hope. The willingness to gamble makes the young people of the nation easy prey to recruiting agents for servants in the West Indies and the Americas and to recruiting sergeants for the British army and for those of the continental countries that still surreptitiously search out Irish marrow for their bloody wars.

The squireen class – Protestants with a horse, a silk waistcoat, mounting debts, high pretensions and no intention of earning a living – have a unique form of gambling: the abduction club. This flourishes in south Leinster and eastern Munster. Young gentlemen with no money of their own join in a club with their fellows and decide upon a suitable victim: a strong farmer's daughter, a Quaker merchant's young treasure, someone with a reasonable fortune in her family, but not from such a grand family that it could exact vengeance. Then, by lot, one of the squireens is chosen to abduct her. The other members of the club throw in their resources: a quality horse, a new pair of boots, a choice cravat, and social introductions to the girl's family, if they have these. The business is decidedly dangerous because, since 1707, it had been a hanging offence to "forcibly" (note that word) abduct a woman. So, the goal is either to capture and bring her around to accepting her captor as her husband voluntarily, or to force her parents to drop any charges and to permit a marriage, since an abducted girl was destined to spend the rest of her life on the shelf, a spinster living on the family capital. This was a big gamble and a few young gentlemen swung by their neck; more, however, celebrated an advantageous marriage by emptying their new father-in-law's wine cellar with their clubmates.

Gambling could be taken so far as to become an art form. That was shown by Buck Whalley who, in 1789 played a game of handball, one of Ireland's favourite sports, against the walls of Jerusalem. He'd walked there on a bet, and a very good game he had.

LIVERPOOL DOCKS. 1752

Dry Numbers

A port official does a tally of the slaving boats that belong to Liverpool. He finds that eighty-seven ships carry on the trade and that in the previous year this Liverpool fleet carried 24,731 Africans into slavery.

He also writes down the names of each of the captains. At least eight of the masters are Irish.

Put it another way: roughly 10 percent of the slave trade was captained by Irishmen.

ST. STEPHEN'S GREEN, DUBLIN. THE PENAL ERA

The Carousel of Life

The habitués of the Irish Parliament and of Dublin Castle may think that they are situated in the pivot of Dublin life, but the real hub is the Green. There, like the figures on a carousel, examples of all levels of humanity pass before one's eyes, revolving in a sequence that has constant motion, but no true progression.

There the entire social order, from rabble to aristocrats, are treated at intervals to executions of society's least acceptable members: Mary Allen, burned on St. Stephen's Green for drowning a child; a gentleman hanged for murdering a city councillor; another for having cut his maid's throat. Darkey Kelley, who kept a bordello, was burned alive on the Green; and there two Irishmen who, in the service of a foreign government, enlisted young men as soldiers, were hanged.

Then there is the Green's bucolic sector. The lord mayor of Dublin is provided with a fenced paddock for his horses and cows.

Race meetings are held on the Green, sometimes on the Sabbath, and everyone from pickpocket to prostitute to squire has a day in the fresh air.

As the century progresses, the Green becomes less dangerous, more carefully policed, more dominated by fashionable homes on its borders and fops on its footpaths. Sunday is the best day for public display of wealth, for carriages and beauties with deep décolletage, but every day a parade of dandies minces up and down Beaux Walk, on the north side of the Green. Unspoken competitions take place according to ornamentation on coats, notably the buttons, on the size of a diamond stickpin that holds white stocks in place and, most especially, the walking stick each dandy carries. They are much closer to a bishop's crosier than to a cane. The impressive ones are held at near-shoulder height and have a gold, or at least silver, figure or emblem on top.

Inside some of these fob-staffs are concealed rapiers or long daggers, for a gentleman never knows when he will need to defend himself against the envious rabblement.

PARIS. 1756

Beware the Honours of Princes

Already a brigadier-general, Count Arthur Lally was made a lieutenant-general by Louis XV and given command of the French army in India. The chalice, handed to Lally by jealous courtiers, was poisoned.

The War of the Austrian Succession had ended in 1748 without the side issue of India being settled. India was a big bauble, but obtaining the cooperation of the notably corrupt French civil servants, the wildcat merchants, and the local military was an impossible task. Lally complained of endemic corruption and made enemies in both India and Paris.

The English took Calcutta, wiped the French at the battle of Plassy, and when Lally tried to take Madras he arrived too late to prevent the English reinforcing the city. His three-month siege was useless. And at the battle of Wandewash, the British commander-in-chief, Sir Eyre

Coote from County Limerick, conquered him. Taken prisoner, Count Lally was brought in 1761 to England and then handed back to the French.

The French ceded almost all their interests in India to the English in 1763 and then they looked for a scapegoat.

Thomas Count Lally de Tollendal.

He was given a parliamentary trial and beheaded in 1766.

In the twentieth century, the French parliament revisited the matter and decided that the trial had been a travesty and that its judgement should be reversed.

Small comfort.

MELIMBA, WEST AFRICA. MARCH 1757

The Black Prince

Heroic, but wasted, so it was universally recognized: Captain William Creevey's patriotic ferocity. He, the Irish master of *The Black Prince* of Chester.

His ship and three others are anchored on the slave coast of Africa. Their holds are full, three to six hundred African men and women stuffed aboard, depending upon each vessel's capacity. Then, a small French squadron jumps them before they can fully set sail.

Instead of surrendering, the captains of the English slave ships run them into the shore. Creevey's *The Black Prince* is hindmost and bears the brunt of the attack.

He and his men fight off two launches full of French marines.

Most of the slaves escape.

The French burn *The Black Prince*.

According to the reports later agreed by the captains of the slave ships, the French permit the blacks to plunder one of the other slave ships. And, while this is in progress, they set a fuse burning so that the powder magazine blows up, killing the Africans as well as destroying the vessel.

The French: perhaps, although it is hard to understand why they would set a trap to punish looters of a ship that they were themselves intending to burn. Certainly under the laws of maritime liability, it was convenient to the vessels' owners that the French enemy, rather than the masters of the slave ships, had intentionally destroyed so much valuable cargo.

HAVANA, CUBA. 1764

Good Postings

Lovely rum. Lovely women, especially the mulatto slaves. Lovely life.

The Spanish general had not been home since he was in his teens. In his mid-forties now, he felt he was finally being justly rewarded for a life of soldiering. Satisfaction in one's calling, a handsome, if jowly face, and now everyone stood to their feet when he entered a room, even the governor's daughters. What more could a man desire?

Alexander O'Reilly, born in County Meath, was lucky and he knew it. As a young officer in the War of the Austrian Succession, he had been slashed severely and abandoned as his regiment retreated before the Austrian infantry. He had fully expected to be gutted, stripped of his valuables, and left as a half-naked corpse for interment in a communal pit.

O'Reilly still had breath and wit left, and when an Austrian infantryman approached to finish him, he husked out in fractured German a story: he was the son of the Duke of Arcos, O'Reilly said in a blood-spattered voice, and a big ransom would be given for him alive. The infantryman spared him and, with his wounds now bound, O'Reilly was taken to the Field Marshal of the Austrian forces.

Who laughed hysterically, and spared his life: Count Maximilian Browne, Irish mercenary, recognized a kindred soul. He sent O'Reilly, once he had healed, back to the Spanish and no charges for the delivery.

The actual Duchess of Arcos liked the story so much that she became Alexander O'Reilly's patroness and he rose quickly. He wasn't a bad officer mind you, but lucky, undeniably. So as a brigadier general, he is spending his time in Cuba organizing the militia, rebuilding the fortress walls, and helping keep up social standards.

His next mission is another bit of good fortune. He is sent to take New Orleans for the Spanish: ceded to them by the French in 1762 along with all French territory west of the Mississippi. General

O'Reilly takes New Orleans with a single frigate and twenty-four small troop transports and forty-eight cannon.

There was no opposition, but that was not O'Reilly's fault. Bored, he responds to local insubordination by torture and brutality and goes down in history as "Bloody O'Reilly," the Torquemada of Spanish rule in Louisiana.

DUBLIN. 1766

Two Trials

"*A Sheehy jury! That's what it was.*" In the last one-third of the eighteenth century, "a Sheehy jury" is a phrase used to refer to a jury rigged well beyond the mere everyday corruption of the Irish judicial process. Of course all county grand juries (which set public policy, provided policing, and raised local taxes) were composed almost entirely of Protestants (they were impaneled by the sheriff of the county who, in this era, always was Protestant), and so too were all petit juries (the trial juries for specific cases). And a property qualification was required in both cases, so even if Catholics had not been filtered off most juries in the high-penal era, only a small minority of persons tried for crimes (those who held significant amounts of property) would have been tried by a jury of their peers.

No one expected it to be otherwise.

The *Sheehy jury* was called into being because a jury in Dublin failed to put policy above justice. The parish priest of Clogheen, County Tipperary was accused of inciting riot and rebellion. Almost certainly Father Nicholas Sheehy (who, incidentally, was a relative of Edmund Burke, Father Sheehy's sister having married Richard Burke, a first-cousin of Edmund), had encouraged resistance to tithe proctors and may have given comfort to Whiteboys. But rebellion, no. He was being prosecuted because of the animus of his rival, the Established Church's rector in the parish, whose tithe revenues were being hurt. The Dublin jury acquitted Father Sheehy.

As he walked out of the courtroom in Dublin, he was re-arrested and this time charged with being part of a Whiteboy murder plot.

The case was moved to Clonmel, to reduce the chances of his innocence being declared. Innocence, certainly: Father Sheehy was not
involved in any Whiteboy murder plot – if such there was – and
indeed no body was ever found. But at Clonmel Gaol he was
dropped into a sink of intimidation. Armed militia surrounded
the courthouse and Sheehy's own attorney had to leave town each
night for fear of being beaten by governmental thugs. In a scandalous trial, Father Sheehy was judged guilty and hanged, drawn
and quartered in mid-March 1766. His grave became a site of
pilgrimage.

DUBLIN. 1772, 1774, 1778

Scholastic Aptitude Test

Take out your special pencils.
Do not open your test booklet until I tell you to do so.
All ... Right ... Now!
**Read the following short selection as quickly as you can. Then
answer the question at the end.**
*The anti-Catholic penal laws in Ireland can be said to have been initiated
in 1692. Their biggest effect was to take land from Catholics: they held
about 22% of Ireland in 1688, 14% in 1705, and 5% in 1776.*
*The Catholic church was persecuted for a brief time, but, by 1714 it was
clear that the last thing the Protestants of Ireland wanted was for the Catholics to convert to Protestantism: for then they could not keep for themselves a
monopoly of the best professions and continue to hold more and more of the
nation's lands.*
Question: *Were the penal laws a success?*
Next selection. *In 1772 and 1774, minor "Catholic relief" acts were
passed by the Irish parliament, allowing Roman Catholics to hold sixty-one
year leases on reclaimed bog land and to enter certain trades and guilds upon
taking an oath of allegiance to the Crown and by disavowing the Pope's right
to depose the King of Ireland and Great Britain. And then, in 1778 a "relief
act" allowed them to lease land for 999 years.*
Question: *Was this a matter of Irish history? or English? Or, perhaps,
French and American?*

THE IRISH SEA. SUMMER 1780

Prudence

Finished linens feed a lot of people.

The finest threads are sent from Ulster to Dublin where they are made into table and dress linens. These are works of art. Women of Huguenot descent are the mainstay of the trade. By some mode of spiritual descent, their refiné personal demeanour is transmitted to their works, so that the result is as intricate as the carpet page of a medieval manuscript, yet peculiarly modest.

So valuable is their output that Dublin linen factors construct special Linen Ships to take these goods to English ports in perfect, unsullied condition.

Now, with England in various stages of war with Holland, Spain, France, and the United States, the Irish Sea is aswarm with privateers, men with letters of marque from England's enemies: licences to steal.

Therefore, each Linen Ship from Dublin, as it leaves port for Chester or Bristol, is joined by a frigate and at least two armed cutters. The delicate cargoes in each transport vessel are worth about £150,000. Renting warships to serve as escorts is a necessary cost of doing business.

The Black Prince is the most feared of the privateers. It sails under French letter of marque, yet is known as "an Irish pirate ship" in newspaper reports, for it is captained by Edward Macartney. The vessel is an accurate symbol of the confusion of the times: French licence, emigré Irish captain, yet the ship was Chester-built and was named for the ill-fated slaveship of Captain Creevey, of the 1757 disaster. Edward Macartney had lived in France since 1768, one of the declassé Irish Catholic gentry who were deprived of land and opportunity by the penal laws.

Life abroad had not made him soft. When he jumped the *John* of Newcastle off the Mull of Galloway, he killed one seaman and severely wounded the captain and the second mate. Fair enough, that was battle. His negotiating technique, however, was noteworthy. He demanded a ransom of £1,000 for the frigate and for sparing the lives of the two wounded. A promissory note from the captain, drawn on the ship's owners, would do. The captain refused, so Macartney let him and the second mate bleed. He watched, they bled. When his own ship's surgeon made as if to help the wounded, he was ordered back. The crew of *The Black Prince* was told to get torches and to burn the *John*.

At that point, the *John*'s master decided that a note for £1,000 was a fair ransom after all, a cost of doing business.

DUNGANNON, COUNTY TYRONE. FEBRUARY 1782 AND DUBLIN. NOV.-DEC. 1783

Seepage

The most ridiculously dressed man in a parade of garish and silly-looking soldier mannequins was Frederick Augustus Hervey, fourth earl of Bristol and Protestant bishop of Derry. He wore a purple uniform of his own design, but with no insignia of rank, as he had yet to raise a corps of followers in the Irish Volunteers.

Dungannon in February 1782 was a town taken over by a circus. The Irish Volunteers were holding their first great convention. One hundred and forty-three corps from Ulster were represented. Since each of the corps was self-formed, they each had their own uniforms, often paid for by the local landlord who named himself captain or major or colonel. These top officers designed their own costumes. When corps of Volunteers congregated, a fair amount of time was spent looking at each other: each Volunteer was both an observer and a specimen in this paramilitary menagerie.

Almost all of the Volunteers were Protestants, but they did not act like it. Granted, they were armed and were quite proficient in their self-taught military arts. And they were seriously committed to defending Ireland against foreign invasion: they had come into being in the later 1770s when regular troops were withdrawn from Ireland to the American colonies and a French invasion therefore seemed possible.

But Protestants were supposed to beat on the Catholics and genuflect towards London and these men in Dungannon do not do that. They have concluded that they are being duped by the English. The Dungannon convention demands operative independence for the Irish parliament, free trade with Britain (a code-phrase for fair competitive access to the slave-sugar economy of the West Indies), various parliamentary reforms and, astoundingly, a relaxation of most of the laws that hamstring their Catholic fellow citizens. With ill grace, but a sense of *realpolitik*, London grants the Irish parliament quasi-independence. Of course the Crown remains (the Volunteers are definitely not republicans) and an immense amount of intermeddling continues at the executive level. But in theory the Irish have self-government for the first time in half a millennium. The Irish parliament removes almost all the disabilities on Catholic landowning and most of the indignities that hindered the Catholic clergy in carrying out their duties.

Not quite enough for the Volunteers, for the Irish parliament remains unreformed, and trade barriers still limit Irish trade with the slave islands.

Thus, the Volunteer national convention in Dublin in the early winter of 1783.

And thus the stately progress of the Earl Bishop from Derry to Dublin. He now has his own troop of dragoons, raised in his diocese, and he is one of the Volunteers' national leaders. He is drawn into Dublin in an open landau. He is dressed entirely in ecclesiastical purple and his six carriage horses are harnessed entirely in purple trappings. Meeting for nearly a month at the Rotunda, Dublin, and parading fearsomely, the Volunteers fail to intimidate the Irish parliament into meeting regularly, holding unpurchased elections, or generally becoming a form of representative government.

The Earl Bishop gives up politics and spends most of the rest of his life in Europe, leaving his diocese to fend for itself.

DUBLIN. 1783

Binocular Vision

John Scott (viscount 1789, earl of Clonmel 1793), longtime chief justice of the Court of King's Bench in Ireland, keeps a diary. He is no more complex than any other Ascendancy figure, only more articulate. He writes:

> **Irish government** resembles extremely the state of the Hottentots in Africa. The common Irish, divided, oppressed, pillaged and abused as they are, are the Hottentots; the English Administration are the Dutch planters; the followers of the Lord Lieutenant are the

bushmen or spies and swindlers ... The man who would live in this country, especially in public station should, like Monsieur Vaillant, the traveller, guard himself hourly against serpents, tigers, hyenas, elephants, jackals, monkey in human form, and against the planters and bushmen inside.

In counsel to himself, Scott writes:

Secure the aid of Women in every scheme ... Carol O'Daly, a famous Irish hero, never went into a house that he did not secure the confidence and affection of some female in it, who constantly supported and befriended him in all his pursuits. Satan found no footing in Paradise, had he not gained over Eve to his part. For ever secure some she-thing to your interest, young or old, high or low, mistress or maid; but your first anchor of flattery should be these.

DUBLIN. 1783

Nomenclature

Recreational gang fights ("faction fights") were one of the Irish peasantry's ways of beating boredom, and each other. Effecting grievous bodily harm was the unofficial national sport.

The same held among the Ascendancy, with the demit that it was not a team sport: solo duelling was à la mode, and there was hardly a member of the Irish parliament or of the judicial bench who had not tried on a handful of occasions to kill another human being.

In 1783, the "Knights of St. Patrick" meet and decide to change their name. As a group of gentlemen who had long desired to suppress duelling, they now change their collective title to the "Knights of Tara." This is necessary because the Dublin and London authorities, anxious to keep Ireland on side in a difficult international situation, had provided a sideboard full of reforms: among them the newest and declared-highest order of Irish chivalry, the Illustrious Order of St. Patrick. This is founded to celebrate Irish and British links.

The gloriously moronic idea behind the activities of these anti-duellists, the sometime Order of St. Patrick, is that they propose to quash duelling by making their members such excellent killers with sword and pistol that all the other gentlemen of Ireland will be afraid to pick a fight with any one of them.

LONDON AND DUBLIN. 1785

Horse Sense

Rarely quick to take in new ideas, the British and Irish military authorities assimilated over fifteen or twenty years the lessons of the 1740s. These were, first, that as Fontenoy painfully taught them, Irish soldiers could be very useful indeed. And, second, the failure of the 1745 Stuart rebellion in Scotland to receive any support from the Catholics of Ireland, said that the days of worrying about their being loyal to the Old Monarchy were over.

Still, the military authorities moved tentatively. In 1758, 1,200 Royal Marines were recruited in Ireland and during the 1760s, English regiments were allowed to recruit all over Ireland, not just in the north. Although, in theory, they were to enlist only Protestants, in practice they picked up thousands of Catholic recruits.

The real turning point was the American rebellion: the shortage of troops to suppress the American colonies led to heavy recruiting of Irish Catholics. They had ties with the American colonists much less frequently that did the northern Protestants, and thus were less squeamish about enforcing imperial loyalty.

From 1787 onwards all regiments, whether based in England and Scotland or in Ireland, were allowed to recruit in Ireland. This made many Protestants swallow hard, because Irish Catholic farm boys were being trained in military discipline which, in Ireland, often became a social and a political skill.

Still, necessity ruled.

Just as the imperial military authorities come to appreciate the value of the Irish Catholics, thousands of Catholics come to see the British military as a machine useful for their own purposes. The clear symbol of the new alliance-of-necessity was the grand old Irish Brigade in France. The scapegoating and judicial murder of Count Lally had left them disillusioned, and then, their remaining loyalty – always dependent upon fealty to a monarch – was destroyed by the Terror. Several of their officers were guillotined. The Irish Brigade broke asunder, some finding a place in the new order once Napoleon came to power, but most abandoning France: the Brigade was assimilated into the English army.

From the mid 1790s until the end of World War II, more Irishmen served the armies of the English empire than fought against it in any kind of military service, foreign or domestic. Not just a few more. Several hundred times more, a fact that should not have embarrassed later southern Irish governments and populace, but did: these soldiers, unlike the Wild Geese, were given few monuments and even fewer songs.

THE DEVIL'S
SUGAR PLANTATION:
THE WEST INDIES, 1690–1785

Sweet Tooth

Watching gentlemen riot is entertaining. Gentlemen don't roll in the dirt. They brandish walking sticks at officials, turn apoplectic, use long words, flip the cravats of those who have offended them and flick index fingers across the enemy's nose, as if to say, I will cut off this tiny protrusion of yours, and then your private parts. Gentlemen when rioting do not take out their swords or pistols, although they place their hands menacingly on them, then remove their hands, bow, and go through it all again, as in a minuet that has no audible music.

The Montserrat gentlemens' riot of 1688. England's slave monopoly supplier, the Royal African Company (founded just after the Restoration by the king's brother, the duke of York, and counting the monarch as one of its chief shareholders), has continually shorted Montserrat on the slaves it needs. Jamaica and Barbados have first crack, then Nevis and Antigua and, finally, Montserrat. It desperately requires slaves as it is the last of the West Indian islands to convert fully to sugar and slavery. And when the Royal African Company does not come through, the Montserratians deal with the Dutch, as they do in their day-to-day smuggling. This time, an official of the Royal African Company catches them and exercises his company's legal right to seize the sixty slaves the Dutch have just delivered.

Watching the gentry barrack the company officials are the small men, former tobacco and indigo planters who own one or two slaves and still hope to expand enough to have half a dozen blacks and thus to run a small cane farm. They are dressed in dirty Osnabrug or coarse linen, and do not carry pistols. Their loose shirts cover the boning knives that each carries sheathed and concealed in the small of his back.

Later, the badly-needed slaves having been taken to Barbados, the gentleman rioters are tried by a local jury of their peers and of course acquitted.

Curdled Milk

By way of a corsair Governor Edwyn Stede receives happy news and bets his career on it. In London, the wife of King James II has had a baby delivered, a son. Some say the delivery was by warming pan and from another than the Queen's womb; others that the birth was the genuine event. Stede stages the biggest celebration yet seen in the West Indies.

The entire white population of Barbados is invited. Stede, in regalia so full that he clanks and sounds like a platoon all on his own, leads a procession that includes every conceivable civic and military officer. He has set a table 250 feet long to serve the 500 gentry who are above the salt. And beneath are sittings for another 2,000 persons. There are more plumped-up bosoms on display than even Captain Morgan had dreamed of, and he dreamed big. The day of feasting and drinking ends with fireworks, salutes fired in the harbour, and so many Loyal Toasts to the king that many of the most loyal guests forget entirely the king's name.

Governor Stede has just ended his career.

THE LEEWARD ISLANDS. 1688–1689

The Biggest Jacobite in All the Americas

In March 1688, Sir Nathaniel Johnson, who had recently taken over the governor-generalship of the Leeward Islands wrote a long and very intelligent letter to the Lords of Trade and Plantations explaining exactly what was wrong with the administration of the Leeward Islands. Sir William Stapleton never would have done this, for ambiguity was his strength: Johnson's appraisal was accurate, transparent and therefore idiotic.

I was petitioned by the Roman Catholics for the free exercise of their religion, which was granted. As the expense of building and decorating chapels, which they have already begun in Montserat and St. Christopher, will be very heavy on them, I have exempted them from contributing towards the support of Protestant ministers. Fair enough. A few middle class Catholics are gratified, such as Nicholas Lynch who is on Montserrat just now, courting the daughter of John Blake.

Ever the well-intentioned fool, Johnson moves the administrative capital of the Leewards from the Russel-family stronghold of Nevis to Antigua where new Irish Catholic gentry are establishing themselves:

the Galway families of Browne, Lynch, Kirwan, Skerret, who have secondary plantations elsewhere in the Leewards, and the Nugents, whose family connections are so wide as to defy geographical detail. Are they pleased with Johnson's new pro-Catholic policy? In fact, no, for the well-intentioned fool calls into question the one thing they value most: their land.

I believe that nearly all the titles in the Leeward Islands are insecure, which is a hindrance of settlement and a loss to the King by the failure of escheets. The only sure way of securing the titles is for the King to grant his letters patent to the proprietors. So everyone in the Leewards who holds even an acre of ground is in trouble, because security will come with a cost. *As to rents, I believe that if the titles were confirmed at a rent of one percent or half per cent on the annual produce of the estates, the revenue would be considerable and the burden very slight.* That is: every settler is to pay a new annual tax. And the model is to be the Irish statute that helped to cause the bloodbath that was the Irish civil war. *An Act confirming the patents granted by governors would also give great satisfaction – such as an Act as passed in Ireland in Lord Strafford's time.*

The high-principled fool thus alienates not only all the Protestants in the Leewards (a majority of the planters), but loses the gentry and merchant class of Irish Catholics, who know exactly where playing pitch-and-toss with land titles leads.

Only the poor Irish, the one-and-two slave settlers caught in pockets of white poverty, follow Sir Nathaniel in a Crown-and-Church crusade. In the name of King James II and holy mother church, they briefly seize Barbuda, join the French on St. Christopher in attacking the English parts of the island, and hold the southern portion of Montserrat as a tiny, though militarily useless Jacobite redoubt. In all these cases, they lose quickly and by the end of 1689 the leaders are in prison in Jamaica or have bolted to some backwater where their names are not known.

For his Irish co-religionists, Sir William Stapleton had understood the primary rule about the Leeward Islands: like an egg balanced on its end, don't push it.

Sir Nathanial Johnson, forced to resign by the gentry of his several islands, took himself and 100 slaves to Carolina, where, in 1703 he became governor, as did his son after him.

PORT ROYAL, JAMAICA. 7 JUNE 1692

How Does One Pronounce Gmrh in Hebrew?

The earth opens and an entire street drops into an abyss. Nearby, a tavern full of roisterers falls into a crack that opens and then closes upon the building, like a sprat being snapped alive by a moray eel. Briefly the bottom of the harbour is visible and sloops and keelboats topple sideways on the ocean floor and then are pitchpoled as the water returns.

The Jamaica earthquake of 1692.

Throughout the island, the homes of substantial planters, built in the English style, are levelled. The flexible wood-frame and thatch houses of the poorer whites and the slaves survive.

Two thousand persons killed immediately and 3,000 more by the epidemic that followed. Not to mention the casualties of the widespread looting.

Port Royal, Gomorrah of the West Indies, remains an abscess on the body of Jamaica, but slowly it seeps away.

It is replaced by a respectable nearby city called, for good luck, King's-town.

BRIDGETOWN, BARBADOS. 24 JANUARY 1693

Humour Them

"She deserves twenty pounds sterling for the lot."

"Indeed, delicate task that."

Laughter.

The Council of Barbados is meeting in a splendid stone building that would be in the Georgian style if that style had yet come into existence. The council chamber would have done well as a debating chamber in a London reading club: a twenty-foot-high ceiling with elaborate moulding made from London patterns; unflinching orpiment walls above rosewood wainscotting. A desk, inkstand, quill and blotter for each councillor.

"I wonder what she will do with the stones."

"Why, lay them on the path, of course."

Laughter.

The councillors are approving the payment to Alice Mills, a mixed-race woman who is a mid-wife, sooth-sayer, herbalist, and, in this case, castrator. Forty-two blacks are to be punished for re-belliousness. They did not go so far as to actually plan a rising, but they spent their free time on Sunday in meeting behind the public market and talking about 'mancipation, a bad word in the planters' opinion. So, they needed to be taught to think more clearly.

"Normal men are they?"

"Oh, yes."

"I mean, two bobs on each one."

"Then, I think the muses demand that we pay Alice Mills in guin-eas, for her services!"

"Whyever so?"

"Thus she will receive a half-crown for a bob. We'll show the world what a great investment Barbados is!"

The councillors laugh uproariously, though a couple have to work out with paper and ink the pun: one half-crown being worth two shil-lings and sixpence.

Then they too join the laughter. Barbados planters are famous for their sense of humour.

THE WEST INDIES. 1690–1713

Cult

Whenever the outside world threatens them, slave owners, small, large, take it out on their human chattel. With brief breaks, 1690–1713 is a time of continual fear: war with France and piracy by bands of 5–600 brigands, a match for most militia units. Planters see African conspiracies everywhere. And short moments of indiscipline and tiny thefts are punished with a severity that can only be judged as crazy: these whites destroy their own property, essential to their economic system, and act as if they are engaged in a votive act before a god that won't tell them its name.

There is no such thing as a nice slave owner: by definition. Ask the male slave found with meat in his possession that he could not account for: he lost an ear and was branded with a hot iron with the mark of the thief. Or interview the wraith of Peter Boone, an African who managed to steal nine pigs. In August 1693 he was hanged, his bowels drawn out and burned, and then he was cut into four quarters and displayed on the main public paths. A traditional punishment for white murderers and mutineers, that, but for pig stealing? Or, worst offence, the black who had nearly beaten his overseer to death: he was suspended in chains without food or water and allowed slowly to expire.

If the gods are angry with the masters, the slaves must pay.

THE WEST INDIES. 1690–1834

Boilerplate

All of the sugar islands have them: laws that are so close to identical that, though each is drawn to fit local circumstances, they could come out of a standard attorney's kitbag: laws concerning "deluding" slaves, and laws providing compensation for slaves that have to be destroyed.

So strongly in demand is labour, that strict penalties have to be enacted against whites who delude slaves away from their rightful owners. Stealing other planters' slaves also had to be banned and so too the harbouring of runaways. Fines of twenty shilling a day were enacted; the problem was serious.

And so too was the danger caused by planters who refused to give up their own slaves for felony punishment. A slave with a hand chopped off lost a good deal of utility, and one hanged was a dead loss, certainly. Every island, therefore, had to introduce generous compensation to planters whose slaves had committed serious felonies. Otherwise, planters would hide their own slaves from the enforcers of civic justice.

Within this bulky boilerplate is found the kernel of the white planters' central problem: the Africans' labour is so valuable that the whites cannot treat them as rigorously, as brutally as the whites' sense of security demands. The planters shuffle nervously along a wobbly plank, economic ruin on one side, slave rebellion on the other.

DOMINICA. 9 JANUARY 1700

Lasting Beauty

The old lady has skin the colour of aged vellum. Once she was a great beauty; now there are scarcely three hairs left on her head. No matter, she is revered. Grandchildren and great-grandchildren arrange themselves around her as if worshipping an idol. She is one of the oldest persons alive in the world.

The French priest who visits her is respectful. He has not come to convert the woman who had a half dozen children by Captain Thomas Warner, founding settler of the British West Indies. He is here to learn from the mother of Indian Warner.

The priest, Father Jean Baptiste Labat, has spent enough time in the tropics not to be put off by her sitting completely naked as she answers his questions. She speaks English, French, and he knows a bit of Carib. She confirms that she is the mother of the late, tragic Indian Warner and she gives Father Labat a comprehensive history of the story of the Carib, from Cristoforo Colombo onward. It is not a happy tale, though Father Labat rejoices in this good woman's remembering one of the first missionaries among the Carib on Dominica. That priest had failed, Father Labat knew, to make a single convert. Yet, with exquisite tact, this ancient savage tells him that Father Raymond would, to the Carib, be always alive.

The matriarch suggests that Father Labat hang his hammock in her family *carbet* and he accepts this honour. The next day she has one of her grandsons take Father Labat to the spot where Indian Warner's life was ended. The Carib, respecting cultural origins, call the place Massacre.

ANTIGUA. 1706–1712

A Terrible Case

The object of this game is simple: determine why Colonel Daniel Parke, who became governor-general of the Leeward Islands in July 1706, was shot, stabbed, and kicked to death by his subjects on Antigua in December 1710.

ITEM. Col. Parke was a Virginian, a member of the council of that plantation, and so violent that he was effectively run out of the colony.

ITEM. He distinguished himself in combat as an aide to the duke of Marlborough and was rewarded with the governorship of the Leeward Islands. This embittered him, for he thought he had been promised the governorship of Virginia.

ITEM. A high and arrogant churchman, he despised both the Scots Presbyterians and the Irish Catholics. Of the Scots, he suggested that London send him 10,000 Scots troops so that they could attack Martinique or Puerto Rico and there settle all the inhabitants of the Leeward Islands. *Send me over ten thousand Scotch with oatmeal enough to keep them for three or four months ... In time the warm sun will exhale all those crudeties that makes them so troublesome and tis not impossible, but it may have the effect to make them of a more sociable religion.*

ITEM. He found capital punishment in the Leewards much too hard to come by. He complained: *A hangman, if found, is like to have but little business in these islands.*

ITEM. He proposed to wipe out smuggling. This affected everyone, but on Antigua the hardscrabble poor and the trading middlemen (Irish families being very strong in both groups) were directly threatened.

ITEM. He seduced the wife of the chief agent for the Royal African Company. He then had this man, who was also speaker of the Antigua assembly, arraigned on a bogus murder charge.

ITEM. He ignored the forewarning he received in September 1709 when an assassination attempt failed. He made a good joke instead: *that men who will not stick at assassination will scarce make any scruples at perjury.*

ITEM. He disregarded an order from the new Tory government in London in 1710 to return to England.

WHY, then was Colonel David Parke lying in the dust in front of Government House, as lifeless and torn as a piece of bait thrown to a pit bull?

And why did Queen Anne issue a general pardon to the inhabitants of Antigua?

Obviously, this was one of the most terrible cases of suicide in recent memory.

THE WEST INDIES. 1700–1834

Toleration and the Thin White Line

After the Royal African Company's monopoly on the English empire's slave trade was abolished in 1698, the pipeline from Africa became a flood plain. The triumph of sugar-capitalism was easily completed in the West Indies, including the clearing of vast areas of the Jamaican bush.

Social balance tips. Constantly, the white line becomes thinner and thinner. Early in the eighteenth century, three blacks to each white was the usual ratio. But even then, in many spots the ratio was 10:1 and as the century wore on, the ratio in some isolated plantations exceeded fifty slaves for each white. Even at ten or twenty to one, the whites were tiptoeing along a series of chthonic waves, any one of which could suddenly swallow them: a potential equivalent of the Port Royal earthquake in social affairs.

Read the law codes of the several sugar islands. They all have desperate schemes, none of which work save for Jamaica's, to draw white servants from the British Isles: bonuses to servant-importers and promises that when a certain number of white servants are congregated, the skilled trades will become whites-only; carpenters, joiners, shipwrights, wheel-welkers, blacksmiths. Instead, the islands make do with a dribble of minor felons, prison-held debtors, and runaway servants; and with their own continually etiolating pockets of white trash, men and women and concave-chested children, the remnants of once self-sufficient, self-enclosed colonies, now barely above subsistence, culturally emaciated: the Redshanks of Jamaica, Montserrat, Antigua, St. Christopher, speaking strange English, and on Montserrat, stranger Irish as well. These are peoples the governors had once feared as rebels, but whom the blacks now fear as the backbone of the islands' militias: bitter, crabbit sadists with a uniform, perhaps with a horse, but always with a horsewhip.

The thinness of the white line is a blessing for the Irish Catholics. Soon after the Glorious Revolution, the several West Indian islands passed anti-Catholic legislation: not full enough to be a penal code in the rebarbarative richness of the Irish term, but a picket line that had to be negotiated cleverly. Quakers and Jews were banned on most islands for a very brief time – brief because either London quashed this, or, on some islands, the assemblies did their sums. Basically, from 1700 onwards Catholics – which really means Irish Catholics – were locked out of the governorships and the legislative councils and assemblies of most islands. The practice of their religion (of which there was very little as the church invested almost nothing in the islands), was not hindered, nor were land titles hashed with nor their trading of goods and property. Just keep your heads down for a while was the message of the early eighteenth century.

And by mid-century, toleration of Catholics was the practice, if not the law, for the simple reason that there weren't enough whites to fill most of the civic and militia posts. Quietly, Catholics came back onto councils and became militia officers and no one asked them to take a noxious oath and everyone realized that the Pope in Rome was a lot less of a danger than the sullen blacks housed within easy striking distance of each planter's home.

The Irish Catholics, even if they have been insulted by the penal legislation, have not the slightest doubt who they are. They are not fellow-victims with the blacks. After 1713, there are no more Irish rebellions. The Irish are whites. And the thinner the line becomes, the whiter become the Irish Catholics.

IRELAND. 1720

Bad Case

Richard Burke, a young Dublin lawyer, has yet to conform to the Established Church. He's a niche lawyer, doing paper work, filing writs, but staying distant from the courts, where Catholics are officially banned: though they're tolerated with a nod-and-wink so long as they stay out of the public eye and act as subordinate clerks.

Burke has been offered a case that is dangerous to his personal safety. He will still be only a supporting solicitor, but this case involves prominent families and his name will get around. Prudence would say that he should refuse the case, but he dares not, for it is tied to his plans for an advantageous marriage.

Bad case it is: James Cotter, heir to the Sir James Cotter who had assassinated the regicide John Lisle in Lausanne in 1664, is charged with a capital crime. The Cotter family is one of the few Catholic gentry clans that has not only survived, but prospered, in the previous two generations. For the murder of John Lisle, James Cotter had been rewarded by King Charles II with sinecure offices in the West Indies. This, combined with his marrying the sister of Sir William Stapleton gave him the opportunity to acquire a fortune in slaves and land. Such resources preserved his Irish estates during the Restoration era.

And, Sir James had been able to hold on to these estates after the Jacobite débacle because he had fought for King James at Limerick and came under the terms of surrender that allowed for the retention of lands by Catholics who had been part of the Jacobite army.

Sir James's son, a flamboyant scapegrace and member of the Hellfire Club, is arrested in 1718 on the charge of raping a Quaker woman. Although the defence brief drawn up by Richard Burke is written with the subtext that Cotter secondus is a Catholic martyr who is being trod beneath the heel of Protestant justice, Cotter in fact is a thoroughly nasty piece of work, a lawyer's nightmare. Already sliding rapidly into an obese and premature middle-age, he is a rich client with an attitude that says I-dare-you-to-hang-me.

Despite the personal risk of appearing too much in public, Richard Burke provides the best aid that he can muster. His motives are purely personal. He is contemplating marrying Mary Nagle of the Blackwater Valley, and the Cotter family is closely intermarried with the Nagles.

The evidence against the rakehell James Cotter is extensive and compelling and his defence is that his victim was drunk and willing. Cotter clearly was guilty of rape, but it was hard luck that the lord lieutenant, who could have commuted the death sentence, was the duke of Bolton: his wife was the granddaughter of the regicide Lord Lisle, whose assassination James Cotter Sr had masterminded.

The rapist Cotter is executed on 7 May 1720, and Richard Burke decides that if he is to be involved in any more widely publicized cases, he will have to turn Protestant.

KINGSTON, JAMAICA. 1720

The Great Cork Exposition

In the tropics, pirates usually fought barefooted and naked to the waist.

Anne Bonney refused to do so and no one dared question her decision. She was Captain Jack Rackham's mot, but that was not in play. Anne carried two pistols, each of which threw a one-ounce ball, a cutlass, and a dirk, and she knew which way each of them pointed. Of Rackham's crew, she had the nastiest tongue: a complete range of demotic curses and, more impressively to her crewmates, a string of Latinate abuses that she had learned from her father, a former attorney in Cork City.

She remembered her father without fondness. The family had moved to Charleston in Carolina when she was a girl, and he had brought Anne along, though she was a brat born of one of her father's housemaids. That was decent enough of him, but when Anne, in her teens, had stabbed to death the family's English maid, he had been small-minded about the incident, so she felt.

At the trial of Jack Rackham and his crew, in Jamaica in October 1720, it becomes clear that Jack is for the drop. "Good," declares Anne, still bitter that when their vessel was boarded by men from a government sloop, Jack had hidden below deck. "If he had fought like a man he need not be hanged like a dog."

Anne remembers enough of her father's table-talk of unusual legal precedents that when she faces the judge, she demurely pleads-her-belly: claims the precedent that a pregnant woman is not to be hanged. She expounds the case law with remarkable facility.

Not only does she not hang, she becomes a heroine to entire flotillas of little English girls, through their surreptitious reading of Captain Charles Johnson's 1724 classic, *A General History of the Robberies and Murders of the Most Notorious Pyrates*.

Captain Johnson, who may have been Daniel Defoe, knew a stirring example when he saw it.

NEVIS AND LONDON. 1726–31

Advanced Management

The manager of his Nevis plantations writes to Sir William Stapleton. There has been a prolonged and debilitating drought on Nevis and water and provisions are critically short. So far, however, Sir William's direct losses are limited to *some old Negroes*.

Sir William is relieved. He has never seen his holdings in the Leeward Islands. He is the grandson of the original Sir William, there having been some brief lives in the family and the hereditary chain has been foreshortened. He desires to be an efficient owner and someday to visit the islands. He reads on, his manager complaining that he has had to waste most of the Nevis plantation's rum supply as bribes *to catch run-away negroes that have plagued everybody this year.* That's how he pays the slave-catchers, poor whites and black informers.

Although his father William (who died, tragically young, in 1699) had been a staunch Catholic, once this young Sir William's mother had removed him and his brother to England, the family became sensibly Protestant. That had to be, if the Stapletons were, in scarcely more than a century, to make their way from Irish rebels to English gentry. Such mobility required money and one could not be too soft on the African drones who produced it. *The Negroes are bare of cloaths and pinch'ed in their belly, having lost abaundance of potatoes by the great rains in August and September,* his manager reported in 1727. Pity. Doubtless the curse of their kind.

Sir William eventually becomes MP for Oxfordshire and his son, Sir Thomas, MP for Oxford City, among the more prestigious seats in the Commons.

There is seldome a weeke but I see your plantation and I do not see that it is better kept and in better order, the manager writes with satisfaction.

I can't tell what occasioned two of your negroes to hang themselves, he adds, genuinely perplexed.

THE BRITISH AMERICAS. C.1750

Intermezzo

You will hear this song again later, in backwoods colonial America, but hear it now. It's not Faith of our Fathers. It's Shall We Gather at the River.

If we listen to the Irish, Protestant and Catholic, and their descendants, who wander, blunder, or thunder into the British West Indies and into the American colonies, as they move around, take care of themselves and their families, it's clear that most of them did not think about religion the way they are supposed to. They are wrong by the standards of religious-war-torn Europe and Ireland; they are wrong by the standards of Irish devotional hagiography as it developed in the second half of the nineteenth century and has been carried on down to us.

These people, out on frontiers, did not see the Catholic-Protestant divide as the most important thing in life. To the rich it was something to be negotiated, like hurdles on a point-to-point race. In the seventeenth and eighteenth centuries, gentry Catholics turned Protestant in the English empire much more often than Protestants became Catholics, and for reasons so obvious as to obviate comment: keeping wealth intact, and advancing socially was a lot easier if one were Reformed. Montserrat, a small set, but one of the few where deep tracing is possible, saw 53 percent of the Catholic gentry families turn Protestant during the late-seventeenth and eighteenth centuries. Fairly typical, one suspects, that about half the rich took up new songs.

We resist accepting how easy this was for most of them, how little crisis of conscience they experienced. Mammon ruled. And all the more easily, because the Catholic church was much less willing to put resources into the British Americas than into the French and Spanish empires; understandably, given anti-Catholic legislation. But it is equally understandable that an unchurched population of the wealthy easily moved from one side of the fence to the other.

Of the average and poor Irish, we have no direct trustworthy news, but one observes the industrious, somewhat melancholy figure of Michael J. O'Brien. Born in County Cork, he emigrates to the USA in 1889 and becomes an accountant for the Western Union Telegraph Company. He travels a lot for Western Union, but he does not drink or play cards in strange towns. Instead, he copies down every tombstone, parish record, municipal list that might have anything to do with the early Irish migrants and their descendants. He keeps working away until the age of ninety and does more to document the early history of the Irish in the thirteen American colonies than anyone ever.

A wonderful obsession, this, yet O'Brien was continually saddened by what he found. What he uncovered in seventeenth-, and, especially in eighteenth- and early nineteenth-century records of Baptist, Methodist, Presbyterian churches was a great cadre of Irish names. O'Brien was a real expert; he knew his Irish families, and masses of them are there: as Protestants. He was too good a scholar, and too honest an accountant, to avoid recognizing the "terrible misfortune" that the early Irish migrants so often came up wrong. Besides the obvious cases flagged by pure Irish names, he sees the Kirwans, become Protestant under their English cognate Whitecombs, the O'Clerys become Clarkes, and so on and on. It's enough to make him cry.

Peace, dear man. These are not turncoats. They are men and women who are vaguely Christian, and desperately in need of comfort on several of the world's roughest frontiers. Most of them are the veterans of more than one frontier and on the North American mainland O'Brien is often observing people who have done their first settling in the West Indies and have moved on. Poor people, hard working people, wives and husbands needing consolation on the death of a child or courage after a bad harvest. They go to the only god-house they can find and almost always in those days it is Protestant. They don't reject their old religion, they simply embrace the only faith that is available.

With their neighbours, they gather at the river.

JAMAICA AND BARBADOS. 1751

Symmatery

Walk for a time in the West Indian burying grounds. They are scattered about the islands. Most often they surround an Anglican church, but there are private burying grounds on several estates. And some of these private grounds are in fact Catholic graveyards. It makes no matter; they are all pleasant enough spots and no one will bother you if you bring a servant along, thus identifying yourself as a solid citizen.

You'll need him anyway. The grass around the gravestones and wooden markers needs to be cleared. And you'll want an umbrella held over you as you decipher the inscriptions, especially if you have to do rubbings to bring up otherwise illegible information. You want to know how long white men and women lived in the islands, so each tombstone of a death from 1650 to 1750 is a small biography.

You will find that white men who made it to age twenty lived an average of another twenty-five years; women sixteen, that is, to thirty-six in the typical case. This is a figure for an elite among the whites: those substantial enough to warrant their family's or friend's paying for a grave memorial. A comparable bit of observation for England and Ireland would find that men on average lived about ten years longer and women twenty. In the West Indies, surviving to age forty, therefore, was a cause for celebration.

Everyone, wealthy whites, black, poor whites, had their lives abbreviated by the world of sugar, slaves, disease and something in the air that can only be termed evil.

LONDON. 1751

Brotherly Feeling at Westminster

The hollow-eyed MP for Bridgeport is arguing in favour of Toleration for Catholics in front of the Commissioners for Trade and Plantations. He refuses to wear a wig and his shiny head is singular in a room full of yellowing judicial topiary.

John Frederick Pinney should have been anti-Catholic. His grandfather, an English Presbyterian, was ejected from his benefice on St. Bartholomew's Day 1662 for refusing to follow the rubrics of the Book of Common Prayer. He viewed the Church of England as halfway to Rome. He served as a cleric in Dublin (the Church of Ireland being more Protestant than that of England) from 1662 to 1688 and then became a lace wholesaler.

Thus non-conformity was the family doctrine, anti-Romanism its inevitable corollary.

Azariah Pinney, the MP's father, had taken part in Monmouth's Rising of 1685, a rebellion of keen Protestants against the government of James II. And Azariah was married to an Irish woman, a very strong Protestant.

Yet John Pinney is for the repeal of anti-Catholic legislation that affects the island of Nevis. For that is where his father went, as a voluntary exile (at the cost of a £65 bribe) after the Monmouth fiasco. And there, using cash from the family lace business and his own skills as a middleman, he built a fortune. He was especially good at lending money, then foreclosing on badly run estates. Not a nice man, really.

In a monotone so dead that it does not produce an echo, John Pinney explains to their lordships that the 1701 Nevis law, *An Act to prevent Papists and reputed Papists from settling in this Island for the future, and for the better governance of those which are already settled* has to be repealed. Only five or six openly-professed Papists live on the island and they are no danger. And the section of the act that requires everyone to take the oath against transubstantiation before beginning any legal proceeding means that Catholics who are owed money cannot collect through the legal system. Pinney explains this in such fine detail that the commissioners' eyes glaze over.

Behind the droning words of the sixty-five year old parliamentarian is the prophecy implied by the human arithmetic of the West Indies: unless Protestants give up their convictions about Catholics, they will find that they have no legal system, no government, and no control over their slaves. Every white is needed.

The Nevis anti-Catholic statute is pronounced repealed.

MONTSERRAT. 17 MARCH 1768

Party Favours

Long before St. Patrick's Day became a civic and secular holiday in the homeland, it was celebrated in far parts of the Empire as an opportunity for Irish Catholics, Protestants, English and Scots to have a party. Even if the Brits didn't turn up, certainly both sorts of Irish would. That's what the black leaders of Montserrat counted on, for the Irish every year were increasingly dominant as slaveholders on the island and incrementally more brutish.

Thus, the plans were that when the planter men and women went inside Government House in Plymouth, they should be allowed to mingle for a time, sup punch and, when the music started, the indoor-slaves were to secure the swords and pistols that the gentlemen had laid aside for the dancing. The slaves would dash outside with the weapons, the doors to Government House would be barred from the outside, the building torched and the entire party would be burned to fine white ash.

As was the case with most slave rebellions, someone talked too much: a female house servant went to her master, and the slave conspirators became the victims of the St. Patrick's Day massacre.

Interesting: this technique had been tried before, on Antigua in 1736 on the occasion of the King's Birthday Ball, when barrels of gunpowder, rather than fire, were to be the active ingredient. The plot discovered, on that occasion six Africans were hanged, five broken on the wheel, scores castrated and seventy-seven burned alive. Lord Londonderry, the governor-general of the Leeward Islands commented on the leniency of the punishment.

And curious: despite the whites' belief that slave rebellion was always imminent, revolts took place rarely in the eighteenth century, if one excludes the constant range-war with maroons and escaped slaves in the hills of Jamaica. This, though, was more of a frontier war than domestic slave revolt.

The really serious revolts only occur in the nineteenth century, when Emancipation was close to hand. Hopelessness, apparently, does not a rebel make.

DUBLIN. 1750–93

Let Ireland Remember

As the pressure within the Irish Catholic world against the penal laws in Ireland grows, so too does Irish involvement in the West Indian slave economy.

Obviously, these are two unrelated phenomena, like the sun spot cycle and your recent toothache.

Maybe.

In the second half of the eighteenth century, a new wave of Irish Catholic merchants and gentry speculators hit the West Indies. They bought up indebted or bankrupt plantations, put in new overseers, bought more and more slaves and drove them hard. New names – Semper, Shiel – are introduced and formerly small Irish Catholic slave owners – Lee, Hussey, Furlonge – become large. Unlike the English, who cannot stand to live in the West Indies, these people manage their own estates and therefore do better than the English absentee planters. Much more importantly, at the same time, what had once been the Cork provision trade to the West Indies expanded into a full-scale slave-based economic system. Limerick in 1784 became a slave trading port. Of greater value, sugar refining became a Dublin industry, and cotton became the basis of a textile revolution: another slave product. Most of the traffic involved Catholic businessmen. The increasing self-confidence of the Catholic middle and gentry classes after mid-century was in large part a result of their economic success; they offset many of the economic handicaps of the anti-Catholic penal code by tapping the slave-based off-shore economies.

Note that the early 1780s Catholic relief agitation included a push for "free trade." This meant something different than it does today: an equalizing of protective barriers so that Irish merchants could trade at no disadvantage with the slave islands. "Free trade" would allow direct trade with the West Indies, involving provisions or slaves on the outward voyage, sugar and cotton back. That, as much as the rights of religion, drove many Catholic merchants and gentlemen to become active in the Catholic relief agitation. Prosperity first, by whatever means, and everything else would follow.

Best Toy Wins

The wills of two Irish Catholics are probated.

Martin Lynch leaves twelve negroes, including "Cork, a good barber," worth £140.

John Dyer's estate totals only £151 2/6d, no slaves, but complete sets of Pope, Shakespeare, seven volumes of Jonathan Swift, and five collections of popular fiction.

Colour Coding

By now, a common vocabulary has developed among the whites in the several islands. It is most precise among those who buy and sell slaves.

Mulatto: child of white man, black woman
Quadroon: child of mulatto woman and white man
Sambo: child of mulatto man/woman and black man/woman
Unspeakable: child of mulatto man and white woman
Mustee: child of quadroon or Indian female and white man
Unspeakable: child of quadroon man and white female
Mustiphini: child of mustee and white man
Unspeakable: child of mustee and white female
Quintoon: child of mustiphini and white male
Unspeakable: child of mustiphini and white woman
Octoroon: child of quintoon and white man
Unspeakable: child of quintoon and white woman

THIRTEEN IS A LUCKY NUMBER
1690–1785

Not the Geneva Convention

The Charter of Rights and Freedoms of all upright pillagers had been quietly drafted in 1690 by the English apostle of Toleration, John Locke. His two Treatises on Government came into the possession of the most variegated collection of readers imaginable: sea captains, colonels, schemers who were arguing with government officials, priests, and the occasional scholar. *God gave the world to men in common*, Locke declared, *but since he gave it to them for their benefit, and the greatest of conveniences of life they were capable to draw from it, it cannot be supposed he meant it should always remain common and uncultivated.* That sentence often was underlined by readers and then the next phrase was double-scored. *He gave it to the use of the industrious and rational ...* There the reader stopped, as after that Locke became all complex and philosophical. No question, though, the Philosopher said that the Almighty had given the commons of the world to us, the rational and industrious.

A century and a half later, on the edge of the massive expansion of the Victorian empire, John Stuart Mill, who revered Locke as "the unquestioned founder of the analytic philosophy of mind," expanded on the duty that God laid on the shoulders of all empire builders. *The sacred duties which civilized nations owe to the independence and nationality of each other, are not binding towards those to whom nationality and independence are certain evil, or at best a questionable good.*

Never mind that this knot might twist a bit around the neck of Irish patriots. If one were out slaughtering the Fuzzy-wuzzies or kicking the Untouchables it was good to know that the finest minds of England sanctioned what the toe of one's boots was doing.

Paranoia

Governor Seymour of Maryland writes to the lords of trade and plantations in London.

Your Lordships will observe a representation relating to Irish servants, who are generally papists; great numbers of which have in late years been imported here, and some hundreds upon a specious, tho' false, encouragment given them in Ireland by Mr. Charles Carroll (one principally concern'd here for Lord Baltimore) or his agents, assuring them of good tracts of land at the head of the Bay, and free toleration and exercise of their superstitious worship.

*And it having been in this provinces complain'ed of and also represented to the House of Delegates how busy those of the Roman Communion were to make proselytes of poor Protestant servants, **gotten into their hands by any sinister means whatever.***

PHILADELPHIA, PENNSYLVANIA. 1708

An Irish Republic?

Captain Charles Gookin, the new deputy governor of Pennsylvania, was a naval officer in his late forties who was good at giving clear orders, and a nimble mathematician. These traits qualified him, as far as William Penn was concerned, for the deputy governorship, a post of greater power than its title suggests, for Penn himself spent only a total of four years (during the years 1682–83 and 1699–1701) in his colony.

Oh. And Gookin was the son of the Charles Gookin, Esq., whom William had settled on the Penns' Shanagarry estate in County Cork in the 1660s.

In one perspective, Gookin and several other leading figures in managing Pennsylvania, including Penn himself, were Irish republicans of very strange form. That is: Cromwellians who opposed monarchy and favoured strong representative government if not full democracy; and, in addition, they were Cromwellians who had learned to buffer their republicanism with a veneer of acceptance of the Restored Monarchy: this is in contrast to the Irish Catholics who seemed to be devoted monarchists.

The first deputy governor had arrived in the colony even before Penn did, and continued in charge after he left: William Markham, Penn's cousin, another former Cromwellian, and a tenant on the Shanagarry estate. Another deputy governor, holding office between Markham and Gookin, was Captain John Blackwell, personal friend of William Penn's from Dublin, formerly a cavalry officer and Cromwell's Irish treasurer for war.

The architect of Philadelphia, Captain Thomas Holme of County Waterford, earned his post through having served faithfully under Admiral Penn, both as a Cromwellian and as a Restorationist. The most capable of Pennsylvania's early statesmen, James Logan, was a Quaker from Lurgan whose father had grabbed Catholic lands in the north of Ireland: he was named secretary of the province, 1700; mayor of Philadelphia, 1722; chief justice of the supreme court, 1731.

The place must have been hell for Catholics: all those Irish planters and, worse, Cromwellians as administrators.

You'd think: especially since the original constitution of Pennsylvania was drawn up when Penn was under the influene of Algernon Sidney, of a long-time family of Anglo land-grabbers in Ireland, and himself, in 1647, the lieutenant-general of horse in Ireland and no friend of the native Irish.

But what a fine constitution of government Pennsylvania adopted.

Absolutely. Best in the New World at the time. Freedom of worship for all monotheists guaranteed. Slaves to be emancipated after twelve years or so of service; this made them indentured labourers with a bad contract, but not really chattel. Lands to be purchased from the natives by treaty, not stolen. Strong system of government. Not a perfect constitution but amazing for its time.

Best place in British North America for Catholics?

Probably. Maryland's toleration eroded as royal governors invoked English precedents against Catholics. In the Carolinas, the toleration promised in John Locke's Fundamental Constitutions was only words. Philadelphia on the other hand accepted a Catholic church in 1733 that was set up by the dreaded Jesuits, bogeymen of Protestants throughout the English-speaking world. No other colony would do that. In most, Catholic worship was illegal, although not usually prosecuted.

What was the catch?

The freedoms given by Pennsylvania's constitution (and by its revision of 1701) were limited by social pressures: such as those Irish Protestant administrators. And Penn in his first thirty years, though he brought in, maybe, 10 percent of the colonists from Irish Catholic sources, flooded the place with Germans and Dutch Protestants, and with Mennonites and Palatines, all from locales on the Continent where Penn had done his missionary tours: not to mention his trying to inveigle any Quaker who said "thee" out loud to migrate.

House Rules, then, were Protestant?

Exactly.

Even before the flood of Ulster Presbyterians?

Even before. So an Irish Catholic gentleman could do well in Pennsylvania. Big Catholic bankers and merchants thrived in Philadelphia. And it was not a bad place for Catholic servants as long as they tugged their forelocks often and were humble as bread pudding.

They didn't have to turn faiths then?

No, fewer did so in Philadelphia and its region than anyplace else in the Thirteen Colonies. Elsewhere, though, in the mainland colonies, it was like the 1600s. In the 1700s , 80–100,000 Irish Catholics came to the colonies and in a generation the families were Protestant, mostly, and intermarried with the American mainstream.

Still the Pennsylvania constitution was a fine thing.

Indeed. We thank God for small blessings.

CHARLES TOWN, SOUTH CAROLINA. DECEMBER 1711

Sage in the Making

Tuscararo Jack returns home a hero. He eventually will become one of the Carolinas' leading statesmen, which says something about the times, as his chief qualification is that he is very good at killing people. He has been in North Carolina, dealing with the Tuscararo, junior partners of the Iroquois.

John Barnwell – Jack – had migrated to the Carolinas just for the hell of it. His father, a Dublin alderman, followed both the Established Church and James II and had been killed in the siege of Derry. A bored young buck, with some family money but only tiresome prospects, Jack chose the Carolinas because several members of his extended family already were there. That was in 1701. He spent the next ten years having bloodthirsty adventures, the sort Irish gentleman enjoyed: fighting the Creek Indians in what is now Georgia in 1702; joining a makeshift naval force defending Charles Town against French attack in 1706; and then campaigning against the Spanish in Florida, where he picked up both reputation and Spanish slaves.

Now Charles Town is full of stories of his blunting the Tuscararo threat. With an army made up of fifty white colonists and 800 natives from tribes that hated the hard-edged Tuscararos, Barnwell had slid north. His big problems were to keep his whites from deserting and his Indians from being insubordinate. He lost more than 300 from his force before any battle. The remainder stayed on, chiefly because they were more afraid of him than of the enemy. That tells a lot, for the Tuscararo, with 2,000 warriors at their disposal, had recently destroyed several small forts and massacred children, women, men. They are responding to the settlers' habit of kidnapping Tuscararo women and children.

Soon the people of Charles Town excitedly tell of Barnwell's victories. At one battle he *carried the day with such fury, that* dear God can this be true? *... after he had killed a great many, in order to stimulate themselves still more they ...* they? yes, Barnwell and his officers and his Indians ... *they cooked the flesh of an Indian in good condition and ate it.* Did they spare anyone? *Oh yes. Of the Tuscararo, thirty men were taken as slaves, but ten women were killed.*

Well done. Men like that make this colony what it is.

Tuscararo Jack belonged to the least-known of all Irish migrant groups. He was one of 15–50,000 (nobody knows) Anglo-Irish who arrived during the 1700s. A collateral ancestor of President Theodore Roosevelt, Jack becomes the London agent in 1720 of the revolutionary group that overthrows the proprietary regime of the colony.

"LONDONDERRY," NEW HAMPSHIRE. 1719

Welcome

A group of Irish Presbyterian migrants moves haltingly from Maine to New Hampshire, like an army in retreat from the snowplains of Russia. They come from the parish of Aghadowy in the barony of Coleraine, county of Londonderry. They have nearly frozen and starved over the Maine winter and they are looking for shelter and a future less harsh. During the winter they questioned why they had made aliyah to America. They knew the answers of course, but the words were less convincing on this side of the Atlantic than on the other. There, in Aghadowy, hard changes were in prospect. The Irish Society, which had held their lands since the early days of the Ulster plantation, was in financial trouble and was selling to the Ironmongers' Company of

London. Upsets were in store: the parish, unenclosed, was to be enclosed; watercourses were to be altered and bleach greens created. A benefit to some, a disturbance to many. Surely the New World would be better. And it would, but not Maine in a damp and cruel winter, with nobody bidding them welcome.

So the families straggle, some few carrying their tools and goods in ox-waggons, most pulling them in man-drawn carts, and a few using the primitive Ulster slipe. They have been told that the tiny town of "Nuffield" was willing to have them.

There they settle and, having been assured that they are well inside the boundaries of Massachusetts, petition the proper authorities of the Massachusetts colony for incorporation as a village.

They are turned down.

Two years later, New Hampshire accepts them as "Londonderry."

ANNAPOLIS, MARYLAND. 1720

Spine

He dies as he lived, a mass of contradictions arranged around a spine of spring steel: Charles Carroll – Carroll the Settler is his name in history. He dies hawking phlegm, cursing barbarically then apologizing elegantly for his crudeness. He dies rich, one of the ten Catholics among the twenty richest men in Maryland, yet as he approaches death Carroll instructs his steward in the minutest details of penny pinching. One moment he recognizes himself as having started as just another Irish gentleman down on his luck and the next he chants hymns of praise to his ancestors, hereditary chiefs with large lands in Offally, on the Leinster-Munster border. He curses King James II for being such a poltroon and King William III for wiping out most of Carroll's family. Carroll hates the English government but remembers London's Inns of Court with affection. Half-hallucinogenically, he re-experiences the taking of dinners and the genteel argument of chambers and he becomes maudlin when he recalls that he had to flee London in 1688. The soul of the old master, the third Lord Baltimore who made Charles Carroll attorney general of Maryland not long before the English crown seized political control of Maryland, is commended to Charles Carroll's priest for special masses, for which the dying man gives him a Spanish dollar; and the Calverts, who in 1715 converted to Protestantism in order to reacquire control of the Maryland government, are consigned to the most fetid regions of hell. In his last ravings, Carroll thanks God loudly that he has had rich wives and sired broods of heirs, and then with equal gratitude he retails the bodily details of his favourite female slaves. Abruptly, he switches to instructing his steward concerning which of his blacks are lazy and should be sold, and the special few who should be manumitted. At the last he puts his shaking hand on an antique short sword that is the only item left from his Gaelic past, and he rattles a stream of invective at the lickspittle servants of the crown in Maryland, who have, in a cascade of bigotry, beginning in 1689, taken away the rights of Catholics to public office, to practise law, to worship publicly, and, in 1718, just as Carroll's health had begun to fail, the right to vote. May they become piles in the devil's asshole, Carroll husks and, that idea bringing a smile to his lips, he dies contentedly.

DUBLIN CASTLE. 1728-29

No Explanation?

Outsiders' view. The Dublin Castle authorities are perplexed. They cannot understand why so many Irish Presbyterians are leaving Ireland, and in many cases, dragging Anglican small farmers along with them. Ulster is the one province in Ireland where the desired Protestant colonization has been successful on a large scale. Why are they leaving? The Castle collects information: not through on-site investigation, but by writing letters to gentry and clergy in Ireland and to some in the Americas. Things do not make sense.

For ... as a group, the Presbyterian farmers and merchants seem to be no better off in the New World than in the Old. Some of them grow rich in America but, then, some do in Ireland. Most of them work long hours as human draught animals in Ireland and equally long hours in the American colonies. They live mostly in small, two-room stone and mud cabins in Ireland and in small two-room log cabins in America. They are surrounded by hostile indigenous peoples in both Ireland and America. Indeed, in the fulcrum colony of Pennsylvania, James Logan, the colony's secretary, has settled them as a buffer between the increasingly-vengeful natives and the pacifist Quaker farmers. As Dissenters, the Presbyterians are tolerated religiously in Ireland: their clergy are given an annual grant by the Irish parliament and the Test Act is negated by an annual Act of Indemnity. So too are they tolerated in the American colonies. Why do they leave?

Insiders' view. An Ulster landowner writes a letter to the Castle and prints the missive as a pamphlet. He has it right: the people are emigrating because of grievances they feel as individuals and predictions they make about their own futures in the New World. They do so as individuals, not as some group average, for even if the lot-in-life of the typical migrant may not improve, these men and women are betting that they can beat the average.

Grievances? They feel hard done by the authorities of the Established Church. *They can never forge that unanimity and good agreement, which subsisted between those of the Established Church and them in the times of their common danger, particularly in the late revolution, when they joined hand in hand against their common enemy, and never parted 'til their country was rescued and delivered from the imminent danger of POPERY and SLAVERY.* Yet, they received none of the compensation for their losses or rewards for their fealty promised by King William III. They hate the Anglican oaths they must take before taking any civil office above that of petty constable; never mind that they receive an annual indemnity, the indignity is galling to proud people. Especially they hate paying tithes to the rectors of the Established Church. *The rectors generally set [sub-contract] their tythes to undertakers, and these often being needy and covetous persons, makes themselves instruments of oppressing the poor people.*

That and land rents that are too high become *the oppression that makes wise men mad.*

Truly oppressed or merely perceiving themselves as oppressed, it makes no difference. They leave in the 1720s in numbers frightening to the Dublin authorities who fear a Popish resurgence in the north. Migration in the 1720s starts a chain of migration that lasts through the century: between 185,000 and 300,000 Ulster Presbyterians emigrate in the eighteenth century (probably closer to the lower number). Mostly they move to the Thirteen Colonies. The exodus became its own cause. *The encouragements and invitations which they receive from those friends of theirs in America, as they represent matters, are very tempting to the people. I have seen some of their letters to their friends here, partic-*

ularly from Pennsylvania and New England; in which after they set forth
and recommend the fruitfulness and commodities of the country, they tell
them that if they will but carry a little money with them they may for a small
sum purchase considerable tracts of land and that these will remain by firm
tenures as a possession to them and their posterity for ever ... and to encour-
age them farther, they impudently tell them that there they have no tythe to
vex or oppress them, nor are they troubled with vexatious suits and prosecu-
tions in spiritual courts ...

You will understand this to be meant of Dissenters, who generally are the
people that are removing ... These letters, which they receive from their friends
in America, in whom they say they have entire confidence, do very much affect
the minds of the people, especially of the better sort.

PHILADELPHIA, PENNSYLVANIA. 1732

Back to the Fold?

Lord, our brethren live roughly, offending against the Almighty's
holy laws; breaking the commandments; blaspheming against thy
holy name; fornication, nay murder, are within their ken.

The Synod of Philadelphia is not yet composed of prigs. It still has
hard-spined ministers and harder-spined elders who understand hard-
ship, hard work, hard hands, and now hard-hearts. The synod members recognize why the small Ulster communities in Lancaster County
– Coleraine, Derry, Donegal, Little Britain, Londonderry and others –
have coalesced, like the bawns and small walled towns in Ulster. They
recognize that these people are the Pennsylvania colony's buffer
against the wild savages. And they understand, with sadness, that
these colonists have been living beyond law, just as surely as those in
the West Indies had once lived Beyond the Line. No civil courts, no
church discipline, only the rule of the knife and the discipline of avoiding starvation by taking, taking, taking.

The synod responds by creating the Presbytery of Donegal and begins what would be called a missionary campaign, though that term is
avoided as being insulting to the separated brethren. And the civil authorities are encouraged to spread the court system over the outlying
districts. It works: within a decade, the frontier people are suing each
other in civil courts and stabbing each other less often; they are bound

into Westminster Confession churches, and are standing before kirk sessions and being properly humiliated for their fornication, out-of-wedlock children, and their perpetual intoxication by strong liquors.

The Ulster settlers are back in the fold. Most of them. But, even as the coopers'-bands of social control are extended, a minority slide out farther, still beyond the law, still beyond the line.

That, for another century-and-a-quarter is the template for the im-perialization of the American continent. Irish men and women and their descendants are always close to the pointed edge, moving be-yond civil law and church influence, serving their own small needs in ways limited only by the laws of biology and ballistics. They succeed on a local scale and then, civilization catching up, they move on. Or, wounded and winded, they reluctantly accept the spancels that the imperial world, directed by men they despise, east coast men in high collars, and soft hands, imposes upon them.

NESHSHAMINY, PENNSYLVANIA. 1735

A Fissure in the Heart

It is not yet Princeton, but the Rev. William Tennent's Log College is nothing to look down on. It is large enough to hold a dozen students, has a central hearth, and, wonderfully, windows of glass, not of the usual greased paper. Tennent has recognized the need for a trained American clergy, for Irish Presbyterian clerics are never in sufficient supply. Tennent teaches his students – who include his three sons – in a formal curriculum of his own devising. It includes standard Westminster Confession doctrine, but something more.

William Tennent, of County Armagh, is perfectly placed to pick up the tectonic stress that is developing as Irish Presbyterians be-come American Presbyterians. He was trained as an Anglican priest in Ireland, but quickly switched to Presbyterianism when he saw the way things worked in Pennsylvania. He recognizes the signs of fracture before they become visible.

Fissure is inevitable, for the core of old-line Irish Presbyterianism is in discord with the New World. Church doctrine holds to every-thing being predestined, but the New World says that everything can be changed by personal will; and church courts try to impose standard doctrines, especially subscription to the Westminster Confession, in a land where, outside of the big settlements, everyone is free to do and believe whatever. How do you keep that together?

Tennent's answer is to teach the Westminster Confession and to undermine it, in a signally American way. He insists on individuality. Each of his students must undergo *the new birth*. This is a spiritual experience that takes them outside the boundaries of the creed, right to God. The new birth takes an outward form that strikes terror into the heart of strict Irish Presbyterian authorities. Tennent is advocating *enthusiasm*.

MASSACHUSETTS AND CONNECTICUT. 1740

Get Right With God

At age thirty-seven Gilbert Tennent is approaching the height of his powers; the chief of these is to scare people to death – or to the New Life. He has trained well. He is a qualified physician who can explain how the human body works and, crucially, can describe its breakdown in stomach-turning detail. And under his father's tutelage at the Log College, he has learned the Bible by memory, acquired the ability to stack dogmas on the head of a pin, and knows the secret fissure that lies at the heart of Irish Presbyterianism.

In Massachusetts and Connecticut, he is doing well, preaching in twenty towns with the enthusiastic approval of the Godfather of the Great Awakening, George Whitfield: a shining light, is what Whitfield calls him.

Gilbert Tennent's preaching in New England is just practice. He knows that his real ministry is in the Middle Colonies, and mostly among Irish Presbyterians. Sometimes, in a vapour of temporary vanity, he tells himself that he, like St. Patrick, is a missionary to the Irish. He should be allowed that fancy, for anyone who could put the fear of the Lord into the frontier savages deserves respect, grudging or full-hearted, depending on your own taste. To watch Tennent march through small towns, hamlets, the occasional city and preach of the *Terrors of an enraged God*, a Lord High Executioner who would *tear you in pieces, except you repent*, is to watch the Slasher Terror centuries before it was invented. He tells how each portion of the human body will be affected by the corruption of the grave and then by the selective torments of Hell. When he preaches, you can actually see each twitch of pain-tormented muscles and of screaming ligaments, and hear the crack of cartilage and bone as the pressures of hell press on them until fractures pierce the skin and the poor sinner loses his voice, for his larynx is sanded bare from screaming in pain and fear. You shut your eyes and the pictures remain; you cover your ears and the groans of Hell's sufferers still can be heard. You suddenly understand that there is only one way to deal with Tennent's message and that is to give in to it: to throw yourself gasping and heaving on the ground, tears streaming and, in paroxysms, repent and seek the forgiveness of Jesus Christ.

The mainline Irish Presbyterians do not know what to do with this bearded holy man who wears his hair halfway down his back and affects the leather waist girdle of the Old Testament prophets. Tennent ignores them and founds his own Presbyterian congregation in Philadelphia in 1743. He wants to purify Presbyterianism, not destroy it and, in fact, he becomes a trustee of his father's old college which, under firm Presbyterian control, becomes the College of New Jersey and, later, Princeton.

All this individual salvation, though, is hard on orthodox Presbyterianism, as it challenges collective kirk discipline and the whole concept of predestination. Just as the Six Mile Water Revival in Ulster had caused waves in Scotland in the 1620s, its eighteenth-century counterpart leads to secondary revivals in Ireland and Scotland. More importantly, unwittingly Gilbert Tennent is the wedge upon which the Presbyterian Church in the Thirteen Colonies begins to rive itself asunder; and he serves as the reagent that, as the chemistry accelerates, produces that most extraordinary of American religious amalgams, the Baptist churches. By the beginning of the nineteenth century, full three-quarters of men and women of Irish Presbyterian heritage are found in one of the variegated forms of the Baptist communions. Individual salvation and local congregationalism fit perfectly with their experience on a frontier where the horizon is always too distant, the enemy ever too close.

NEW YORK. 1741

About Time

They deserve this show, the anti-papists of New York. Ever since the Glorious Revolution they have been waiting for a grand garotting of their nemeses. Now they have a whole gantlet of executions, satisfying in the extreme. Entire families watch the cascade of death, mothers holding young children up so they can see the spectacle. Broadsheets are sold with the schedule of executions on them. The procedures take several days, and one does not want to miss a single last gasp, eh?

From the viewpoint of most spectators, the lovely thing about this cascade of diverting events is that it is a twofor: both Africans and Irish Catholics. The Negroes are a bit of a sidebar, of course, but they die with such excellent facial gestures, especially the whites of their eyes. A Negro Arson Plot has been discovered, so a score of blacks are strung high, and their twisting forms are pelted with garbage. The main executions, however, are those of eight Irish Catholics who are accused and easily convicted of aiding the conspirators. And, most delicious of all, an Irish Catholic priest is hanged, simply for being what he is. His execution draws the largest crowd and several of the women and children in the front rows are injured by the press of the onlookers as they try to obtain closer views of the man in the strange long skirt. They want to look under it, for they know that the devil and his demons have tails.

HUDSON'S BAY. 1741–42

The Fog Drifts in from Castle Dobbs

In an era when there was a lot of good writing being done, Arthur Dobbs of Castle Dobbs, County Antrim, was a wonder. He was a fog-making machine. Here is one of the best one or two sentences from a memorial he wrote in 1731 on the subject of the Northwest Passage:

You may be Surpriz'd that I should endeavour to revive an attempt to discover the Northwest passage to the great Southern and Western Ocean of America, which has in Manner been Explored since the year 1621 ... Since that time, it has been reviv'd but once, by Zacharaiah Gillam commander of the Nonsuch Ketch in the year 1667, who pass'ed Hudsons Straits, went into Baffins Bay to the latitude of 75 degrees and from thence returned to the Bottom of Hudson's Bay to the latitude of 51 degrees or thereabouts ...

and on and on, as Dobbs blathers for page after page, his precise meaning unclear, but his general intent undeniable. He is convinced that the Hudson's Bay Company, chartered in 1670, has been doing nothing to find the way to Asia and that this fabled path lies in their domain.

Dobbs addresses his memorial to Colonel Martin Bladen who is one of the lords commissioners of Trade and Plantations and also to Sir Charles Wager, first lord of the Admiralty. And then he hawks copies of the document around the world of maritime England and Ireland, seeking supporters for an expedition under crown patronage, by which he means Royal Navy approval and equipment.

Dobbs's long memorial contains a good deal of arcane argument about tidal flows in Hudson's Bay, almost all of which turns out to be wrong; but Dobbs actually understands very well how the Empire works at this time – and that strings pulled in Ireland can produce movements among marionettes half-way round the world.

Dobbs, round-faced and irritatingly self-confident, comes of an Ulster family, Established Church, accustomed to hard-grabbed privilege and to acting venomously against those who diminish it. In his thirties, he sat for nearby Carrickfergus as an MP in the Irish House of Commons and then in 1730 acquired the plum patronage post of surveyor general for Ireland.

... Another presumption for a Passage is from the time of the flood at Ne Ultra and the Tides flowing later as it went to the Southwards towards Port Nelson, for a W.S.W Moon (or when corrected) a S.W. Moon ...

Not all of his ideas were dotty. Dobbs wanted tenant reforms for Ireland and economic improvements that actually did not occur until the second half of the nineteenth century: he saw things close to home quite clearly.

But concerning the route to Asia he is a monomaniac and when he reads an article in the *Philosophical Transactions of the Royal Society* by one of the Hudson's Bay Company's captains, an Englishman, Christopher Middleton, he knows he has the helmsman for his great expedition. Middleton possesses a very nimble mind and his scientific work earned him election to the Royal Society. Dobbs engages him in correspondence concerning the Northwest Passage and holds out the plum of an exploration to be conducted under Royal Navy commission.

Alas for Middleton, the dream came true. Dobbs gained royal patronage in 1740 and in 1741–42 Middleton commanded an expedition. His ships were named, naively, *Discovery* and, proleptically for his ambitions, *Furnace*.

He found a lot of ice and not much else. Upon Middleton's return, Dobbs veered between accusing him of incompetence and the antithetical suspicion that Middleton had found the long-sought passage to Asia and was keeping it secret. A pamphlet war between the two men followed.

Captain Middleton, though honest and competent in his observations and reports, was broken. He never commanded a vessel again.

Dobbs marched ever-energetically onward, one long foot-step after another into his self-made fog. His crown-favoured expedition having failed, he put together a syndicate of Irish and English backers for another trip to Hudson's Bay. This one, 1746–47, was led by Commander William More, who was the cousin of Christopher Middleton. It yielded no results except that the expedition proved yet again that where the eighteenth-century Empire was concerned, the English could be the puppets of the Irish.

And, finally, the fog led Dobbs to his own Grand Bank. He was appointed governor of North Carolina in 1754, a post worth £1,000 annually in English currency. There he forced his retainers to listen to his endless theories until they too could scarcely see out of a window, even on a bright day.

RAMELTON, COUNTY DONEGAL. 1750

Star Power?

Wonderful beauty. Fine name. Great frame. No fame.

This is not the Jane Russell whose beauty launched a million bombs in World War II, but a worthy predecessor. And she is crying.

Jane Russell, daughter of the owner of "Big Airds" is marrying beneath her station. Her elderly parents are certain of this and although they do not disown her, they give her no dowry. They are among the Anglo-Irish who live amongst Presbyterians on the far northwestern edge of the Ulster plantation. Their farm, forty acres of thin soil and grass over impervious rock, is hardly rich, but by Donegal standards it is solidly middle class. The land drains well as it slopes towards the river Lenon and to Lough Swilly, and the Russells have grazing for several cows. They are miles away socially from the Catholic mountainy people, who practise spade husbandry and live on potatoes. And, in their own minds, they are a social caste above the Presbyterians, with their constant grabbing for pennies, their rough manners, and their brutal attacks upon the English language, if that is actually what they are speaking.

Jane is a prize beauty, no doubting that. If only she had married John Buchanan in a ceremony conducted by a proper Church of Ireland rector, the old couple would not have let her drop into the charmless world of those cold Presbyterians without the usual dowry: a cow, a decent bed, domestic linens, and household utensils.

Still, when children come along, at each birth the Old People slip Jane a guinea or two. The Russells understand the concept of family loyalty even if they disapprove of her husband. The last child of Jane Russell and John Buchanan was born in 1761. Soon after that his mother died and his father – ah, we knew what he was all along – disappears. No raising a brood of children for him.

The infant, who bears the name James Buchanan, is taken in by his uncle Samuel Russell (as are his brothers and sisters). Samuel has now taken over the family farm from the Old People. The Buchanan children are well looked after. They grow up more Anglo-Irish than Ulster-Scots, and they grow to adulthood with no illusions. Each of them works hard on the farm, herding sheep and cattle, marling gardens, moving middens. They eat well, but they are given no hopes of inheriting the property. That will go to real Russells. The Buchanans will have to find their own way once they are adults.

One by one the Buchanan children drift off from their adopted parents' farm. James, the youngest, is treated most indulgently, though by no means softly. He is given a small wage by his uncle, and he saves it. Then, his uncle Samuel proposes that he will call in a social debt to help James, now aged 22, on his way. There is another Russell uncle, a hotel-tavern keeper who lives near Gettysburg in Pennsylvania: earlier Russells had been on the cutting edge of Irish migration to the American colonies. In 1783, then, James Buchanan sails from Londonderry to Philadelphia where his uncle Joshua Russell meets him and brings him to the then-back country. Uncle Joshua, it turns out, is a shrewd man of business: he has a tavern, forty acres of cleared land, and eight slaves.

The new USA is made for James Buchanan. Within four years he has 100 acres of decent land of his own and sets up a provisionary-hotel-tavern near the gap through the Allegheny Mountains. He marries a fiercely Presbyterian woman (from thence the misapprehension that the Buchanans were full-line Ulster-Scots rather than Anglo-Irish) and the first child of this marriage who survives childbirth is named James, after his father.

James Buchanan, who had never known his own father and who had led a necessarily harsh life as a youth, swears the oath that so many men, conscious of some deprivation in their own youth have uttered, and forever down-the-generations will keep on swearing: *my son will have all the advantages I never had.*

TIMAHOE, COUNTY KILDARE, AND CAMDEN, SOUTH CAROLINA. 1751

Length

Irish Quakers, like those in England, disapprove strongly of Roman Catholics; the Irish Quakers not only disapprove of Catholics in principle, but hate them in practice. None felt that way more than those of the parish of Timahoe, County Kildare. Here was one of the several small Quaker colonies that dotted Munster and Leinster, made up of pacifist families who had been granted Catholic lands conquered by more militarily inclined Protestants. They lived in Timahoe surrounded and infiltrated by a Catholic populace that loathed them as grabbers. Beginning in the 1720s the Catholics increasingly took vengeance on those who held their family lands: thatch-burning, cattle-maiming, and the occasional thumping of one of the men and boys in black hats.

These Quakers are hard-working people and fairly easy to govern; they pay their rents on time and don't steal. They are just the sort of people Arthur Dobbs wants on his North Carolina estates. He has a half-interest in almost 500,000 acres, empty acres. The Quakers of Timahoe, after searching their collective conscience, decide to move there.

But the Divine Will intervenes. The vessel's captain makes a navigational error and lands them in South Carolina. The Quakers pray, consult, improvise, and obtain lands at what is now Camden. Even

amidst the flux of the New World and the upset of subsequent movements across the North American continent, these Timahoe Quakers
are extraordinarily inward looking. They work and live in the New
World, but are not of it. For a generation their children marry only
with other Timahoe Quakers. After that, as they scatter, most families
produce Birthright Quakers: that is children, both of whose parents
are Friends. Irish Quaker attitudes, especially their virulent anti-Catholicism, are maintained long after their source is forgotten.

This is especially notable among the descendants of a couple married in Timahoe in 1721, who migrate to South Carolina with their
children in 1751: Sarah Miller and John Milhous, the key in the taut
genealogical-cultural chain that produces that most uneven and angular of personalities, Richard Milhous Nixon.

RHODE ISLAND, IRELAND, AFRICA. 1752–58

An Ordinary Mind

*Some people may think of scruple of conscience in the human trade, but it is
very seldom minded by our European merchants.*

Nicholas Owen, a young Anglo-Irish gentleman down on his luck
(a spendthrift father had drunk most of the family estate and spent
the rest on lawyers), takes to the sea to repair his fortune. He never
rises above first mate, for he has no special talent. His commonplace
book of recollections of several round trips between the British Isles,
the American mainland and West Indian colonies, and Africa is a
masterpiece of banality, a template of the white mind of its time.

He does no slave catching, for by the 1750s the trade is so well organized that one only has to deal with African tribal leaders. Yet that,
Owen recalls, is extremely tiresome. *In the first place, you are obliged to
treat them all to liquor before you purchase anything or not; at the same
time, you are liable to their noise and bad language without any satisfaction.
You are obliged to take all advantage and leave all bounds of justice when
trading with these creatures as they do by you —otherwise your goods won't
fetch their starting price at home.*

As for the West Africans: *The character of these people is certainly very
bad; they are maliciously given, in all their dealings deceitful, great drunkards, seldom at peace with their neighbours or themselves, expert in war yet*

ignorant of discipline; their weapons: guns, swords, bows and arrows, clubs; their chief commodities: elephants' teeth, slaves and rice; they receive in return: guns, powder, ball, dry goods, pewter, brass kettles, pans, iron bars and India goods.

Slave trading to Nicholas Owen is merely business. The only time in his career that he becomes morally exercised occurs when a tyrannical captain and set of officers lock down the ship in port and keep the men working at meaningless tasks, like convicts on a treadmill. Owen and five others desert in a lifeboat, using *that method to obtain that liberty to which every European is entitled.*

At age twenty-six, Nicholas Owen dies in West Africa, apparently none the wiser than when he had entered the human trade.

ANNAPOLIS, MARYLAND. FEBRUARY 1757

Strategy

The wedding of Elizabeth Brooke and Charles Carroll, 15 February 1757, was a small affair, with only a Jesuit priest and the necessary witnesses present. The son of the marriage was nearly twenty years of age.

A tactical move by a fine strategic thinker.

Charles Carroll of Annapolis (son of Charles the Settler) had taken the substantial estate his father had left him and expanded it into one of the largest personal fortunes in mainland America. His chief, but not sole tactic, was to turn vast empty land grants into cultivated and improved land. Irish and German farmers were recruited directly from the Old World for his own estates. Tenants of rented estates were required to clear and improve the land.

As an Irish Catholic, Carroll was ever-aware of his vulnerability. Locked out of direct participation in the political system, he had to be wary of his fortune being attacked.

He needed, above all else, an heir who was a solid, trustworthy Catholic and who was not a complete dunderhead. It was a terrible risk to give birth to an heir, for under primogeniture, one is stuck with a lad who may look perfect in the cradle but has a long time to turn rotten.

So, Charles Carroll of Annapolis has an heir out-of-wedlock. That allows him to be sure his first son has turned out Catholic and responsible as an adult. Carroll and Miss Brooke live together as man and wife while the lad is growing up, but do not marry. The Church is more than tolerant; it is complicitous. Carroll is an extremely rich man.

Therefore, only when it is clear that young Charles (the family has a propensity to use the same name over and over for its eldest males) is sound value, do his father and mother marry. The heir to the Carroll fortune is made legitimate in his twentieth year, not long before he comes of legal age. Everyone breathes a sigh of relief.

FORT PITT, THE OHIO RIVER. 1758

Suspicion

The most influential Indian trader and Indian agent for the Middle Colonies is in trouble. In the midst of the French and Indian War, he comes under suspicion of disloyalty.

This is not because George Croghan (he spells his name half a dozen different ways) is too close with the indigène, although he gets along with them and understands their style of diplomacy. One of his daughters by his Indian wife (he also keeps a white one) eventually marries Thayendanegea – also known as Joseph Brant, probably the most successful of North America's native leaders in protecting his people against white aggression. Croghan is at ease with the natives – *you'l excusing my writing and paper,* he casually scribbles to a correspondent, *for I have this minitt twenty drunken Indians about me.* No, that was not why his loyalty was now being questioned.

Nor was it because he spends on his family a goodly portion of the official salary of £1,000 a year he receives for representing Pennsylvania's interests west of the Appalachians. Of course he puts his own relatives on the payroll, people whose background is just like his own; his nephew John Conolly, his brother-in-law William Trent, his half-brother Edward Ward, and cousins Daniel Clark, William Powell, and Thomas Smallman. Everybody does that. Indeed, no one would trust a man who did not keep faith with his own kin.

No, the trouble is that Croghan is suspected of being a Papist. This suspicion tells everything about the Middle Colonies and nothing about Croghan: for Croghan is a Dublin-born Anglo-Irishman, barely literate, but thoroughly Church of Ireland, meaning Established Church. Anglican. As are his relatives. So unusual is it on the western frontier of the Middle Colonies to find an Irishman who is not an Ulster Presbyterian, that Croghan and family are taken to be Catholics. He has to explain carefully that his Prayer Book is not the dreaded Missal of the Papishes and that kneeling at prayer does not necessarily mean one is bending one's knee to Rome. Croghan is given his full freedom only when authorities in Philadelphia confirm to his accusers that, yes, there is such a thing as a third sort of Irishman, and you really should let him get on with his business.

THE SOUTH CAROLINA-GEORGIA BACKCOUNTRY. 1760

Too, Too Far

Pressing farther and farther beyond the line of civilization, the Irish Presbyterians and their outriders sometimes go too far. Thus the 300 settlers of the Long Canes region of the Carolinas are way beyond help when, in 1760, the Cherokee decide that they have had enough of their theft, killing of game, desecrating the land. The settlers retreat, trying to make harbour in Augusta. Early in their march, forty settlers are killed or captured by Cherokee cavalry (to give the mounted force its European name). Two days later, the warriors return and hack to pieces another twenty-three. This time the victims are all women and children.

The Irish Presbyterians are great holders of grudges and this generation in the American backlands transfers their former frontier-hatred of Irish Papists – ignorant, superstitious, bloodthirsty savages – to their New World equivalent: ignorant, superstitious, bloodthirsty Amerindian savages.

That is why the Ulster people are the backbone of the American wars of the 1760s against the aboriginal peoples. For them it is not a matter of military necessity. They believe in cleansing the land.

PHILADELPHIA, PENNSYLVANIA. DECEMBER 1763

Vexed and Determined

Two hundred armed white men, dressed as Indians, careen through the streets of Philadelphia: 199 of them have taken at least a quart of whiskey apiece, but that does not impair their ability to yell, taunt and threaten the locals.

The Irish Presbyterians of outland Pennsylvania are sick of taking shit from Indians, from English, and especially from Quakers. We are the ones who carry the weight of protecting the seaboard cities, they say, and all we get is grief. Whine. Complaint. Sanctimony. No gratitude. Even Ben Franklin is saying we are Christian Savages!

So, they invade Philadelphia, though not before doing some housecleaning.

The men and boys of Pextang in Lancaster County (it comes out "Paxton" in the Ulster-Pennsylvania accent), have recently dealt with a bit of the aboriginal problem and haven't taken well to criticism of their methods. The Paxton Boys had learned that a group of four dozen Indians living at Conestoga Manor included some natives who had helped their western cousins in attacking frontier settlements. Need disciplining: so, the Paxton rangers burned their cabins, killing six of them. The remainder of the Indians found shelter in the Lancaster workhouse. The Paxton Boys collected at an inn on the Donegal Road and, using mostly hatchets and scalping knifes, raided the workhouse and killed fourteen. They scalped two children of three years of age and some women as well as warriors.

You would not believe the complaint we received from those hypocrite Quakers! for housecleaning.

Indeed, the Quakers of Philadelphia send out emissaries to bring local natives into the city where they can be protected.

Protected! It's us, the frontier people, and those that are even farther out than us, what need protecting!

The Paxton Boys could, and would, have kicked every Quaker and other Indian-lover through the streets, and then turned to the joys of arson, in which they were well practised.

Only Ben Franklin in best voice, false bonhomie, and insincere sincerity, can calm them. He promises to bring their grievances about insufficient protection from marauding natives to the attention of the government. He finds it impossible to convince any of them that not all Indians are murderers-in-waiting. He settles for their agreement to disband quietly and even offers to stand them a couple firkins of whiskey.

And as they disperse, Franklin, for one of the few times in his life, says a deep prayer of thanksgiving to a personal God.

LARNE, COUNTY ANTRIM. 1765

Face

It is the opposite of the British and Irish way. Face: in the British Isles, one shows wealth in public and lives in chilblain cold in private without a ha'penny's worth of coal for the grate. In later eighteenth- and early nineteenth-century America, the custom will be to plead a poverty-stricken childhood, and to live like a pasha behind the family walls. At least if one wants political power.

Andrew Jackson spends all his life talking log-cabin in America and victimization in Ireland.

Bollocks.

The parents of the future-Andrew had shipped from Larne in a party that his father, a weaver, and merchant in Carrickfergus, had organized. In later years, young Andrew's grandfather, a large merchant in Carrickfergus, leaves the lad in America a legacy worth £300, a fortune in the Thirteen Colonies.

Young Jackson is taught to think of himself as someone special, a cut above the common ruck, but always to plead humble origins. An American template.

NEW YORK CITY. 1766

Origin Myth

One of the largest and the most influential denominations in America in the last quarter of the eighteenth century and the first half of the nineteenth was the Methodist Episcopal Church. (The more-numerous Baptists were active as mosquitoes in those years, but had no more organizational coherence than their etymological counterparts.) Methodism, although it had bishops and a centrally directed set of pastoral arrangements, flexed with the moving frontier; it was local enough to meet the requirements of hamlets and homesteads. Assiduous scholars show that 60 percent of the Methodist clergy in that era were of Irish background, and not all of those had Protestant origins.

New World, new origin myth required. So with scarcely a bow to the Rev. Mr Wesley, the American Methodist Church decrees that the foundress is the Irish Palatine, Barbara Heck. She of constant prayer and unremitting righteousness who finds some of her friends playing cards of an autumn evening. An innocent occupation? No! These are the devil's calling cards, and she seizes the deck, and throws it into her cooking fire.

Then she seeks out a holy Wesleyan, Mr. Philip Embury, another Irish Palatine, and implores him to preach. *Preach, dear woman, I cannot; There is neither house nor congregation.* Barbara Heck is undeterred, *Preach in your own house to your own company!* and thus begins American Methodism.

So they say.

DRUMBO, COUNTY DOWN; SOUTH CAROLINA; GEORGIA. 1765–1775

That Old Sweet Song

Exporting solid Protestants to the Thirteen Colonies was a good business to be in, especially if one had trustworthy family on both sides of the ocean. Matthew Rea, who never sets foot outside of Ireland, had a vocation: shipping emigrants to his brother John. At first he collected indentured servants and sent them to his brother's estate in South Carolina. It was not a hard sale to make, for South Carolina had a generous bounty system: indentures were limited to four years, the master had to pay £20 sterling to the worker at the end of the period, and the colony's government added a bounty of £4 and 100 acres of land. When the colony ended the scheme in 1768, the brothers took to filling a 50,000-acre estate in Queensborough Township, Georgia.

Much harder to sell: there was no regular trade between Georgia and Ireland and the gossip network said it was not such a wonderful place. Nevertheless, Matthew is able to send seven boatloads of Protestants to Savannah in the years just preceding the American revolution. Everyone sixteen years of age or over is promised 100 acres from John Rea's massive estate, the only cost being ship's fare and two shillings quit-rent for each 100-acre plot: provided the migrants come armed with a certificate from their Presbyterian minister or Church of Ireland rector attesting to their not being Papists.

The brothers would have done even better had not some of their settlers written home, singing the woes of Georgia. *Savannah: a woeful place, a poor hole ... Full of pride and wickedness ... The home of high prices ... inhabited by a few Irish and some runaways from all parts of America.* And the virtuous Irish Protestant settlers on John Rea's Queensborough estate: eighteen of them were up on charges in 1769 for stealing their neighbours' horses and cows. *John Rea: a liar and a cheat.* He was using his Irish migrants *as a hedge* between his own plantation and the ferocious local Indians.

The migrant-stream slowed for a bit, and then resurged: people hear the song they want to hear.

THE OHIO RIVER VALLEY, KENTUCKY. SPRING 1774

Patriotic Acts

They are way past the Proclamation Line – the London-declared limit to white aggression – which is just where George Washington has told them to be. The American imperium proceeds even before Independence is achieved. Surveyors from Virginia stake out lands that they intend to seize. Among them is Patrick Henry, whose motto at this period of his life is Give me Liberty or Give me Kentucky.

The Shawnee have several times given notice that they are becoming vexed at this continual scarring of their lands by the pissing of such surveyor-dogs. They capture several of the land-defilers and their equipment.

They make a pyre while the trespassers wet themselves. The Shawnee speak quietly as they decide what to do. At last an elder stands up, picks up a theodolite and throws it on the fire. All the other equipment is burned, bashed, buried.

Then, dismissively, the same elder signals for the surveyors to leave.

PHILADELPHIA, PENNSYLVANIA. 2 AUGUST 1776

Prudence

On a hot sticky day in Philadelphia, Charles Carroll of Carrollton – called Charley by his family – signs the American Declaration of Independence. It is a rich white man's document, but no less resounding for that. And Charley, as a very rich white man, places all the family chips – which include the largest slave holdings in Maryland – the only place he can. His move may look risky, but his strategy is prudential. That is family tradition.

This 5'6" dandy, in his late thirties, educated in France and London, signs with the tough kids because he knows that a union of the American colonies is the only way his family will escape from the vexatious penal laws of provincial Maryland. As Catholics, they cannot vote, hold most public office, or practise law. And the laws have become worse in Charley's own lifetime: in 1756, Maryland requires that Roman Catholics pay double the annual land tax demanded of Protestants. Not what a large Catholic landowner wants to hear.

Charley is the only Catholic to sign the Declaration of Independence. In later years he explains that he knew that toleration for all Christians would become part of the rules for the united colonies and that equal rights for all would follow. That was later: at the time he kept silent about his hopes and tried to breathe quietly.

CARROLLTON, MARYLAND. 1777

Distance

Charles Carroll of Carrollton, son of Charles Carroll of Annapolis, grandson of Charles Carroll the Settler, is worried. About his dining arrangements. He has hired a new Irish slave overseer and counting room clerk, William Skerrett, who comes of an Irish Catholic merchant family. They were successful merchant traders in the early West Indian trade and now manage plantations and train slaves. Skerrett, at present on his way to Carrollton, is well-recommended and doubtlessly is a charming young chap. But there are principles. The great landowner makes it clear that the new overseer must understand his duties in advance and *not expect to be admitted to my table.*

Charles Carroll of Carrollton never confused American Independence with social democracy: equality before the law for white people and toleration for the Catholic religion, yes, but the social classes are to keep apart.

Charley keeps in touch with the distant Irish world: the top end. In his old age he has the pleasure of seeing three of his granddaughters marry men with Irish or English titles. And one of them in 1825 marries Richard Colley Wellesley, first Marquis of Wellesley, and lord lieutenant of Ireland, 1821–28. She reigns happily as consort of the king's representative in Ireland. Sadly for old Charley, in late 1828 the couple must leave the vice-regal lodge: the brother of Wellesley, the Duke of Wellington, has just become prime minister of Great Britain and Ireland and he asks for Wellesley's resignation, as the Duke finds him soft on Catholics. Wellington is about to engage in battle against Daniel O'Connell and his demand for Roman Catholics to be seated in the United Kingdom's parliament.

THE THIRTEEN COLONIES. 1776–1781

Coils

The General Orders to Officers issued to the units dealing with the American rebellion were very specific on everything from the angle at which a shako was to be worn to drill formations to be employed in training. In addition, apparently there existed an invisible regulation: "Thou Shalt not Get Anything Quite Right. Close is enough; anything more is Bad Taste and unbefitting an Officer and a Gentleman."

So the blurt of an officer who wrote the following was close, but off. *Call this war by whatever name you call it, but it is nothing more than a Scotch-Irish Presbyterian rebellion.*

Close, but not entirely right. Men and boys of Irish Presbyterian heritage were very active –40 percent of the serious fighters in the colonial army it is estimated – but by now most of them were not Presbyterian. Half or more were Baptists or Methodists or wild frontier Jesus-jumpers. The middle class stayed Presbyterian. Yet even they had trouble with the language of American politics which, elevated and sublimated by men who had drunk deeply of the Enlightenment, yielded documents that are among the most dazzling political literature produced by humankind. Sublime as they are, from the Irish viewpoint these documents are imperfect as revolutionary literature because they don't tell whom to thump and why.

The down-class portion of the Ulster-Irish filled the void with their emotional energy and willingness to stay staunch on the long slog, as

fetid summers turned to frost-biting winters, and the stomachs of the
fighters were filled more with fear than food. Attitude: no one wins a
close-run war without serious attitude. The Irish Presbyterians, Baptists,
Methodists, snake handlers and Second-Coming apocalyptists had that
in plenty. Forget all the high-floating phrases of the Declaration and the
draft articles for confederation and, later, the federal constitution, noble
though they are. What these people really hated was corn-holers. And
the British, with their foppy uniforms, too-polished cavalry boots, and
their treat-them-like-servants style, crossed the indignity line. So, from
being universally loyal to the Crown in the wars of the 1750s and 1760s,
most of these Protestant Irish decide that, sod-me, those cunts have to
go. The way they fight is not pretty, and the way they celebrate victory
is not kosher: scalping white people, even foreign mercenaries, is not
anything their officers wish to have recorded.

In the fulcrum of the American War of Independence, the Middle
Colonies, the Irish are the majority of foot soldiers and they seem almost entirely to have been on side (apart from a few who, influenced
by the Philadelphia Quakers, had taken to fluttering their handkerchiefs and trying to bring peace and light).

To the north and south, matters were more complex. From New
York northward and from South Carolina southward, pockets of serious Irish Protestants remain committed to the Crown. Nasty in-
ternecine and intra-family battles ensue, most of them lost to
history: the winners do not wish to memorialize their victimization
of dissidents, and the losers either surrender quietly, or straggle to
the Maritimes or the Canadas, there to create for themselves yet another New World.

Ah, the other side. Of the forty-six British and Irish battalions in the
Empire's army, fourteen are Irish units whose infantrymen were Irish
Catholics. Thus, in the cockpit battles, the sons of the Irish Catholic
peasantry worked at defending the Empire by killing off the descendants of the Irish Presbyterian tenantry who were striking for what
they called American Freedom.

Thirty percent, roughly, of the officer corps of the Empire's army
were Irish Protestants, mostly Anglo-Irish. Men like the leader of the
surrender party at Yorktown, the Anglo-Irishman Charles O'Hara of
County Sligo. And, serving with distinction against the republicans
of the New World was Lord Edward Fitzgerald, two decades away
from becoming a martyr for Irish republicanism.

WAXHAW SETTLEMENT, THE CAROLINAS. 1781

Cherché the Mother

An Englishman, he was certain of it. Even though he had a habit of drooling when speaking, young Andrew Jackson had an ear for spoken language. The English bastard had slashed the fourteen-year-old, an awe-struck hanger-on of some American patriots. Granted, Andrew had been stupid to be cheeky when the officer had told him to clean the mud off his cavalry boots. But slashing the lad all the way down to the cheekbone was excessive and left a scar on his face and a bitterness in Jackson's heart that lasted his lifetime.

Deciding whom to hate was probably the biggest decision in Andrew Jackson's life. Everything else followed from it. Free-floating animus was already part of Andrew's personality; his mother had made certain of that.

A good mother in her way, Elizabeth Hutchinson Jackson, but she knew there were only two sides to any issue, hers and the wrong one. She often told Andrew of seeing Ireland for the last time in 1765, of catching a glimpse of Carrickfergus as the ship eased out past Island-magee, and then everything was lost in a blur. A few warm memories, but mostly she taught Andrew the people to hate: first, Papishes, the servants of the Great Whore of Babylon, and second, English landlords who had pinched down on the Ulster people and reduced the future for people like the Jacksons. Young Andrew was puzzled by the Papish problem as they were very scarce on the ground in his part of the Carolinas and the few he encountered were just like everyone else. All that hatred going to waste. And who were the landlords in a land where no one, not even the government, knew who held title to what?

The deep cistern of hatred that Andrew Jackson's mother had filled might have eased slowly away, had not that English officer been so demeaningly cruel. To a lad who already was an expert on the protocols of the cock-fight, the humiliation of the back-handed slash was as wounding as the actual cut. From now on he would hate things English – and forms and government and manners and ways of speaking that resembled those of the English. The English became for Andrew Jackson what the landlords were to his mother.

And, later, the Indians become the focus of his white hot temper; he does to Indians what his mother told him should be done to Papishes.

Andrew's mother: her husband had been nearly two months dead when Elizabeth Jackson gave birth to Andrew. She raised the lad. And she died just six months after Andrew received his sabre slash; she was nursing wounded American prisoners in Charleston at the time.

BLUE LICKS, KENTUCKY. 1782

America's Thirty Years' War

"Trail's still hot."

"I discern a trap."

"Old man."

"Young fool."

Daniel Boone, the greybeard of the party of 180 men who are chasing several hundred Shawnee, is arguing with Captain Hugh McGary. They are on the edge of a narrow ravine and the Indians they have been chasing since the Shawnee raided Bryan's Fort, Kentucky, have disappeared into the valley. There is no obvious way out, so a good day's slaughter is at hand.

"Easy pickings," says McGary decisively.

"Too easy," replies Boone who has fought Indians most of his life.

However this turns out, it will be just another battle in the first year of the Thirty Years' War of the soon-to-be United States of America. Already this year there have been at least two dozen serious encounters, including the levelling of several peaceful villages and the burning, shooting, scalping (a favourite activity of the settlers), rape, and final destruction of their inhabitants. The natives are beginning to fight back and skilfully.

"Blatherer," says Boone, nettled.

"Bleater," replies McGary and moves his hand to his knife. This opposition by the old man is undermining his command.

The Thirty Years' War was a nearly inevitable result of the creation of the American republic. When they were in control, the British had partially limited inland infiltration of white settlers. The Proclamation Line of 1763 ran from mid-New York down the peaks of the Appalachians all the way to Georgia. The Six Nations of the

Iroquois confederacy were supposed to act as a coordinating network, encouraging the southern tribes to police the line, but to keep on the inland side. That half-worked, about half the time. No one could keep all the unlicensed fur traders or the rabid land-seekers at bay, but the presumption of right was on the side of the native inhabitants. The tribes, plus London-decreed penalties for apprehended offenders, kept the Proclamation Line from becoming completely porous.

All that changed with U.S. Independence. The British withdrew north of the St. Lawrence, and brought with them the most effective of the Iroquois, notably the Mohawk. They made treaties with these tribes as sovereign nations, and these arrangements they honoured, mostly: if for no other reason than that they desperately needed the natives as allies.

In the U.S, matters were different. No one needed the Indians to do anything more than get out of the way. From George Washington's administration onwards, federal policy, interrupted only by a thousand official lies, was to move the natives west of the Mississippi: and to abandon any idea of containing the pent-up energies of the land-hungry eastern population, especially not the Irish.

Hugh McGary has lost all patience with Daniel Boone. "Poltroon, Coward. Old Teat." He'll skin Boone if necessary.

"Right. I'll give chase with you, Captain."

Of course Daniel Boone was right. Of the 180 men who spurred their horses down the ravine, a scant 100 returned.

The battle meant nothing, save as a conspectus of the horizon of this long conflict.

Captain Hugh McGary, more savage than any he called savage, survived. When, four years later, he meets an old redman who says something unintelligible, he takes it as a reference to Blue Licks and he belts him with a hatchet and then uses his long knife to cut off the old man's scalp. Tried for murder, he is found guilty and also guilty of disorderly behaviour. As punishment he is suspended from his captain's rank in the militia for one year and then, punishment served, is immediately promoted to major.

Daniel Boone also escapes.

He comes home slowly, for he is leading a second, burdened mount. Tied across that horse, like an old saddle blanket, is the body of his son Isaac who perished in the ambush.

And at Blue Licks a young Indian warrior had engaged in his first offensive actions against the invaders. He is Tekamthi – whom the whites call Tecumseh, and come to fear as an Indian Caesar.

Only after Tecumseh's death in late 1813 at the Battle of Thames, Upper Canada, fighting in alliance with the Upper Canadians, the British, and the Mohawk, does the USA's concerted Thirty Years' War on the people of the land come to an end.

AN IRISH HISTORY OF CIVILIZATION

Book Two

Kings of the Wild Frontiers?

OFF THEIR KNEES.
IRELAND
1785–1830

Banna's Banks

Shepherds, I have lost my love, –
Have you seen my Anna?
Pride of every shady grove
On the banks of Banna.
I for her my home forsook,
Near yon misty mountain,
Left my flocks, my pipe, my crook,
Greenwood shade, and fountain.

Not a bad song. It, and some other standard ballads of the time, were written by George Ogle, a member of the Irish privy council and MP for County Wexford. In his mixing of melody and political malfeasance, he resembles several latter-day governors of the state of Tennessee, where a number of his people settled.

Now, though, he's in no singing mood. Ogle has been challenged by the Catholic whiskey distiller, Barny Coyle. Perhaps Ogle might have slipped out sidewise, by claiming that he would duel only with a fellow gentleman, but Coyle is a very big whiskey distiller and, besides, Ogle had initiated the tilt by stating that the Romanist Coyle "would as soon break an oath as swallow a poached egg," and to move to the heart of the matter, Ogle really wants to kill Coyle.

A mutual inflammation society: the two men fire four braces of pistols at each other, well beyond anything honour required. They wanted blood.

Bad shots, though; all eight go wide.

The seconds for these two leaders of Irish society, Catholic and Protestant, take to their heels when the duel turns into a fire-fight.

The only victim is one of the seconds who falls into a potato trench and breaks his arm.

Never shall I see them more
Until her returning;
All the joys of life are o'er –
Gladness changed to mourning.
Whither is my charmer flown?
Shepherds, tell me whither?
Woe is me, perhaps she's gone
For ever and for ever!

DUBLIN. APRIL 1793

Fire Sale

In the face of yet-more foreign danger, the Irish parliament, composed solely of Protestants, removes almost all the remaining Catholic disabilities, and London agrees. The most important exception is the right to sit in parliament. Catholics can vote now, but only for Protestants.

Ireland, perhaps, was on the road to religious accommodation.

Still, it might have been taken as a portent of the pyrrhic nature of any advance that, in February 1792, the commons chamber of the Irish parliament had been gutted by fire. It did not re-open until October 1796.

DUBLIN. 19 MAY 1798

Upstream

Like a salmon leaping upstream, Lord Edward Fitzgerald has eluded his captors by one spectacular jump after another. He is the senior United Irishman still at large in Ireland. The rest are in prison or have fled abroad. Fitzgerald has the prestige of one of Ireland's greatest aristocratic families and the useful virtue of being Protestant: a virtue because the northern Presbyterian radicals are uneasy at their being a minority in the increasingly-Catholic revolutionary movement.

The revolution will begin, Lord Edward decides, on the twenty-third of May. Having just eluded capture, he is hiding in the Thomas Street house of a friend.

As leader of the revolution, he must be properly dressed: he has his self-designed commanding-general's uniform brought to his hiding place.

The authorities receive word of his hiding place through the hand of Francis Higgins, proprietor of the *Freeman's Journal*. Lord Edward is surprised in his bed by two military officers and nine soldiers.

A salmon in a shallow pool, he thrashes about wildly. He wields a dagger with deadly effect and, though shot in the shoulder, is captured only because one of his pursuers sacrifices his life by clinging to Lord Edward's leg even as his own blood drains away.

Lord Edward dies on the fourth of June and with him dies the chance of the 1798 Rising being *a* rising. No leader remains in Ireland who commands the respect of both Catholic and Protestant revolutionaries, or who can knit together the thousands of local grievances into a united movement. There will be several 1798 Risings, but their multiplicity guarantees their failure.

Lord Edward's bedizened uniform was kept as a curiosity by his captors. Like the scales of a salmon clawed from the water, it lost its shimmer as soon as the life seeped out of its wearer.

DUBLIN. 19 MAY 1798

The Future

At the same moment the Castle authorities are planning the capture of Lord Edward Fitzgerald, a Catholic attorney, round-faced and in his early twenties, is being admitted to the Irish bar.

Daniel O'Connell.

SCULLABOGUE, COUNTY WEXFORD. 5 JUNE 1798

No Act Too Vile

"The chiyill. Mind the chiyill!" The harpie pointed at a two-year old who had crept under the door of the burning barn. A pikeman came running and skewered the infant. Half a dozen women, camp followers of the revolution, screamed approval.

The revolution in Leinster, and most especially in County Wexford, had become a sectarian war, with Catholic small farmers and labourers fighting hamlet by hamlet, townland by townland, against Protestant small farmers and labourers. Liberty, equality, and fraternity had nothing to do with this.

What made this war so frightening was the women. Hundreds of camp followers accompanied the Catholic insurrectionary forces. They cooked, carried fuel, made bullets, but mostly they moved ceaselessly, speeding with the random energy that violence, hatred and vengeance bring. Though some of the rebel contingents were headed by priests, and all of them had some clerical participation, that made no difference: women coupled behind stone fences and hedge rows with their men and often with their men's fellow warriors. The adrenaline of blood lust and the lust in the blood are closely related, the one triggering the other.

The fighting men feared these women. Their ridicule could be scalding. Their desire to see vengeance written in Protestant blood was greater than that of all save the most fervent insurgents.

After the rebel setback at New Ross, County Wexford, it is the women who, first, keen, and then begin an ululation that is a cry from the underworld of the human heart.

The opportunity for revenge comes at the small town of Scullabogue. There more than 200 Protestants, and a few Catholic loyalists, are penned in a barn located at the foot of a steep and rocky hill. Mostly they are women and children, but men as well: entire families have been swept up by the rebels.

In groups of half-a-dozen, thirty-seven of the men are brought out. They stand at the foot of Carrigburn hill and are shot. The women, screaming as banshees, descend on the corpses like crows on an orphan lamb. They take everything of value and vent their own war lust by poking the now-dead enemy with small knives and needles. One woman finds her joy in popping the eyes of the Protestants with a sharpened crochet hook.

This is too slow for some and too gentle for most: dead bodies don't feel pain. So the barn, containing 184 persons, is set afire. The doors are barred from the outside and the building is surrounded by men with pikes and by women who dance wildly, calling down the powers of gods who reigned long before that of St. Patrick became dominant.

Similar events occur every place in the south of Ireland where the Rising flames. Only in scale is Scullabogue unique.

BALLYCARRY, COUNTY ANTRIM. 7 JUNE 1798

Wailin' and Willie and the Boys

Word of the Scullabogue atrocity did not reach the north of Ireland until the eighth of June. If it had arrived a day earlier, no Protestant would have turned out.

Willie Nelson, scarce seventeen, and his brother, only a year older, are awakened before sunrise and told to raise the troops. Deeply enthused with the American revolution, as are many northern Presbyterians, they are honoured to be told, "Be Paul Revere."

The Nelson boys are from a family that has lived in Ballycarry and Islandmagee since the first Presbyterian settlement. Ballycarry-Islandmagee is a set of two contiguous communities twenty miles north of Belfast, bordering on the muddy tidal flats of Larne Lough. It was in Ballycarry in 1613 that the Reverend Edward Brice began the first Presbyterian ministry in Ireland, and he preached alternately in Ballycarry and in Islandmagee. This is the cockpit of Ulster Presbyterian identity. So strong is that identity that the only members of the Established Church are foreigners – mostly English members of the Coast Guard – and they are viewed as only one step away from being Papists.

The locals are neither gentlefolk nor gentle folk.

They muster at Knowehead Brae, Islandmagee, behind William McClelland, the twenty-two-year-old son of a substantial farmer; and in Ballycarry village they form behind James Orr, a hump-backed weaver who has a mesmerizing facility with words and a fire in his eye that can be diminished only by drink. The two platoons join and attack Redhall, the only gentry house in the area, seizing arms and thus insulting the dignity of the owner, R.G. Ker, Esq. This affront eventually proves fatal for Willie Nelson.

Swords, pikes, pitchforks, improvised weapons of all sorts are the revolutionaries' armoury. Several carry from Redhall's armoury flint-locks that lack flints and would be better used as firewood. The rebels march through Larne and towards Donegore Hill, near Antrim town, there to join forces under Henry Joy McCracken. As they march, they are accompanied by their womenfolk. Some of the wives plead with the men to come home; others tell them to come home, like Spartans, either victorious or on their shields.

They arrive too late for the battle.

And the fight has been lost, or at least decisively not-won.

James Orr joined Henry Joy McCracken and the shirttail of his force in the Slemish Mountains. Captured, the poet Orr was permitted exile in the United States.

William McClelland moved quickly, and made Islandmagee before the government troops. He hid in a cave on a small isle, Portmuck, just off Islandmagee. Ground water dripping on him, hungry, he was not solaced by a nautical panorama that had remained unchanged since St. Patrick had sailed by, a slave, more than thirteen centuries earlier. McClelland survives and becomes a successful smuggler.

Willie Nelson and his brother are not so lucky. Captured on the information of local touts, and lodged in Carrickfergus gaol, the brothers are both sentenced to be hanged. At the end of June 1798, they are placed in a cart and drawn to Ballycarry, where, within sight of their mother's window, stands an ancient oak. The yeomanry who bring the lads home are under the command of the local landlord, R.G. Ker of Redhall, and he is a man of bitter subtlety. As the mother of the two young rebels pleads for their lives he sits silent, like Solomon, and then makes the most stiletto-sharp of decisions.

He neither pardons them nor condemns them.

Instead, he frees the elder and condemns the younger.

Willie Nelson swings, a human pendulum, pointing directly to the depths of God's earth.

The landlord explains: "This will show that I have the power of both life and death."

VINEGAR HILL, COUNTY WEXFORD. 21 JUNE 1798

Spectrum Shift

The colours of Irish allegiance change.

Both before and after the 1798 Rising, blue is the official national colour. But it becomes a Protestant colour. The local instance of this is that one of the gangs in the Wexford civil war becomes known as "Ogle's True Blues." They are named in honour of George Ogle, Wexford landlord and former MP for the county. A strong opponent of Catholic Emancipation, he sits now for Dublin, since there was no chance that the mostly-Catholic electorate of Wexford would give him their vote. Blue.

And a new colour, also Protestant: Orange. The counter-revolutionary Protestant force, the Orange Order, had become a national organization in early March 1798. Blue and Orange, then, are the Protestant colours in Wexford. Since there are no more than 500 regular army troops in south Leinster, it is bands of true-blue Orangemen, regularized as yeomanry, who try to hold off the century-savoured revenge of their Catholic neighbours. They are heavily outnumbered – Catholic armies of 15,000 and 20,000 form – but the most active of the Protestant bands blunts the revolution. Among the most effective Protestants is Hunter Gowan, of Mount Nebo, Wexford. He commands Ogle's True Blues and his troops hit the workshops of Catholic blacksmiths and cottages where picks and scythes are hidden. And chapels. They strike with the swiftness of banditti. The summer of 1798 is unusually hot and dry and these apocalyptic riders appear and disappear in a cloud of dust. Hunter Gowan becomes a Wexford legend by returning from one of his sorties and from the saddle ordering a bowl of whiskey punch from the terrified landlord of a public house. When it is brought to him, Gowan directs the landlord to hold the bowl up. When he does so, Gowan takes a finger from his bullet pouch. It has been recently severed from a stubbornly silent Catholic blacksmith. Still dripping vermillion, it is used by Hunter Gowan to stir his drink.

The Catholic colours are not yet agreed, but they are shifting towards the dark end of the spectrum. At the turn-point battle of Vinegar Hill several flags compete. They are mostly black. That is the colour of revolution. Some of them have icons crudely embroidered on them – the harp is the favourite – but most are staunchly and unflinchingly black. Fewer in number are dark green devices. Green is not yet Catholic Ireland's emotive hue.

At Vinegar Hill, where 300–400 Protestant "loyalists" have been "tried" and executed, an army of nearly 20,000 Catholics (and a very few Protestants) has, through amazingly incompetent leadership, found itself surrounded by a mélange of nearly 10,000 yeomanry, vengeful gentry, and a spine of regular army troops, commanded with modest incompetence by General Gerard Lake. What should have been an epic bloodletting turns into a nasty, but not terminal, defeat for the rebels when Lake leaves a defile open and most of the rebels pour out, racing in full retreat towards Wexford Town.

There begins the final spectrum shift, to the vermillion and incarnadine, that becomes the Irish nation's true hue. The bitter and defeated rebels complete a sadistic circus that has been running since Wexford City had been taken a month earlier. The killing of nearly 500 men, women and children is completed: Protestants and a few Catholic loyalists. Show killings. Sequential woundings of prisoners with one additional body part cut, burned, stabbed each day. Blindings. And the drollery of having four men piking a victim aloft on their upraised weapons, and then tossing him about like Chinese acrobats twirling plates on the top of long bamboo sticks.

The revenge of the government and of the Protestant small farmers as they gain control of Wexford is equally imaginative. Captured Catholic rebels are capped with hot pitch. That alone would kill a man; set alight, the victim provides a useful, if animated torch. The infamous Heppenstall, the Walking Gallows: tall, broad, zombie-like: Lieutenant Heppenstall walked the countryside, hanging over his own broad back persons he took to be rebels. They choked, plunged, kicked, turned first red and then suddenly grey. Instead of a rope, Heppenstall often used his own silk cravat.

The colours of Ireland: Orange, Blue, Green, Black. A spectrum that shifts ineluctably towards the cruelest of hues, the congealing hematitic swirl of the jasper spots in bloodstone.

DUBLIN. 11 NOVEMBER 1798

Etching

Theobald Wolfe Tone had committed to suicide well before he committed suicide. Before joining a small French fleet that sailed from Brest for the far north of Ireland in early September 1798, he had taken care of his temporal affairs the way a dying man does: he gave his wife power of attorney over his property, wrote letters to friends, and examined his principles. *I will never suffer a public execution* he swears. To Tone that means he will not accept being hanged in front of a jeering crowd. Death by a military firing squad is acceptable. Tone knows that he will be apprehended in Ireland, so his resolve is not a mere dramatic statement, but rather a First Principle.

Tone's vessel, the *Hoche*, has fearful luck, running into foul weather and a picket of British ships, and is captured. Tone is immediately recognized and taken ashore at Buncrana as a prisoner. This on the third of November. Transported swiftly to Dublin, he is sentenced to death. This he had expected. The question remained: what sort?

On the evening of Sunday, 11 November, Theobald Wolfe Tone is told that he is not to die as a soldier facing a firing squad, but as a common criminal in the yard of Newgate Prison, Dublin. Against the advice of the court, Lord Cornwallis, lord lieutenant of Ireland, decides that Tone's head need not be removed after the hanging and exhibited on the end of pike.

Tone, true to his principles, cuts his throat, and that was the trouble: instead of solely severing his carotid artery, he digs so deeply into his throat with his penknife that he half-severs his windpipe. Instead of easing into a swift and terminal somnambulance, he lives on, in excruciating pain for another eight days, his neck sewn together with sutures of catgut. He dies, delirious but unbroken 19 November 1798.

No one of stature equal to Tone ever committed his life to melding Catholic and Protestant into one Irish national movement; from then on, Irish nationalism and Irish anti-nationalism were each vulnerable to the oppressions of the sectarian extremes.

MAYNOOTH SEMINARY. 1800

Acts of Union (1)

It's all so confusing.

John Butler becomes thirteenth Baron Dunboyne in 1785. He is sixty-eight years of age and his succession to the peerage comes unexpectedly: his nephew, the twelfth Lord Dunboyne, has died without heir and there are no other males in the line.

A problem. Butler has for twenty-three years been the Roman Catholic bishop of Cork.

He ponders. He seeks Papal dispensation from his priestly vows.

This denied, he engages in a formal ceremony of recantation, turns Protestant and in 1787 marries a distant cousin.

Lord Dunboyne's union is barren.

So, in 1800, approaching death, the barren baron returns to the Catholic faith. He leaves his fortune to Maynooth Seminary. After a bit of bargaining with Dunboyne's enraged Protestant heirs, the Roman Catholic bishops obtain £10,000 from his estate and this they use to establish an institution of advanced study at Maynooth.

DUBLIN. L JANUARY 1801

Acts of Union (2)

It really *is* very confusing.

On the first of January 1801 Ireland as a nation-state ceases to exist. It becomes part of the United Kingdom of Great Britain and Ireland.

This is neither the first time that England has tried to solve its problems by constitutional mergers (Scotland in 1707) nor will it be the last (French Canada in 1867). It's not a dumb idea, merely a wrong one: this time.

For contemporaries, the confusion is that there's no clear pattern of for-or-against the Union with Great Britain. The Catholic bishops favoured it; the Whigs opposed. The Catholic aristocracy favoured it, Protestant loyalists opposed. Protestant gentry were split; Dublin lawyers, sensing loss of pelf to London, opposed. Yet Daniel O'Connell disapproved. Within every interest group, fissures were common, and the common people cared not a farthing one way or the other. So very confusing.

And made more so by the Union bill's being lost in the Irish parliament the first time through and being passed the second time only by golden shovelfuls of compensation. That is, by bribes that were not exactly bribes because they were offered in public and because the compensation for lost civic offices and parliamentary seats went to everyone – including those parliamentarians who voted against the Union.

The Irish parliament voted itself out of existence with a mixture of greed, shell-shock (the Rising was still a fresh memory) and bemusement.

John Toler, who as Irish attorney general prosecuted many of the rebels of 1798, was rewarded for supporting the Union by being created first Baron Norbury and made chief justice of the court of common pleas.

Barracked by a female heckler – "You have sold your country!" – he replied with unnecessary candour: "It is very lucky, Madame, that I have a country to sell."

DUBLIN AND BELFAST. 1803

Two Songs

By one of history's mean jokes, Lord Norbury, the cruelest joker ever to sit on the Irish bench, presided over the trial of the patriot Robert Emmet, author of the 1803 Rebellion. With wild puns, songs, incoherent harangues, Norbury ran Dublin's court of common pleas as if he were in charge of a marionette theatre and drunk besides. On his best day on the bench, in terms of productivity, he sentenced ninety-seven persons to death.

Somehow Robert Emmet, twenty-five, blindly idealistic, heroically articulate, used Norbury's court to redeem in Catholic folk-memory the 1798 Rising from what it had been. His own 1803 Rising had been a minor and failed affair, but his demeanour in court rewrote nationalist history: his Speech from the Dock was not so much a speech as a song, so vibrant that it was still being memorized by schoolchildren 150 years later, and quoted in bars by their maudlin parents. After declaring that his Irish revolution would never have exchanged a French tyranny for an English one, and that his people had a competence and a right to take their place among independent nations, Emmet concluded with a startling recitative, in a low and dead-slow Sprachgesang.

Let no man write my epitaph ... And when I am prevented from vindicating myself, let no man dare to calumniate me. Let my character and my motives lie in obscurity and peace, till other times and other men can do them justice; Then shall my character be vindicated. Then may my epitaph be written. I HAVE DONE.

Shortly after Robert Emmet was executed in Dublin in mid-September 1803, another veteran of the 1798 Rising, James Orr, was returning to Ireland. Orr, a poet of facility in the Ullans tongue of the Presbyterian north, had spent his exile in Delaware and now returned home under a general amnesty. America, though hallowed in Ulster-Scots thought, was a disappointment to him. However, it had given him plenty of time for thought and the more he reflected on the 1798 Rising in the north of Ireland, the more he realized it had been a mug's game and that his fellow rebels had been mostly blowhards and runners-in. Orr's sarcastic epic "Donegore Hill" was a biting anti-war song, directed at the audience that knew its vocabulary, the Ulster Presbyerians. He reminded them that on the morning of 7 June 1798,

> *... close-leagu'd crappies rais'd the hoards*
> *O' pikes, pike-shafts, forks, firelocks,*
> *Some melted lead some saw'd deal-boards –*
> *Some hade, like hens in byre-neuks:*

But not all those who turned out were enthusiastic:

> *Now* Leaders, *laith to lea the rigs*
> *Whase leash they fear'd was broken*
> *An'* Privates, *cursin' purse-proud prigs,*
> *Wha brought 'em ball to sloken;*
> *Repentant Painites at their pray'rs,*

An' dastards crousely craikin',
Move on, heroic to the wars
They meant na to partake in,
    By night, or day.

And, not surprisingly, the corps begins to melt away:

Some lettin' on their burn to mak',
The rear-guard, goadin', hasten'd;
Some hunk'rin at a lee dyke back,
Boost houghel on, ere fasten'd
    Their breeks, that day.

But the remainder reached the field:

When to the tap o'Donegore
Braid-islan' corps cam' posting',
The red-wud, warpin, wild uproar,
Was like a bee scap castin';

And retreated:

the pale-fac'd randies
    Took leg, that day.

Two songs, which one to sing? In December 1803, Michael Dwyer, the last remaining guerilla warrior from the 1798 Rising, surrenders. He is transported to New South Wales and there he sings neither. Instead, having served his time, he begins a successful, if uncomfortable career in law enforcement. He becomes the embodiment of the Irish revolutionary tradition in the Antipodes.

IRELAND. 1800–45

Wholesome Diet

Black
Apple
Dough Black
Hamper

Cup

Lumper

These and dozen of other names of potato-varieties were as well known to nineteenth-century Irish folk as were the names of their own children.

They could have been the names of angels for they kept a burgeoning population alive and very healthy. A diet that included ten to fourteen pounds of potatoes a day may have been boring, but the Irish peasantry were among the largest and healthiest in Europe. James Orr wrote a fourteen stanza ode to the potato, beginning:

I ledge we'd fen gif fairly quat o'
The weed we smoke, an chow the fat o';
An wadna grudge to want the wat o'
    Wealth-wastin' Tea;
But leeze me on the precious Pratoe,
    My country's stay!

Or, they could have been the secret name of seducing demons: for not only did the potato feed the burgeoning population, as pastoral or grain-farming never could have done, but it encouraged that burgeoning to become an explosion. Collectively, the Irish went way beyond the 2.1 child-per-family rate that yields equilibrium. In the sixty years between 1781 and 1841 the population of Ireland doubled and was shooting ever-upward.

A countryside that was highly productive – potatoes are immensely productive; a family can live on two acres – was an ecological ruin. Any monoculture is a worry; one that feeds most of a population is actively dangerous. By the early 1840s, Ireland was a massive rural slum. Mud cabins stood cheek-to-jowl; in much of the countryside, trees and wildlife had vanished, save on landlords' plantations.

That the physical environment was abused and the population out of balance with its ecosystem was no secret to the people of the time, though they expressed it differently. Major, but survivable famines in 1816, 1821, 1831, were harbingers of the future. Like men and women living along an earthquake line, the Irish peasantry awaited the Big One, while trying hard not to think about it.

Later, lazy historians are to argue that the Great Famine when it arrives is a piece of bad luck and that it really did not need to happen. Indeed it did not, for nothing is inevitable; but when the earth is so badly abused, it usually swallows its tormentors.

Miracles could have saved Ireland: fatal fungi could have been confined to North America (by force of God, one assumes); Irish landlords could have refused to allow the land to be hacked into tiny potato plots (thus forcing either the starvation or the emigration of literally millions of the rural poor); or Holy Mother Church could have encouraged population limitation (birth spacing was already common in rural populations in regions of France and in some districts of Quebec).

No.

The signal point we must honour about the Irish peasantry of the early nineteenth century is that they knew. They knew they were living on the edge; they lived with the constant electromagnet hum of risk and the bee-scapping drone of disaster, everywhere, every minute.

Somehow, they did not all go mad.

MORLAIX, FRANCE; DUBLIN, IRELAND. 1803

Uniform Standards

When the French delivered the green uniforms to the rank-and-file Irishmen of the Irish Legion, they discovered the same problem in the Napoleonic era that earlier revolutionaries had encountered: the Irish were too big.

Nothing fit.

This had been the case when the French had landed near Killala, County Mayo, in August 1798. At that time General Humbert had brought with him bales of uniforms for the Irish, mostly to raise morale, but also to impose discipline. The uniforms were cut to the standard size of French infantrymen. That is: they fit the small, wiry bodies of Marseille guttersnipes just fine, but when the Irish countrymen put on the uniforms, they could not be buttoned at the chest and great white patches of forearm and shin stuck out from the sleeves and legs.

The same thing happened in 1803 with the clothes for the lower ranks of the Irish Brigade. They were handed out to the infantrymen and the green of the new uniforms was scarcely enough to cover all the important parts of these Irish volunteers.

The fact was that the Irish peasant was the largest in Europe save, perhaps, for the Scandinavian countries. Your average soldier may have led a life of nutritional monotony before his enlistment, but the potato diet of the Irish peasantry was much more nutritious than that of the European grain-eaters. If the average height and size of every army was small by modern standards, nevertheless the Irish were big Europeans.

The other regiment to wear green throughout the Napoleonic wars was in the United Kingdom's army: the 95th Irish Rifle Brigade was dressed in forester-green, with the collar facings lined with black, and these uniforms fit. Their tailors worked to Irish standards.

The 95th was an experimental unit. Formed in 1800, it consisted only of riflemen, no artillery, and it was expected that its men would disperse over a wide front on a hit-and-run basis. Therefore, unusually, it carried no battle flag.

And, unlike almost every other infantry unit in the British army, the 95th did not march to battle with a drum. Instead, the "bugle-horn," which had begun to be used in some British units in the late 1770s, was the regiment's official signal. Because it carried farther and was more variable in pitch, the bugle's notes were much better for getting a message to riflemen than were drums.

This would not have been acceptable to the high command, however, had not the Austrian composer, Franz Joseph Haydn, in the 1790s composed a set of bugle calls that so engaged George III that he permitted them to be used in the British forces.

FRANCE. 1803–15

Carpe Diem

Yes, they were given green uniforms, but that was about all that even came close to being right.

For, of all the days to seize, the volunteers for Napoleon's Irish Legion seized the worst: time and time again. The Irish Legion, founded with the intention of providing leaders for an invasion of Ireland and a mass popular uprising, never got as close as Brest. Its original officers were former leaders of the United Irishmen and its foot soldiers were supposed to be Defenders or others who had fought in '98.

Based first at Morlaix, sixty kilometres from Brest, the legion was from its first day wracked with politics, split between the followers of Thomas Addis Emmet and Arthur O'Connor (brother of the highwayman Roger O'Connor and uncle of the Chartist Feargus O'Connor).

Eventually, O'Connor won and became a French general, and Emmet lost and became a successful U.S. lawyer, a lesson for everyone.

The Irish stay at Morlaix for two years as one invasion of Ireland after another is postponed. The rank-and-file begin to desert and the officers to moot resigning. Talented, unusual men: such as Captain Valentine Derry, a Defender from County Louth and cousin of the redoubtable Fr. Quigley of Forkhill, he had taught English for a time at St. Cyr, and in later life would open his own academy in New York. Now, 22 May 1805, he spends the day drafting a letter of resignation, the heart of which speaks for many of his compatriots: *After a long wait in vain, I see that I cannot render any service to my country by remaining a part of the Irish legion.*

Eventually, Napoleon turned the Irish Legion into a small unit – five battalions at its peak – of his European army. The officers still are Irish, but now there are not enough Irish solders and the ranks are filled with prisoners-of-war, mostly Poles, and deserters from the enemy. This legion was bulked by some new Irish recruits from Silesia – they were rebels of 1798 who had been held on prison ships and, instead of being shipped to Australia, had been sold by the English to the King of Prussia to work in the Silesian coal mines. When liberated, they were very pleased to fight against the Prussians.

Next, in Spain, they fought the Spanish guerillas and the best of English generals. The desertion rate was 10 percent a year, high.

After the French defeat at Waterloo, the remaining Irish legionnaires – mostly officers with non-Irish troops – were required to swear a new oath of allegiance: to King Louis XVIII. This in 1815: on the twelfth of July.

Though the remaining Irish legionnaires were ready to be as staunch Bourbon monarchists as once they had been Irish revolutionaries, their legion was disbanded 28 September 1815.

They were allowed to keep their green uniforms.

DUBLIN. 1804

Defence of the Realm

As the head clerk of the Irish yeomanry hands over the figures for the previous year, he takes the liberty of looking the under-secretary for

Ireland directly in the face. He is waiting for the smile that will result from his seeing the totals: at the end of 1803, the Yeomanry Corps had 83,000 on the active duty roster, including 7,000 officers.

During the long war with France, home defence was assigned to the militia and to the yeomanry. The militia, formed in 1793, was made up mostly of small farmers and labourers and was liable for service anywhere in the British Isles. Increasingly, it was used as a feeder to provide foot soldiers for the regular army. If a local area did not produce sufficient militia men, a ballot was held – a lottery for the unlucky.

The yeomanry were all volunteers. Middle and large farmers, gentry, aristocrats, professional men. Founded in 1796, they represented property, both Protestant and Catholic, though mostly Protestant. Given the yeomanry's ferocious reputation for their part in defeating the '98 Rising, they were, by 1800, looked at as the only real line of defence against the French, should an invasion occur.

Still, what attracted many volunteers was the uniform. Each unit had its own – tunics of scarlet or blue, a wide range of epaulettes, breeches of black, scarlet or, in one case, white leather. In the yeomanry, one was among gentlemen.

Marking oneself off from the ordinary populace was important and that is why Daniel O'Connell joined the Lawyer's Artillery company of the yeomanry in 1797. Anything was better than *the disgrace of being forced to march as a common solder*, he said, and that was the fate that could fall on anyone who risked the militia lottery. O'Connell and his fellow lawyers paraded in blue uniforms, that being the official colour of Ireland, and he wore it proudly.

IRELAND. 1800–45

Just Watch

John Revans, sometime secretary to the English Poor Law Commissioners and later secretary to the Irish Poor Law Inquiry, was the kind of Englishman who was loathed by the Irish: for his long frock coat and his starched wing-collar and his pursed lips, certainly, but mostly because he watched the Irish with an unblinking gaze and reported accurately.

Revans, as part of the Poor Law Inquiry, stood quietly as Irish women served the mid-day meal to their men. Unlike the English agricultural labouring class, Irish women and girls did not eat until the men and boys were finished. Irish women had shorter life expectancies than did men, which is a sure sign of hard treatment for, biologically, human females have a longer life than men, everything being equal.

Revans listens as young men and women explain why, despite the harshness of family life in the potato-culture, they see marriage as their only hope of survival. *The life of a vagrant is the prospect of the Irish peasant, unless he has children able and willing to support him. Every prudent peasant therefore marries ... His children are thus a savings bank ... They are the only property which cannot get taken under the landlord's rent.*

Revans, unusually for his time, pays attention to girls and women, for he recognizes that they are the most vulnerable members of a vulnerable society. No woman, he observes, can expect to make a living on her own. *The inability of a woman at any age to get her own subsistence, makes her most desirous to be married. They require a husband to maintain them whilst young and children to maintain them when old.* That necessity is why Irish peasant women accept more domestic domination, more abuse, less nutrition, than elsewhere in Europe: no bargaining power. *It is evident, therefore, that besides the usual motives of marriage, there are in Ireland many powerful additional.*

And Revans dares to observe something about pre-Famine women that the Church later does everything possible to erase from the historical record. He sees that they use pre-marital sexual activity as a way of obtaining the key to a lifetime above the starvation line: *The peasant women constantly seek illicit intercourse with a view to inducing marriage.* Later work in the fugitive records available suggest that roughly one-in-five rural women, Catholic and Protestant, came to the altar with a baby-in-belly.

Pregnancies usually lead to what the clergy call "subsequent marriages." *The clergy of all persuasions seem invariably to recommend (which is equivalent to enforcing) marriage in all cases of previous intercourse, provided the woman has previously borne a good character.*

And what if the young man refuses? The girl's brothers or other male relatives call round and threaten him or simply kick him until he is either amenable or unconscious. Usually that works. That failing, *the woman has still another resource – she swears or threatens to swear a rape against him. This practice is extremely common in Ireland and is mostly successful.* Often the landlord or his agent is the local magistrate and he, like the parish priest, wants the social fabric to be maintained. *Yet some men do not yield till they are held in prison; whilst a few do not consent until the trial has commenced or even til the verdict is given against them.* Given that rape was a capital charge, marriage was a reasonable plea bargain.

John Revans makes few judgements, save the obvious one: to be a peasant woman in Ireland was to be in a desperate situation. Desperation is the mother of invention and, here, the invention of mothers.

TUNBRIDGE WELLS, ENGLAND. 1810

All Those Endearing Young Charms

Although only thirty-five years of age, the dowager marchioness of Donegall had already been a widow for ten long years: long because her step-son, the second marquis of Donegall, though he held title to Belfast and to huge pieces of the north of Ireland, was mortaged to the hilt and was constantly behind in the payments on her jointure. A widow's bench can be uncomfortable and boring. So she kept a pet.

The gnome poet Thomas Moore had a genius for friendship and, besides, he had the trick of being in and out of a hole faster than a ferret. He tried out his verses and their associated tunes, mostly adapted from the Belfast Harp Festival of 1792, in her drawing room and was able to mount the marchioness and tickle her fancy all within the space of sixty ticks of the metronome. A really amusing pet to have about. He dedicated his 1810 volume of Irish Melodies to her and she stood godmother to his eldest daughter.

Moore's poetic genius flowed in a sentimental vein that post-Victorian audiences have found hard to thole, and more loss to them. In the nineteenth century, any place in the world an Irish audience congregated, Moore's songs were something they had in common. And tears flowed.

Chased by creditors, Moore fled to Italy in 1819 in the companionship of Lord John Russell, the future prime minister. In Venice they spent time with Lord Byron, an intimate of Moore's. The three of them played horse-and-rider and as always the Irish poet was in and out like a flash. And good company besides.

That's why Lord Byron left Moore his memoirs and made him his literary executor. And the reason that Lord John Russell, after retiring as prime minister, produced eight volumes of Moore's journals and correspondence.

He was the most endearing charmer.

THE PENINSULAR WAR. NOVEMBER 1811-JANUARY 1812

Good Honest Lads

William Grattan, a distant cousin of the parliamentary patriot Henry Grattan, disapproved of Arthur Wellesley: not socially, for the future Iron Duke was impeccably bred even if he denied his Irish background. No, militarily, for Wellesley frequently expressed his disdain for Irish troops and said they scared him as much as they did the enemy. That was all wrong, Grattan felt. As a lieutenant in the 88th Regiment, the Connaught Rangers, he found his men to be good honest lads and he dealt with them the way an indulgent uncle treats a pack of nephews.

He could only laugh at the way the boys, headed by Corporal Owen Mackguekin, had simply walked out of their quarters one night, armed only with their bayonets. They were starved for a good feed and the hills were full of sheep and goats and only a few Portuguese shepherds – civilians – were left to protect the animals. Hadn't his lads, just as clever as could be, slipped up on a sheepfold, bayoneted the five Portuguese, and then performed an amusing joke? They tied the arms and legs of the now-dead shepherds together, so that they formed a dead-man's circle. That was "to keep them aisy," Corporal Mackguekin later said, breaking into tears of laughter, and then the boys had performed a similar rite on three of the sheep. Oh, it was a bit naughty of them, but soldiers in war need fresh meat. And when the local Portuguese complained, he had the men tried and flogged but, really, his heart wasn't in it.

Grattan did not much mind when his men pillaged a Spanish town in mid-January of the next year. How could he begrudge the boys having a bit of a spree, after what they had been through, short rations and hard marches. The wine they stole, why it was good for their stomachs, even the Apostle Paul had said that. The difficulty with the Connaught Rangers, Grattan later admitted, was that as men they were more enthusiastic than as soldiers, so the lads had to be let off their leash now and again.

Thus, in the sack of this Spanish town, the officers of the Rangers kept prudently aside. The men, showing their usual initiative, formed themselves into parties of four or five and attacked the heavy doors that defended the gentry houses. Big doors, like those of a prison, Grattan later recalled. The soldiers, instead of banging away with battering rams, worked out a method of simultaneously firing two or three muskets all around the key hole and then, the lock blown clear off, the door swung open. Churches, provisioning shops, and big houses were their favourite targets and then they turned to the women. The lucky females, stripped half naked and raped or not – Grattan never knew and did not want to know – huddled around the officers and were kept safe from further attention. The unlucky ones, caught upstairs in a house, were used until they could be used no more. This was terrible, William Grattan knew, but, really chaps, a war was on and these were foreign women and when the drums rattled for real battle, his boys of Connaught, good honest lads, always formed up and went forward like heroes.

ST. PIERRE, FRANCE. 1813

A Strong Broad Back

"M' back is nearly broke, but none knows why."

"So, tell us Mrs. Skiddy." The young ensign, George Bell of County Fermanagh, was not being sarcastic. "I really wish to know."

"It was broke, so I can scarcely stand, from ... from helping himself out of Spain. You see, one of those French villains shot our poor donkeys."

"Yes?"

Silence

"Was there a special problem, Mother Skiddy?" The term was one of respect and affection. Mrs. Skiddy was the self-declared head of the female camp-followers of the 34th. She was also known as "Commissary-General Mrs. Skiddy" and, like most of the followers, was very useful to the army. She did washing and mending for the officers (paid) and for the men (unpaid) and she and her gang foraged for food, made bandages, cooked extra rations for their men and sometimes tended the wounded. They were not ever admitted to exist in official reports, save as a bearable nuisance, but camp followers were a necessary and useful arm of the British army. And none more faithful to the regiment than the Irish women.

"It's when we were leaving Portugal and then Spain and then coming into this Atty-istic country that I had Dan Skiddy on m' back. Sure the march was halfways an attack and halfways a retreat and we never knew what was coming. Or what ways the compass read."

Ensign Bell grimaced in remembrance of a winter in hell.

"It was a time of great confusion. No question there."

"An' on one of the spins of the compass we were chased by the French. 'O! Dan, jewel,' says I, 'I'll help you on a bit. Take a holt of me arm an' throw away your knapsack.' 'I niver will,' says he, 'nor my firelock, while I'm a sodjger.' Och, sure, but later didn't the brave craither drop on the ground an' not have the spirit to move. An' the French coming on. So I picked him up onto a bank. Knapsack, gun an' all. I draws him onto my back and, Holy Mother of God, I was so afraid that I walked two miles with him and his knapsack an' his firelock. That's why my back is broad as a turtle's and is all crulged over."

"You're a wonderful woman, Mrs. Skiddy."

"There's just one thing, sir."

"Yes?"

"Could you be payin' your account for the last year's washing and darnin'?"

TOULOUSE, FRANCE. 1814

The Mummers' Parade

"Sergeant! Line the men up for the Mummers' Parade."

That was the term used in the Irish Rifle Brigade for the post-battle accounting. It was never a pretty sight. The term came not from a black-humour reference to Christmas mumming, but was an Irish corruption, or, really correction, of what had originally been termed "the Mother's Parade."

Technically, it helped the officers to reassess their company's strength. But primarily it was held for the benefit of the camp followers. It permitted them to see if their husbands or lovers (and, in a few cases, sons) were still alive and ambulatory.

Assembling the men for the Mummers' Parade was among every sergeant's most-disliked duties. He had to have one-legged men dragged from their beds, men with bad head wounds propped erect between two comrades, and worse. The men then stood in staggered rows and answered when their names were called. The camp followers were allowed to stand on the edge of the makeshift parade square. They listened intently as each name was called. If a name was missing, they clustered around the sergeant and then he queried the company as to who had any knowledge of the missing man.

"Joseph Cochran. Does anyone have any knowledge of Private Joseph Cochran?"

"Aye, Sir." A private stepped forward. "I saw him die, sir."

"Know the spot?"

"I do Sir."

"Take Mrs. Cochran there."

So an already-grieving widow is taken to view the remains of her husband. She sees a body with its head half vanished. She falls on the body anyway.

"He died bravely, ma'am." She would be told that even if he were bayonetted in the back: some civilities war cannot destroy. "He was standing up like a hero, fighting the Frenchie and in the heat of the action, why what did your man do? He stood up straight, held up his canteen in the face of the Frenchie and said in a brave voice to the enemy, 'Here's to you, old boy,' just like an officer at the mess. Oh, he was a fine man entirely."

Private Cochran's mate continued quickly, sliding over the idiocy and unnecessary bravado of his friend as fast as possible. "And just after he'd defied the Frenchie in that way, why didn't a ball the size of a cannon, take him in an instant to the God's heaven. And with no pain." That was an another agreed lie for the Mummers' Parade: nobody died painfully.

Mrs. Cochran clung to her man's corpse for the rest of the day, keening wildly, and only when the swampers came to bury the body did she go back to the other females who laid her down near a fire and comforted her.

As was not uncommon, another private solder soon offered to marry the Widow Cochran. Although there was nothing in the King's Regulations on the topic, an unwritten Levirate Marriage clause ran through tight units like the Irish Rifles. The Widow Cochran declined, with gratitude for the respect. No, she said, she was returning to Ireland where men lasted longer.

CASTLE DANGAN, CO. MEATH. MARCH 1815

What Godfathers Are For

When a messenger brings news to Castle Dangan of the escape of Napoleon from Elba and of his march on Paris, the courier has a hard time distinguishing the main entrance from the servants' entrance. Castle Dangan was not much of a castle, more a collection of outbuildings, since Roger O'Connor had torched it for the insurance money. The family had yet to move to its nearly derelict second home, Connorville.

Before the insurance fire, Castle Dangan had been one of the finest houses in Ireland, the seat of the Wellesley family, and the place where the young Arthur Wellesley, now Napoleon's matched opposite, had spent his holidays.

The news of Napoleon's escape galvanizes Francis Burdett O'Connor, second of Roger O'Connor's sons, into action. He decides to go to France as quickly as possible to help not Wellington, but Buonaparte. He wishes to serve under his uncle, the French general Arthur O'Connor. At age twenty-six, Francis feels he has been cheated of action in life. He rides as fast as he can to Dublin, sells his horse, and heads to England with the naive idea of catching a ship for France: as if one took a ferry boat to the enemy's lines and simply joined up.

Fortunately, he calls on his godfather, Francis Burdett, MP. Burdett is a longtime radical and a hero of Francis's father, and the senior O'Connor had dedicated to him his imaginative forgery *The Chronicles of Eri*. He is now an MP for Westminster, a prime seat, and he has been an opponent of the ruinous expense of the European war. Still, when young Francis asks for cash to travel to France, the MP does his godfatherly duty: he explains to his namesake that, son, there is a naval blockade in place and you have more chance of successfully sailing to Egypt than you have of making the French shore, much less reaching Napoleon's lines.

Dejected, Francis takes the few pounds that Burdett gives him and returns home. He is terrified that his father's violent temper will greet him, so in Cork City he visits his father's steward and asks for passage money to the United States. Again, wisdom of the elders prevails: the steward tells him to wait a bit, and soon news of Waterloo arrives. Francis Burdett O'Connor goes home and instead of being horsewhipped, merely has to attend a long sermon delivered by his father. His brother Feargus listens to the rant and is barely able to keep from breaking into laughter.

In 1821, this time with the blessing of his godfather, who gives him an expensive sword, Francis Burdett O'Connor joins an Irish regiment of lancers that will fight in South America for the independence of several countries from Spain or Spanish proxies. He fights in Venezuela, Colombia, Peru, and finally Bolivia, where he becomes a major-general under Bolivar.

Thanks to his godfather's advice, he lived into his eighty-first year and, in the twentieth century, became the subject of a handsome Bolivian commemorative postage stamp.

ULSTER. 22 DECEMBER 1824

Not a Superstitious People

The reason that this tune called York
I never yet could know:
They might as well have called it Cork,
Carnmoney or Raphoe.

These are not nonsense phrases. They are the pattern-phrases used to teach the metrics of the holy psalms. John McKinney, an ancient veteran of 1798 – he had brought word to Henry Joy Mccracken at Templepatrick of the approach of the military – now is drilling a small choir. He is called a cantor or a precentor. Since no musical instruments are allowed in strict Presbyterian churches, the small choir needs to be note perfect if it is to lead the congregation in singing the Psalms of David.

In Ireland doth fair Dublin stand,
The chief city therein ...

The Irish Presbyterians pride themselves on not being at all superstitious. That is a term they apply to the Papishes, with all their plaster saints and priests in skirts and ridiculous pilgrimages. No, we're not like them.

That being the case, it is hard to see why they feel it's very bad luck to chant the psalms outside of kirk. They resemble foreign tribes who won't say the name of their god except in their special god-house.

... And is said by many men
The chief city for sin.

And if they are not superstitious then why, as Christmas 1824 approaches, are so many Presbyterians in Ulster (and Anglicans in Ulster and the rest of Ireland) so worried about a superstitious Catholic prophecy, the Pastorini Utterance? This was derived from a book published in 1771 by an English Catholic bishop, Charles Walmesly, using the pseudonym, Signor Pastorini. It was an elaborate interpretation of the apocalyptic end to the Christian scriptures, the Book of the Revelation of St. John. In substance it was nothing that keen Protestant Bible readers hadn't been doing for centuries – figuring out when the world would end. This Catholic version circulated among the Irish peasantry and in mud cottages visions of the end-times, when God would rid the earth of the evil of heresy, and would do so in a spate of blood, became hearthside tales.

Of course we don't believe such Papish nonsense, the kirk elders affirmed. But throughout Ulster, the Christmas service of 1824 was notable for armed men, standing outside each church. Just in case.

DUBLIN. 1827

And a Revelation

In the low mountains and the valleys of County Wicklow, a Church of Ireland curate works feverishly. He has the bearded, thin face of an ancient anchorite, the broken gait of someone who has been trampled, and the emaciated body of a warrior who wears starvation as his armour. This cleric follows Jesus' dictate of eating only what his listeners will provide. He wears only clothes they give him and the cast-offs of the Irish peasantry are truly cast-off: he is sometimes mistaken for a beggar and given a shilling by the Quality. He teaches the Bible and offers prayer in any mud cabin or byre where someone will listen. His listeners, almost all Catholics, revere him as a holy man.

John Nelson Darby has come by his vocation directly from God. Certainly not from his comfortable King's County family: Admiral Lord Nelson was his godfather; he had attended Westminster School, then Worcester College, Oxford, obtained a double first and joined the Dublin Bar. His conscience, however, would not let him practice law because, in the nature of legal procedures, he would inevitably be defending the wrong side, morally speaking, in many of his cases. So John Darby studied theology at Trinity College, Dublin, and took holy orders.

From the very first, his superior, William Magee, archbishop of Dublin, did not know what to do with this young man with the hollow eyes, who, even in his TCD days, wore clothes that had the shine of extensive wear, and who prayed alone much too often for his own well being. The Church of Ireland was not accustomed to such enthusiasm, ascetic and self-effacing though it was.

The Rev. John Darby came down from the Wicklow mountains several times a year to raise funds for his mission. He was convinced that throughout Ireland the Catholics were turning to the Protestant state church at the rate of 7–800 a week, a delusional belief, but also a goal.

Then, almost simultaneously in 1827, two traumas propel Darby out of the Church of Ireland. His archbishop condemns Catholic Emancipation, something that as a Bible-Christian Darby sees as a just goal: after all, in Christ there is neither Jew nor Greek, all are one. And, in weak health, Darby had been unable to control his horse and, being underfed, it had taken him through the entrance of a stable, and broken several of the holy man's bones on the doorpost.

Darby convalesces and in that time he realizes that his holy orders are vanity; the Established Church a vain pomp. He has nothing less than a revelation: that only by reprising the primitive church can the Christian god be found. No more organized ministry and men in holy orders; all believers are priests; a weekly fellowship meal; business and medical practices must be compatible with New Testament examples; a literal reading of the Bible; and a setting-aside of Believers from the rest of a society that is unholy. Thus, the Brethren are born in Dublin.

The spiritual world of Dublin being heavily roiled by the Catholic Emancipation fight, Darby moves to Plymouth, England: hence the everyday name for the new religion, the Plymouth Brethren. Because each congregation is defined as being completely autonomous, they fight among themselves in their solemn, highly judgmental way. Darby himself leads a congerie of worshippers in 1849 who become the Exclusive Brethren, as distinct from the Open Brethren. The Exclusives will not even chew a crust of bread in the same room with someone who is not one of their own – did not our Lord forbid breaking bread with unbelievers?

The Brethren, in their various forms, spread throughout the English-speaking world and, in the latter half of the nineteenth century, begin to be very active missionaries in India and, a little later, central Africa and South America. They are a strangely quiet religion. They are not showy or effusive, but are like the hard kernels of some desert plant that can remain hidden for decades and then, under the right conditions, briefly flower, produce another generation of rock-hard seeds, and thus continue the life cycle.

They, like all religions, are an imperium, but one whose members are in a near-secret service. In any collection of people, any governmental office, any file of voters, there are many more Brethren than one would guess.

They behave modestly and are careful not to catch each other's eye.

COUNTY CLARE. JULY, 1828

Off Their Knees

The Protestants need not have worried about Pastorini's prophecies. They should have heeded those of Daniel O'Connell. When he was done, he said, the Irish nation and the Catholic nation would be one. Ultimately, he is wrong, but he comes close.

Catholic Emancipation – the grand term for the simple right of Catholics to sit in parliament of the (now) United Kingdom – is the last consequential hurdle left: once achieved, the Penal Laws will have been undone. After that the next step will be to undo the conquest of Ireland.

O'Connell's genius is multi-faceted, but its jewel is his creation of the first grass-roots political movement in the British Isles. From 1826 onwards, at every Catholic parish church in Ireland, a collection is made. One penny is enough to bond a pauper to the cause, so long as it is given monthly. More from the wealthy. A parish-by-parish political organization that unites people of all classes has never before been seen, and it is another thirty years before the English political parties catch on to the method.

The Irish Catholics, previously a congerie of local loyalties, conceive of themselves as a nation. Before O'Connell if, say, an average west Cork tenant farmer was asked what he was, he might, if he had broad personal horizons, have said, "a Munster man," but that was as far as he would have gone. If someone had told him that he was of the same nation as somebody from Connaught, he would have been incensed.

Daniel O'Connell changed that.

Everything of political importance in subsequent Irish history follows from this one epochal achievement.

When, in 1828, O'Connell wins Clare, he and the hatchet-faced Duke of Wellington – Anglo-Irish and England's greatest living military hero – face each other in a duel of wills. Both realize that if Wellington as the United Kingdom's prime minister refuses to let the Catholic O'Connell sit in parliament, Ireland will break into a civil war that will make 1798 appear to have been a dancing class.

Wellington, wisely, backs away, and in February 1830 Daniel O'Connell is in parliament and the Roman Catholics of the British Isles have their civil rights.

O'Connell knew that he was not effecting a revolution. Just before the Clare election he told the agricultural labourers on his Kerry estate, "Lads, whatever happens, you will still be breaking stones."

PORTMUCK HARBOUR, ISLANDMAGEE, COUNTY ANTRIM.
1829–30

Solid Citizen

As he watches the hand-operated winches on the dredges clear the stones from Portmuck Harbour, William McClelland has sharp memories and few reflections. Under his supervision, the Irish Fisheries Board is making a harbour on the northeast side of Islandmagee, scarcely 300 yards from where McClelland, as a rebel of '98, had hidden from the Yeomanry.

The harbour takes all summer to build. Large boulders, capped with mortar form a wall around three sides of a harbour that is now large enough to take cattle and coal coasters. Trade with Scotland will become much easier for the Islandmagee folk. McClelland recalls the details of his own smuggling career, when he plied between the Low Countries and County Antrim. That was before he returned to Island-magee and became a solid citizen. This transformation he accomplished by visiting the local magistrates, pleading remorse, and then joining the Yeomanry.

William McClelland has turned from being a radical democrat who believes that revolution will yield freedom into a radical democrat who believes that revolution will lead to tyranny; the more so now that Daniel O'Connell has turned the Catholics into an army that, Mc-Clelland believes, could crush the Protestants of Ireland at any time.

In erecting a strong, though not unbreachable, barricade around his home harbour, William McClelland is doing physically what most Irish Presbyterians do in spirit after Catholic Emancipation. They remain strongly assertive of their own culture and religion, but now they trust for their defence only to themselves.

CRY NOT FOR COOK'S WAKE
1768–1793

From Sea to Sea to See

To a real empire careerist, doing well in the Canadas meant winning the privilege of leaving. James Cook understood this very well, but it still required a dozen years before he broke tether and went on to glory.

Cook, talented, extremely ambitious, was also workmanlike, a zealot for detail. He rose from able seaman to gain his master's ticket in June 1757 and was given command of a gunship that was present when the French surrendered to General Amherst at Louisbourg in July 1758. Being on the winning side always helps a career.

As preparation for the British assault on Quebec City, Cook prepared meticulous maps of the St. Lawrence Gulf and River: without these the victory by General Wolfe would have been unlikely, if not impossible.

The war with the French in the New World temporarily won, Cook was given a decade of mapping work, charting previously unknown shores of Newfoundland, Nova Scotia and the St. Lawrence River valley. Interesting work and useful, for his maps were on the table during the negotiations that eventually severed British North America from the American colonies: but not the Big Chance.

Finally, in 1768 London commissions him to look for the Holy Grail of European explorers, an easy maritime road to Asia.

Still Worshipping the Old God

Able seaman Joseph Childs, who gives his home port as Dublin, is one of the first to sign on with the crew of Lieutenant (not yet Captain) Cook's boat *Endeavour Barque*. That's the official name, to distinguish it from the Royal Navy vessel the *Endeavour*, but in later memory, Cook's vessel becomes the real "Endeavour." Childs has a good disciplinary record and some useful secondary skills and, eventually, in February 1771 when the ship's cook goes incompetent, he takes over. For the rest of his life he tells strangers in dockside taverns that he has served as "Cook's cook," and usually he gets a free dram or two based on that fact and upon his stories.

Childs, unlike everyone else on the vessel, understands the primary mission of the voyage: to observe the transit of Venus – that is, the march of Venus across the face of the sun – from an ideal vantage point, in this case the island of Otaheite – that is, Tahiti – in what was known to English-speakers as the Society Islands. His fellow below-deck crewmen see Tahiti only as a land of pear-shaped breasts and wide-legged native women – at least if Cook will let them off *Endeavour* long enough to get their tools to digging. And the scientists above deck are nothing if not exactly the opposite; ascetically rigorous. They are part of a globe-circling scientific venture being coordinated by the Royal Society: observations were being made at Fort Churchill in Hudson's Bay and at the North Cape in Africa, two locations that were about as uncomfortable as one could find. The third location, in the Pacific, was originally to be set up in the Solomon Islands. The difficulty there, however, was that navigators had lost the exact location of the Solomons so that would have to be rediscovered, and even sitting in London, the savants of the Royal Society saw this as a drawback. Thus Tahiti. Cook and his scientific observers set up a telescope on a sheltered coral rock 150 yards off shore. They show the locals the path of the planet across the sun, but that is something these people knew of already. The male indigènes are more interested in nicking small items from the Europeans (Cook views the Tahitians as the most nimble thieves in the world) and the women in spending nights in shore tents with the sailors. The actual observations made by the scientists are clear enough, but eventually worthless, since one cannot make precise celestial calibrations unless one knows accurately where one's observation point is located and that precision was way beyond contemporary instruments.

Still, Joseph Childs knows that the effort has been successful because the gods have been served. He knows not the names of these deities but, then, he has almost lost memory of his own name. When he signed on to his first ship in Dublin, years ago, he hardly spoke English and the Ulster-bred master simply wrote down "chiel," meaning young man, and that migrated into Childs on successive voyages. He remembers clearly, though, the circular stone carvings he viewed as a youngster, the spiralling patterns on stones now cast up as boundary walls in close-grazed fields.

He looks at the sun intersecting a celestial body, and acquires the same knowledge that the builders of Knowth, Howth, and New Grange possessed, that the sun could dance and that every item it embraced was only its temporary partner.

RAITEA, SOCIETY ISLANDS. NEAR TAHITI, 21 JULY 1769

Aggrandisement

"Truly, the man loves possessions."

"That is only his duty. It is for the Crown."

Two able seamen are intently watching Lieutenant James Cook. The possessions he loves are not artifacts, textiles, spices, the usual booty of explorers of his time; he loves possessing entire islands, archipelagos and, if possible, continents. They're not for himself, but for his country and its Empire.

Cook is just completing an involved ceremony with the native leaders of the southern half of the largest of the Society Islands. He does so with the help of a Tahitian of chiefly rank, one Tupaea, whom the ship's naturalist, Joseph Banks, has been teaching English. Whether or not he is able to translate accurately is open to question and, quite possibly, the words of James Cook and of his indigenous counterpart slide by each other like blots of ink on parallel plates of glass.

Still, the elaborate ceremony goes on. The native chief strips to the waist as a sign of his pacific intent, and Cook directs a senior member of his own party to do the same. Long ritual speeches follow, their specific meaning unclear on both sides, but their intention peaceful. Cloth is exchanged and plantain plants and feathers. The prize item given the foreigners is a pig. Cook responds with a small brass engraving and some English coins.

Then Cook has the Royal Ensign hoisted on a pole and he takes possession of the island in the name of his Brittanic Majesty.

He does the same thing in another land in November 1769. Now according to his secret instructions, he is free to explore south, and westward, the transit of Venus having been recorded. At Mercury Bay in the North Island of New Zealand he plants a flag. He does so in a medieval manner. Instead of rigging a flag pole, he thrusts a long lance into the earth, as if killing a giant enemy; atop the lance is the ensign, and he claims the country around him for the united Crown of England, Scotland, and Ireland.

And, again, in January 1770, in Queen Charlotte Sound in the South Island, he performs the same spear-thrusting gesture and announces "I take possession of this land."

The action, in each case, exceeds the explanatory powers of his Tahitian translator, who can only half-communicate with the Maori observers of these events.

"I wonder where he is taking his possessions?" one of the Maori elders comments with a half smile.

CAPE KIDNAPPERS, NORTH ISLAND, NEW ZEALAND.
7 OCTOBER 1769

Ethnographer in Training

Ethnographer. Anthropologist. Call him what you wish: Joseph Banks was the first of the sort in the English-speaking world. And the first one to cry.

A first-rate naturalist, Banks had all the credentials and then some. Educated at Harrow and Christ Church, Oxford. Independently wealthy. Experienced: he had accompanied Cook on one of his Newfoundland mapping expeditions.

In the round-the-world *Endeavour* expedition of 1768–71 he made meticulous notes of flora, and when he returned to England, this led to an honorary D.C.L. at Oxford, a knighthood, and the presidency of the Royal Society, the highest scientific honour of the time.

As a sideline, Banks fills the interstices of his journals with observations of fauna – human fauna. With the naive eye of the naturalist, he views the complexity of human societies.

Take the events on 7 October 1769. Lieutenant Cook has anchored off a modest cape inside Hawke's Bay. The local Maori come in canoes to trade. Despite their experience in the Society Islands, Cook and his officers have yet to gain control of the grammar of Polynesian trading – not the words, it's the rules they are too inflexible to understand. As a result they always feel they have been cheated. Today, for example, they bargain for baskets of one sort of fish but, being paid, the Maori send up baskets of other species and a few stones in the bottom of the containers. And, when one of the locals offers to sell a very desirable dog-skin cloak to Cook, the mariner agrees to trade a piece of red baize for it. Then, when the huckster gets hold of the baize, he simply puts it in his basket and calmly paddles off with both his purchase and his own dog-skin cloak.

Infuriating, certainly, but by now anyone with a stroke of wit would understand the rules of trade as they then held: physical possession gave ownership, so don't take your hands off your own trade goods until the other party does the same with his. Easy, really, and not beyond two children trading polished stones behind a school house.

Cook misses every lesson. He permits the boy Tayeto, who is a ward of the translator Tupaiea, to trade small goods from deck to fishermen. No one asks, no one knows, whether he is the translator's acolyte or catamite, but he is some form of property and therefore vulnerable. One of the Maori men in the canoes grabs the lad and he is sped away in a six-man canoe. In immediate response, Cook has his marines fire into the canoe. They kill one Maori and Tayeto leaps out and swims to safety. Cook lowers a boat with marine marksmen and they kill a number of Maori, not just those who did the kidnapping.

Joseph Banks watches all this with his scientist's eye. But it is as an ethnographer that he appreciates the small ceremony, where the kidnapped boy, now safely on the *Endeavour*, offers a fish to his god, a thanksgiving token that he returns to the sea. Banks rubs back tears, for the beauty of that small ceremony.

QUEEN CHARLOTTE SOUND, SOUTH ISLAND,
NEW ZEALAND. JANUARY 1770

Gambler's Luck

James Cook is anchored in a large bay, a perfect harbour: calm, with fresh water easily available. The indigène are moderately friendly, despite a bit of stone throwing. One of Cook's officers is able to trade for a human head. And some of the crew find human remains that have recently been gnawed upon. Cook takes one of his able seamen and climbs the hills behind the harbour. He comes down so exhilarated that his crew wonders if he has been drinking.

Cook has seen that the bay he is in is, most likely, a passage of open water and, therefore, this New Land he is charting is not a continent but a set of islands. Joseph Banks, one of the two naturalists on the voyage, says Cook is dreaming. When the *Endeavour* lifts anchor on 7 February, Cook sails far enough into the strait to convince even the skeptical scientist. Banks is a good enough loser to insist that this be called Cook Strait, and, after ritual modesty, Cook agrees and the name is inscribed on the chart he is making.

A great honour, but considering that the Maori cook whom the expedition had picked up knew about the strait, and confirmed Cook's supposition, not exactly a discovery.

The Maori term for the strait, "Raukawa," would have done just as well.

And Cook still could have maintained his immortality: for in one school of New Zealand poker, a unique hand is recognized, the Cook Straight. It is a Queen, King, Jack, and Ten of hearts, with the Ace missing. It ranks just below a Busted Flush.

38 DEGREES LATITUDE, THE EAST COAST OF AUSTRALIA.
22 AUGUST 1770

Taking it All In

Like a giant caterpillar, Lieutenant Cook and his crew have been moving northwards, up the east coast of Australia, assimilating everything they come upon and leaving behind little castings that reveal their passage. At several points, Cook stops and goes through the elaborate pantomime the crew now know by heart: he takes possession of a piece of land for King George of England, Scotland, and Ireland.

At Stingray Harbour, the crew had especially enjoyed the capering of Joseph Banks, who had collected enough previously unknown specimens to revolutionize the science of Botany. He had done so in such a fever of excitement that he had paid no attention to the darts directed at him by some very brown-coloured naked men. In this bay, Cook had incised an inscription on a large tree, memorializing his presence and, of course, had displayed the Royal Ensign.

The botanist Banks was especially pleased that Cook immediately changed the name of the place from Stingray Harbour to Botanist Bay. Later, it became Botany Bay.

A bay to the north was christened Port Jackson after one of the secretaries to the admiralty, and it eventually became Sydney Harbour.

Thus the *Endeavour* proceeds northwards, the scientist Banks taking in bales of botanic specimens and the explorer Cook taking in millions of hectares of land. Of course, it is empty land, or virtually so, he asserts, so it is being redeemed.

At a place that he aptly names Possession Island, Cook stabs the earth with another lance bearing the Royal Ensign and then announces that all the land south of 38 degrees belongs to His Britannic Majesty and that it shall be called New South Wales.

Much later, when Banks is Sir Joseph Banks, president of the Royal Society and a Privy Councillor, he is an influential advisor on the settlement of Australia. He argues strongly and convincingly that New South Wales would best be used as a penal colony and, consequently, Botany Bay becomes a place to discard, rather than to discover, unusual specimens.

THE ANTARCTIC CIRCLE. JANUARY 1773

The Public's Right to Know

"Tied a sheep-shank lately, Gunner?"

Most of the ordinary seaman believe that John Marra, gunner's mate on the *Resolution* on now-Commander Cook's second expedition, spends all his spare time playing with his rope, and they make pointed remarks about it.

"Terribly hard work below decks. Am I right about that Gunner?"

They're careful, though. Marra, a red-haired Cork man, has a reputation for violence. Still, it's hard to ignore his drawing himself into a fetal position in his berth, and pulling a blanket over his head and body, and then busying himself with a project that they all understand only too well. Even the officers are aware of his predilection and Marra is sometimes referred to by them as the Furtive Firbolg.

Everyone is wrong.

Marra is keeping a journal. Somehow in the near-darkness he scratches away for an hour or more each day, filling a tiny bundle of notebooks with his own log of the great expedition. It is his, his alone, and he understands that being notorious as a pudding-puller is the price he has to pay for his writing. Were any of the officers to suspect the art that he was really practising, his jottings would have been confiscated and he probably would have been up on disciplinary charges before Commander Cook himself.

Cook understood well the advantage of controlling what was reported concerning his voyages. The ground-rules had been set before the first of his three expeditions. All the log books and any journals kept by his officers were to be surrendered to him. Further, none of the crew was permitted to divulge where the expedition had been, much less profit by writing about it in the public press or in books: not until official permission was given and that would not be forthcoming until Cook's own version of events was spread far and wide as the Gospel truth. Certainly this protected any national interests, but also Cook's; it's easier to become a national hero if one controls what the public knows, and it's easier to gain monies for further expeditions.

Marra scribbled on. He was not caught and when, in July 1775, the expedition returned to England, he secretly made his way to the London publisher, Newberry, who bought the journals and surreptitiously began setting them in type. They appeared late in the year and made Marra a few guineas. A bit later, Cook was elected a Fellow of the Royal Society and, as the nation's most celebrated navigator, was assigned another expedition: perhaps this time he will obtain the alchemist's goal, the discovery of the Northwest Passage to Asia.

John Marra, having done what few men of his time had done – been around the world, literally – went home briefly to Cork and then sailed to Port Jackson, choosing a future as far away from home as possible.

THE HERVEY ISLANDS. LATE SEPTEMBER, 1773

Honorifics

Captain James Cook, midway through his second voyage into the Pacific, hedges his bets for the time when he will need high political friends at home. He sails near a covey of islands in mid-Pacific, but they lack natural harbours and he is unable to land. Still, no use wasting them. Cook is aware that he missed a big chance in dealing with the largest islands in Polynesia, Aoteraoa – the land of the long white cloud in Maori – and that he should not have left them with its Dutch name, Zeeland, pendant: it would have been a great place to hang the name of a royal duke or, at minimum, a prime minister.

The present small group of islands is about right for a middleregister personage. So Cook announces, as he marks them on his ever-infilling chart, that they are the "Hervey Islands."

This is a piece of sycophancy that looks more shrewd than it really is, for it ties Cook's efforts not only to Augustus John Hervey, third earl of Bristol and one of the lords of the admiralty, but also to the entire Hervey clan, some of them barely housebroken. Thus, George William, second earl of Bristol, after a life of undemanding diplomatic plums, had been named Lord Lieutenant of Ireland in October 1766, just at the time his son Augustus John (third earl in 1775) was named Chief Secretary for Ireland. Nice, that, a father-and-son team holding the two chief offices of Irish state. Except that neither bothered to show up in Dublin and both *père et fils* resigned within a year, having done nothing at all.

And, indelible in the folk memory of several Irish counties and European cities was Frederick Augustus Hervey, destined to become the fourth earl of Bristol in 1779. At the time Captain Cook was counting as many of the Hervey Islands as he could (he missed quite a few), Frederick Augustus Hervey, D.D., bishop of the Protestant diocese of Derry, was presiding as the most worldly, most eccentric, most talked-about priest in the Church of Ireland. Immensely wealthy, and incapable of taking direction from his ecclesiastical superiors, the Bishop of Derry spent most of his time on the Continent where, after his rise to the earldom, "Hotel Bristol" became the name of the flash hotel in many cities. Particularly fond of Rome, this Protestant cleric went about that city in red plush breeches, a broad-brimmed white hat, and enough chains and gee-gaws to lead the Catholic authorities to conclude that, compared to their Irish Protestant rivals, they were liturgically outclassed. Frederick Augustus Hervey spent a fortune on good works in his diocese, ranging from a notable folly that made jobs for hundreds, to more sensible projects, such as draining waste land for the peasantry. His high point came in 1783 when, backing Catholic Emancipation, he joined the Volunteer Movement. He journeyed down to Dublin attended by a troop of dragoons from his own diocese. He himself was dressed entirely in purple and entered Dublin in an open landau drawn by six horses, each in purple livery.

That the Herveys were as different from the prudent, responsible, predictable Captain Cook as chalk is from cheese is manifest. It was only justice that in popular usage among mariners and, increasingly among governmental officials, the Hervey Islands came to be called the "Cook Islands," and in 1888, when a British protectorate was declared, they officially took that name.

MANGAIA, THE COOK ISLANDS. 29 AND 30 MARCH 1777

Leverage

How right the ancients were, when they asserted that anyone could move the earth, given a long enough lever! On his way home (so he hopes) from his third Pacific voyage, Captain Cook again passes through the group of islands he calls "the Herveys," this time with two ships under his command. Previously he had sighted Manuae and "Palmerston," small, barely inhabited atolls. Now he finds a gem, Mangaia, that rises from the Pacific like a fortified medieval town. Surrounded by coral that has been raised by geological forces, from a distance it seems to have walls whitewashed with lime, and these are surmounted with a lush green plateau.

The island's rich volcanic soil supports three villages and the Mangahians are a confident people, curious and cunning. "The big canoes must come from the spirit world," one chief surmises.

"Such a waka must carry a god," another agrees.

"Perhaps gods, perhaps men, who cares!" Mourua, a notoriously impetuous warrior cries, and runs to his outrigger. His mate Makatu follows and they skim right up to the largest of the two vessels. Some nails and a handful of blue beads are passed down to them. Makatu wants to leave, but Mourua swings himself aboard and there he and Cook face each other.

Each is impressed: two warriors in their prime.

Cook gives Mourua a knife, which he later carries in a long slit he makes in his ear.

Mourua has seen that the gods in the waka are merely men, but he is not disappointed, for if they are not deities they still would make excellent relatives: dynastic marriages in Polynesia are as important as they ever were in the Holy Roman Empire. He orders his daughter Kurakaau polished. "Make her fit for an ariki," he orders his wife, for he understands Cook to be a king or, at minimum, a very high chief. At first light the women of the family groom the daughter, oil her breasts, dress her in bark skirts of the most elaborate design. Then she is sent to saunter slowly down the beach.

With immense and respectful gravity, Captain Cook declines the offer. It is a proposition so obvious that he does not need his interpreter to explain it to him. In declining, Cook gives Mourua a skein of printed cotton in recognition of the girl's great beauty. And he provides the warrior with a fine English hatchet.

The gods have allocated Mourua a short future. His head is split by a stone adze two or three years later, during the endemic warfare that runs through almost all the Polynesian islands. And Cook has less time than that.

Yet, Cook, in a single motion, by leaning, apparently without aforethought, on a giant cultural lever, has moved these islanders from the stone age to the iron age, and in a single day.

More than six decades later the details of Cook's visit are still fresh on the tongues of the people of Mangaia, the memory of the boats and the cloth and the knives and the axe clear, and the items themselves so valuable that they became gravegoods, to be buried with the most revered elders. A white missionary, upon being told of the tradition of Cook's visit, commented gravely: "An important step had thus been taken in civilization: they had become acquainted with the existence of a race different from all that they had hitherto seen or heard of, wiser, stronger, and more benevolent than themselves."

LONDON. 1779

A Single Myth Will Serve

Joseph Banks is plump and shiny as a salmon-fed otter. London suits him. He enjoys his fame. Though only in his mid-thirties, he has already been named president of the Royal Society, and thus is the intellectual heir of Sir Isaac Newton, who had held the presidency for twenty-five years. Banks soon will receive a knighthood, for that is automatically given to England's ranking scientist. Were he indeed a musteline carnivore, Banks would spend most of his time grooming his glistening fur and taking occasional breaks to admire his reflection in a quiet pool.

As it is, he must be satisfied with employing audiences of politicians and of amateur scientists to serve as mirrors to his vanity.

There will, I assure you, be no opposition from the natives. Banks is testifying before a parliamentary committee that is considering what to do with the criminals that are piling up like cord wood, now that the revolution in the American colonies has stopped transportation of felons to that New World. *Gentlemen, I assure you, as one who himself studied most carefully the topography, botany, and fauna of New Holland in my voyage in 1770 with the peerless Captain Cook* (oh, how pleasant it is to be an authority) *that there is little probability of opposition from the natives to any settlement that we might make.* Banks pauses long enough to make his inquisitors silently ask why he believes this to be the case. *In the entire region of Botanist's Bay (named for my own modest contributions to science), there are only fifty of the naked savages and that might be a high count.* Banks knows his politicians: a little vivid, slightly salacious, detail will keep their attention. *Yes, naked, both men and women. Not so much as a stitch of clothes on their bodies, except some of them wear a woven flax belt that serves them as a cincture to hold small utensils. The women are passable, but never bathe and are covered in dust and grease. The men are the most contemptible creatures. Cowardly, given to stealthy attacks, but always run away when confronted by the countenance of an honest Briton.* Banks realizes that he had better assure the parliamentarians that the naked natives can never be a problem. *In any case, no matter how treacherous they are, it makes no difference. There are so few of them as to make a trifle only. Gentlemen, an entire vast continent is empty. Therefore it is rightfully ours, if we so desire.*

Thus, Joseph Banks became the "father of Australia," at least in nineteenth- and twentieth-century histories. Banks was a singular man, one of great ability in his way, but his Founding Myth came out of the imperial forge. It was the same myth that justified the conquest of Ireland, the rape of the Americas, and the despoiling of Africa, and like all durable myths it was simple:
– the natives are uncivilized at best, sub-human at worst.
– the land is empty: either literally, because there are so few of the natives or, metaphorically, because the indigène waste the land, rather than use it efficiently as Europeans would.
– therefore we have every right to take the place.
Few moving parts: the Founding Myth works almost anywhere.

At the time Banks is giving his testimony to parliament, there are perhaps 300,000 indigène in Australia (no one knows for sure) and they maintain roughly 200 cultures that are strong enough to have their own separate languages.

Not one of the languages has a word for what Banks represents.

KEALAKEKUA BAY, THE SANDWICH ISLANDS (HAWAI'I).
17 FEBRUARY, 1779

Some God

Midshipman George Gilbert watches with vicarious pleasure as the two Irishmen run amok. He does not know their names. Gilbert, a product of a proud naval family – his father had been a ship's master on Cook's second expedition – had found a berth on now-Captain Cook's third voyage almost by hereditary right. The Irish seamen are, in his view, little better than the savages they now were slaughtering. But, oh, he envies them. Two days previously, Captain Cook's inability to comprehend even the simplest rules of indigenous societies had cost Cook his life.

When Cook had first encountered the Hawai'ians (he named their islands the Sandwich group, after yet-another English politician), the natives had prostrated themselves before him. They did so to show him the respect they would give to any great chief. Cook, however, took this greeting, and the elaborate ceremonies associated with it, to mean that the natives believed him to be a god. This is the sort of mistake some Europeans still make.

Thus divinized, Cook left Hawai'i and searched the northwest coast of North America, the Bering Straits, and the coast of Siberia, searching for the Northwest Passage. He then returned to Hawai'i to reprovision.

There, a god or not, he once again failed to understand the rules. Wherever he met Polynesians, he was cheated, because he did not understand that property exists when someone has his hands on it; otherwise it doesn't. So he frequently had been beaten in trading with natives and his response, several times, had been to take a chief hostage until the goods that he defined as stolen were returned. All over the Pacific Ocean he had practised this strategy and it had worked.

The Hawai'ians were a bit different, however. They did not cheat him in trades; he found them the finest, most upright people in all the great ocean. But one night they took a six-oared cutter, which had been left unguarded and, hence, become a free-good.

Furious, Captain Cook had the mouth of the harbour picketed, and then took three cutters full of marines to shore and marched with his three-dozen or so men to the house of the high chief. Cook invited the chief to come on board his vessel, an invitation that was declined. The chief was surrounded by between two and three thousand of his men so, when Cook, unused to having his will frustrated by any human being, lost control of himself, it was ill-advised, extremely. A small fire-fight with the Hawai'ians began and Cook, retreating to the water's edge, caught a metal dagger (one he had traded to the Hawai'ians) in the shoulder and then was clubbed on the head. Immediately his opponents jumped on him and held his head under water for several minutes and then they beat his head upon the rocks. His lifeless form was taken away as a trophy.

Dead silence for half an hour followed among Cook's men when news from shore came of their captain's death. He may not have been a god to the Hawai'ians, but he was some sort of divinity to his officers and men. When one of the Hawai'ians appeared on the beach wearing Cook's jacket and trousers and making obscene gestures, it was barely within the power of the officers to keep the crew from rowing ashore and seeking tribal vengeance.

The Captain's body was distributed to several chiefs on the island: a prize worth sharing. The next day, one group of Hawai'ians with whom the Europeans had been particularly friendly, brought to the ship a peace offering: a basket that contained about five pounds of Captain Cook's flesh.

Two days later, needing to fill their water casks, the crew of the *Discovery* was pelted with rocks as they approached a well. Their officers decided to have the nearby native dwellings burned, as they gave cover to the stone-throwers.

That is the moment when the marines, and especially the two unnamed Irishmen, went berserk. Thirty houses were burned and six Hawai'ians killed.

The two Irishmen cut heads from two of the dead, but still warm, bodies.

They fix the heads to the sterns of two of their six-oared cutters. The heads stare out, with the same blank yet all-seeing eyes that were found in the household gods carved into Polynesian war canoes.

LONDON. 1783

Bow Waves Batter Shoreline

Long after he has left the vicinity, the bow waves of James Cook's 1770 voyage up the east coast of Australia are still striking the shore, some harmlessly and others with unexpected force.

Take the fancy of James Maria Matra. He had been a midshipman on the *Endeavour*, and he sees New South Wales as payback-land for an oppressed people: his own, for Matra was New York-born, one of the thousands of colonists in America who remained loyal to the Crown. What he observes after 1775 is a cruel, mob-driven persecution of the Loyalists. In colony after colony in America, their houses are burned; mobs pelt the men with stones and the women and children with dung; justices of the peace clap Loyalists into gaol for no other reason than their political opinions. Many Loyalists dare not show their faces even in church for fear of public denunciation. Eventually, 80,000 to 100,000 are forced to flee the new republic. But where should they settle permanently? The Crown owes them recompense for their support, surely. Would New South Wales not be perfect? Matra in 1783 writes a pamphlet arguing that southwestern Australia is empty, an immense tract of more than 2,000 miles of shoreline, a land "peopled only by a few black inhabitants," who lead "a mere animal existence." And what a glorious place! Why, with a bit of Chinese or English-poor labour, silk would grow and spices and tobacco and coffee, all in abundance. And, with the coast of Australia peopled by gentry Loyalists from the American colonies and by hard-working, durable peasants, this would be a perfect base to harass England's enemies and, perhaps, even to invade South America.

The other bow-wave from Cook's voyages has real force. Ever since his 1779 appearance before the parliamentary Committee on Transportation, Joseph Banks had pressed for a colony of felons to be created at Botany Bay. As Banks described it, the climate was similar to that of the south of France and the colony would be self-supporting after a year or so.

That was the key, and this idea, like Matra's, was also a result of the American revolution. For the past sixty years, England, Scotland and Ireland had been dumping an average of roughly six to seven hundred felons a year into the American colonies, and now these felons were piling up in disused hulks of ships in various British harbours. That need not be a crisis, for the British Isles had a population of roughly 16,000,000, growing steadily, and could easily have paid for satisfactory land-based prisons. And, if cost were the sole problem, the six or seven hundred felons could have been shipped to the British colonies in the West Indies where the demand for labour was prodigious and where systems of labour supervision (perfected upon slaves) were sufficiently strict.

Banks's plan wins, for he is a skilled advocate. The America Loyalists, roughly 50,000 of them, are offered grants of land in the Canadas, although some choose to return to the British Isles, or to roll down the coast to the Caribbean and try their hand at plantation life.

In 1786 the London government chooses Botany Bay as its solution to felonry in the British Isles. It is the start of a network of colonies in Australia that are founded on meanness of spirit and that yield a culture of resentment. Between the First Fleet's arrival in 1788 and the end of transportation in 1868, roughly 162,000 men, women, and, occasionally, children were shipped involuntarily to Australia.

Captain's Cook's bow-wave abraded the natural shoreline, bared jagged, skin-ripping volcanic out-croppings, destroyed the natural ecology and left ashore the most carnivorous of fauna: felons and their equally ravenous keepers.

AITUTAKI, THE COOK ISLANDS. 11 APRIL 1789

"Wiser, Stronger, and More Benevolent"

"Slavery merely produces more slaves, not more goods for the rest of us." Thus asserted the sailing master.

"You're wrong there, Mr. Christian," his first mate declared. "With respect: it also produces more slave masters."

"And prisons simply yield more prisoners."

"Wrong again: they create places for warders, and that's something I might try in Botany Bay."

Fletcher Christian said nothing. His heart ached. He hungered for his Tahitian "wife": that is what he called her, though they had taken no formal vows, and he meant the term reverently. The recent brief respite, occurring when the *Bounty* had sighted Aitutaki, only made Christian lonelier. The island was quickly added to an admiralty chart – "discovered," in the language of the time. Its name, learned from natives in their small boats, was recorded phonetically: plenty of time to re-name it later, the captain had said. Aitutaki was heartbreaking to Christian, its protected lagoon and miles of white sand reminding him of the out-islands in the Society Group, the British name for what eventually became the centre of French Polynesia.

Christian loathed his present duty. The *Bounty*'s task was to help to shore-up the slave system in the West Indies, which was slipping badly: cane profits dropped after the American revolution opened the way for cut-throat competition, and the damned slaves, they cost too much to maintain, the West Indian plantation owners complained. Have to feed the brutes, even if they're not working. Thus, with the advice of the world's most famous botanist, Sir Joseph Banks (and with his investment as well, for Banks was a wealthy man and intended to become more so), the *Bounty* was detailed to solve this problem.

Breadfruit trees, that was Sir Joseph's answer. One of these South Pacific trees, when transplanted to the West Indies would produce enough to feed a slave for six months. Lovely fruit, Banks asserted, sweet, yellow, soft if picked when ripe. And it could be baked if picked early and turned into the equivalent of a loaf of bread just by being heated. Sovereign stuff, entirely.

The *Bounty* therefore was packed to the gunwales with a thousand or more of these plants, acquired in Tahiti. She was making for the West Indies by way of Cape Horn, and even a hardened soul would have felt fear of that passage and thought of the recent delights of Tahiti. Fletcher Christian was as soft in his centre as a ripe bread fruit. He came of a too-wealthy Isle of Man family – Fletcher's father had been brought up in a forty-two bedroom ramble – and even if slightly reduced in circumstances, Christian had been overly educated for the sea: his schoolmates in the north of England included William Wordsworth. Classically-trained schoolmasters had tuned young Christian to the nuances of words.

"Dog, suttler's whore, duffer's rag, rampike," were words Christian had to endure on this voyage, all barked at close range by Captain William Bligh, whose vocabulary of abuse rivalled any officer in the Royal Navy. Bligh, in his early thirties, was only a dozen years senior to Christian, but he lived in a different universe. Bligh had made his mark as a midshipman in his early twenties by serving on a pirate-and smuggler-catcher in the Irish Sea, and he'd learned not only summary punishment as a nautical policy, but also a fair bit of Irish and Manx abuse. "Feamnach!" he would scream at Christian, comparing him to the common bladderwrack, a seaweed that with its long, drooling chain of bubbles trailed ignominiously across Celtic beaches. Coming from another man, this might have been bearable, even diverting. Bligh, however, possessed an intensity that made him impossible to ignore. Square built in face and body, his skin was unnaturally white and his eyes were an equally unnatural deep blue. Men who had sailed with him on Cook's voyage up the western coast of North America compared Bligh's visage to that of an ice-wolf, white, bare, unblinking.

Fletcher Christian endures for two weeks more, and then the mutiny occurs. Subsequently he and his fellow escapees from Bligh's floating prison wander the Pacific, picking up loved ones in Tahiti and eventually settling on Pitcairn Island, as yet unknown to the mariners of Europe.

By 1808, when American whalers discover the island, only one of the original crew is found alive. Christian, in 1809, is said to have been seen in England, but most likely he was killed earlier in communal strife that spasmodically ran through the little community, like rabies in a population of carnivorous mammals.

Breadfruit, when it eventually is tried on the slaves of the West Indies, is a complete failure. They would rather starve than eat such pap, and several do so before their masters, wisely and benevolently, give up the experiment.

NORFOLK ISLAND. APRIL 1793

Just Business

It was their own choice. The two Maori men were given the alternative of staying aboard the *Shah Hormuzear*, sailing from New South Wales to Calcutta, India, or disembarking at Norfolk Island and doing the job they had been kidnapped to do: they chose to stay near home. And, thereafter, they behaved as model prisoners, although they were not really part of the Pakeha thug and harlot population that was being built on Norfolk.

In fact, they were slaves, and in an Empire that permitted the business of slavery, the capturing of slaves was sometimes a necessary piece of business.

Why, why? they asked each other, what god have we offended, what tapu have we broken? Cousins, in their mid-twenties, both with spiral moko covering their face and bodies, they were fine specimens.

But of what? Why did the white-faced people want these two men? Huru, the taller of the two, was related to the principal chief of Rawhiti, Bay of Islands, and had two wives and a child. The sturdier, Tuki, was from Oruru in the Doubtless Bay area and had a wife and a child and was marked out to be the future tohunga of his iwi. Active, intelligent, young men, they had been visiting below decks on the vessel *Daedalus* when they realized that the ship was sailing. They tried to kick out the aft cabin windows and escape, but were pinioned and bound. As far as they knew, they would never see their land again. They could only hope for a quick death.

Why taken? Because Sir Joseph Banks, the great naturalist, had observed that the Maori were skilled as flax dressers and that there were several places in the Pacific where flax usefully could be grown. Why taken? Because in 1791 George Vancouver, once a midshipman on Cook's second and third voyages, and now an explorer in his own right, sheltered at the tip of Africa just at the moment the Third Fleet on its way to Australia anchored at the Cape of Good Hope. There the new governor of what would become the Norfolk Island penal colony offered Vancouver £100 if he could deliver two Maori to teach flax-working to the convicts. That would keep the convicts busy and would turn a profit for the penal colony. So, Captain Vancouver had his supply ship, the *Daedalus*, which was taking some cattle and other things to Port Jackson, New South Wales, grab the first two Maori its crew members could put their hands on.

Huru and Tuki behaved with dignity beyond heroism. They were shipped to Botany Bay and then transhipped to Norfolk Island. There they taught flax-dressing and learned enough English to be able to explain some aspects of their world to their masters. Each word must have cut them, shards of glass in the mouth, for they believed that they were telling of a land and of families they would never again see.

When, after only six months on Norfolk Island, the two men were returned home, their warders agreed that the captives had been treated kindly.

MEASURING THE LAND OF RESENTMENT.
AUSTRALIA 1768–1793

Contact

"Runs like a filly at a point-to-point."

"That one's more like a bitch in heat."

"I wonder if they spread their tail-feathers like a duck ..."

"And flap their wings, the way a turkey does when it's mounted."

This was one of the few agreeable moments the officers of the First Fleet had: they were watching a covey of young native women who were cavorting before them in a mixture of coquettishness and ridicule. The officers had spent eight months at sea, in filthy tubs of ships, and since their landing in late January 1788, they had little to do except watch the marines watch the convicts who, in turn, watched the ground. It was a sullen place, and anyone with an ounce of sanity stayed as drunk as possible and seized on any amusement the land provided. The Iora people of the coast were worth the naval gents' attention, for they had some interesting ways of spearing fish and of collecting edible crustaceans. And, of course, their daughters ran around buck naked.

Unlike the officers, the convicts were not content to watch the indigène as if they were observing specimens in a zoological garden. Late in May, some convicts killed an Iora tribesman and a week later, two convicts who were cutting rushes for roof-thatch, were speared to death in revenge. Thus the contact-cycle began.

When he goes to recover the bodies of the convicts and the metal tools the men had been using, Governor Arthur Phillip learns quickly that Sir Joseph Banks had been a blatherskite when it came to the Aboriginals. Phillip is met by more than 200 hundred armed black men and they show little fear.

That becomes the pattern. Frequently the officers of the First Fleet and their servants encounter two or three hundred armed Iora. The warriors step silently aside in these confrontations and let the white people pass, but the message is clear: the natives are doing so in courtesy only.

Governor Phillip concludes that there probably are 1,500 natives in the Port Jackson-Botany Bay region. More importantly, he observes smoke as far as fifty miles inland. Cook and Banks were wrong, this is not an empty land.

PORT JACKSON. 25 NOVEMBER 1789

Prize Speciman

Governor Phillip is happy. He now has another indigenous specimen. His previous item had died in May from smallpox. A great pity, that, for the specimen had been perfectly reconciled to being fed and kept by the white men.

Now, Lieutenant William Bradley, a navigator and cartographer by training, has captured two excellent males, fine examples of their sort. Bradley has achieved this by using two large fish as bait. At Collins Flat, Manly, he and some marines in a rowing boat approached several natives on the beach. The two fish were offered as a peace token, and when two of the males bravely stepped forward, the marines seized them, stuffed them into the boat and rowed like fury.

The two native males are fitted with leg irons and each is tethered to a convict. At first they seem content enough, consuming huge amounts of food: twelve pounds of fish at one sitting was the mark each set. One of the natives, a male in his thirties, lulls his keeper to inattention and escapes.

The other, however, stays in custody and seems to love it. His name, Bennelong. He becomes, after Governor Phillip, the best-known character in the penal colony. A stout (and ever-stouter) man of 5'6", in his mid-twenties, he takes to European clothes and European liquor with immense enthusiasm. He acquires western manners quickly and learns English tolerably well. He speaks it better than some of the convicts. Bennelong escapes briefly, but returns of his own accord.

Governor Phillip enjoys Bennelong more than anything or anyone else on this hideous continent. When Bennelong becomes drunk and does acrobatic dances upon the sand, Phillip laughs and says "Go to it old son, dance for the both of us."

Bennelong's head and body are etched with scars, some ornamental, others from battle. Bennelong makes no distinction between domestic and military conflicts: he is especially proud of a set of teeth marks on the back of his neck, where a woman he was stealing from another tribe suddenly became animated and sank her teeth nearly into his spine. "And what did you do then?" Governor Phillip asks. "I knocked her down, beat her senseless, and then carried her home."

Phillip requires that Bennelong sit for long periods at sunset, so that the governor can watch the way the pattern of scars and etching on the black skin varies as the light slowly fails, and, finally, Bennelong is one dark block on a lightless horizon.

NORFOLK ISLAND. AUGUST 1790

Pride of the Second Fleet

Catherine Crowley rocks her baby with a rhythm that duplicates the below-decks roll of an ocean-going sailing ship. She is on land, but for the rest of her life her soul will never leave the fetid hold of the Second Fleet.

She is still a pretty woman, but when she walks she has the spread-legged gait of a drunk: she never loses the sea-legs she acquired in the almost unendurable passage round half the world. Still, Catherine had done better than most. Hasn't she picked up a gentleman for a husband and has a baby boy as well?

In truth, not a husband, for he never marries her, but he does visit her occasionally while they are on Norfolk Island.

He, D'Arcy Wentworth, is not a prisoner, although he came very close to being one. Descended from Protestant colonizers who had jumped into the Irish midlands during the reign of King Charles II, he counted among his present day relatives (distant ones to be sure) the Marquis of Rockingham, the Earl of Strafford, and the Earl Fitzwilliam. "A great people, we are," D'Arcy Wentworth often said and on Norfolk Island there were not many with comparable bloodlines.

Wentworth is the surgeon for the penal island, despite decidedly thin medical qualifications. "What does it take to remove a leg, anyway?" he had once asked. "Give me a saw for my hand and a bullet for the patient to bite on."

D'Arcy Wentworth's family had been on a long slide. His grandfather was a failed barrister who had lost the family lands and his own father had been reduced to running a public house in Portadown. D'Arcy Wentworth's sole capital in the world was his imposing height, good looks, and natural charm. He had learned his medicine in his early twenties in the First Armagh Company of the Irish Volunteers, an almost-entirely Protestant regiment that favoured Catholic Emancipation and a medley of other semi-radical causes. The Volunteers had given Wentworth shirt-tail membership in decent society, and when in the mid 1780s he went to London to finish his medical apprenticeship, he traded on these connections and on his distant kinship with the noble Fitzwilliams.

The expenses of even a medical-gentleman were excessive and he took to highway robbery to cover his shortfall. Of amazingly cheerful disposition, D'Arcy was caught and charged three times in 1787. He took it all as just part of the dance of life and was two times acquitted and the third time let go for lack of prosecutorial evidence.

And he went back to the pistol and the silk handkerchief over his face, and was caught again in 1789. This time the evidence was strong enough that he was forced to cut a deal: he agreed to sail as surgeon with the Second Fleet of felons being sent to Australia. In return, he would go as a free man, with no criminal past. En route to Australia he enjoyed Catherine Crowley, a lovely and lively twenty-one-year-old English shoplifter, and who knows how many other female prisoners.

Settled on Norfolk Island, D'Arcy Wentworth lived in the officers' quarters and drew full rations. Catherine and her growing brood were housed separately and drew prisoners' victuals. She gives birth to two more sons.

D'Arcy Wentworth loved more than anything his own family lineage. When he was appointed to serve as prison surgeon at Parramatta on the mainland, he took Catherine and his three sons with him. She died in 1800 and D'Arcy started a second family with another mistress.

Soon thereafter, the three Wentworth sons were sent to England to be educated as gentlemen.

They were not told of their father's near-felon past, nor of their own illegitimacy, nor of their mother's felonry. They were told only of the ancestral glories of the Wentworths and of the Fitzwilliams and that this glory was theirs to recover.

PORT STEPHENS. SEPTEMBER 1790

Flying Squadron

The sun cracks the skin of the men rowing. The backs of their hands reticulate with tiny fissures through which blood seeps, forms tiny scabs, then seeps again. Their foreheads have peeled so completely that their colour resembles that of boiled lobsters. Despite their tying kerchiefs around their necks, like the hackles of a domestic rooster, the unforgiving sun has turned their necks and throats livid.

These five men are among the first successful escapees from Parramatta. They have seized a six-oared boat that some marines left unguarded and with no food and no navigational equipment have rowed in a hallucinogenic fury northwards. North, indeed, but it could have been any direction, anything away from constant abuse and the promise of slow starvation. Somehow they make it past Port Stephens and find a safe harbour that they perceive to be uninhabited. Exhausted, they let the tide carry them ashore.

The two leaders, George Lee and George Connoway are Irish. One of the other three soon dies. The four convicts who remain are barely alive and no threat to anyone.

Five years later, an English ship, the *Providence*, sailing from Brazil to Port Jackson, is driven off course and makes Port Stephens. A rowing boat with four naked white men comes out to the anchored vessel and they are let on board. They are unwashed, their skin the colour of dried meat and they give off such a feff that the English captain insists on their remaining on deck and downwind.

The ability of the men to speak English has diminished somewhat and they speak a dialect of their own, comprised of English as they had foreshortened it among themselves, interlarded with scores of aboriginal words. As the captain of the *Providence* slowly winkled their story out of them, it was simplicity itself, despite its bizarre details. The escapees had been fed and protected for five years by the members of a seashore tribe. This with no hesitation by the natives: the refugees had been thrown upon the shore from the mouth of the sea and that made their protection an imperative. So the refugees had been given wives, and food (which, being alien in character almost killed them at first), and tribal names. The white men lived with the tribe in amity and came to admire the peaceful nature of this seashore clan: and when hostilities with other tribes occurred, the white men were told to keep out of harm's way.

Soon thereafter, the four escapees were shipped to Norfolk Island. There they were rarely allowed to speak to each other, but occasionally they would encounter one another out of range of a guard, and in their private creole they would murmur brief words about the good old days.

DUBLIN. 4 JUNE 1793

Cold Type

The editor of the Dublin *Chronicle* knows what his readers want: a front page full of advertisements and inside pages full of English gossip. The Irish news they can obtain elsewhere. He picks out from the London broadsheets an item concerning Governor Arthur Phillip who had left Australia in December 1792, glad to never again have to see an endless beach or to be served by any functionary more frightening than a bath chair attendant. The *Chronicle*'s editor senses that the following London news item will be found amusing in Dublin drawing rooms and coffee houses. "Governor Phillip has brought home with him two of the natives of New Holland, a man and a boy, and brought them to town. The *Atlantic* has also on board four kangaroos, lively and healthy, and some other animals peculiar to that country."

There the original item ends, but the Irish middle class needs a bit more to chew on. The editor adds his own commentary. "From the description given of the natives of Port Jackson, they appear to be a race totally incapable of civilisation, every attempt to that end having proved ineffectual and yet they discover an astonishing art and cunning in their mode of fishing and entrapping the kangaroo and birds, the only animals found there."

Part of the story was true. Bennelong had been brought to England by Governor Phillip. It was only for a year's stay, the governor promised. A youth also accompanied them, Yemmerrawanie.

Bennelong was introduced to King George III. He found St. James Palace cold and draughty, just like everyplace else in England. He and Yemmerrawanie were quartered in London, Bath, Eltham in Kent, and, finally, for six months aboard the ship that was supposed to take them home.

Yemmerrawanie never left England. The damp and cold overcame him and he died in May 1794 of a pulmonary condition. His burial place was the parish church yard in Eltham.

There the excessive amount of cold-chiselling required to incise his name on his gravestone later was a matter of some bemusement to Charles Stewart Parnell who, in the 1880s spent a good deal of time walking about Eltham, waiting for the husband of Mrs O'Shea, his mistress, to leave "Wonersh Lodge," the family home.

Attention Deficit

Richard Bourke, eighteen years of age, listens to two men argue. He is in the London house of one of his relatives and the study door is open and there, throughout the night, two lions roar at each other. One is James Mackintosh, Scottish intellectual in an age when that was a compliment, and now a London barrister. Four years earlier he had vigorously written against Edmund Burke's *Reflections on the French Revolution*, and now he is arguing, with less and less conviction, against Burke in person.

Richard Bourke, as befits a man who eventually will become governor of New South Wales, falls asleep and misses one of the great intellectual conversions of the era. Macintosh, a big man intellectually, recognizes that Burke is a giant. He leaves Burke's house shortly before dawn, convinced of the great Irishman's view that violent revolution is a mistake.

Return of the Native

Bennelong steps onto the lighter that transports passengers from Governor John Hunter's ship to the shore. He is in the second cohort to be brought ashore. He sits alongside the ship's surgeon, George Bass, and each is in full dress uniform, Bennelong's being an unofficial version of royal navy wear. A notable difference is that as the lighter is being rowed ashore, Bennelong takes off his shoes and stockings.

"He conducts himself as a man of consequence," a sympathetic observer wrote. Perhaps, but Bennelong was a man being chased by an avalanche of consequences. He was given a room at the governor's house and for his first weeks home was frequently at table and his European manners were excellent.

With his brothers and sisters he is at first imperious, lecturing them on being peaceful and on the need for cleanliness. He goes to find his wife and discovers that she is under the protection of another man.

The two men argue, and Bennelong gets his wife back, and a spear in his back as well. Drink, one of the reasons he had been willing to live with Europeans, remains his tether.

Increasingly, however, he slurs his words. Now, each day he takes off all his clothes and goes away with his family. At night he returns, dresses carefully, and takes as much drink as he can.

Soon he is staying in the bush for days on end, and then he returns to "civilization" for several days' bingeing. In the autumn of 1796 he turns up at the governor's residence with his face deformed: he had lost a fight with his former best-friend. His mouth is cruelly misshaped, his front teeth missing and his upper lip permanently split.

Bennelong, a walking victim, spent the rest of his life alternating, like the phases of the moon. He would spend weeks in the bush, where he maintained a family, and then would return to Sydney, put on clothes and demand food and rum. His demands were always met, despite his becoming aggressive and menacing when in his cups. When he died in January 1813, no European had much good to say for him and he was used as a proof that the natives could never be civilized.

He was buried in the garden of the proprietor of the Colonial Brewery, which seemed fair enough.

SYDNEY. FEBRUARY 1796

Just Grievances

"There, that's done with. They'll always try to cheat an Irishman. God knows they'll try." Michael Hogan, a stocky man in his mid-thirties, was walking victorious out of the government building. "And the acquittal was so obvious that we scarce needed to meet. They only charged me because they cannot tolerate an Irishman being successful."

That was Hogan's perpetual phrase – "they'll always try to cheat an Irishman" – and he repeated it more often than he did his prayers. In his native Cork, he had uttered it whenever he talked about the convict trade with Australia. Why, he wanted to know, were the authorities in London transporting to Australia all those English convicts and so few Irish? He counted only three ships of thirty-eight having been from Irish ports. Why couldn't he, a master mariner, obtain one of those profitable commands? "They always try to cheat the Irish."

Finally, Hogan was named master of the *Marquis Cornwallis* and he sailed, with his wife and two children, in mid-1795. He was a harsh captain, so rough that a sergeant and some of the soldiers of the New South Wales Corps joined the convicts in a mutiny. Hogan unhesitatingly used grape shot and put the sergeant and others he wounded into chains. They died. "As so they should," Hogan later told the inquiry held into his behaviour. "They thought they could cheat me because I am Irish. Ha!"

After his exoneration, Michael Hogan obtained a lucrative contract with the London authorities, taking cattle from the Cape of Good Hope in Africa to Sydney. Then, using Cape Town as his base, he became a partner in a big firm of British merchants engaged in a quasi-legal slave trade. In 1800 he showed up in Cape Town with four shiploads of slaves, and claimed that these had been captured from the French. That was legal under the rules of war but, in fact, Hogan had bought the slaves in Mozambique, and that was not. Again, Hogan went before an official inquiry and again he escaped punishment.

Michael Hogan, having worn out the Southern Hemisphere – they always try to cheat the Irish there – made one last run to Peru and then settled in New York, where he died in 1833.

His son became a New York congressman whose political career was based on representing the immigrant Irish. He warned them that they had to be on their guard constantly, "Otherwise, they'll always cheat the Irish."

THE SOUTH PACIFIC. 1797–99

More Dry Numbers

Fine. So, perhaps one out of every ten captains in slave trade was Irish. And that was the top end of the eighteenth-century trade: very profitable indeed. The proportion in the less-remunerative maritime sectors probably was higher.

Fine again. But the really important numbers are big and invisible. For every Irish captain in the imperial commercial web there were many ordinary seaman, able seamen, carpenters, cooks, cabin boys and mates. What was the multiple? Call it ten, call it twenty, there is no way of knowing.

Of the captains we know something. In the usual case they returned to their home port at the end of a voyage, so usually their stories have a collective and cyclical quality. The everyday stories of the Irish crewmen, however, were part of a pattern whose coordinates were known only by each individual.

Take two straightforward seamen. They are Munstermen, ordinary seaman Michael Murphy and able seaman Thomas Lee. They sail out of Bristol in one of the scores of ventures to scoop the treasures of the South Pacific which follow upon Captain Cook's voyages. Murphy and Lee sail under Captain Charles Bishop and they sign on for a trip that will centre on Norfolk Island. The captain's goal is to gain a cargo of oil rendered from seals and also the seal pelts. Murphy signs on for 1/140th of the total value of the cargo, Lee for 1/120th.

The two Irishmen are just as much gamblers in commerce and speculators in empire as are the Bristol ship owners. They, and tens of thousands of Irish merchant seamen over the eighteenth and nineteenth centuries, bet their lives, and that is as high a wager as a gambler can lay.

Lee and Murphy are good seamen and they are given their discharge and pay-off without difficulties or deductions. But why do they choose to take their rewards in Port Jackson (soon to be renamed Sydney), Australia? This in late 1798 (in Lee's case) and in the spring of 1799 (Murphy's.) Are they waiting for another vessel to sign on to? Or are they among the earliest European prospectors for fortune in Australia – those who understand that, for free men, the penal colonies in Australia offer great opportunities, not least because small kingdoms can be built with convict labour?

COUNTY WEXFORD. 1798

One Tune Playing

The sound, once heard, is never forgotten.

It cannot be reproduced, only remembered.

The scraping of a surgeon's saw as it amputates a shattered leg, accompanied by the inarticulate gurgling harmony of the victim's throat-sounds. The patient bites on a spoon. Otherwise, in his pain, he would amputate his own tongue.

Thomas Murray has been taken to a small cabin by his comrades. A yeomanry musket ball has shattered his leg and it has to be sawn off if he is to live. Terence Murray, his youngest son, holds a lantern, but he is so stricken by his father's condition that the lantern wavers, as if on a ship at sea, and the small blocks of light it casts swirl from wall, to floor, to wall inside the mud cabin.

Thomas Murray reaches out and takes the lantern from his son. He holds it steady for the duration of the operation.

SYDNEY COVE. 1799

The Laws of the Bazaar Are Bizarre

Two old sergeants of the Rum Corps watch a quayside auction. Officially, they are in the New South Wales Corps, the British army unit that keeps order in the colony. Everyone knows the soldiery as the Rum Corps because, for a brief time in the 1790s the administration was so impoverished that the soldiers received their pay in alcohol. ("Rum" covers every kind of fortified or distilled liquor). And now the Corps controls the illegal spirits trade.

The old veterans are observing just for entertainment. They are already well supplied with the product on sale. The crowd's comments and bidding are good for a laugh.

One of bidders comments sardonically, "that one has a Tipperary Dowry." Everyone laughs. This is an auction of women. Those who don't wish to be put out to domestic service or to work carding and spinning wool in the Female Factory at Parramatta, have an alternative: they can rent or sell themselves to the highest bidder or to a male syndicate. "Too right: a Tipperary Dowry: two townlands, stream's town and ballinocack; that's her fortune."

Such auctions, though never officially sanctioned, continue until 1810 when most of the officers and many of the men of the Rum Corps return to England. The basic situation, though, changes little for decades, because men outnumber women roughly three-to-one in the convict population and when free immigration becomes important, mostly single males choose to come to Australia.

"Peculiar thing," one of the old sergeants muses, "If there were more women, they'd be worth less, but be a lot happier."

"Oh?"

"I mean, were there more women, there wouldn't be so much mott-jumping and passing them around like valuable trinkets."

He is right: it might be a good thing for a woman to be a slightly-scarce entity, for that would improve her bargaining position in choosing a mate and in household arrangements and the like. But once a certain threshold is reached, women become rare enough to be treated like any other valuable commodity: bid for, stolen, bought collectively. A woman without a male protector in Australia was as vulnerable as a jade vase in a glass window.

"The Irish girls, they're the most value. It's all such a surprise to them." Almost 60 percent of the female convicts sent to New South Wales were Irish (Irish men were less than one-third of the felons).

The "surprise," if such it was, started on the long journey. Each sailor was permitted, as if by common law right, one women convict for his use. On shore, the eight companies of the Rum Corps were each allotted ten women to serve the lower ranks and ten more were allocated to the officers.

Other women who were sent out to domestic service often were abused and instances of their being traded for £5 sterling or for a gallon of rum were recorded. None of this, of course, went into the official reports that were sent to London.

The colonial administration desperately wanted women, as a means of civilizing the men. A convict woman who showed she had any personal fortune at all – a few pounds – usually was given her ticket of leave immediately upon arrival. Normally when a female convict married a fellow convict, they both were given their tickets of leave. And male convicts could have their wives from the Old Country join them, always provided they could afford passage.

The few middle class women in the free population (the daughters or sisters of various officials, usually) were treated like royalty.

Irish girls and women, if they were lucky, found space in the Female Factory. Even then, it was a risky business, for dormitory space existed for only a third of the prisoners. The remainder had to earn the cost of their private lodging by selling themselves.

NEW SOUTH WALES. 1800

The Physics of the Land of Resentment

Essay two successive thought-experiments, each with only one conjectural part.

The first: a 1959 graduate of Fordham University Law School, a founder of a local chapter of the Capital Punishment Society, is sent to study the sentencing and incarceration principles of New South Wales in the year 1800. To his surprise, he finds them much softer than those prevailing in his own state and in U.S. federal legislation and practice. He is surprised to find that most of the Australian felons, though they are multiple offenders, are sentenced only for their final crime (grabbing a watch or whatever) and that they receive short sentences: seven years, with the possibility of commutation to ticket-of-leave after four years of good behaviour. When fully emancipated three years later, they are eligible for forty acres of free land. And these felons spend most of their time in the open air. Most of them aren't incarcerated. Mostly, they work for local farmers, though a minority are kept on government projects, such as roads. And though a quarter of the convicts are lifers, they are usually given tickets-of-leave after eight years of satisfactory behaviour. Scores of the offenders – especially the Irish who arrive in 1800 and after – would have been hanged for treason if they had lived in the U.S. in the era of Joseph McCarthy of blessed memory. What a soft system! The place is speckled with men (always it's men) who have plea-bargained their way out of treason charges and, by agreeing to be taken to New South Wales, arrive without a conviction on their record. Upon arrival in Australia they have the legal right to be treated as free men, to obtain land grants and to mix with the quality, if such there be. Talk about a country-club prison! And forget the usual restrictions on conjugal visits. Prisoners can bring their wives and families with them, and just getting married usually gets a seven-year man his ticket. These people should see Attica! And even the lifers are constantly receiving full pardons from the governors for doing some administrative job or other that really should be done by a paid federal employee. Executive summary: this soft a system won't cut down on crime at all.

The second. Envision one of those revolving bird-cages that were used in eighteenth-century gaming houses to play an early form of Lotto. One could bet on the colour of ball to come out or the number on a ball or sequence of balls. Naturally, the odds on what would come out were influenced by what one put in (if five out of six balls were red, probably a red ball would be the winner), but nothing is certain. That's the way Australia as a prison system worked: you knew what you were supposed to get, but the odds could desert you and almost anything could be your fate. The system was insanely badly managed in its first decade: near starvation for the inmates (now where was that on the sentencing menu?) and records were so badly kept that a person could serve a full-seven year sentence and then be told that there was no record of his being here, much less having done his time. When the administration straightened out, it was replaced by efficient random terror. What your life was like depended largely on the luck-of-the-draw: were you assigned to a reasonable farmer or a decent construction boss, or did you become the pissing post for a real sadist? Did you mock too obviously the governor and his social circle? That, or a thousand other petty infractions could get you sent to Norfolk Island which was used (from 1788–1813 and from 1825-to-the-1850s) as a Devil's Island. There the level of official sadism was so great that prisoners sometimes made judicial suicide pacts: one would agree to kill the other, the first man finding immediate release through death, the second his own through the hangman.

Soft time? Hard time?

Both, actually, depending on the draw.

To create a system that prescribed a condign and predictable punishment, and then altered it by arbitrary and random means, was a perfect recipe for rebellion in the short run; and a prescription in the longer run for a national culture of resentment.

SYDNEY. JANUARY 1800

A Nose for Sedition

The New South Wales Corps had seen enough convicts stagger ashore to be accustomed to the spectacle. Now, though, they watched attentively. The first ship containing Irish rebels, transported for being part of the 1798 Rising, had arrived. Three hundred, roughly, (all men) arrive in 1800 and a total of 500 Irish political prisoners by 1806, their highpoint in the colony. Most Irish transportees to Australia were decent ordinary criminals – a close tally has found that fewer than 600 political prisoners were sent in the entire history of Australia as a penal colony. That is, 1 ½ percent of the Irish total.

The authorities smelled trouble, however; literally, according to the Rev. Samuel Marsden, Church of England chaplain of New South Wales. He watched the *Minerva* unload its human cargo, and he stood as close as he could to the Irish convicts as they shuffled on to land, and he sniffed. Not tentatively, but the way a bloodhound does when it is casting for a trail. There was a miasma of evil coming off these men. Of course they were wrapped in an olfactory fog of unwashed human odours, ammoniac smells of urine, and tattered clothes half-rotted by the half year or so at sea. Behind all that, Marsden scented sedition.

The chaplain pressed the governor and the military to be vigilant. By mid-August, he had witnessed several shiploads arrive and had heard from his informers that a rebellion was afoot.

It should have been, at least among the Irish ordinary-decent-criminals already in New South Wales, for the records of the seven-year criminals who had been sent out in 1791–93 from Ireland had been lost. They all should have served out their sentences, but were kept in the system, and very bitter they were.

The flint to spark this tinder was missing. The Irish political prisoners were a disparate group and their long voyages had neither enspirited nor united them. They ranged from red-hot sectarians who had been in the Wexford Rising merely as a chance to kill Protestants, to the Protestant "General" Joseph Holt who came with his wife and family and, as a gentleman, was not expected to be flogged or made to act in a servile fashion; three Catholic priests were included, plus schoolmasters, several graduates of Trinity College, Dublin, as well as a mob of illiterate farmers' labourers. It was too soon for these men to coalesce, if ever they would.

As chief inquisitor, the Rev. Mr. Marsden was a small-time Torquemada. His method was to listen to informants (any prison system will produce inmates who are willing to tell the authorities whatever they want to hear), and then to have the Irish suspects flogged. Men such as William Maum, Maurice Fitzgerald, Patrick Galvin, received three to five hundred lashes with the cat. At times Joseph Holt, Richard

Dry and other suspects, were made to watch the proceedings, to encourage their own volubility. Holt recalled being fifteen yards downwind of Fitzgerald, and as the man's shoulders were flayed into mince, skin, blood, and chunks of flesh blew into Holt's face.

It smelled for all the world like fate.

CORK CITY. 10 AUGUST 1801

Sentimental Journey

"The condition upon which God hath given liberty to man is eternal vigilance." So spoke the great Irish barrister and defender of liberty, John Philpot Curran, in 1790.

A bit more than ten years later he is involved in a case in which an Irish judge sentences a man to death, but commutes the sentence to transportation to New South Wales. This is the John Philpot Curran who served as defence counsel for Wolfe Tone, William Drennan and other United Irishmen of 1798. Has he lost another stacked case? another instance of imperial justice crushing an Irish hero?

Indeed not. Curran is delighted with the verdict. He has been acting as the lead barrister in a squad of seven prosecutors, who have been battling a team of nine defending barristers. And Curran has brought down Sir Henry Browne Hayes, Ireland's most famous non-political criminal of the day.

Just at the time in 1790 when Curran was fighting for the city of Dublin's historical political rights, Henry Hayes was selected sheriff of the city of Cork. He became thereby a High Sheriff of the County and was given a knighthood. Hayes was twenty-eight at the time and had been married for six years to a one-eyed heiress who rejoiced in a considerable fortune and a family house named, transAtlantically, "Mount Vernon."

Sir Henry's lady wife died in 1794, leaving him with four children. Sir Henry, still in his early thirties, set out to find another heiress. Unhappily, as John Philpot Curran scathingly explained, in 1797 Sir Henry took a shortcut in his courting, and kidnapped a Quaker heiress, worth £20,000. (Rich Quakers were fairly thick on the ground in County Cork.) He put her through a mock wedding and then assaulted her.

In court, John Philpot Curran was too circumspect to state whether or not the attempted rape was successful, but Miss Pike (such was her name) was emotionally smashed. She fled to England for two years. Whatever the physical events, she was ruined for life.

Sir Henry is everything Curran despises. Boastful, bullying, an officer in the local militia, one of the enemies of 1798. So secure is the Protestant Ascendancy after 1798 that Sir Henry, despite a £1,000 reward on his head (half put up by the Pike family) walks about Cork City unmolested until, in a moment of extreme hubris, he decides that, since he certainly will be acquitted by a jury of his peers, he might as well turn himself in.

"In faith my good fellow, why don't you turn me up and have the £1,000." So suggests Sir Henry to his barber. "You've always given me a close shave."

John Philpot Curran is too much of a gentleman to smile when he later reads that Sir Henry, like many an Irish rebel, has been transported to the Antipodes for having had a Pike in his possession.

NORFOLK ISLAND. 1802

The Silent Brotherhood

No birds' songs could be heard in the prisoners' barracks. The pine forest had been cleared far back, so that the sounds of incarceration were all artificial: metal grinding on metal; doors being slammed and latched; the heels of the guards' boots on gravel.

On work details, the men were forbidden to speak to each other and any human contact, such as passing a plug of tobacco to a mate, produced 100 lashes on the triangle. Work began at 5: 00 a.m and twenty-five lashes met anyone who was a moment late. Letters to and from the outside world were prohibited.

For five years, 1800 through 1804, Joseph Foveaux ran the island as lieutenant-governor in title and as the most sadistic of gods in practice. He had found pikes, a hundred or so, in December of 1800 and this was evidence of a real Irish rebellion in the making (the Sydney authorities having packed the island with those they feared most). Foveaux devoted his term of office to breaking every man (and the few unfortunate women) in the population, and, if necessary killing them inch by inch.

A brotherhood emerges, not always predictable. D'Arcy Went-worth, gentleman highway robber and surgeon on the island, saves the life of "General" Joseph Holt who was being killed by overwork. Patrick Galvin, Maurice Fitzgerald, Richard Dry, nearly flogged to death in Sydney, now silently break rocks and occasionally catch each other's eye. Later, just after Foveaux returns to England for a sabbati-cal, they are joined by William Maum.

Norfolk Island slowly runs down and is closed, in 1813. It is re-placed as a locale for "secondary punishments" (read: very hard time) by Van Diemen's Land.

Nobody who has been ensilenced on Norfolk Island ever is the same. The men who have survived it go their separate ways, and keep their scars covered, out of sight of the generality. When they en-counter each other, they do not talk of their hard times, but instead salute each other with the quick, sidelong glance that they learned in the silent prison.

"VAUCLUSE," NEW SOUTH WALES. 1803

Levitation

He has no idea that he is heading for Norfolk Island. Instead, Sir Henry Brown Hayes, conscious more than ever that he is an Irish gentleman, rusticates. He has built one of the premier residences in New South Wales. Though still a convict – a term he refuses to allow to be applied to himself: he is "suffering under law," he says – he has purchased 150 acres and is spending over £2,000 constructing his residence. Right now he is watching his workmen deal with the snake problem.

Sir Henry is a great worry to the authorities: mostly because he re-fuses to grant them authority. He protests whenever he is referred to as a felon and he makes it clear that he believes the governor and his staff are mere tradesman. He has the ability to levitate above reality that distinguishes the Anglo-Irish gentry at their apogee.

Residual money helps, of course. Sir Henry had given £200 to the cap-tain of the ship that transported him to New South Wales and that permit-ted him to bring as many of his possessions as he wished, to have private accommodation shipboard, and to dine and drink with the captain throughout the voyage. Sir Henry did not speak to the felons on board.

With about £5,000 in specie in pocket, Sir Henry lives well enough, for he spreads his money about shrewdly. No revolutionary, certainly, but still a worry to the authorities: the more so because Sir Henry is a Free Mason, and he has a warrant from the Irish grand-lodge to start a lodge in the Antipodes. He asks for permission to do so from the governor and is told, no, absolutely not. And quite rightly, for Irish masonry in 1803 was not the anti-revolutionary body it became in the 1830s. True, many masons were influential and respectable gentle-man and government officials (no comfort there for someone trying to run a penal colony and to avoid outside criticism). Yet the Masons were also the home of many front edge political critics, and, this was in the days before the Pope condemned the organization. Daniel O'Connell was a Mason, and so were many Protestant businessmen of the radical sort: men who had founded the United Irishmen.

Sir Henry ignores the penal authorities' disapproval and his Free Mason's lodge becomes a talking shop for some of the best educated of the colony's prisoners and emancipists. Sir Henry pays the govern-ment no more mind than he would a gorse hedge that one would jump on a west Munster fox hunt.

For the moment, he concentrates intensely on his system of snake-proofing. All around Vauclause House he has had the convicts whom he employs dig a trench, six feet wide and two feet deep. Seventy-five men are employed at this, hired from the Superintendent of Convicts.

Now they are completing the job. Sir Henry has had a shipload of turf sent from Ireland. It costs him a fair bit of his capital, but he knows it will be worth it. The convicts are filling in the moat with the snake-repellant soil of Ireland, and Sir Henry believes that when they are done his life will be in order.

NR. PARRAMATTA. APRIL 1804

Family Names

Major George Johnston, English, the most competent officer in the Rum Corps, looks into the eyes of William Johnston, Irish, the most courageous of the rebels who, in March 1804, make into a unique reality the dozens of plans for a rising that float around the penal colonies.

The Irish rise in early March, and lose in a fashion that is virtually liturgical and unconsciously suicidal. Why else would they call the place of battle "Vinegar Hill," after the site in County Wexford of the decisive rebel defeat in 1798? Why, though holding the tactical high ground and outnumbering the government forces (two thirds of whom are untrained volunteers) roughly three-to-one, do the Irish parlay rather than fight?

George Johnston had first looked into the eyes of William Johnston when two men had come forward at Vinegar Hill as spokesmen for the rebels. The major saw indecision. He immediately pulled a pistol, as did his aide, and William Johnston and his mate were marched to the government lines. Major Johnston understood full well that a snake without a head is just a piece of rope. When the two Irish rebel leaders were captured, the men on Vinegar Hill did nothing to save them. Major Johnston then ordered his own men to fire and the battle turned into the sport of hare coursing.

Four days later, Major Johnston again looks into the eyes of William Johnston and this time he sees courage: at court martial, Johnston is the only one of ten captured rebels who does not whine or deny. He states in a clear voice exactly what he had done and why. The major admires that.

In respect, therefore, Major Johnston has several times come to the spot outside Parramatta where from a tree the body of William Johnston has been suspended in chains, following his execution by the hangman. The stench is ferocious, but nothing that a veteran soldier isn't accustomed to. Major Johnston looks into the eyes of his close acquaintance and reflects that it's a wonder, really, that the birds haven't broken the panes of those clear, unblinking windows.

SYDNEY AND DUBLIN. 1805

No Fares Are Charged

The Shipping News:

13 July 1805: three troublemakers are sentenced to a stint on Norfolk Island: Sir Henry Browne Hayes; William Maum, who had been flailed almost to death after the putative 1800 Irish prisoners' rising but had kept clear of the authorities since then; and Maurice Margarot, a Scottish republican radical who was a member of Sir Henry's

Free Mason lodge. The magistrates cannot find direct evidence of these three having been involved in planning the 1804 Vinegar Hill Rising, but surmise, rightly, that they had been all in favour of it and had encouraged the participants. Of course there's no charge for shipping them to Norfolk, but the authorities specify that these men are not to be maintained at government expense: a euphemism for sentencing them to forced labour. The trio's only good fortune is that all of them are off the island in less than a year.

25 July 1805. Michael Dwyer, destined to be celebrated as the greatest Irish patriot to be buried in Australia, boards a small convict ship in Dublin Bay. He and a handful of his followers are taken to Cork and transferred to a larger convict ship. Dwyer has been the most successful of all the leaders of the 1798 Rising, for he did not surrender until late 1803. For more than four years he and a score of followers continued a guerilla war in the Wicklow Mountains. When he surrenders, it is part of an elaborate plea-bargain. He agrees to be transported to the United States of America, but as a free man, not as a felon. And his family is to accompany him. Further, while waiting in Kilmainham gaol he is to have his own first class cell, his family with him, and a pint of spirits a day. The Irish government, of course, breaks its agreement. First, Dwyer's spirits allowance is cut in half and then (as they did earlier with "General" Joseph Holt who also had been promised America) the authorities don't send him to America after all, but to Australia. Still, he and his wife and his five followers and their spouses are not berthed with the convicts. And, as free men, each of the Wicklow men is granted 100 acres of land west of Sydney. It's hard land, granted, and the former-guerillas are not accustomed to regular manual labour. Fortunately, "General" Joseph Holt comes out to teach them farming. And each of the republican patriots is given two convicts to do the really hard labour for them.

NEW SOUTH WALES. 1806–10

Bonding Agent

Say what you like, Captain William Bligh brought people together. He arrived as governor of New South Wales 7 August 1806 and did a lovely job of welding fragmented enemies into opposition phalanxes. He did this with the Irish Catholics by buying the Rev. Samuel Marsden's line that all Irish Catholics were a cabal of drunkenness, riot, and sedition. Never mind that four of the nine rebel leaders hanged for the 1804 rebellion, including William Johnston, were Protestant. Although Michael Dwyer and his compatriots were staying out of politics and trying to earn a quiet living in May 1807, he charged them with treasonable conspiracy. So weak was the case that a jury composed of the Judge Advocate of the New South Wales Corps and six officers declared the charges "perfectly false," about as powerful an acquittal as one can obtain this side of heaven. Again, never mind: Bligh had Dwyer and the others transported to Norfolk Island and then to Van Diemen's Land.

And Bligh bonded the other side as well. The New South Wales Corps was knee deep in corruption, certainly, and it had a near-monopoly on most of the black economy of the colony, but at least it supported the governmental authorities. Until Bligh. So roughly does he move on their trade, especially in spirits, that the unthinkable occurs: the Corps arrests him and takes over government of the colony. This in January 1808.

The Fletcher Christian of this coup was George Johnston (recently promoted to lieutenant-colonel), who had saved the colony during the Irish rebellion of 1804.

Bligh, the fabulous psychopath, not only converted the colony's best soldier into a revolutionary, he somehow managed to turn Sir Henry Browne Hayes from being a full-time troublemaker into a paladin of authority. Sir Henry, back from Norfolk Island and Van Diemen's Land, defended the governor and for his troubles the Rum Corps sends Hayes to digging coal in the Newcastle prison mines. (Eventually, when the Rum Corps were brought to heel, Bligh granted Hayes a full pardon, one that permitted him to return to Ireland.)

Although Captain Bligh never regained full control of New South Wales (other officials ran satrapies until a new governor arrived in 1810), he was rewarded by being promoted rear-admiral in 1811: thus confirming that if one cannot be highly successful, the next best thing is to be a huge failure.

William Bligh's greatest legacy to New South Wales was his daughter, a military widow. She was famous in Sydney society for wearing dresses cut so low that she frequently had to pop a breast back under cover. Brassy, argumentative, beautiful, she was unwilling to admit that her father had ever made a mistake. Just before she was to return with her father to England in May 1810, she accepted a proposal of marriage from the lieutenant-governor of the colony, Colonel Maurice O'Connell.

Yes. Maurice O'Connell of the Kerry clan, distant cousin of Daniel O'Connell, the Liberator. Maurice O'Connell whose education in France had been paid for by General Count Daniel O'Connell, one of the great Catholic resisters to the Irish penal laws. Major-General (1830) Sir (1834) Maurice O'Connell who spent his life furthering the Empire, and during three tours of command in New South Wales did a fine job of keeping the croppies quiet.

William Bligh brought people together: didn't he just.

GEORGE'S RIVER DISTRICT, NSW. 1810

Cultural Camouflage

A great pity that Charles Darwin, who later traverses one of the farms that Michael Dwyer had owned, never met the man. They could have had a fine discussion of the concepts of protective cover and of adaptive colouration. Dwyer had been a successful guerilla leader in Ireland because he always fit in and every reminiscence of him is the same: "a fine man;" "decent;" "never did any harm that wasn't required"; "you could trust him with the Crown jewels." Yet, details just slipped away. He was like a snowy owl on a winter hillside, all outline and no details.

Dwyer had stood before Lieutenant Col. George Johnston twice and each time Johnston had seen an honest and principled man, much like he believed himself to be. The first time, Dwyer was shackled, and was being tried by a court martial convened by Captain-Governor Bligh. There Dwyer had talked quietly, sensibly, about why the evidence of his heading an Irish conspiracy was false-knit. No histrionics, just the good sense of a man of character, and Johnston had led his fellow martial-jurors to declare Dwyer innocent. And then, after Johnston seized government from Bligh, he had the Irishman brought back from Van Diemen's land and allowed him to settle with his family on the mainland. The two had talked and Johnston had been left with the distinct impression that Dwyer approved of the Rum Rebellion, but not of any future Irish one; Johnston, though, could not remember Dwyer's exact words.

Protective colouration meant obtaining patronage, for what is a patron but an overhanging rock to shelter beneath? D'Arcy Wentworth, former highwayman and now the principal surgeon of New South Wales, and well on his way to controlling both the civilian police and half the petty cash of the colonial government, saw Dwyer as a useful tool: someone who could handle the hard-types, but who was loyal to his protectors and therefore a good acolyte.

So, with Wentworth's recommendation, in 1810 the greatest Irish rebel in Australia becomes a police constable. He farms in the George's River District, an area thick with former Irish rebels, and he agrees to keep them in order.

What Michael Dwyer could have told Charles Darwin is that developing protective colouration comes at a cost. Changing plumage from season to season may be adaptive in the short run, but it places a heavy drain on life's energy and a frightful strain on the nerves.

SYDNEY, NSW. 1811

Mature Reflection

"After being rolled on a deal beach, you're certainly in Rome Villa, Mr. Wentworth."

"As are you, Mr Riley. And our friend Blaxcell." D'Arcy Wentworth, Irish gentleman, English highwayman, Australian surgeon, was accustomed to spending time with those beneath his social class. Courtly, handsome, given to wearing waistcoats of shimmering silk, he found most of his friends and business partners in the rougher elements. This was not his preference, but he had been ruled unacceptable by Sydney society on the undeniable grounds that he was spreading his seed around the colony at an alarming rate: he already had ten children by several women.

"That Scots git has turned out to be trumps for you, wouldn't you say, Wentworth?" The reference was to Lachlan Macquarie, who had arrived to sort out New South Wales and did so with a strong hand, serving as a virtual czar until 1821.

"Yes, Riley," Wentworth replied and drank deeply. He was a claret man, an expensive habit in this part of the world. "I rather like Macquarie, and that is in addition to all the good he has done me."

"Better for you than old Bligh!"

"Indeed." Bligh had tried to court martial Wentworth for conspiracy to rebel, with no success. "It's useful being the Governor's personal physician, especially now that you've built him such a fine hospital, Riley."

The hospital was an amazing project, even for New South Wales. Soon after Macquarie had arrived, Alexander Riley, bigtime contractor and user of convict labour, and Garnham Blaxcell, sometime secretary to Bligh's predecessor, Governor King, had offered to erect a hospital large enough to serve the needs of the growing colony and to do it free. The only cost would be that the contractors would receive the right to import 45,000 gallons of spirits ("rum") and a monopoly of spirit importation for three years, plus the labour of twenty convicts and 20 draught bullocks. The moment the contract was signed, D'Arcy Wentworth came forward and joined the syndicate and it was clear that he had been the mastermind from the beginning. In the end, Riley made a fortune and ended up with a huge landed estate; Blaxcell blew his money and absconded in 1817 to avoid debtors' prison; and Wentworth made a bit and in 1811 was named as head of the hospital and remained as principal surgeon of the entire medical system of the Australian colonies.

"Still, I'll warrant the police lark will be your ticket to the land of the Pashas."

Wentworth smiled and stopped looking at the barmaid's tits. He has been wondering if they had names. "A deep responsibility." D'Arcy Wentworth had been made chief police magistrate for Sydney as part of Governor Macquarie's reform of the police service. Then, even before the year 1810 was out, the governor named him the Police Fund's treasurer. The fund paid for public works, maintaining gaols, police salaries and for all sorts of items that weren't underwritten by London. Three-quarters-plus of the colonial customs revenues ran through the Police Fund. More than £10,000 a year was to pass through the hands of the former highwayman, and if not quite all of it passed through, well, he was not greedy. When, in 1817 the Bank of New South Wales was formed, he was the second largest investor. He explained this affluence to one inquirer by noting that he had given up both tobacco and married women.

Wentworth retired from public life in 1820 and, in his declining years, raised race horses and arranged for the maintenance of his many offspring. One of the few truly amiable men in the first fifty years of the Australian colonies, he died in 1827: his train of mourners was nearly a mile long and his epitaph, self-chosen, admirably summarized the good times he had had: "In My Father's House are Many Mansions."

HOBART TOWN, VAN DIEMEN'S LAND, 1812

Parallel Lives – I

Two government storekeepers, each dressed in the respectable black coats of men of business, walk the Hobart Town waterfront. They are passing time, waiting for a shipment of goods from Sydney. Occasionally they note a wattle-and-daub hut of the sort that had been the homes of the guards and marines who had brought the first convicts in 1804. The two survey the mountains behind Hobart and the Derwent River that cuts through them. Mostly, though, they watch seaward, preferring to look to their own future, rather than to the island's past.

William Maum and Richard Dry had not known each other until their shared hell on the *Minerva* in 1799–1800. They were Irish Protestant veterans of the revolutionary 1790s. Dry, the son of a gentleman farmer, had become a Wexford wool draper and local radical. He was convicted of sedition in 1797, before the Rising, a rare distinction. Maum, from County Cork, had been educated at Trinity College, Dublin, a hotbed of conspiracy, and was transported for his political beliefs. Maum and Dry had been lashed on the same triangle during the inquisition into the non-existent 1800 conspiracy in New South Wales. Their blood had watered the same ground, literally. Each had served time on Norfolk Island.

"Perhaps it is the gods who wish us to walk abreast," Maum suggests. He is still the keen classicist: Trinity had taught him more than sedition.

"So long as it is profitable."

Quite accidentally, the two men live parallel lives. Richard Dry, now a fully-pardoned emancipist, serves as a storekeeper in Launceston, and William Maum, still unpardoned, as assistant in the commissariat at Hobart Town. These are good posts, and the opportunity for profit is considerable.

"Perhaps we shall regain some recompense for our pain."

"Yes, Maum." A vessel becomes visible in the Derwent estuary.

"Perhaps that is our ship."

William Maum receives a conditional pardon in 1813, and does well for himself, becoming chief governmental store-keeper in Hobart. He is dismissed for embezzlement in 1816, but has set enough aside to farm comfortably. He moves to New South Wales for a time and receives an absolute pardon and then returns to Van Diemen's Land. There, like an Irish squire, he trains race horses, some of the best in Australia.

Richard Dry also does well. He stays in the commissariat in Launceston until 1817 and leaves with a reputation for honesty. No one questions how a man whose annual salary had been £50 managed to farm, with his tenant, 300 acres. In 1817 he had 7,000 sheep and 4,000 cattle. By 1827 Dry has 12,000 acres and a year later he becomes one of the founders of the Cornwall Bank. "God blessed me," he asserts in later life. In witness to God's glory, Dry becomes the assistant secretary of the British and Foreign Bible Society in Van Diemen's Land and is very proud when one of his two sons becomes the first person born in Van Diemen's Land to take Anglican holy orders. After Dry's death in 1843, his other son is nominated to the Legislative Council, becomes a leading figure in the anti-transportation movement, and is knighted.

EAGLE ISLAND, THE FALKLAND ISLANDS.
FEBRUARY 1813

Parallel Lives – II

Two men, each in solid middle age, sit with their backs to each other. They are not friends, or even friendly, but talking relieves the tedium of the scenery.

"Ah, that it should have come to this."

"A soulless place to die."

"A worse place to live."

They are seated in a natural alcove on a promontory overlooking the endless sea. The hateful breakers that kick up below them, saliva in the mouth of some unseen Leviathan, are no comfort.

"Pity we had no charts."

"Pity the captain was drunk."

"Pity he didn't die before we left port."

Sir Henry Browne Hayes and "General" Joseph Holt have so much in common that they repel each other, like magnets that have the same polarity. Irish Protestants, each sentenced to transportation as an alternative to hanging, each feeling himself to be a gentleman, well above the common ruck of felons, each briefly tasting the pain of Norfolk Island and Van Diemen's Land, each pardoned conditionally before Governor Macquarie arrived and each pardoned absolutely by him.

"Always hated islands."

"Only certain ones."

"Ireland's satisfactory, I grant."

"No, not really."

"More of a place, than an island, I'd say."

"And not so windy. Get windy don't you?"

The last comment was hostile and was not a reference to the winds that blew across the Falkland Islands, continual westerlies that never abated and drove quiet men mad and mad men violent. In point, the comment was directed at Sir Henry's having reacted to their ship's hitting rocks by jumping into the only rowboat on board and making for the shore along with his servant and three seamen. Later he claimed that he was hurrying to shore to find ways to save everyone's life.

Sir Henry had boarded the Isabella in Sydney Cove with his manservant (whom Joseph Holt referred to as Sir Henry's "fancy man"), and a ton of luggage. Joseph Holt, with his wife, son, and three servants shipped almost as much luggage. Both Holt and Hayes had sold estates of several hundred acres, well-stocked, and they left as gentlemen: just before they sailed, Governor Macquarie came on board to wish them a safe passage.

"Generous man, the Governor."

"Should have pardoned us sooner."

"Aye. No need for that formal hearing."

"Damned impertinence."

The Isabella's company rescued most of the provisions and allocated them so that the survivors could last for a year. The question of who would have dined on whom after a year was fortuitously avoided for in April they were rescued, left at Rio de Janeiro, and from there shipped to Liverpool, arriving in 1814.

Joseph Holt tried to keep a tavern in Dublin but failed miserably. The remainder of his money he put into houses in Kingstown, south of Dublin, and lived off the rents, all the while regretting having left New South Wales. Sir Henry went home to Cork City, did nothing, became rotund, affected a straw hat of the shape of those the convicts made from native flax, and never admitted to regret about anything.

THE BLUE MOUNTAINS, NSW. MAY 1813

Road to China

The prison colony of New South Wales had itself always been imprisoned by the Great Blue Wall. Seventy kilometres westward, the inland mysteries of Australia are blocked by a range of hills that transform themselves into mountains as high as 1,100 metres. From a distance they are a disquieting blue in colour, for a thin cobalt-coloured haze envelops them, formed by fine mist as it dances around eucalyptus trees. As one approaches this wall, the chill of apprehension is reinforced by temperature: it is chilly even on the misty mountain tops; and the deep valleys, which sometimes have only an hour or two of sunlight a day, are painfully cold to anyone accustomed to a coastal climate. Prisoners have long believed that beyond the Blue Mountains lies China. Through the years, scores of escapees have lost their lives trying to break through the wall.

In May 1813, William Charles Wentworth succeeds. Twenty-three years of age, he is one of the most privileged young people in the colony, and no one can deny his talent, strength, and energy. One of the three semi-legitimate sons of D'Arcy Wentworth (the three from his first Australian liaison, whom he declared to be true Wentworths), William had been sent to England for education at age thirteen. There he had learned his classics and had kept up the family ties with William Wentworth Fitzwilliam, second Earl Fitzwilliam, a former viceroy of Ireland (1795), and head of the privy council in 1806–07. So, despite his youth, in 1811 Governor Macquarie appointed William acting provost-marshal for New South Wales and gave him an estate of 1,750 acres. Young W.C. Wentworth was as tall as his father – well over six feet – but not so handsome. He was broader of shoulder and had a leonine head and a perpetual untidiness. Physically courageous (he was a famously daring hunt jockey) and strong beyond most men, he was the perfect explorer to break open the inside of the continent. In an expedition of twenty-one days, he and six other men, keeping to the ridges, proved it was possible to enter the interior of Australia, and on a path broad enough to allow cattle to pass. This was the first great Australian exploration venture to succeed, and the settlement of the continent depended upon it.

W.C. Wentworth returned to receive another 1,000 acres from the government as his reward, but the Blue Mountains nearly proved fatal to him. He returned with a cough that threatened to turn into rheumatic fever or tuberculosis.

As cure, his father sets him up as first mate on a small schooner that is out to scavenge sandalwood any place it can be found in the Pacific Islands. It is this vessel, under Captain Goodenough, that provokes the first violent encounter with the Cook Islanders. He has no hesitation in kidnapping men and women from the Cook Islands.

Young Wentworth is a feral child, the embodiment of the second generation of Australians: at once innocent and brutal. He has not yet been told of his own illegitimacy or of his father's past as a highwayman, but only of his romantic and noble Irish roots. Young Wentworth quotes classics and writes satires against oppressive officials. He is headstrong, physically intimidating, and he follows his father's path in fornicating with anything that crosses his path. He is a mammalian precursor to the Australian cane toad.

William Charles Wentworth decides that, if he is to master Australia, as he fully intends to do, he must become proficient in the law. In 1816 he leaves again for England and a year later puts his name down at the Middle Temple.

SYDNEY COVE. MAY 1813

Timing

At exactly the same time William C. Wentworth is chipping his way through the Blue Mountains, George Johnston, scourge of the Irish rebellion of 1804 and usurper of Governor Bligh in the Rum Rebellion of 1808, returns to New South Wales. Now he is George Johnston, Esq., not lieutenant-colonel, for he had returned to England and put his behaviour before a court martial. He came within an ace of being hanged for mutiny, but former-Governor John Hunter spoke on his behalf and he lost not his life, but his commission (a saleable piece of property in those days) and therefore most of his life savings.

He returns to New South Wales to wed Esther Abrahams, the Jewish convict woman he had lived with since 1788, and to support their brood of children. To his credit, Governor Macquarie treats him not as a threat, but as another settler in a land that can use all the yeomen it can attract. In fact, Johnston and Macquarie strike up a sensible friendship: after all, how many men can Macquarie talk to who have had the experience of being in charge of the whole colony?

George Johnston successfully farms at a gentry level and when he dies in 1823, he is interred in a specially-designed vault on his property.

Later his body was re-interred at Waverly Cemetery, where many Irish rebels rest. Despite Johnston's have suppressed the first real rebellion in Australian history, this should not be read as irony: Johnston had a lot more in common with the Irish rebels than he did with the ramrod correctness of the Imperial government.

NAAS, COUNTY KILDARE. 1815

This Is Revenge?

Terence Murray – known for most of his life as "Paymaster Murray" – settles into his new post as paymaster of the Forty-Eighth Regiment of Foot. Now that Napoleon is no longer a threat, occupying Ireland is a useful army activity. This Terence Murray is the same person who, as a lad, had watched his rebel father have his shattered leg amputated. "Remember the enemy," was a phrase the family had been told, daily, from that day onwards.

The young men of the family did remember – and joined them. Terence in 1805 married a fellow-Catholic, Ellen Fitzgerald of old-gentry connections. She and her sisters were pets of Mrs. Maria Fitzherbert who, in 1785 had become the morganatic wife of the Prince of Wales (the future George IV). Mrs. Fitzherbert was a Catholic and promoted worthy Catholics in a small way: nothing to shake the constitution of the country, just good posts. So Terence found himself in 1811 suddenly made paymaster in the Second Brigade of Guards. One brother was appointed an army surgeon, another a naval surgeon and two others become low-ranking officers. The family kept its Catholic faith, but turned from fighting the Empire to defending it, a turnabout much more common in Irish Catholic families than is conveniently remembered.

Paymaster Murray's unit shipped to New South Wales in 1817 and, in the usual rotation, to India seven years later. The paymaster so liked the opportunities for land and cheap convict labour in New South Wales that he returned on half-pay in 1827. He farmed as a gentleman and he produced one son who became an army surgeon, a daughter who married a military captain, and another son who became a noteworthy, if volatile, Australian politician. None of them had anything good to say for violent revolution.

SYDNEY, NSW. 1819

Small Crimes

Laurence Hynes Halloran passes idle moments by composing his own epitaph.

Here rests, at length, by Heaven's kind will,
"A strange Compound of Good and Ill:"

Halloran has plenty of idle moments, for he is the founder and headmaster of the first secondary school in Australia, the Sydney Grammar School, and he has the lads copy out Latin paradigms and do Euclid for one or two hours each day. Though much better educated than the average convict, Halloran is typical in believing that he has been hard done by:

Who little rest enjoy'd on Earth.
Doom'd. from the aera of his birth.
Griefs and Vicissitudes to know –
Some Comforts, but more Cares, and Woe!

And, typically, later observers have seen the charge sheets and agreed with the convict. Halloran, after all, was transported for forging a ten-penny frank for a letter! Tenpenny! And the records show women transported for stealing a handkerchief, men for a watch or for maiming a cow. All gross injustices.

No, just bad historical records. Except for the one or two in-a-hundred of the Irish convicts who were political prisoners, felons were sent from the British Isles because they were repeat offenders, usually habitual, and were often violent; and they received shorter sentences and softer time than they would today. Later observers naively take the absence of sound criminal records as an indication of the absence of a bad criminal history.

Take Halloran, who did indeed leave a trail. He was a Catholic, from a family that jumped back and forth over the religious divide, the son of a West Indian slave owner who died a year after Laurence's birth. Born in County Meath, Halloran's mother was from decayed gentry stock and when she was widowed in 1772, she took Laurence and his four sisters to England.

Some Comforts, but more Cares, and Woe!
Tho' not a Saint, (Truth now may speak,)
He was less vicious far, than weak!

In England he was hardly a deprived child, for a great uncle (on his mother's side) took over his guardianship. This uncle had been chief justice of the Province of Quebec (a job he lost in part because he did not know French) and in 1774, became a justice of the Supreme Court of Carolina, then still within the Empire. When this uncle went to the American colonies, Halloran, aged eight, was placed in Christ's Hospital, London. This was an excellent school, established by King Charles II to train navigators and surveyors for the expanding empire. Halloran boarded there. He not only received a fine technical schooling, but, at age fifteen, was apprenticed to a captain in the Royal Navy.

His Course, oft steer'd by Passions strong,
By sad fatality was wrong.

Laurence, still less than eighteen years of age, deserted his original captain, but managed to sign on with another one.

In Plymouth he engaged in a "duel" with a midshipman whom he killed. This duel must have been conducted under very unusual rules, for the midshipman died from a sword strike that entered from the back and came out through his abdomen.

Yet, to Philanthropy inclined,
His heart embraced all Human Kind!

Here Halloran's naval career ended (killing crew members, even if passed off as a duel, was not on).

He took up the normal pursuit of those who love mankind, school teaching. After ten years or so of this, he declared himself to have seen the virtue of the Established Church. He converted, and then declared himself to be an Anglican divine – this based on a forged ordination certificate from the Bishop of Ossory in Ireland. In 1800, King's College, Aberdeen, awarded him a genuine Doctor of Divinity degree based on testimonials and credentials he submitted.

And tho' he felt Ingratitude,
Which still his thorny path pursued;
Tho' persecuted, wrong'd, betray'd,
None ever vainly claim'd his Aid!

His large heart permitted him to declare the daughter of his own sister to be his wife. This incestuous relationship eventually yielded twelve children. In any case, as a clergyman he found his idiom in the forces. He served as chaplain of the *HMS Britannia* and was on her at the epic battle of Trafalgar, 1805, praying like a true Christian. Two years later he was promoted to principal chaplain of the army and navy at the Cape of Good Hope at £1,200 per annum, a large enough sum to permit him to keep his niece and her incestuously-conceived children in one ménage and a mistress and her children in another.

To Woe, even to the last sincere,
He gave, (all else was lost,) a tear!

Had Halloran possessed any self-control at all he would have been safe the rest of his days but, no, his temper led him first to argue with the commanding general of the Cape and then to libel the same man in print.

Turfed from the forces, the Rev. Dr. Halloran served as a curate in several English parishes. When finally caught out, he was discovered to have copper plates in his possession for uttering high-quality documents. This was a capital offence, but calling his career to public attention would have produced several hundred invalid marriages and perhaps a thousand thus-illegitimate children, a ripe mess for both church and state.

So, as in the case of wholesale thieves who were sentenced for stealing a single pound of butter, his charge was reduced to the minimum needed for transportation.

And, to Life's close from its beginning,
'Was still more sinn'd against than sinning!

Was Laurence Hynes Halloran transported to Australia for uttering a tenpenny forgery? Please!

CABRAMATTA, NSW. 1820

Equipoise?

The night sweats have stopped and so too have the voices. Michael Dwyer has survived for almost eleven years in a mountain range of ambiguity that makes the Blue Mountains seem to be only foothills. He has been a farmer during these years, a period of drought and of low prices; simultaneously he has been, since 1810, the constable in charge of the George's River district, an area populated mostly by Irish ex-rebels who are trying to scratch out a living on small farms. And Dwyer, of course, is the most famous Irish guerilla leader ever to land on the Australian continent.

Dwyer has spent a decade in hell, keenly aware that he needs to support his family and also that social order is no bad thing: but he hates having to arrest the occasional old ally and, more often, one of their sons. The whole district is a web of intermarriage between the children of 1798 rebels, and they are forever getting into scrapes.

Michael Dwyer has dealt with his painful position in two traditional Irish ways. He drinks heavily. At night he can be heard talking to people who aren't there, arguing about what is right and wrong with a phantom jury of his peers.

And he has turned very religious, a leading crusader for a Catholic priesthood for the colony. In 1817, he almost wins, and what a balm that would have been to Dwyer's soul. An Irish Franciscan who has done missionary work in the West Indies arrives in Sydney, without either governmental or ecclesiastical approval from the English Catholic authorities, under whom Australia falls. He is badly needed, for there has been no priest in Australia for seven years and then the priest was a convict and was not permitted to perform his duties openly. The Franciscan Father Jeremiah O'Flynn is semi-literate and able to speak only halting English (these being the reasons the English Catholic authorities refused to approve his mission), but he speaks Irish fluently.

Father O'Flynn adopts the pray-say-and-disappear mode that distinguished the Irish Catholic church in the penal era. He preaches and says mass publicly. Then, ordered by Governor Macquarie to leave New South Wales, he hides in the bush, going from cabin to cabin among the faithful, just as the penal-era priests had done.

He surrenders in 1818 and is deported.

In classic Faith-of-Our-Fathers fashion, the Church wins by its virtuous defeat. Michael Dwyer is one of the band of laymen in the Cabramatta area who form a "Council for the Protection of the Blessed Sacrament," because Father O'Flynn has left a pyx with the consecrated host in it. And throughout New South Wales, a petition circulates among the Roman Catholics asking for the appointment of Catholic clergy.

Victory. In 1820 the government agrees to fund two Catholic priests, the lead figure being Father Joseph Therry. He and the Dwyer family become close and Michael Dwyer is one of the first contributors to the building of St. Mary's Cathedral in Sydney.

And, in secular balance to this spiritual blessing, in 1820 Michael Dwyer is promoted to chief constable of Liverpool, a new settlement within easy ride of his farm.

NEW SOUTH WALES. 1822

Spiritual Mysteries

Father John Joseph Therry spent more than four decades building for the future and feeling inadequate in the present. Scant wonder: his senior colleague, Father Philip Connolly, with whom he arrived as the official Catholic chaplains, took himself off to Van Diemen's Land in 1821 and for the next five years Father Therry was the only priest on the Australian mainland. In 1822, he wrote:

It requires at least seven priests to discharge in a proper and regular manner the duties which devolve on me, but which I perform in a very irregular and superficial manner.

Yet Therry, more than anyone else, established the Irish Catholic as a special kind of Australian. Before he arrived the term "Irish Catholic" was a slur, implying sedition and disorder. Within a dozen years of his arrival, it referred to a recognizable community, one that could not be ignored or kicked about like a stray dog. If there were 6,000 Irish Catholics in 1821, there were 16,000-and-rising in 1833. And they knew they were a people, not randomly collected social detritus.

Father Therry spent an immense amount of time in the saddle, moving slowly and wearily from one hamlet to another. His flock was mostly bush farmers, self-sufficient families, settled on blocks of land they had received upon being pardoned, or had purchased with money saved while labouring. Mostly the Irish Catholic settlers (like those of all backgrounds) lived in primitive conditions. Their first homes were a sheet of canvas, then a low house made from slabs of wood slashed from the surrounding bush. The walls usually were bark, and the roof overlapping slabs that leaked rivulets during any rain. Many of the Irish settlers had one or two convicts assigned to them, but in any case, the first years were spent clearing land, perch and rod by aching acre. Women spent their days keeping cooking fires alight, guarding the domestic animals (a decent milking cow was a treasure to be protected with one's life). And always, children were aborning. The struggle to maintain minimum standards of decency wore heavily. Thus, a visit to the neighbourhood by Father Therry was a lifeline; he was a much better priest than he knew.

Two mysteries that, perhaps, have a spiritual explanation. The first is that, when a census was taken in 1818, the authorities found that about one-fifth of the Irish Catholics were free-born in the colony; a third were convicts, and the rest were former convicts. These people were doing as well as any other identifiable group, in terms of garnering land, livestock, real wealth. How?

And, how did it come to be that, by the mid-1820s, a successful, if angular, society had emerged in Australia – constructed from some of the most twisted pieces of humanity one can encounter, men and women who were so brutalized as to have lost the outward evidences of their humanity? By what miracle do these people and their children and their keepers and rulers knit together a world that, though spikey and still bent by its convict origins, begins to resemble a civil society? Man proposes; God disposes? Perhaps Father Therry knew.

SYDNEY HARBOUR. JULY 1824

Big Parcel Travelling

"What in the name of Christ is that?"

"An ignorant mallicker of a crate, obviously."

Two foremen watch as a massive crate is swung from shipside to quayside and then trundled on dollies into the customs shed.

"If you weren't as lazy as Ludlum's dog, we'd know soon enough." The reference was to a hound so lazy it leaned against a wall to bark. "Grab your spud bar and we'll have a wee look."

"Me, lazy? When we were in the marines you'd lay down your musket to fart." This argument was a pantomime they'd been doing for a dozen years, first as marines in South Africa, and now, mustered out in New South Wales, as minor customs officials and foremen of a gang of dockside navvies. "Right, we'll inspect the cargo."

Inside the customs shed they stand on a sawhorse and pop the lid.

"Merciful Jesus, it must be a wine press."

"Biggest one I've ever seen. Wouldn't want to catch my hand in that yoke."

"Aye. It would press a boulder into a pebble."

"Maybe this effort's a wool baler. You know, press the fleeces into tight blocks for shipping."

"Aye, that's what it would be."

"Well, that's settled. Like to talk to its owner, mind you."

"That would be me." The voice that surprised them had a mixture of authority and contempt that journeyman veterans of the British Empire knew all too well. Whether in a line regiment or in a clerk's office, the tone of the captain, governor, or bishop was always the same and, whatever the words uttered audibly, they were transmitted in a tone that said you-will-do-what-I-say-and-by-the-way-you're-shite. "Or, more, correctly, I am the co-owner with Dr Robert Wardell." The voice was very forceful. "Now, kindly have it cleared and delivered to Wardell's office."

"Aye, sir, it's the biggest one of these we've seen."

"Yes, it's a bigger printing press than the government has." William Charles Wentworth was returning to Australia with a vengeance, and among other things, he was to be a co-owner of the *Australian*, the country's first uncensored newspaper. And this without governmental approval.

William Wentworth was a bigger parcel than even his printing press. He had indeed qualified as a lawyer in England, and become a man of the world: thanks in part to a year in France supported reluctantly by his kinsman Lord Fitzwilliam. There he had learned a lot about wine and a lot more about brothels, knowledge he soon was to apply assiduously in New South Wales. Always a man of great energy and application when required – he had, after all, conquered the Blue Mountain range – he now was motivated by a hard, burning fire. While in England he had learned his family's secret – that his father, D'Arcy Wentworth, had been a highwayman – and this hardened his pride, like a blacksmith's hammer banging on a steel blade. He returned to Australia with a passionate commitment to assert his family's standing as against the "exclusives" of Sydney society. And, since these exclusives were usually hyper-English in affectation, if not always in origin, he came home an Australian patriot.

Whereas in his youth, D'Arcy Wentworth had been so handsome that one could not avoid looking at him with admiration of his beauty, his son William demanded one's attention because of a menacing ugliness. Well over six feet tall, very heavy set, he walked with a club-footed gait that made him appear always drunk and always on the edge of falling over. When he harangued someone, it was from a superior height but, confusingly, with a visage whose eyes did not quite meet. He had a cast in one eye and it was impossible to know exactly where to look when he was instructing you.

Australian patriotism to W.C. Wentworth was simple enough: it meant that all free immigrants and all emancipists should have the same privileges as citizens of the United Kingdom. His great triumphs were the introduction of the free press and, after a legal war with the authorities, in 1830 the introduction of trial by civilian, not military, juries.

A big package was W.C. Wentworth. In 1827 his father D'Arcy died, leaving a large estate, and William bought "Vaucluse," the estate that Sir Henry Browne Hayes had built. This uniquely snake-proofed residence was expanded into one of the largest country houses in Australia. W.C. married in 1829 at "Vaucluse" and had three sons and seven daughters. A year after his marriage, he had a child with an Irish widow, and, over the years, several other by-blows were spawned with various women. His best moment, though, was in 1841, when he had more than 4,000 guests to "Vaucluse" to celebrate the departure of one of his chief enemies, Governor Sir Ralph Darling.

LIVERPOOL, NSW. 1825

Awake

"He looks very good, doesn't he now?"
"Ah, the very best, as if he could come awake any minute."
"And the best of company he'd be."
"Aye. Pity about the last five years."
"Just when things were going well. Chief Constable of Liverpool and more posts on the hob for the future."
"Chief Constable Michael Dwyer. Never sounded right, somehow."
"That's how he felt, too."
"After Molloy was arrested on charges of bushranging."
"Old friends. That was hard on Michael. And then Molloy being executed, that broke it. I saw him that night, coming home loaded in a cart like a sack of flour, so taken with drink was he. Never stopped with the drink after that."
"That's why he lost those documents, the ones with the official seals on them. And then was dismissed as chief constable."
"Still, wasn't he the best of publicans? Better than he ever was a constable?"
"True. How many publicans do you know would throw away the key to the front door of his tavern?"
"Great heart, there."
"Too many took advantage."
"Isn't that the way of it, always?"

"Bankruptcy and then debtors' prison. Not the right ending for an Irish republican hero."

"No. And dysentery's no dignified path to the next land, priest present or no."

"Still, Father Therry was a rock. Stayed with him 'till the end."

"Yes, a good priest. And now he's taken the widow and the three daughters into his house. Says he's thinking of using the girls as the start of a new order of nuns."

"That would make Michael proud."

THE BLUE MOUNTAINS, NSW. 1827

Inventing Jesus

John Donohue huddled out of the fine, cold rain and planned. He should have been scheming how to make a bit of dishonest money, but his mind kept returning to the warm fire of future fame: the way he would be remembered for generations to come as bold Jack Donohue.

Oh, my lass,
He kicked their ass.
The Bold Colonial Boy.

Needed work, but he had time. Donohue decided he had better do the crime and then do the rhyme.

As a teen-age bandit, Donohue had done some competent highway robberies before being apprehended, in 1823, aged seventeen, and sentenced to New South Wales. Assigned to a settler, he had problems, was put on a government road gang and then sent to another settler. From there he took off.

"Bush-ranging" was common, had been since the first days of Port Jackson. It was not an act of free men, but of convicts who refused confinement and who mostly stole food and clothing, the requisites of a dicey existence. Mostly unskilled in bushcraft, frequently lost, the bushrangers were the nightmare of small holders. Large landholders had defendable enclosures; small holders only a leather-hinged door and bark walls between their families and the half-starved, half-crazed roaming convicts.

John Donohue and two confederates took to highway robbery. They were somewhat limited in what they could rob, since they were on foot and most people travelling with valuables were not. So, they tried to hold up a line of supply carts being pulled by oxen, reckoning that they had the advantage in foot speed. They did, but Donohue would have done well to calculate his method of escape a bit more precisely, since scarpering with a train of ox wagons has its disadvantages. Caught, sentenced to hang – two sentences for hanging, actually – he worked on his legend. He wrote:

Though I be a Bushranger
You still are the stranger,
And I'm Donohue!

Still needed work. His brilliant escape from the very foot of the gallows, however, was what counted. And he put together a serious gang, English and Irish, mounted banditti. For a year-and-a-half the gang had all of New South Wales in apprehension. Their work-rate was prodigious, at least one hold-up a week. And Bold Jack, knowing that the greatest danger to his freedom came from informers, worked hard to transform himself into a legend: he gave or traded stolen goods to bush farmers, and became, if not Robin Hood, at least a wronged, and therefore sympathetic, Irishman:

Then hurl me to crime and brand me with shame
But think not to bulk me, my spirit to tame,
For I'll fight to the last in old Ireland's name.

There, that was good. Bold Jack had completed that bit before he was surrounded at Campbelltown, near Sydney, and, in September 1830, took a trooper's musket ball clean through his head.

Had he not invented himself, John Donohue would have been invented. As it was, "J.D." becomes the Australian-Irish version of "J.C." A score of ballads in his honour appeared, and if sometimes they were about Jack Duggan or Jim Doolan, or John Dowling, they were all about the same figure: not the low-rent sociopath from Ireland, but about a figure who personified resistance to authority: specifically, Irish resistance to British authority. Heroic, romantic and, of course, unsuccessful. That was the rule of nineteenth-century Irish myth-making: heroes, if they were the real item, had to be martyrs.

SWAN RIVER, WESTERN AUSTRALIA. 1830

Some Swans Are Geese

Mrs. William Shaw – Eliza, daughter of a wealthy Dublin merchant and the wife of an army officer – wrote letters with the sting of a wasp. She chronicled the gentry settlement in recently-annexed Western Australia with an eye that missed nothing and forgave little. Letters from her early days in the colony circulated in Dublin, and one sequence gave special pleasure to Daniel O'Connell, for they involved the relatives of Robert Peel, his longtime enemy and ultimate nemesis. Peel and O'Connell had almost fought a duel in 1815 when Peel was chief secretary for Ireland. In 1829, Peel as home secretary in Wellington's government, had surrendered Catholic Emancipation in the face of O'Connell's massive national movement.

Now O'Connell was passed the letters describing the demise of the corrupt Peel-family business in the Swan River colony. At the time when Robert Peel was home secretary, his cousin Thomas Peel was allocated 150,000 acres of prime land between the Swan and Canning Rivers, provided he settled it with a virtually-medieval band of retainers. Trouble was, Thomas Peel and his illegitimate son (and seneschal) arrived a bit late in 1829 and had to select their vast acres in poorer land than they had intended, to the south of Fremantle. His 180 tenants and their families were enough to start a small city had the Peels not chosen a site distinguished by bad soil and high winds.

Thomas Peel retreated into a mixture of upper class hauteur and ill-health. His roughly 500 dependents were allocated in their first seven months of settlement only four cattle, three pigs and two sheep as rations, and no vegetables or anti-scurvy nutrition. So bad were conditions that the local magistrates – men with Peel's outlook on social gradations – nevertheless freed the servants and tenants from their indentures to the great pillock. Most left, and in a world where labour was desperately needed, they had no trouble signing on with other gentry settlers. Eventually Peel moved his few remaining servants to a spot about fifty miles from Perth and a small bit of arable farming began.

In July 1830, one of Peel's tenants, who was putting a roof on a house, was approached by natives. The spear one of them fired at him went clean through his chest. He was the first white casualty in the western range war with the indigenous people. He might as well have had a note pinned to his chest: "Coming Attractions."

HOBART, VAN DIEMEN'S LAND. 1 OCT. 1830

The Magna Carta

Whereas, by my proclamation, bearing date the 1st day of November, 1828, reciting (among other things) that the black or aboriginal natives of this land had for a considerable time carried on a series of indiscriminate attacks upon the persons and property of His Majesty's subjects, and that repeated inroads were made daily by such natives into the settled districts ...

Col. George Arthur reads his proclamation in a loud drone. He is the sort of colonial administrator who inevitably does the wrong thing, while having decent intentions. His rigid efficiency is made all the more irritating by his evangelical smarm. He governs Van Diemen's Land from 1824 to 1836, and is the first to have it as an independent satrapy, for the island is broken off from New South Wales in 1825. He has just come from the British settlement in Belize, where, in 1820, he crushed a slave revolt and this, having aroused his humanitarian instincts, led him to introduce into Honduras the Jamaican Slave Code, which gave the human chattels some few rights. And there he let the Miskito Indians, illegally enslaved, go free. In sum, he managed both to vex the slave owners and to kill quite a few of the African slaves who had rebelled.

... I, the said Lieutenant Governor, did declare and proclaim that from the date of my proclamation [1 Nov 1828], and until the cessation of hostilities, Martial Law was, and should continue to be in force against the said black or aboriginal natives within this Island ...

As prison administrators went, Col. Arthur was a model, of a nineteenth-century sort of course. With a convict population at 6,000, and this growing by a thousand each year as New South Wales authorities directed more and more of the hard cases to Van Diemen's Land, the island was a problem. Arthur replaced the disorder and random brutality of his predecessor with a system of graduated punishments: there was a system of rewards for good behaviour and one of deterrence for bad. The system's working was visible and tightly rule-defined. Col. Arthur believed that transportation was the most humane punishment and the most effective one that human wit had yet designed.

But, dear Lord, he hated disorder.

That's why he reaffirms martial law and begins the Black War that leads to the virtual extinction of the Tasmanian Aborigines. In his evangelical fashion, he wants it done gently:

But I do nevertheless, hereby strictly order, enjoin and command, that the actual use of arms be in no case resorted to, by firing against any of the natives or otherwise, if they can by other means be captured, that bloodshed be invariably checked as much as possible ...

Pious hope. A local guerilla war against the indigène has been going on since 1803, and the 4,000 or so original inhabitants were now cut in half. Free settlers and escaped convicts shot or poisoned them just as they dealt with any other species of vermin. The Aborigines, in 1828, had writhed into a final spasm of resistance, raiding quickly, then disappearing. This was the disorder Col. Arthur could not tolerate. Still, he did not want to kill them all. His solution was to designate an isolated peninsula as an Aboriginal reserve and then drive them into it. Thus the spectacle of a seven-weeks long Black Line sweeping the island. Every free male settler and every emancipist (about a third of them Irish) was involved, and prison warders, redcoats, half-pay pensioners, tramped alongside former Whiteboys from Tipperary, Heart of Oak Boys from Ulster, and men whose fathers had fought and been transported in '98. They combed the island and, when the several lines joined together, they discovered they had caught two blacks and killed two more. The rest had slipped through.

... and that any tribes or individuals captured or voluntarily surrendering themselves up, be treated with the utmost care and humanity ...

Col. Arthur decided that in trapping these black beasts he might do better to use honey. He employed a "conciliator," George Robinson, who was a failed evangelical missionary, but a very good negotiator. Robinson visited every tribe, clan, extended family, and, in the company of "tame" Aborigines, he convinced them to settle in a reserve on Flinders Island in Bass Strait. There they were given food, rudimentary shelter, and contempt. They just died, for they had no future and knew it. In 1846, with fewer than fifty still alive, they were brought to a camp near Hobart and, in filth and drunken stupor, encouraged to pass quietly away.

The last full-blooded Tasmanian Aboriginal man died in 1869. The last woman died in 1876; after allowing her body a brief peace in the grave, the Royal Society of Tasmania dug her up, bleached her bones, reassembled her skeleton on a wire frame and placed her on public display. Two to three thousand mixed-bloods survive, although throughout the nineteenth and twentieth centuries they were declared non-existent by successive Tasmanian governments.

Col. George Arthur was among the first of her subjects to be knighted by Queen Victoria, and in 1837 he was sent out to govern Upper Canada.

THE LONG WHITE SHROUD.
NEW ZEALAND
1792–1830

Empires Recycle

Pelf. Bodies. So much goes round and round.

William Hobson, destined to become the first governor of New Zealand, is born into the family of a minor Waterford barrister.

What little wealth the family possesses is recycled slave money. It comes, very indirectly, from the intermarried family of plantation owners: Thomas Meade (Protestant) and Peter Hussey (Catholic) of Montserrat. United under the Meade name, the family owned 340 slaves, three plantations, including the "Waterworkes," the island's most prestigious. The money came home to Ireland when Thomas Meade retired in the late 1740s, and the pelf was spread among family members who had backed the slave investments.

At the same time, the Hobsons, a group of Protestant adventurers who go back to the Civil War, were marrying their son to "Angel," daughter of the Laundys of Muckridge, County Cork. To this young couple, the heirless Dr. John Meade leaves his fortune.

Confiscated Irish lands; coerced African bodies. It all gives the Hobson family a modest stake to chance on the roulette wheel of empire.

Hobson's Choice

At the Deptford naval station, a ten-year-old boy signs on as a second-class volunteer. He gives his age as twelve, but he is lying. Only a few days later, the ship is away, cruising the North Sea, escorting merchant ships in the Anglo-French Wars.

Don't pity the lad. He has made an excellent career choice. He has enlisted in a firm that does not exist on paper, but which has its own army, navy, and church.

It's the Irish army, navy, and church, southern branch: or, more precisely, it is the visible portion of the massive, and mostly invisible influence machine of the Beresford family, the most powerful family in the country, centred in County Waterford. That's what young William Hobson, himself a Waterford lad, was joining.

The firm was as follows: the godfather was Lord John Beresford (1738–1805), the most powerful Irish politician of the 1790s and principal advisor to William Pitt on Irish policy. In 1800 he quietly pocketed a fortune to support the union of Great Britain and Ireland. His brother, George de la Poer Beresford, Marquis of Waterford (1735–1800) was distinguished by his wealth, prodigality, and ability to foster children in and out of wedlock. One of his legitimate offspring, Lord John George (1773–1862) assumed the throne of St. Patrick in 1822 – that is, became Protestant archbishop of Armagh. There, for four decades, he fought every reform he saw: especially giving Catholics the right to sit in parliament. Of course he opposed the reduction of the privileges of the Anglican state church. His great enemy was Richard Whately, archbishop of Dublin, whom he hated for being English, liberal, and, most especially, for wishing to provide state funds for the education of Roman Catholic children.

One of the bastard sons of the first Marquis of Waterford, William Carr Beresford (1768–1854), had a truly brilliant military career, and was one of the leading generals in the Peninsular War. Created a baron in 1814 and a viscount in 1823, William Beresford ended his career as master-general of ordnance.

And, then, the naval branch. Another bastard son of the first Marquis of Waterford, John Poo Beresford (1766–1844), was already a full captain by 1795, this being the early trajectory of a career that eventually led to his being knighted, given flag rank and, after he entered parliament, to being one of the lords of the admiralty.

That is the man under whom William Hobson enlists. Though only ten, this is not a case of some lad running away to sea. Hobson's father is a Waterford barrister, and the apprenticeship that is arranged is part of the patronage network, whereby Protestant families of southeastern Ireland look after each other. It's not much different than fosterage in ancient Ireland.

The *Virginie*, which Hobson joins, is under Beresford's direct command, so he has a protector of sorts. Over a period of years, Beresford makes sure that Hobson is formally educated, but it's a hard school. In later life, Hobson remembered Beresford as genial and kind, by which he probably meant that he was not buggered and was not frequently beaten. However, one of Captain Beresford's ways of passing the time was to have Hobson and some other boy-volunteer drink a lot of rum and then set them to punching each other senseless. That helped Beresford and his officers pass an otherwise boring evening.

By age nineteen, Hobson was an acting lieutenant, and a year later a lieutenant in his own right. That on the recommendation of Captain Beresford who, whatever his vices, took care of his own boys.

PORT DALRYMPLE, TASMANIA. 17 JUNE 1806

Founding Mother

One of the men with a gun is a woman. She and the first mate, Benjamin Kelly, are pistol-whipping the captain. Charlotte Badger has the forearms of a stevedore and she follows through with her stroke like a professional boxer. The captain loses teeth, and his left eye is shifted from its socket. Soon he resembles some as-yet-unidentified insect, a round palette of oozing vermillion surmounted by a retina on a stalk.

The vessel is the *Venus*, from Port Jackson, and it has been ordered to take Charlotte, her child, an Irish woman Catherine Hegarty, and some male prisoners to Tasmania. Charlotte, having served in Parramatta most of her sentence for housebreaking, was being paroled to a good job, as a domestic servant, in Tasmania. The convicts, led by Benjamin Kelly, and his paramour Catherine, easily seize the ship. They head for the Bay of Islands, New Zealand.

The others leave New Zealand after a year or so, but Charlotte and her daughter stay on.

She is the first white woman to make her home in the land of the long white cloud.

LONDON. 1809

Missionary Training

In the grey light of dawn, the Thames would not reflect his face. He leaned over and vomited a mixture a blood and sputum into the flow, and there it was indistinguishable from the waste and sewerage that floated into the tidal wash. This curiously twisted figure, torqued with the pain of broken bones and internal injuries, was destined to be leader of the Nga Pahi. Wrapped in a long blanket, he would appear to anyone who encountered him to be a corpse walking, shroud carefully tucked in to preserve life's remaining warmth.

Thus began Ruatara's lucky day. This was the day when he would cease being an old man, near death through physical and moral wounding, and return to his own real age: he was in fact only twenty-two years of age.

Four years earlier, he had signed on with one of the dozens of whaling ships that used New Zealand as a base. He had only one goal: to go to England and to meet the great king – George III. Through four years of extreme abuse – buggery, beatings by his ship-mates, theft of his pay – intermixed with occasional kindness by crew who took pity, through all that Ruatara had bobbed to and fro across the Pacific until he finally found a berth to England. There, he discovered, he had as much chance of meeting the Pakeha monarch as he had of becoming Archbishop of Canterbury.

Having failed in his quest, Ruatara was on the verge of willing himself to death: no violence, no physical suicide: he was strong enough of character to withdraw life from his body.

That he did not do so occurred because, visiting a low tavern where he was permitted to sit silently in a corner, he heard two words: "Ann," the name of a convict ship that was heading for Botany Bay, and "Marsden," a priest of some sort. He put the two together.

A round-faced mixture of pomposity, greed, generosity, spirituality, cruelty, realism and idealism, the Reverend Samuel Marsden was the leading Anglican clergyman in the convict world of New South Wales, a magistrate and a shrewd land speculator as well. He had become interested in spreading his good works and temporal power to New Zealand, and had been home in England successfully pleading for funds from the Church Missionary Society to undertake that new work. Ruatara came to him as a gift from the Almighty.

Marsden took Ruatara into his home in Port Jackson, New South Wales. There, for eight months, Marsden tried to teach him Christianity, and Ruatara, instead, learned European agriculture.

He was converted: to wheat. It was to him one of the world's great wonders and he spent the remaining years of his short life (he died before he was thirty), trying to show his people the virtues of this amazing crop. They laughed; he planted. They harvested the stems and threw away the seeds; he told of biscuits, bread. They made sleeping mats of the stems; he obtained a small grinding mill and made flour. He planted and planted and planted, ruining his health in heavy weather.

When he died in 1815, the missionary Marsden was in attendance and bread was being baked in an earthen oven.

LONDON. 1812

Paying Attention

Did you need to know the standard weight of a barrel of potatoes? It wasn't the same in Mullingar as in Bandon.

So, you checked Mr. Wakefield's book.

Were you comparing bushels of oats produced in lands you owned in Donegal and in Tipperary? Not the same at all.

Edward Wakefield, that's your man.

Were you trying to expand upon the one single sure thing you know about weights and measures in Ireland – that an hundredweight of anything *never* weighs a hundred pounds – you opened your copy of the volume that Edward Wakefield painstakingly produced in 1812, *An Account of Ireland, Statistical and Political*, and you'd discover that an hundredweight of turnips would not balance the scales with an hundredweight of praties, nor could you equate Dublin with Donaghadee.

Small facts, collected by a man who paid attention. A London businessman whose Quaker family, like so many of that sect, had grabbed land from the Irish peasantry during the wars of religion and had done well, all with the absolutely clear and untroubled conscience that encircled them, like a cloud by day and a pillar of fire at night. Still, generations removed from that unpleasantness and now a London philanthropist, Edward Wakefield paid attention to Ireland and to its tiny details. He visited each market town and, ankle-deep in mud and dung, noted how business was done.

His wife told him that he should pay more attention to his family than to those creatures across the water. Oh yes, he was right: Ireland was overpopulated and heading for a disaster. But he should spend less time in the company of men such as James Mill and Francis Place and control his ménage, for his own boys were even more out of control than were the Irish.

NEW ZEALAND. 1815

Mixed Perspectives

From Day One, the Europeans who encountered the Maori saw them either as worthy enemies or as noble savages. This in sharp contrast to their view of most other native peoples, whom they despised.

The Maori were less sure of what they saw when Europeans began disembarking, in tentative squads, obviously afraid, obviously assertive, manifestly rich. By 1815 they had a collective name for these people – Pakeha – and probably it meant people who resembled men, but who really weren't, like the tough angels in Semitic myths of the Ancient Near East.

Their social observations concerning the Pakeha were often inaccurate, if sensibly so. Given that the explorers and the whalers travelled in village-sized vessels and did so without women, it was natural to infer they were homosexuals. Even after the crewmen of several vessels had coupled with Maori women, it remained a custom to offer important Pakeha visitors their choice of young men or young women.

TUNBRIDGE WELLS, ENGLAND. JUNE 1816

Acquiring Technique

The cockfight is nothing unusual: metal-spurred blurs of aggression slashing each other until one dies. It is the kind of sport humanity has always loved to watch. A smooth-faced young man in his early twenties is shouting encouragement loudly. When the bird he has bet on wins, he thumps his companions on the back and says, what a great time all this is.

He hates it, actually.

He is on a mission, however, and though he can momentarily hide from the stench of the cockpit and its noisome crowd by putting his scented silk kerchief to his nose, it is only momentary respite. He must assiduously cultivate the two older men he is with. They are the uncles of a sixteen-year-old ward of the court of chancery, Miss Eliza Pattle. She is the daughter of a late East India merchant and possesses a fortune. The uncles control access to this treasure.

Edward Gibbon Wakefield is not yet awake to the world-shaking ambitions that lie just beneath his consciousness. The family is distantly related to the great Gibbon and eventually Edward Gibbon Wakefield paints on a canvas as big as his namesake. Now, however, he is just working on technique.

He worms himself into the interstices of the social wall that protects his heiress and professes his love to her. Soon, still in high summer, a well-schemed elopement occurs. Two identical carriages career out of the residence at Tunbridge Wells. The two uncles follow the wrong one, as Wakefield has planned, and he and Miss Pattle jounce on corrugated roads to Edinburgh where they undergo a civil marriage. Then they return to England. In London, Wakefield takes out an insurance policy: he marries his heiress again, this time in a Church of England ceremony.

Elopement with a ward of chancery was in theory a capital crime. Edward Gibbon Wakefield, however, negotiates well. Both he and the uncles understand that, even if Wakefield were to be convicted, the uncles still would have an unsaleable property on their hands. Those are Wakefield's words and the uncles swallow hard, knowing he is right. They accept reality and agree to the largest settlement ever granted to-that-date to a husband from the inheritance of his wife: nearly £2,000 a year and he is given a swish job as a secretary in the English legation in Turin, Italy.

Instinctively, he has practised the basic technique of imperialising anything, man, beast, land: gain it, claim it, drain it. Before his child bride dies in 1820, she bears him a girl and a boy. For the remainder of his life Edward Gibbon Wakefield always says he had eloped for love, but he never said love of what, exactly.

MURIHIKU, NEW ZEALAND. 1817

The Foot Soldiers of Empire

"Sit in cold water. Up to your neck."

The first case of measles has hit the South Island and the tohunga is trying to cure something he never before has seen.

"Do not move. Be still or the spirits cannot heal."

Unlike the European population, whose biological resistance has reduced measles to a child's disease, among the Maori it strikes all ages.

Tuberculosis becomes frequent in the 1820s among Maori who have contact with outsiders.

An influenza epidemic ricochets through the population in the 1830s.

The spirits cannot heal. These and other European diseases weaken the social fabric and reduce the credibility of the ancient system of beliefs. Mortality among Maori in many areas is proportionately as great as that in Europe during the Black Death. Maori culture does not break; the old gods are not buried. But, as an advanced military people, steeped in tactical thinking, the Maori recognize that they require reinforcements. They will have to fight the enemy with weapons taken from that enemy: Pakeha medicine, muskets, religion, boats, beliefs.

Whatever is required.

KORORAREKA, NORTH ISLAND, NEW ZEALAND. 1820

Fine Tuning

"Repair. You. Repair."

The Irish sailor is surprised. Why is the tattooed native holding out a flintlock to him?

"Repair. Not work. Repair."

The seaman shakes his head and steps around his petitioner. The mariner enters a slab-built trading shop. He turns and looks out the doorway. The native is approaching another European: "Repair. You. Repair."

Flintlock muskets, the power-sticks of the Pakeha, are coming into Maori hands. They are untrustworthy devices at best, and the European traders never sell the best to the natives. The sticks often need repair, the more frequently because their new owners embrace them too enthusiastically. The Maori are forever cleaning the flintlocks, taking them apart, loosening and tightening the screws that hold the firing pieces in alignment. Then, their treasures not working, they approach the nearest Pakeha. They are convinced that every European knows how to field strip a firearm and believe it is only churlishness that makes the Pakeha refuse their simple request: "Repair. You. Repair."

Muskets spread. They are a Pakeha innovation that could be used against the Pakeha. Some future day. Now, however, they are a new virus in the Maori population, one without an antigen. The flintlocks are used to settle old scores and to lever new ambitions. For a decade and a half, a series of internal wars rage among several of the major Maori tribes. These musket wars end not by any formal armistice, but through simple exhaustion. No audit is possible: certainly, however, more human lives were ended than in any other conflict on New Zealand soil and undoubtedly more men of New Zealand died in these wars than were killed in World War I.

Twenty thousand lives?

"Repair. You. Repair."

STEWART ISLAND, NEW ZEALAND. 1822

Connect the Dots

Captain W.L. Edwardson, master of the *Snapper*, peers assiduously through his magnifying glass. He is amazed at the careful artistry he observes on the face and body of a man who stands patiently as he is examined. The complex patterns, the mixture of symmetrical motifs with limning that accentuate the man's individuality, leaves Edwardson awestruck and uneasy. They involve a form of primary artistry that Europeans had given up the best part of a thousand years earlier, an art that eschews the representational and searches, in pattern, for the eternal.

"Are you done, so?" the man asks.

Edwardson is not merely taken with the overall artistry of Maori tattooing, he is fascinated by its technical complexity. Under his strong reading glass he can see that each curve, line, swirl, and arabesque is comprised of hundreds and hundreds of tiny dots. He marvels at this and wants to keep looking, the same way, later in his own century, viewers of the first rotogravure pictures in newspapers are to spend hours examining the little dots that make the big pictures.

"Och, now you must be." The accent is Irish, the man's name, James Caddell, or Caddle: it matters not, he can no longer write it.

A dozen years earlier, Caddell had been a sixteen-year old cabin boy on a sealing ship that put into Stewart Island. When a six-oared boat was sent to shore, a Maori war party jumped the crew and five of the six seamen were killed. Caddell, the sixth, was saved when, in a gloriously romantic gesture, the chief's niece threw her cloak over him, thus instantly granting him asylum and simultaneously claiming him as her own. They married, and Caddell gained chiefly rank, largely because of his ability to fight.

Caddell is a Connacht name, imported into Ireland by Anglo-Normans who pushed aside the local Irish and then became as Hibernian as those they displaced. A Richard Caddell was sheriff of Connaught in 1306, and from him directly descend not only the Caddells, but the Blakes, major players in Irish history the world around.

Richard Caddell. James Caddell.

If we could fully connect those two dots, the pattern would be exponentially more complex than any moko, than any illuminated manuscript, and we would be the richer, the wiser.

ST. ALBAN'S HALL, OXFORD UNIVERSITY, 1825

Tutoring

The Rev. Richard Whately, D.D., principal of St. Alban's Hall, Oxford: at this time he was writing his *Logic* and his *Rhetoric*, works that made him the leading logician in the British Isles until John Stuart Mills' *System of Logic* appeared in 1843. And, Whately was trying to revive the smallest Oxford hall of its day, to which he had just been appointed. St. Alban's Hall was known as the Botany Bay of Oxford. It had been filled by the previous master with men thrown out of other colleges. With no endowments, no permanent fellowships, St. Alban's was an academic reform school for the upper classes.

That explains why Whately was teaching a young Anglo-Irish gentleman, of county Westmeath roots on his mother's side, how to get into Sandhurst. Most Oxford tutors of this era made more money by taking private pupils than they received from their college stipend, and Whately, despite his title as principal, needed money. His teaching style was eccentric, but effective. He received his pupil in his study and immediately Whately stretched out on an enormous chesterfield, and started to smoke a pipe. He would quiz the pupil on what he knew, and then on what he wanted to know and why. Then a lecture would pour forth and the young man eventually would be sent away with an assignment for the next supervision.

George Grey has been tutored off and on by Whately since 1820, when Whately was an unmarried fellow of Oriel College. Having run away at age eight from his boarding school because of its strict discipline, Grey did not at all mind learning under the negligent gaze of the Rev. Mr. Whately, for he was treated as a mind and as an independent human being. Whately took Grey for walks in the Oxford meadows and there the Principal threw stones and jumped puddles with a lack of concern for academic dignity. Whately had been doing that sort of thing for years, and his young men had prospered: for example, Nassau Senior and John Henry Newman, who, as a young fellow of Oriel College had been assigned to Whately (then an Oriel fellow) for polishing.

Whately's method subtly turned George Grey on his head: from being a scapegrace, he transformed himself into a young man responsible for his own future. In tutorials he frequently reminded Dr. Whately that he was preparing for the Royal Military College examinations, and could he please have more practical assignments?

In June 1821 Whately had married George Grey's aunt, Elizabeth Pope. Grey, a young man of good manners whatever his problems at boarding school, was included in the Whately family visits with their closest friends, the Thomas Arnold family. Arnold had been elected to an Oriel fellowship in 1815 through Whately's influence. Now, both he and Whately were married and the two families visited each other on holiday and named their children after each other. Arnold, in 1828, became the headmaster of Rugby.

For Grey, these connections had long-term benefits, but for the moment his triumph was entry into Sandhurst in 1826. Better still, he was eventually commended for academic excellence. In 1830 he was commissioned. His regiment, the Eighty-Third Foot, was stationed in Ireland for six years.

In 1831, Richard Whately, D.D., accepted appointment as the Protestant archbishop of Dublin. He remained in Ireland for the rest of his life, thirty-two years.

Grey and Whately met occasionally. As each became knowledgeable about the hideous state of Irish life, they came independently to the same conclusion: only heavy emigration, underwritten by the government, could prevent disaster.

Another Colony

Edward Gibbon Wakefield is about to take his second colony. The first, Miss Eliza Anne Frances Pattle, had seen him right – he had lived in Paris on a high scale: her inheritance following her death in childbirth in 1820 had provided him with, well, with a widower's bench. That's what he termed it, with obvious pleasure. Although his new position as secretary of the English embassy in Paris was a respectable enough post, his being able to live well above his station was the gift of a colony to its metropole.

But move on he must. That is the rule of the true imperialist: before one colony runs dry, find another one. And now he has a beauty and she is only fifteen, an heiress worth £600,000, or so rumours say, and ah, dear Lord, he never has had such ... such pleasure, such power.

Edward Gibbon Wakefield and his brother William (always ask twice, with someone named Billy or Liam – is there any evidence he is not a fool?) have kidnapped this lissome daughter of a Macclesfield silk manufacturer from her school. It is all Edward's plan, of course, and it reads like the end papers of a three-volume romance, where the publisher tells his palpitating audience the outline of his next breast-boiler. God, Wakefield loves it.

He sends his French servant up to the boarding school door. This lumpkin pretends to be the new butler of William Turner, the Macclesfield silk magnate, and the headmistress and the poor distressed girl are given a note that purports that Miss Turner's mother is dangerously ill. Ellen is taken to a hotel, where Edward Wakefield calls himself "Captain Wilson" and he somehow gets her into a coach, which heads north, brother William in attendance. On the way, Edward convinces Ellen Turner that her father is about to go bankrupt and that marrying "Captain Wilson" will solve this problem.

Yes, granted: it is total rubbish. As a melodrama, it would have made even Dion Boucicault laugh. Wakefield loves it, and as the coach jogs north he has to put his hat over his male member: it's so gloriously, favourably, unambiguously wonderful to have power over another entity, to have so much power than one can reel the trophy in slowly, savouring the moment, tasting the surrender.

Never mind that the service took place in Gretna Green, Scotland, a freeport for dodgy marriages; or that it was conducted by a blacksmith; or that immediately after the service, Edward Gibbon Wakefield, learning that his putative father-in-law (who also happened to be a county sheriff, an honorific office that, on occasion, gave real clout) was on his trail, hied away to Calais as fast as he could. He was nabbed by hard men, hired by Ellen's distraught mother and very angry father. Don't even pay attention to the three years Edward and his slow-witted brother William are sentenced to serve in Lancaster prison.

Recognize: Wakefield did not mind, for he had raised to a conscious level the pleasure that the narcotic of colonial power could provide. From now on, he stays away from tiny islands, such as teenage girls, and proposes plans to colonize entire continents. While still in prison he writes colonization plans, pamphlets that are taken seriously by civil servants and junior ministers in government. Edward Gibbon Wakefield is on the road to becoming the nineteenth century's most influential theorist and lobbyist for the colonial settlement of the Second British Empire.

THE BAY OF ISLANDS, NEW ZEALAND. 1827

Bewilderment

The elders of the Nga Puhi see a world that is out of control and can give no reason. Dwelling in and around the Bay of Islands, the Nga Puhi see and feel the impact of the Pakeha well before most other tribes.

New diseases arrive, but no new cures. New methods of warfare emerge, but no ways of making peace. Slavery follows the new musket warfare the same way that dysentery and typhus follow a famine. Battles had always produced slaves, but now nearly one-tenth of New Zealand's population is held as chattel: mostly these slaves are women and young people, for the men who are captured in the musket wars usually are killed and, frequently, ritually eaten.

Disoriented, no compass to be found, a group of Nga Puhi elders tells the leading Pakeha that they strongly desire to emigrate to some distant island.

There they could be free of the oppression of their countrymen.

Then, and only then, could they live in peace.

HOKIANGA, NEW ZEALAND. 1828

Official Origins

The first respectable, middle-class, craw-thumping, clergy-revering
Irish Catholic to arrive in New Zealand did so in 1828. This is known
for a certainty, because he was so-declared in 1897 by Patrick Francis
Cardinal Moran, archbishop of Sydney and the first historian of the
church in Australia and New Zealand. Thomas Poynton, from Ireland, was a major timber merchant and his wife was the Sydney-born
daughter of Thomas Kennedy of County Wexford.

To be fair, Cardinal Moran simply denominated Poynton as the
first Irish Catholic settler in New Zealand. Full stop: no qualifiers.
Apparently all those Irish sealers, whalers, sharp traders, musket-
sellers, and gone-Maori predecessors of Poynton were Protestants.

That's a comfort. You can look it up in Moran's history of the
church. And it's all in the prophecies of Saint Malachy.

ROME. 1829

God's Sharp Cleaver

Captain Peter Dillon wrote a fine hand and a seductive sentence. His two-
volume story of his twenty years sailing in the south Pacific sold well in
London. More importantly, his correspondence with various ecclesiastics
sold the south Pacific well in Rome. Wisely, he accepted the coaching of the
rector of the Irish College in Rome as to whom to deal with, and how. So,
the authorities of the Sacred Congregation for the Propagation of the Faith
passed from hand to hand a letter of his, written from Paris, 7 September
1829. Dillon described in mouth-watering detail the souls to be won in
"Oceania," and the route to winning them. He was himself an adopted
son of the "princess of Tahiti," so he claimed, and was a revered figure in
Tonga "where several of the natives are deeply attached to me, and have
joined me in my sea voyages." And, additionally, "the last time I visited
the Fiji Islands the excellent prince there sent his three brothers a distance
of 200 miles in order to congratulate me on my arrival and to beg me to
come to live near him, offering me his own daughter in marriage."

Rich fare, that, for Captain Dillon reports that at each of these sites the tribal leaders are calling for missionaries.

To those hungry for souls, Dillon is judged to have been provided to the Church by divine providence. On 22 December 1829 the Sacred Congregation approves plans to evangelize the whole south Pacific.

Pope Gregory XVI, previous to his elevation in 1831, was prefect of the Sacred Congregation, so he knew what a tempting territory this was: perhaps the last, easiest frontier for the Church to conquer. And, as a shrewd Vatican politician, he knew that this prize was too lush to be run as a single religious satrapy. So, looking at history, he reflected on what one of his predecessors had done in dividing the world between the Spanish and the Portuguese. Gregory XVI split the Polynesian world, giving "Eastern Oceania" – from Tahiti eastward – to the Picpus Fathers and "Western Oceania" – running from the Cook Islands to New Zealand, to the Society of Mary. Thus a French order, the Marist Fathers, became spiritual proprietors of lands that spoke several languages, though none of them French.

KAPITI ISLAND, NEW ZEALAND. NOVEMBER, 1830

Useful Tools

"White People. They are very useful if one uses magic words. You have to tell them what they want to hear."

One of the first Maori leaders to overcome the shock of European incursion and to turn individual Pakeha into instruments of Maori intentions was Te Rauparaha, leader of the Ngati Toa. His tribe had been forced out of the midlands of the North Island, and had finally come to rest on Kapiti Island. This is a good defensive location and economically fortunate: Kapiti Island is the centre of the New Zealand flax trade and ships to and from Australia call in frequently.

"We require help," Te Rauparaha explains to Captain John Stewart of the *Elizabeth*, a brig of 236 tons. "The fight is your fight too." He explains to Captain Stewart that the Ngati Tahu, who reside on the eastern coast of the South Island, have killed several Europeans; a trader named Smith, a Captain Dawson and five of his crew, and a midshipman and longboat crew from the *H.M.S Warspite*.

The Englishman buys this, which is unfortunate. Granted, the deaths were real, but are not chargeable to the Ngati Tahu. This is tribal war, pure and simple, and the Pakeha are useful tools.

Piloted by Te Rauparaha's forceful personality, Captain Stewart sails to Akaroa. There, with Te Rauparaha's war party concealed beneath decks, the Pakeha captain goes on shore and invites the Ngati Tahu chief, his young daughter and three or four others on board. Once on ship, they are locked in the brig and then, by cover of night, Te Rauparaha and his warriors launch a surprise attack. The vessel holds 120 men, and the raid is remarkably successful. The night becomes luminous with burning whares, their inhabitants sometimes left inside. The butchery is so efficient that the raiders are able to bring back to the ship nearly five score baskets of human flesh. As a precaution against spoilage, the flesh is cooked for half an hour or so on shore, before loading.

The chief of the Ngati Tahu and his principal wife, knowing that their own lives will be a slow ritual of torture, parades of humiliation, broken bones, deformity and finally death, spare their eleven year-old daughter from this.

They strangle her.

ALBION, HIBERNIA'S
BENT OLD DARLING
1715–1830

Wisdom and the Big Picture

Just jack it in.

Forever, throughout eternity, courtiers, counsellors, civil servants have loved categories, because lines and boxes and definitions and prescriptions give them the illusion that what they can categorize they can control.

In June 1394, on his way to thump the Irish chiefs in Leinster, Richard II decides that it would be a good idea to require all the Irish in England to return to Ireland within the coming year.

They don't, and they last longer in England than he does.

In 1413, just days after Henry V accedes to the throne, the Westminster parliament requires that by Christmas day all Irish-born persons are to return to their homeland. Few leave and in 1431, '32 and '39 the royal counsellors issue further expulsion orders. The Irish wriggle through the cracks in the categories.

In December 1442 the campaign is abandoned.

Later attempts to exclude from England specific categories of Irish people – beggars, Jesuits – are attempted, yet never again do the English assert anything but a theoretical right to keep the Irish, as a national group, out of the country.

Westminster, 1949: the one possible guillotine-moment occurs. A stream of black and brown people from the Commonwealth is making white England nervous. And southern Ireland has just declared itself a republic, totally separate from the United Kingdom and the Commonwealth. This would be the time to lump the citizens of the Republic with all those coloured foreigners and keep them at home.

Wisdom prevails. War-groggy England, critically short of work power, needs Irish men and women to rebuild itself. The southern Irish, though no longer in the Commonwealth, are provided with a special status. They can enter, take jobs, and they receive health, unemployment and welfare benefits.

And they can vote in British elections.

LIVERPOOL. 1715

The Liverpool Machine

Was it a gantry? Or a catapult? Few said, for the machinery being built was unknown to most.

The first dock at Liverpool was nearly ready for opening. The dock itself, with massive windlass apparatuses and pivoting cargo-loaders, was one of the wonders of the age. The dock can be taken as one large machine, designed to revolutionize ocean transport.

And so too can the entire city of Liverpool. Already it was rising to dominance in the slave trade and it held a prime place in the provisions business. As Liverpool transformed itself during the eighteenth century into a giant maritime machine, with dockage that made export and import of everything from timber to human bodies quick and cheap, it became the world port of England.

The English empire already was profiting from the slave trade. Now that triangular trade came to have Liverpool as its apex, the coast of Africa as one corner, the Caribbean or the American colonies as another, vessels sailed around the triangle and ended back in Liverpool as the offloading and auction point for raw materials from the New World.

This machine – indeed, was it a gantry or was it a catapult? – became, after the Napoleonic Wars, as ingenious at moving masses of migrants on and off the ships as it was with cattle or bales of cotton. By the 1830s most Irish people shipping to North America did so from Liverpool. And hundreds of thousands of Europeans made the voyage to the east coast of England, then travelled to Liverpool, for in the mid-Victorian years it was northern Europe's cheapest route to the New World. People out, goods home. A fine machine.

And, for those Irish who work, settle, prosper in England it is the most-used port of entry. Ships from Derry, Newry and Belfast would make the Clydeside in Scotland or the Cumbria coast of England: Cobh or Dublin to Cardiff was popular with transient labourers; but Liverpool, whether for entry into England or for escape to a New World was used by most.

Such a gigantic, complicated, unpredictable invention. Often it disregarded the intentions of those who tried to use it. Would it sling a migrant seawards, towards America; or inland to Manchester or even London? or back to Ireland? or, leave the migrant for long years, stripped of resources and trapped among the rookeries and labyrinthine alleyways that reticulated along the base of that giant Liverpool machine?

LIVERPOOL. JUNE 1757

I Saw the Light

The crew of the *Liverpool*, a privateer under Captain Hutchinson, did not merely prey, as did other privateers, on the defenceless. They prayed.

The captain insisted that his men attend daily religious services. They had the Prayer Book rammed down their throats with the same threatening enthusiasm that the King's regulations were read to royal seamen, and then they had Captain Hutchinson's own rules chanted at them: steal anything for yourself, fail to put anything into the common treasure purse, and you are dead.

On this cruise from its home port, the *Liverpool* takes two French vessels and frees a number of English and Irish sailors held prisoner by the French.

Unhappily, the captain became obsessed with the French and could see or hear little else. Sailing in a light fog, he took the *H.M.S. Antelope* for a French vessel and hailed it in French, demanding surrender. The *Antelope*'s captain, reasonably assuming that he was meeting the old enemy, replied by raking the *Liverpool* with a full broadside. She lost her top-gallant mast, but survived to make port.

Captain Hutchinson, realizing the limits of his own naval vision, took up the post of dock-master for the harbour of Liverpool. There he invented the reflecting mirror for lighthouses, a monument to his perspicacity while on land.

OLNEY. 1770

Jesus the Very Thought

John Newton's maritime career was chequered. As a youth, a Liverpool press-gang grabbed him on the street and dragged him down to the docks for service in the Royal Navy.

Later, he was flogged through the same streets for his chronic indiscipline.

He found his home in the merchant navy and rose from ordinary seaman to command and ownership of his own slave ship. He was a proud captain in the armada that made Liverpool a wonder of the world: wet docks and sleek merchants, made possible by the trade in woolly heads: abolition of the slave trade in 1807 was a time of mourning.

Before then, Newton found Jesus, an unsettling discovery. He renounced his former life; he became a clergyman, took the curacy of Olney, and wrote one of the most peaceful and comforting English hymns of the century: **Jesus the very ...**

THE LIVERPOOL BRIDEWELL. NOVEMBER 1775

A Clean Breast

Brigid McCarthy, also known as Brigid O'Donnell, is observed carefully by the pioneer prison reformer John Howard. She is undergoing her first hygienic bath since arrival in Liverpool and subsequent arrest as a small-time thief.

In her turn among the women prisoners, she is tied into a large chair that is attached to a long pole. A counterweight at the opposite end balances the device and makes it easy to revolve the pole on its axis.

As part of her weekly education in becoming a decent women, Brigid is placed in a flannel shift and then the pole is rotated until the chair bearing Brigid is over a huge bath. She is ducked three times and Mr. Howard is convinced that she comes out of this baptism a much better person.

LIVERPOOL. 1793

User

William Barton (later Sir William) is the sort of Liverpool man-of-commerce who is loved as being a hearty and True Briton.

At the moment, he is nearly blind-drunk at table, but not yet deaf-drunk. He can hear the toasts that ramble continously as one more merchant chief after another slurs his way into unconsciousness. An ambitious fellow merchant addresses Barton. "I pay my respects, deeply to you, sir ..." and he continues on.

Barton goes red and tries to stand. That failing, he rails incoherently. "You sir ..." is all the company can make out, save that he is obviously furious.

Finally one of the junior members, recently back from the West Indies, explains that in Barbados, where Barton had been a very vigorous slave owner, "You sir," was the phrase of mixed authority and contempt a master uses to his male indoor slaves.

Barton, the True Briton, in his cups believes that he has been addressed as a slave and if he could rise to his feet he would challenge his detractor to a duel.

LONDON. 1802

Transhumance

More than ever has been calculated, the Irish Rising of 1798 enriched the social and economic life of England – with men and women from both sides, who had to scramble to stay ahead of their own pasts.

For burned-out loyalists, it was often no more than their come-down in life, from shirttail- or real-gentry to merchants, traders, economic chance-takers. Former rebels, who in Anglo-Irish circles often were from the same family as the loyalists, had economic problems and the additional one of being liable to prosecution if they had been too far in front of the rebel van. Eventually, an informal statute-of-limitations came into effect. Irishmen on the re-make in England, if they acted as gentlefolk, were allowed to pretend to have no past worth enquiring about and, later, to be vaguely identified as formerly-Irish gentry.

Nathaniel Grogan settled in London in 1802 as a small trader in wines (a commodity his family knew all too well). When navigating the fringes of London society, he was careful to maintain his mask as a well-mannered gentry-merchant. And never to give a clue to what he had been in Ireland: the rebel son of Cornelius Grogan whose head was last seen in Wexford City in 1798, and a goodly distance from his body. Grogan Sr.'s head sat for months on a pike over the gate of Wexford and served as a strong reminder that the decision to rebel or to be a loyalist should not be taken lightly.

Nathaniel's problems were tougher than those of most Irish on the-remake, for he was most likely the illegitimate son of the much-piked Cornelius Grogan by his housekeeper: by-blows were fairly standard among Anglo-Irish in Wexford, Waterford, Cork. For instance, the Grogans' prime enemy, Hunter Gowan of Mount Nebo had children by his female servants as naturally as a ram tups a ewe.

Illegitimacy, though vexing, was less a problem for Nathaniel than the well-known tale in the south of Ireland of how his father had ineptly engineered his own death, havering at a dinner party of fashionable radicals and then deciding to lead the mostly-Catholic peasantry for fear of having their pikes enter his spine from behind. He became a minor official of the Committee of Public Safety of Wexford Town, and when the Loyalists recaptured the town he was hanged on the town bridge and his body dropped into the river: but not before his head was severed and placed on a spike at the courthouse. So Cornelius Grogan had ended dead and the centre of a folktale about inefficacy.

As did so many of the former Irish gentry, Nathaniel found his own tiny niche in London and, like a whelk on a piece of wave-washed basalt, used it to expand. Of course it took more than one generation and he did not see the end – the Grogans eventually claiming an empire in Africa in the late nineteenth century the way their ancestors had claimed one (albeit smaller) in Ireland in the seventeenth – but he saw the trend and was pleased.

His son Nicholas took over the wine merchancy and purchased a house in St. James, and was married in St. George's Church, Hanover Square.

What Nathaniel Grogan found especially admirable about his son Nicholas, wine-merchant-on-the-rise, was that when it came to selecting a mother for his children he did not mess about with any nonsense about politesse: a quality English woman was beyond this generation's reach. Young Nicholas married what he needed, an illiterate English woman who was to be the brood mare for his family and produce a platoon of healthy and aggressive offspring.

BRNO, MORAVIA. 1804

Espionage

Two Irish spinners, their names forever unknown, smuggle crucial intelligence to the officials of the Habsburg empire. They have been working in Nottingham, where Richard Arkwright has married his spinning machines to James Watt's best steam engine. English officials have managed to keep the details out of foreign hands, but now a full set of drawings is made available to the Habsburg government and their empire begins to mechanize wool spinning and, soon thereafter, cloth manufacture.

THE THEATRE ROYAL, LIVERPOOL. JANUARY 1805

Fair Comment

The popular tragedian George Frederick Cooke frequently appeared on stage drunk and incoherent.

Usually his audiences put up with it, for seeing the ruins of a great monument is better than looking at a pillar of salt. But this night the Liverpool audience hissed him. The noise to his ears was the sound of a thousand geese, and he snapped into consciousness. He steadied himself and then rounded on his critics.

"I have not come here," he told the burghers of Liverpool, "to be insulted by a set of wretches, every brick in whose town is cemented with an African's blood."

THE ATLANTIC TRIANGLE. 1807

Farsighted

Before they became shore-bound businessmen, the Tobin brothers of Liverpool were master mariners. They were famous for a genetic trait inherited from a grandfather, a Dublin wig-maker-to-the-Quality: they could see farther with the naked eye than most mariners could see with a spy glass. In their early life as privateers and as slavers this ability served them well. Now, in 1807, Thomas and John (the strongest and brightest of seventeen children), foresaw what the abolition of the British slave trade would do to the port of Liverpool.

"Nothing, I should say."

"Aye, save we will not have to lash down the cargo quite so tightly."

Carrying human bodies had been the high-profit end of the Liverpool shipping industry – first Africans and, from the 1820s onwards,

Irish people – but the everyday overheads were covered by a mundane, but very large, trade in everything from English soap to Canadian timber to American cotton.

"We shall trade with the same places in Africa and buy from the same people."

"Palm oil. That's the answer."

And it was. The same ships that had carried slaves now took merchandise, soap, and especially, Manchester cotton goods down the west coast of Africa. The Tobins's companies worked as far south as Angola. The indigenous chiefs who had sold human beings to the Liverpool slavers now demanded palm from their subjects, and what once was slavery simply became capitalism. The oil either went back to England or, more often, to the USA, where the chief product of the American slave economy – cotton – was picked up and brought to England to be woven into textiles, some of which went back to Africa to keep the wheel spinning. Unlike the other main African trading family of the nineteenth century, the Horsfalls (who were caught running slaves in the 1840s), the Tobins kept their slate clean and made more from the new and sanitary version of the slave system than from the old one, with all those messy bodies to be disposed of.

By the mid-1850s, Liverpool as a port was handling one-third of the United Kingdom's imports and one-half of the exports, a triumph of vision, if not of virtue.

HYTHE, KENT. MAY 1808

True Romance

England was as good a place to rehabilitate an Irish girl's reputation after a dangerous flirtation as it was to resuscitate the fortunes of the male victims of 1798, both sides.

Sarah Curran, to whom the myth-burnished hero of his own 1803 Rising, Robert Emmet, was supposed to be inconsolably attached, knew that. Later myth had her dying in Sicily of a broken heart over Emmet's martyred memory. Sarah, although not a hard person, knew better than to spend her life grieving.

She was the daughter of the political philosopher, pre-Union MP and serial adulterer John Philpot Curran and his merely adulterous wife Sarah Creagh, who in 1792 had blown the family apart by becoming pregnant by the local Anglican clergyman. So, Sarah, age ten, was sent away to be raised by a respectable family, who showed her the social graces but little love. It was hardly surprising, then, that when at age eighteen she met Robert Emmet, a gilded TCD student, she found him attractive. She came to idolize him in the way that schoolgirls later romanticized popular singers, constructing an imaginary set of architectural drawings of the life together they would never have. Emmet, for his part, became interested in her only in the autumn of 1802 and wrote her letters that, though warm, bear the signs of a man who had more important things on his mind.

To his great credit, though his letters could be read as showing that she knew of the planned 1803 insurrection (and thus was complicitous), he lied convincingly during his trial and saved her from charges: treason being at least theoretically possible, since a French invasion had been mooted by Emmet.

Sarah Curran, though she genuinely, if formulaicly, loved Emmet, was a practical gel and knew that mourning for a hanged felon was not a good career choice.

She cried deeply and a bit more than two years after her own last letter to Robert Emmet, she married in County Cork, a Captain R. Henry Sturgeon of the Royal Engineers, a promising officer and, not incidentally, a nephew of the late marquis of Rockingham, some-time British prime minister. They settled first at Hythe, Kent, and then the regiment moved on to Sicily where Sarah wrote of the land and people in a mixture of evocative and, often, very shrewd prose. The British army, as so often, was saving an Irish soul from its troubles.

The demise of Sarah Curran was sad, but not unusual for the time: childbirth trauma. Pregnant in the summer of 1807 and on her way back to England, she experienced a viciously difficult delivery. Her infant son died, and she never recovered physically or mentally.

She died, not in Sicily and not mourning Robert Emmet, but in Hythe, Kent, grieving her wee baby, child of the Sicilian sun.

THE IRISH SEA. 1818

Act of Union

The first regularly running steam packet across the Irish Sea begins to operate in 1818 between Belfast and Glasgow. Soon it has several imitators sailing to ports in England. This in addition to the older, un-predictable, sailing ferries.

Prices drop and three decades later a cabin on a Dublin-Liverpool boat costs ten shillings and the standard deck rate on a steamer is 5 shillings. But anything can be bargained, and 2/6d is not uncommon. Some do even better, especially in the winter months.

In 1836, a woman in Londonderry who has nine shillings owed to her in Dublin, worries about it. She cannot afford to lose the sum. She frets. She cannot sleep.

Choosing her moment, she ships from Derry to Liverpool and then to Dublin, where she collects the nine shillings owing.

Then she takes passage back to Liverpool and back to Derry.

It's a good investment: collecting her 9s has cost her a total of 1/6d – eighteen pence! – that's how close are England and Ireland.

LIVERPOOL. 12 JULY 1819

Season's Opener

England, with its own ripe history of sectarian violence, sees its first piece of Irish sectarian display: institutionalized, predictable, end-lessly repeatable, and, alas, portable.

Ninety Orangemen, mostly Irish in background, but English and Scots among them, perform the prescribed march to a church near Dale Street. They begin at the town centre and have a band leading them. The church they are heading for is in the settlement range of the quickly-infilling Catholic poor, abutting the quays.

Everything could have been rehearsed: the march announced weeks in advance; Catholic plans to attack put in place almost at once; warnings in the public press from concerned citizens who know what each side has in mind; and, finally, 2,000 or more Catholics at-tacking the Orangemen at Dale Street, leaving many of the marchers seriously injured.

In Liverpool, over time, the only thing that changes is that the Prot-estant party (increasingly English, not Irish, in origin) learn not to pick fights when they are outnumbered.

LIVERPOOL. 1820S

St. Patrick's Purge

The one place in Ireland's spiritual empire where St. Patrick's Day is a Catholics-only affair is Liverpool. Elsewhere it's genuinely mixed or, at minimum, token efforts at inviting Irish Protestants to join in any public celebrations that are planned. None of that here.

Throughout the 1820s, an annual St. Patrick's Day parade is held. It is never attacked by Protestants.

Because: 10- to 12,000 marchers are in the van each year, and inciting them by attack would be equivalent to igniting Liverpool by fire.

Vent, volcano, vent.

"CONNORVILLE," COUNTY CORK. 1822

A Very Literary Year

Roger O'Connor is arranging the final details of the publication of his major creation, the *Chronicles of Eri, being the History of the Gaal, Sciot Iber or Irish People*. O'Connor is a zealous patriot and wishes the Irish people to have as long and rich a history as those of the other islands surrounding the Irish sea. That's why he works so hard on the maps and parchment shards that he will pass off as ancient. O'Connor, at sixty, is still a formidable bulk of a man, though now he must bend close over the parchment and use thick spectacles as he engrosses the fine details.

The Connors, a Protestant family of reasonable lineage – Roger Connor's uncle was Richard Viscount Longueville – had split in the 1790s. Roger and his brother Arthur had been fierce rebels and the three other brothers scorched-earth Orange. Roger and Arthur both had been arrested, but escaped the treason charge. Arthur, deported to France, became one of Napoleon's generals. Roger, after serving time at Fort George, was freed. He added the Gaelic prefix to his name as being the original form, and lived the rest of his life as a chieftain.

In another wing of the square-built, fortress-like house, another literary work is in progress. O'Connor's twenty-eight-year-old son is writing a pamphlet. It's a curious effort, dedicated to defending "my slandered, sainted sire."

Feargus O'Connor is correct in feeling that his father requires defending. There are, for example, the continuing complaints by the officials of the Insurance Office that they really should not have paid Roger Connor £7,000 in insurance money in 1809 when his then-home Dangan Castle went up in flames. The building had been insured for only months, not even a year. More to the point is the universal belief, all the more damaging for being accurate, that Feargus's father had, in October 1812, accomplished the best Irish mail robbery of the age. He and six subordinates had robbed the Galway mail coach at a time when it was full of remittances from England and of drover's funds for the market fair at Ballinasloe. So stuffed with booty was the coach that the highwaymen had to use barrows to cart away the scores of sacks. The subordinates' share was over £500 per man. Amazingly, when five of them were caught, they chose to stay silent and hang, rather than take a pardon for informing.

All that, the trial of Feargus's father in 1817, his suborning of witnesses, his acquittal, and the niggling matter of other mail coach robberies, required refutation. The best route was to present all the matters as part of a governmental conspiracy to besmirch an incorruptible patriot of 1798.

Back in the library, Roger O'Connor, never one to hold back in anything, goes the whole route in his literary efforts. *A Translation from the Original Manuscripts in the Phoenician Dialect of the Scythian Language.*

KENYON: BETWEEN LIVERPOOL AND MANCHESTER.
SEPTEMBER 1830

Virgin Rail

Prime minister the Duke of Wellington takes his seat beside the Marchioness of Salisbury in a specially-constructed car. It is one of three dignitaries' carriages pulled by George Stephenson's *Rocket*. Five additional wagons carry second-line political and business notables, a brass band and assorted clergy.

This highly-publicized journey between Liverpool and Manchester is intended to open the new age of travel, one that will eventually subordinate Liverpool and its associated waterways as the hub of England's transportation system.

Half way to Manchester, the cars are uncoupled so that water can be added to the locomotive's steam boilers.

Wellington, who loves being a general as much as he hates being Irish, insists that those who wish to pay their courtesies to him during this stop should come to his carriage, like beggars at the back door of a Big House.

One of the MPs for Liverpool, William Huskisson, makes the obligatory journey to scrape before England's Saviour and unfortunately does not hear the whistle as the *Rocket* moves to re-couple with the wagons. Huskisson slips.

The *Rocket*, portent of the future, crushes his leg and he dies within a few hours, wondering if rail travel really is the answer.

ST. PAUL COMES
TO POLYNESIA
1795–1830

Received Texts

"Christians, St. Paul says, are distinguished by their vision." This was the favourite phrase of the Rev. Dr. Haweis, chaplain to the Countess of Huntingdon. "And our vision reaches as far as the thousands, nay, tens of thousands of Christians that will some day be the harvest of souls in the South Seas." Haweis knew of Fletcher Christian, of course, but he counted him as a lost sheep. What he saw was a huge flock of Pacific natives, all requiring to be brought to the good shepherd.

The "Connexion" of the Countess of Huntingdon was a strange pantechnicon of Wesleyanism and evangelical clergy of the Church of England and of the Church of Ireland. It served as a bridge between the several branches of Protestantism in the British Isles, and negotiated a religious convention among Protestants that was similar to the Rules of War drawn up much later in Geneva, Switzerland. Now, in the mid 1790s, the English nation in mortal military combat, its enthusiasts turned their faces away from the Continent and decided to fight the legions of the devil in far distant lands.

That London in their era might reasonably be seen as the world's centre of heathendom, and thus a curious place from which to Christianize a quarter or so of the world's surface, did not strike the Rev. Dr. Haweis and his followers as noteworthy. They lived in a world of glowing texts, St. Paul's epistles, mostly, but also their newest inspiration: the journals of Captain Cook, published between 1771 and 1782. The noble savages of the South Pacific were engraved there, souls begging to be plucked from Satan's burning: so the animated clergy inferred from Cook's descriptions.

Thus in a series of meetings that began on Monday, 21 September, a clerical hysteria grew, one that fed on visions of a pan-Protestant conquest of millions of acres, and whose rolling, romantic, enspiriting chant was a collectanea that became the new litany: St. Paul, his charges, comminations, jeremiads, and the report of dangerous, mysterious, god-needing savages taken from Cook's works, their mephitic figures made all the more commanding by their being so solemnly reported by Cook.

The intoxicating incense, thick as the cloud that led the Chosen People by day, was inhaled first in the function room of the Castle and Falcon Inn by scores of London's ministers who in their enthusiasm subscribed £740 to the as-yet-vague project. In the evening of the same day, an inaugural general meeting was held, with influential and wealthy laymen and clergy from the countryside attending. The next day a service was held in the dissenting chapel in Spa Field, where 200 leading clergy heard the Rev. Dr. Hawies tell them of all the savages that needed saving. Thereafter, they formed a "Missionary society"– soon to be renamed the "London Missionary Society"–whose goal was "to spread the knowledge of Christ among heathen and other unenlightened nations." They meant, of course, foreign nations.

THE TONGAN ISLANDS. 1799

The Reception of Guests

Occasionally, modern ethnographers use the right words. "Precontact" is a good example.

The adult females of the islands of Tonga in the late eighteenth century marked their daughters according to their physical state, the same way that, in a later era when a market economy arose, they marked their livestock.

Girls who were no longer virgins had a small vertical slash cut in their foreheads. Sometimes this gash was blackened by tattooing. This practice only slightly affected the girls' worth in Tongan society, for the locals were no Puritans. Its main, if unintended effect was to make contact with the Europeans easier, for now the outsiders knew exactly what the score was.

English captains sought out girls with clear foreheads. Their crews did otherwise.

THE TONGAN ISLANDS. JANUARY, 1800

Nomenclature

Early English-speaking navigators and cartographers almost always got the names wrong. The Tongan Islands, for example, were called "the Friendly Islands," a cavalier act of name dropping that brought no end of bitterness to the first London Missionary Society representatives on those islands.

There five missionaries huddled together, and spent equal amounts of time praying that they would not be prey, and fortifying the hill-side caves where they sought shelter. Only two flintlock fusils kept the Friendly Islanders from their refuge.

All had seemed so sublime, so god-intended, and the holy messengers had sung hymns and prayed spontaneously when, in April 1797, they had first seen Nuka'alofa. Nine of them disembarked from the *Duff*, an unfortunately accurate name for a vessel delivering heaven's emissaries. All of them were male, and that may have been the London Missionary Society's main mistake. Bands of men are easily seen as constituting war parties, especially in a place such as Tonga where, as the missionaries learned, tribal warfare was the national pastime. And then there were all those clearly-labelled young women: soon one of the missionaries joined the natives in a life of cat's cream concupiscence. One down, eight left.

To make matters worse, one of their two faith-texts failed them. Cook's journals now were dangerously out-of-date. Thanks to the enthusiasms of Sir Joseph Banks and his "Botanist's Bay," the coast of Australia now was a penal colony and demons who escaped from that hell skittered across Polynesia, inciting the natives against anything smacking of official British virtue.

Five of the missionaries, having the courage to be craven, fled to seaside cliffs, there to await deliverance.

And now their second text, the Bible, failed their three stauncher colleagues. They refused to hide, for they read aloud the portions of the book of Daniel where Shadrach, Meshach and Abednego stand forth in the fiery furnace against King Nebuchadnezzar and triumphantly survive. Thus, when a band of warriors approached the mission station, the missionaries brazenly went out to meet them, heads high, no trace of fear on their faces. Encountering such disrespectful people, the warriors had no choice but to club them to death.

The five survivors' nightmare ended in January 1800, when a commercial vessel, passing by, saw the missionaries and took them to Port Jackson, Australia.

The mission in the Friendly Islands was suspended.

MANGAIA, THE COOK ISLANDS. 1801

Local Vocabulary

Weep for Tairoa, who was first to fall
By the weapon of the Papaa.

Papaa. It is an old word with a new meaning. It fills a need, for creatures have appeared that never before were seen and therefore have
no name. White people. In the Cook Islands they are *Papaa.* In the Samoan group *Pa'plagi.* In the Tongas, *Pao'longi.* The languages are related and the local vocabularies are similar responses to the same
problem: what to call those European creatures. The various words
are translated as "pale ghosts," "angels," "spirit messengers," "pale
devils," and a score more, none of the translations being very infor-
mative or stable over time: "white people" covers it.

By what mysterious method
Was Tairoa made from a distance
    Stone dead?

The lament, written by a sister of the young warrior Tairoa, commemorated an event that was so shocking to the Cook Islanders that,
despite their retentive memories, they recalled only the horror, and
not the name of the ship, nor the details of the Papaa involved.

Sometime, soon after the start of the nineteenth century in the
western reckoning of time, a whaling ship called at Mangaia. Remembering Captain Cook's felicific trade, the Mangahians immediately
sent their waka out to greet the whaler. Business was good and,
equally, it was an adventure. Real warrior action. A local chief, Koroa,
had just made a major trade – an octopus for a tenpenny nail (the basis for a bradawl) and for a knife when a young warrior, Tairoa, wild,
brave, ambitious, grabbed for fame. He paddled his canoe close to the
ship of the Papaa and fatally speared one of the pale angels. Then he
paddled a bit away and enjoyed the consternation that his conquering of the Papaa produced. Certainly he would become a warrior of
legend.
Tairoa was puzzled when a long bamboo stick was pointed at him
from the foreigners' vessel. He saw a light and heard a noise only a

decasecond before his world exploded into searing pain, blinding sunshine, and a roaring of reef-shredded breakers. He fell dead in the bottom of his canoe.

Everyone fled, and the Papaa took the body of Tairoa, for perhaps it would have value to some of the scientific mob that were constantly being sent out from London.

Thy body was abandoned by Koroa;
It was left in the hands of thy foes.

RAROTANGA. THE COOK ISLANDS. 1814

Sandalwood

The first Papaa woman to be eaten by the Cook Islanders had sometimes called herself Mary Butcher, because that was easier for the English to remember. In fact, she and her Huguenot grandparents had fled to Ireland during the persecution of Protestants by Louis XIV. Having gotten herself into legal trouble in London, she had been transported to Australia, and then became the mistress of William Wentworth, the 22-year-old son of one of the wealthier men in New South Wales: the Principal Surgeon of the colony, d'Arcy Wentworth. He has sent his son to sea to clear up a tubercular-sounding cough and the young man is now the first mate on a small vessel that scoured the South Pacific for items to steal.

"Bouchier," she had often told Wentworth. "I am called Bouchier, not Butcher, and I will thank you to remember."

Now, she was being called sweet-pork by the Rarotongans. The local method of cooking a person was to insert a long spear in the rectum and continue pressing it upward until the spear's sharp point emerged somewhere in the region of the neck. In Mary's case, rictus of her neck left her mouth conveniently agape, so that the lance emerged without breaking any skin. The spear served as a spit, and its ends were lodged on two solid piles of stones. The carcase was rotated on this spit, and practised butchers removed all the body's hair, cuticles, and other inedible outer parts. Mary Bouchier's intestines were then removed and washed in sea water, before being set aside in banana leaves for future use, either as storage skins or as crisp-cooked delicacies for the children. Then the body was buried in a large earthen oven, similar to that used to cook wild pigs, although considerably larger, and eventually the meal was ready. Because Mary Bouchier was female, and thus not a trophy of war, she was divided among the entire tribe. Men killed in battle were reserved for males, and a fearsome ritual was performed in their dismemberment and ingestion. Mary was simply tasty protein, which is not to say that she was not highly appreciated in her final earthly role.

Sandalwood had brought about the discovery of Rarotonga by Philip Goodenough, captain of the ship on which Mary Bouchier and William Wentworth sailed. The vessel had as officers Goodenough and Wentworth (whom the captain kept deriding as a "half-marrow," meaning that though he had spent plenty of sea time, he was an incompetent seaman), and as crew three other white men, three Lascars, two New Zealand Maori, Goodenough's whore and two Tahitian women who served the carnal needs of the crew.

Sandalwood, the fragrant heartwood of the genus *Santalum*, prized for carving, or burned as incense, had drawn Goodenough and his *Cumberland* on a prospecting mission. By accident, he found the third point in the golden triangle of the Cook Islands: he added Rarotonga to Aitutaki and Mangaia, and thus robbed some Royal Navy captain of becoming a famous discoverer. Goodenough cared not at all for filling in the world's map; he wanted sandalwood and he was furious to find that there was none. Still, a man of adaptable greed, he calculated that the local *Nono* tree, a small dark-green plant, might be valuable, for the Rarotongans used the bark and root to make a yellow dye.

Anchored at Ngatangiia harbour on the eastern coast of the island, Captain Goodenough formed the first European-style work gangs in the Cook Islands. The islanders were set to digging the *Nono* and for a while things went swimmingly. The Rarotongans received small trinkets, the traders food and women. Gradually, however, too much kava, fornication, and reciprocal thefts of women (before her murder, Mary Bouchier was abducted and used sexually, in recompense for the traders doing the same thing with Rarotongan women), led to a fracture. The men of Ngatangiia snapped: and on a single day they killed, and subsequently ate, four of the foreign men, plus Mary.

Curiously, once a week of intermittent battle was done, everybody made peace. Captain Goodenough rubbed noses with the chief of eastern Rarotonga and loading of the boat was completed.

As they sailed away, Goodenough and Wentworth grabbed two women and a man. The women were left on Aitutaki, and the man was taken to Botany Bay.

The cargo of *Nono* turned out to be commercially useless.

RAITEA, NR TAHITI, THE SOCIETY ISLANDS. 1821

The Apostle Papehia

"Lord, if it is thy will, keep this bucket away from me." Thus prayed Papehia. His mission-school training was a bit off-kilter, for he meant to be quoting the words of Jesus Christ before his crucifixion. No matter, he knew that glory often was obtained by way of a cup of gall.

The London Missionary Society liked to pretend that it had a successful mission going in "Tahiti," but that was words-as-wishes, if not downright lying. In fact, the Tahitian mission was barely back on its knees after being knocked flat by the hurricanes of local reality. Tahiti was intended as their beachhead, but the first decade, beginning in 1798, had produced eleven missionary defections to New South Wales, one murdered preacher, a passing familiarity with Tahitian (the first Polynesian language that they seriously studied), disarray, near-nakedness, conflicts with shipwrecked sailors, losing arguments with Tahitian leaders about the practice of infanticide, and, finally in 1809, withdrawal in complete defeat.

So very unlike the Catholic priests, French and French-trained Irishmen, whom Herman Melville encountered a couple of decades later: dark, sepulchral Frenchman in black canonicals and three-cornered hats who had no more interest in the natives than they did in the life cycle of sand termites, and the occasional Irish priest who got on a treat with the sailors, beachcombers and ship-jumpers and, though ignoring the natives, ministered to tainted souls, even if they were ingloriously European.

The London Missionary Society had regrouped and sent out more missionaries in 1812 and some of them were smart enough to bet on the winner in a local war on Tahiti. That helped, but most of the real conversions were made on Raiatea, where Tamatoa, a high chief, was captivated by John Williams, a former ironmonger, who not only burned with God's incandescence, but could perform a skein of apparent miracles with wood and iron, by employing various skills he had acquired in his old trade in England. Soon idols were burning all over Raiatea.

So, it was from that island that the first, crucial stone that was to become the avalanche of pan-Polynesian Christianity began to roll. It was a fortuitous place to start, for in several Polynesian legends, Raiatea is identified as "Havai'i," the mythological origin-place of all of the Polynesian peoples.

And John Williams was more culturally acute than all the doctors of divinity who stood behind the London Missionary Society. He intuited one thing perfectly: Europeans later, natives first.

Meaning: train and send some keen locals. More effective and a long-chalk safer.

Thus, in December 1821, Papehia and an assistant were taken on a sailing vessel by John Williams to Aitutaki in the Cook Islands. The Raiatean native was thirty or so years old, of average build, and possessed a complete confidence in his god and in himself.

The vessel that delivered him to Aitutaki could not broach the reefs surrounding the island and she stood off, while dozens of native canoes surrounded her. Tamatoa Ariki, one of the Aitutakian chiefs, was invited on board, and to John Williams he promised that the two teachers would not be harmed. Soon, the two brown Christian missionaries disappeared in Tamatoa's large waka, along with clothes, small tools, and other items donated by the Christians on Raiatea.

Poor Papehia! He knew of St. Paul's refusal to accept anything to do with heathen idols – he'd memorized that part in "Corinthians" dead right – but he also wished to stay alive. So, when in proper etiquette, Chief Tamotoa took him to the local marae, home of the carved gods of the island and prayer-home of the Aitutakian people, he shuddered. He knew no local words, only cognate vocabulary from his homeland, and he had not words to protest. Ah, pagan gods! For the moment, Papehia deserted Paul: he put up with them.

A year later, when John Williams dropped off another native preacher to help him, Papehia had not done much, at least not to Williams' industrial-English eye. He had, however, won, by slow and moderate converse, by strong and quiet dealing, by showing no fear in the face of danger, a constituency, one that started with the ariki, the aristocracy of the island. For, whatever rank he may have been born, Papehia was one of god's aristocrats. Thus, stimulated by John Williams' visit, he started his campaign. Within the next fifteen months, all the marae on Aitutuaki had been destroyed, burned down to the ground, and the idols, piled up as cordwood, had been burned.

That's what he called them: idols, for that is the word of the white man's Bible. It means every god but one's own.

MANGAIA, THE COOK ISLANDS. 1823

No Joy

Papehia leaps into the foam. Because the forbidding reefs around Mangaia are close to shore, he has shouted to the warriors drawn up on the beach.

"Bind up your spears and I will come ashore," he called from a clunky home-made vessel that John Williams had designed. Williams, as the Wellington of the Christian march on Polynesia, had added another tenet to his strategy: not only should the invasion-wave consist of native Polynesians, but the point of attack – the breakthrough location from whence all Polynesia would be Christianized – should be the Cook Islands. Williams had brought native missionaries and their wives with him, and, after having picked up Papehia from Aitutaki, he searched for Rarotonga.

Williams navigated and prayed, while the Polynesians prayed and looked for signs. They could not find Rarotonga, but they came upon Mangaia.

The Mangahians remembered their last fatal encounter with Papaa who arrive in big canoes and they stood on the beach, shaking their spears, ready to repel any invasion.

"Bind up your spears and I will come ashore!" Papehia's words sound slightly stilted to the locals, for he is a Tahitian and he has been on Aitutaki, but, clearly, he is brown and he is unarmed. They comply.

Papehia, with the courage that distinguishes his entire life, dives in and expertly surfs over the reef. He and the Mangahians parley satisfactorily and he returns to the ship to pick up his assistants: two Tahitian missionaries and their wives return with him, thrashing through the surf. This party will convert the heathen.

Immediately the islanders invoke the customary law of the beach: people and property who are washed ashore belong to the finders.

The missionary wives are especially desirable, lithe girls barely in their twenties, soaked and now virtually naked. The Mangahians grab the women and take them into the woods. Whether they will become the property of the ariki or will suffer rotation rape is an open question, but certainly nothing pleasant awaits them.

Papehia tries to prevent the abductions but a piece of cloth is slipped over his head and a warrior twists it hard. This garroting would have quickly succeeded, had Papehia not managed to force his hand into the aperture at his throat.

Thus, the chief voice of the Gospel in Polynesia neared silence. Only John Williams's firing the ship's cannon frightens away the Mangahians, who have a long memory of fire-sticks. The native missionaries regroup on shore and swim out to the waiting ship. John Williams, who has not so much as got his feet wet, later records, "We left the island with feelings of deep regret."

RAROTONGA, THE COOK ISLANDS. 1823

Arrivistes

I, Maretua, was in my twenty-first year when the missionary first tried to come among us. Not the Papaa. They commanded the ship that brought the brown men who knew the sacred word. It pains me to my bones that we did not welcome them properly.

Three men and two wifes arrived. They were very excited and we had difficulty understanding the language they spoke. Then they caught their dignity and one of them, from Aitutaki, explained very clearly why they were among us. They were here to tell us of their generous god, Jesus-Tangaroa.

Makea, the ariki of our district, visited the missionaries' ship and promised the white master of the missionaries that he would treat the visitors well and that they could safely spend the night ashore. That evening, the missionaries were separated, the single male, whom we later knew as Papehia, slept in one dwelling. The other two men and their wifes slept in another.

To our shame, in the morning we found that a band of warriors had planned to kill the two men and to take their wifes. One of the wife fought off rape, and the other had her clothes ripped from her. Their husbands had argued and fought in their defence, but it was Jesus-Tangaroa who protected them all.

The missionaries gathered on the beach at sunrise and signalled to the white man on ship and paddled out to that vessel. The two men who had wifes wanted to leave immediately and the white master agreed that Rarotonga should be left in darkness.

But one of the brown man came back. It was Papehia. He placed his trust in god and said he would stay on our island alone. That evening, when the mission ship was on its way back to Raiatea, he mounted a tree stump and began to tell us of the true god.

MANGAIA, THE COOK ISLANDS. JUNE 1824

Were the Old Gods Dying?

At last the white mission-masters were able to land two of their men successfully on Mangaia. These two Tahitians were not the best the London Missionary Society had on offer: the junior figure, Tiere, was in poor health and survived only eighteen months as a preacher. The other, Davida, was strong and fat in the way the Polynesian aristocracy admired, but he was the slowest student the Papaa masters ever had taught. He could argue well enough, and remember whatever he heard, but he could scarcely read, so his knowledge of the new god grew little, if at all.

Carrying as a talisman the New Testament in Tahitian, Davida led the way, pulling Tiere forcibly when necessary. Having been let off a sailing ship that was on its way to Sydney, they stumbled painfully onto the reef at Mangaia with the sacred text tied to Davida's head, wrapped in his shirt to keep it dry.

Before jumping into the surf, the native missionaries had repeated Davida's favourite prayer. "Oh Lord, let me never be confounded." Davida was not sure if "confounded" was a place or a mental state, though he suspected it was what happened if one did not preach the gospel properly.

Immediately he caught his breath, Davida thought he had been confounded. A spear was pointed at his chest by a warrior with a sinister smile. "You won't catch many sharks here, brother," he said and cocked his arm.

For the rest of his life, Davida would say "But then his arm was confounded by the strength of the Lord." Actually, one of the local aristocrats, standing behind the warrior, had gripped the spear's shaft. Davida's salvation was no less miraculous for that.

"The old gods are dying," Davida told the island's ranking chief at a feast that was prepared for the visitors: the Mangahians had only two modes of greeting visitors, killing them or treating them as visiting princes, and Davida and Tiere, having been saved from the former now were on more comfortable ground. "Jehovah is the true god's name," Davida intoned. He was interrogated for an entire evening by a skein of chiefs:
– where does your god live?
– does he have many wives?
– who was your god's father?
– has your god many children?
– how can a man be made out of a rib?
– how does Jesus fly up to the sky?
Davida's greatest assets were his complete self-confidence and his ignorance of anything that remotely resembled theology. He told his version of the Christian story in exactly the same way he had learned the sacred story of the gods of the Tahitian islands. And, when the natives built him and Tiere a grass hut, he used it as a school room, and there he explained with satisfying literalism the miracles Jehovah had done and the conclusion these miracles always led to: "The old gods are now confounded. They are dying." Always he said this solemnly, with never a triumphal note in his voice. He was telling a sad and ineluctable truth.

Were the old gods really dying? – before the native missioners and their white masters arrived? No, they were doomed, not dying. Polynesian societies were not falling apart, were not losing their sacred sense, not erasing their rules of conduct. Of course the old gods were foredoomed, for we now know of the tsunami of economic and social re-configurations that followed in the wake of the industrial revolution, and few, if any, of the ancient deities could have been adapted to the new order.

But these foredoomed gods were dead before that wave struck. Christianity thrust a spear through their belly.

Davida knew that he would be victorious on Mangaia the day two warriors came to see him. In the prime of life, they were specimens the ancient Greeks would have admired. The crowning glory of Polynesian warriors in the pre-missionary days was their hair, grown to waist-length, oiled and brushed to the sheen of a fine stallion. The men offered to imitate Davida and have their hair cut short. It would be a sacrifice such as the Chosen People put onto Jehovah's altar. Thereafter, the revolutionary party on the island grew and, like the enthusiasts of the Revolution in France and the 1798 Rising in Ireland, the soldiers of the new faith marched with cropped hair.

Within two years of his arrival, Davida had convinced the Mangahians to burn their *marae* – these being their god-houses – and he had collected the images of all thirteen deities that made up the island pantheon. These figures – he called them idols – were lodged in Davida's house.

When a white missionary vessel eventually called, the figures were taken on board. For a time they were displayed in the headquarters of the London Missionary Society.

Now, in the British Museum, they are venerated, a bit.

RAROTONGA, THE COOK ISLANDS. 1825

Family Pride

My father, now resting in the arms of Jehovah, was one of Papehia's first converts. "Maretua," he told me," our family will become follower of the god of Papehia." He treated Papehia as an ariki and when a teacher called Tiberio later came to aid Papehia, he too was given respect by my father.

We are an island of rows and ranks, no less now than before we saw god's great light. Six ariki for our entire island; then forty sub-chiefs and then many minor-chiefs and finally the commoners. Each ariki had its own territory, and they jostled for precedence. Too often we fought and my own father, before his following Jesus-Tangaroa, had his own earth oven and there I tasted the flesh of the long pig.

Papehia understood our rows and ranks. He sought and gained the favour of Tinomana Enururutine, the ariki of Avarua. Papehia had great conviction and Tinomana was the first ariki to allow his marae to be burned and the gods of the Tinomana tribe destroyed by holy fire. The Rev. John Williams, the missionary-master of Papehia, later told me that Papehia recalled to his mind the magnificent Christian King-hero, Henry, number VIII of England. He had burned the idols and the false gods of the people of England and Papehia did the same for our people: six of the seven marae on the island were purified by fire and their gods became as dust in the wind.

Papehia understood holy war and Jehovah tells us such wars are necessary if the Land he gives us is to be made holy. Papehia brought all the Christian people into the village of Avarua and there they were able to defend themselves against the heathen. As many as one thousand men were sworn to protect the people of god. Papehia took god's war to the heathen. I joined him, his students and a band of warriors and, Jehovah be praised, we ambushed a pack of heathen. We threw them into a stream, reddening it with their blood. All their idols we took and their pigs and everything they own. More and more the people of our island began to respect the Word of God.

Peace descends when God is honoured. That is the lesson I have learned throughout my life. Every place where Christianity rules now has fewer wars than before. That is true here and on other islands and the Rev. Mr. Williams tells me it is also true in his land, the Isles of Britain.

The apostle Papehia married the favourite daughter of Tinomana. Papehia's assistant took as a wife the daughter of another ariki. They did so because it was only right that the messengers of Jehovah should be in the front row of our people. It was right too, that Papehia for his own family-land took land that had once belonged to heathen.

RAROTONGA. THE COOK ISLANDS. 1825

Distinguishing Sheep from Goat

Papehia passes the word that a missionary-master will visit the island. He will baptize those who have become true followers of Jesus-Tangaroa.

A new church must be built. Already the one he constructed in Avaroa is too small. The Papaa must see a fine new structure and know that Jehovah-god is winning the battle on Rarotonga.

Papehia is a man of ambition. He plans a building that will be one hundred metres long and fifteen metres across. He knows only Polynesian structural tricks, so this is a vaulting ambition, without any knowledge of how vaults are actually constructed. God will provide.

Many of the workers that swarm to the site are heathen, false converts. Papehia knows this. But how can he tell the two species apart? He is not so doctrinaire as to refuse the help of the unrighteous, for did not Our Lord accept the aid of publicans, whatever they are? A difficult concept in a world that has yet to discover alcohol, much less public houses. So, Papehia accepts the centre-posts that are carved with the figure of the god Tangaroa, who has a phallus that droops to his knees. And one of the king posts is adorned by a narwhal tusk, carved with the figure of a god who looks like a malevolent banyan tree. Papehia hates the squid-like visage of this demon-god, but he has been told that the ivory comes from the spiral tusk of a beast that lives in the northern seas where the Papaa originate. Perhaps it is not a false god, after all, but one about which he is yet to be informed.

How can he separate the unbelievers? For if the missionary-master arrives and baptizes unbelievers, Papehia's whole ministry will have been a false vanity. His answer is to teach. Not Jehovah, but plastering. He assembles the builders. Mostly they are long-haired warriors, but among them, sitting comfortably fanning themselves in the shade, are the sons of ariki. One of them, Makea Daniela, though only in his youth, is already beyond six feet in height. He will be a prodigious man, for his eldest brother weighs 312 lbs (white missionaries later weighed him) and their father nearly five hundred weight. This crew, working by rules of rank and region that defy the demands of mere architectural necessity, build a church. Papehia, when he assembles them, talks only of plaster. They know how to do the rest.

But he explains carefully something he learned on his home island from the white people: how to make really good plaster using burned coral to form a coat of white lime that is impervious to everything but earthquake.

Then he watches.

The real Christians do as he has suggested, but the false-converts just mix sand and water. When completed, the church appears as if it has leprosy, but Papehia knows who has done what: and so he decides accurately who can be baptized, and who not.

RAROTONGA. THE COOK ISLANDS. MAY 1827

Owning a European

As the strategist-commander of the spiritual conquest of most of Polynesia, the Rev. John Williams acknowledged that he and his aide-de-camp, the Rev. Charles Pitman, were worthy of respect by the islanders. The fulness of their reception, however, unsettled Williams.

He and Pitman, their wives, and Williams's two children, arrived at Avarua on a Saturday, but a fierce rainstorm prevented their landing until Monday. Waiting on the shore for two full days were the six ariki of the island and the two spiritual ariki, the Tahitian teachers Papehia and Tiberio, and hundreds of onlookers.

In a gesture reserved only for the highest chiefs, the missionaries were carried on wooden platforms for eight miles on twisting, muddy trails to Ngantagiia. Williams immediately understood that the site of the disastrous first full encounter between Cook Islanders and Europeans was a fine symbolic place to carry him, a king in victory.

John Williams was an immensely talented man – he designed and constructed his own ocean-going schooner and he translated large portions of the scriptures into several Polynesian languages; yet he always wore the uncomfortable hair-shirt of Dissenting Protestantism, the feeling that all men were as mud before God, and that pride was the sinuous and secret sin that most frequently brought down even the most saintly.

Thus, his first Rarotongan sermon, given very slowly in Tahitian, was based on John 3: 14, a text of double-deep abasement. "And as Moses lifted up the serpent in the wilderness, even so must the Son of man be lifted up."

Lifted up? From selfless sacrifice to finding oneself worshipped, Williams encountered continual temptation. On Rarotonga, three of the six ariki were paramount, and each of them wanted to own a missionary. That is the word used, in several languages, all across Polynesia: "own." Williams was forced to satisfy the islanders by assigning himself and the Rev. Mr. Pitman to separate ariki and in naming Papehia an honorary white missionary. This satisfied the third high-chief only because Williams promised to find him a real Papaa missionary as soon as possible.

Owned? Williams and his conscience struggled even more with this idea. It was selfless to be owned, granted; yet the missionaries were slotted into the strict social hierarchy at the level of a high-chief. As a covenant-of-convenience it worked: the old rulers kept their temporal power and the representative of the new god controlled spiritual matters. It was as yet unclear what would happen if the two powers clashed, but Williams knew enough religious history to worry about the apparent parallels to the Holy Roman Empire.

John Williams spent the next dozen years in a pattern: sending out over wide stretches of Polynesia brown teachers as the point-men, the danger-takers in the enterprise. If they failed, he sorrowed. If they succeeded, he followed up their beachhead. Never did the successful brown teachers deal with the common people. Always they found a patron among the local aristocracy and then became high ranking personages themselves. The arrival of the white missionary capped the process. Comfortable with it or not, Williams entered the various islands as a papal figure.

The Samoan and the Tongan Islands. The outer islands of the Tahitian group. More islands in the Cook group.

On most of the islands they invaded, Williams's forces preceded significant European contact with indigène, so Christianity became a form of maritime varnish, a limitation on the worst damage that subsequent white visitors would do: not a perfect preventative, but a limitation.

Williams's method became the model for the conversion of most of the peoples of Polynesia, and a generation after his death, most of the major island groups were, in their own ways, Christian.

Only once, in a fit of self-abasement, did Williams approach a native society without his brown teachers as an advanced guard. This was on 20 November 1839, at Erromanga in the New Hebrides. Williams and two white missionaries went on shore from a large schooner, leaving their wives and children to observe from the ship. The three men went up the beach, bearing presents, a method of showing respect and also of igniting the greed that would lead the natives to want to own a European. The white men disappeared from sight for a moment and then were seen running back along the beach, pursued by brown people with spears and stone hatchets. Mrs. Williams and her nearly-adult children saw the great white missionary cut down in the water as he tried to swim for his life.

Later, it was established that all three missionaries had been cooked and, as in the eucharist, reverently consumed.

TAHITI. NOVEMBER 1827

Missionary Stealing

"Mind if we sits bodkin, dearie?" That query came in the midst of a nightmarish voyage from London. The inquirer was an old slattern who claimed to be on her way to meet her "husband" in Australia. "Me and the Mr. used to sit this way on the coach from York."

The Rev. Aaron Buzacott, prim, pale, proper, in his late twenties, stood quickly and replied with, he hoped, Christian forbearance. "Not at all. Indeed, we were just to go below. Come along, Mrs. Buzacott, my dear." He almost called his wife "Miss Hitchcock," so recently had they been married. The couple had been trying to find a few moments alone together on the only piece of deck structure that wasn't either crammed with gear or splintered by the storms they had been through. Travelling to the South Pacific by way of the Cape of Good Hope and Australia took five months and even then they would not be at their own missionary station. They would be dropped at Tahiti and later taken to Rarotonga. Buzacott was the new white missionary that John Williams had promised the Rarotongan chiefs.

Missionary wives, scarcely remembered in the memoirs of the heroic age of nineteenth-century Christian expansion, save in a few platitudinous sentences about "helpmeets," had the worst position on the planet. They followed god-drunk zealots around the globe, watched the men break their health, nursed them, bore children, taught native children's and women's classes, and tried to hold on to their own sanity as their husbands oscillated between being almost divine figures to the natives and desperate, fearful, infantile in the bosom of their own family. This, and most of them pass into official histories without even their own Christian name being known.

The Buzacotts had a lot to learn. The heady days of the London Missionary Society's having its own ship to ply the Plymouth-South Pacific routes were gone. Instead, the sympathetic owner of a shipping company had given them free passage and the Society had paid the captain and crew handsome tips to take good care of the young couple. Some care: the functionaries of English commerce disliked missionaries intensely, for they were great interferers with business. So, immediately the vessel was at sea, the captain took for himself the special provision of meat and water that had been put on board for the Buzacotts, and issued them with stale water and salted meat so hard it could have been used to make ornamental carvings. And, torture to the young couple, the decks leaked severely and the ship's carpenter fixed only the portion over the captain's berth. The captain found it hilarious that in rough weather "the holy family," as he called them, were constantly soaked. Poor Buzacott only managed to make life bearable by nailing folded blankets over his wife's berth and by rigging a runoff trough made from bamboo to protect his own berth. Not a honeymoon.

Ah, but Tahiti! Their perseverance now surely must be rewarded. The visual splash of an island that appeared royal purple from a distance, interspersed with deep green mountains rising several thousand feet, coral reefs close to shore and placid lagoons with safe harbours: like the Chosen People, Buzacott told his wife, we are viewing a Promised Land.

Six white missionaries already were at work on the island – that's if one does not count the Catholics, and the LMS preachers certainly did not. They were cordiality itself, and everything augured well for a productive season of holy labour before the Buzacotts moved on to Rarotonga. Some small problems, however. In London the Buzacotts had been promised that furniture would be provided for them in Tahiti. Now they discovered that they had to make their own. Wisely, the training college in London did not point out to aspiring missionaries that they would have to perform in the mission field most of the tasks that artisans and workers did in the British Isles: this was not something to tell to young men who, in most instances, were moving out of those social classes and prized a clean pair of hands as much as a spotless soul.

Even here, God seemed to provide. A group of Tahitians helped. They refused payment. They were from a distant part of the island, and, in fact, were recruiting.

– "For you, we will build a church."

– "For you, we will fence a garden. No payment."

– "For you, a schoolhouse, and a fine dwelling, and pigs, and chickens. You will be our priest and king."

Buzacott declined. He was promised to Rarotonga. "Oh, but the people of Rarotonga are savages," he was told. "And they are terrible cannibals." Still Buzacott declined. He did not consult his wife in doing so, for of course she would have agreed with him.

The importuning Tahitians waited, and on a day when the resident missionaries were away, a large canoe was sent with a false messenger.

"Come and join your friends." The Buzacotts went along and soon found they were being kidnapped. An elaborate and cunning plan was in train, involving not only stealing the missionaries for the distant village, but plans of ambush and counter-attack, if the plan was violently opposed. What saved the young couple was their implacable innocence. "We are promised to Rarotonga, and that is where we will go." Over and over the young cleric repeated this phrase in his basic-Tahitian.

The missionary stealers returned them.

In January 1828 Mr. and Mrs. Buzacott were taken to Rarotonga on a schooner, named *Industry*. They already had learned that they were less respected by persons of British commerce than they were by people they had been trained to refer to as heathen and as savages.

SOMOSOMO. FIJI. 1830

Functional Design

Even white trash were useful, provided they did not come in job-lots. For example, a single European beachcomber, no matter how raddled with pox pustules and desiccated from consumption, could be a very useful device for a Polynesian chief to own. This because the European had immunity from *tapu* and could do some dirty jobs – say, burn down an enemy's dwelling located on a sacred site, something that anyone under *tapu* either could not accomplish, or would be forever punished for by the gods.

Only one was required, and that was the difficulty for James Magoun and his fellow crew members, who struggled ashore from the wrecked brig, the *Fawn*. The Fijian tribe that met the several sailors on the shore took them to a nearby settlement and then debated their fate.

"Knock the salt from their eyes," some of the elders suggested, referring to the traditional method of clubbing unwelcome strangers to death. "Besides, they are the property of the gods."

Others pointed out that the shipwreck had already been stripped and that the gods had done pretty well out of the business.

"Then they can serve us as long pigs," the traditionalists argued.

The reply to this was that the tribe's recent military successes had provided as much human flesh as anybody had a taste for, and argued in effect that it would be healthier to get back to a traditional high-fibre diet.

Good sense and compromise prevailed. One of the men would be kept as a useful instrument; but the others were surplus to requirements and, besides, if half-a-dozen were kept alive, one of them would eventually fall into the hands of our enemies.

By whatever mode of evaluation, the chief chose wisely. James Magoun turned out to be much more useful than mere white trash. He had been a farrier in northwest Ulster and had served as a ship's blacksmith and mechanic for several years before coming ashore in the Fijian Islands. His name, "Magoun" was the Ulster dialect for his trade – "Gowan": smith or armourer. And that's what he became to his proud owners. He directed Fijian divers as to where in the sunken ship to uncover his metal working tools. He rigged a block-and-tackle that allowed the raising of the brig's anchor. This he turned into a bick-airn, a two-horned anvil on which he hammered out spear points and pieces of body armour.

His owners understood his value and he was given respect: land, a dwelling, eight wives.

In 1835, the white community at Levuka heard of Magoun and offered to buy him, or ransom him in European terminology. Negotiations were complex, and were completed only when it was clear that the armourer would not go to any rival tribe but would live among white people. And even then his price was high: a dozen knives, six muskets, two rolls of lead for making musket balls, two kegs of gunpowder, a bundle of hoop-iron, two bolts of red cloth, twenty pounds of red paint, two large iron pots, twenty pounds of beads. And one Tongan girl.

THE CANADAS
1770–1830

Modes of Exchange

"And how would you say, 'And immediately the spirith driveth him into the wilderness'?"

"Now, what about 'and the wind ceased: and they were sore amazed in themselves beyond measure, and wondered'?"

"And here, my friend, is a very hard matter. However do we render 'the abomination of desolation, spoken of by Daniel the prophet ... '?"

John Stuart, one of the strongest moral spines in North America, is conferring with Thayendanegea, one of the nimblest of North American minds. Stuart, the Philadelphia-born son of hard Ulster Presbyterians, has converted himself to Anglicanism and become a missionary for the Society for the Propagation of the Gospel. He is translating the Bible into Mohawk and other languages of the Six Nations. Thayendanegea – who goes by the name of Joseph Brant when he must deal with people who are linguistically limited – helps him. They have almost finished the Gospel of Mark in Mohawk and are about to move on to the catechism. The Mohawk, like most of the people of the Six Nations, are very loyal to the English crown and those that take up a European religion almost always join the Church of England.

The Rev. Mr. Stuart is no soft touch. When Thayendanegea asks for permission to marry his late wife's half-sister, Stuart rules against it on canonical grounds. Later he does sanction Thayendanegea's marriage to a Mohawk-Irish beauty, the daughter of the Indian agent George Croghan.

Alliances

The Rev. John Stuart is one of those tall men who carries his height as if it is a responsibility. Well over six feet tall, he looms even larger because he, like several of the natives in his community, wears a Caroline hat: a felted version of a stove pipe, and that makes him loom, sticklike, a giant preying mantis. In preaching and formal meetings he uses his height to advantage: commanding the high ground, he realizes, is as useful socially as it is militarily.

Shrewdly, whenever he deals privately or with the Mohawk in small groups, he removes his headgear, and as soon as manners permit, he seats himself on the ground. That way he is an equal and, he hopes, a partner.

This day he carefully removes his hat outside of a native dwelling and politely enquires if he may have permission to enter. He is on a most delicate mission.

Seated, he explains to a woman of thirty his problem. She is nursing and that is why Stuart is here. His own dear wife, he explains hesitantly, is unable to nurse their first-born child, a son. Would the dear Christian woman consent to share her milk with his own infant son?

Stuart starts to quote a few Bible verses in Mohawk, but she interrupts. Of course she will: her own infant daughter would welcome the white boy as her brother.

The missionary child survives and after the American Rebellion is taken with his father to Kingston, on the north side of the St. Lawrence River. There the father is a missionary and rector. The son, christened George O'Kill Stuart, succeeds his father in 1812 and eventually becomes archdeacon of Kingston. His incumbency includes being chaplain to the Mohawk living to the west of Kingston.

Each year he makes a pastoral visit. He preaches a sermon and performs his liturgical duties reverently; but, actually he is there to see the sister whom he loves.

HERKIMER COUNTY, NEW YORK. 1777

Family Treaties

The local store keeper is a woman and she owns the place outright, not as a front for some man. Most of her customers are Six Nations, but she sells rum and blankets to anyone. And is equally feared by white and red: she is formidable.

Molly Brant, as she is known among the whites (her Mohawk name is Konwatsi'tsiaienni), is the older sister of Joseph Brant, and he too finds her fearsome. Iroquois society is matrilineal and this throws a lot of power to women, who become the bearers of genealogy and as-

sociated traditions. Molly Brant is the head of the Six Nations matrons. If they had a society by that name, she'd be president. She
possesses such force that she was included in a delegation of Six Nations chiefs who dealt with the crown authorities in Philadelphia in
an attempt to stop bogus purchase-and-sale of their lands.

"And" she is saying to a trio of three young men, two Mohawk and
one white, "it is yourselves that will get to Fort Stanwix." This she
quickly translates into Mohawk. She is telling them that they must
warn the British and Indian forces who are surrounding the fort that
an American band is coming to relieve it. "If you don't arrange an
ambush for those rebels, I'll do an ambush on you; and that I will."

Molly Brant speaks one of the thousands of mini-dialects that glow
briefly on the contact-frontier and then die, fireflies in the night. A native speaker of Mohawk, educated for some years in white schools,
she had become the second consort of Sir William Johnson of Dun-
shaughlin, County Meath. Johnson had begun as a landlord's agent
in Ireland, had continued the profession in New York and had made
himself, by the time of his death in 1774, into one of the richest men in
British America. He was knighted for his influence with the local
tribes, especially the Six Nations, and was credited (perhaps over-
credited) with keeping them on-side during the hideous French-In-
dian Wars. As superintendent of Indians for New York for twenty
years, he had slept with scores of his wards. Never marrying, he had
lived with a white woman (a runaway indentured servant) and had
three children with her and then, after her death, eight children with
Molly Brant, all of whom were given his family name. Besides the
children and some property, Sir William had bequeathed to Molly a
manner of speaking that combined the flat-line timbre of the Mohawk
with the syntax of the Anglo-Irish world of his own youth. This, if
anything, made her more formidable, especially when her fierce temper set her tongue going.

Molly Brant, like most of the Six Nations, and all of the Mohawk, is
deeply loyal to the Crown. She is delighted to learn that the rebel
forces were successfully decimated in an ambush and when her three
young warriors return, she gives them store-made hats and a gallon
of rum each.

Later, with sadness she learns of loyalist defeats, and she never recovers fully from the sorrow of the Mohawk being pushed by the rebels
from their ancestral lands. She settles in Kingston and most of her people set down a bit further west, on the north shores of the inland seas.

In Kingston, she lives in a house built for her by the government and has a pension of £100 annually, more than the British give to any war chief. Each Sunday she attends St. George's, Kingston, where the Reverend John Stuart, who had officiated at the burial of her beloved Sir William, is now rector. She reads her prayers in a loud voice, as if broadcasting defiance to the enemies of her people.

BALLYMENA, COUNTY ANTRIM. 1782

Tariff

"Lafayette!" The name is uttered as a curse by a wiry man, who, though not yet thirty, appears to be late middle-aged.

"De Kalb!" As he utters the cursed name, he whacks with a knotted rope the donkey he is unloading: not hard enough to hurt the animal, but with enough emphasis to make himself feel better.

"Gates!" The man is a grocer and he is just setting up shop in Bally-mena, the home district that he had left in 1772 when his parents, farming people, had taken him and his seven brothers and sisters to South Carolina. They had been part of the Ulster outflow to North America and, more precisely, a link in a chain of relatives and neigh-bours who had settled north of Charleston on the Packolet River. The family was not at all political, but was vulnerable when the American rebellion broke out: family members had good land and they hadn't been in the colony long enough to develop a protective envelope of alliances among the vulpine. They were easy pickings.

"Washington!" Young Alexander Chesney, age twenty at the time, had been arrested on the pretext of his having sheltered loyalists. A drumhead trial gave him the choice of a full military trial or of enlisting in the rebel army; which is to say, of shooting with us or being shot by us. He chose enlistment and spent three years fighting the Creek Indians who were allied with the British, as were most Native American tribes. Then he had escaped and fought for the loyalists until taken prisoner.

He remembers little of the worst days of his life: being taken pris-oner by the revolutionaries and forced, though wounded in the knee, to march for three days. Before the march, the rebels stole his shoes.

"Be-God-Damned Cornwallis!" This time he whacks the poor don-key with real force. Alexander Chesney, though stirring the bitter dregs of his own grievance, is notably different from thousands of loyalists in only one way. Most of them remained in the Americas. Like him, they had their property stolen (several hundred acres of family land, in Chesney's case, much of it cleared) and their bodies abused. And, like Chesney, most eventually received some compensation for their hardships.

But, Lord, becoming a grocer in Ballymena?

THE BAY OF QUINTE, [UPPER CANADA]. 1783

Nation

After moving through the woods separately, a dozen Mohawk, elders and selected warriors, meet at a designated spot. They can see the bay through the trees from here, but the spot has no special geological features. That's the point. Something really valuable has to be hidden in a place so ordinary that no one looks there.

Silently, two of them dig and turn up first a tattered piece of cloth. This one of them holds up resignedly. It is a communion cloth and has rotted. Then they return to digging.

They are seeking some of the most valuable relics of the Mohawk nation, ones that guarantee their nationhood in the world of the Europeans.

A metallic sound: this is what they seek. Now the diggers proceed using only their hands.

Finally, they find the items. These treasures had been buried during the American rebellion when, given promises of Mohawk lands and goods, members of the Oneida tribe had abandoned the Six Nations' loyalism and gone over to the rebels. As defence against the perfidious Oneida, the Mohawk elders had buried their most important items, their grail.

In 1710 a Six Nations' delegation of four chiefs had visited the court of St. James. As delegates of an independent nation, they had pledged loyalty to Queen Anne and her successors. As witness of mutual alliance, she had given them a communion set, the one they now held up to the light as one of the mission-educated warriors reads its words:

The gift of her Majesty, Queen Anne by Grace of God of Great Britain, France and Ireland, of her Plantations in North America, Queen of Her Indian Chappel of the Mohawk

There. Loyalist, certainly. A nation, undeniably.

ST. LAWRENCE RIVER AND LAKE ONTARIO. 1784

Vigour

Sir John Johnson, the man in charge of settling the loyalist refugees north of the St. Lawrence, would have been more comfortable at the head of an army. The son of old Sir William Johnson, at age thirteen he had fought under his father's command against the French. And it was he who, when Molly Brant had sent word of a rebel force approaching, had commanded the successful ambush.

Molly Brant was his step-mother, her children his half-brothers and half-sisters, and he now was both the superintendent of the Six Nations and also the chief officer for settling loyalists displaced by the American revolution.

Both the loyalists and the Indians sheltered behind his mixture of Anglo-Irish grace and sometimes-eccentric manners: he defends them well, and makes London pay attention. Neither group minds that he picks up several thousand acres of land for himself.

Despite being a demi-god in the upper St. Lawrence, Sir John settles in the Montreal region where he acquires a seigneury and more than 100,000 acres.

At age eighty-nine, shortly before his death, Sir John is seen vaulting a six-foot fence, in much the same style that a gymnast goes over a pummel horse. Having dropped to his knees he exclaims, surprised, "By God! I believe I am getting old."

LONDON. 1785

Was it Diplomacy or Raw Courage?

Being presented at St. James Palace was something Thayendanegea long had anticipated. Having spent much of his life in the company of members of the aristocratic Johnson family, he had more social graces than most of the white soldiers who had served under his command in the unsuccessful attempt to suppress the American insurrection. Still, he always wanted to learn more and he was curious about royalty.

When he appeared before George III, Thayendanegea was in standard court dress, save that he did not wear a periwig, but rather his own long hair in a single braid. The various royal courtiers were disappointed, as they had hoped for a noble savage with beads and feathers, and maybe a scalp hanging from his belt.

"Vee are glot to encounter you, Mr. Brant." George III was not about to attempt an Indian name.

"Your servant indeed, your Majesty." Thayendanegea bowed with a grace that would have done credit to a veteran courtier. Acute of ear, he was already forming the impression that he spoke English better than did the English king.

Thayendanegea had come to London to present claims for Mohawk war losses, and this he already had done to Lord Sydney, the Home Secretary. An audience with the monarch was ceremonial, though still an honour.

Thayendanegea stood, composed. The king shifted, cleared his throat, and suggested the next move in this regnal dance.

"Wenn you wish," George III suggested with unusual tact, "you may kneel bevore us ..." Thayendanegea did not move ... "Und dann you will be permitted to kiss our royal hand."

From the corner of his eye, the Mohawk chief caught sight of the Queen, Charlotte Sophia of Mecklenburg-Strelitz, forty years of age and monumentally ugly, even by the standards of the Hanoverian monarchs of England, who had a Teutonic affection for large gargoyles.

This offered Thayendanegea, who had no intention of kneeling and kissing the hand of any man, a glide. "No, your Majesty, I cannot." Silence. "But gladly would I kneel and kiss the hand of your Queen."

King George motioned dismissively. "Dann do so."

When Thayendanegea gently presses his lips to the Queen's hand, she smiles so broadly that her lady-in-waiting must deftly wipe away the drool that issues from the royal lips.

MAITLAND [UPPER CANADA]. 1787

The Starving Time

Truly hungry people, having little to taste, develop a preternatural sense of smell. It's a small evolutionary device that goes back to the days before the invention of agriculture. Under the right conditions of wind and humidity, berries, spruce buds, carrion, can be detected from miles away, and this by persons who normally could not tell if the fry-up on the fire was bacon or goose.

Hence the starving wend their way to a field near Maitland. They are loyalists, stripped of most of their possessions by the American rebels, and provided with too little aid, and that much too late, by the imperial government. These starving men, women, children, are for the moment feral humans, temporary throwbacks: they scent something and move towards it. They follow a trail they cannot identify, but it is food: that knowledge comes from some place below their line of consciousness. As they move forward they walk for a few rods, stop and sniff the air just as their hunter-gatherer ancestors had done. Then they proceed.

From all directions, families make their way through heavy woods, swamps, across pre-Cambrian rock cuts and finally they emerge from the bush into a five-acre field. It is not much, but when one has nothing, not-much is a lot.

The field, a natural clearing, was planted to wheat early in the spring; somehow it has escaped the killer-frosts that hit early in the summer.

The kernels are not yet ripe.

No matter. The milk-heads are stripped by the starving and boiled into a gruel. Young children stop crying. Nursing women again are able to take their babies to breast. Men tell each other that there is hope.

Momentarily satisfied, the feral-people rest, then stand and again begin to search the air for invisible information.

AUGUSTA TOWNSHIP [UPPER CANADA]. 1788

Totem

Only in mid-summer 1788, when the first crops could be harvested, did the starving time of the St. Lawrence loyalists come to an end. Starvations, like wars, produce folk memory, and under the torsion of time, folklore.

The loyalists of Augusta township, in origin rational, substantial bourgeoisie, remember two totem animals and tell their children and grandchildren about them.

Rabbit. Cat.

Obadiah Reed, forced to find food for his wife and two children, journeyed by boat up the St. Lawrence, and into Lake Ontario, all the way to the far end of the lake. There he had friends who would lend him food.

He left his family with two weeks' provisions, and after more than three weeks of his absence the wife and children were nearly dead.

The morning after their food was entirely exhausted, the poor woman opened the cabin door and found that the family cat had brought back a rabbit, something it had never done before.

It did so the next day. And the next, and on. These were enough to keep the three humans alive.

Obadiah Reed finally returned home with food.

The cat never caught a rabbit again.

UPPER CANADA. 1791

Strange Refuge

That Upper Canada, broken off from Quebec in 1791, was the best domain in the English-speaking world for Irish migrants, and especially for Irish Catholics, was providential.

In the aftermath of the American revolution, the loyalists had been dealt out along the St. Lawrence River like cards on a bezique table. Some cunning was involved: closest to the French Canadians were placed Gaelic Scots, most of whom shared Catholicism with the French *habitants*. Next, upstream, were German-derived loyalists. Only farther upstream were English-speaking loyalists of British Isles background settled. Keep the French and the British apart.

Sir John Johnson deserves partial credit for the next step. As early as 1785 he had represented the St. Lawrence loyalists' demand that they be given a separate province of their own. That way English freehold land possession would prevail and so too would English common law, instead of the French system. Sir John also assumes, wrongly, that he would be named governor of the new province.

When in 1791 Upper Canada is created, the loyalists win. They have their own world.

But it's a better-crafted world than they had demanded, for the religious and civil rights of Catholics are protected. That follows from the precedents already set in French Canada.

So, long before full civil rights are given to Catholics in Ireland, they can migrate to a new world where they can vote, hold elective office, and farm without a system of landlordism weighing them down. Of course in Upper Canada they have to be content with being a minority, but that's a nuisance compared to what they have to put up with elsewhere.

YORK, UPPER CANADA. 1800

The Name Game

As a natural aristocrat, Thayendanegea was a political conservative. In his English-language mode, as Joseph Brant, he particularly admired two Irishmen. One of these was Edmund Burke and it was one of Brant's deep regrets that when in London in 1785 he had not met the great man.

The other conservative he deeply admires is: Edmund Burke, in this case a French-trained priest from Maryborough in the Irish midlands. Burke was the first priest to work more than thirty miles west of the border with Lower Canada and he had been sent to the far west of Upper Canada at the request of Governor Simcoe to fight Jacobin influences among the French Catholic population.

Joseph Brant left his estate in the Grand River settlement rarely. He preferred to be a host rather than a guest. He maintained a score of servants and the black ones were dressed in full livery when guests were present. So, Brant's journeying to York for the sole purpose of meeting with Father Burke was significant.

Brant pleaded with Father Burke, who was also the vicar-general and superior of missions for Upper Canada, to appoint a priest to his village in the Niagara Peninsula. He even told Father Burke that he was himself a Roman Catholic, a whopping lie. What Brant wanted, clearly, was a force for order and white respectability among his Mohawk.

To the disappointment of both Thayendanegea and Edmund Burke, the French-dominated hierarchy will not release another priest to work in Upper Canada.

Providence, however, has compensation in store for Father Burke. He is appointed vicar-general of Nova Scotia in 1801.

He succeeds another Irishman, a Dominican from County Tipperary. That man's name: Edmund Burke.

PORT TALBOT, UPPER CANADA. 1803

Artificial Insemination

"I may boast," declared Colonel Thomas Talbot later in life, "like the Irishman in the farce, of having peopled a whole country with my own hands." He said this with a modest irony that Victorian ears never picked up. Talbot, a life-long homosexual, was well-known for his aversion to women, though he could be charming to the rich or the powerful among them. Eventually, Talbot was to introduce settlement in twenty-nine townships on, or near, the northern shore of Lake Erie, and to acquire more than 65,000 acres for himself. As many as 20,000 settlers found land under his patronage.

A master of the theatrical gesture, Talbot lands in May 1803, aged thirty-one, at a spot on Lake Erie that is sixty miles from the nearest settlement. Talbot jumps ashore with an axe in his hand and immediately attacks the virgin forest. A tree falls and Talbot announces that here the future Port Talbot will begin. He has only his own servants to listen to him, but he makes a florid speech, full of Latinate words that most of them do not understand.

Talbot is the sort of settler whom the London authorities desperately desired. The fourth son of the Talbots of Malahide, County Dublin, he had a commission purchased for him in the Sixty-Sixth Foot when he was eleven years of age. At age sixteen, his distant relative, the Marquis of Buckingham, lord lieutenant of Ireland, made him one of his brace of youthful aides-de-camp. The other, with whom he shared a bedroom and an occasional round of buggery, was Arthur Wellesley. "Ah, the Iron Duke," Talbot would say in his later years, in one of those private jokes his guests always missed, "Quite the Iron Duke was Arthur Wellesley before he became Wellington."

The manic activity of 1803 was part of Talbot's recovery from having his heart broken two years earlier. Talbot had been to Quebec City in 1790, and he saw British North America as a field of dreams. Through the influence of Lord Buckingham, he became private secretary to John Graves Simcoe, lieutenant governor of Upper Canada. Then he had fought the French in Holland. When peace seemed to break out, he had sold his commission – now a lieutenant colonelcy: sold it on Christmas Day, 1800, the day he and his lover had decided they would begin life in their own Eden in Upper Canada.

Talbot's heart was given to a son of the English aristocracy, an unusually intelligent, well educated and idealistic member of the Brand family who held title to the Dacre baronage. This beautiful lad had studied in Germany, was deeply attached to Kantian philosophy and to political liberty and to something resembling democracy, though not continental French democracy. Oh, just to listen to him go on gave Talbot the same frisson that Verdi's freedom operas later gave to Italians. Such high ideals, such lovely eyes.

Young Brand will accompany Talbot and be his helpmeet and their colony in the New World will avoid all the errors of the Old. This they agree. And, army commission sold, they plan their voyage. They are almost ready to sail when a messenger brings word that the mother of the Kantian enthusiast has died. Immediately he disembarks; he promises to follow Talbot at first opportunity, but the necessary funeral obsequies must be observed.

Talbot sails. He retches several times before the vessel is out of sight of land, not from seasickness but from sickness of the heart. He knows the idyll is over. In fact, his companion settles into English country life, marries, becomes the twenty-second Baron Dacre, and forgets all about Utopian experiments. He breeds roses.

Until his death in 1853, Thomas Talbot pursues his own increasingly wobbly course, mostly with the approval of successive governments who desperately wish to fill Upper Canada with settlers as a defence against aggression from the American states. Talbot builds a cliffside estate on Lake Erie that he calls the Castle of Malahide. Unlike the gentry residences of his Irish youth, however, it consists of an interlocking set of low buildings, modelled on the French-Canadian farms he had seen as a young officer. He kept his settlers well away, not wanting their cabins near enough that he can ever see the smoke of their hearths. Until the last months of his life, he walked daily in the clement seasons in his two-acre formal garden and his sixteen acres of orchard. Always he was alone: even when he permitted a man-servant to accompany him.

THE ST. LAWRENCE RIVER. 1804

The Visible Irish Man

Though not yet the most-beloved Irishman of the nineteenth century, the gnome-poet already is a presence. He drops verse wherever he goes, like Salome dropping veils. Even his worst work is good, if a bit over-egged.

Thomas Moore is ferried across the St. Lawrence River and he cannot help writing a song about it.

Why should we yet our sail unfurl?
There is not a breath the blue wave to curl.

Moore, the son of a Dublin grocer, had charmed his way into appointment as the registrar for admiralty prizes in Bermuda. Such a post many men dream of, for there were no ships being seized as prizes anywhere near Bermuda and the job was a complete sinecure.

But, when the wind blows off the shore,
O, sweetly we'll rest our weary oar.

Moore was bored to death. He craved social attention, so he decided to quit. He went back to the British Isles by the only sensible route: a tour of the northern part of the United States and of the Canadas.

Blow, breezes, blow, the stream runs fast.
The rapids are near and the daylight's past.

There are several more verses. Generations of Canadian school children come to hate his name, for they are forced to learn the song, the ominous tap-tap-tap of the teacher's cane replicating the rhythm of the boatmen's oars as they row the poet across the St. Lawrence and he briefly dreams that he is in Venice.

AUGUSTA TOWNSHIP, UPPER CANADA. 1804

The Invisible Irish Woman

Just two months before she died, Thayendanegea paid the biggest compliment he could to the woman who was the most influential female in the history of Upper Canada: he travelled from his estate to speak with her, a journey of one day by land and three more by boat. She had a reputation of being a spirit-mother and he was deeply aware that his people needed to learn about the whites' spirit world if they were to survive in their temporal world.

He introduced himself, as he usually did when dealing with Europeans, as Joseph Brant.

She said she was Mrs. Heck. Barbara Ruckle Heck. And would he please permit a prayer before they talked? Her bony hand seized Thayendanegea's as she talked directly to God, her eyes shut, the words unrehearsed, easy, intimate. She was talking to an old friend. Her hand was surprisingly strong and Thayendanegea wondered if she was trying to pull him directly to heaven.

He noticed that her English was very much like that of King George III. This confirmed her status, he concluded.

Over tea they talk. She says she is a Palatine, and Irish. He says he is Mohawk and half his family is Irish. She talks of her people, 10,000 of them at least, fleeing the Rhine river Palatinate, persecuted Protestants, mostly Lutherans, under siege by a French king. He talks of the Six Nations being forced from their homeland. She tells him of her people's dispersal. Most of the Protestant refugees passed through England to the American colonies, but some thousands stayed in England and Ireland. Two hundred families were settled in County Limerick, in a community the government hoped would bolster the Protestant interest. There they kept their old customs alive. They spoke the old language as well as the new; they appointed a *burgomeister*, and maintained their own domestic customs. We always had two beds, Mrs. Heck tells her visitor, one for the man and one for the woman. Thayendanegea is puzzled by this practice but tells her that it is always good to keep the old customs.

She is such a stubby old woman. So ordinary. Finally Thayendanegea puts the question he had come all the way down Lake Ontario to ask. "How did you come to possess spiritual ... spiritual ..." He does not want to offend her. "... spiritual awareness?" Suddenly Barbara Heck is an incandescent figure. In a flow of narrative, mixed with Bible verses and phrases from hymns, she tells him of John Wesley's visit to Ireland in 1748 and of the conversion to Methodism of half the Palatines in a single week. St. Paul never spoke with more enthusiasm about Jesus of Nazareth than did Barbara Heck of John Wesley. She had touched the hem of his garment.

At some points she cannot find the right word in English and uses archaic *Plattdeutsch*, but her meaning is clear. She describes purely in terms of God's-will-being-done, her family's migration to New York

City, and, at her fierce insistence, the formation of the first Wesleyan church in America. She is, she sadly reports, nettled when she is called the Mother of American Methodism. She approves neither of vanity nor of the United States. But even there the faith can work wonders.

Of course her husband had enlisted in a loyalist regiment, for who could not be grateful to the Crown for protecting our people from the French devil-kings?

Thayendanegea thinks: and of course you lost your American property. Indeed: as loyalists the Hecks only received land in Augusta Township in 1785, after the starving time was over. Palatine families, almost all of them Methodists, settled in Augusta and further upriver, on the Bay of Quinte, near where half the Mohawk are settled.

After another hour's talk, Thayendanegea leaves, politely bowing his head while Mrs. Heck says a prayer for the safety of his body and soul. Something big is happening, he realizes.

In August 1804, Barbara Heck dies: holding a Bible. By the middle of the century, Methodism is the unofficial state religion of Upper Canada. It's the common denominator of Protestantisms and, if the culture of Upper Canada and, later, Ontario, is the tiresome rectitude of the Methodist Bicycle Company at prayer, it had to start somewhere. Of course Barbara Heck was only a catalyst; of course she left no papers or collected correspondence; of course she was just a frontier woman.

Bite your silly tongue.

THE EASTERN DISTRICTS OF UPPER CANADA. 1812-14

No Great Sincerity

"Fetlock covers."
  "Here."
  "Tandem Harness."
  "Just as ordered."
  "Two driving bits."
  "Could find one only."
  "And a stallion bridle."
  "Yours. We're even now."

A horse-dealer from the Lansdowne area has just delivered five horses to an American drover. Usually he takes payment in American money, but he needs tack and war encourages barter: never know when the currency might be altered.

All through the war of 1812–14, a smuggling corridor ran from the Rideau country down into the States. It was well-travelled before the war and would be after. No reason for governmental incivilities to stop business. The loyalists are great ones for talking about the republican devils to the south, but many of the leading loyalists are willing to sup with these devils and never mind using a long spoon.

Neither the Canadians nor the Americans won the war of 1812–14, although both wrote their history books as if they had. The British, who had the only real victory of the time, burning Washington, D.C., simply forgot the whole mess happened.

In the equivalent of an opinion poll, three companies of the Second Leeds Regiment, from a core loyalist area, hold a formal muster and discover that more than one-quarter of the men have deserted.

THE NIAGARA PENINSULA, UPPER CANADA. JUNE 1813

Who's the Hero?

Not much glory and a ton of aching bones, scalded hands, nicked shins, and one leg that will scarcely bear her weight. Laura Ingersoll Secord's life is in no significant way different from that of other frontier women. She tries to keep her seven children alive (six daughters, how did that happen? she often wonders), she feeds her husband two large meals and one light one a day, and in summer she fights unsuccessfully to keep flies out of the combination shop and farm house from which the family makes a just-above-subsistence living. In winter she fights the frost and snow with equally indecisive results: on windy nights tiny drifts are formed under the door. She's in charge of the family cow, a good-tempered scrub Durham that is kept tethered near the house. The two moments each day that Laura looks forward to are when she can set her three-legged milking stool down and rest her forehead against the animal's soft and comforting flanks. Briefly, she has the feeling that she too is being mothered.

Laura's companion in destiny, a man she meets only four times in her life, is James FitzGibbon and he's cut from chevalier cloth. This despite his coming from a fifteen-acre farm near Glin, County Limerick, close to the River Shannon. As a lad he had dug potatoes barefoot and if there's one thing that wholesome manual labour taught him it was that there's nothing all that wholesome in manual labour. His family was poor, but always looking for the edge: his grandfather had turned Protestant in the 1760s, and James's own father made side-money weaving. He pushed his sons to read and write and stay in school, which in Glin meant to age eleven. It worked: James's brother, Gerald, became a rich Dublin lawyer and receiver-master in chancery for Ireland.

Able Irishmen on the make. The key, of course was patronage, for ability in late eighteenth-century Ireland was never a sufficient passport. The FitzGibbons' luck was that their landlord, the Knight of Glin, needed Protestant tenants to protect him and his estate against the sullen Catholics, people whose memory was too long for comfort. In young James FitzGibbon's case the patronage was garnered in 1795 when, at age fifteen, he enlisted in the Knight of Glin's Yeomanry Corp, a bulwark against the revolution that the Ascendancy rightly fear. In 1798, with the Knight's blessing, he joined a Fencible regiment, which was real soldiering, and then was recruited to the 49th regiment of the British army.

FitzGibbon fights in Holland. He is a very good soldier and is decorated and becomes a sergeant-major. When the 49th moves to Canada in 1802, he catches the attention of Isaac Brock who marks him for promotion to officer.

That's what FitzGibbon wants more than anything else: to be a real officer.

Laura Secord just wants a few moments peace and for her bones to stop hurting. American soldiers move back and forth across the Niagara frontier pretty much at will and one big-mouth bunch stays with her family. They brag about the surprise attack they are planning on a Canadian-British outpost at a place imaginatively named Beaver Dams. She takes off on a journey through unmarked bush, swamp, deer-flies, mosquitoes, unrecognizable sounds and, worse, recognizable ones. She will warn the garrison.

Her piece of luck is that she comes across a band of nearly 400 Indians, loyal and ready for combat.

FitzGibbon's luck is that he is in charge of an elite force of 46 men and three officers and has licence to freelance along the frontier: a commando unit it would be called later. The Green Tigers, mostly Irish. He is given the chance for glory.

The Americans, roughly 500 of them, hardened veterans, walk into a trap. They are surrounded by 400 Indians who seem to them to be 4,000. And then, under flag of truce, FitzGibbon cons the Yankees, masterfully. He takes the American commander up to his men, whom he has arranged so that they are visible, all forty-nine of them. He tells the Yankee that there are several times more, rifles ready, in the woods. The American is conned. Five hundred American soldiers surrender to one-tenth the number of Canadians.

FitzGibbon takes all the credit and becomes a national hero. The Indians receive no credit and are bitter.

Laura Secord receives no credit and she does not bother being bitter, but just gets on with being poor. Years later, she asks FitzGibbon for help and he writes testimonials for her in 1820, 1827, and 1837, but these are all ignored by the government. Only in her mid-eighties, does she receive a pension of £100 and some attention. Posthumously, she becomes a great national hero.

When asked why, at the time, he had taken all the credit for himself, James FitzGibbon answers with a candour that tells exactly who and what he is.

"I knew all along the Yankees were coming. And anyway, I wanted my captaincy."

JOHNSTOWN DISTRICT, UPPER CANADA. JULY 1813

The Silent People

The new people who come into the back concessions of the settlements at the eastern end of Lake Ontario are different. Unlike the original loyalists, they have no personal bitterness against the former American colonies, and they see the American revolution as an abstract mistake, not a personal tragedy. Yet, unlike the "late loyalists," most of whom arrived in Canada two decades or more after the American revolution and were not loyalists, just Americans looking for empty land, these new people have a fierce loyalty to the Crown and a detestation of republicanism that runs far beyond the rational. They are Protestant families from Wexford and Wicklow and they've seen too much strife in their lives ever to be open-minded.

Even while the war of 1812–14 was in mid spasm, the Upper Canadian authorities realized that something had to be done about the communities at the top end of the St. Lawrence River and the outfall of Lake Ontario: there were too many Yanks in the back townships and the loyalists in the river-front settlements were losing their phobia towards the Republic. They might not be keen on it, but they'd trade with its citizens even during wartime.

The new incomers, the silent people, have their own folklore, their own system of beliefs. *My father, the head of a household of nineteen children and our mother was killed in the bloodthirsty strife between Catholics and Protestants.* They are of two sorts: Anglicans and a small body of Methodists. They have in common their having been small farmers – ten to fifteen acres – in Wexford and Wicklow and having gone through the 1798 Rising. The Methodists had been especially brutally treated, as they were a small colony of Palatines that the Irish government had settled in the mid-eighteenth century, on a Protestant-Catholic fault line. People who speak strangely are treated even more severely than others when it comes time to crop ears, remove eyes, cut out tongues, pitchfork babies. None of the families had pleasant memories. *The night our house was broken into a farm labourer of ours was leading the mob and he drove a pitchfork at my father's head.* In using these people as back-stiffening agents in Upper Canada, the authorities are being opportunistic to the point of cynicism. But it works, because these people cannot forget. *For two days and nights our family, clad only in our nightclothes, hid in hedges and ditches. We all but were overcome by hunger, thirst, and exposure. We tried to walk to Wexford, only six miles away. We were crossing the Slaney bridge at Enniscorthy when the rebels surrounded us. Father was carrying four-year-old Nathanial. He was ordered to put down the child and to open his waistcoat. He stood there as seven of them piked his body and finally, hoisting him on their pikes and holding him above their head, like they'd just piked a pig, they threw him into the river.* These Protestant families with 1798-memories filter into Augusta, Elizabethtown, Leeds, Kitley, and they begin a chain-migration that continues into the 1830s: tough Protestant farmers who want out of southeastern Ireland. The Palatines among them spread the stories of persecution quickly to the Bay of Quinte settlers. This base for Irish migration to

Upper Canada, later swallowed by massive numbers from elsewhere in Ireland, is easily missed: hard, bitter people who vow that
they will not be run on again by Catholics or by republicans. Since
the Catholics of Canada – overwhelmingly French – are not an immediate danger, the government is using the newcomers as a spiked
fence against the real danger: republicans to the south. These people, after all, could give as well as take punishment. *My brother, a
yeomanry major, rushed to save what he could of the family. He and his
men captured a band of the rebels. My brother condemned eleven of them to
be hanged in Wexford at midnight and that, praise God, was done.*

HOLLAND. MARCH 1814

Forearmed

He is destined to be 0.5 of the future All-Canadian Victorian Champion Invitational Writing Team, but you would never know. He is
arse deep, and worse, in ice-water. This gentleman officer is strug-
gling to lead his men as part of a combined British and Russian attack
on the French who hold Bergen op-Zoom in Holland. It's been an intensely cold winter and even in March the canals and rivers freeze
over at night; and then the ice cracks during the day and won't bear a
human's weight. He and his men are making their way up a river
whose ice won't support them and whose water-course is formed of
mud. They sink to their waists in ooze. Each man then has to free one
leg and put it forward into the mire. Sometimes they sink to shoul-
der-depth in this slough. One regiment gets mixed with another;
weapons are soaked and powder rendered useless. All this occurs
with excruciating slowness, for thrashing about or moving quickly is
a sure way to die of drowning.

An Irish general called Skerret has them in this mess, but 0.5 has no
national animosity towards him, for 0.5 has soldiered enough to
know that almost all generals are fools.

As 0.5 moves along he flashes in and out of reverie: he's one of
God's durable souls, and he's capable of entertaining distracting
memories, while leading a company towards a fight-to-the-death. He
laughs to himself as he remembers a few days earlier coming upon a
Russian regiment, and being taken to see its colonel-in-charge. An

aide had conducted him to the colonel's bedroom where 0.5 observed two people lying in bed in flannel nightshirts. The elder was a massive man with an unpleasant countenance; he seemed to be a Cossack with bowel complaints. The other, whom 0.5 at first took to be the colonel's wife, turned out to be a lad of seventeen, handsome, with a most delicate complexion. Ah, the life of a Russian officer.

Mostly 0.5 keeps his spirits up by thinking of a young Dutch widow in the town of Tholen. He had been billeted with her parents and the little dumpling was a very welcome added amenity. He's fallen in love, so he thinks, and well may have, for 0.5 had taken to studying Dutch grammar, something that no Briton has ever done unless in a very tight circumstance.

Finally, 0.5 and his men escape the ooze and engage the French who outnumber them three-to-one and possess the tactical advantage of having a competent commanding general. Rather than surrender, 0.5 leads his men to flee by jumping onto the ice floes in the harbour. He moves from floe to floe until he has the bad luck to have his left wrist shattered by a musket-ball. Then he surrenders to the French who, after a decent interval, let the British shuffle back to their own lines.

Nearly naked, weak from loss of blood, 0.5 keeps his spirits up by imagining life in a warm climate, say, southern Africa.

REYDON, SUFFOLK. 1816

The Other Half

To the intense embarrassment of his second wife and six daughters, Thomas Strickland loved the Norwich coach building shop in which he was co-partner. The wife and girls (all the product of Strickland's second marriage, as well as two boys who were born last and were supernumerary appendages in this female colony) lived at Strickland's estate in Suffolk and were terrified that he would do something that would drop them from their newly-minted gentry status. They collected wild flowers, learned needle-point, and tried to avoid letting the subject of Mr. Strickland's means of earning a living – in trade – arise in conversation. For his part, Strickland wasn't at all embarrassed about work: he'd started as a penniless Londoner whose parents had come south from Lancashire and he'd risen to running one of the east London docks. Nothing wrong with honest trade so far as he was concerned, though he'd moved to the country to keep his wife happy.

Thomas Strickland spent half his time in Norwich and each morning he walked with steps of anticipation to his factory from the house, a *pied-à-terre* he'd bought there. Directing skilled craftsmen as each applied his art in producing a single elegant item was pure joy. It wasn't the power over workmen he enjoyed, but the blending of skill and creativity into a collective work. The pleasure began even as he approached the shop, for he could smell the library of hardwoods that were being aged, each for a different part of the coach. These were closely monitored and moved weekly so that they neither warped nor bowed; "casting," he called it and a year of seasoning for each inch of thickness was his rule. Strickland always found his men at work. That was another rule: have things in order for the governor. The older hands needed no instructions, except a word or two once a week. The most skilled were the wheelwrights. Somehow, by a magic Thomas Strickland understood in his head but not in his hands, these men took dissimilar blocks of wood and made felloes, hubs, and formed them into the perfectly-curved pieces that fitted together and made a wheel. Strickland saw it all as a moral lesson of great beauty: imperfect individual pieces of wood, with burls, gall-spots, wavy edges, turned into collective perfection. And then locked there by the lead blacksmith, the only one trusted to beat into place around the wheel, a hot rim of iron. As it cooled, the iron tightened every single piece of wood into place: provided each piece was indeed perfectly crafted. But the blacksmith could ruin perfection if he left the rim too loose; worse yet, if he calculated wrongly and put it on too tightly, the cooling would bring so much force onto the wooden pieces that they would crack or, sometimes, explode and be tossed into the air as worthless splinters. Strickland never tired of the drama and risk involved in finishing a wheel. Then there was bodywork. On a fine carriage the curves were as delicate and sensuous as on a violin. Working with a bank of chisels and hand-planes, the finishing-men built the body to each customer's specifications. To allow the body to flex under uneven road conditions, they glued successive layers of ash together. The body was then covered in tanned leathers, horsehide for the exterior, cowhide for most of the interior, and kid leather for the portions that would come in contact with a lady's body. Finally, the front apparatus, attaching this chariot of the gods to an earthly animal, was effected. This involved forming a hames to marry with the horse's collar. Not a great moment, one might think, but the curved pieces, turned from the toughest ash butt, were always in delicate curves. When held in hand they assumed exactly the form that Thomas Strickland visualized as the lyre of Orpheus.

Although at home he was not permitted to talk of his manufactory, and certainly not of the joy it gave him, Thomas Strickland had a second factory and this one his second wife approved. They were great admirers of Richard Lovell Edgeworth of Edgeworthstown, County Longford. He had a large family and had worn out more than one wife and was deeply interested in the proper education of his children. Unusually for his time, Edgeworth had set up a system of humane home education, one that gave as much attention to the intellectual development of the girls as to the boys. The system gained attention in progressive circles and in 1798 his daughter, Maria, had co-written *Practical Education* with her father. Central to the Edgeworth Plan was serious attention to expressive writing. Thomas Strickland embraces this plan because it has the same social beauty as does his carriage factory. He sets pieces of work for his daughters; his wife acts as shop foreman. (The two boys receive a traditional education in Norwich.) Reading, and especially writing, are the main elements of the girls' curriculum, for too much arithmetic and calculation are not right for a lady's education. Each child receives her own set of assignments each week. The key is that the entire enterprise is cooperative. The older girls help the younger ones and many of the tasks set by Thomas Strickland involve two or three of the sisters completing a single enterprise. Like his carriage factory, the pattern is: direction from the top, cooperative craftsmanship on the shop floor, and a final product that is the work of many hands.

The only sins are slacking and doing a project solo: no divas allowed.

Susanna Strickland, aged thirteen, breaks the no-diva rule only once in her life, and even then she needs a doppelganger. She and her one-year-older sister Catherine decide that each will write her own novel – from foundation idea to first word to last word and her own name, solo, on the title page.

Disaster. Their mother and their eldest sister discover this breach of collective production and Susanna's work ends up in the fire and Catherine's as papers for the curling iron.

Lesson learned: never again will Susanna Strickland produce a literary piece of work on her own. She will write hymns, patriotic poems, pastoral verse, children's stories, rustic sketches, political pamphlets, all with wonderful facility. She will put her own name on these works in most instances, but she will never again give herself her own assignment.

Like even the most skilled hand in Thomas Strickland's carriage factory, someone has to tell her what to do – and help her a little if she needs it, and praise the final product.

LIVERPOOL, ENGLAND. 1822

Well, at Least He's Not ...

The future leader of the Orange Order in central Canada takes his first step in that direction. He is inducted into the order in a staunchly Protestant ward of Liverpool. He's a good catch for orangeism: twenty-three years old, smart as a whip, fluent in half a dozen languages. To his advantage, the order will provide him customers and, more importantly, protection in the Protestant-Catholic troubles that increasingly disturb Liverpool.

His initiation into the order has taken till midnight, but he knows that his nine friends will wait for him. He is needed.

Slightly drunk, he knocks on the door of a four-storey house on Hope Street and is quickly admitted.

"Shalom" he says, but offers no explanation for being so late. "Shabbat Shalom."

Moses Cohen now calls himself George Benjamin and, though he may be catholic, he certainly isn't Roman Catholic.

UPPER CANADA, 1815–45

Report from the Front

Marriage, in Canada, is invariably a matter of necessity and expedience, and not of mere choice or taste. The affections are seldom engaged and it is indeed almost impossible that they should: for no sooner do the females of this coun-

try throw off the frock of childhood, and assume the important looks and con-
sequential attitudes of matrimonial candidates, than, like fresh-blown roses,
they are snatched from the parent stem, and pressed to the bosom of some
waiting swain ... They are children today, women tomorrow, wives the next
day, and frequently mothers ere a week expires.

In late 1823, the Irishman Edward Allen Talbot (no relative of the
eponymous Colonel Thomas Talbot, although Edward likes to obscure that point), manages to make it back to Ireland with his notes
on life in Upper Canada. Having spent two years farming woefully in
London township, he had left for home, but it took him three years to
arrive. He is the sort of man who is interested in everything he sees
and he never has the good sense to let his own failures get him down.
So, he'd gone slowly down to Montreal, gostering and taking notes
on everything, and there he saw an Irish girl whom he instantly
adored and soon married. That took time and then there was the matter of his perpetual motion machine. It absorbed a lot of time and
never came quite right. And then he returned to London township to
set up his wife and now-two children on a new hundred-acre farm
before he finally left for his Old Country home. He'll restore his fortunes and be back to Upper Canada, so he promises.

In Ireland, Talbot writes a graceful, deceptively casual book about
Upper Canada, two volumes that are packed with shrewd sightings,
and without the veneer of mahogany morality that makes most later
travel books, the truly Victorian ones, so oppressive. Talbot's is valuable because he does what Victorians never permitted themselves to
do: he peaks behind the bedroom curtains. And tells.

The influence of climate may unquestionably have some effect in forming the
character, and determining the conduct of women as well as of men ... I see
this strikingly exemplified, whenever I contrast the females of Ireland with
those of Canada. [In the Canadas, lack] of chastity is not considered a crime
of the first magnitude, and so far is this from being the case in Upper Canada
or in the United States that an unmarried female with a baby in arms is
much respected, and as little obnoxious to public animadversion, as she
would be had she preserved her virtue with a Vestal's fidelity.

What Talbot observes holds true for all the in-migrating groups,
not just the Irish: for the first two or three decades on the frontier – at
least to 1830 along the front and to mid-century in the back bush –
there aren't enough people, packed close enough together, to enforce

domestic morality the way it was done in the home countries. Besides, Upper Canada is desperately short of labour, so breeding one's
own workers was the best strategy for a frontier farmer. And a girl
with a bairn at the breast demonstrated that she would be a satisfactory breeder.

*The Canadians are ... the most indulgent husbands imaginable ... A respect-
able farmer, with whom I am well acquainted, on his return from a journey of
some hundred miles, surprised his wife in the arms of an old friend, who had
endeavoured, kind man, to console her in the absence of her husband ... The
injured husband, with a meekness above that of the Stoic Philosophy, addressed the usurper of his being in the following sentimental language:
"Neighbour you and I have, I guess, long lived on terms of intimacy, and
God forbid that any event should ever dissolve the bond of friendship which
has so long united us! ... The laws of our country would, you know, give us
redress if so be we were to appeal to them, but I calculate that law is a bad
speculation, and I do not see why two old friends might not settle a trifling
affair of this kind without throwing away $200 or $300 to a set of rascally
lawyers." ... An armistice was immediately agreed to and in a short time it
was settled, "that, within two weeks the injured party should receive two
well-fatted hogs of no less than four hundredweight as a full and fair compensation for the injuries he had received ..."*

After the end of the Napoleonic Wars, the people coming into this
strange, and quickly-to-vanish, New World are overwhelmingly from
the British Isles, with a few former Americans thrown in. For the
Irish, British North America is their favourite destination: up to 1845
about three-quarters of the overseas emigrants head there, an average
of 20,000 persons annually between 1815 and 1845. Almost all of Upper Canada's Irish immigrants are from the eastern half of Ireland
where the market economy is most advanced.

The Irish are formative for the Canadas, especially Upper Canada.
They form the largest ethnic group, roughly half of the British-Isles
derived population. Two-thirds of the Irish are Protestant, which
means that even if one splits them from the Catholics, they are as numerous as are the English or the Scots. Upper Canada is an Irish land.

*"This," you will say, "is a bounce!" But, believe me, it is a real fact, as well
known to hundreds as it is to me; and singular though it may appear, I could
tell you many anecdotes equally true and equally shocking.*

YORK, UPPER CANADA. JUNE 1827

All Sorts

Veteran loungers on the York waterfront agreed that it was the biggest load of personal baggage they had ever seen come off the Durham boats: seven tons, three hundred weight. The property of a fifty-eight-year-old Church of Ireland cleric, the Rev. James Magrath.

Most immigrants to Upper Canada disembarked from their transatlantic vessel in Quebec City or Montreal and took smaller boats upstream. Past Montreal, broad, flat-bottomed Durham boats were employed. The average Irish immigrant family had a set of trunks and money in hand, but not more than £100 in the usual case. Poorer individuals often worked for a year or two in Montreal before moving on, either to Upper Canada or to the States.

If the former rector of the Parish of Shankill, straddling the border of counties Down and Armagh, was unusual in both his advanced age and in his material goods, his motives were those of the everyday immigrant. Despite a parish in Ireland that grossed over £500 per annum and provided a stately manse as well, Magrath left because he saw that Ireland offered little opportunity for his four sons. So he offered his services to the Society for the Propation of the Gospel in Foreign Parts and he and his wife, eighteen-year-old daughter, four sons, and a nephew chanced their hand in the New World lottery. He won: almost immediately upon his arrival at York, Magrath lobbied the lieutenant-governor and the bishop for a parish and he was given the Toronto mission, eighteen miles from York, a salary of £150 annually from the London mission people and 700 acres of land at a bargain price.

The Toronto parish was like a diorama. Within a ten mile radius of the rector's new home – "Erindale" – could be seen everything from bush-breaking that differed little from the loyalists' efforts in the 1780s to, at the other extreme, gentry-esque farms with whitewashed fences surrounding mock-Georgian houses. The Rev. Mr. Magrath was surprised and repulsed by the wildness, drunkenness, cursing, and sexual liberty he encountered, but fascinated by the ingenuity of the immigrants and their offspring in making a living. In a few instances, his parishioners were living in tents on the edge of their bush lots. They then built shanties of rounded logs, chinked with moss: no hearth; the cooking was done on a fire in the centre of the hovel. A hole in the roof let the smoke escape. Magrath had seen plenty of these shelters in Ireland, except that there they were built of mud. The next step up was a squared-log cabin, and an immigrant with £100 in pocket could skip to this stage quickly and begin with an operating farm, having maybe ten acres already cleared. And on: immigrants, Scots, Irish, English, moved up the ladder. Richer ones bought in higher at arrival: half-cleared farms, and, for the well-off, stone houses. What was missing, an Irish clergyman had to note, was paupers: anyone who could and did work had a livelihood.

The Church of England had no future as a state church in Upper Canada: already in 1830, Rev. Magrath was noting that most of the population, to the extent it was religious, was Free Church – or as Magrath called them, "Sectarians." James Magrath laboured in God's vineyard until his death at age eighty-two. His sons became a lawyer, a prosperous store-keeper, an estate manager, and a turf-and-yachting gentleman. Magrath was not a bad clergyman for his new world. He took care of his family, didn't raise religious arguments, and looked after his parish – a parish made up of all classes of persons, but like himself, most of them were hopeful immigrants.

THE RIDEAU CANAL, UPPER CANADA. 1828

The First Epidemic

"They deserve the last rites."

"Too true, your worship."

"And a proper burial."

"Yes, your lordship. The medicals, though, say the plague can be stopped only by quick burial."

The Most Rev. Alexander Macdonnell, Roman Catholic bishop of Kingston and its hinterland, is discussing with his chaplain the victims of the first epidemic to hit the Irish of Upper Canada: malaria. Three to four thousand labourers, about one-third of them Irish Catholics, were engaged to do the donkey-labour of building a canal from Kingston to Bytown (later, Ottawa) to the north. It was a defensive measure against American invasion. The men had entered the army of diggers as their first step in building a stake in the New World, and all they ever saw, poor souls, was swamp, limestone, tree stumps.

Sleeping six to eight to a tent, they fell asleep exhausted and were attacked by clouds of mosquitoes.

A dozen years later the nature of malarial transmission is discovered, the mosquito being the vector. In this earlier era, the best physicians believe that human-to-human transmission is responsible, so within an hour of a sick man's stopping breathing, his corpse is in a communal grave.

"Shame that our Faithful have to be left in unconsecrated ground and with heretics," notes the chaplain.

"Unconsecrated ground: that is sad," agrees Bishop Macdonnell. He remembers earlier burial grounds, when he was chaplain of the Glengarry Fencibles, a regiment of Highland Catholics who helped quell the 1798 Rising in Ireland. He had stayed on with the occupying army until 1802. Macdonnell had seen many men die, good and bad, Catholic and Protestant, and he had learned that sometimes the beginning of wisdom is to suspend human judgement.

Gently, he rebukes his chaplain. "As for sorting out the faithful and the heretical, I think God will be able do it all later."

COBH HARBOUR, COUNTY CORK. JUNE 1829

Sic Transit

A group of nine people stands on the breakwater of Cobh and surveys a ship in the harbour. The craft, a moderately-sized vessel of 550-ton, is scheduled to sail for Quebec City and Montreal within three days, winds permitting. This is an ordinary emigrant ship, but these people do not consider themselves ordinary. A domineering young man in his mid-twenties is the obvious head of the party. He appears to be assessing the ship the way he would examine a horse: looking at her lines and conformation, as if he could buy the vessel if he had the mind to.

Ogle Robert Gowan, accompanied by his wife, his mother, two female servants and four children under ten years of age, is emigrating for reasons he would prefer not to discuss. His strut borders on truculence. Constant self-assertion will, for a time, make Ogle Gowan the best-known Irishman in Upper Canada and one of the most influential. Never, however, one of the most loved.

Gowan is about five feet, nine inches in height, solidly built, with long side whiskers that have a ginger sheen. His nose, which has been broken twice, is broad and bent slightly to one side. Gowan, in herding his small flock of emigrants, several times flaps open and closed the double breasted greatcoat that he wears despite the mild weather, making himself appear like a large greyling gander bristling about the barnyard. Under the greatcoat he bears colourful plumage: a modish morning coat with padded shoulders and a Paisley-fronted waistcoat and harmonizing cravat. A bit glossy, but if your eye isn't too keen he does appear to be a gentleman.

As a son of the legendary Catholic-killer of 1798, Hunter Gowan, and a namesake of the Catholics' bête noir, George Ogle, MP, Ogle has had a good run in Ireland: access to top-line Protestant attorneys, editors, and employment by the Orange Order as a factotum. His own profession was anti-Catholicism.

On board ship, the Gowan entourage lives well, although not up to the standard of those Irish migrants, the Blakes and their associates who, three years later, sail from Cork to North America with fine linen tablecloths and their own silver for proper dining. The Gowan party has two state rooms. One is occupied by Gowan and his wife Frances and the other by his mother, the children and the servants. The party has access to a large dining room for cabin passengers and, weather permitting, the run of the ship.

On deck, Ogle Gowan rehearses his grievances. Of course he doesn't see them straight-on, but in fact they are simple. Life went downhill when his father died in 1825 and his last will and testament was contested by various family members. In a ripe chancery suit it came out that Ogle Gowan was illegitimate and that he had tried to forge a codicil to his father's will. One of Gowan's political enemies had printed the trial-testimony in a pamphlet and it was so damning that Gowan had been dismissed from his position in the Orange Order. All this at a time when the very devil himself, Daniel O'Connell, was taking over the Irish countryside and making it clear that there was not going to be an easy future for professional Catholic haters: certainly not in south Leinster and Munster. Time to go.

In each stateroom of the ship is a drop-leaf desk and Ogle has two crew members move the desk from the children's cabin into his own. There the two desks, placed side by side, make a large enough surface for him to read and write on and he soon has them covered with books, bundles of foolscap and various documents engrossed with official-looking seals. These are authentic warrants and certificates of the Orange Order. Gowan had stolen these when he was dismissed by the Order. He intends to put them to use in Upper Canada.

NEAR PRESCOTT, LANARK COUNTY, UPPER CANADA.
12 JULY 1829

The Seven Irishmen

It's a mockery. They've been doing it since they arrived in 1820 as seven lads in their late teens and early twenties, full of life, and very social. One is from County Limerick – James Carberry – and the rest from County Waterford: John and Patrick Quinn, John Cullen, Terence Doyle, James Power, William Scanlen. They'd all been on the same boat over and had decided to stick together. Their first decent job was clearing land for the military settlement at Perth.

They're drunk as lords right now and have been since well before noon. These men, Catholics who'd encountered the Orange Order in various unpleasant ways in the Old Country, had celebrated their first year in Upper Canada by holding their own Glorious Twelfth, a parody of the Orange version, with the exception of their becoming legless, which was authentic enough. Over their nine years in Canada, they had collected their own toasts:

> Up the Long Ladder,
> Down the Short Rope.
> To Hell with King Billy,
> And up with the Pope.

Items of that sort. These became funnier to them with each passing year.

Because of their good record as bush workers, the seven had been granted 200 acres each and these in a block, so that they could forever be neighbours. For the first half-dozen years they had lived together in a large log house, taking turns doing the cooking. They worked together, clearing bush and doing field work on the original farm. When a second lot was sufficiently cleared to be a liveable farm, a small log house was built and one of the men moved to it. And so on until all seven had a workable farm and a house.

None of them married. They continued to do all their field work together and were famous for their hospitality. They'd play music, dance, drink at any reasonable provocation, even the anniversary of the Battle of the Boyne.

QUEBEC CITY, LOWER CANADA. 28 JULY 1829

First Impression

The vessel with Ogle R. Gowan and his family aboard is anchored before Quebec City. All the passengers are impatient to touch land, but there are port formalities to complete. These are nothing like the quarantine that the migrants of later years experienced, but bothersome nonetheless.

Gowan loudly insists that the port officials deal first with the cabin class passengers and thus he and his entourage are the first onshore. They are continuing up-river to Montreal, but after fifty-eight days at sea even a brief call on land seems a holiday.

Once on shore, Gowan gives his wife, mother, children and servants strict instructions not to stray more than fifteen minutes from the quayside.

He proceeds briskly away from the wharf. Soon he is on a crowded thoroughfare and immediately he learns something important about the New World – it is different. That does not sound like much, but it is a truth many British Isles gentlemen never pick up. Gowan, though, listens. In shop fronts and squares he hears few words of English. He watches people closely and he sees in this commercial area black, brown, yellow people and all varieties of white persons.

Gowan leaves this cosmopolitan bazaar and proceeds to the centre of the city. There he runs into the captain of his ship and accepts an invitation to a hotel, meaning a drinking spot. There they are each served an enormous tumbler of cognac and given a pipe, three feet in length, and a paper of Virginian tobacco. The sea captain grows expansive; Gowan listens, asks questions, listens some more.

Two massive cognacs later, the captain suggests that they walk a bit or they shall fall asleep. He kindly offers to show Ogle the summit of the city and the celebrated Plains of Abraham. To both Gowan and the captain the fortifications of the city are of great interest, particularly the citadel that stands on Cape Diamond, 350 feet above the St. Lawrence. The captain, having sailed in and out of harbours all over the world is something of an authority on maritime redoubts and Gowan, raised on dinner table conversation of the need for stout defensive positions, always has had an interest in such things.

Their walking tour proceeds amiably, if slightly drunkenly, until they come upon a memorial to General Wolfe.

Gowan becomes visibly upset. "By God, will you look at that!"

"Yes, Mr. Gowan, it is a monument to a great man."

"Monument!"

Gowan points with disgust. "You call *that* a monument to a man who, by his skill and valour annexed the vast territory of the Canadas to the British Empire?" He spits. "*That* is a pitiable tribute. If that is the gratitude of the people of Quebec, then hell roast them."

Ogle Gowan has been incensed by a wooden sculpture, about four-and-a-half feet high, apparently hatchet-carved. The figure is painted red, white, and black with the name JAMES WOLFE incised on its wooden pedestal.

"You expected, Mr. Gowan, the people of Quebec to raise a bronze statue; Wolfe on a charger perhaps?"

Gowan glares at the captain, but holds himself in check. "My dear sir,"he says abruptly," I find that I am feeling a bit ill. All that cognac and smoke I fear has upset me. I shall return to the ship."

As Ogle Gowan descends through the centre of the city he notes and marks well that almost all of the churches are Roman Catholic.

THE AMERICAN EVOLUTION
1785–1830

Dominion Over God's Earth

Four years after the Articles of Confederation were framed and two years after the Treaty of Paris was signed, the American colonies achieve true independence. It is gained not by their casting off their chains, but by embracing them.

The chains are those of surveyors, twenty-two yards in length. They are the simple device that lies at the heart of the U.S. imperium on the American continent. They are wonderful implements, having the same power and elegance to move social and economic mountains that the simple lever has to move physical ones. Just twenty-two yards. Placed at right angles to each other, twenty chains by twenty chains form precisely forty acres. And just make a square of sixteen forty-acre parcels and one has a square mile – 640 acres – exactly one mile on each side: later to be called a "section." The geometry is beautiful and all the more so for being non-metric and decidedly human in scale: farms are described in sequences: forty-acres, quarter-sections, sections.

The measuring of America begins at an arbitrary point in the Ohio territory on lands that are those of the federal government. That Land Ordnance of 1785 has affirmed the United States' collective ownership of all lands between the Appalachian Mountains and the Mississippi River. The ceding of their western reserves by the seaboard colonies was not an amiable business and would not have occurred except that Maryland refused to ratify the Articles of Confederation until the demits were promised. (Even then, Georgia did not actually give up its claim until 1804.) But now, the central authorities have begun to turn all that land into a human-defined grid, not out of any sense of mission: they are broke and need to sell the lands.

Such mundane causes begin the most hubristic and most successfully pharonic taming of nature and brutalization of the natural world that any agricultural society had yet assayed. The lines drawn on the land – indicated at distant intervals by cairns, deep-driven iron bars, and the occasional masonry-mounted brass plate – created an invisible web that asserted man's dominion over God's natural world. No longer were natural features the primary descriptors of the shape of America, but rather map references, numbers finding place in a system. Conceptual triumph.

The grid, invisible as a radar beam as it leaps from point to point, eventually stretches all the way to the Pacific Ocean, south to Mexico, north to British North America. It teaches.

It teaches that God may propose but that man disposes, as far as the American earth is concerned.

It teaches that land can be owned, for the U.S. government uses its grid to demark saleable spaces of earth and there the purchasers are told that they are freeholders – meaning owners. Never mind that no human being can ever own land. (Show me men and women who have lived longer than their land; any real farmer knows that the land owns him.) The fantasy becomes a bedrock belief of the new culture. The belief is a magnet for immigrants. They can own the earth! and receive a piece of paper to prove it.

The twenty-two yard chain, as much as the Constitution of 1787, is the foundation of the United States of America.

NR CADIZ. 1786

The Shores of Tripoli

In usual circumstances, James Leander Cathcart was not a forgetful man. If he placed something out of mind it was an intentional act. Strangely, as a trader in the Mediterranean and north coast of Africa, he forgot two crucial bits of information: that, though Irish-born, he was a self-declared American and, secondly, that the Thirteen Colonies' victory in the war of independence meant that the Royal Navy was no longer protecting American-flagged vessels or American crewmen. So, at age twenty-one, Cathcart was caught up in a dragnet of Algerian xebecs. The Barbary coast principalities of Tripoli, Tunis, Algiers and Morocco swept the Mediterranean, taking seamen as if they were seining sardines. Cathcart spent three miserable years as a latrine slave in Algiers, emptying night soil, catching several loathsome communicable diseases, yet somehow surviving.

Late in the 1790s, he becomes a garden slave of the Dey of Algiers. The Dey was impressed both with his assiduous attention to detail and his intelligence. Cathcart, good at languages, knew Spanish before his capture and also the lingua franca of the Mediterranean maritime world. In captivity he added Arabic. The Dey made Cathcart his personal coffee-server, a risky and unpleasant post in some regards: the Dey was terrified of being poisoned and, according to Cathcart's later record, had a habit of using his coffee-server as a human spittal-post. However, the Dey was princely in providing his personal servants with gifts and James Cathcart became moderately wealthy. When the Dey died in 1791, Cathcart was freed and he became a civic official – the Overseer of Christians – for his successor. He was particularly good at keeping the new Bashaw from being overcharged by Jewish moneylenders, whom Cathcart called Christ-killers. On the side, Cathcart became the leaseholder of seven tavern-brothels.

The United States, desperate to cease losing ships and sailors, sent an envoy to Algiers in November 1793 to seek a truce. The Dey loftily refused to meet the man. The U.S. persisted, however, and James Cathcart was appointed the diplomatic representative of the North African states. He successfully negotiated a peace treaty, and this despite John Quincy Adams labelling him a Troublesome Irishman.

Then, in a lovely arabesque, James Leander Cathcart becomes the United State's consul in Tripoli. He serves later in Cadiz, Madeira and Lisbon, before settling in Washington where he passes the last twenty years of his life as the Second Comptroller of the U.S. Treasury.

PHILADELPHIA, PENNSYLVANIA. 1791

Big Numbers

There are no founding mothers; only Founding Fathers. When the first generation of American legislators meet in Philadelphia in 1791 (previously they had convened in New York City), they are interested in big numbers. They await the results of the first census in the English-speaking world, that of 1790.

Big numbers only. The Fathers do not wish to be reminded of some embarrassingly small ones: that the constitution of 1787 (ratified in 1788) was drafted by fifty-five men, of whom only thirty-nine actually signed it. And those men were chosen by state electors that did not reach a total of 2,000, all of them white males.

Much better to fasten upon the burgeoning population of the new American empire. The Fathers learned the good news that the USA had a white population of about 3.2 million; curiously, they did not count unmarried individuals who lived alone, so the real total was closer to 4.0 million. Of course African slaves were not officially counted; and the elusive and sometimes nomadic Amerindians could not have been enumerated even if they had been thought worthy. A reasonable guess of the time was that, east of the Mississippi, there were about four-and-a-half million human beings, if one included non-whites, which some did.

This was the most Irish moment in American history. Between 3–400,000 individuals were of Irish background, the overwhelming majority immigrants or second generation. Never again will the USA have so large a portion of its population with such close ties to its Irish roots. Larger numbers, yes, but not so large a proportion of the USA's peoples so recently a product of the Irish homeland.

DAVIDSON COUNTY, TENNESSEE. 17 JANUARY 1794

Mother Substitute

Rachel Donelson, a pale, fine-boned lady who looks as if she has been crying, marries for the third time. The Rev. Thomas Craighead solemnizes the union. For Andrew Jackson it is the second time.

Yet Andrew's only marriage partner has been Rachel; and Rachel has married Andrew twice, and no divorce in between.

Here was the problem. The legal system of the frontier was medieval and slow; the demands of everyday life were immediate and demanded quickness.

In 1791, near Natchez, the first time Rachel and Andrew married, the ceremony had been a joyous one. She was not pale then, but a vibrant, sun-browned woman whose body still held the lines of her tomboy upbringing. Age twenty-five, a year older than Andrew.

Neither partner was naïve. Andrew, on the basis of a £300 bequest from a relative in Ireland, had apprenticed as a lawyer and become the attorney general of the Mero district, south of the Ohio River, a judicial office that meant he delivered writs with a pistol in his belt. When, at twenty-two years of age, he had taken this post, he had purchased, as preparation for his trip from the Carolinas, a black girl. From his middle teens onward, Jackson had understood the need to clear his sinuses frequently, and using Indian and African women was the accepted practice of his time: just don't flaunt it or talk about such things before ladies. One acquired a lady wife and of course one kept something on the side, at least if one aspired to planter status.

And Rachel, at age nineteen, had been married – her first, if one is keeping count – to a man who turfed her out because he believed (probably wrongly) that she was seeing someone else. They had reconciled, and then she had fallen in love with Andrew Jackson. Her husband had gone four-fifths of the way towards completing the divorce process, which involved the legislature of Virginia and was truly complex. Maybe Rachel's husband never completed the process; the records are unclear. But Andrew and Rachel married the first time and then, when gossip began to flow that she had eloped from her husband, they married again. Odd morality, but a double standard of course: a bit on the side for the man, but a lady's reputation was ruined if she played around. This in the land of the Cowans, McGarys, McKees, respectable frontier Irish who knew about wearing the good Presbyterian face.

For the rest of his life, Andrew Jackson defends his wife's honour. He has a chivalric side and, besides, protecting his wife's good name was similar to his growing up as a boy, when he had to protect his husbandless mother who was, of course, also protecting him. Andrew wears for the remainder of his life a locket around his neck. It contains a cameo of Rachel and no Arthurian knight ever carried a lock of his love's hair with more constancy. As he rises politically, the slanders against his darling increase. Duels. Lawsuits.

Rachel increasingly withdraws and becomes the Silent Madonna. Andrew, with a plantation of two score slaves does not suffer sexual deprivation, but he worships Rachel and it is all he can do to withstand her entreaties to give up his political ambitions and remain with her at their home, the Hermitage. *They talk of his being President ... In this as all else I can say only, the Lord's will be done. But I hope he may not be called again to the strife and honours of public place.* Jackson indeed is elected president of the United States in November 1828. Will Rachel reside in Washington? Will she even come out from behind the curtains and attend the Inauguration? During the election campaign, pamphleteers have called her names she cannot even read without crying, and the real gutter stuff is kept from her.

Immediately after Andrew's electoral victory, Rachel takes an un-defined illness and has to be bled. That settles her for a while and she reads her Bible in a heavily-curtained room and prays and prays. *I as-sure you I had rather be a doorkeeper in the house of God than to live in that palace in Washington.* She takes ill again after discovering one of the fouler printed slanders about her past which Andrew had kept from her. She is taken with seizures, and is terror-stricken with the thought of the Inauguration festivities. She so wants God's peace, not the strife of American political life, and she finds it. She dies 22 December. She had willed herself into God's arms.

Thus the strand of chivalry in Andrew Jackson's soul is cauterized, ended forever. Inaugurated as the seventh president of the USA in March 1829, he cuts a fine public figure. But he has once again be-come an orphan, as at the moment in the American Revolution when his mother took ill and died. He is bereft both of a protector (as his mother and Rachel had been) but, more importantly, robbed of some one, some thing, pure to protect. Now, as in 1781, he is left with roil-ing hate. *May God Almighty forgive her murderers, as I know she forgave them. I never can.*

PHILADELPIA, USA. AUGUST 1795

Roses in Summer

No one except the world's champion romantic would have sought the grail that Theobald Wolfe Tone pursued in the 1790s: the concen-tration into a single political force of the Presbyterians of Ulster and the Catholics of the whole of Ireland. In his explaining to Presbyteri-ans the justice of Catholic claims for civil rights and, later, in preach-ing to Catholics the radical democratic ideals of the Belfast merchants who founded the United Irishmen, he was trying to use the heat of their common dislike of the British crown to form a social weld, one that would join them into a single, scythe-sharp instrument.

A romantic task: made possible in large part by his being of neither group and thus able to idealize each. Tone was nominally a member of the Established Church, but actually a deist. His fine, almost femi-nine features, expensive cravats, extravagant waistcoats and flighty motions with his hands made a distracting initial impression, but were a necessary part of his persona. If he sniffed at the world through a perfumed handkerchief, he nevertheless struggled to bring it up to his expectations, and noble these truly were.

The life of a romantic, even a genuinely heroic one such as Tone, was inevitably hard. Not because of persecution by the enemies of virtue (that was to be expected, indeed, desired), but because the forces of right often were so very awkward and aesthetically unpleasing.

In Paris, in one of the most lubricious moments in French history, the height of the revolution, Tone keeps himself pure for his own wife, but it is no trouble: French women are terribly ugly, he adjudges, and their fashions remarkably unattractive, especially their wigs.

In Philadelphia, where he meets with other leaders of the United Irishmen, he is predictably disappointed with the Irish migrants to the New World. In the USA, they had picked up all the worst habits of the Americans. *They are as boorish and ignorant as the Germans, as uncivil and uncouth as the Quakers, and as they have ten times more animal spirits than both, they are much more actively troublesome.*

Tone, his scented handkerchief dabbing frequently, decides that he and his wife could never raise their children in the American republic where, because of *the boorish ignorance of the peasants about us, they would encounter a society wherein learning and talents were useless.*

FEDERAL AMERICA. 1790–1830

The Book No One Rights

Go to any Baptist or Methodist or Presbyterian or Episcopalian graveyard where grave markers cover the early years of the United States. Each marker is a page in a collective book, the biography of the early state. Take along Patrick Woulfe's classic *Sloinnte Gaedeal/ Gall* which gives most Irish names in play in the eighteenth and nineteenth centuries and their variant Anglicized forms. Only a mule will miss the fact that in thousands of tiny Protestant cemeteries of the early USA there lie buried tens of thousands of men, women, and children who had begun life as Catholics *pur laine*. This is not a new pattern in the American mainland, but a continuation of the colonial experience.

That is unsettling, for was not the new, free, united America supposed to rewrite the book of old injustices?

Not really. Read the Constitution of 1787 and the Bill of Rights just like you do those gravestones: put a piece of paper on those monumental legal documents and do a charcoal rubbing: hidden patterns emerge just as they do on the individual memorials: and strange blank spaces.

As a document written from the top down, the Constitution was careful to avoid items on which rich men (and men not yet rich who believed they soon would be) might deeply disagree. The text is a charter of class unity, upper class, and its genius is that any time a matter divisive of that unity comes close to the page, a display of verbal pyrotechnics distracts the reader and the dangerous moment passes. The most obvious of these issues is slavery which could not be reconciled with the notion of individual human rights, so it was slipped silently into those topics on which each state could decide. And so too America's anti-Catholic penal code, and this was handled with even more finesse.

Apparently the U.S. Declaration of Independence and first two constitutions provided for freedom of religion. Sorely needed indeed: in only two of the original Thirteen Colonies were Catholic priests explicitly given the freedom to serve their faith, and in some, such as Massachusetts, they were proscribed until 1780. Virginia abandoned its Anglican State church in 1786 and passed a statue of Religious Liberty. Was not that sort of thing unnecessary after 1787–90? Did not the U.S. Constitution and subsequent Bill of Rights make any religious discrimination illegal?

No. It was a federal document and, true to their practice with slavery, rather than fight among themselves the framers looked away from the core issue of full toleration for Catholics. The federal Constitution gave freedom to worship and prohibited an established church, but that was all: the states were free to legislate as they wished on civil matters. So – this cruel point is almost universally avoided by historians – anti-Catholic penal laws survived in several states of America considerably longer than they did in Ireland itself. New Jersey kept Catholics from voting and from holding state civic offices until 1844. And not until 1878 could Catholics hold state office in New Hampshire.

Back to the burying-grounds. They are the resting places of the widening and deepening stream of migration from 1790–1830 that encompassed Germans, Britons, Irish. In the early nineteenth century, more Irish than ever came to America, but their pattern was the same as in the eighteenth century. Very roughly: three-quarters Ulster-Scots, and the remaining quarter split between Anglicans and Catholics. The real number that counts is those remaining Catholics: few. If as many as one in twenty Irish persons was Catholic at the end of their life in America, it was a triumph for the faith. When the Catholic Church finally becomes functional in America in the 1830s, the first bishop of Charleston estimates that three million Irish Catholics have turned Protestant while in America. His figures are figurative, his way of saying, "almost all of them left us."

That's what America did. No surprise, then, that no competent scholar has detailed and explained the nature of America's penal code, 1607–1878. As was the case with the Founding Fathers, there are some things we just do not wish to see.

LONDON AND DUBLIN. OCTOBER 1798

Opinions

A shared problem, but radically different views: the Dublin authorities have several hundred rebel prisoners from the '98 Rising in custody. They have hanged those they can with any propriety execute, but the rest are a problem, especially eighty United Irishmen, prominent in the failed Rising.

Word reaches Rufus King, the U.S. representative in London, that these radical democrats will be sent to his country (or "allowed to emigrate thereto," which is really the same thing). America does not need political radicals, especially Irish ones, for they tend *to act in concert and under artful leaders may be, as they have been, enlisted in mischievious combinations against our government.* The sort of people who threatened the rule of Dublin Castle would threaten the rule of the American upper class. *The danger of this was even greater when the emigrants were United Irishmen.*

Lord Castlereagh, chief secretary for Ireland, disagrees. He wants the trouble-makers banished but does not see the Irish patriots as any great threat to anybody. *The majority of our prisoners are not more dangerous than the general class of America settlers.* Ah, there's a point. *Were it not that the loyal would be disgusted and indignant at their being at large in this kingdom [of Ireland], the greater part of them might be discharged without much danger to the state.*

Still, Castlereagh understands why the American ruling class might not want the United Irishmen. *The Directors in Kilmainham [Gaol] describe the tyranny of the American government as not less grievous than their own, and speak of [President] Adams and [Prime Minister] Pitt in terms of equal disrespect.*

CANE RIDGE, KENTUCKY. 1801

Natural Market

Although the Great Awakening was a touch rumbustious, it gained a subsequent respectability that made discussing it in public a possibility; few, however, have talked loudly about the great frontier Jesus Jumping that began in 1799. That revival was such a howling at the moon that even its spiritual heirs do not wish to mention it: whole families taking seizures, speaking in tongues, frothing at the mouth, hallucinating and chasing the devil, repenting so hard that blood spurted from their noses. It had several apostles, the most affecting being an Irish farmer in Kentucky: James McGready, who had seen himself sitting at Jehovah's right hand, just a little down the table from Jesus of Nazareth.

The emaciated McGready looked as if he had been run over by a large road-roller. The crucified Jesus emanated from his every breath. What a man! In August 1801 he drew a crowd of 25,000 – most of the ambulatory population of the southern frontier – to a small town in Kentucky and there, without benefit of anything save his own miraculous voice, struck them down in the Spirit. Lord, to have seen that!

The revival affects all sorts in the south and especially settlers on the frontier. The best natural market is the Irish who, outside of Pennsylvania, are settled largely in the south: the Carolinas, Georgia, Kentucky, Tennessee, and even Virginia, are on average 20 percent Irish, mostly of Presbyterian background.

With this revival, Presbyterianism, south of Pennsylvania, is shattered. By 1815, most of the old Ulster-Scots are Methodists or, more often, Baptists.

Worth noting, for eventually the Southern Baptist Convention becomes one of the two unofficial established churches of the United States of America.

EAST TENNESSEE. 1802

Peculiar People

"To thee, young David, be protection, as from Jehoaikim who slew Urijah."

"Amen," says David Crockett, sixteen years of age and totally illiterate. He has no idea what his master is referring to, but he reckons it has to do with protection from Indians, as he is being sent through the woods to a mill with a hundredweight sack of grain on his back.

John Kennedy, Crockett's master, is a Quaker from North Carolina and David is working off a forty dollar debt that his own father owed Kennedy. The backwoods holds a surprising number of Quakers from southern Ireland: William Penn had favoured them in his plantation schemes and, like everyone else, they multiplied on the frontier. Something about all that fresh air. Young Crockett thinks they are strange indeed, but he quickly learns how to imitate their mixture of Irish language, perpetual proverbs, and willingness to drive hard bargains.

David Crockett cannot read, but he has grown up working around his father's forever-failing tavern, and he has learned how to make sounds that keep happy any of the dozen sorts of fortune-seekers that slash their way into the interior of the continent. And as a young boy he has watched men fighting outside his father's shebeen. He learns the tricks that later keep him alive among mountain men: how to put a finger into an eye and pull it out of the socket entirely; the value of teeth in fighting, especially in severing a nose clean off and thus, through copious haemorrhaging, filling the opponent's lungs with his own blood; how to detect a knife hidden inside the sleeve of a deerskin jacket; and, most importantly, how to escape from a stacked fight by making jokes that distract the on-lookers and allow an honourable climb-down.

When David's compulsory time with Kennedy is done, he stays on because he has fallen in lust with a local girl, Mary Finley, nicknamed

"Polly." She is an Irish girl. That's how he describes her, although only her mother is directly from the old country. And the mother is a termagant. First the old dear encourages David's attention to Polly, then warns him off as she's found a better suitor, and, Lord, doesn't that woman have a way with words. Speaks faster than anyone David has ever met.

He stays on with the Quaker, however, and part of his payment is that he learns elementary reading and writing; and he wins out. In 1806 he weds his Irish Polly. All that the new couple receive as a marriage portion is two springer heifers.

And from John Kennedy a fifteen dollar credit at the nearest store.

WASHINGTON, D.C. 1803

Virginia Gentleman

Thomas Jefferson, who always kept a decanter of brandy handy, knew his Napoleon. Consequently, he feared that a French empire on the western side of the Mississippi River might pen in the American empire. He wished to buy the vast Louisiana Territory from the French, who had acquired it from the Spanish only in 1800. Fortunately for Jefferson, Buonaparte's adventures in conquering Hispaniola chilled him on the idea of a western French empire and the U.S. acquired for $15 million, more than 800,000 square miles of land. The size of the U.S. was almost doubled, running now to the Rockies in the north and through Louisiana in the south, with big patches of undefined territory overlapping with the lands claimed by Mexico.

Jefferson, an excellent gentleman scientist, understands classical physics very well. He knows that the purchase makes a war with the United Kingdom inevitable: the northern boundary is a messy business. He knows that his new lands must be staked out quickly by settlers allegiant to the U.S., and this will require heavy immigration from Germany, Ireland, and Great Britain. And, he certainly knows that the aboriginal inhabitants will be displaced, but he cares not a tithe, for they are scarcely human.

His knowledge comes together in a single Unified Field Theory of Aboriginal Rights during the War of 1812, when some of the natives choose to resist the American empire. *This unfortunate race, whom we*

have been taking so much pains to save and to civilize, have by their unex-
pected desertion and ferocious barbarities justified extermination, and now
await our decision on their fate.

THE GREAT LAKES BASIN AND ST. LAWRENCE
WATERSHED. 1812–14

Simple Query

Riddle this.

Why did the USA, which should have won in a walk, not win the War of 1812–14? (Mind you, it did not lose either, just didn't win.) The sums make it obvious. The USA had at least six million white citizens, the Canadas, half a million and many of those disaffected *habitants*. The British army, mostly locked into the Maritime ports and Quebec City, boasted 8,000 men; the Americans 7,000. The multiple militias of the USA fielded more than half a million men and those of the Canadas, one-tenth that number, plus Indians with whom the British had treaty relations, notably the Mohawk.

Thus and all, it should have been a piece of piss: six months at most.

The answer to the riddle is Tecumseh. He and his mantle of leadership were the balance weight that kept the scales from tipping in the USA's favour. Easily the shrewdest military leader of the 1812–14 war – even cannier than his partner Sir Isaac Brock – he out-generalled his vastly better-armed and more numerous opponents.

To the credit of the Americans, they later recognized him as an authentic, if ill-fated, colossus. Towns, counties and, most tellingly, children were named after him.

Take the implacable William Tecumseh Sherman for example.

THAMES RIVER, UPPER CANADA. 1813

Primitive Magic

Sorting through the bodies of the losers, the U.S. soldiers look for that of Tecumseh. Unlike many military leaders, he had worn simple buckskin and is therefore hard to identify. During the battle, Col. Richard M. Johnson of the Kentucky militia killed a warrior at close quarter, but he had no idea who it was. Eventually a body is found that fits Tecumseh's description, and a later autopsy shows that it is indeed the Indian Caesar, for a broken leg bone tallies with knowledge of Tecumseh's military career.

The American soldiers are too civilized to take the heart or to drink the blood of their enemies, but it is perfectly acceptable to assume the spiritual power of the dead unto oneself.

Col. Johnson declares that he killed Tecumseh. This claim – for who knows if it was true? at least a dozen others claimed the credit – opens the way to Johnson's becoming first a congressman and then a senator and then the ninth vice president of the USA. How can the conqueror of a great man not himself be great?

NEW ORLEANS. 23 DECEMBER 1813 – 8 JANUARY 1814

Old Hickory

Andrew Jackson possessed an amazingly steep learning curve, especially when it involved killing people. He had spent most of the War of 1812–14 hunting down the indigène in Tennessee, the Mississipi Territory, and parts of Florida, with such success that he was named Major-General. He was no arm-chair general. He prepared his men for battle personally. Just before his greatest triumph against the Creek, the Battle of Tohopeka (Horseshoe Bend, the Mississippi Territory), he was planning his strategy with his chief scout, John Coffee, when a seventeen-year-old lad, a new recruit to the militia, was brought to him. "He's been defying his officers, sir."

"Shoot him. Shoot him!" replied Jackson immediately and two days later the lad was. That encouraged the others and they killed 650 savages at the cost of only forty-nine of their own. Jackson, who already knew that his future lay not in the law but in politics, expressed regrets about having to shoot the disobedient militia-boy and having to kill some Creek women and children.

So, it was appropriate and fortunate for the U.S. side that Jackson was the American general in the only encounter in the War of 1812–14 that was fought by the rules and customs of eighteenth-century

European warfare: conventional warfare involving fixed positions, classical battle plans employing artillery, cavalry and infantry; and, as frequently was the case in European warfare, Irish generals in command of each side. Here it was an American-Irishman, Jackson, against two competent, but not exceptional, Irishmen, Generals Keane and Pakenham. And Jackson who had never fought on a military game board by European rules learned quickly, almost instantaneously. He responded to a well-crafted surprise attack by the U.K. forces with a manic, and totally surprising, attack of his own.

The full Battle of New Orleans lasted just over two weeks.

Technically, it was not really part of the War of 1812–14: Jackson's victory came two weeks after the treaty ending the war had been signed, far away.

DANIEL BOONE'S PALATINATE NR THE MISSOURI RIVER. 1817

Imprinting

"Show it to me again, father."

"Ah, sure." Lindsey Carson stopped hoeing and held out his left hand. Two of the fingers were missing. The stubs stood like stumps in a partially-cleared forest. Kit wondered if they would grow back.

"And tell me how you lost them, Sir." Kit had been raised to be mannerly. His father did not at all mind going through the details of the way the War of 1812–14 had flashed across the Missouri frontier, like heat lightning. British and loyalists and *Canadiens* and Indians had fought U.S. citizens and Indians in battles that were unpredictable, brief, and lacked any strategic sense. The part of the story that Kit, aged eight, liked best was the way that a bullet from a large bore rifle had clean removed his Da's fingers while his hand was grasping the stock of his own rifle. And the good part was that his father told in detail – always the same, the tale never grew – how he had shot one of the Indian attackers and killed the other one in hand-to-hand combat. Lindsey Carson's left hand, diminished, had nevertheless wrested the Indian's own knife from him and thrust it into his bowels and twisted and twisted until the life had drained completely out of him.

The glory of victory over the savages and the sacrifice necessary for such victory was imprinted on Kit Carson.

That was why in 1831 Kit joined the Rocky Mountain Fur Company, a band of beaver-trappers who were working in New Mexico and northwards, in competition with the Hudson's Bay Company. He was recruited by Tom Fitzpatrick, whom he never had previously met. The decision to join was immediate on Carson's part and he never questioned it.

Fitzpatrick simply talked to him for a while about the men he was losing to the Comanches and then gestured with his arm. Not his hand. He was known as Broken Hand by the several Indian tribes he dealt with and his left hand curled under itself. It had been nearly severed by a tomahawk and now, folded under, was a gnarled stub, an ancient cypress whose dangled roots awaited regeneration.

Of course Kit Carson said yes.

SAVANNAH, GEORGIA TO PHILADELPHIA,
PENNSYLVANIA. 1818

Dust Clouds

The long-long-trail-awinding begins early in the history of the U.S. It is marked by dust clouds kicked up by thousands, sometimes tens of thousands of animals. Each autumn it begins and the herds are driven to the cities of the southern and middle states seaboard. People living along a transport artery see the dust that swirls a day before the drovers and their charges appear. Then, two hours or more before they appear, the sounds of animal noise grow, blurred by distance at first, and then the identifiable complaints and grunts of individual animals are distinguishable as they come around the bend and then, for hours, walk, limp, occasionally scamper by. They push outside the lines of the road and citizens lock their doors and guard their gardens until the last of the beasts, always foraging, always being yelled at or prodded by the drovers, moves past and disappears into the cloud of their own creation.

This is the start of the tradition of the Long Trail.

It begins in the South, not the West.

And the animals are pigs.

Squealing, snorting pigs that still have their tusks and can dig up a hedge or collapse a ditch in search of worms, roots, anything. They are not welcome but are a fact of life. Collected from the southern and middle-states' inland areas they are the annual cash crop of the everyday farmer. Not plantation owners, everyday farmers. The pigs widen the roads as they go and leave behind a trail of urine and slimey shite that only the winter sleets finally rinse away.

The drovers' capital, the biggest receptor of these tough four-legged, strong-necked, razor-toothed barrels, is Philadelphia. During the annual autumn hog-drive it is said that if you follow the herd down into the city, you are in danger of sliding all the way into the harbour.

DANIEL BOONE'S PALATINATE. 1819

Mentor

Observing the ten-year old spend his days with the most famous frontiersmen in America, you would have thought them to be grandfather and grandson. Young Kit Carson was wiry, middle-sized, agile and surprisingly strong, as Daniel Boone had been at the same age. Boone, who now skittered rather than ran, moved through the woods behind little Carson, who already knew how to move without really touching the ground. Silently they would track game and later Boone would watch young Carson skin a rabbit or a fawn deer and help him a bit when he had trouble.

Some days back in the Boone hamlet, the old man sits in the sun and shows Kit how to resharpen a knife when no whetstone is to hand. And they spend hours on firearms: disassembling them, mixing powder, shooting. Boone needs a student as badly as Carson requires a mentor: Boone's children are all grown, his grandchildren scattered, and Carson's father has recently died: a falling tree limb had crushed his skull.

Although Boone has conquered more land than had most of Caesar's generals, it mostly has been the inadvertent results of his prodigious wanderings, and the occasional necessity of killing those who impeded his meanderings. Unlike ancient generals, Daniel Boone accepts that as a man grows old he grows smaller and he does not raise any statues to himself to hide that fact. In his prime he had been 5'8"and 175 pounds, with a strong upper body and thighs like young oak trees. Now, in his eighties, he weighs 155, if that, and is stooped, his once-massive torso bent over, as if some invisible rope were twining him to the earth.

He is neither happy nor unhappy. Sooner or later a man encounters a gantlet he cannot run. Boone is still bitter that his land claims in Kentucky have come to nothing. He had filed decent stand-up claims to 28,000 acres of Kentucky land – why, he easily could have claimed 100,000! – and most of it was contested by later blow-ins and, though he probably would have done well in court, he had no patience with organized dishonesty, lawyers and the like. So, in 1799, he had accepted a seigneury from the Spanish government and settled beyond the U.S. borders. It was not a big palatinate he was to govern – and he received just 1,000 arpents (800 acres) for himself – but it was a good title: for a brief time. Trouble was, the Spanish transferred this part of "Upper Louisiana" to the French and the French passed it on to the U.S. government and Boone was right back to holding land but not being sure how clear his title actually was. Vexing, certainly, in a locale where at times half the men still had to stand guard against Indians while the other half worked the land. In his old age, Boone no longer raged against governments; he merely spat contemptuously and turned to filling his mind with things he enjoyed.

Kit Carson came of an Irish family that had hit America about 1720 and had rolled from Pennsylvania through the Shenandoah Valley, into the Carolinas and then Kentucky and in 1811 into Daniel Boone's little principality. The Carsons and Boones were already joined by intermarriage and following the great patriarch made sense. Mind you, with or without the Boone affiliation, the Carsons would have kept moving, seeking for things to seize. They came of a culture that said "what we take, we deserve." It had been well-practised in Ulster and the American version was simply the Presbyterian Scots' conquest of Antrim and Down written on a much larger scale. They had Right and that was the end of the matter.

A lifetime later, in 1868, Kit Carson, now a brevet brigadier-general and renowned Indian killer, meets the grandson of Daniel Boone and they travel together by train from St. Louis to Washington. There Carson testifies in favour of a treaty with the Ute, whom he respects, settling them on a reservation of more than 15 million acres in western Colorado. Carson at the time is in ill-health and, just as his mentor had done, is shrinking in size. He coughs terribly, but manages to put forward an argument that had been best articulated in the early seventeenth century, during the plantation of Ulster: "the natives must have some lands within which they can provide for their subsistence and obey our laws; or they must be exterminated, a policy expensive of attainment."

MONTICELLO, VIRGINIA.1820; BETHANY,
WEST VIRGINIA. 1841

Same Book, Different God

At age seventy-seven, Thomas Jefferson wearily sits down to correct the Christian scriptures. The result, published as *The Life and Morals of Jesus of Nazareth*, is usually known as the Jefferson Bible. It is a rewrite of the New Testament that aims to get behind the myths of the Gospels and show Yeshua of Nazareth as he really was. For Jefferson that means no dumb stuff, like the Virgin Birth, miracles, or the Resurrection. Jesus becomes a rabbi who, in line with Jefferson's predilections, is not at all Jewish.

At age fifty-three, Alexander Campbell walks excitedly around his frame house and plans to correct all previous courses of Christian education. Born in County Antrim and trained in Glasgow as a Presbyterian minister, in America he joined the Baptists. Then, in 1827, he founded his own denomination, based on baptism by total immersion, a faith in the imminent Second Coming of Jesus, and a perception of the futility of all church creeds: the Bible alone was enough. In 1841, he founds Bethany College. There the only textbook for every subject is the Bible.

Jefferson's Bible is moderately popular and, beginning in 1904, it has been given to every new member of the U.S. senate upon swearing in. Campbell's denomination – the Disciples of Christ – is more popular. It claims in the later nineteenth century nearly one million adherents.

MURFREESBOROUGH, CENTRAL TENNESSEE. 1822

Stump Carvings

As a seat of government, Murfreesborough had little to say for itself except that it was in between Knoxville and Nashville and was spelled phonetically. The legislators who met there were nearly all literate, but letters like the "ph" in Murphy gave some of them, David Crockett included, trouble. Good thing, then, one member of the Murphy tribe had changed his name a little, to Murfree.

Crockett still is David Crockett, but he has taken the first steps towards becoming the legend: Davy Crockett, King of the Wild ... you know.

David, in his mid-thirties, has already moved twice since his marriage. First to Middle Tennessee and now further west. He's lost a wife (in child-birth) and married another one and has kept siring children and is becoming well-known for his hunting skills, his ruthlessness with Indians, and his ability to drink whiskey all night and work all day.

When friends josh him into running for the legislature, he resists and then, when they print up fake election posters for him, he takes the joke to heart and goes at electioneering full-bore. Crockett has a Lawrenceburg tailor run him up a special electioneering vest. This waistcoat has big pockets, almost the size of those in a shooting coat, and Crockett keeps these filled with plugs of tobacco. When he calls on an elector, usually the elector spits out the tobacco he is chewing and they talk a while and then maybe have a slug of whiskey or two and then Candidate Crockett goes on his way. Except just before he does so he pulls out a fresh plug of tobacco and gives it to the voter. So every elector that David Crockett visits is a bit better off than when he called in.

On the stump – much of the time all the candidates travel together, both for safety and efficiency – he develops the I-may-be-unschooled-but-I'm-smart-enough routine for debates. He turns his near-illiteracy and misuse of language (wild even by frontier standards) into a virtue. He sure won't cheat you and he don't like them rich folks in the east any more than you do. And he tells jokes and tales about Andrew Jackson, bears, new settlers, and Indian enemies.

In fact, that's his platform.

And he's hell to run against, because he's homey, funny, and beyond rational discussion. Besides stories about Jackson (whom he now admires but later will turn against), he is especially good on the stump about wolves. Need a bigger bounty on each wolf scalp? And bears? He advises his audience to hunt bears in winter. Easier to get them when you poke them out of hibernation, and, why, Candidate Crockett had himself killed 105 in his best half-year's hunting and you folks can do the same. How does any electoral opponent argue against that? Can't, really. Nor against his denunciation of anything that gets in the way of settlers moving where they wanted. Set-asides for things like colleges (as North Carolina had done) were a swindle and pre-emptions for public purposes were really a front for eastern bumstickers to grab land without having to perform any settlement duties. Oh, you know that my friends, you know that.

Having fought in half a dozen "Indian wars," Crockett hits a sympathetic nerve he shares with his listeners, most of whom would have lost at least one family member to the heathen. More federal troops if possible. More protection by the state militia if Washington won't help. When Crockett begins on the Indians, it is the only time he abandons his molasses-slow mountain delivery and talks fast, almost barks. For he hits that nerve in himself: his grandparents had been "massacreed" by Creek and Cherokee in North Carolina in the late 1770s; his great-grandfather had been born on a boat coming from southern Ireland where the natives there, like savages here, made life for the family impossible; and his great-great (or was it great-great great? he could never remember) grandparents had been run out of France by Louis XIV, or somebody like that, because they were Protestant, Huguenots. (The family name had been de Crocketayne. David could not pronounce it, so he left that part out of his family history.) After expulsion from France, the family had been forced to live among savages in "Battery Bay," in Ulster, where they had been battered by the local heathen until they had to leave for America. Never mind that Crockett referred to the Munster plantation and to Bantry Bay; no one hearing him knew the difference, but what they understood clearly was that righteous people, men with families and children, had always been hindered in their search for a decent life by tribes that were backward, ignorant, and who refused to share their lands and thus stood in the path of God's own peoples as they marched forward.

Elected to the legislature, Crockett goes to Murfreesborough and swears he'll do all he can to set things right.

NR. FAIRFIELD, VERMONT. 1827–30

Shock! Horror!

In a partially empty barn, William Arthur preaches the Word and even dances while he does so. The son of a sombre Anglican family from The Draens (pronounced Dray-uns) near Ballymena, County Antrim,

William had emigrated to Quebec, and then, like tens of thousands of his countrymen, dropped into the USA. An educated man (he had attended the Royal Belfast Academical Institution), he was apprenticed to a Burlington, Vermont, lawyer when the Holy Spirit grabbed him and he started preaching and dancing for the Lord. Not a lot of Baptists did that, so, after his ordination in 1827, he is a big draw.

When the fifth child and first son of his marriage is born, he dances with the infant in his arms through the main street of the town of Fairfield, where he did most of his preaching. His own congregation was accustomed by now to his terpsichorean ways, but the local Presbyterians and Congregationalists were shocked.

The real shock and horror, however, came more than fifty years later, when the Rev. Mr. Arthur's son becomes the twenty-first president of the United States. A scurrilous pamphleteer, noting that the senior Mr. Arthur had lived for a time in the Canadas, suggests that Chester A. Arthur had been born in Quebec and thus is ineligible for the presidency.

Shock; horror. And quite untrue. Really, how low can a yellow journalist go? *Canadien!* I ask you!

GENTRYVILLE, INDIANA. 1828

Lincoln's Gentryville Address

His neighbours say that Abraham Lincoln, age nineteen, is lazy. He likes to hang around the Gentryville General Store and Spirit Grocery and talk to the old boys, the ones who had been on the frontier when it was still a mystery, not just big woods to cut down, wretched tree by tree. The craic is good, and it gets better when drovers are in town, drinking and telling lies.

Young Lincoln is not the shape of person most people want to mess about. He's awkward, but at 6'4"his long, heavily muscled arms and his huge hands are not a bramble bush to tangle with: except for the occasional drunken drover who considers that a bare-knuckle beating of the rube would be good fun.

Occasionally Lincoln has to fight, but nineteen times out of twenty, he makes a joke, tells a story, diverts attention, and the moment of ignition passes.

People like having the lad around; he's good for a laugh even if it's hard to know what to make of him.

One of Lincoln's pet pieces, one that he has to be ritually begged over and over to do, is an amazing speech he has off by heart. It is long, but despite that, he and dozens of ambitious young orators in back country America know it.

Abraham Lincoln stands on the steps of the Gentryville store and declaims to a score of farmers, drovers and several drovers' dogs: *Let no man dare, when I am dead, to charge me with dishonour; let no man attaint my memory by believing that I could have engaged in any cause but of my country's liberty and independence.*

Much later, at Gettysburg, the metrics and timbre of Robert Emmet's 1803 speech-from-the-dock will reappear. There they will not be the drone notes of a threnody but instead will undergird an ode to the resurrection of the American soul.

THE EDGE. IRELAND
1830–1845

Poor Health

Bad news and ill-health march faster than armies.

In March 1832, cholera was reported in Belfast. The disease had escaped from the slums of India in 1826, moved through Russia and then into central Europe. A line of fever-flags, placed on a map of the western hemisphere, would have shown it conquering the West like some previously unknown eastern warlord.

The virulent march from Belfast to Dublin required only a week, and three days later, cases were reported in Cork. Two months after that, cholera had appeared in every Irish county.

Its symptoms were gut-twisting vomiting and the expulsion of "rice water" – diarrhoea – and, usually, a complete collapse within a few hours and then death.

No population, even the most medically savvy, could be anything but terrified by such a silent enemy, and Ireland in 1832 was overwhelmingly illiterate and located in a world of magic, and unseen spirits.

Thus the blessed turf.

In early June, the Blessed Virgin Mary appeared to a woman at the chapel in Charleville, County Cork. The Virgin left behind some ashes that were a certain protection against cholera. These ashes, the Blessed Mother directed, were to be tied into small parcels and taken to cottages in the Charleville area and there hidden in the rafters or in the chimneys. This would save the cottagers.

Virtue, being the direct opposite of vice, had to march, to be an army on the move against evil. Each now-protected cottager was to take the holy ashes from the rafters or chimney and give them to four vulnerable families. And so on.

The limit to the magic was that the blessed ashes soon diminished to a few particles. The solution to this problem was their transformation into a "blessed turf," for turf could be turned into an infinite supply of ashes that would then be mixed with the ever-diminishing original sacred item.

Virtue marched swiftly. Within the span of a single week, three-quarters of Ireland had been covered by this network of magic prophylaxis. It worked as well against cholera as did any of the scientific medicine of the day.

IRELAND. THE 1830S

Pure Choice

You are a young man or young woman and you won't be inheriting a farm, because your parents have none to leave to you, and you have to eat. You enter the free market, and a mart it certainly is. Each little town has a fair or market at yearly or half-yearly intervals, sometimes more often. You'll know. Twice a year in most place these markets include a hiring fair. There you stand in a straggly line with all your competitors, arranged around the town square or ankle-deep in mud on the main street. You bring a bundle holding your clothes with you and, if you have them, you wear boots: that shows you have worked and saved in the past. And hob-nailed boots are good agricultural implements. The farmers – men who rent five to fifteen acres – walk up and down, inspecting you and your competitors. If they favour you, they'll ask you to show your hands, and to walk around a bit to be sure you don't have a gimpy leg or some injury you're trying to hide. Then they'll name a price for six months' labour and if you agree, the two of you spit on your hands and lock grips. The farmer gives you a shilling as earnest-money and you give him your clothing bundle. You'll wait for him and when his other dealing is done, he'll take you someplace for the next half-year of your life.

Or you're a married man with a family and a bit of land too small to feed them and your wife is pregnant again. If you live within reach of the coast, your best bet is to become a spalpeen: you beg a few pennies and from Donegal Town, Belfast, Dublin, Cork, you ship on deck to England or lowland Scotland. Irish labour contractors – lords of the harvest – will fit you into a gang and you work your way through the British harvest season. Potatoes, grain, hay, whatever. Twelve hours work a day and sleep in a barn at night. Food provided. And, if you don't have a weakness for the drink, you return home by Christmas with three, four, maybe even seven guineas in your pocket, enough to pay the landlord and buy necessities and supplementary food for the family. There's a floating bridge between Ireland and Britain and you use it.

That's how it all starts: the great exodus from Ireland. Once ablebodied men and women become accustomed to leaving their home parish and to participating in the cruel auction that is the "free" market of the English-speaking world, they consider the next logical step: leaving Ireland forever.

Sooner Than We Remember

The great Irish exodus did not begin with the Famine of the mid-1840s.

The minute the Napoleonic war was over, the conduit opened. Families, mostly, and the occasional felon transported in chains.

During the 1830s the viaduct widened dramatically. The lucky and the smart got out and the former always said they were the latter.

Full records aren't there. But in the 1830s easily 60,000 persons were leaving Ireland in a typical year. Alert people. Tough. Informed about their chances and willing to risk their lives in the big casino. Women, men, teenagers, heroes in their way, for they bet their lives on achieving a better future. They loved Ireland, they hated it, God knows what each calculus was: but each left because of a calculation that life would be better elsewhere.

Sometimes right; sometimes wrong. But respect their agency. They weren't flotsam.

The choice of roughly half of them was British North America, which makes sense: that's where they knew how things worked and Catholic rights were protected there in a way they weren't in the USA. And one-fifth or so settled in Britain, although that's a hard thing to calculate because the ports kept sloppy records, and who knows, anyway, if a spalpeen came home at the end of his labours or stayed in, say, Liverpool or Manchester and became a permanent resident?

Had the Famine not happened, Ireland still would have emptied itself of the young, able, aggressive, ambitious.

They weren't abandoning Ireland; they were embracing hope.

Mass Education

The United Kingdom government was never forgiven for the single best thing it ever did for the Irish people: in 1831, Edward Stanley, the chief secretary for Ireland, set up a national system of education for the common people. This, four decades ahead of similar efforts in England and Scotland. By mid-century, most Irish people could read and the proportion was rising sharply. Of course they were reading in English, but that was the primary language of most of the Irish population, and had been since roughly the beginning of the nineteenth century. Most importantly, the young men and women who left Ireland for Canada and the USA had a major advantage over their competitors from other European countries: literacy in English.

The Catholic church fought the system from its earliest days, the premise of the system (abandoned by the mid-1840s) being that Catholic and Protestant children would be educated together. The Presbyterians at first fought the system because it gave Catholics the right to use school buildings after school hours to teach the Roman catechism. And the clergy of the Established Church were opposed to it because they thought, unrealistically, that they should control all popular education.

Without the protection of a holy trinity: Daniel Murray, the saintly Catholic archbishop of Dublin, Richard Whately, an Englishman newly arrived in Dublin as Protestant archbishop of Dublin, and the Rev. James Carlile, a Presbyterian cleric of distinction, the effort would have been strangled at birth. They fought for the system, and by the mid-1840s, the school books of the Irish national school system were the most widely used in the English-speaking world. Throughout the empire, master teachers from the Irish national system were in demand and they demonstrated how to set up a mass education system.

The imperial government insists that the Irish invest heavily in their children and the parents readily agree. It's the professionally religious who see this sort of venture as a moral danger.

IRELAND. 1838–40

Dates That Count

– *"I swear my family remembers it perfectly. Not a doubt. My Da was at the very first meeting of Father Mathew's temperance crusade. In Cork it was. And mother left at home give birth to me. In April, it was, 1838."*
– *"I do solemnly swear or affirm that my birth was in the year 1839. It was in January, on the day of the Big Wind in Ireland, and the thatch was blown off our cot and my family talked of it many times."*

– *"It is my solemn oath that I was born in the archdiocese of Armagh. My baptism was on St. Patrick's day, 1840. That was the same day the cornerstone to the new cathedral was laid and I was named Patrick after the saint."*

Those years, 1838, 1839, and 1840, were the ones that Irish people in the twentieth century professed to remember most clearly from the nineteenth: not the date of the Union, not Emmet's Rebellion, not the Great Famine, not any political event.

These were truly magic numbers.

Because, an act of the United Kingdom parliament (8 Edward VII, cap. 40) provided for pensions for persons seventy years and over. Most Catholic records before, roughly, 1860, were badly kept and governmental registration of births did not begin until 1864.

So, every duffer fifty years of age or more went before the governmental commissioners and swore to events that verified their age as being at least seventy. They practised a lot before seeing the commissioners, so that they got the details right.

The Big Wind indeed.

PARISH OF TULLOGHOBEGLY, COUNTY DONEGAL. 1844

Prepared for the Worst

The inhabitants of the purest, most perfectly Irish parish in all of Ireland remember the generosity of an anonymous English benefactor with the same reverence Micronesian cargo cults are later to recall the gifts from the gods that were brought to them by crashing airplanes. Inexplicable bounty.

Tulloghobegly preserves a form of economic, and therefore social, organization that disappeared elsewhere in Ireland as English law was inserted into the Celtic world, beginning in the twelfth century. Now only a few parishes in the entire country practise the ancient system of communal landholding. The peasantry holds land from an outside landlord, of course, but then the old Celtic system usually had some neighbouring rí who had to be paid off. Rundale, runrig, the system has several names, but in Tulloghobegly everyone shared in the decent land and the waste, pasture, bog, rock, and whins.

But not much was there to share. In 1837 the teacher of the national school, Patrick McKye, wrote to the lord lieutenant of Ireland. He told his lordship that 4,000 persons lived in the parish (he underestimated by half, actually), all Catholic. McKye had been around: through nine counties of Ireland, had visited England and Scotland, been to British North America and seven states of the United States of America, *and never witnessed the tenth part of such hunger, hardships, and nakedness.*

The people have between them, one sliding cart, but no wheeled cart, or any other vehicle; one plough, 16 barrows, 8 saddles, 2 pillions, 11 bridles, 20 shovels, 32 rakes, 37 table forks, 93 chairs, 243 stools, 10 iron grates, no pigs, 27 geese, 3 turkeys, 2 feather beds, 8 chaff beds, 2 stables, 6 cow houses, one national school, one priest, one policeman, no gentry, no bonnet, no clock, 32 latches, 8 brass candlesticks, no fruit trees, no turnips, no parsnips, no carrots, no vegetable except cabbage and potatoes.

None of their either married or unmarried women can afford more than one shift, and some cannot afford any, and more than one half of both men and women cannot afford shoes to their feet, nor can many of them afford a second bed, but whole families of sons and daughters of mature age indiscriminately ly together with their parents, and all in the bare buff.

That reached the English press and, horrified at their nakedness, an English gentlemen sends the parish a supply of shirts for the men, shifts and flannel petticoats for the women, and bed-ticking so that families could have more than one bed and not sleep together in a pile.

A sovereign gift, surely, and it gives the people of Tulloghobegly faith that, should they ever again face truly trying times, Providence will send them relief.

DUBLIN. 1845

Edge

The *Nation*, founded by Charles Gavan Duffy in 1845, appoints a new leader writer, John Mitchel. He, Duffy, Thomas Davis, and a score of fine and finely romantic minds, are distancing themselves from Daniel O'Connell who is aging and will not risk a civil war.

Mitchel's editorials are brilliant in the jagged way that industrial diamonds are: abrasive and wearing.

Privately he writes a letter to O'Connell, whom he despises. "I don't know how you can lower yourself to treat with the bishops and with the government."

"You dance at all the weddings."

Vital Signs

The tall men walk slowly through the clachans, hamlets, towns, villages. They take notes. The same men, now mounted on heavy hunters, ride the countryside, slowly, making notations.

They are the only national institution that affects everyone in the country: the Irish constabulary. The poverty of Ireland is not economic only, but institutional. Ireland lacks the webbing to hold a nation together. The parish system of government that had worked in rural England had no purchase here: how could it, when there was no single faith, merely multiple religious hatreds? What passed for local government was a country-wide set of grand juries run by the gentry. A network of poor law unions, on the English model, was decreed in 1838, but was not yet more than a skeleton without joints and ligaments.

That is why the tall men are the only succour Dublin Castle can turn to when, in early September, reports of a potato blight appear in the Dublin papers. They are ordered to report on the local crops and to do so each week. So they begin their regular rogations, like mounted priests beating the bounds of their parishes.

REGARDING THE CROWN JEWEL.
INDIA
1785–1845

Is This the Start of Ireland's Immigration Problem?

Right. Granted. It doesn't look dangerous.

The seneschal (he loved the old title bestowed on him by his superior) opened the account books of the gentleman Godfrey Evan Baker. "We must have a talk, sir." Baker, of a solid Anglo-Irish gentry family and a returned-officer from India, had recently married the second daughter of Baron Massey, a large Cork landlord. "I suggest that you order a trinket for your lady wife. Just a bauble from London. But you know how women are, sir."

"Go to it."

Now, you see, that is how it all starts. Ireland's modern immigration problem. You know. You agree, but don't dare say so in Dublin 4 or in Trinity. It's the start of all those sharp foreigners, coming here, sponging off us, taking our women (oh, sorry, I mean, intermarrying with our young people), and then, when they've gotten as much from us as they can, and without breaking into a sweat, these cadgers, dodgers, slaggards, go off to England and do the same thing all over again and all the while saying that they're Irish, which is some laugh. It gives us all a bad name, so it does.

Dean Mahomet, the nut-brown, five-foot tall man in question was one of Ireland's first imperial immigrants, maybe the very first from the Second British Empire. As an Islamic child in the India that the East India Company colonized, he had made a decision very early in life. Rather than stay with his own north Indian family, civil servants in a crumbling bureaucracy, and rather than try his hand in the court of any of the 600 or so independent princedoms that fractured India, he saw that the future lay with the English. At age eleven, in 1769, he turned up at the barracks of one of the company's brigades and made himself so useful that he was soon an accredited camp follower. His big break came when Godfrey Evan Baker appointed him his personal servant and took him under his wing.

And not just his wing. Mahomet became Baker's catamite as he was a handy size and was most anxious to please. The relationship was more difficult for the brown man than the white, because the Islamic concept of the Forbidden Hole clashed with the Anglo-Irish notion of any-port-in-a-storm. This was eventually solved by Dean Mahomet's embracing the Church of England.

Mahomet followed Baker faithfully as he rose from a new cadet in the third Brigade of the Bengal Army to a full lieutenancy. Gradually the relationship changed and they tacitly agreed that they really were not men who loved men, but men who preferred women who loved men. They became as brothers and, in 1781, Dean Mahomet was made a subaltern in the Bengal army in tandem with Godfrey Baker's promotion to a captaincy. They did hard duty together, with Mahomet frequently in command of a sepoy company in hand-to-hand fighting.

How far the pair would have risen can be only speculation for, in 1782, Baker, in his drawling Anglo-Irish way, misconstrued the instructions of Governor-General Warren Hastings to seize three men who had murdered a Brahmin and instead simply seized their village and held the whole population to ransom. This occasioned some complaint. Baker was allowed to resign.

And so, Dean Mahomet, accompanying his white brother, came to County Cork in 1784, just as the First British Empire was ending and the Second was, quite unconsciously, beginning.

Mahomet ran the Baker household efficiently and life could have been perfect, except that in 1786 his patron died. Almost immediately Mahomet married Jane Daly, a local Catholic. This was a dicey business as marriages conducted by Anglican parsons between Catholics (as Jane was) and Protestants (as Mahomet was, at least by Irish standards, for he certainly was not Roman Catholic) were still illegal. Mahomet posted a special bond in case the rector was prosecuted. But he wasn't and Mr. and Mrs. Mahomet lived comfortably in Cork while he did man-of-business services for the Baker family, and wrote his two-volume autobiography, published in 1794 and notable both for its evocative description of India and its being in parts plagiarized.

Isn't that the way with them though? They'll take everything, even our ideas. Still and so, the worst of them bring in their own ideas and there's real trouble, unChristian, infidel ideas, like eating vegetables and burning their wives, and wearing funny things on their head.

When the Baker family's patronage wore thin and the proceeds from his book were spent, Dean and his-now expanding mocha-coloured family moved to London. There he stayed, for five years, 1807–12, first as a practitioner of Oriental medicine and then as the owner of a coffee house where the ambience, if not the coffee, had an Oriental flavour. Not doing so well, he moved to Brighton ...

You expected he'd take himself to Leeds?

… to Brighton and built a fashionable practice as a Far Eastern masseur among the quality. They needed him and he kneaded them. Several members of the Royal Family came under his thumbs and for a man the size of a large pepper mill he had great force. Working on the spraddling bodies of the English aristocracy, listening to the usually-corseted men and the unusually-corseted women retail the most intimate gossip gave him a purchase within English society that few foreigners, let alone brown ones, had. He was a font of knowledge on many things, including architecture, and consulted with the Prince of Wales, the future George IV, on ways to improve the Royal Pavilion so that it could include a truly therapeutic bath house. And he taught the principles of the sari to several of the Prince's mistresses, so that their breasts, even if uncorseted, did not fall beneath the Plimsoll Line.

Ah, the man did humanity a wheen of good, you're saying?

And then, well past middle age, he wrote a second autobiography, stuffed with big slugs of information on the ways that Western and Oriental medicine could be – should be – combined.

Isn't that just the way with them? Writing two autobiographies when most of us can scarcely get our names in the Irish Press.

HANSI, HARIAN DISTRICT, INDIA. 1801

A Fair Reach

As his palanquin approaches the market place, *Jowruj Jung* orders his bearers to stop. He pulls back the curtains and scatters handfuls of coin and watches with satisfaction as the poor of the town scramble on the ground like geese at feeding time. The coins are of his own minting, as money of any sort is in short supply on the outskirts of the territory directly controlled by the East India Company.

Jowruj Jung means "George the Conqueror" and it is the title borne by George Thomas, a tall, mustached Irishman in full military uniform that he has designed himself. It is based on the Hussar's uniform of the Hungarian cavalry with details added, such as several medals that he has awarded to himself.

George the Conqueror is now in his mid-forties and a long reach from his family's mud cabin in Tipperary. He had taken to the sea as a lad and, having risen to quartermaster, jumped ship at Madras in the early 1780s. He joined the private army of an Indian prince and rose rapidly until in 1787 he was commander of the forces of the famous female ruler, the Begum Sumroo of Sardhana, a former dancing girl and now fanatical Roman Catholic monarch. Soon George Thomas became both her chief military and civil administrator, a considerable achievement for a man who, at the time, could barely read and write English. He was, however, a quick student and became not just literate, but fluent in Persian, the court language, and Hindi.

George Thomas did not mind the Begum scattering her domain with chapels. What bothered him was the Begum, a widow, taking as her second husband (the first had been German) a Frenchman. Thomas led a rebellion against her. It failed, but she spared his life. Next, he briefly soldiered for Appao Rao, a middle level prince, from whom in the mid-1790s he broke free and started to conquer large territories, mostly Sikh, in his own name.

That is the purpose of his present appearance in the market. As part of maintaining his authority over the 800 to 1,000 towns that he has brought within his own kingdom (the number was ever-reducing, as he kept burning any village that rebelled), George the Conqueror is ritually humiliating some Sikh leaders. This he does by a method that harks back to his own days as a young seaman. When his vessel had crossed the Tropic of Cancer he, and all the other maiden-crew, were bound, covered with cooking grease and shaved with a razor made from a portion of an old cooper's hoop. This was followed by their heads being bobbed in a tub of salt water until they nearly drowned, and finally the flowing cuts and seeping abrasions on their faces were covered with tar to staunch the flow.

This humiliation he now visited upon five Sikh generals and princes. To the accompaniment of a single military snare drum, he has their beards removed and, as the ultimate insult to their religious purity, their heads shaved into a patchwork of bare skin and tufty leftovers.

George the Conqueror is planning his next venture: the conquest of the Punjab. All this is in the name of "planting the British standard."

The lunacy of attacking the entire western frontier of India with only a private army does not occur to George Thomas, but it does to the officials of the East Indian Company and to the British governmental administrators, particularly the Marquis of Wellesley. They

quietly permit the Sikhs to form an alliance with one of the few remaining French forces in India. George Thomas is beaten and surrenders his capital at Hansi.

George the Conqueror was on his way by river to Calcutta, intending to retire with his family and considerable fortune to Ireland when
reality finally caught him; in August, 1802, he died of a fever, brought
on by war wounds and the knowledge that his reach would always
exceed his grasp.

DELHI, INDIA. 1803–04

Brother Act

In the defeat of the Maratha confederacy, Major-General Arthur
Wellesley (on his way to becoming the Duke of Wellington) served ef-
ficiently under his brother, the Governor-General, Richard Colley,
Marquis Wellesley.

However, the major battle, the taking of Delhi, was won by General
Gerard Lake whose previous experience made him particularly useful in dealing with indigenous peoples: he had been in charge of
breaking the United Irishmen in Ulster in 1797 and he knew the value
of relentless repression.

One of Lake's chief staff officers in his scarifying the earth of India
was an Irishman who, though he had an illustrious brother, refused
to refer to him in any way whatsoever: Major William Tone, eldest
brother of Theobald Wolfe Tone.

DUBLIN. 1825

An Incarnation

Not often are we permitted to see a god of India in his young days.

Shield your eyes and squint: John Nicholson, three years old, is
playing with a knotted handkerchief. His mother is a Lisburn Protestant Dissenter of the Bible-quoting, devil-fearing, silence-is-kept sort.
She comes from substantial linen merchants, recently down on their

luck, and is married to a physician who practises at the Dublin Lying-In Hospital. He is a dis-fellowshipped Quaker and is rarely home.

The young god is flicking at something with his handkerchief. He is absorbed totally, as if in a contest with an invisible enemy.

"John, what are you doing?"

With all the gravity of a high court judge pronouncing a capital sentence, he says "I am trying to get in a blow at the Devil."

"You can see the Devil?"

"Oh yes, and he wishes me to be bad. I shall not have that."

Very portentous sentences from a three-year-old. "How will you stop him from making you bad?"

"I shall get him down. And then I shall kill him."

John Nicholson: certainly a peculiar child, but destined within three decades to be worshipped as a god on the Indian subcontinent. Literally. He will become the first Irishman since the beginning of the Christian era to be raised to the godhead.

DUBLIN, IRELAND AND BENARES, INDIA. OCTOBER 1839

Year of the Blessed

All crusaders give and receive blessings. The Liberator is still postponing his last crusade: the Repeal of the Union of Great Britain and Ireland. All that will tie together the two nations will be the Crown. If he succeeds.

The Crown: in the form of the iridescent, still-virgin Queen Victoria. She has recently announced her engagement to Albert Francis Charles Augustus Emmanuel of Saxe-Coburg-Gotha. Critics, especially ostentatiously loyal Tories, have dared to criticize this alliance with a foreigner, as if the English have seldom within the previous millennium had a non-native monarch or consort. The union receives Daniel O'Connell's blessing. *Oh! If I be not greatly mistaken, I'd get, in one day, 500,000 brave Irishmen to defend the life, the honour, and the person of the beloved young lady by whom England's throne is now filled.*

At the same time, the Irish god-in-waiting John Nicholson is learning Hindi and wandering among the mosques, pagodas, groves, ghats, interspersed incongruously with state buildings. He had been intended for Trinity, Dublin, but his uncle, an old and very rich India

hand, was on the verge of being elected one of the twenty-four na-
bobs who ran the East India Company from India House, Leadenhall
Street, London. "Forget Trinity" he told his nephew. With his uncle's
powerful blessing, John Nicholson bypasses the usual entrance examination and the tiresome interviews and becomes a "direct cadet" in
the company's service.

   At age sixteen, modestly prepared, he is sent to be one of the masters of an empire of millions. Most of his skills he is expected to acquire on the job. Nicholson's response is to decipher local customs,
study languages, and to read at least a chapter of the Bible each day.
He is virtually silent in the mess, avoids wine, retires early to study,
and makes few friends. In his own way, he is preparing.

GHAZNI, NR. KABUL, AFGHANISTAN. MARCH 1842

Voices in the Wilderness

Take heed, ye unwise among the people: O ye fools, when will ye
understand?
   The unrighteous shall be destroyed forever; as for the seed of the
ungodly, it shall be rooted out.

The voices first came to John Nicholson while he was a prisoner of
the Afghani. As an ensign in the Bengal Army he had been assigned
to the 27th Native Infantry, consisting of three sepoy regiments. He
had spent the winter of 1839–40 in huttings on a treeless plain in the
Punjab. Provisions were spare and he found that flogging the occasional native made all of them much more generous in their tithes for
the army. Nicholson is a quick learner as a young officer, but he is
known as a cold fellow, spending his leisure time by himself. Besides
the Bible and grammar books, he is ingesting big chunks of a book
entitled *Fulfilment of the Scriptural Prophecies*. This regimen suits him,
for he has grown two inches since arriving in India and, as he writes
to his mother, he expects that though he is now six feet tall, he will
grow another three or four inches.

To me belongeth vengeance and recompense.
The day of their calamity is at hand.

Nicholson had served with efficiency, but no special distinction, as the 27th Native Infantry had moved across the Punjab in November 1840, and through the Khyber Pass. The British were on their way to teach the Khan of the Afghani a lesson.

Along the march, Nicholson makes his only real friend in the service, a subaltern, Neville Chamberlain (later Sir Neville) of the 16th Bengal Native Infantry. Chamberlain, a reflective, pacific man, listens attentively as Nicholson tells him of the prophetic map of world history that is being unrolled for him by his biblical studies. As yet, no voices.

They come to Nicholson after he, his commanding officer, and their native troops surrender to the Afghani to whom they are supposed to be teaching a lesson. These Afghani from the neighbourhood of Ghazni promise that if the British surrender, all their men will be spared and the officers will be treated with respect. Immediately upon the surrender, most of the sepoys are slaughtered and the remainder are sold as slaves. The white officers are stripped of their valuables, kept on short rations, and some of them tortured. The officer commanding was a particular target of non-lethal abuse. The Afghani enjoyed tying a rope around his leg and then using a tent peg to tighten it, cutting off all circulation and nearly severing tendons. Then they would release the pressure and with great merriment watch him lurch about in an uncontrollable fashion.

It is now that Nicholson's voices start. *The cities that are inhabited shall be laid waste, and the land shall be desolate.* His captors have taken from him his Bible, his notebook, even the locket with his mother's hair that he had kept around his neck. The voices become more frequent, louder, sometimes when other officers are nearby, so that he has to concentrate on not betraying his receipt of auditory intelligence inaudible to everyone else. He tells no one.

Finally, in late August, the prisoners are marched through the Hindu Kush to another set of captors who, by way of a Persian intermediary, sell their freedom to British representatives. The army pretends that they have been rescued, but really they were ransomed.

Nicholson, at twenty-one years of age, has become convinced that he is the holder of the sword of the Lord and of Gideon.

He returns to India and by June 1847 he is in charge of Amritsar, the Sikhs' holy city, and of vast territory around it.

By that time, he has, as he promised his mother, grown to be six feet, three inches in height.

PUNJAB, INDIA. 1845–49

Piercing the Veil

Even before the Second Sikh War, John Nicholson was spoken of with awe.

Nikkul Seyn: his street name. Locals averted their eyes as he passed, for to look him in the face would be to show disrespect to a man behind whom the sun rose. He was not yet a god, but no longer a simple mortal.

Nicholson ruled a thinly settled area of diverse tribes, Rajputs, Ghakkars, Pathans, and these peoples were themselves under Sikh rule. The British, economical with resources as usual, kept control of the Sikhs with a handful of their own officials; big sahibs. Keeping the Sikhs in line required immense character, for the Sikhs used plunder and random killing as a means of enforcing order on those lower down the tree. John Nicholson responded by being harder, haughtier, colder, more reserved, more mercurial than any Sikh warlord. He rode out hawking with their chiefs in the wild hill country and jumped ravines and assayed hillsides they would not themselves touch. He kept his own troops, now mostly Sikh, at a high state of preparedness and they protected the smaller, vulnerable groups, the Gujars, and the Jats and others. When a handful of his men deserted, Nicholson rode after them, cutting down one sepoy after another with his cavalry sword, all the time roaring incantations that no one who heard them understood, but everyone remembered.

His fearlessness and predilection for violence might have engendered only fear, had it not been coupled with habits and rituals that the locals whispered about in the street. They were the habits of a holy man. He would sit cross-legged on the floor of his bungalow, fanned by his sole servant, and not move for hours and hours. He fasted frequently. When the cold of winter came, he went to the hills and spent days alone, wearing only a linen robe. He talked to the stars, the people in the street said. His reputation spread from village to village. *Nikkul Seyn.*

Reputation. On the eve of the Second Sikh War of 1848–49, Nicholson took control of an entire village of rebel Sikhs by riding to the town at breakneck speed with only thirty men, and he rode up so swiftly to the fortified gates that the Sikh defenders could not close them. Once inside, he jumped off his horse and approached the first

Sikh who put his hand on his sword. No weapon was drawn by Nicholson. He approached the man slowly, his index finger pointing at the guard's heart. He was daring the defender to attack him; the sentry saw not a British officer, but a man with the piercing eyes of a hawk, the fearlessness of a god, the incarnation of some higher power. Nicholson ordered the sentry to gather his fellow sentries and to go and arrest their own officers. This they did, and within the hour the entire band of rebels was marching, head down, into the dusty countryside.

When full-scale warfare later broke out, John Nicholson spent two years engaging forces greatly superior in number, and not at all cowardly. Impossible victories followed improbable victories and the notion grew that he could not be killed by a bullet. Nicholson led every charge in person, walked through hails of bullets, and then slaughtered the opposition in a berserker frenzy that even the Sikhs rarely had encountered. Life was his to take and to give. When the Sikh chiefs submitted to the British, Nicholson returned to his home bungalow and there discovered, sitting worshipfully, the first of his disciples.

NOT THE DARKEST
OF CONTINENTS.
AFRICA 1805–1845

Commitment

As the British troops disembark at Table Bay, they meet token resistance from the Batavian forces. Ten days later they are in full control. There is no conscious commitment to taking over southern Africa. It is nearly another ten years before the Cape Colony is formally annexed. Yet, the British were stuck with the place much earlier than they consciously perceived for, in the days before the Suez Canal, the passage to India by way of the Cape was strategically necessary. India, if it was the jewel of empire, required this. And, later, minerals are found inland in southern Africa and that makes expansion of the British rule desirable. So, always as an afterthought, the dominion over the Cape Colony grows, through successive stages into control of the entire southeastern tip of Africa, and only ends when the apartheid state, the Republic of South Africa, becomes independent and leaves the Commonwealth in 1961.

At the beginning, though, the British administration of the Cape is more suitable for a borstal or a brothel than for a colony. The governor, the earl of Caledon, had unfettered despotic powers. The Dutch, the mass of the white population, were treated with contempt and responded in kind; an attempt to make the Cape the world's first free port, where goods from India could be bought, failed, and Cape Town became a tiny sink of Sodom, tempered only by official despotism.

It was the perfect home for many: such as the fraud-chaplain, the Rev. Dr. O'Halloran, spiritual leader of the 93rd Regiment. He witnessed a duel on Christmas Day, 1809, between the paymaster of the regiment and his own prospective son-in-law, a Captain Ryan. Irish Protestants stick together, and the chaplain acted as the captain's legal defence. This was successful, but in further argument the chaplain managed to have himself banned from Cape Town for two years for his use of obscene language, an achievement equivalent to being thrown out of the Hell's Angels for excessive violence.

LONDON. FEBRUARY 1810

Communications Gap

An earthquake of significant magnitude has hit the Cape of Good Hope. That much the *Morning Chronicle* of London gets right in its issue of 8 February 1810.

What it reports wrongly is a perfect encapsulation of how much the metropole of empire knew about the extremities: the *Chronicle* reports that Robben Island had completely and totally disappeared.

Dear God, if only it had.

CAPE TOWN, SOUTHERN AFRICA. APRIL 1814

Slightly Strange

As he rose higher in public office, it became increasingly clear that Lord Charles Somerset was slightly strange. And it was inevitable that he would rise: the second son of the fifth Duke of Beaufort; born at the family seat, Badminton; a direct descendant of the Plantagenets. He would inevitably rise and his oddness would become more apparent.

As he steps ashore, the new governor of the Cape of Good Hope, commander of its armed forces, judge of the court of appeals, seems at first viewing to be impressive. He easily swings himself into the saddle, and on a large black gelding he takes a run up and down the strand. A man of trim figure in middle age, he wears a hat of the same shape and cut as that favoured by Napoleon. Somerset is ahead of Napoleon in that he takes over the Cape colony even before the peace at the end of the Napoleonic War transfers it formally from the Netherlands to the United Kingdom.

Even on that first ride, close observers note something strange. Somerset frequently twitches his head, quite violently. The motion is obvious because he has an enormous nose and, wearing the Napoleonic headgear, his twitching is like a still weathervane suddenly being dunted by a stone from a youth's slingshot. He has neurological problems.

These stem from his being too enthusiastic a patriot and having spent too much time in Ireland. As colonel of the Royal Bristol Regiment of Foot, he had taken his corps to Clonmel in the mid-1790s, as part of the defence against French invasion and Irish insurrection. He enjoyed himself, riding and drinking with the Irish gentry and not worrying much about military matters. He fell afoul, however, of good fun. After a successful hunt, or during the middle of a good midday drunk, the Anglo-Irish were in the habit of firing pistols and muskets into the air. Good fun and the balls dropped harmlessly to the ground, didn't they?

Not that day: Lord Charles, galloping near a stone wall, had the incredible misfortune of having his horse catch a descending pistol ball in the head, and then to crash into the stone barrier. Somerset's leg was shattered and something happened to his spine that left him forever not-quite-right.

Still, he was a Beaufort, and he rose: paymaster general of the armed forces, and later governor of the Cape of Good Hope. There he followed two courses: Anglicize everything; courts, legislature, everything official, leaving nothing in Dutch; and bring in as many settlers from the British Isles as possible, especially those who will settle in the eastern Cape and thus provide a buffer for Cape Town from the fearsome tribes to the east.

The twitches became worse after his wife died in September 1815. They were somewhat relieved, however, by Somerset's quickly bringing to the Cape Dr. James Barry, then twenty-one years of age. Barry arrived in 1816 with the official title of Assistant Surgeon to the Forces, but in fact he was largely there to serve the needs of the governor.

The strange intimacy with Dr. Barry pacified Somerset, although the sight of the governor walking alongside Dr. Barry, who wore high-heeled boots and a massive cocked hat to compensate for his diminutive size, caused comment: the more so when Dr. Barry perambulated with his black poodle in tow and was accompanied by a servant with a large umbrella to keep the sun from Barry's translucent white skin.

Not altogether strange was the small hermaphroditic medical doctor's leaving the Cape of Good Hope eleven years later, just a season after Lord Charles himself returned to England.

EMBOMMA, THE CONGO RIVER. OCTOBER 1816

A Viral Affection

The initial stage of Ireland's long and inexplicable entanglement with the Congo ends with the burial at Embomma, the Congo River's chief port, of commander James H. Tuckey, R.N. Tuckey, of Mallow, Co.

Cork, was uniquely qualified to deal with the Royal Navy's obsession with the rivers of Africa. Were the Niger and the Congo joined? Did the Congo run southwards into the far south of Africa? Was there any tie to the Nile? Tuckey's qualifications were that he had been a serving officer in battle, had spent time in India, had been in charge of the survey of Port Phillip harbour in Australia, and had been with Captain Flinders in the first circumnavigation of the Australian continent. All this before the age of thirty.

Yet, in his quiet way, Tuckey was also one of the unluckiest officers in the Royal Navy, and Irishmen who later entered the Congo had scarcely more pleasant experiences. While in India Tuckey had picked up several tropical diseases from which he never fully recovered, malaria and chronic diarrhea being the least exotic. Then, in 1805, he had been captured by the French (in a battle with no name, for the R.N. gives names only to victories, apparently) and kept captive until the end of the war. As an officer, he was treated reasonably and allowed to receive money from home, so that he bought minimal comfort. Another prisoner of the French was a Miss Stuart, of mysterious origin, and Tuckey fell in love with her and they had several children. Just as the war was coming to crisis, in 1814, the family was forced inland and one daughter died and Tuckey's youngest son was lost and never found.

At age forty, Tuckey received a command appointment to explore the Congo River: with his luck it would turn out to be a sewer.

And it was. The navy's specially equipped *Congo* made it 300 kilometres upriver, past slave-trading tribes, starving populations, to a set of minor cataracts. From thence, Tuckey and his men started to march. They made only a few days' progress before yellow fever struck them, one by one. The lucky ones, Tuckey included, made it back to their ship to die. Their bodies, taken downriver by the two crew members who were immune to the fever, were buried at Embomma. For a time the Irish forgot the Congo.

THE OVERBERG, NR SWELLENDAM,
SOUTHERN AFRICA. 1817–19

Moodie Blues

Elephants. Not something that Lord Charles Somerset had thought much about. J.W.D. Moodie had: *A large female, accompanied by three others of a smaller size, issued from the jungle which skirted the river margin ... Being alone in the middle of a little open plain, I saw that I must inevitably be caught, should I fire in this position and my shot not take effect. I therefore retreated hastily out of their direct path ... until I should find a better opportunity to attack them.*

The first significant cadre of new settlers, the human building stones of Lord Charles's fence against the Kaffirs and Hottentots (in the vocabulary of the time), arrives in 1817. Captain Benjamin Moodie, a half-pay officer and eldest son of a down-at-heel Orkney laird, recoups his family's fortunes by bringing to southern Africa in 1817 three shiploads of Scottish settlers. They spend their first months working as a labour gang in Cape Town under the semi-feudal eye of Captain Moodie. The party then moves to the Swellendam district, 100 miles east of the Cape, by twisting paths. There, at Grootvadersbosch in 1819, John Wedderburn Dunbar Moodie joins them.

On looking back, I perceived to my dismay, that they had left their former course and were rapidly pursuing and gaining ground on me. Under these circumstances, I determined to reserve my fire as a last resource ... I made for the bank of the small river.

Lieutenant J.W.D. Moodie, also a half-pay officer, has joined his older brother in 1819 (and soon a third brother will become part of the group). John Moodie immediately is given half-share of the massive family farm (massive, but mostly bush) and becomes its manager. In this part of the country, it's elephants, not natives, who have to be cleared off, which explains his present problem.

Before I got within fifty yards of the river, the elephants were within twenty paces of me. But the gun, unfortunately, from the powder being damp, hung fire ... Halting only for an instant, the animal rushed furiously forward. I fell. She then made a thrust at me with her tusk. Fortunately for me she had only one, which, still more luckily missed its mark. Seizing me with her trunk by the middle, she threw me beneath her fore-feet and knocked me about between them for a little space ... once she pressed her foot on my chest with such force, that I felt the bones bending under the weight.

Moodie is rescued by a passing member of the Royal African Corps. He returns, unflapped, to being a farm manager. Over the next ten years, he moves farms several times, going generally westward and finally settling in Grahamstown.

In that district, the danger is not elephants, but lions and Xhosa. They, like the elephants, are viewed as exterminable, but dangerous, pests.

THE EASTERN CAPE, SOUTHERN AFRICA. 1819-23

Markedly Overqualified

Algoa Bay (soon renamed Port Elizabeth) was a tent city in the early
1820s, filled with shipload after shipload of migrants. They were on
their way to being settled in the "Albany District," a name that does
not last long, but refers to great chunks of land between the Bush-
man's River and the Great Fish River, roughly 300 miles east of Cape
Town by direct reckoning. There they are to keep the Xhosa at bay, so
says Lord Charles Somerset.

A measure of the economic desperation in the British Isles after the
end of the wars with France is that nearly 40,000 souls applied for the
privilege of bobbing for months on vessels of less than 500 tons,
cramped, though not ill fed. They were promised farms and hope.
These were not the immiserated poor, but shop owners, artisans, and
a minority of small farmers. They all had good character references
from their clergy and were considered safe imperial investments.
Even so, Lord Charles did not let their vessels land at Cape Town, for
fear of their deciding to stay in the capital; he kept them on board
and, having had the credentials of each party checked, he made them
sail up to Algoa Bay. There they went ashore, unloaded their worldly
goods, and excitedly planned their new life. They did not talk much
about the danger from the native population, nor that Grahamstown,
a frontier fort in 1819, had been nearly destroyed by Makanda, a
Xhosa prophet, though the affray's being called the Fifth Kaffir War
should have given them pause.

Each party was led by an entrepreneur who had put them together,
and each group was allocated land in a batch.

Not a bad idea.

The bad idea was that the 4,000 or so persons selected, and the 1,000 or
so who came out independently (or as indentured servants) to southern
Africa at the same time, were not hard enough to do well. Not at first.

Witness three women, aspiring middle-class matrons, trying to do
basic farm tasks when their husbands are away. The government provides them with rations in the form of live sheep and they, who have
never even watched an animal be butchered, try to kill it. They tie up
the animal and, not knowing how to kill anything humanely, they stab
away at the animal until it finally dies. Then, they do not know enough
to bleed it, and instead hack off the skin with wasteful slashes of a carving knife. Finally, they have enough meat so that they can cook. The

battered slabs of sheep flesh, still full of blood, are heated over a fire and eaten too quickly. The children have desperate stomach aches.

Or watch a former carpenter as he tries to plant his first kitchen garden. He has never used a hoe or a spade before and has to be taught by his neighbours not to place all the seeds at the same depth. And not to think that the deeper the seed is buried, the greater will be the crop.

The theory of this buffer colony was that they would prosper by raising crops, a governmental calculation made without any knowledge of the soil structure of the area. But this was cattle country, ill-suited for intensive cultivation. So, eventually the settlers turn to livestock raising and the minute they do this they stimulate the Xhosa to raid their stock. Because most of these "1820 settlers" (a slightly misleading label, but customary) were not hard rural farmers (unlike those from Ulster who went to the American colonies), but too urban or too respectable; they had no experience of serious fighting. So, in their early days, rather than serving as a defensive barrier against the Xhosa and other natives, they required defending by government forces.

Slowly, they hardened. Or died. Or were killed. Or returned to the British Isles. Their hardening was best observed in their clothing. The stout woollens and well-cut clothes they brought with them were gradually replaced among the men by short jackets that ended at the waist and did not impair movement. And for hunting they took to homemade trousers and an adaptation of the workingman's frock, much like the buckskin shirt of the American frontiersmen of the same period. The women went to simple fabrics, muslin dresses, with long sleeves. And they wore shoes that anyone at home would have called boots.

These, the ones who could adapt, were the ones who survived.

THE NORTHWEST CAPE. 1820–21

Pretty Much the Shaft (1)

"So, yourself is selling me to the man over there?" This is asked in Irish. "So and all, it is for your own good, and a fair man he looks, so he does," is the reply.

John Ingram, who has headed one of the seven Irish parties that went to southern Africa in 1820 had, in 1823, filled a ship with 352 destitute Cork Catholics and was hawking them around Cape Town. In his cargo were 186 men, and 59 women. They went quickly. The remainder of his shipload, mostly children, took longer. A year later he still had 106 on his hands and eventually he kept fifty-one for himself, rather than let them go at knockdown prices.

Ingram's party and the other six Irish parties that arrived in 1820 had come mostly from counties Cork and Wexford, where population pressure made it clear to small farmers that their children would never hold land and that in order to provide for their offspring's futures, they should leave. The same pressures were manifest elsewhere in Ireland, but the southeastern corner had a long tradition of emigration and it was an easier decision for these sea-coasters.

These, and one Irish party drawn up in London, comprised 350 people, and, with a few Irish in other parties and arriving independently, plus the indentured servants, 800–1,000 Irish were settled in the Cape of Good Hope by the mid-1820s.

The Irish parties mostly took the shaft. Though they were led in each case by Protestants (and in the case of William Parker, by a zealot), they were half and half Catholic-Protestant. And nobody trusted the Irish, especially the Catholics, less than did Lord Charles Somerset. Thus, five of the Irish parties were sent 150 miles north of Cape Town to an area called "Clanwilliam," after the first earl of that name.

The Clanwilliam district is a semi-desert, best suited to raising dust. With the exception of one party (Parker's), the group was entirely made up of families, most of them with children. Allotments, which ranged from 6 to 250 acres of this land, were useless. The Church of Ireland lay preacher, Francis McClelland, wrote to the Bishop of Waterford that they had a large band of people in a place *which is barely sufficient for the competent subsistence of two Boer families. There do not appear to me to be above forty acres of land fit for cultivation in the whole place.*

The Irish are transferred within a year to the eastern Cape, there to join the other 1820 settlers. They are a year behind their compatriots in the Albany district, but several years the wiser.

NR. THE KOWRIE RIVER, EASTERN CAPE,
SOUTHERN AFRICA. JULY 1820

Learning the Score

The social geography of southern Africa was harder to learn than was the physical.

A forty-waggon parade, pulled by oxen, has crossed the Kowrie and is headed for its designated location west of Grahamstown. The party, that of Thomas Mahoney, has been recruited in London and the home counties and consists mostly of Irish families that have already been once-displaced: from Ireland to England. That should make them quick learners.

As they wind their dusty way forward, they are observed by several "Hottentots." The natives immensely enjoy watching the white people struggle over land that if the white people only had the sense, they could walk over, like skittle-bugs on a pond.

The observers come close and they are friendly. Their linguistics reveal the social geography that the Irish have to understand if they are to survive in this new land. The natives first say a few words to each other in their own tongue, then direct some sentences in Dutch at the settlers. When the settlers look puzzled, they go into a third language. "Ha, ha ha!" they laugh. "Englis setlars!"

That is the score: uniquely in south Africa, among all the places in the British empire that the Irish settle in significant numbers, they are a triple minority: a minority, as usual, among the British Isles peoples; a second minority, for another European culture, the Dutch, is numerically preponderant; and a third, for only in southern Africa do the European peoples not destroy the indigenous peoples at least to the point that they out-number them.

In other words, the whole game will be played by other people's rules.

EAST OF GRAHAMSTOWN, THE EASTERN CAPE,
SOUTHERN AFRICA. 1820–24

Pretty Much the Shaft (2)

Admittedly, Thomas Mahoney's party of Irish-English slum rats were not the ideal colonists, but they had their character references, just like everyone else. Their real references, though, were the elbows-out assertiveness that frightened the other passengers on the *Northampton*, their emigrant ship. Mahoney himself quarrelled continually with the ship's captain. Two of Mahoney's followers had to be handcuffed for punching the captain. And below deck, disagreements with the other passengers brought out Irish knives.

So, the Cape administration made sure that they received the most dangerous placement on the eastern frontier: the red clay pits on the far side of the Kap (or Coombs) River. This was not a bad place for farming, as there was plenty of water and pockets of good soil.

The clay pits, though, were sacred to the Xhosa, who used the red clay in body painting. The Irish came under frequent attack and were the first of the 1820 settlers to be killed by natives.

Tough as the Irish were, they were no match. Thomas Mahoney himself fetched up in Grahamstown in late December 1821, in full terror, after having spent the previous days hiding in a combe from the Xhosa.

Mahoney, looking out for himself, became a building contractor and left his settlers to learn on their own the difficulties of stealing land from people who were as bad-tempered as they themselves were. Gradually, his party melted away, taking labouring jobs in the settlements or working for other settlers who had received better locations.

CAPE TOWN, SOUTHERN AFRICA. 1824

Niche Markets

Revan Matthews (of Scanlan's party) and Bridget Murphy (of Porter's), both in their early twenties, had been with the Irish parties sent to the northwest Cape. When that desert became unbearable, they both took French leave; instead of accepting relocation to the eastern frontier, they came to Cape Town and took up cabinet making and prostitution, respectively.

Now, two years later, they are slowly walking between taverns, advertising their wares in their own way. Revan has failed as a carpenter and consequently is dressed in full black, as if attending a funeral. He is an undischarged bankrupt, and wearing funeral garb is one of the few Dutch customs that is still enforced by the English courts. He is taking up a new career and wears a sign board over his mourning garb.

Bridget carries a large white parasol and wears a frilly dress that certainly is not designed for warmth. If she breathes deeply, a breast pops out and she giggles as if this is the biggest surprise in all the southern hemisphere.

Revan has found a trade in which the patron pays immediately, not late, or never, as in cabinet making for the gentry. He carries a sign board proclaiming:

To Lovers of Good Eating
TURTLE SOUP
At the London Hotel, Hout Street.
Fresh turtles, just arrived from the Island
of Ascension, will be dressed this evening
by R. Matthews, Esq.,
formerly turtle dresser to His Excellency
the late acting governor.
And will be sold at three rands per pint.
The public is invited.

Adaptability is everything in a new land and Revan and Bridget, one a professional dresser, the other an undresser, thank their lucky stars that they are young and have what the quality really wants.

LONDON. 1826

Lame Poet

Thomas Pringle is back in London and he intends to abolish slavery. Not just slave trading by sea, but the whole practice of chattel slavery within the British empire. He has been in Africa for six years and knows what he is talking about. He has developed a show-and-tell routine that he uses in England when convening meetings. The introduction of his presentation involves his setting the stage with depictions of the emigrants' life in southern Africa, such as:

First, here's our broad-tailed mutton, small and fine
The dish on which nine days in ten we dine;
Next, roasted springbok, spiced and larded well;
A haunch of hartebeest from Hyndhope Fell:
A paauw, which beats your Norfolk turkey hollow;
Korhaan, and guinea-fowl, and pheasant follow;
Kid carbonadjes, à-la-Hottentot,
Broiled on a forked twig, and, peppered hot

With chili pods, a dish called Kaffir-stew;
Smoked tongue of porcupine, and tongue of gnu

Usually that catches the interest of the gourmands, if not the poets, in his audience.

Despite his handicaps, Thomas Pringle, southern Africa's first English-language poet, took big strides socially. In 1819, with the recommendation of Sir Walter Scott, whom he had cultivated, he was named head of a party of twenty-four persons who sailed to southern Africa. As a farmer's son, Pringle was physically fit, though hampered by a limp that he acquired in infancy when his nurse dropped him awkwardly on the floor. Thomas Pringle's party was given a decent location on the Baviaans River. Actually, Thomas had never really intended to be a frontier settler, and, by virtue of some recommendations he had brought with him, including another one from Sir Walter, he became in 1822 the government librarian. He and his wife moved to Cape Town and left his brother William in charge of the family's small frontier settlement.

Pringle tells his London audience of the first time he had seen the effects of the law restricting natives from entering certain areas. *A Kaffir woman, accompanied by a little girl and having an infant strapped on her back came from the district town of Uitenhage under the custody of a female constable. She was one of a number of Kaffir females who had been made prisoners by order of the Commandant of the frontier, for crossing the line of prescribed demarcation without permission; and they were now to be given out in servitude among the white inhabitants of this district.*

In Cape Town, despite his soft job as librarian, Pringle had started a periodical and in his writing bit the hand that appointed him. The last thing Sir Charles Somerset wanted to hear was the plain truth, that his eastern Cape strategy was failing. *The emigrants who have abandoned their locations, consist of all ranks and classes, but more especially of mechanics and labourers.* To replace them, the British adopt the same slave-holding practices as the Afrikaaners. *The British Settlers had now become active competitors with the Boers for native labourers, and in placing themselves in a similar position, the majority had with lamentable facility adopted similar sentiments.*

In the London drawing rooms where he was organizing his antislavery campaign, Pringle lightened the tone by re-enacting a famous interview he had with Lord Charles Somerset, who, upon reading Pringle's views, became apoplectic.

Lord Charles summoned me. I found him with a copy of my writings in front of him. No, not my humble poetry, but the commentary upon settlers and settlement in the periodical press. Nearby sat the Chief Justice of the Cape of Good Hope, Sir John Truter, and he was there to frighten me, I dare say.

"So, Sir," said Lord Charles. "You are one of those who dare to insult me. And to oppose my government! Arrogant! Halt and blind librarian! Comforter of our enemies! Ingrate!"

Pringle rolls on, and after a two-hour sermon, he hits his one simple point, the one so simple it cannot be debated. *To end slavery in the empire, we must not trust to local governors, no matter how noble. Only our Imperial Parliament can end this abomination to all that is good and holy in our civilisation.*

The lame poet works feverishly as secretary, the main organizer, of the Anti-Slavery Society.

In 1834, the day after the Emancipation Act passes parliament, he begins to spit blood in dangerous quantities. He has advanced tuberculosis, and has kept his own mortality at bay only through a zeal no less effective for being kindly.

NR. GRAHAMSTOWN, SOUTHERN AFRICA. 1828

Passage, Right?

"My God, look at that kraal of Kaffirs," observed Major-General Richard Bourke. "They look like cattle."

"Boney cattle, not too well fed, I should say," added John W.D. Moodie.

This 1828 tour by Bourke, governor of the eastern Cape, is more of a farewell inspection than a serious administrative examination. He has been in office only three years but has done well: so well that he is being posted to the governorship of New South Wales. Hence, his last round before sailing.

"Must sting when they do that."

"Makes men of them, so they say."

Moodie was showing Bourke something new: a Xhosa circumcision camp. Among the Xhosa, this rite was conducted after puberty. The youths and young men were housed together in a bush kraal for ten days, and were taught the lore of manhood. A daub and wattle hut was attached to the kraal and there each young man had a long interview with a wise man who determined if the lad was spiritually ready for this step.

"Not at all like our schools," Bourke observed. He was fanatic on education and the chief achievement of his administration was to extend the school system by employing dozens of teachers, paying them decently to teach reading, writing, and loyalty. This was in English of course and was intended to keep the British Isles settlers from going Dutch, and, if the Dutch wanted, for them to have their children learn English, the language of power.

Bourke and Moodie had arrived at the isolated kraal at a propitious moment. The youths were now being carefully daubed with sacred red and white clay and a bundle of reeds was tied around their waists, a thick, dangly sporran. Then each of them was led into the little hut and, after a cry of pain, let back into the kraal. Those who had just been circumcised were given a wad of moss by one of the male elders.

Richard Bourke, a kinsmen of the great Edmund Burke, was well read on such African practices even before he had arrived at the Cape. He was acquainted with Lieut. Moodie's reputation because he had read Moodie's famous story of being stomped by a female elephant in *The Library of Entertaining Knowledge*, to which Moodie and his friend Thomas Pringle had submitted several African animal anecdotes under the title "Menageries." Moodie and Bourke had gotten along well from the first. Both were well read and enthusiastic about the emigration theories of the Rev. Dr. Richard Whately, and both believed in the absolute need to abolish all forms of slavery: not so much to protect the native, but to cease the debasement of the Noble Britons, as Bourke called them, optimistically.

"Oh dear, that one has passed out," observed Bourke as one of the young Xhosa crumpled to the dust. Another one was immobile in a fetal position, jamming the wad of wet moss onto his private parts, and a third was writhing in the dust like an expiring snake.

Eventually, all the circumcised youths pulled themselves together enough to be led back to the village. Each was given a long wand to symbolize his new manhood and their heads were wrapped in flowing bits of decorated cloth. Crowds of children alternately teased and praised them as they waddled into the village, legs spread apart. There the women beat drums and sang of the lads' future virility.

"Are you staying here, Moodie?" Bourke asked as he turned to leave.

Misunderstanding the question, John Moodie replied, "Yes, I think so. This is a good colony for the right man. First, though, I'm thinking of returning to England to find a wife."

"Mind you don't find a gel who'll do anything surgical to you." Moodie winced. "No chance of that. None at all."

THE OVERBERG, SOUTHERN AFRICA. 1831

Jonah and His Brothers

Like sailors swallowed up by the sea and somehow vomited forth on dry land, the Emmet brothers do their patriotic duty world wide as barristers, pamphleteers, lawyers and, of course, as martyrs: in Ireland, France, the USA and southern Africa. They submerge for long periods and suddenly bob up, riding the crest of some new historical wave.

Fifty years of age, Edwin Emmet appears in the section of the Overberg that is an English-speaking island among the Dutch majority. It is a community dominated by an Irish landholding family, the Barrys, and by the Moodie family which has several estates in the region. Through his Irish connections, John Emmet has been promised the appointment of private clerk to the local magistrate who, under the Cape's legal system, is a tiny czar. He brings two sons and they practise law and one of them marries into the Barry clan.

This younger Emmet, John, moves north and in the mid-1880s his own daughter marries Louis Botha, destined to be both an Afrikaner general fighting the U.K. forces in the Anglo-Boer War, and then, with Westminster's blessing, the first premier of the unified South Africa.

SOUTHERN AFRICA. 1834–38

Bible Reading: No Help Here

The British and Irish settlers outside of Cape Town, like settlers in difficult positions throughout the empire, spend a lot of time getting right with Jesus. The experience of epidemics of wheat rust, elephant trampling, pissed off indigène, obdurate Dutch neighbours, and arrogant colonial governors does that: makes a family read the Bible after the evening meal and leads to a great deal of silent praying in the night as twigs snap, cattle bawl unexpectedly, and dawn takes eons to arrive. Trouble is, too much Bible reading confuses the British Isles settlers, for half the time they seem to be on the wrong side of the Good Book.

Oh, they can buy the abolition of slavery in December 1834, for hadn't Saint Paul said, *There is neither bond nor free ... for ye are all one in Christ Jesus* (Galatians 3: 28)? Besides, hiring black and coloured labourers only during the busy times of the year was cheaper than supporting them all year round.

Their deepest problem was that the Great God Jehovah clearly told the Chosen People to fight their enemies; *and when the Lord your God give them unto thee, thou shalt smite them and utterly destroy them. Thou shalt make no covenant with them nor show mercy unto them* (Deut. 7: 2). This ran counter to the way the Cape government tried to make treaties on the eastern frontier with the Xhosa and instead ended up in mid-1830s with the Sixth Kaffir War (later delicately called the Sixth Frontier War, but you should read the tombstones of the dead settlers: no polite euphemisms there). The biblical adepts among the settlers point out that the successors of Joshua were punished for not wiping out their enemies and that those who were not killed would in future, *be as thorns in your sides* (Judges 2: 3).

Then there was the matter of the Great Trek and the victorious border wars of the Dutch farmers and cattlemen, 1835–38. Like the Chosen People fleeing Egypt, as many as 10,000 of them, in two main parties, had headed north to the Transvaal and northeast to Zululand and Natal.

If they are acting like the Chosen People, then are we the Egyptians?

The English-speaking peoples of southern Africa never quite get it right: never quite develop a sense of communal settler identity, or an agreed moral and political purpose that they can wear comfortably. White tribe lost.

ALGIERS, NORTH AFRICA. 1843

Stoners

No one needed to speak French to cut blocks of stone, but a few words might have helped when dealing with the French authorities. A small regiment of Irish stone masons had been assembled to work on the fortifications of Paris in the late 1830s. The job done, twenty-one of them, some with family, were recruited to sort out the crumbling governmental buildings and fortress walls of Algiers. They arrived in March 1843, their passage and housing and food provided in full by the French government: at first.

None of them could speak French or Arabic, or much English for that matter. What they knew was how to spot the fissure lines in a large rock and turn it into a quorn or a segment of an archway. They spoke to rocks, really, a silent and secret language.

The colonial government of Algiers runs out of money soon after they arrive and only a few obtained skilled jobs and within five months most of the Irish were poorer than the local peasantry.

Only the Old Fool Tie saved them. The French governor-general of Algeria, a man called Bugeaud, revered the memory of his mother, who was part of an Irish Jacobite family from near Clonard who had followed James II to France generations earlier.

In honour of his mother's memory, he provides from his own pocket funds for the liberation of these Irish stone masons from the serfdom that would soon be their fate.

He ships them to Gibraltar.

KURUMAN, SOUTHERN AFRICA. 1845

Rural Smarts

The Very Rev., the Rector, All Hallows College, Ireland possessed the rural smarts of the son of a large farmer, which he was. He subscribed to the annual printed report of the interdenominational Protestant group, the London Missionary Society. The report was a printed volume, several hundred pages in length, and it detailed with an admirable, if sometimes self-defeating, honesty the efforts of Protestant missionaries to convert indigenous peoples all around the earth. The rector always read it with a smile for, shorn of their heretical notions, the Protestant efforts were often quite amusing.

For example, in the 1840s, the mission of the Rev. Robert Moffat to southern Africa was detailed. He had worked for twenty years to promote on the edge of the Kalahari Desert his own New Jerusalem. In that time he had converted forty natives, and half of these had gone back to being, alas, natives. Early in 1841 he had received the help of a young Scottish doctor who, after four years, married the Rev

Mr. Moffat's daughter. The man was Dr. David Livingstone and he was a sincere minister of the Gospel.

In the first four years as a missionary, David Livingstone converted exactly one indigenous person: only to see this rare sheep leave the fold and choose instead animism and, more piquantly, polygamy. Dr. Livingstone, realizing that there was more empty land than receptive souls in the African universe, took to exploring.

That, and hundreds of similar stories explain why the Catholic Church in Ireland did not spend its money on attempting to convert natives until the end of Victoria's reign, when it finally had too many priests to stable in Ireland. Although founded in 1842 to supply priests to foreign missions, All Hallows College sent its priests to minister around the world to white people and especially to Irish emigrants. They needed improving, and, after the Devotional Revolution of the 1850s, most of them were far below the Irish Church's standards of minimal Christian practice. So, it was not callousness but a sense of priorities that left the dark peoples of the world to themselves.

Still, one had to admire the plucky, gormless Protestants. On special evenings in winter, the rector would sit and read to his college staff the dafter items of Protestant missionary enthusiasm. Sometimes the rector wondered what Dr. Livingstone was up to now.

THE END OF EASY MONEY.
THE WEST INDIES
1800–1865

Flexible to the End

I would rather live a Savage
Than be born:
   A New Gent.

Insult poetry, an Irish art, and the Nugents and the Savages families were forever at each other's throats. Or feasting at each other's hearths. It was a volatile relationship.

The verse above comes from the mid sixteenth century when Christopher Nugent was earning his knighthood by fighting against Shane O'Neill.

Unlike most Irishmen who did well in the West Indies, the Nugents and the Savages were from the north of Ireland. Like most successful Irish gentry, they played both sides of the political net and had done so for centuries. Patrick Savage, made seneschal of the Ards peninsula in the north of Ireland in the 1570s, inspired this:

High Ulster, destitute, starving,
   A district without delight, without mass;
Where the son of Savage, the English hangman;
   Slaughters barnacles with a mallet.

Members of both families were on several sides during the Irish Civil War and the Jacobite affray, but by the eighteenth century the successful ones are solidly Protestant and pro-Empire. In the West Indies, both Savages and Nugents build solar systems of slave estates; and one Nugent holds the governorship during the eighteenth and early nineteenth centuries, of Jamaica, and another of Tortola, a new plum in the Leeward Islands.

When the will of the Hon. John Nugent, of Tortola and of Dysart, county Westmeath, is probated, it divides his estate between his nephews, all of them Savages, in at least one sense of the word.

BARBADOS. 14 APRIL 1816

The Easter Rising

The big social explosions always happen after oppression is eased. From the viewpoint of self-interest, the best policy if one is an occupying power or a dominant social group is either to be unremittingly ruthless or to cut-and-run as fast as one can. The United Kingdom in the early nineteenth century is still a century-and-a-half away from that knowledge. In 1807 the legislature of the new (since 1801) United Kingdom of Great Britain and Ireland abolishes the slave trade in vessels that they control and in colonies that they govern. But slavery itself is not abolished. Instead the legislators begin to "ameliorate" slavery.

Slavery cannot be ameliorated. It is like a guillotine. Either it slices or it doesn't: one's head, half severed, is not ameliorated.

The Easter rising in Barbados – "Bussa's Rising" – was four days of arson and combat. From a military point of view, Barbados is the wrong place for such an effort, for it lacks deep forests and mountain ranges and troops can move about it easily. A quarter of the sugarcane crop went up in flames; probably as many as 1,000 slaves were killed, mostly in battle, and one militiaman and two regular army soldiers lost their lives in combat, and an untold number of elderly whites died of fright.

Demerara, taken over by the British in 1814, was the site of a rebellion in 1823 and Jamaica had a big rising in 1831–32.

Hope: the cause.

THE WEST INDIES. 1834–38

Non-Reactive Measurement in the Social Sciences

Almost everybody at one time has been rated by one of the standard social scales: maybe the Taylor Manifest Anxiety Scale, or the Stanford Dogmatix Index (or, one wonders, is it the other way around?) or the implement that made members of my own extended family prosperous beyond wit's end, the Minnesota Multiphasic Personality Inventory.

If one wanted to rate the nastiness of any group of slave owners, and do so from a satellite that does not allow them to avoid assessment, one would work out the West Indies White Sonofabitch Scale and it would have two scalular elements:

1. The degree to which a slave owner's cohort of blacks *increased* between the abolition of the external slave trade and slave emancipation in 1834–38. The real bastards among the slaveholders bet that there would be a sackful of compensation paid by the London government for the loss of their human properties and they stocked up on slaves from among their neighbours (or smuggled them from other islands or from abroad). These investment pieces were not needed for work, so they were housed and fed worse than any slave cohort since sugar began.

2. And, which slave owners let their slaves emancipate *early*? The legislation of 1833 provided for formal emancipation on 1 August 1834, followed by a period of "apprenticeship" (set at four years), which meant four more years of slavery. But owners could emancipate their slaves early. Watch those that do: they are not being liberal, but nasty. Most of the West Indian Islands experienced a drought that began soon after Emancipation Day and it was cheaper for many slave owners to free their slaves than to feed them. So thousands of blacks were suddenly cast on their own resources. The owners took their compensation and got on a boat.

These scalular observations can be made on any of the sugar islands, but there is only one where it is possible to cross-ruff the information with that on religion and ethnicity – namely, Montserrat. On that, the only economic Irish-dominated island, the number of slaves grew by 7 percent in the last ten years of slavery. Five Irish Catholic families owned one-third of the island's slaves and, taken together, Irish Catholics had about half the island's human chattels. As emancipation approached, all save one of the big slave owners of Irish Catholic background bought into slaves. They stayed right to the end, buying slaves at knock-down prices from the planters who left early and then making their profit via governmental compensation.

And then in 1837, the Montserrat legislature, now controlled by Irish Catholics, ended apprenticeship a year early: it was too expensive to feed the blacks.

MONTSERRAT, BARBADOS, JAMAICA. 1852

Gaeltacht and Beyond

The last known Irish-language speaker on Montserrat was recorded in 1852 by one John Donovan. As a native of Ring in the Munster Gaeltacht, Donovan knew his Irish well. While serving as mate on the brig *Kaloolah* he landed a cargo on Montserrat, probably at Kingsale or Plymouth. There he began chatting with several of the black wharf-men in a language they thought was secret to their own island: Irish.

"I come from Cork," he told them in Irish.

"Ah, that would be Cork of the harbours," was the reply. This knocked Donovan back, for "Cork of the harbours" was a phrase that he had only heard old people use to distinguish Cork City from its surrounding county. In fact it went back to the mid-seventeenth century. For the Montserratians it was a live phrase, because their island held a small inland village called Cork and this had to be distinguished from the port in Ireland from which, until recent times, so much trade to Montserrat had originated.

By the time of Donovan's visit, the only Irish speakers on Montserrat were former slaves who had been owned by small farmers in an impacted poor-Irish enclave on the far south of the island. With emancipation, the poor whites filtered away, leaving few traces.

In contrast, on Barbados and Jamaica, the groups of poor whites were large enough to be communally self-sustaining, in an inbred fashion. A mixture of English, Scots, Irish, the "Redshanks" or "Redlegs" became small ethnic groups of their own, fiercely proud of their non-black bloodlines, economically backward, educationally resistant. When Samuel Taylor Coleridge visited Barbados in 1825, he observed: *The greatest part of them live in a state of complete idleness, and are usually ignorant and debauched to the last degree. They will often walk half over the island to demand alms, and if you question them about their mode of life and habits of daily labour, they stare in your face as if they were actually unable to comprehend the meaning of your discourse.*

If anything, they became less acute as the nineteenth century wore on. Their inbreeding left them physically feeble, and less than fully alert mentally. The women wore loose shifts and dragged their feet in the dust as they moved, the men and youths had a mode of ambling that involved almost no motion of the arms. This, when combined with their habit of wearing trousers that ended in the middle of their shinbone made them appear as if they were practising to be mimes in some sad rural circus.

In contrast, at the north end of Montserrat was an alert, proud, tiny elite, the "Black Irish." They were light-skinned blacks whose origins went back to the mid-eighteenth century. They were the product of white-male, black-female unions (not legal at the time), and their lighter colour was a sign of higher status. They were universally Church of England as it was the Established Church that permitted their children to be baptized, at a time when the Catholic church was limiting itself to whites-only. These Black Irish were an exclusive set of families – Daly, Gibbons, Ryan, Sweeney and Allen being the most important – and these went back to Irish families who in the eighteenth century had been Protestant on Montserrat. The Black Irish of Montserrat were flourishing as late as the 1960s.

REDONDA. JULY 1865

Phantasy Island?

The appropriately-christened Dowdy Shiell always loved monarchy. He was the sole bit of driftwood left on Montserrat by the Shiell family, who had come to Montserrat at mid-eighteenth century. By the 1820s the family held more slaves than anybody on the island.

The white exodus after emancipation left, by 1850, only 150 whites and the number was dropping fast. Dowdy Shiell had given up any pretence of farming and presented himself to the world as a sea-trader. He talked widely of being descended from the ancient Irish kings of Tara.

Joyfully, in mid-1865, he learned that his wife had produced a son: after eight daughters.

To celebrate the boy's birth and to provide him with a rich heritage, Shiell and a few friends sailed to nearby Redonda and, since it had never been formally claimed by any country, declared it to be his own kingdom.

He became a king and when his son, Matthew Phipps Shiell, reached fifteen years of age, King Dowdy abdicated in his son's favour. The lad's coronation was held on the island 21 July 1880.

The ceremony must have been brief: Redonda at that time was a massive rounded mountain of sea-birds' guano and could be smelled, when the winds were just wrong, as far away as Antigua.

ADVANCE AUSTRALIA FAIR, OR FOUL

1830–45

Old Boys Network

The Chief – that's what he calls himself – takes delivery of seven convicts. They'll work for him and work hard. The next year he is allocated six more. They'll call him "Sir," or "Chief," and if they don't,
either he gives them a drubbing or sets the English law on them, and
then they're back on a road gang near Sydney.

Ned Ryan. Forty-six years old and hard as nails. He's only 5'6½",
but he demands that his tribe look up to him. Even with hob-nailed
boots, he can still kick the top jamb of any door on his property, and
that's higher than any man's jaw. The romance of his successfully in-
stalling himself as a Gaelic Chief in the great expanse beyond the Blue
Mountains obscures two things. The first is that he is a man of immense ability, with a desperate need for success and a ravenous hunger to hold land.

And, secondly, his spacious personality appears more unusual than
it really is. There exists, quiet and unspoken, in early Australia, an
Irish Catholic Old-Boys network that is parallel to the classic English
one of Eton-Christ Church-House of Commons-Prime Minister. It is
this Irish network that makes possible his achievement, and if that
network is lost to historians, it certainly was known at the time.

So watch: the code word for the first portion – the Eton of Irish-
Australians – was either "Tipperary" or "Whiteboy." To graduate
from Whiteboyism, which mostly flourished in Tipperary, was to be
the product of one of Ireland's hardest environments. Whiteboys
went back to the middle years of the eighteenth century and they
mixed patriotism and sectarianism with local clan wars. They were
gangs, hard men who fought regularly at markets and fairs, whirling
in the dervish-joy of recreational violence. But they also enforced an
unspoken moral economy, shooting and sometimes killing landlords'
agents. Or tithe proctors who pushed too hard were "carded," that is,
had their naked backs raked by the long sharp spikes that were used
to straighten out a wool-clip before it was sent to market. And, crucially, Whiteboy gangs protected themselves against "jumpers," the
poor, near-starving wretches who would bid up the price of tenancies
and thus take them over. Price control through terror was a large part
of this curriculum. Ned Ryan, as a strong farmer of thirty acres, had a
keen interest in maintaining the status quo, for he and his family

were doing well. Of course he was a Whiteboy. And when, in September 1815, his gang decided on a semi-patriotic venture, he went along: the infirmary in Ballagh, Clonoulty, County Tipperary, that was run for the local poor was being turned into a temporary barracks for the militia. The Whiteboys' demolition of the place went well enough, but they were turned in by a publican named Michael Dwyer. Another case of the Old Enemy corrupting a native and making him turn informer? No, just the opposite: a native using the government for his own ends. The "informer" Michael Dwyer belonged to one of two gangs in the area that split the community like a deep crevasse: the Whiteboys vs the "Shanavests"; the Ryans vs the Dwyers, and Michael Dwyer's brother was a tithe proctor who had been killed by Whiteboys a month earlier. So, in one efficient move, Michael Dwyer's gang got even with the Ryan gang by turning them in. One of the Ryans' set of Whiteboys was hanged and thirteen were transported for fourteen years to eastern Australia.

Next code: James Meehan. A 1798 rebel. He possessed one of the skills desperately needed in the prison colony; he was a surveyor. He arrived in 1800 and by 1801, was assigned as a convict to the surveyor-general of the colony. He took part in the earliest expeditions of exploration and, in 1803, while still a convict, became the chief official of the surveying department: of course he did not have that title. He measured farms and he had a great influence over who was granted what piece of land. Given his absolute pardon in 1806, he not only surveyed a large part of Van Diemen's Land and of New South Wales, but worked his way up to the official post of surveyor-general for the Australian colonies and superintendent of roads and bridges. All this was a licence to print money, and Meehan discreetly put together a large estate for himself. And, quietly, he settled those Irishmen of whom he approved, in tight little settlements, on decent land, in the southwest sector of New South Wales. Ned Ryan's being assigned to James Meehan in 1816 was no accident: Meehan took the ablest convicts for himself, and Ryan was soon an overseer. He stayed on with Meehan after getting his ticket-of-leave in 1822, and was superintendent of the Meehan estate when it moved to Goulburn. Meehan died in 1826, but by then he had given Ned Ryan his master's degree: experience in handling large flocks of sheep and herds of cattle, and in keeping in order lazy and cheeky labourers, and in clearing off Aboriginals, by poisoning, shooting or whatever was necessary.

Next: squatter. Illegally occupying land and holding it by brute force was the road to riches, once the mountains had been breached.

To limit this activity, in October 1829 Governor Ralph Darling defined the "nineteen counties" areas of lawful settlement. These were in roughly a 200 mile radius of Sydney. Ned Ryan received his absolute pardon in June 1830 and a year later he was squatting on lands at Galong, fifteen miles beyond the legal line. To be a successful squatter in the early 1830s took an immense amount of will. The squatters held land by the force of their own hand, and experience in gang warfare was a definite advantage. This first generation of squatters picked up retainers who would serve as henchmen, and bullied, maimed, or burned-out those settlers who would not. To seize vast expanses of land, they had to drive out the indigenous blacks, and a frontier war, no less vicious for being recorded only in fragments, raged: squatters and their flocks against Aborigines and their ancestral lands. Between fighting off rival settlers and clearing the Aborigines, Ned Ryan had his hands full: a visitor to his expanding fiefdom found the shacks and huts fortified. Later, in 1836, in an attempt to control squatting, the government issued annual grazing rights to the squatters, and in 1847 they received preferential, though not exclusive, rights to purchase freeholds. In the early 1830s, however, when Ned Ryan marched through the "Lachlan Pastoral District," as it was later called – from Galong to Boorowa on one flank and Yass on another – he did so as a Celtic chief cutting out a kingdom, and devil take anything in his way. One thousand square kilometres is an estimate of his kingdom. If, unlike a seventeenth-century Irish chieftain, Ned Ryan did not appear on his threshold carrying the head of his vanquished enemy, it was because it was not necessary to do so: after 1836 he could use the Imperial legal system to protect his grazing rights as far as whites were concerned, and with the blacks, his outriders did the necessary, so that his own hands remained clean.

The result: like W.E. Gladstone's passage up the English Old Boy network, from Eton to Christ Church, Oxford, to the Commons, to the prime ministership, Ned Ryan had done the Irish Old Boys version: Whiteboy – client of James Meehan – aggressive squatter, and finally, Gaelic chieftain and the biggest Irish-born landholder in Australia. In chiefly fashion, he built a castle, patronized blind Irish musicians, and practised public generosity, all the while treating his workers as if they were churls in a far off land and time.

It is a sign of his shrewd recognition of the insecurity of the life of a frontier ganglord, that only in 1848, after the law gave squatters real security, did Ned Ryan permit his wife and children to leave Ireland and join him in his self-constructed kingdom.

LONDON. 26 FEBRUARY 1833

Investment

Edward Foster, chairman of the Emigration Committee founded under authority of the under-secretary of state for the Colonial Office, distributes a notice to parish ministers and poor law guardians throughout England:

NOTICE

TO

YOUNG WOMEN

desirous of bettering their condition by an

EMIGRATION TO NEW SOUTH WALES

In New South Wales and Van Diemen's Land there are very few Women compared with the whole number of People, so that it is impossible to get Women enough as Female Servants or for other Female Employments. The consequence is, the desirable situations with good wages, are easily obtained by Females in those countries; but the Passage is so long that few can pay the expense of it without help. There is now, however, the following favourable opportunity of going to New South Wales.

The package is attractive: if a woman is between 18 and 30, of good character (a clergyman's letter is required), is willing to pay £6, the scheme will pay the rest of the passage. And if she needs a safe and comfortable place to stay in London awaiting the departing of "the fine teak-built ship, *Bussorah Mercant*," due to sail on 3 April, the Emigration Committee will arrange this.

A serious investment.

MORETON BAY, NSW. NOVEMBER 1833

Miscalculation

John Graham is thoroughly brassed off. He's a tiny man, 5' 2"with no meat on his bones. Now that he's wearing clothes he looks a little bigger than when he returned to Moreton Bay penal colony, buck naked, covered in ochre, his hair bleached blond by the sun. Then he had resembled a lawn ornament.

Now, in his convict's canvas garb, he marches himself in a large circle outside the governor's barracks, kicking up little trails of dust as he does so. He curses, kicks the ground frequently. The warders watch, amused.

As a twenty-one-year-old apprentice in a rope works in Newry, County Down, Graham had ripped off his employer – ropes were easy to turn into cash in the coastal community around Newry, Dundalk, and Strangford Lough – but eventually he was caught and sentenced to seven years transportation. As a labourer in Sydney, John Graham used some of his spare time for theft. He was lucky when apprehended, for he was charged only with pilfering, not with burglary, which he was indeed practising. A repeat offender ("secondary offender" was the term of the time), he was sent to the Moreton Bay penal settlement, founded in 1824, where the heat, humidity, and heavy labour were supposed to wilt the starch out of the most awkward characters. His sentence was to be completed 28 October 1833.

So why is he wearing a hole in the earth as he paces endlessly like a Tasmanian Devil in a circular cage? Because the devil's spawn, Captain Patrick Logan – ah Jesus, the Irish warders are always the cutest whores – had changed the rules.

For John Graham, after six months of Moreton Bay had taken to the bush and had been adopted by an Aboriginal clan that accepted him as the resurrection of a dead family member. Even the dead man's wife declared him to be the genuine article. So, carefully calculating the passage of days, months, and years, Graham had lived with his new family until his sentence was completed. He stayed out an extra four days, just to be sure. Then he walked into the governor's office and announced that he was now a free man.

Indeed, he might have been, but while Graham was out in the bush, Captain Logan had moved the goal line: so many men were taking to the bush and then returning with at least part of their time filled that he had ruled that time in the outback didn't count.

Now, however, there is a new Irishman in charge, a man named Clunie, and he debates with himself the issue for sixteen days before telling Graham that he will not be let out until May 1837.

"Will I put him in irons, Sergeant?" asks one of the warders who was watching John Graham gyrate.

"No, I think a word in his ear will be enough." The sergeant put himself in pedestrian orbit with Graham for thirty seconds, said half a dozen sentences: Graham stopped walking and broke into delighted, helpless laughter.

"What'd you say, Sarge?"

"I just told him the truth – the sad fact that while he was on his walkabout, our Captain Patrick Logan mounted an exploring expedition, fully provisioned and well armed."

Graham was still laughing hysterically.

"And didn't the black fellas put enough pointed sticks into our dear governor that when he was found he looked like a giant anemone. Terrible way to go, really."

In the background, John Graham stopped laughing and rendered his own lapidary judgement: "A man should respect the rules, even those of blacks and convicts, and shouldn't change the way things are done."

"I'll report for work tomorrow, "he tells the sergeant.

"REDESDALE," STILLORGAN, NR. DUBLIN. 1834

Sarcasm

Ireland's most effective campaigner against transportation for criminal offenses, Richard Whately, Protestant archbishop of Dublin, never met Ned Ryan. A pity.

In 1832, and again in 1834, Whately publishes public letters directed to the prime minister, Lord Grey. Whately puts the case against transportation. It's simple enough: transportation is too brutal for soft men, too soft for brutal ones, and it makes the society of the Australian colonies unstable and excessively repressive.

To the great bulk of those, therefore, who are sentenced to transportation, the "punishment" amounts to this, that they are carried to a country whose climate is delightful ... that they have a certainty of maintenance, instead of an uncertainty ... and if their conduct is not intolerably bad, are permitted, even before the expiration of their term, to become settlers on a fertile farm, which with very moderate industry they may transmit as a sure and plentiful provision to their children.

Whatever other advantages this system may possess, it certainly does not look like a very terrific punishment.

KING ISLAND, BASS STRAIT NR. VAN DIEMEN'S LAND.
13 MAY 1835

Precious Cargo

Women are more valuable to the government authorities than any other mammals, save pedigreed stallions. Even if they have to accept barge loads of Irish convict women: more than half of the female convicts sent to New South Wales before 1830 were Irish, and they turned out all right for the most part. Thus, the authorities look forward to the arrival of the *Neva* from Cork City, for it was full of social ballast and not just convicts: the *Neva* carries 150 female prisoners, accompanied by thirty-three of their children, plus nine free women with their twenty-six children.

Bodies to help civilize the body politic, Governor Bourke philosophizes.

The distressing news is that the vessel, bound for Sydney, had veered ninety miles off its reckoned course and had hit a reef just before four o'clock of a dark morning. Lifeboats were lowered, but they upset when the hawsers holding them caught in the davits, and the *Neva* was broken into pieces before they could be set right.

Twenty-two persons clung to flotsam and made shore on King's Island. There seven died from exhaustion and at least one from gulping long draughts from casks of spirits that washed ashore. The survivors: nine of the crew and six convict women.

The government ship despatched to rescue them from King's Island was named the *Shamrock*.

NEW SOUTH WALES, 1830–37

The Irish Whig Network

The wisest governor New South Wales ever had could hardly speak: he had taken severe wounds to his jaw in the war in the Netherlands in 1799.

He could not think for more than an instant of his wife, who died at Parramatta in 1832, without tears running down his cheeks.

By the time he resigned office in 1837 he was almost blind from nights spent working through piles of official reports, letters, briefs.

Richard Bourke's memory was a bit fuzzy, and he often said that he wished he had paid more attention when, as a young man, he had stayed with his kinsmen, Edmund Burke, then at the height of his powers. Still, he kept a selection of the great Burke's speeches in his portmanteau, and they had been a guide when Richard was governor of the Eastern Cape, South Africa, before he took over New South Wales. Edmund Burke's views on the great subjects of his own day – America, India, Ireland – yielded principles that the Whigs of Richard Bourke's day embraced: ease up on the colonies; cut back on special privileges for any colonial group; introduce visible justice and decent education; but don't push too hard: make haste slowly.

So Richard Bourke fought the "Exclusives" by bringing in the extension of jury trials that W.C. Wentworth had so strongly demanded, and by cutting back the power of country magistrates to flog and incarcerate virtually at will. When a syndicate under one John Batman in 1835 traded a pile of blankets, canvas shirts, axes and rum to the few bedraggled surviving natives in the area that became Melbourne – traded these inconsequentials for roughly 600,000 square acres – Bourke invalidated the transactions.

Like so many persons in Australia in the nineteenth century, Bourke was part of an invisible Irish circle, and not solely because of his spiritual godfather Edmund Burke who was deeply, if privately, Irish. Richard Bourke's best friend, a man to whom he wrote weekly letters, was Thomas Spring-Rice (later Lord Monteagle), of a liberal Co. Kerry Protestant family and, conveniently, secretary of state for war and the colonies in the Whig administrations of Earl Grey and of Viscount Melbourne.

And both Bourke and Monteagle were under the influence of the Protestant archbishop of Dublin, Richard Whately, the only Whig on the entire Irish bench of bishops. Whately was a virtual machine, pumping out pamphlets and making speeches against transportation, in favour of aided emigration of free persons, in favour of peaceful accommodation between Irish religious denominations and most importantly, for popular schools, mostly state supported, to be attended by both Protestants and Catholics alike. Bourke adopted and adapted this Whatelyian program. He had to accept transportation, but he created a "bounty system," essentially a plan of government aid to free settlers who wished to migrate to New South Wales. He refused to let the Anglicans become a dominant church and he provided annual grants to all the major denominations. His chief failing was one that was to dog statesmen all over the world – when he tried to create a system of national schools, modelled on those of Ireland, he was baulked: neither the Catholics nor the Protestants wanted their children educated together.

Richard Bourke was as undramatic a man as one can have in charge of a government, and that is why he (like Ned Ryan, his Catholic counterpart) is such a good illustration of a signal characteristic of Irish men and women in the Empire before, roughly, 1850. Whatever they do, it cannot be adequately explained either by appeal to some heavy principle or by big, general statistical trends. They acted the way they did in large part because of tight and tiny relationships, influence of their friends, and because of the character of the social circle wherein their minds were continuously shaped, constricted, energized.

Bourke eventually returned from New South Wales to his estate, "Thornfield," in County Limerick. There, despite his bad eyesight, he began a massive literary project with his friend Charles William Wentworth, the third Earl Fitzwilliam – and son of the second Earl Fitzwilliam who had given financial support to the two Australian political nonconformists, the highwayman D'Arcy Wentworth and his son William Charles Wentworth.

The project they worked on was an edition of the correspondence of Edmund Burke.

BATHURST VIA THE BLUE MOUNTAINS, NSW.
JANUARY 1836

Wedgwood Dish

Charles Darwin has spent most of his time since December 1831 at sea, with breaks to look at strange things. He would like to hie back to London and sleep in a decent bed and have servants bring him the newspapers, but he knows he has the best part of a year to wait. Now, in Sydney, he does his duty by hiring a man and two horses to take him over the Blue Mountains to Bathurst. It's a fair ride – about 120 miles – and takes a full week. There's a lot to see, but Darwin has pretty much gone stale on vegetation. His chief comment is on the "extreme uniformity" of the botanicals. To him, that apparent uniformity "is the most remarkable feature in the landscape of the greater part of New South Wales." Also, his guide is a pest and wants to know how he can afford to wander the entire world looking at oddities. Irritated, Darwin tells him the truth. "If you ever are served tea in a proper drawing room – and I doubt that you will be – discreetly turn the saucer over and read the maker's mark. Josiah Wedgwood was my grandfather."

The only species that fully engages Charles Darwin's attention is a band of "black aborigines" passing by, carrying spears. He has his guide give a shilling to the headman and the blacks put on a spear-throwing demonstration for his amusement. This band was partly dressed in European clothing and some spoke a little English. On the basis of this meeting and of stories he has heard of their tracking ability, Darwin judges that on the "scale of civilisation" they stand a few degrees higher than the Fuegians of South America.

This Olympian conclusion being achieved, Darwin collects information that he later includes in his journal to explain why the indigenous peoples of Australia are declining: the availability of distilled liquors, the introduction of European diseases and the increasing scarcity of wild animals are his three points of explanation, and he articulates them well.

Curiously, it never occurs to Darwin that being shoved from their homelands, being shot, and being poisoned, might also have some demographic impact upon this population group: which, actually, he refrains from referring to as human, although he probably accepted that these "harmless savages" were in some manner related to the descendants of Josiah Wedgwood, even.

BRUSH FARM, NR SYDNEY, NSW. 1837

Diction

"They read the book for to know the law."
"Yes, but better to say 'they read the book in order to know the law.'"

Had the officers and gentry of New South Wales named one of their innumerable point-to-points or steeplechases after the most culturally adaptable citizen of the colony, it would have been engraved with the name of Mark O. Pong, the first Chinese person to become an Australian landholder and the first to be married in the colony.

"I am after doing the laundry."
"Good, my dear. However, we usually say, 'I have finished the laundry.'"

Born in Canton in 1798, Pong had made his way to Sydney in 1817 as a free settler. Then he had fewer words of English than most people have teeth. Pong laboured, learned bits of the language and studied the rules for land allocation. Thus in 1821 he was given thirty acres at Brush Farm and in 1823 he married in the Church of England church, Parramatta, an English woman, Sarah Jane Thompson.

Together they work relentlessly on his English and he soon is both more articulate and more literate than most of the population, which, admittedly, was a disadvantaged group.

"I do be reading books."
"And proud we are of you, though I wish you would say 'I am continually reading.'"

Pong left his wife Sarah and four daughters behind in 1832 and went back to Canton where he had assets and money-owed. He arrived back in New South Wales in 1837, cash in hand, but his darling Sarah had died a year earlier and the persons appointed as guardians of his children had bilked the family of their small farm. He started over, and five years later he was well enough fixed to marry Bridget Gillorly, a west Donegal Catholic. Eight years older than Pong and well past the age when European marriage was a reasonable possibility, Bridget was quite willing to marry a Chinese man in a Protestant church, and to take seriously his endless English lessons. Having grown up speaking Irish, her English embodied scores of Ulster Gaelicisms that Pong laboured hard to correct.

"It's to Sydney we need to be going."
"Yes Bridget: now repeat: 'We need to visit Sydney.'"

Later, during the gold rush, hundreds of Chinese men married Irish women. None of them, however, took the time to improve their wife's diction the way Mark O. Pong had done.

LONDON. 1838

Australian Mateship

Archbishop Whately's pamphleteering and lobbying the government against transportation of criminals gains momentum. In 1840 his motion in the House of Lords for the abolition of transportation was enough to force the authorities to stop sending criminals to New South Wales: diversion was a first step towards complete abolition.

But even that step was heavy work, and here Whately picked up the perfect disciple: Sir William Molesworth, still in his twenties and not only energetic but discriminating. He had been sent down from Trinity College, Cambridge for challenging his tutor to a duel. He'd finished his education at Edinburgh and then, after a European tour, had been elected MP for East Cornwall and had founded the *London Review*.

On the evils of transportation and on the necessity of colonial self-government, Molesworth was like a rat terrier in a competition box. Not much walked away unwounded.

With Whately's urging, the prime minister, Viscount Melbourne, appointed Molesworth head of a royal commission on transportation, and rarely has there been a less dispassionate bit of investigation. Enough material on the horrors of Norfolk Island (re-opened to prisoners in 1825) and to a lesser extent Van Diemen's Land and New South Wales was produced to fill a dozen Victorian three-volume novels. Australian society was presented as often-brutal (which it was) and as permanently limited by its convict past (which it most definitely was not.)

Like most royal commission reports, the best parts were left out. They had to be, or the final version would have had to be sold beneath book store counters. For the one matter that the evidence was unambiguous on was the issue that prison reformers cannot deal with even in our own day: men in worlds without women will sleep with each other. Men in constricted environments, such as prisons, will rape the young, exchange sexual favours for food and tobacco, will suck off overseers and guards in order to draw soft jobs or to avoid punishment. Men assigned to farmers and ranchers will serve them as required to avoid being sent back to chain gangs, and mates, sleeping together in the bush, will of a frosty night, keep their private parts warm. Buggery was the Australian national sport: at least that's what one would have concluded if the evidence and conclusions of the Molesworth Report had not been heavily censored.

The evidence was strong: Catholic prelates, surgeons, judges, warders, former convicts, reported the same thing: that sexual abuse was an integral part of the punishment of many, if not most, of the men who went through the system.

WELLINGTON PASTORAL DISTRICT, NSW. 1838

Child Care

The baby's mother does not look back. She knows that if she does, she will see that her child is already turning grey and that the spirits are assembling to welcome it. That is a moment no human can share.

Perhaps it is a gentle way to die, but the infant does not think so. She cries as the mid-day heat and a blanket of flies torment her. Eventually, her voice cracks and she makes no more sound than does an insect digging a burrow in the sand. By the time she falls silent, her mother is far away.

This event occurs a few miles from a white settlement on the Darling River that will soon be named Fort Bourke.

Governor Richard Bourke was deeply worried that a race war would envelop the back country and that the dry tinder of hatred would be ignited by the whites' habit of grabbing for themselves any native women they fancied. In 1837 he had prohibited whites from forcibly detaining Aboriginal women.

Sadly, the results were that white stockmen were afraid to bring the women to their huts, so they made them live in the bush nearby.

And the stockmen, worried about legal evidence, insisted that the women kill their half-caste infants.

LIVERPOOL PLAINS PASTORAL DISTRICT, NSW.
JANUARY 1838

Yet Another Vinegar Hill

Blacks steal sheep. Blacks run cattle. Blacks spear station hands. All blacks' fault.

The race war that takes place in the massive squatting districts – Murrumbidgee, Lachlan, Wellington, Bligh, Liverpool Plains – is only a tithe recorded and then in wildly contradictory fashion, and that's among the whites. The blacks' versions are equally confused and confusing and that, like the whites', is the hallmark of authenticity. Real wars makes messy histories.

No squatter of any size was unbloodied; and all had blood on their hands. The squatters, seizing immense tracts of lands, employed anyone they could find as a station hand, and easily nine-of-ten stockmen were ex-convicts. The deepest enmity in all of Australian history was between former convicts and Aborigines and you don't need a psychologist to tell you why: the last curs to be fed are the ones that tear most fiercely at each other.

Major James W. Nunn celebrates the fiftieth anniversary of the first settlement of New South Wales by protecting the interests of the squatters and their employees. He is a major in the Eightieth Regiment of Foot in the regular army and has been seconded to command the Mounted Police. This makes him the third-ranking military officer in the government. Nunn is a career-officer, a veteran of the Napoleonic Wars. His career has been stalled because he is too financially straitened to purchase rank. He has to rise by ability and by self-advertising heroism. The one advantage he has is that he is very dashing, and now in his late-forties, bears a striking resemblance to the Duke of Wellington, but younger.

With only twenty-two troopers, he is on a mission that he hopes will be conspicuously heroic: to protect the squatters and station hands of the Liverpool Plains Pastoral District from the blacks. He'd like a victory that would raise him to a lieutenant-colonelcy.

Somewhere on the Liverpool Plains – it's either at the place that whites later call Slaughterhouse Creek or at Snodgrass Lagoon – Major Nunn has his Australia Day battle. One of his scouts discovers an unusually large Aboriginal encampment. Nunn and his troops creep through thick brush and surprise them, shooting men, women, and children at will. Some of the blacks scramble up trees and squatters who later visit the site of the battle find them still lodged there, "shot like crows in the trees."

Major Nunn's own estimate of his bag for the day is sixty to seventy Aboriginals. A later white official checks the site and reckons 200 is a minimum count.

Nunn and his men refer to their victory as the Battle of Vinegar Hill.

God, that's strange. The convicts of the 1804 rebellion used the same term to refer to their own doom-washed knob of history. Was Nunn remembering them, even sarcastically?

Hardly.

Major James Winniett Nunn came of a family that had been in County Wexford since an ancestor, a captain in Ireton's dragoons during the Cromwellian invasion of Ireland, had settled there.

So, while the convicts of the 1804 Australian rebellion had been identifying with the rebels of the 1798 battle of Vinegar Hill, County Wexford, Nunn and his men are placing themselves in history alongside the yeomanry and the regular army troops who crushed the Irish Rising.

History apparently was on Major Nunn's side, for eventually he was promoted lieutenant-colonel.

SEVEN HUNDRED MILES NORTH OF PERTH,
WESTERN AUSTRALIA, 11 FEBRUARY 1838

Needle Point

The liberalism of Richard Whately's tutee, Lieutenant (soon to be Captain) George Grey, is being severely tested.

In the wilderness of Western Australia, he and two outriders suddenly find themselves surrounded by a group of Aborigines. These are not people interested in conversation. One comes at Grey with a spear fixed on a throwing-stick, and Grey shoots him in the arm. Others press in and Grey and his companions take cover and consult their own tribal gods.

This, if he survives, will yield a good indication of how strong his core beliefs really are. While serving in Ireland from 1830–36, Grey had come to know the state of that country almost as well as did Archbishop Whately, whom he occasionally encountered. Grey came to share four beliefs with Whately: that large, ill-run absentee land-holdings were a cause of great misery; that keeping Irish Catholics and Protestants apart was, in the long run, insane: social amalgamation or "assimilation" was the best answer; that emigration from overbrimming to empty lands was a benefit to both sending and receiving countries; and that, eventually, at home the Irish should run their own local affairs: what in a colonial situation was called responsible government.

Grey realizes that if he and his men remain in a defensive position, they are slated to die. Each time they examine a new bit of rock, they discover that an Aboriginal spear-chucker is behind it. Grey jumps out to attack one of his tormenters and immediately is struck by three spears, one of which enters the fleshy part of his hip. He pulls out the shaft, fortunate that it is a throwing spear and thus leaves no head to embed in the wound. He pulls his haversack over the wound, so that neither his enemies nor his two shite-scared companions can see it and he continues to advance. The lead attacker turns and runs and as he does so, Grey shoots him in the back. The Aboriginal party dissolves.

Grey never again killed a man. Nor did he hide from the fact that he had taken an Aboriginal spear in the arse (a subject of mess humour in any soldier's company), nor that he had killed the man with a back-shot. That had been necessary and Grey did not flinch from reporting events straight.

After two exploring trips in Western Australia, Grey, in October 1840 was appointed governor of South Australia. He became a strong advocate for "assimilating" native groups throughout the Empire, mostly through education. That was the only way to end strife. Well and good: he remained a Whatelian liberal. If his idea of assimilating the indigenous and the European peoples in colonial settings through schooling was naive and not a little patronizing, consider the assumption it was based on: that native peoples are as capable of civilization as are Europeans. And remember what the alternative was in his own day: that the indigène were destined to be perpetual savages, hunted as vermin, their lands declared empty and hence open to confiscation.

PORT PHILLIP DISTRICT. AUGUST 1838

Natural Law

William Bowen, an illiterate Irish convict, is found in the records of the Port Phillip District which, in 1851, is separated from New South Wales and becomes the colony of Victoria.

Since he cannot spell, his name is recorded just as he pronounces it: B-O-N-E. He is a labourer on a survey gang.

Surveyors use convict labour to do the chopping, clearing, and carrying required for topographical work. The district expands continually into Aboriginal territories. To keep the convicts from mutinying, the chiefs of survey parties frequently permit them to drag along some comfort: that is to capture an Aboriginal woman and share her among themselves.

In August 1838, William Bone is admitted to hospital in the recently-named settlement of Melbourne. He is suffering from such severe sexually transmitted diseases that his penis must be amputated.

SYDNEY GAOL. 18 DECEMBER 1838

Hanging About

Four government officials attend the hangings. Soon seven corpses are twisting slowly, first in one direction, then in the opposite, as if they are experiments in a ghoulish branch of physics. The officials are old hands in the world of justice and they have seen enough executions so as not to find the spectacle of great interest. They are attending in order to keep their eyes on the small crowd permitted into the gaol compound and on the larger one outside. This is a very political moment. They are relieved to see that there is no trouble from the crowd.

This is the first time that the government of New South Wales has made it absolutely clear to the white population that one cannot massacre blacks at will: there are limits.

The seven men executed, all ex-convicts, were stockmen, the unlucky members of a band of twelve, who had killed twenty-eight "tame" (that is, peaceable) Aboriginals who were living quietly on the massive Myall Creek Estate in the Liverpool Plains district. This in June 1838.

The stockmen would have not even drawn comment, had they been satisfied with half a dozen deaths, or so, or if they had been less sadistic. The bulk of the twenty-eight victims had been collected from their camp and tied together and shuffled away to be slaughtered. A few others were picked up elsewhere. They were shot, stabbed, mutilated using "cobawn knives" (an Irish soldier's term for a cutlass) and hatchets. Only one young woman was saved and also two little girls about seven years of age: for sexual purposes. The reprieve for the girls was brief, however. Their orifices proved too small to permit sexual entry, so they were enlarged with stock-knifes, utilized, and then killed. The young woman was saved for rotation rape.

A day or two later, the stockmen began to worry that they might have crossed the line and they returned to the site of their massacre. They put the bodies and the often-separate heads in a big pile and built a large triangular pyre around the bodies and body-parts. Then they burned the victims beyond recognition. The smell of this amount of flesh, first burning, then being rendered down to ash, must have been recognizable miles and miles away.

Too big for the authorities to ignore. That is why the four government officials are standing together, chatting softly while the hangman finishes his job: he pulls each man's boots off, and then he lowers the corpses to the ground. The four men do not pretend they are viewing a tragedy. These trash deserved.

The officials have a lot in common, not just their being the agents of justice;

Edward Denny Day. A hero: he was sent to apprehend the miscreants and he captured eleven of the twelve. The son of an Anglican clergyman, he had spent his youth in the kingdom of Kerry, the remote land run by the O'Connells, and home of the Liberator. After fourteen years in the 46th Regiment of Foot, he migrated to Sydney and was clerk of the executive council. Though he was not political, he was deeply loyal to Governor Richard Bourke, to whom he owed his various promotions and his becoming a police magistrate. When Bourke left in December 1837, Day considered resigning, but stayed on under Governor George Gipps.

Roger Therry. Second barrister for the prosecution of the Myall Creek killers. Voluble, aggressive, entertaining, he was one of the first generation of Irish Catholics to benefit by the abolition of the penal laws. Educated by the Jesuits at Clongowes Wood and then at Trinity College, Dublin, he qualified for both the Irish and the English bars. He was a close associate of Daniel O'Connell in the Liberator's fight for Catholic Emancipation. As part of the Whigs' pay-out, in 1829 he was appointed commissioner of the Court of Requests in New South Wales and permitted to practise privately as well. His devotion to Governor Bourke was both familial and personal: his own father had been a ward of Edmund Burke.

John Hubert Plunkett. Lead barrister in the prosecution. Of a Catholic family that had kept much of its wealth intact during the penal era, he too was educated at Trinity College, Dublin, and qualified for both the Irish and English bars. He practised on the Connacht court circuit and Daniel O'Connell credited him with swinging Connacht to the Whigs in the 1830 election. Plunkett's pay-out was to become solicitor-general for New South Wales and then, in 1836, simultaneously to hold the attorney-generalship: Bourke was his patron.

Let the fourth man slide out of our vision for a moment. Irishmen of a certain sort – Whigs (or if you prefer, liberals), jointly influenced by the world of Daniel O'Connell and by their debts to Richard Bourke, have been pushing Australia over a watershed, a big step in the rule of law.

They almost failed. The eleven men captured by Edward Day almost escaped punishment. Plunkett's opening argument that "the life of a black is as precious and valuable in the eyes of the law, as that of the highest noble in the land," was fine, but he and Therry ran on too much. Legalese fell on the jury's ears like a thundering waterfall; perspicacity the barristers possessed, perspicuity not. The result was that the jury took fifteen minutes and acquitted the men.

The decision was highly popular. The stockmen's defence, involving three top-rank barristers, had been paid for by a general subscription of graziers, squatters and, oh, magistrates.

Plunkett and Therry prosecuted again, on a charge of seven of the men's having killed one child, and this time they won.

The fourth observer at the hanging was the highest ranking government official present. He was the newly-appointed commander of the military forces in New South Wales. A major-general, he arrived on 6 December, not long before the execution. He has been away from Australia on military duties for nearly twenty-four years, but he still knows his place: at the top. *General (and now Sir) Maurice Charles Philip O'Connell.*

SYDNEY, NSW. 24 DECEMBER 1838

No Real Reckoning

"Nigger-hunting" (one of the local terms) continued in the outback through the 1950s, but by then it was just a sport. The really large-scale race wars and territorial wars (the same thing, almost) were finished a hundred years earlier. The score was reckoned at roughly 20,000 blacks killed and perhaps one-tenth as many whites.

A body of folklore developed in the mid-years of Queen Victoria's century, celebrating the victory of the Europeans:

A tribe entire, with many a shriek,
Was pent, and held at bay,
Till there, like sheep, in one close heap,
Their slaughtered bodies lay.

But the hanging of the Myall Creek massacrers modified the behaviour of some, as noted in the Sydney *Monitor.* Two substantial gentlemen are talking:
– *So, I find they have hanged these men?*
– *They have.*
– *Ah … we are going on a safer game now.*
– *Safer game? How do you mean?*
– *Why, we are poisoning the blacks, which is much safer; and serve them right too.*
That is: add prussic acid, arsenic, or virtually any sheep-dipping compound to dampfer and give it to the starving wretches when they come around begging.

LONDON. 26 DECEMBER 1838

Solar Systems

Empires are like solar systems: things revolve around each other and each satrapy, each tiny polity has its own pull and can affect any of the others.

Sir George Grey, under-secretary for the Colonies, writes from London to James Croke in Dublin. Croke, an Irish Catholic barrister of eighteen years standing, has been appointed clerk of the Crown for the Port Phillip district which officially is still in New South Wales, but is on its way to becoming a separate colony. Croke's move to Australia, it appears, is a simple one, directed from the metropole and involving his translation from one colony to another.

Perhaps, except that James Croke initiated the proceedings himself and used as his referees four O'Connellite MPs, all of whom called on Sir George and pressed Croke's claims. Nationalist Ireland demanded its share of the colonial pickings.

More explicitly, another deputation, headed by Richard Lalor Sheil, MP for Tipperary and campaigner with Daniel O'Connell for Catholic Emancipation, told the chief secretary for Ireland that members of the Irish bar were not receiving their "fair proportion of colonial patronage."

The point is clear; if Ireland is to be colonized, it acquires the right to be a colonizer, to take as much as anyone else the spoils of the Antipodes, of Africa, of the Canadas.

SYDNEY, NSW. 7 FEBRUARY 1840

Quiet Allies

In public, the Protestant Empire and Holy Mother Church often vilipend each other, but they are allies and the power-brokers in each hierarchy know that.

Thus, the colonial secretary for New South Wales writes to the Rt. Rev. J.B. Polding. He tells the bishop that, under a statute enacted late in Governor Bourke's regime, the Catholic Church will receive £150 a year for a priest to reside in Melbourne, specifically, the Irishman Patrick Bonaventure Geoghegan.

And, throughout the colony, when an amount in the range of £50 to £100 is raised for the erection of a church, the government grants an equal sum.

In Ireland, the bishops had refused to have anything to do with funding of the clergy or of contributions to building Catholic chapels by the state.

In the Empire, by contrast, it's clear that the state and the church are on the same side.

SYDNEY HARBOUR. 28 FEBRUARY 1840

Real Patriotes

In the hold of the *Buffalo*, Bishop Polding says mass. The ship bobs in the slight swell of the harbour and the light from the overhead hatch moves correspondingly. To some of the men listening to the bishop, it is a cathedral window, to others the sign that a benevolent hand finally is on the frail cradle of their lives.

These men are part of the only shipment of purely political rebels ever sent to Australia: the rebels of the 1837–38 Rebellions in Upper and Lower Canada. No petty thieves, forgers, burglars, cut-purses, or criminal felons among them. They have been sent here upon the recommendation of Sir George Arthur, lieutenant-governor of Upper Canada. After his time governing Van Diemen's Land, Sir George remained an enthusiast of transportation, especially because of its humane nature.

The Anglo rebels have been left at Hobart, Van Diemen's Land, and the *Canadiens* are brought on to Sydney: fifty-eight men.

Bishop Polding and his Irish-born secretary both speak French. They meet the ship when it anchors and converse with the *patriotes*. Polding is impressed with the sincerity and religious commitment of these men and with their desire to hear mass as soon as possible. They had been five months at sea, and no priest has been sent with them.

The *patriotes* spend one year of hard labour. They quarry stone and build the Victoria Barracks at Paddington. They make and put down the first wooden paving blocks in the streets of Sydney.

They do this on two meals a day, breakfast porridge and midday meat. Two die of this treatment. After this hard year the *patriotes* are given tickets-of-leave and, since they are mostly skilled artisans or clerks or merchants or medical men, they are valuable employees. They are the sort of individuals the government would like to have settle permanently.

After seven years they are granted a free pardon.

All but one return to French Canada.

THE MURRAY RIVER. SEPTEMBER 1840

Critical Response

As the first commissioner of police, Thomas O'Halloran was a success. His twenty years of army service in India gave him a brass neck, and the sale of his commission made him a small capitalist. He bought four sections of land and set up as a grazier. Appointed as the commissioner of police, he sorted out an undisciplined and corrupt force ruthlessly.

The Milmenrura tribe and O'Halloran collide. The natives, who live near the mouth of the Murray River, are among the most feared in Australia, for they have been dealing with whalers and, having been victimized in the past, are now proficient at defending themselves against white interlopers. In September 1840, a ship founders on a reef near the mouth of the Murray River. None of the twenty-six passengers and crew survive and ten bodies are found, mutilated, showing all the signs of native attack.

Major O'Halloran takes a squad and confronts the tribe. He really is not interested in forensic or judicial matters: he hangs two at random, and the tribe gets the message. This is the most important step in making the Murray River the Mississippi River of Australia, and O'Halloran is widely praised. His superiors, however, tell him to be a bit more respectful next time about evidence.

Hence, nine months later when he goes far up the Murray to rescue some stolen property and to find the murderer of a white stockman, he returns without firing a shot, since he had no means of identifying the robbers or the killers. His superiors approve, but he takes a terrible roasting in the public press.

Two years later, Governor George Grey cuts heavily into the police force and complains of inefficiency. He suggests that O'Halloran double up and be not just police commissioner, but serve as a magistrate as well.

Major Thomas O'Halloran has not come to Australia to be a whipping post, and he resigns.

No more criticism. Instead, he takes to grain farming, imports one of the first mechanical grain harvesters and becomes one of the largest wheat farmers in the land.

SYDNEY, NSW. 17 MARCH 1841

In the Footsteps of St. Patrick – I

The first formal St. Patrick's Day procession to be held in Australia was respectable and that was the point. Previously there had been convivial annual dinners and, once or twice, processions staggering from one hotel to another, with musical accompaniment. This time, a priest was in charge and there was good order.

The vicar general of New South Wales, Father Francis Murphy, was taking advantage of his religious superiors' being out of the country and was melding Irish nationalism and Irish Catholicism in a way the Australian church later would use to great effect.

Sydney, even in the early 1840s, was still a waterside town, scattered widely over hills, rolling lowland and patches of reclaimed slobland, so a procession was hard to direct: where should it go? Because most of Father Murphy's marchers were former convicts, he had them form up at King's Wharf (where they each had been at least once, on unhappier occasions), and then march the length of the main thoroughfare, George Street, less than two miles. A set of pipers played national airs, and the men (no females were permitted to march) tried to keep in rank. They wore their best clothes, in most cases woolen jackets and trousers. The procession worked its way to St. Mary's Cathedral and there Father Murphy celebrated High Mass. Dinner for a hundred "gentlemen" followed, with eireinic toasts to some Protestant Irish guests present, a loyal toast to the Queen and brief mentions of Daniel O'Connell.

Father Francis Murphy's purpose was to harness Irish national feeling to his own clerical ends. In point, he wanted an Irish church to rival the English Benedictine cathedral, St. Mary's. Of course it would be called St. Patrick's.

To that end a St. Patrick's Society had been formed a year earlier to raise money to memorialize Ireland's patron saint. A veteran of the 1798 Rising, William Davis, now wealthy and ageing, donated a building site.

For this and for other dances with Irish nationalism, mild by any standard, but not quite respectable, Father Murphy is punished by his metropolitan.

He is promoted in 1844. He becomes the first bishop of Adelaide, South Australia, a vast area with about 1,200 Catholics, no church, no schoolhouse. Try organizing a parade there.

FREMANTLE, WESTERN AUSTRALIA. OCTOBER 1841

In the Footsteps of St. Patrick – II

His soul sings: the Rev. George King has just begun the first school for native children in Western Australia and, maybe, in the entire country. Fremantle is such a strange place for this effort: only 400 inhabitants (and dropping, as South Australia's copper mines draw away population). And the colonial chaplain, who lives upstream in Perth, has not visited Fremantle for seven years as the locals won't pay his expenses.

George King bubbles with such energy that he handles it all: builds three churches to serve Fremantle and the country districts and also establishes his native school. He is a missionary of the Society for the Propagation of the Gospel in Foreign Parts and has an annual salary of only £250, less than a labourer's wage, and he has a wife and family. The love of God will provide, he believes, and he is right.

King was given the song in his heart by St. Patrick. Young King was cut from the right social cloth for Irish Anglicanism, Portora School and Trinity College, Dublin, but that background rarely led to the god-drunk buoyancy King shows in Western Australia. One of the Fellows of Trinity Dublin had control of a curacy in Larne, Co.

Antrim, and in that grim, Scottish Presbyterian town, the Rev. George King began his career. The rector of the parish had lost his voice, and the young King, as curate, had to become the voice of the church. King became keenly aware of St. Patrick by walking the paths of his neighbouring parish Islandmagee – which St. Patrick had known as Rinn Semhne. Of course he knew of the bilious public argument the Church of Ireland and the Roman Catholic Church in Ireland were forever having about who was the real heir of St. Patrick, but this was of no interest, a fight about bones. George King had encountered St. Patrick at the Ballylumford Dolmen on Islandmagee; no visual apparition, but a voice that repeated the ancient hymn "St. Patrick's Breastplate" till King's spirit was borne by the harmonics of a thousand voices into a joy he had never previously experienced and thereafter never completely lost.

Volunteering for Western Australia was his version of St. Patrick's going on mission to Ireland. King knew he had to convert natives, for hadn't his spiritual patron done just that?

The native children are intelligent and apt to learn. He is careful to respect Aboriginal sensibilities, or at least he tries hard. He obtains parental consent for each pupil to attend school. And when, later, he discovers that some of the girls have been betrothed since infancy, he summons their future husbands and buys their freedom for a few shillings. These transactions are scrupulously written out before a magistrate and all parties concerned make their marks on a piece of paper.

Is this generous, ethical, red-haired dust-devil of religious energy doing good? No one can deny that he is doing his best. He is attempting to do for the Aborigine what St. Patrick did for the Irish: change their view of the future world, and thus of the present one. *We have reason to conclude that they have no vague idea of a future state.* To teach this was an imperative. *To the Aborigines we owe, and England, whose subjects they have now become, owes a debt of which nothing less than the bread of eternal life can be an equivalent: [for] we have usurped their well-stocked hunting grounds; taken possession of their fisheries; and ploughed up the very staff of life, which the rich valleys naturally yielded in the bulbs and roots so congenial to native life.* He works hard, but almost alone. The government at first gives him a few pounds, then withdraws support, and the citizens of Fremantle are not keen on having literate natives around. A pound of bread a day and a bit of milk and fish now-and-then were all the aid George King received. After four years of experience: *I have no hesitation in stating my conviction that in moral sentiment, as well as in the ordinary attainments, as well as in the attainment of ordinary humble tuition, they are not one degree inferior to the common average of European children.*

With no sense that Christ's love and English civilization could be anything but a godsend, George King innocently observes from his ever-growing bank of experience that Aboriginal children can be educated to take their place in civilized society only by separating the children from their parents.

MUSTON'S CREEK, THE PORT PHILLIP DISTRICT [NSW].
FEBRUARY 1842

Colonial Experience

Later, in colonial Africa, it will become the glory of big-game hunters to bag the Big-5, or sometimes the Big-7, the really big trophy animals. The hunters often are military, or ex-military men, but need not be: all of them share a secret – that the really big bag is the Big-1. Baden-Powell, founder of the Boy Scouts, will put it bluntly: of all the sports, the greatest is man-hunting.

Killing a human being.

That's one reason Australia is so attractive to transient gentlemen from the British Isles; it gives them a shot at the big trophy.

At Muston's Creek, squatters and their employees are on the alert for bands of marauding blacks. The honest-to-god squatters don't want trouble, but others enjoy it, including four gentlemen who are here for the experience. One of them is working as a station hand – rather like "cadets" later do in New Zealand – picking up a bit of exotic experience. He is Richard Guinness Hill, and he trades on being the nephew of Sir Richard Guinness of the Dublin brewing family.

A bottom-level employee, a hut-keeper, has borrowed a gun from a nearby station. He has asked that it be loaded with heavy ball, as he is intending to shoot some kangaroos. However, he tells the visiting gentlemen of his actual plans and they join him. They mount and ride down Muston Creek until they come to a stand of trees where some indistinct black figures are huddled. They circle, fire into the copse, and leave, pleased with themselves.

A good manhunt, except in fact no men were killed: a male baby, three black women, one of them hugely pregnant, and one with a gunshot wound in the back who, two days later, was still agonizingly dying.

Charles La Trobe, superintendent of the Port Phillip district offers a £100 reward for information and the murderers are arrested. There is, however, no chance of a guilty verdict. One jury member says that he would have eaten his boots before he would have voted "guilty." The shooters all are acquitted. In a private letter, Sir George Gipps, governor of New South Wales, says that had he been on the jury, he would have found guilty two of the gentlemen in the affair, including Richard Guinness Hill.

There was a term employed at the time for men such as Hill who were knocking about the colonies as a way of broadening their own horizons: they were referred to, respectfully, as "colonial experiencers."

EASTERN GIPPSLAND, (THEN-NSW). 1844

Chivalry

Saving maidens has always been an acceptable excuse for male violence.

Saving white women from being touched by blacks has been a universal licence in European-derived civilizations for heroic mayhem. Like saving Jerusalem from the Musselman hordes, it's been a Christian duty.

In eastern Gippsland several expeditions have been mounted to save a white woman who is said to be living with Aboriginals. Obviously she would not do so by choice and certainly she requires saving.

She proves hard to find, despite some satisfying killing of blacks who will not divulge her whereabouts.

Finally, she is found.

She is the well-preserved carving of a woman, the figurehead of the wreck of the ship *Britannia*.

SYDNEY. 9 JUNE 1846

Principles

The grandson of the 1798 veteran Thomas Murray, the son of "Pay-master" Murray, rises in the legislative council to state his principles.

Terence Aubrey Murray is known after one of his immense estates as "Murray of Yarralumla." He and his family have long abandoned any respect for the principles of the '98 Rising. Though Gaelic Catholics in background, they now are thought of as Anglo-Irish and are pleased with that. Terence, baptized Catholic, married in an Anglican church and in public claims to be a Unitarian.

A large man, given to wearing knee-length riding boots even in the city, he shakes the windows of the council chamber with his deep voice. The most iniquitous legislation is in passage and must be stopped: the governor is trying to renew an act that requires licences for squatters. Terence Murray declares that, though he has hundreds of thousand of acres, he will abandon squatting because he cannot accept any government interference. The wilderness is like the ocean, he says, and it should be open and free to anyone who wishes to occupy it.

Murray concludes his speech by reading to the assembly the American Declaration of Independence.

TREATY NEGOTIATIONS?
NEW ZEALAND
1830–1845

New Fences

Several senior chiefs, among them Moetara Motu Tongaporuta, leader of the Nga Puhi, meet with the Protestant missionaries. Both groups are worried. They have heard rumours that the French have designs upon New Zealand. In part they are picking up subsonic vibrations from the ambitions of the Vatican, where spiritual capture of all of Polynesia is a major topic of discussion. French holy orders will be in the vanguard. And several French civil figures, including the preposterous "Baron" Charles Philippe Hippolyte de Thierry (who believes he owns most of New Zealand) are discussing New Zealand's place as part of the natural Gallic order of the universe.

In response, the chiefs and the missionaries petition the government of the United Kingdom of Great Britain and Ireland for protection.

TE PUNA, BAY OF PLENTY. 1832

Modest Ambitions

"I am Papahurihia. The name of the son of god is Papahurihia. I am the son of god."

No one should have been surprised. The young tohunga, scarcely in his thirties, was doing for the Maori what Saul of Tarsus had done in his day: steal Judaism.

"You are the Chosen People. You are called 'Hurai' – or, in the tongue of Jehovah, 'Jews.'"

Papahurihia, who could read Maori, knew his Bible well, as much of it as was available. To him, the Hebrew scriptures were just fine: heroic tales, primary literature, like the mythology of his own people.

"You will follow my standard, for Jehovah wills it." This standard was modelled on that of Moses, the scriptural personage with whom he most identified: a snake held aloft on a vividly-tinctured rod. Papahurihia's people worshipped on the Hebrew sabbath, Saturday, and not on the Christian Sunday.

Papahurihia had a solid career as a Jewish god. With great relief the government learned that in 1856 he converted to Wesleyan Methodism. Somewhat misreading the story of Jesus of Nazareth and the toll-collector Zacchaeus, the grateful authorities appointed him as a tax assessor.

Home Stay

What can he do to get back to sea? William Hobson has been beached since 1828 and he understands why, but that does not make it any easier. He spends most of his time – oh, there's so much time, and it moves so slowly – with his wife and young family. Now he is paying respects to old family friends in Waterford, and seeing if there are any strings that can be pulled.

Ever since he was commissioned a lieutenant, Hobson had a varied and distinguished career: he served in a naval support group for an invasion of the state of Maine in 1813; was selected to serve in the flotilla that took Napoleon Buonaparte to St. Helena in 1815; was on pirate chasers in the Mediterranean and the West Indies, and was promoted to commander in 1824 and given his own vessel. The problem, however, was that the Royal Navy was shrinking in the late 1820s, and Hobson no longer had any useful patrons.

That was what he was confirming in his melancholy visit to his home city. The Catholics had humiliated the Beresfords in Daniel O'Connell's march toward Catholic Emancipation. The Beresfords still had wealth, but shrinking influence. The archbishop of Armagh was fighting a rearguard action against church reform; the old general was retired and the admiral was now spending all his time playing parliamentary politics and had no time for his old boy-sailor.

Most distressingly, no new godfather was coming to the fore. Hobson learns in Waterford that the present Marquis of Waterford (he is the third Marquis, born in 1811), the natural defender of the Protestant interests in southeastern Ireland, is as profligate as his grandfather, and twice as thick as his father. He is spending his way through the family fortune in Dublin, in London, and on his English and Irish estates in a manner perfectly designed to humiliate the Protestant Ascendancy. That is, unless one considers normal his maintaining one of the world's largest collection of bellpulls and door knockers. Or unless his shooting the eyes out of the portraits of his ancestors is considered balanced. Or, unless his passionate desire to see two train engines crash head-on is viewed as sensible.

In pursuit of the latter diversion, Lord Waterford builds a long piece of track on his estate at Curraghmore, County Waterford, and purchases two steam engines. His wee bit of the apocalypse will be when the two engines, running at full speed, round a corner and crash in front of a viewing platform that he has constructed on the slopes of a gentle hill. As the social event of the year, this is marred only by the trains' speed being unequal, so that the first train appears, makes it all the way past the spectators, only to disappear around the far curve before the other engine is in view.

Evidently the wreck was impressive, but all the Marquis and his guests heard was a loud metallic bong.

William Hobson, who has already had three attacks of yellow fever while in the West Indies, and who consequently suffers from severe migraine headaches, hears these details with intense pain. He spends the next week in a darkened room, with cold compresses as his medication.

LONDON. 18 AUGUST 1834

An I.O.U.

The rehabilitation of Edward Gibbon Wakefield would have made any prison reformer proud. And it brought especial pride to his cousin, the Quaker prison campaigner Elizabeth Fry. In Lancaster Prison Wakefield spent his time teaching his own children their elementary school lessons (they were housed around the corner from the prison) and writing articles and pamphlets on emigration. One of these pieces was picked up by the *Spectator*, and Wakefield was back into his career as a colonizer, even before he was back on the street.

No one has ever described adequately where Wakefield's force came from, but one acquaintance, who advised that the only way to resist Wakefield was to "hate him like the devil," was probably right. He had a power that came from some Faustian covenant. How else is a man, in 1831, less than a year out of prison, a convicted kidnapper and cradle robber, able to bring about the cessation of free land grants in New South Wales? Of course, he used an organizational front as a cat's-paw, but even to put together a body of highly respectable associates to pressure parliament was a piece of black magic.

Wakefield's dark power enabled him to appeal to the worst in the nineteenth-century ruling and middle classes, but to do so in the vocabulary of virtue. Colonies, which previously were going out of fashion – all that pessimism of Bentham and Mill, who said they were expensive – now were to be self-financing. And, to pay for coloniza-tion, land was no longer to be "free" to every rag-tag-and-bobtail who came down the pike. Settlers would pay for land (Wakefield originally suggested £2 an acre, but later shrewdly befogged it by saying the "sufficient price" should be set locally). Thus, only capital-ists could arrive and immediately buy land. The drones would have to spend time in hard labour in the colony before amassing enough money to purchase it. And so, a nice hierarchy of labour exploitation would emerge, all of it justified by the refusal to make colonial land free, which obviously was morally bad for those paupers who wished to emigrate.

KORORAREKA. 24 NOVEMBER 1834

A Decent Arrangement

The missionary of the United Church of England and Ireland is so good that the Anglican communion is known by the place where he serves: it is called by the Maori, "the church of Paihia," to distinguish it from the Wesleyan Methodists.

Henry Williams, the priest in charge of Paihia, is rowing across the bay to choose land at Kororareka for a church. Land had been spoken for by an earlier missionary, but it had never been plotted out or paid for. So the Rev. Mr. Williams is to meet with two Kororareka chiefs, Rewa and Wharerahi, and also with Moka of the Ngai Tawake. The meeting goes well.

And so it should, for Henry Williams is not the usual missionary. Following his father's death, in 1804 he had entered the Royal Navy where he had served, from age fourteen onwards, ten years during the Napoleonic wars. And he came of a Dissenting family, so his ver-sion of Anglicanism was less formal and more democratic than that of most Church Missionary Society pastors.

Site and price having been agreed, the parties cut one further cove-nant: Maori and Pakeha shall have equal rights of burial in the churchyard, an agreement that is honoured until 1970, when the burying ground is filled, and therefore closed.

HOKIANGA, NEW ZEALAND. 21 SEPTEMBER 1835

Self Control

As worldly resumés go, that of Thomas McDonnell, of County Antrim Protestant origin, was average. He'd been around, but had no medals to show for it, just experience. As a young man he had fought in the British navy in the Napoleonic wars. Of middling family, he had been an officer, but of the junior ranks. Like so many Royal Navy officers, he hadn't found any place for his talents in the British Isles during peacetime, so he had joined the East India Company as a ship's captain. He made enough to become owner of his own vessel. His trade was various. The most profitable, albeit risky item, was Chinese opium.

So, his serving as the chair of a meeting demanded by the local Maori required a new attitude on his part. The Maori leaders around Hokianga were becoming worried about European drunkenness being transferred to their own people. They understood social contagion clearly. And, because the Maori were one of the few cultures in the world that had not discovered how to brew alcoholic beverages, the danger was the same, they believed, as smallpox, measles, or tuberculosis.

McDonnell, who since 1831 has been running a trading and timber milling business in Hokianga, is also the deputy British Resident, a title without a stipend, but a bit of local dignity. McDonnell listens gravely as the locals spell out their worries. He keeps his face impassive, but he is impatient: like most Pakeha, it drives him nearly crazy to adapt to the slow and ritualized pace of formal Maori petitioning and debate. God, why don't they just say what they want?

Temperance. Grog control. The searching of all ships that enter the Hokianga. Prohibition on the sale of ardent spirits within the area. That is what they want.

McDonnell appoints two local Pakeha and Moetara Motu Tongaporuta, one of the 1831 petitioners for British protection against the French, as inspectors of all in-coming vessels. As an experienced smuggler himself, McDonnell knows that it won't work: that no one can stop dealers in any trade from selling anything to purchasers who want it. Badly.

PAIHIA. 26 NOVEMBER 1835

Tyndale, Luther, Maunsell

From England, via Sydney, arrives a Church Missionary Society couple who do not look to have staying power. She is very delicate, from the genteel edges of Camberwell, then a London out-village, with leafy meadows, well-maintained carriages and, in summer, flocks of the Camberwell Beauty. He is an Irishman, stooped from too much scholarship, and soft of hand. The seventh son of one of the partners of Maunsell's Bank, Limerick, he traces his roots in Ireland back to the Norman invasion. Susan Pigott and Robert Maunsell.

They are tougher than they look and are excellent missionaries, Susan markedly determined and Robert passionate and absolutely dogged in a dispute. Robert Maunsell has a gift for languages – he won the Hebrew medal at Trinity College, Dublin and honours in classics. His goal is to learn Maori so well that he can compile a complete Maori dictionary and grammar and a full translation of the Old Testament, which the people take to more than the New.

The couple moves to Maraetai at the Waikato Heads and there, besides the usual schools and preaching, Maunsell masters Maori. Not learns a bit of it: masters it. Frequently he gathers around him a group of indigène, especially the older ones, whose tongue has not been corrupted by European usage, and he goes over words and constructions with them. He offers a rope of tobacco to anyone who can catch him in a mistake and convince him that it is indeed an error.

Working only in a rush whare, with an earthen floor and a hole in the wall for a window, Maunsell plows on year after year. In 1842 he is half done with his philological work: his grammar is published. Finally, in July 1843, he and his wife move into a better house. On 21 July it burns and with it are incinerated the materials for Maunsell's dictionary of Maori and his nearly-completed translation of the Old Testament.

He abandons the dictionary but starts again on the Old Testament.

His wife dies in 1851. He remarries, to a missionary lady, in 1852. He keeps toiling at his translation. He is not cheating: he translates from Hebrew directly into Maori.

Finally, in 1857, his Old Testament is in print.

PAIHIA. DECEMBER 1835

Same Coordinates, Different Journeys

When Robert Maunsell and Susan Pigott Maunsell arrived at Paihia, they received less than the usual courtesies from their Church Missionary Society colleagues. A demanding visitor was taking everyone's time. Most of the Anglicans went inland to Waimate with this character, Charles Darwin, who wanted to see how vegetable gardens and orchards fared in this new world. His ship, the *Beagle*, was anchored in the Bay of Islands.

Not much of New Zealand garnered Darwin's approval. As he confided to his diary on 30 December 1835, "I believe we were all glad to leave New Zealand. It is not a pleasant place."

Maunsell stayed, Darwin left. Under the harshest of conditions, Maunsell slaved at his scholarship. Under the softest of conditions, Darwin puttered. In 1857, Maunsell staggered to the finish line, his Old Testament in Maori completed. In 1857, Darwin, pushed momentarily out of his cosseted indolence by friends and, more importantly, competitors, dashed off a sketch of his theory in a letter to Asa Gray.

No one remembers Maunsell, everyone knows Darwin.

Is that really survival-of-the-fittest?

DUBLIN. 1833–36

Vision

He is on his way to being the most unpopular man in the Irish middle and upper classes: Richard Whately, the Church of Ireland's archbishop of Dublin. The country, especially the metropolis, can tolerate his roaring jokes, love of outrageous puns, and a preaching style so variable that he frequently gives sermons with one leg looped outside the pulpit. In the latter instance, he gives the impression of being a ventriloquist's agent, a torso and body that is animated and controlled by the dangling extremity.

No, Dublin is full of truly deep-dish lunatics, and a few ecclesiastical foibles can easily be accepted. The real problem is that many of the clergy of the Anglican communion hate Whately (hate is not too strong a word) because he is cooperating with the only moderate among the Catholic archepiscopate (Daniel Murray of Dublin) and with a sensible Presbyterian clergyman (the Rev. James Carlile) in trying to create a national system of popular education that will not only teach literacy to all Irish children, but will help them to learn toleration. This by their going to school with children of opposite faiths. The Anglican clergy, who still are the servants of an Established Church, denounce Whately for giving up their church's monopoly on state funds. The Catholic clergy denounce Whately's system as a stalking horse for Protestantism. And the Presbyterians see it as a cover for Papacy and all its vices.

Then, in 1833–36, Archbishop Whately brings into agreement the Protestant and the Catholic land-owning classes who had not been together on any issue since they were threatened by the 1798 Rising. He chairs a commission on the state of the Irish poor, one that produces ten volumes of evidence, all systematically collected in a way that would make a modern social scientist proud (Whately had been Drummond Professor of Political Economy in his last years at Oxford). No one in Ireland is more knowledgeable about the poverty of the peasantry than Whately, which is why the landowners come to hate him so deeply. He puts forward the case that one-third of the people of Ireland are destitute, and that they cannot be made whole by the workhouse system. They must be given massive amounts of social aid; public works schemes are essential, and state aid for emigration has to be provided. All this if Ireland is not to be swamped in a tidal wave of poverty, national in scope, permanent in effect.

The landlords will not pay for this and Whately is treated as a naive blow-in from England. He watches sadly and prays that there will not be a famine.

LONDON. DECEMBER 1836

Justifiable Pride

The Irish gentleman naval officer, in his early thirties, occupies the study of his mother's London house. She is Lady Frances Anne Stewart, eldest daughter of the Marquis of Londonderry. Though privileged by birth, Robert FitzRoy is also hard working and talented. He had received the first prize medal at the Naval College and there earned the highest examination marks yet seen. This, and his birth, had led to his receiving his first command in August 1828.

The *Beagle* was an ideal command, the more so because its naturalist had suggested all manner of interesting diversions ostensibly for scientific purposes. If only Charles Darwin were not so lazy!

Thus, Robert FitzRoy works, surrounded by journals, logs, odd bits of papers, writing the Narrative of the *Beagle*. Occasionally Darwin calls in, but the visits always produce the impression that someone left the window open.

In early December, FitzRoy marries Mary Henrietta O'Brien, daughter of a major-general, and keeps on writing. By early the next year two of the volumes are ready, and Darwin completes the third. Fitzroy is deservedly proud to be awarded in 1837 the Gold Medal of the Royal Geographical Society for his achievement.

SAINT JOHN, NEW BRUNSWICK. 9 SEPTEMBER 1837

White Tribes Streaming

Sometimes a pane of glass is a mirror.

Throughout the nineteenth century, alert Pakeha in New Zealand watch apprehensively as Maori tribes make and break alliances; hapu shear off from one tribal group and join another; great leaders come and go; identity, sense of self, changes. This the Pakeha see vaguely, through a distorted and filmy pane of bubble glass.

The same thing is happening to the Pakeha, and they would see it, if only they possessed a mirror. In New Zealand, in North America, in the British Islands, and throughout the Empire, the hapu of the Pakeha are shifting, the tendrils of new connections are interlacing, new tribes being formed out of alliances of old ones.

Take a simple case, a metonym only.

In September 1837 in a wind-blown New Brunswick harbour, a stiff-backed girl, Sarah Macauley, is married before a Justice of the Peace to a widower, a sea captain whose broad, weather-beaten face is a map of the continents he has visited.

A simple event.

She was born in County Londonderry, her parents part of a tiny, willful, unrealistic migration of Presbyterians from Aberdeen who thought to better themselves and didn't. In the mid 1820s, several of the families forming this small hapu moved to New Brunswick.

The litmus-question is: why was Sarah Macauley being married before a JP – that is, in a civil ceremony?

Because she is marrying a Roman Catholic. He, the son of a rebel who had been out in 1798 and had fled to the United States. This rebel's son, Daniel Dougherty, was born in New Orleans, 1804, not long after it became U.S. territory through the Louisiana Purchase. Dougherty has been every kind of seaman in the whaling trade and has risen to ship's master.

The new couple become one particle in the flux of religion, ethnicity, nationality that streams around the globe: a child is born in the Bay of Islands, then they are back to Canada, then to London, then back to New Zealand to an isolated whaling station, finally to Wellington, where Dougherty becomes the master pilot for a difficult, busy harbour.

Nothing unusual really, but impressive certainly. After Daniel's death in 1857, Sarah runs a boarding house in Ghuznee Street, Wellington, and becomes a successful minor capitalist.

Long cross-tribal tendrils: Thomas Arnold the younger, who as a child had played happily in Richard Whately's garden with the Whately children, encounters Sarah in Wellington. He finds her intelligent and well-informed, by standards that are quite high.

HOKIANGA, NEW ZEALAND. 10 JANUARY 1838

Another True Faith

The tall, princely looking man is something New Zealand has not before seen. He steps ashore in black canonicals and a garment that observers take to be an ornate cape. He is attended by seven acolytes and he speaks to them in a language not immediately familiar to the gawking locals.

Jean Baptiste François Pompallier has been sent to organize the Roman Catholic church in New Zealand. Despite his regal bearing, he is a man of great charm and of genuine spiritual humility.

He and his party pass the shipyard of Thomas McDonnell, who, by virtue of his Irish Protestant heritage, knows a Popish demon when he sees one. Pompallier proceeds through the zone of influence of Frederick Maning, Pakeha-Maori, who is also Irish Protestant, but not concerned with the subtleties of European god-politics. The Vicar Apostolic of Western Oceania comes finally to the house of Thomas and Mary Poynton, devout Catholic lay persons. The Poyntons vacate their own cottage. The bishop moves in and immediately turns the cottage into a temporary chapel. He has brought with him a portable altar and on 13 January 1838, mass is first said in New Zealand.

Then Pompallier and his men begin in earnest to learn English and Maori.

QUEBEC CITY, LOWER CANADA. 29 MAY 1838

It's All in the Gaze

Mesmerism: hypnosis. Edward Gibbon Wakefield is a very gifted practitioner. All across the Atlantic he has amused his colleagues and their fellow top deck passengers with hypnosis as a post-prandial entertainment. It is all done in good spirit and Wakefield does not take advantage of his powers.

He arrives in Quebec City in good spirits, indeed, for he is in distinguished company and he has been promised a post as commissioner of Crown lands, a position that will, he believes, allow him to leave an imprint on the better part of a continent. Wakefield is travelling as part of the suite of John George Lambton, first earl of Durham who, following the Canadian rebellions of 1837, has been given virtually tyrannical powers over the Canadas. Durham is a pox doctor to humanity: he is a mixture of extreme aristocratic arrogance and liberal-to-radical political ideals, and thus he has both the answer to all problems referred to him and the rudeness to override even the strongest of objections. Shrewd political observers see him as a likely Whig prime minister.

Great times for Edward Gibbon Wakefield, who is well on his way to being one of the few figures in the Empire who will be better known to later generations than he ought to be.

But before Wakefield can assume his office, Lord Durham receives a letter from the prime minister, Lord Melbourne, who decrees that a convicted felon and child abductor is not to be an official of His Majesty's government. Durham accepts this, but keeps Wakefield on as an unofficial advisor. He accompanies Durham everywhere and he acts the part of someone who indeed has a real appointment. Wakefield views the Canadians as uncivilized and fears that they will be forever backward, since already they have spread too widely on the ground. For civilization to emerge, they would have to be herded together. Sharp control over future grants of Crown lands, combined with heavy taxes on undeveloped lands in private hands might accomplish this, he suggests.

The Durham mission lasts little more than four months before Durham, incensed at being criticized for sending a band of political prisoners off to Bermuda without having them tried first, resigns. The party returns to England and rapidly writes a report covering every big question in the Canadian polity. The parts on land, settlement, and colonization are by Wakefield, although his name never appears.

Indeed, Lord Durham's report almost did not appear. Given to the cabinet in late January 1839, it probably would not have been made public. Except: it began to appear in *The Times*, and thus the government was forced to print the full text.

Question: which mesmerist provided the newspaper with this material?

PLYMOUTH, ENGLAND. 12 FEBRUARY 1839

Two Envelopes

The second envelope is handed by Captain William Hobson to a state messenger. His wife Eliza looks on proudly. It is Shrove Tuesday and Hobson is accepting the first governorship of New Zealand. Admittedly, his official instructions are so muddy that it's hard to tell exactly what he will be. His title, it seems, will be lieutenant-governor and he will report to the governor of New South Wales. He is to keep the peace but he is not provided with any military force and is, in fact, prohibited from raising a militia. Strangest of all, he is to recognize that Maori sovereignty and land titles are indisputable; and yet he is to uphold the Crown's right of land pre-emption.

The first envelope was the one that put Hobson on the trail of this patronage plum, if such it is. In 1834, George Eden, earl of Auckland, became first lord of the Admiralty. He was impressed by Hobson's pleas for a sea command and in mid-1834 offered him the *Rattlesnake*, a vessel of the sort the British Navy used as a work horse, doing the everyday task of Empire. Hobson was so pleased to receive Lord Auckland's letter of appointment that he promised himself never to forget this man: which explains why, when Hobson selects a site for a new city, one that is intended to be the focal point of the North Island, he promises himself that it will be called Auckland.

BAY OF ISLANDS, NEW ZEALAND. MARCH 1839

The Tourist Makes Two Fundamental Observations

In those days, anyone who stayed less than six months was just passing by: a curiosity-seeker. The twenty-four-year-old English botanist, John Carne Bidwell, would have accepted this designation. He has already been to the Canadas and to Australia and now he will spend a little time in New Zealand. For all his flightiness, he is a good botanist and a shrewd social observer. In his diary, he observes two basic fissures in this new world:

There is a terrible dislike amongst the low Europeans generally to the missionaries ... The generality of them are great rascals, runaway convicts, sailors etc, who, with the ordinary rancour of low minds, dislike people superior to themselves in intelligence and respectability.

And:

I can state that I have met with but one person, and never heard of more than four, in all the country, who could speak Maori so perfectly as to be able to ask even the simplest question not connected with their trade, in such a manner as immediately to make the Maoris understand what they said; and the greater part of them, including men who have been many years in the country are incapable of speaking more than a couple of sentences and those not correctly. Of course I do not include the missionaries ...

QUEEN CHARLOTTE SOUND, SOUTH ISLAND.
17 AUGUST 1839

Invasion of the Pod People

The ship, a fast-sailing armed merchantman, the *Tory*, had sailed from Plymouth, England, in a desperate race with the government of the United Kingdom. The New Zealand Company – a joint stock company formed after parliament rejected the colonization schemes of the New Zealand Association – was determined to reach New Zealand and grab as much land as it could before the government's representative, William Hobson, arrived in the country. This was an expensive gamble: a 400-ton vessel, twenty-eight crew members and only eight passengers.

Two of them looked alike, fruit from the same pod, which had ripened at a slightly different rate. Colonel William Wakefield, leader of the party, was the spitting image of his famous brother Edward Gibbon Wakefield. He was a modest height – 5 feet, six inches – but broad as a stevedore, with an enormous head, out of all proportion to his body. His nephew Edward Jerningham Wakefield – the spawn of Edward Gibbon Wakefield's first abduction of an heiress – was a younger copy of the family form. These two intended to be marcher lords, creating a kingdom of Norman proportions. Accompanying them was Colonel Wakefield's valet, and a Maori translator, a botanist, a storekeeper, a surgeon, and a draughtsman-surveyor. After a month getting organized, the party sailed across Cook Strait to Port Nicholson.

Colonel Wakefield did not share the family gene for sharpness, but his nephew more than made up for it. He was calculation, aggressiveness, and tactlessness personified. The two Wakefields negotiated with the Ngati Awa for 1,100 acres of land around the port and for an additional 110,000 acres elsewhere. Colonel Wakefield presided in these negotiations in a somewhat doited, indeed puzzled, fashion, while his nephew worked out the details. The colonel's chief contribution was to ensure that the port would be renamed "Wellington," thus paying off one debt his brother owed to the Iron Duke for his support in creating South Australia, another of Edward's projects.

WAITANGI, NEW ZEALAND. 5 FEBRUARY 1840

Cross Talk

There should have been a mild and common joke, an agreed reference and thus the basis of amity.

All day long, the players had been arriving. Lieutenant Governor William Hobson came early, well before noon, for he wished to show respect to those with whom he was negotiating. The day was dazzlingly fine, and the dories of the Wesleyan and the Church Missionary Society representatives, as they were rowed in from their stations around the Bay of Islands, resembled water beetles skittering to shore. Interspersed among them were Maori canoes, each a throne for a chief. Eventually, the players converged at a large marquee which the British Resident had set on a lawn that had been cropped short by a small flock of ewes. The marquee had flags streaming from each corner, like something from a nineteenth-century re-enactment of a mediaeval tournament. On the lawn, Lieutenant Governor Hobson chatted in English with the Europeans, moving from group to group as if at a garden party. The Maori chiefs squatted in small groups on the ground and watched with a mixture of interest and apprehension the social practices of this foreign tribe. Despite the fineness of the day and the diverting setting, everyone was nervous.

Which is why a mild joke might have helped.

Hobson signalled that he was going inside the marquee and that serious talks would start.

Immediately Jean Pompallier, Roman Catholic bishop of Western Oceania, and his attendant priest swung in behind Hobson. As a long-time veteran of Vatican protocol-wars, Pompallier knew that proximity in these matters was power, and that precedence paid dividends. And, besides, he enjoyed the simple pleasure of forcing the Protestant clergy to walk behind him, sealed off from His Britannic Majesty's chief representative.

"Brethren," William Colenso, printer to the Church Missionary Society, announced, "this will not do ..."

"No," agreed the Rev. Richard Taylor, a CMS missionary, and added, "I will never follow Rome!"

That should have been a nice ironic comment, a light sandpapering of Pompallier's sharp-elbowed behaviour.

The next day, several of the Maori chiefs signed the treaty, but most held back. Bishop Pompallier made a point of being seen to leave the marquee before anyone signed, and he later claimed that he had been neutral: in fact, he had advised against the natives' signing: as did, in later consultation, the two Irish Pakeha-Maori, Frederick Maning (a Protestant) and John Marmon (a Catholic). Eventually, forty-five chiefs signed, and Hobson had various officials and missionaries scour the rest of the North Island and part of the South, explaining the text and gaining more chiefly marks.

Heaven only knows what they thought they were affirming, but it was enough to allow Hobson to proclaim, on 21 May 1840, Crown sovereignty over all of New Zealand. Were the Maori chiefs like the Irish chiefs who met Henry II?: did they believe that any covenant they made was valid only so long as the covenant-maker was in the country? Could the late medieval practice of surrender-and-regrant of lands to the Crown make any sense to the Maori, any more than it had made sense to the inhabitants of Connaught? There were no exact Maori-language cognates for the treaty concepts whose meaning was defined clearly only in the context of English civil law. Even had the translation of the Treaty of Waitangi into Maori been done by the one linguist able to do so – Robert Maunsell, rather than the Henry Williams who fudged the English meanings into baby-talk – it still would have been a phantom.

Treaties, like jokes, require good will and a willingness to draw out commonalities of meanings. Covenants, like conversations, are protean, the meaning of vocabulary, voice and attitude being determined by continual mutual feedback, each party educating the other. That is why any complaint about the Maori- and English-language texts being different is interesting, but epiphenomenal. That is why any attempt to draw out the "original" or "true" meaning of the treaty, as if it were scripture, is to wallow in a culture's juvenilia.

Even in the very best of circumstances, the meaning of the Treaty of Waitangi would not have been made final in February 1840, but only have been defined in embryo. Every living covenant is drawn anew every day and is outlined in the future and articulated in the present.

The treaty: for the two cultures, it should have been a mild and common yoke, an agreed reference for covenantal conversation, and thus the basis of comity. Should.

Names

The first abstract mental function that disappears when a person has a cerebral stroke is the ability to find names. That is why someone who has had a stroke, though apparently physically recovered, often has a vexed and disconcerted look, as if shuffling through a deck of index cards that are smudged and out of order.

On board the *Herald*, which was making a preliminary survey for a new town, William Hobson felt pins-and-needles in his right arm and leg. He assumed that one of his periodic migraine headaches was in train, and he went to his cabin and took a heavy dose of laudanum. The migraine did not follow. Instead, his vision blurred, his tongue seemed to bloat and turn itself into blotting paper. His entire right side lost its ability to follow his orders. An invisible plane had bisected his body, incapacitating one side, leaving the other untouched. Using his left arm and leg, Hobson levered himself into a sitting position and called for help. His voice was that of a man wrapped in a heavy winter scarf.

For nine days a series of strokes marched across his brain, reaching a climax on the first of March. Then they stopped.

William Hobson was no giant of body (he was a slender, smallish man, as if designed for life in the cramped confines of a Royal Navy vessel) nor was he a towering intelligence. However, he had an immense reservoir of character: in his pirate-hunting days in the West Indies he had once been taken prisoner, and, rather than give up a ring with his family crest upon it, had had his ring finger almost amputated. Now, Hobson teaches himself to write, to walk, to think. It is a ceaseless task, for each small victory opens the door to another dragon to be slain. Hobson is perpetually exhausted by the effort and he cries a lot, but only when he is alone. He uses a diary as his barometer-of-progress, and the entries take the form of an extended letter to his wife who, with his children, is in Sydney, New South Wales.

Although Hobson never recovers full strength, he rapidly recovers command of all his mental abilities and also his command of the New Zealand mission. He is especially pleased when full and immediate recognition of names is again at his call and recall.

Now, indeed, naming things gives him the greatest pleasure. Especially new names. In April he ratifies the purchase of a block of land from an early Pakeha settler and sets up a new government station in the Bay of Islands. It is called Russell, after Lord John Russell, now colonial secretary under Lord Melbourne. In September he formally names the site where New Zealand's capital will sit, Auckland. This recognizes his patron, who is now governor-general of India. He is able to permit himself an ironic smile when he learns that the directors of the New Zealand company in November 1840 had renamed Port Nicholson, in honour of Wellington: beat them to the punch. And when, in May 1841, a Royal charter was proclaimed, giving New Zealand a government of its own, separate from New South Wales, Hobson was sworn in as governor and commander-in-chief of a colony that according to the charter was to have its components renamed. The three islands – North, South, and Stewart – were henceforth to be called, respectively, New Ulster, New Munster, and New Leinster.

AUCKLAND, NEW ZEALAND. 8 SEPTEMBER 1841

Fosterage Survives

Fosterage as an Irish form continued long after the Gaelic aristocracy were broken. As a survival practice, it spread (as did so many aristocratic social customs) downward into the peasantry. And, like a drop of oil in a bowl of water, it covered a large surface; the practice was not limited by religion or geography.

No one could have known by looking at him that James Dilworth, a long, weedy, twenty-six-year-old in a brought-from-abroad tweed suit was the product of fosterage. He stood, silently and extremely attentively, watching the second auction of lots held in Captain Hobson's new capital, Auckland. He had a great memory for figures and could keep the entire auction in his head. He did so for a full year, and during that time he collected information on how much each lot brought when it was resold. Dilworth took a day job as an accountant, but his mind was always on speculation. In 1842 he bought his first block.

James Dilworth was the sock into which an entire family put its social capital, and that is what fosterage had become to the Irish tenantry. His family in Ireland ran back to land hungry seventeenth-century Quakers who, despite their late nineteenth- and twentieth-century image as meek-and-mild, were among the most rapacious land grabbers in Ireland, Papists not being human beings in their books. By the late eighteenth century, his branch of the Dilworths were Anglican and concentrated in County Tyrone, small-to-strong tenants, but no more. James, who was good with a plough, probably would have spent his life walking behind one, had not his father's unmarried cousin, a woman holding thirty-six acres of good land on a long lease, offered to bring James up. This was genuine fosterage, plus family-survival, for this female cousin ran the land with her two brothers as her junior partners. So, from eight years of age onwards, James was fostered by a family collective, and they sent him to Dungannon Royal School, where he boarded. And then the family paid his way to the New World of his choice. These people, looking at rural Ireland in the late 1830s, knew that the future was limited for a bright lad and for almost everyone else, for that matter.

Irish fosterage, because it had become invisible by the nineteenth century (no poets remained to celebrate its tangled glories), is a social arrangement – an effect – that is rarely noticed. Even less so is fosterage as a cause of some Irish person's later behaviour. Take James Dilworth who, incidentally, all his life refused to do what so many Irish Protestants did and mumble that he was British. He was proudly and ecumenically Irish. Dilworth was one of his generation's great men of business. Yet, he remembered who he was and how he came to be. So, when he was doing his final accounts, death approaching, he created the Dilworth Ulster Institute Trust. Its purpose was to board and educate bright boys whose families were in tight circumstances.

THE LOWER HUTT VALLEY, NORTH ISLAND,
NEW ZEALAND. FEBRUARY 1843

Long Wait

Neither of the neighbouring slab whares is large enough to hold the congregation.

Father O'Reilly, an Irish Capuchin, has appeared almost magically in Wellington. He was sent by Lord Petre, a director of the New Zealand Company, and he arrives without either the permission or, indeed, the knowledge of Bishop Pompallier. He is thirty-seven years old, well educated and an experienced pastor. Wisely, Pompallier permits him to serve. Father O'Reilly's first mass is in a waterfront hotel. Nearly 100 persons attend.

Now he is ministering in the Hutt Valley, where there are twenty Catholics and a good deal of catching up to do. Members of three separate families, twenty children have yet to be baptized. They are offspring of new Irish *perigrini*, now composed of lay persons who travel any and every place in hope of a decent livelihood. These three families had fetched up in Scotland where they did Paisley weaving, a high skill that slipped ever lower in demand as machinery displaced handwork. No priest had been in their town, and none of the childer had been received into the Faith.

Father O'Reilly decides to use the nearby river as the Jordan. He takes all twenty children down to its banks and there he sprinkles them in the name of the Father, Son, and Holy Ghost.

NEWRY, COUNTY ARMAGH, 29 SEPTEMBER 1838

Women. Family

The army of the Second British Empire made a great deal of family and of women, albeit in a strange way. John O'Hara, not-quite eighteen years old, understands this. He goes through the ritual of accepting into his hand the Queen's Shilling from the recruiting sergeant, but unlike most of the other strapping farm lads, he has a father who had been a Redcoat. So he has been tutored in the ways of the military: how to stay out of trouble, how to call attention to one's virtues, and where the edge lies and the quiet privileges are hidden.

The families of Irish small farmers, just as much as those of the Anglo-Irish gentry, had traditions of using the military as a means of keeping family together; these are rarely recorded, because little of individual peasant life was recorded in any way – and after the Irish revolution, the oral memory of these family traditions was quietly silenced. Young John O'Hara has no doubt about the whole business. He's well aware that he's not just getting the Queen's Shilling. He receives the full fifty shillings from the sergeant that a good recruit commands. And almost exactly a year later, when the annual swing of the recruiting sergeant comes again to Newry, Patrick O'Hara,

John's younger brother, joins the same regiment. He's a canny lad and picks up an extra penny a day for being able to beat a drum competently. That doubles his daily beer money.

The scarlet jacket is as handsome an infantryman's uniform as ever was created and John O'Hara loves it. Because he has been tutored by his father, his pleasure in the uniform is not diminished by the heavy garment's high, neck-chaffing collar, nor the board-like quality of the cloth. Just as well: the enlistment papers he has signed are for fifteen years. The Fifty-Eighth Foot spend the first five years of John's enlistment guarding military depots in Ireland and England: not high adventure. Then, in 1843, the regiment is sent to the far side of the world. In retrospect, it is not a bad time to be leaving Ireland.

Guarding convicts being transported to Norfolk Island is John and brother Patrick's first foreign duty. Then to Parramatta, Australia, where the 58th is created a special detail to search out bushrangers and to put down any civil unrest. Interesting tasks, real men's work. The intriguing point is that their mother and sister join them in Australia under a military-passages arrangement for wives and family. The two women stay in the Parramatta complex for a time. Then, when the regiment is shipped to New Zealand in 1845 to suppress a Maori uprising, the women follow, at government expense.

Eventually, sister Mary dies of an unknown disease, brother Patrick becomes a drunk, mother Margaret acquires two freehold lots and settles in Auckland, and John, discharged from the army with a spotless record in 1852, marries a twenty-one year-old from County Cavan.

Bishop Pompallier himself performs the marriage.

CUTTERS' BAY WHALING STATION.
SOUTH ISLAND. 18 JUNE 1843

Location

"Go outside," she tells the young Maori man who has stumbled, exhausted, into her three-roomed slab house.

Sarah Macauley Dougherty presides with Presbyterian solemnity over a community that is visited frequently by every kind of fornicator, atheist, and rough-neck who sails. Her husband, Captain Daniel

Dougherty, has established his own whaling station, a mixture of trading post and abattoir. His physical strength and force of personality keep the station from falling into anarchy, but it is Sarah who raises it above the threshold of civilization.

"You must excuse me, Colonel," she tells her guest. "I shall deal with this." She steps outside with the sort of authority one associates with large castles and harsh, cheerless moors.

"Now, you: what do you ..." She moves into a slanguage made of English, Maori, American, and a bit of French, the transitory creole of the shore-workers of the whaling station. As the only European woman in Cutters' Bay, she has spent enough time with the Maori consorts of the shore workers to be able to understand, if not speak, idiomatic Maori. She pales as she hears the message that is being relayed. A careful person, she has the information repeated twice before she lets the exhausted messenger slide to the ground. She does not offer him any aid.

Inside, Captain Dougherty and Colonel William Wakefield continue to smoke their pipes. They pride themselves on being unflappable men of the world, and between them they have seen most of it and done most things twice that few men do once. Colonel Wakefield, a younger brother of Edward Gibbon Wakefield, had spent his three years in Lancaster prison for helping his brother to kidnap Ellen Turner, and then had served in the Portuguese army, where he was knighted for bravery. Then he went into the Spanish service, where he became a lieutenant colonel. Like his older brother, he was rehabilitated and then some. Even so, it was extremely convenient that his wife had died while he was in prison: for their marriage had come about through his forcibly abducting her, not long before his older brother tried the same trick with his heiress. A gentleman does not wish to be reminded of such youthful indiscretions.

Sarah Dougherty re-entered the small house and immediately held out her hand in a grand duchess's gesture. "Colonel, you have my deepest sympathy."

He looked up, puzzled, a condition he had frequently been in since taking up his post in 1839 as the Principal Agent of the New Zealand Company.

"Your brother's death will be a loss to us all, "she continued. "Would you like more tea?" Sarah added, as if she had just brought word of a change in the weather.

The colonel started to remark, or to question, but then thought better of it. Sarah, recognizing that she was being unnecessarily cryptic, explained. "Your brother, the Captain. He was killed yesterday at Wairau."

Captain Arthur Wakefield, agent of the New Zealand Company at Nelson, was a legitimate captain: he held that rank in the Royal Navy. And he was the only one of his immediate family who could be left in a room with decent silverware. He had retired from the Mediterranean command of the Royal Navy in 1841 and was brought into the family project, the colonization of New Zealand. He and twenty-one other Pakeha were massacred while trying to enforce a warrant against two Maori chiefs, one of whom was Te Rauparaha, whom no one sane approached without either large gifts or larger ordnance.

"Why Arthur?" Colonel Wakefield asks.

"Family ties?" Sarah suggests. She has Macbeth in the back of her mind.

"Doubt that," the colonel replies and then falls silent. It takes this bullock of a man several weeks to realize that Captain Dougherty's wife is right, although for the wrong reason. Arthur Wakefield had become ensnared in the Wairau disaster because the Europeans believed, wrongly, that lands had been purchased from Te Rauparaha by Colonel Wakefield.

Purchases of this consequence were something that a competent principal agent would have defined precisely.

"Pity about Arthur," Colonel Wakefield concludes, before moving the conversation to other topics.

KAUAERNGA, NORTH ISLAND. 1844

Fond Memories

The Pakeha call the stooped chief Old Hooknose. It is an affectionate term, for he has been patron, first, to the American trader William Webster and later to the traders and timber workers who followed. Now, in his late eighties, he likes to reminisce. His memories are hopes for the future, expressed in terms of a rose-tinted past. Te Horeta, a leader of the Ngati Whanaunga, has ever been an optimist. Maori and Pakeha can and will live in peace. He has always believed that.

Frequently he retells his favourite memory, a tale that now is burnished like a copper bowl that has been passed from hand to hand so frequently that it shines of its own accord. This memory is of his meeting Captain James Cook, and it was a real event. The tale has acquired great power, because Te Horeta is the only person now alive in New Zealand, Maori or Pakeha, who met Cook.

The memory gives Te Horeta a soft warm glow, similar to the warmth he gets from the thick dark rum his trader clients bring to him. As a lad of twelve, he saw Cook's expedition enter Mercury Bay in November 1769. Terrified at first, he and some other children eventually overcome their fright and accept Cook's invitation to scramble aboard the *Endeavour*. The high chief, Cook, is kind to them.

Te Horeta, in passing on this memory, always emphasizes the blessing that came from Cook. The great captain gave to the Ngati Whanaunga seed potatoes and in a few years they were part of the people's diet.

In the vicinity of Sir Walter Raleigh's old estate, near Youghal in the far south of Ireland, a similar story is told, albeit with less historical accuracy: that Raleigh introduced the potato into Ireland. Like Te Horeta's story, it is an analgesic, a suggestion that an invader could produce a blessing and an implication that the gods had not yet totally turned their backs on their people.

WELLINGTON, NEW ZEALAND. LATE JUNE 1844

Clearing the Deck

Governor William Hobson, weak, but able to look a snake in the eye, had visited Wellington in August 1841. There, the ship *Victoria* at his back, he had stayed in a waterfront hotel and forced the locals to come to him. Colonel Wakefield, accompanied by his nephew, Edward Jerningham Wakefield, was punctilious about recognizing the sovereignty of the United Kingdom over their settlement. The colonel even flew the Union Jack over his own house and he had several of the flags placed strategically along the shore line. That was as far as civility went. Hobson objected to the spread of satellite settlements, and the Wakefields ignored him – with fatal effects in the case of Arthur Wakefield in the South Island.

Hobson died of yet-another stroke in September 1842, and the Wakefields did not mourn.

His successor, another Irishman of naval experience, Captain Robert FitzRoy, of Darwin's *Beagle*, harassed the Wakefields like a ferret down a drain. FitzRoy was a dead loss as a national administrator, but he knew how to chase down enemies. His view of the increasingly crapulous Edward Jerningham Wakefield was that, in his dealing with the Maori on land, he was "the devil's missionary."

Meanwhile, Colonel William Wakefield, while still large of voice and leonine of head, was losing some of his credibility, not least because of the way his own incompetence had led to his brother Arthur's death. And his boon drinking companion, Michael Murphy, chief police magistrate of Wellington, took up defending Maori rights, was detected cheating at cards, and was found in bed with the wife of one of his constables, the first of these three sins being mortal.

Recognizing that the Wellington beachhead had expanded as far as it could go in the face of official opposition, Edward Jerningham Wakefield shipped home in June 1844, there to seek his charismatic father's aid. He was by now a prodigious drinker and stayed virtually unconscious all the way to Valparaiso, Chile.

KORORAREKA, NORTH ISLAND. 8 JULY 1844

The Lads Have a Pissing Contest

The classical Maori tongue – that is, the early nineteenth-century language, before it was corrupted by extensive loan words from English – was formal, stylized, and elegant. It lacked, however, the power of trashtalk which distinguishes English from virtually every other demotic tongue, save Irish, from which the English took lessons in slag. In particular, Maori lacked the plastic idioms of shoulder-shrugging resignation that are employed when someone is either about to do something irrevocable or, alternately, to walk away and not do something irrevocable. Phrases such as "ah, fuck it."

Hone Heke, a young Nga Puhi chief, decided to distinguish himself from all his rivals and to put a finger in the eye of Pakeha officialdom as well. Before daybreak on 8 July 1844, he and a band of young warriors climbed through dense bush to the top of a hill that overlooked the sheebeen- and sharp-trade town of Kororareka. There, Governor FitzRoy had erected a flagpole and there the Union flag hung, slack in the pre-dawn stillness. The flagpole had no strategic significance and was unguarded. Hone understood that it was a symbolic ornament, nothing more: but not any less meaningful for that. Symbols count, especially those that implicitly proclaim overlordship.

Hone and his men took turns pissing on the flagpole and then they chopped it down.

Had any other naked, branchless tree in the forest been felled, Governor FitzRoy could have ignored it. FitzRoy, despite his navy background, was a pacific man. He was a devout adherent of the evangelical wing of the United Church of England and Ireland and in part he owed his appointment in New Zealand to Church Missionary Society influences: the missionaries believed the Maori were being hard done by and wanted a governor who would not slice every tort to suit the taste of the colonizers.

Still, FitzRoy had to do something, for both he and Hone implicitly agreed on what the game was.

Hone took to being transported around the islands in a canoe that flew from its stern the Stars and Stripes.

FitzRoy began to assemble a militia (his powers as governor were severely restricted in that regard), and Hone calculated that an apology was in order on his part. He had some ambiguous words written in his name and promised to replace the flag pole.

This he did, but in a manner that was brilliantly defiant. He and his band found the straightest, tallest specimen they could, then felled and peeled it and by brute force brought it through the bush, up several hundred feet to the top of Flagstaff Hill. The Lord giveth, Hone seemed to say.

Then, after the soldiery had erected the pole and put the Jack upon it, Hone and his men waited until it was time for them to again piss on the pole and chop it down. The Lord taketh away, Hone seemed to say.

Governor FitzRoy, a mild-mannered man in an unmannerly situation, had to do something. He offered a £100 reward for Hone's capture.

Hone, in turn, offered a £100 reward for the governor's capture.

Meanwhile, the damnable flag pole had to go back up and in January 1845 a detachment of thirty soldiers and a band of Maori who were allied with the government put up a third flagpole. This one was sheathed in iron and it was guarded.

Hone, alone, moved through the bush on Flagstaff Hill and through the pickets surrounding the flag. He considered his tactics for a moment and then moved to the guy-wires that served as backstays, keeping the pole upright. It was at that instant, when the richness of the English language would have been a benison: "ah, fuck it."

He chopped through one of the three taut backstays and the pole came down as if it had been shot from a catapult. Hone walked into the bush and became invisible.

Poor FitzRoy. His fourth flagpole was guarded by a blockhouse and below that installation was another blockhouse that incorporated a gun battery and had a potentially devastating field of fire. No one was getting this flagpole.

Except Hone. He effected an alliance with another chief, who diverted the guards and while the soldiers were chasing these false attackers, Hone and his warriors performed their by-now familiar ritual micturition on the flag pole and crashed it to earth.

Then, bored with pissing around, they burned most of the town of Kororareka. Hone exhibited his control even in doing this. He drew a line in the dirt where the destruction was to stop: he preserved both the Catholic and the Anglican churches.

DUBLIN. OCTOBER 1845

More Chopping

A casual visitor to "Redesdale," the residence outside Dublin of the Lord Primate of Ireland, would have mistaken the man with an axe for a workingman. In fact, it was the archbishop, Richard Whately, and he battered away at a beech tree with an energy and work-rate that made it clear he was not doing this for a living: he was putting too much into it. Dropping a large tree was one of Whately's favourite ways to clear his heart of his own anger and his head of someone else's bad ideas.

Whately had just spent a long morning, a slow luncheon, and an afternoon with two men, one of whom he loathed, the other he admired. The one he admired was Samuel Hinds, a prebendary of St. Patrick's cathedral in Dublin and Whately's domestic chaplain.

Whately and Hinds were intimates from the days when Hinds was under Whately's tutorship at Oxford. There the two had spend many hours informally, walking the river, Whately in a long white coat and Hinds dressed completely in black: they came to be known as the White Bear and the Black Bear. Hinds, like another of Whately's protegées, John Henry Newman, served for a time as vice principal of St. Alban's Hall, Whately's project in academic slum clearance. Hinds was a fine logician and good pastor and was on his way to becoming bishop of Norwich.

Hinds's abilities and good will made his blindness on the big issue especially vexing to the archbishop.

That big issue was emigration and the state of Ireland. It was splitting the two men because of their visitor: as an emissary of his father, Edward Jerningham Wakefield had been sent to Dublin. His task was to sell what his father called a "Church of England settlement" in New Zealand. Whately carried a good deal of influence on the emigration question and his help in the House of Lords would be valuable. The archbishop remained politely distant for as long as he could, but when Hinds started to take the hook, Whately became the coldly logical don, a side of his personality he tried to keep hidden when being pastoral.

"Do you not see what is happening in the countryside?" he asks Hinds, and himself answers, "The people are digging black potatoes."

"Surely that must pass, Archbishop."

"Surely, but when?" No one in Ireland foresees that this is the first of four years of famine, but already invitations are out for a Mansion House conference in Dublin, at month's end, to assay the damage. In London, Sir Robert Peel is gathering information on the price of maize in the American market. Whately continues. "The one thing I know for certain from heading the Poor Law investigation is that one-third of our people are close to starvation every year. How many more this year?"

"Indeed, Archbishop, but what has this to do with a Church of England colony half-way across ... "

"Our major premise, Hinds, is that the Irish people are close to starvation; our minor premise, Hinds, is that large scale emigration, funded by government and landlords could reduce the misery." Whately turns to Edward Jerningham Wakefield, whose massive head seems to sit like a bust of some second-line Roman emperor, smug, immobile. "Therefore the idea of supporting a settlement in New Zealand that severely limits the number of the peasantry it will accept, and which, indeed, wants few Irish and no Irish Catholics, is a violation of your and my duty as pastors." Whately glares at Wakefield. "In fact, to do so would be an immorality."

That was his view and six hours of honeyed words from Wakefield and genteel nudging from Hinds did not move him. Whately remained civil, but when the two visitors left, he was a coiled spring.

He chopped away until nightfall. Then, soaking wet with perspiration, his hands raw, he returned to the episcopal palace and, briefly, tried to pray.

PEBBLES IN GOD'S HAND.
POLYNESIA
1830–1845

Dancing Fool

Just as the Word was brought to the South Pacific, so, in counter-current, word of the Pacific was carried to the British Isles.

Observe one of these messengers, now on Ponape, one of the Caroline Islands. He places a set of worn logs, flat on top, on the beach and then he tries to clog dance for a visitor, the captain of the *Spy*. James O'Connell is a terrible dancer, but desperately energetic. He and a mate, another Irishman, George Keenan, have been here for three years. They have been on various island beaches since 1820 and this is the best place they have found. It's paradise, he tells the visiting American captain and his crew: food easily available, women easily obtainable, and the local chiefs prize white men and fight over their ownership. Paradise or not, the two Irishmen want to leave.

By his dancing O'Connell is demonstrating how, when he and Keenan arrived as escapees from the world of Australian prisons, he had mesmerized the native chiefs and thus saved their own lives. Ponape had been a great place, he tells the captain, but now at least thirty white beachcombers have joined them: escaped criminals, mutineers, lunatics. The whites in this little Pacific world are a lot more frightening than are the natives.

The American captain slips the two Irishmen aboard his vessel and sails quietly away.

O'Connell spends the rest of his life exhibiting his native tattoos, dictating a book on his adventures, and lecturing. The high point of his lecture is when he shows how his dancing saved his life.

Never included is mention that he left a wife and two children behind.

Sometimes when he is dancing, however, he recalls that his son would be of the age to submit to the Ponapian puberty ritual of having one testicle crushed. When that enters O'Connell's mind, he dances faster and faster.

NGATANGIIA, RAROTONGA, THE COOK ISLANDS. 1834

It's Not Simple

Few missionaries were more than two steps from a nervous collapse, and throughout Polynesia, the leading problem was sin: the native peoples affirmed Christianity with an alacrity that was unsettling, yet they did not evince any sense of sin-against-God. The missionaries mastered the several indigenous languages required, but everywhere the frustration was the same: the tongues had no concept for the aching sense of inadequacy and the guilt for betrayal of Jehovah that the missionaries themselves felt. Could these people really be Christians? Was our work all a sham, a delusion set before us by the Arch Deceiver? Long sleepless nights were lost as these thoughts skittered across the atolls and volcanic islets of the South Pacific, affecting only Papaa who served Jesus.

One trick – oh, is it a trick? Lord forgive us if that is all we are doing – was to start an inner-church. On Rarotonga this was called an "Eklasia," a word hobbled together from bad Greek and incomprehensible Rarotongan. Formed in 1833 by the Rev. Mr. Pitman, it had ten members. (One of them was Maretua, whose family had been declared Christian by his father soon after the apostle Papehia had appeared.) These ten at least seemed to have a sense of sin and of God's forgiveness of it through Jesus-Tangaroa. Pitman sent them throughout the island, inculcating guilt, remorse, relief and redemption, and perhaps they made some progress in undermining the primordial innocence of their compatriots.

A more effective means was shame. That was the Polynesian instrument of social control and its operation explained why there was no need for police before the Papaa arrived. If there were no sense of guilt before God, at least fear of being shamed before one's fellows could produce the same results. So, early on, John Williams convened a meeting of the ariki and the white and brown missionaries and together they agreed to promulgate some new laws:

– no idols. This caused surprisingly little problem in its enforcement.
– only one wife per each male. Here was grinding of teeth and tears, for the men loved their wives and the second and third wives did not understand why Jehovah did not want them to have a high-status male protector.

– no eating raw fish. The Rarotongans could not for the life of them understand what this was about, but the missionaries read to them a long paraphrase of the book of Leviticus, and this made it clear that Jehovah cared a lot about proper food, even if the Papaa could not tell a crustacean from a piscine.

– And avoid gluttony. This, like the raw-fish proviso, was an imposition of English taste, not divine will, for the missionaries were offended by the girth cultivated by the children of the aristocracy, especially, the cracking of the skin as the fattest – and thus the fairest – grew ever larger.

To all this and more the ariki agreed, and their subjects accepted, with the reservation that Jehovah's time might be better spent than in worrying about the small details.

Thus arise both police and also the most pivotal moral moment in the post-contact history of the Cook Islands. One of the informers at Ngatangiia (probably Maretua, who was now serving there as a deacon), reports that Pori, the chief of the place, has taken back one of his former wives. His justification is that he had believed the prohibition on multiple wives was only temporary and if he had known it was permanent he would have considered his selection more carefully.

Tribal war almost follows, for the primary wife goes back to her own people, powerful aristocrats, who jeer at Pori. Nevertheless he decides to avoid war and goes back to monogamy.

Momentarily: but as solace, he soon takes two more wives. This time the Rev. Mr. Pitman intervenes. He sends five deacons and the chief judge of the new law code to Ngatangiia. They travel in Pitman's boat, a nice bit of intimidation. They say three prayers while at sea and a fourth as they arrive in the harbour. People from all over the island are on hand, for this is an amazing moment: never in this history of the island has an ariki been judged before the law: always, previously, judgements were the personal power of the chief.

Pori is treated respectfully – the visitors accept his food – but he is lectured at great length about King Saul and the other kings of Israel and shown that when they did not obey Jehovah, they experienced calamities. "The same will happen to you. God will abandon you if you abandon him."

The chief judge then pronounces a fine.

Pori accepts it.

The people of Ngatangiia grieve and wail. No ariki has ever been so shamed and if he deserves the shame, then it is theirs to share.

They run to their houses and bring out their own treasures to pay their chief's fine.

A master-moment, one that is repeated over and over on the various islands: abstract law comes to stand outside personality and, therefore, the strong are subservient to it. Unlike *tapu*, it is supposed to apply evenly, to everyone.

Not simple, though. The shrewder missionaries understand that controlling the native leaders by shame pinions the missionaries themselves on a wheel that could spin out of control. In this era the chiefs own the missionaries; but, since Jehovah owns everyone and the Papaa missionaries are his messengers, then the missionaries can direct the behaviour of the chiefs, subject to the limit that the chiefs own the missionaries and can destroy them at any moment.

Ah, the nightmares. Across the South Pacific, white missionaries share a common night-vision, one that arises like an archtype. They see themselves far off-shore on a fast-sailing outrigger canoe. The boat is running down wind dangerously fast, and is doing so on the curl of a massive wave. The canoe moves so swiftly under these conditions that its stern creates a white swirl. Cavitation. The spiralling formation of brief bubbles of life-supporting oxygen is followed almost instantly by the collapse of these vapour pockets through the force of the deep blue Pacific as it rushes past.

UPOLU, THE SAMOAN ISLANDS. 1835

More Powerful Than the Fire Stick

"Joe Gimlet" his shipmates on small island-trading vessels called him. In his native Samoa, he was "Siovili," and a very shrewd man he was. He understood that the power of the Europeans was not in their guns, their iron, their clothes, but in their knowledge. The Pa'plagi had a useful god and an even more useful secret: they knew how to store words so that the words thundered on and on even after the speakers' voices were still.

Siovili saw the people's thirst for a new god and for the new power that was bound up in sheets of paper. So, he gave it to them, founding a Christian-manqué sect that lasted for three decades. Like the missionaries, he held services and healed the sick. Like the white angels of god, he built churches. All this he had seen done on various islands he had visited in his coasting career.

He did well, the more so because he knew that he had to have a box of words, stored between covers. These he possessed in the form of a bound number of *The Rambler*, decades old. This he would raise with vigour whenever he needed to make an especially important point; Siovili had seen plenty of white missionaries and could mimic them perfectly.

His flock knew that this word-box was power and they respected him for owning it. Even more were they convinced of Siovili's spiritual authority when he traded *The Rambler* to a British naval officer for a copy of *Treatise on Railroads* which had a deep crimson cover and therefore much enhanced sacramental power.

RAROTONGA, THE COOK ISLANDS. 1838

Metonym

Sitting on the thatched veranda of his house, pages of precious foolscap by his side, an English text before him, the Rev. Aaron Buzacott feels full peace. He has put the Gospel of Matthew and St. Paul's First Letter to the Corinthians into Rarotongan, and now he has time to do something less demanding, though still serious. He polishes Watts's *Scripture Catechism* so that it can be used here in the Cook Islands and, because it is in an easy question-and-answer form, it will, he believes, be imitated all over Polynesia.

Now that he is a veteran missionary and has had the opportunity to talk with others who have laboured for the Lord's harvest, he has become convinced that all of the South Pacific will respond to writing on paper more fervently than to spoken words: not at once, but when it comes time to obtain true lifetime commitments from the natives.

So, as a parable, he has written to the secretary of the London Missionary Society at home, embodying this truth.

Every few months, he tells the London people, a ship calls at Rarotonga and we receive communications from home. It is a great moment for the entire island and it has become a badge of honour for one of the local young men to be chosen to bring to us our mail. The natives choose among themselves, and often the young man selected cannot read or write.

It is touching, Buzacott reports, to see the admixture of reverence and curiosity with which the letters are carried to us. The youths are greatly puzzled as to how letters allow Europeans to communicate with each other without making a sound. "Yesterday, I observed two youths intercept our letter carrier. They all held the envelope to their ears to see if they could hear the contents."

MANGAIA, THE COOK ISLANDS. 1839

Market Conditions

Maretua, now in his mid-thirties, is finally given his own charge. For years he has been the acolyte of the Rev. Mr. Pitman and he knows he is ready to step into his own mission, even if this is intended to be only temporary. Mangaia, from a spiritual viewpoint, is in trouble. Davida, its heroic early godspeaker, is old and the Tahitian teachers that have been sent to help him are fighting among themselves. A strong new force is needed.

The Rev. Mr. Pitman, unwilling to let full control of his protégé lapse, tells Maretua that he must go alone. However, the Rev. John Williams, in the last months of his foredoomed life, is kinder. "Where's your wife?" he inquires.

"I'm told that she is not allowed to go."

Williams is the ranking missionary. "Take your wife and child," he tells Maretua. "You never know what could happen."

Maretua and his family march up the beach at Mangaia with two large boxes. These are to be the source of his power on the island. In one of them are separately bound copies, small tracts really, of the books of Matthew and of Acts. These have been available since 1831, when John Williams fully cracked the Rarotongan language.

Williams, Buzacott, and Pitman have been labouring away at the New Testament and they print it piece by piece. Now, the full edition just completed, Maretua is given as armament the full Christian scriptures in Rarotongan. These fill his second box.

The language of Mangaia is not the same as that of Rarotonga, but it is a lot closer to Rarotongan than to Tahitian. So, Maretua's first task is to fight an early and miniature version of the Latin-Vernacular war of the Reformation. The Tahitian missionaries try to keep services in Tahitian, which they hold to be a sacred language. Maretua, amiable and able to drop into the Mangaian tongue with ease, charms the people and shows them how closely Jesus-Tangaroa spoke to their own tongue.

Sales of scripture are not merely brisk, but almost violent. The Acts of the Apostles and the Gospel of Matthew each go for six lengths of fishing net. The entire New Testament costs many times more and is paid for in tara starch, netting, bark-cloth. All these things are sent back to Rarotonga, where, in turn, they are transhipped by the LMS missionaries and sold. Maretua's entire stock of holy literature goes quickly.

The same holds all over those of the Cook Islands that understand the Rarotonga dialect, Aitutaki, Mitiaro, Mauke, Atiu, as well as Mangaia and, of course, Rarotonga. Near the end of his life, the Rev. Aaron Buzacott reflected on this moment. Five thousand copies of the New Testament had been sold in the Cook Islands almost overnight. This was "the first grant made by the Bible Society to the heathen, the complete cost of which was repaid by the natives into the coffers of the society."

And, he added, the pattern was soon followed in many other places in Polynesia. In the train of Bible-owning came literacy. On Mangaia much of the teaching was done without benefit of paper, pens or ink. The people learned to write on sand and on fronds.

So successful is Maretua's tour of duty on Mangaia that when he went on mission business to Rarotonga in February 1841, the Mangaians sent a deacon to accompany him to ask the white missionaries to let Maretua be their permanent pastor. And the islanders kept his wife and son as hostages: in "safekeeping," as they termed it. The Papaa missionaries accepted the local will and Maretua served the Mangaians until mid-1845, when a white missionary replaced him. That, of course, was the sign that he had fully succeeded.

APIA, UPOLU, THE SAMOAN ISLANDS. 1839

The Royal Palm

The first printing press comes ashore in Apia, Samoa and the whole settlement rings with shouting and traditional songs of welcome. The machine is treated as if it is a visiting chieftain and a canopy of royal palm leaves is constructed for it. Warriors carry it up the surf and then into the village; they carry it high on their shoulders, just as if it is a visiting dignitary.

The brand name of the press is "Albion."

The missionaries set up shop and each day permit a few selected natives to watch as the lead type is put in place, the paper inserted, the big printing blocks screwed down upon the pieces of paper. The watchers report faithfully to those outside and the entire island of Upolu knows how the work is progressing.

Waka songs and honour chants are composed in the press's honour and the printed pages, when they are hung up in large sheets prior to binding, are approached reverently, but not touched. They are *tapu*, though the missionaries have not actually used that word.

Finally, the first folded-and-bound pages are ready and these go to the main chiefs of the island. Care is taken not to offend any aristocrat's sense of honour. In each village, the small bound portion of the Christian Bible is greeted with dancing, feasting.

There was no Samoan word for printing press; it acquired its title from the people, "The Spring from Whence the Word of God Flows throughout the length and breadth of Samoa."

Literacy. It followed in the train of conversion of the islanders to Christianity and it was one of the missionaries' great sources of pride. And worry. The Samoans, like all the other central and western Polynesians, not only took to reading the Bible with enthusiasm, but when they received the Old Testament, they began to study it with unsettling intensity. The complexity of the laws given by Jehovah to the Chosen People provided an endless source of debate. Comparison with the law code introduced by the Christian church was constant. The manner in which the god Jehovah had arranged the tribes and ranks of princes and priests and people in ancient times was similar to the hierarchy by which Polynesian societies operated. And, most importantly, heroic figures such as King David, and Daniel in the Lion's Den, fit with the almost-Odyssean sense of self that is found in so many Polynesian legends. The missionaries began to worry that they had made a mistake in letting literacy get out of hand. Jesus-meek-and-mild made for easier social control, but the god of ancient Israel was a danger, if accepted undiluted.

Oh, the missionaries worried. Had they gone too far in extending literacy to anyone who would be baptized and would sit quietly in class? Even those who did not come to class learned their letters from someone who did. It all was out of control and as one canny observer later noted, "in this way, the visible church in Oceania was condemned to a state of virtual universality which the missionaries had neither sought nor desired, but which for the sake of peace they were obliged to accept."

Hard lines, that: developing a doctrine of divine selection and then discovering that everyone is selected.

The white missionaries ran their race and if they won a different crown of laurels than they had intended, no shame be on them. In the face of immense difficulties they had cracked and recorded a dozen major Polynesian tongues. This had been done, as the veteran translators ruefully admitted, more than once for most languages since, out of sheer mischief, the Polynesians had taught them obscenities, fake-idioms, and sometimes entirely bogus paradigms. All these the white missionaries later had to unlearn. This sly sense of devilment, of satirizing the white foreigner, was something the missionaries forgave, but which later ethnographers completely forgot.

Translating the various Polynesian languages not only preserved them at a near-pure pre-contact level but, by the end of the reign of Queen Victoria, most of the larger islands in central and western Polynesia had nearly universal literacy in the ethnic language of the respective islands: more than could be said for the British Isles.

RAROTONGA, THE COOK ISLANDS. 1830–45

The Rabbinics of Polynesian "Missionary Law"

Patronizing. Self-congratulatory. Smug. Such is the tone of early twentieth-century white administrators as they look at the older law codes of their respective island communities. So too, later anthropologists. And, later still, the indigenous leaders that take over the islands as independent domains. They all patronize the past. Patronizing, self-congratulatory, smug, and in each case cocksure that they have come so much farther themselves.

They are also short-sighted, impercipient, and far wide of the mark. God, however, is good, for, whenever there is a handicap, He provides compensation: as, for example, have you not noticed that a man with a shortened leg is also given a longer one? So, there meets in the heavens a *beth dinn*, a court perpetually in session that forever reviews human law codes, parses them according to Divine principles, and announces whether or not they fit Torah, the notion of God's law that runs from Mount Sinai down to the present moment, and thus corrects their human shortcomings. There sit Akiba, Hillel, Gamaliel III, Yeshua of Nazaraeth, Saul of Tarsus, Maimonides, Blackstone and, surprisingly, Jefferson. Those are the big names. Mostly, the everyday commentary and correction are by Teachers whose names are known only to students of the more obscure portions of the Babylonian Talmud, experts on such things as the extraordinarily difficult portion of the Bavli that deals with the proper preparation of pigeons for sacrifice.

Our law is no respector of persons. So reads the primary article of the code drawn up jointly by the ariki and the missionaries of Rarotonga.

R[abbi] Zera. Who can fault that? God makes law and all men are under the law.

R. Simeon ben Gamaliel. And what of foreigners?

The penalty, from the chief to the least, from the native to the foreigner, is the same.

R. Mari bar Rabel. If an aristocrat disturbs the peace, what is his penalty?

When an ariki quarrels with another, or with a subchief, or with a common man, and if he is judged to be wrong, then he must build a stone wall equivalent to $100 in money.

R. Nahman. It is a principle of the Almighty, that everything in His universe has rank.

R. Jose. And, hence, penalties for those of lower rank should be lower than for chiefs.

R. Nahman. If the crime be not too high.

R. Maimonides. And what are these $$$?

R. Jefferson. Shekels used in the South Pacific.

If a man drinks till he is drunk, he will be fined five dollars.

R. Akiba. That is harsh; even students are permitted drunkenness at Purim.

If anyone drink bush beer the fine shall be, for the maker $10 and for the drinker $5.

R. Saul of Tarsus. Certainly they could allow a bit of bush beer for the stomach's sake.

R. Zera. So long as it does not, in its making, profane the Sabbath.

If drunk on the Sabbath, the fine shall be $15.

R. Zera. Excellent.

R Simeon ben Laish. Do these laws hold the Sabbath truly holy?

No trading on the Sabbath. All avoidable work is to be left undone. No one is to walk about from house to house while people are at worship …

R. Judah. With no exceptions? Always there must be exceptions.

… except to visit a sick friend. Or to help strengthen the house against a hurricane.

R. Nahman. What is a hurricane?

R. Jefferson. A natural act.

R. Hillel. A hurricane is God's will.

He who strikes a man, and that man dies shall be judged. He also shall die.

R. Ashi. Sound: Exodus 21: 12.

If any man wilfuly and of intent cause the death of another he too shall die.

R. Ashi. Sound as well: Exodus 21: 14.

If a man slay another in self-defence, he shall not be judged.

R. Blackstone. Tricky, that one.

If a man throws a stone at a pig and it strikes a person and death follows, without evil intention on the part of the thrower, he shall be fined $20, half of which shall be paid to the friends of the deceased.

R. Akiba. Subtle.

R. Ashi. Fine sense of intent and detail.

R. Zera. Is throwing stones at pigs wrong?

Thou shalt not commit adultery. Thou shalt not bear false witness. Thou shalt not steal. For stealing a turkey a man shall repay fourfold. For stealing bananas, kumaras, taro …

R. Simeon ben Laish. Could we take the specific penalties as read? I have a divorce court to attend.

R. Akiba. Indeed: the code has twenty provisions on the spearing and stealing of pigs.

R. Zera. All this concern for pigs seems unholy.

R. Yeshua of Nazareth. Show a little tolerance.

Rebellious children. Children who strike a father or mother will be made to do ten fathoms of stone wall and be put for two months in the stocks. If they repent they may be released.

R. Ashi. Sound: it follows the Commandment, Honour thy father and thy mother.

When a father has lectured his child for wrongdoing and the child does not pay attention, let the child do five fathoms of stone wall, a yard-and-a half high.

R. Jefferson. Ah, if only I had heard that a century ago!

NEIGHBOUR. ENGLAND
1830–1845

Mikveh

The entire downstairs of the tenement of Kitty Wilkerson and her husband is full of steam. Near-boiling water is brought from a fire in the yard and is poured over the sick who, one after another, enter the bath. A special soap, made with so much lye that it stings even the callouses of their feet, cleanses them. After a few have been immersed, the tub is emptied onto the cobbles outside and the whole process starts anew.

This is the cholera epidemic of 1832 and Kitty not only washes the suffering, but produces porridge for at least five dozen feeble sufferers each morning. She has some financial help from the Rathbone family, who were always leading Liverpool philanthropists and, generation after generation, worried about the Almighty's judgement on the source of their income. This is the first bathhouse in Liverpool and, if we now forget such amenities, their importance to public health, especially for the urban poor, should be recalled.

Kitty Wilkerson, an Anglican who migrated to Liverpool from Londonderry in her youth, spent a life of equal parts impoverishment and generosity. The vessel that she, her mother and her sister-in-arms travelled to Liverpool on, experienced such a violent storm that her infant sister was swept from her mother's arms and drowned. Kitty's mother went mad, completely, permanently. Kitty somehow held herself together and became the Victorian equivalent of a Block Mother to scores of troubled immigrant children. Her work in the cholera epidemic of 1832 would, on its own, have produced sainthood had she been a Catholic.

Her bathhouse charity shamed the Corporation, and in the next epidemic, caused by the Irish Famine of 1846, the Liverpool authorities finance a municipal bath and as many Irish immigrants are saved by their being cleansed of ticks, lice and other parasites as by gifts of food.

Kitty and her husband run this new municipal mission, but he dies within a few months.

She carries on and eventually a window is dedicated to her in the Lady Chapel of the Liverpool Cathedral. Without a trace of self-criticism, the burghers of Liverpool call down God's blessing on "ALL POOR HELPERS OF THE POOR."

Maiden Speech

In his own later years, William Ewart Gladstone was tearful about the virtues of his father. *He could not understand nor tolerate those who, perceiving an object to be good, did not at once and actively pursue it.* This in reference to John Gladstones (he informally dropped the plural in 1787 and did so formally in 1837), who had moved from Leith in Scotland to Liverpool before the wars with France, and had done brilliantly as a Liverpool merchant. He so actively pursued what he thought was good – money – that by the time of his death he was worth over £600,000, one of the richest men in Liverpool when it was the merchant casino of the entire Empire.

None but his children know what torrents of tenderness flowed from his heart, his most famous son recalled, and that without irony. In point, the Gladstone family fortune was at least half-founded on slaves and very hard dealing in that commodity. When, in 1807, the senior Gladstone was forced out of the direct slave business (the trade was now illegal, but not overseas slave holding), he did what the hardest of those in the slave business did: he did not sell out his overseas holdings, but instead bought more West Indian plantations with their attached slaves. This was a canny move, for Africans were being sold very cheaply by some West Indian planters who reckoned that they could not replace worn out slaves and thus their plantations would run down and become unprofitable. So, buy human beings at fire-sale prices, and then – here was the real warmth of the Gladstone heart revealed – make money on them in one of three ways: hold them like any speculative item, with the hope that an increasing shortage of slaves in the British West Indies would drive up their worth locally; or, second, quietly and illegally ship them to the USA; or, thirdly, work them to death, the way one would beat the last mile out of an old dray horse.

A savage's head, affronté, distilling drops of blood. That was the symbol the senior Gladstone accepted when his family became armigerous. A more appropriate symbol is hard to imagine. In 1823, a massive slave outbreak occurred in Demerara, where Gladstone had one of his plantations, and his place was the centre of the revolt. A five-month jungle war followed. Fifty Africans were hanged and others shot in the back country or, when captured, whipped to death. Within a year of these events, John Gladstone had no qualms about accepting silver plate worth £1,200 from the merchants of Liverpool for his vigorous defence of slavery in the Liverpool and London press: sanctioned by providence, slavery was, and the difficulties of slave emancipation were impossible, so Gladstone argued. When Emancipation eventually occurred, John Gladstone received a bit more than £50 for each of the 1,609 slaves he individually owned, plus smaller amounts for those he held in partnership.

In the first reformed parliament, when the twenty-three year old William Ewart Gladstone made his maiden speech (electoral laws may have been regularized, but money still bought a seat), it was in a debate on slave emancipation. His father had been accused of working his slaves systematically to death and William, ever the good son, declared his father on this charge to be wholly innocent.

MANCHESTER. 1833

Reserve Army

John Potter, owner of a textile factory, has recently discharged almost all of his Irish hands. There had been thirty and he kept only two or three. He is a man of strong opinions. The Irish, he says, are as quick as the English to learn how to operate the power looms. And the best of them make fine mechanics, bobbin turners, swingmen. The general run of Irish workers, though, are untidy and slovenly in their work and turn out second-quality products.

Potter, however, understands why having the Irish available is important. *Ten or twelve years ago we could not have done without Irish: the demand for labour in Manchester could not have been satisfied without them. Not only was there a real scarcity of hands, but the English were so mutinous that nothing could be done with them.*

He could have been reading from the as-yet-unwritten text of "Capital." *The Irish were employed as a check on the combination of the English. Now there is an abundance of English hands and we could dispense with the Irish.*

KILCREA, COUNTY CORK. 30 JANUARY 1835

Recessional

Feargus O'Connor, now an O'Connelite member of parliament for County Cork, walks in solemn procession as his father's remains are taken to the tomb of the MacCarthys, with whom the O'Connors have a relationship that stretches almost to time-out-of-mind. The cortege and its followers form a long black ribbon that, on this sunless day, almost disappears into the dark grey of the horizon.

The death of his father does not leave Feargus bereft, for the old man had enjoyed a fine run of days and, as Himself had often said, had deserved to be hanged at least a dozen times. No, the issue that weighs on the radical MP is the more practical matter: how much did the old hero leave? This is more than a financial matter to O'Connor, for the requirement for anyone to hold a parliamentary seat for an Irish county is that he have property worth £600 a year. Feargus has been keeping up a stout front, renting "Fortrobert House" from his sister-in-law, but in fact he owns only the furniture and has debts. He needs an inheritance.

When the lawyers finish their accounting of the late Roger O'Connor's estate, it makes an interesting narrative, but provides Feargus with no financial comfort. His father had served as agent for the Irish estate of his exiled brother, General Arthur O'Connor, and, it turns out, had embezzled so much from the estate that his brother finally had lodged a decree-of-sale against Roger O'Connor's real property. Nothing, save trinkets, remains.

Expelled from parliament for failure to meet the property requirement, Feargus O'Connor does what so many of his former constituents already had done: he moves to England to alleviate his distress.

MANCHESTER. 1836

Prescription

As a witness before the Royal Commission on the Poorer Classes in Ireland, Dr. James Kay mouths the proper economic words of his time. *It is of the utmost importance to the successful employment of capital that manufactures should enjoy an unlimited command of labour.* Kay's younger brother is an early Oxford economist and he has passed along the right technical terms. Kay, an Edinburgh-trained medical doctor, needs these gnostic formulae because in fact he wishes to undermine economic orthodoxy. *And therefore the immigration of the Irish [into England] has been of service to the trade of this town.*

James Kay is no fool, but rather an ambitious, God-bothering zealot for health, education, high morality and racial purity. He has spent his time in the trenches. In 1828 he became senior physician at the Ancoats and Ardwick dispensary in Manchester and in 1831 became secretary to the local health board that fought cholera. His special expertise is Little Ireland, the worst Irish immigrant settlement in all England. Located on the edge of the parish of Chorlton-upon-Medlock on the south side of Manchester, Little Ireland has a population of 21,000 living in toxic poverty. The Irish settlement, situated on low riverbank land, is waterlogged in good times and flooded in bad. Surrounding this inhabited semi-swamp are more than a dozen factories that send their flammable waste up nearby chimneys and their solubles into the River Medlock and thence into the rise and fall of Little Ireland's water table. In 1832, Dr Kay publishes a pamphlet that is a national sensation: *The Moral and Physical Condition of the Working Classes employed in the Cotton Manufacture in Manchester.*

He cares.

He also illustrates the melancholy fact that being in opposition to something that is wrong does not necessarily make one right. Granted, he argues that economic gain is not all-important and that the immiseration of the English working class has to be stopped.

And, for Dr. Kay, one way is to stop the Irish. *The effect of the colonisation of a barbarous race on the habits of the people of this country must be considered apart from the economical questions,* he tells the royal commissioners. *And provided the trade of the country did not require the importation of cheap labour from Ireland, the moral condition of the labouring classes of this country might be more easily ameliorated **if unaffected by the example of the Irish with whom they are now mingled.***

LIVERPOOL. 1837

Some Cod

"You dropped your glove, my dear."
   "Indeed. Thank you. Such a fine lecture, was it not?"
   "The very model of learned declamation."
   "And spiritual depths as well."
   "Yes. Spiritual depths."
The May meeting of the Ladies' Irish Island Society of Liverpool had passed off most improvingly. The Ladies especially appreciated a lecture such as this afternoon's, when a long oration precluded their having to speak to each other too much. Conversation among them was always socially risky, as they had so many different Irish regional accents that they could not always understand each other. And, as they all mimicked Received English, with uneven effectiveness, every one had the sinking feeling that she was not doing it quite correctly. Today's lecture, "The Cult of the Virgin Mary on the Far Irish Islands" had been especially satisfactory as each Lady left the hall feeling decidedly superior to most of the Irish wherever they might be encountered, except of course real Ladies and their Gentlemen.

That the Protestants and Catholics of Lancashire did not entirely understand each other is only to be expected, but it is hard to see how amity could have been helped by the Ladies' speaker explaining in detail that the Catholics of the western islands worshipped the Blessed Virgin Mary not as a spiritual figure but as a fish. A large one, actually.

AINTREE, LIVERPOOL. 1837

The Road to Clontarf

The second annual running of what eventually became the Grand National was neither grand nor national. So badly managed and ill-advertised was it that only four runners entered.

The favourite was "Dan O'Connell" and he made the early running. His main rival was "The Duke," and if O'Connell and Wellington were to re-run their previous Catholic Emancipation Handicap, then this was the right place: the course was brutal.

One of the chase obstacles was a massive ditch with six feet of thorn in front of it.

All four runners refused: horse sense.

"The Duke" was brought around again and he made it, as did two of the remaining three runners.

Not "Dan O'Connell." He refused twice and called it a day.

LONDON. 1839

Forgiveness

Why is this Scot-git, brothel keeper to the imagination of the English middle classes, not on the Geneva Convention's list of all-time racist assholes? He lacks the imagination of Nietzsche, the music of Wagner but, from his very pores, he distills proto-Fascism, power worship, Aryanism before it is invented. Cromwell and Frederick the Great are his historical mind mates and he writes and talks of them at interminable length. Scant wonder that, as the sum total of his life's work, he is awarded in 1872 the Prussian Order of Merit.

Hear him on anything and cringe. Hear him on the Irishman. *He is the sorest evil this country has to strive with. In his rags and laughing savagery, he is there to undertake all work that can be done by mere strength of hand and back – for wages that will purchase him potatoes.* This is deposed in a broad Scots accent and in a tone that is as insistent as a surgeon's saw. *He needs only salt for his condiment, he lodges to his mind in any pig-hutch or dog-hutch, roosts in out-houses, and wears a suit of tatters, the getting on and off of which is said to be a difficult operation ...* He overbears opposition as much by assertive force as by wit, though he declares himself to be a man of genius so often that periodicals adopt it as a catch phrase attached to his name, as Homer did with his more worthy subjects. *... said to be a difficult operation transacted only in festivals and the high tides of the calendar.* His audiences claim to see in his eye the true index of his genius, a wild and mystic fire that breaks through the dark surface of his countenance. *The Saxon man, if he cannot work on these terms, finds no work. The uncivilised Irishman, not by his strength, but by the opposite of strength, drives the Saxon native out, takes possession in his room.*

Thomas Carlyle utters these words two years before he organizes the foundation of the London Library, the most amiable reading room in the world, and his ticket out of the lowest circles of hell.

BIRMINGHAM. 22 JUNE 1841

Stained-Glass Ceiling

St. Chad in the seventh century journeyed to Ireland to improve his knowledge of sacred texts and to deepen his contemplation of the divine. The Catholics of Birmingham, who are present at the consecration of St. Chad's Cathedral, are proud that this is the first house of worship to be built specifically as a cathedral in England since the Reformation. Most of the money for the construction has come from English Catholics, but the congregation waiting outside the new cathedral is largely Irish.

That, in miniature, is how it stays. English Catholics look down not just upon the Irish, but upon the various Protestantisms. They identify themselves with the Catholic aristocracy, the hermetic, exclusive set of families that had kept both wealth and faith. Still, the English Catholics know their duty to the poor and they quietly underwrite church buildings in Irish settlements and provide priests, fine ones. The bulk of the English Catholic laity may avoid worshipping alongside Irish immigrants, but the priests who live among them in Lancashire, Yorkshire, London, are held up as local saints.

The doors to the new Birmingham cathedral are sealed until the relics of St. Chad are carried in from the Lady Chapel. They had been held translated from Oscott two days earlier and prayed over day and night by the brothers of the Guild of St. Chad. In consecrating the cathedral, the bishop blesses a spot over the high altar where in future the relics are to be enshrined. This done, the massive doors are thrown open and the cathedral fills quickly for its inaugural mass.

The Catholic church in England opens the doors of the parish ministry to Irish Catholic priests, especially from the mid-1840s onwards. Most are temporary appointments, young clerics from the diocesan seminaries at Carlow and Kilkenny and some from Maynooth. All Hallows College, Dublin, is founded in 1842 to train priests for overseas, and this includes Great Britain. These priests serve successfully in England, but they have the same problem their parishioners do: as immigrants, they can rise only so far.

For priests of Irish birth who are trained in Ireland, a stained-glass ceiling exists. They do not, save in the rarest cases, obtain promotion, much less bishoprics.

The Roman Catholic Church in England and Scotland is the only one in the English-speaking world that the Irish do not capture for their own. Prelates with Irish-origin names eventually rise, but that is a century later and they are men who are second, third, and fourth generation in Britain, and Irish in name only.

LONDON. JUNE 1843

Letter to Zurich

The only thing that excites Frederick Engels more than Irish servant girls in England is Irish men in Ireland. *Two hundred thousand men – and what men! People who have nothing to lose, two-thirds of whom are clothed in rags, genuine proletarians and sanscullotes and, moreover, Irishmen, wild, headstrong, fanatical Gaels.* Engels's father, a wealthy German textile manufacturer, has sent him to England to the Manchester branch of the family firm, Ermen and Engels. Instead of learning how to manage textile workers, Frederick spends two years travelling about England, studying the sordid side of the industrial world. He writes letters for the radical Zurich journal *Schweizarischer Republikaner* and, eventually, a classic book, *The Condition of the Working Class in England*. But it's the Irish men who excite him. *One who has never seen Irishmen cannot know them. Give me two hundred thousand Irishmen and I will overthrow the entire British monarchy.* The idea makes him so animated that he has to find a prostitute. She smiles knowingly as he spasms and hisses in her ear. *Give me two hundred thousand Irishmen!*

UPPER CANADA. IRELAND'S COLD DOMINION

1830–1845

The Union of the Canadas

Finally, destiny is served. At the home of the antislavery campaigner Thomas Pringle, the members of the future All-Canadian Victorian Champion Invitational Writing Team meet each other. Each of the eventual-partners is clinging desperately to a gentry status that neither can afford. It's a case of self-interest at first sight, but later it becomes a deep love.

The canonically-anonymous 0.5 of the team – John Wedderburn Dunbar Moodie – had retired as a half-pay lieutenant after the Napoleonic Wars and spent three years being bored to death. He is the fourth, and youngest, son of the ninth Laird of Melsetter in the Orkneys, an inheritance that sounded greater than it was, for his father had to sell most of the rocky estate in order to pay his debts. The sons went into the military, and in 1817 Captain Benjamin Moodie, the eldest son, led the first band of Scottish settlers to South Africa. Running out of future, Lieut J.W.D. Moodie joined his brother in 1819 in Grootvadersbosch, near Swellendam. He became manager of a farm on a half-share basis and was no dilettante settler: he knew what he was doing. He and a third brother, Donald, moved through a succession of farms. They were successful, but loneliness, not economic failure, was their enemy. In August 1829, John W.D. Moodie sails from Algoa Bay for England. He's certain that he can make a fortune in the Cape Colony if he has a wife and can raise a family; otherwise, he's uncertain. With a withered left arm, his old war wound, and a face creased and browned by the sun, he presents himself in the London marriage market as a slightly exotic, strong-backed, durable officer, and thus a gentleman.

Susanna Strickland confuses him. She is bouncing between two extremes like a gutta-percha ball. She has just renounced her allegiance to the Church of England and has taken up Congregationalism. That is not something a truly genteel lady does. On the other hand, she is courting every small-time publisher and middle-level literary lion who might help her writing career. So, while talking to Moodie in the sombre tones of a truly-redeemed Congregationalist, she wears a flirtatious outfit: a frock with gigot sleeves, a plunging neckline whose lace barely provides decency, and a set of slippers suitable to dancing, not walking. Confusing and charming to a man who has just spent ten years in South Africa, much of it alone.

Susanna Strickland needs a partner as badly as does John W.D. Moodie.

Her family has been holding on to their position as semi-gentry since 1818, when Thomas Strickland had died. That was trouble enough, but worse, it was found that since the end of the Napoleonic War, his beloved coach manufactory had been on the way downhill. There is nothing left to support Mrs. Strickland, her six daughters and two sons. Like limpets, they cling to Reydon Hall, their increasingly run-down late seventeenth-century Suffolk home. Most of the servants are let go and those that remain receive their wages late and often in coppers.

The problem of course is the girls. The two boys are bright and have received standard secondary school educations, so they can be expected eventually to take care of themselves. But how does one keep six daughters until they – oh dear God, please let it be! – they are married?

In response to their problem, the Strickland women do something amazing, if far from original: they adapt the factory system to writing. This is, after all, the era of the industrial revolution, and in his craft-oriented way, their father had been part of it. He had taught them how to simultaneously maintain separation-of-crafts and yet conjoin collective effort. So, they save themselves and their place in the world, one poem, one vignette, one pamphlet, one literary sketch, one hymn, one historical piece, at a time. They are lucky, for the age kicks up new middle class readers who are hungry for assembly line books, just as they are for material products. There are a dozen-and-a-half "annuals" in operation in the 1820s and in the same period "gift books" become immensely popular. These are the equivalent of the boxes of assorted sweetmeats that are the vogue in the same era, tinselled cardboard boxes with marzipan, various chocolates, cremes, all different, small, all sweet. Catherine becomes adept at children's books, a feature of the new middle-class literary market. And Agnes does false-epic poetry very well and in later years becomes a royal biographer and adopts a monarchical arrogance towards her own family.

Ah, Susanna. "Suzie" to the increasingly-besotted Lieut. John Moodie. She is on the edge of big literary success, she feels. Lately she's been producing a good deal. In the early 1820s sister Catherine had found the formula for children's books and she subcontracts to Susanna parts of them. They usually go out under Catherine's name, but she does not want to flood the market, so sometimes they are anonymous and occasionally Susanna has her name on the title page: *Spartacus. A Roman Story* (1822); *The Little Quaker, or the Triumph of Virtue. A Tale for the Instruction of Youth.* (1825); *Hugh Latimer; or, the School-Boy's Friendship* (1828).

In 1822, Susanna had met a family of printers, the Childs of Bungay, and they proved very useful, if forceful, for they were strong religious non-conformists. They pushed her to write a volume of psalms and hymns and these she had completed by 1828, through the expedient of lumping together poetic work she had done since age fourteen onwards. The result, *Enthusiasm*, was published in 1831, with the Childs's firm being the printers.

Susanna responds equally well to the coaching of another East Anglian printer-cum-publisher, Thomas Harral, an old friend of the Strickland family. He published briefly the *East Anglian*, a local literary magazine, and two local newspapers before becoming the editor of the aspiring London *La Belle Assemblée, or Court and Fashionable Magazine*. There Susanna is assigned to do four narrative sketches of Suffolk life and they are gooey even by the standards of *La Belle Assemblée*. Her editor tells her to concentrate on the marzipan items she does so well – religious poems, vignettes about duty and virtue, the occasional patriotic verse. Susanna listens well and is continually published. By 1830 she is in several annuals and gift books. Venues such as: *Lady's Magazine; Pledge of Friendship; Forget Me Not; Juvenile Forget Me Not; Iris: a Literary and Religious Offering*. And on and on, the titles changing each year, the items pretty much the same. She still cannot write more than 300 words of narrative for adults without help.

Lieutenant Moodie and Susanna Strickland fall in love and then she falls out. She does her sums and finds that she is earning about £12 pounds a year by her writing and calculates that she can triple that easily, and thus earn about as much as a skilled wheelwright in her late father's factory.

Passing rich in her imagination, Susanna declares herself to be a blue-stocking, breaks off her engagement to Moodie and moves into London in early 1831. She uses Thomas Pringle to introduce her to editors and third-line writers, the sort who can be helpful in selling her material. She calls Pringle "Papa" and she happily goes to work in his propaganda factory. There she, Pringle, and various drop-ins, turn out pamphlets for the Anti-Slavery Society, of which Pringle was secretary from 1827 until his death in 1834.

As John Moodie frets, in Pringle's manufactory Susanna takes from dictation two long narratives. One is the autobiography of Mary Prince, a former slave, and the second is that of Ashton Warner, another African slave. "Papa" Thomas Pringle does not trust Susanna to edit the narratives for publication. He does that himself and the volumes appear before the year 1831 is out.

Meanwhile, John Moodie accidentally does the one thing that will win the respect of the bluestocking-Susanna: he shows that he can write better than she. Far from being a threatening rival, she immediately perceives him as a potential protector and a director for her own work. Moodie in late 1830 has a long essay, 25,000 words, published in *The United Service Journal*. This was a demanding location, for the periodical was aimed at career officers, politicians, and professionals who were interested in military affairs. Moodie writes a seemingly-effortless narrative of the 1814 campaign in Holland. In it he moves easily from his own evocative memories to matters of larger strategy, and back to the telling personal anecdote. It's a lovely piece of prose. The readers' response was so strong that Henry Colburn and Richard Bentley – high status London publishers, way above the job-publishers with whom Susanna dealt – brought it out early in 1831 as the second half of a volume on the campaign in Portugal and in Holland in the recent war. Lieut. Moodie's share of the royalties was just under £65 pounds, more than Susanna had made in total by her writing during the decade of the 1820s.

This, she decides, is her sort of man.

BROCKVILLE, UPPER CANADA. 1830

The Big Bang

Better tell a big lie than a little one, Ogle Gowan believed: little ones invite investigation, while big ones fully engage the imagination. So, having booked the Brockville Court House, he now will invent both himself and the Canadian Orange Order. Brockville was a good place for such self assertions: in 1813 when two loyalist families were scrapping about which one of them the jurisdiction should be named after, Sir Isaac Brock rode into town to decide the issue. "Brockville," he snapped and rode out.

"I am here as a representative plenipotentiary ..." Gowan loved big words and they always worked on yokels "... of the Grand Lodge of Ireland and of England." This was patently untrue. "I bring with me warrants for the creation of Orange Lodges ..." True enough, though they were all purloined. "... And I have the direct approval of the Worshipful Grand Master, his royal Highness, Prince Ernest Augustus, Duke of Cumberland ... and also of the Duke of Gordon ... and of the Honourable the Earl O'Neill, and the Earl of Enniskillen." None of them would have recognized Gowan at a levee, or even in a brothel, but they were famous Orange names.

Gowan does not need to sell hard. Half his audience is from the back country of eastern Upper Canada and most of these are Wexford or Waterford families. The rest are Presbyterians and Anglicans from Ulster who have started filing into Upper Canada and these people know the Order. His audience is keen to buy what Gowan has for sale.

He's providing the answer to a problem they didn't have in the Old Country. Oh, indeed, they love the traditional anti-Catholic oath, *I swear that I am not, was not, nor ever will be a Roman Catholic or Papist,* but it has little to do with their problems in Upper Canada: they are not greatly troubled by Catholics but rather by the old loyalists who, having had parents or grandparents who suffered under the republicans of the American colonies, are convinced they have an hereditary right to every decent governmental job, from pound keeper to customs collector. They're impossible to deal with on land matters, like registering titles, and that counts for near-everything in a place where land is livelihood.

Gowan has the meeting arranged so that at the end, he is elected deputy grand master for the Canadas, meaning that he is in charge. He accepts modestly.

Within four years, the Order has 144 lodges and nearly 13,000 members in Upper Canada: one of every twelve males above the age of sixteen: far-and-away Upper Canada's biggest non-religious organization. It flies upwards so quickly because English and Scots small farmers, labourers, artisans join this Irish Protestant body – and they do so because it meets their needs just as much as it does the Irish Protestants'. In the 1830s, the Orange Order is the closest thing Canada ever has to the One Big Union.

Entrenched loyalists, not Papists, are its real target. In eastern Upper Canada, where their numbers are strongest, the Orangemen break the loyalists in 1834 by a mixture of superpatriotic rhetoric, shrewd electoral strategy, and heavy thuggery.

"Yankees!"

"Traders with the enemy!"

"Militia Deserters."

The vilification of the loyalists is easy for the Orange and their associates, because the one thing the Orange are is hyperloyal. They outflank the loyalists where it is least expected, on the patriotism issue.

Patriotism, actually, is often the first resort of the scoundrel. When the 1834 election is called, Ogle Gowan puts himself forward as a candidate. That's easy enough. His real coup is to convince the attorney general of Upper Canada to run with him; all the electoral contests were for two seats and having a respectable running-mate in harness helped the vote. By tradition the attorney general, though appointed by London, also had to win a seat in the provincial parliament. The new attorney general, Robert Jameson, was either the coldest fish in all of Upper Ontario (his well-published wife's view) or a warm, decent, hardworking, and egregiously cuckolded public servant (his friends'). But in either case he was highly respectable and he gave Gowan just the patina of legitimacy he needed in running against the local loyalists. (That some of the old loyalist families were now presenting themselves as advanced Reformers is a complication that need not detain us, for it certainly didn't detain Gowan.)

Public elections at the time were held in the open, the balloting was not secret and was held over a several day period, an invitation to intimidation. This one was in the back of Leeds township in a town then called Beverly, the heart of an Irish Protestant area. On 6 October, the hustings were opened by the county's sheriff in archaic language that hadn't changed since used in England in the 1660s. Scarcely fifty voters cast their ballots the first day. Gowan's people challenged the qualifications of every voter whom they did not trust.

On the second day, Gowan's forces surrounded the hustings and when a hostile voter approached, they let him part way through the crowd, then closed on him, cutting him off from his friends. He'd be punched where it wouldn't show blood: in the ribs, elbowed in the kidneys, or kneed in the thigh or stuck with a hat pin.

The third day an organized gang fight broke out. The Irish won.

That evening Gowan and Jameson were declared winners.

The election was protested and thrown out, but Gowan in 1836 won again.

This pattern was imitated throughout Upper Canada, and save in Toronto (the new name for York and environs), the old families no longer had life entirely their own way.

Think this was a social-class movement? Think it was merely sectarian? Reply: in 1836 an alliance between the Orangemen and the Roman Catholic Bishop, Alexander Macdonnell, threw six races to the representatives of immigrants. The Orange-Catholic alliance was limited, temporary, surely, but speaks volumes about who the real enemy was.

LONDON AND SUFFOLK. 1831–32

Just Let Them Be

Inquisitor: Shall we begin?

Outside observer: Are you the Grand Inquisitor?

In: Good heavens, no. He's retired. I'm the Less Grand Inquisitor's ... godson, actually.

Out: Get along, shall we?

In: Why do we care about the cloth heads?

Out: The Moodies you mean?

In: They're so mundane. Tiresome. Hardly worth fate's punishing them.

Out: Point given. Point for you lost there too.

In: Oh?

Out: They're like flies, crabs, voles, wheat rust: something most of the old immigrants had to deal with in the Empire, not just Upper Canada.

In: Charming.

Out: You know: the jumped-up, pain-in-the arse English who leave the Old Country in tattered shape and try to assert gentility and even feudal rights in some New World. Wear silly hats all the time and won't raise the cloth from their head save in the face of royalty.

In: The world's full of Scots, Irish, and English working class who testify to these sort of ...

Out: But hearing things from the side of the cloth heads has value. The Moodies are articulate. And they're basically decent people.

In: Decent has never counted for much in my business.

Out: Should do. Anyway, they're a bargain, a twofer. Sweet, isn't it, how they marry in April 1831 and in July are expecting a wee one?

In: Yeah, very Niagara Falls.

Out: And, how Susanna becomes a good wife and gives up writing: doesn't even want to do it. Not a bluestocking anymore, she says.

In: Pity. She wrote some dandy hymns. I like the one about the lake of salvation's-blood.

Out: Very Lake Erie.

In: Why'd they inflict themselves on the Empire?

Out: Little capital. Peacetime. No gentleman's employment. Only a half-pay officer's salary. The usual reasons.

In: Why Upper Canada?

Out: Their big mistake. Lieutenant Moodie wants to go back to South Africa. He knows the place and has connections. His wife is afraid of wild animals.

In: Really.

Out. Really. As if there're none in the Canadian bush. And she has family who've already left for Upper Canada and thinks it will be friendlier. She thinks they can form a little world of gentry.

In: God help them.

Out: He didn't much. At first, though, they had Providence on their side. Bentley, a big English publisher, buys John's proposal that he write a big – very big – book on his ten years in South Africa. That way he can make money during their first year or two in the Canadas. And start his gentry farm.

In: Why not write about Upper Canada?

Out: Lieutenant Moodie pitched the idea to Bentley. Gave him a whole outline on making it in the backwoods. Bentley said books on Canada wouldn't sell.

In: Comforting to know that some things never change.

Out: They sailed from Edinburgh in July 1832.

In: And the rest is herstory.

Out: So they say.

THE CANADAS. 1832

The Second Epidemic

Called "the emigrant disease." Cholera. Totally unfair. It's been slouching its way from the villages of the Indian subcontinent for six years and would spread even if there were no migrants, just temporary travellers. Papers report it. Comes closer to Europe and overruns Britain and then Ireland. An Irish ship from Dublin, the *Carrick*, brings it to Grosse Île, the new quarantine station just outside Quebec City in June 1832. Quarantine not very strict.

Violent cramps. Severe diarrhoea. More cramps, wrenching. "Rice water" expelled with great force from the rectum. Dehydration. Collapse. Delirium. Death.

Quick burial. Public policy that.

Towns along St. Lawrence create local health boards and most residents move to the countryside for the summer.

Methodist churches embrace 3,652 new members, triple the previous year's candidates.

Twenty years on, it will be discovered that poor sanitation is the vector: sewers save.

Right now, 1832, not the best time to settle in Upper Canada.

COBURG, UPPER CANADA. 1832

September's Song

If half of good luck is missing bad, then the Moodies were lucky. Arriving in Quebec City in late August of the year of the cholera epidemic, they had no oceanic contact with the disease and their ship was cleared for Montreal just three days after arrival. They transhipped upriver from Montreal as quickly as they could, for they had read of the unpredictability of the Upper Canadian winters. They arrived in Coburg, all their goods intact, and no brush with the epidemic.

Lieutenant John Moodie leaves Susanna in a Coburg hotel and goes prospecting for land. He has enough cash in hand to buy several decent half-cleared properties; of course he only needs one and he promises his gravid wife that he will consult her: she is pregnant again. The unjustness of Nature made Susanna's pregnancies extremely enervating and the post-partum slough of melancholy a time to fear: she can see it approaching already. Eventually Susanna has six children, and each birth leeches the energy from her soul.

Here, in Coburg, she stays in her hotel room and cries. She sleeps only fitfully, awakes, cries, tries to read the Bible, cries, passes judgement on herself and her weaknesses, cries. Susanna's only moments of vigour are when she uses pride and prejudice, her own, to lift her into anger. She rehearses her hates and these are the constants that are to keep her going in Upper Canada. She hates emigration. An "infection" she later calls it. She hates Upper Canada. Probably she would hate Lower Canada too, but she never spends any time there. Upper Canada is a land of swindlers and ruffians, she sees that already, and twenty years later she is barely able to cover her contempt when writing of the place, and then only for money. Susanna has run into Yankees and already hates them. As for the local lower classes (her term), they are poorly disciplined and excessively democratic. She knows, though, she cannot live without them and never does so: even when huddled in a 20' x 20' log cabin with a dirt floor, she keeps a female servant and Lieutenant Moodie usually keeps a hired man. Already among the locals she has had a bad time with the Irish and Susanna is forming in chrysallis her fierce hatred of all things Irish, Protestant and Catholic alike. Later, when she writes about them, she is unable to distinguish an Ulster from a Munster accent, and all her Irish people speak in the dialect of the Victorian English novel. As for other groups: the Jews she hates most of all and hopes she never will meet one in this new world. Negroes, she knows, have been badly treated, poor dears, but she understands she won't encounter any. The only people she would like to meet, besides English persons of gentility, and at a stretch the occasional civilized Scot, are the Noble Savages. Otherwise, oh dear Lord, I am a stranger in a barren and heathen land.

Lieutenant Moodie returns full of enthusiasm for several pieces of property. He is thirty-eight, nearly thirty-nine, years of age and Susannah is ten years younger, but one would think their ages were reversed, so full of energy is he.

Before the winter settles in, the Moodies are in their own small cabin on a cleared farm in Hamilton Township, near Coburg: they and their two servants and expanding family. The winter of 1832–33 is one of the coldest on record. Susanna huddles by the fire, day after day mewling to herself, remembering her glorious Suffolk childhood when heaven and earth were one. John Moodie cheers her by playing the flute. And to make money, he begins to write the book he has promised Bentley, his English publisher. It will be a two-volume work. Some mornings, his inkstand is frozen, and he has to heat it near the fire, as if it were a kettle of frozen water.

BROCKVILLE, UPPER CANADA. APRIL 1834

Moses Visits the Mountain

"May I see your certificate of Kashruth?" Ogle Gowan is enjoying himself a great deal. He is holding an audience with George Benjamin who wants his approval to form an Orange Lodge in Belleville, ninety miles up Lake Ontario, where he intends to settle. The interview takes place in a Brockville hotel because, although Gowan calls the farm he owns in Leeds County "Escott Park" and claims to be a gentleman farmer, he does not like to be visited there: it is a bush farm with a slab-sided house and very little genteel about it, save some of the family furniture that his mother brought from Ireland.

"You may indeed, your Reverence," says Benjamin, as he hands over his certificate from the Liverpool lodge that had initiated him into Orangeism. Benjamin is no fool. He knows that Gowan knows he is Jewish and also knows that Gowan does not care. The two men have taken to each other. Each recognizes the other as that rare form of art, the spectacular fake.

Gowan examines the certificate very carefully. "Definitely Kosher," he announced.

"Thank you, your Holiness." Benjamin's using Roman Catholic terms and Gowan's using Jewish ones was a private game whose rules they were developing even as they spoke. That Benjamin understood the unstated rules was a sign to Gowan that his visitor was the right sort.

Right sort, but an original fabrication, Gowan realizes. Unlike almost everyone who flowed into Canada in the 1830s, Benjamin had sailed from Philadelphia and that explains why he arrived when the ice was barely out of the river, and in advance of most emigration ships from the Old World. The stubby, portly Benjamin was on his way to Toronto to arrange some financial matters and then was coming back to Belleville where he had agreed on the purchase of a printing plant. There he would run a newspaper called *The Belleville Intelligencer*. It would be the right sort of paper, he told Gowan, unblinkingly conservative, loyal to the Crown, anti-Yankee, and would provide support for the Orange cause.

"I warrant it will," said Gowan, laughing. He reaches into his satchel and takes out a piece of parchment that already has a wax seal affixed. "And this warrant will allow you to form a lodge and be its Worshipful Master."

Thus George Benjamin is enabled to become the most important Orangeman between Brockville and Toronto. He begins weekly production of his newspaper in August and inaugurates his Orange lodge soon after. Benjamin keeps his public and private life strictly separate. He has a fifteen-year-old wife, whose maiden name was Isabella Jacobs. She came of a New Orleans Jewish family and he had married her shortly before her thirteenth birthday. That was during the four years he spent in the United States, mostly in North Carolina, before moving north. Isabella is aided by a black woman, a slave in the States, who now, in the British Empire is immediately a former slave. A nursemaid is a necessity, as Isabella eventually has twelve children, one every eighteen months.

If Ogle Gowan does not mind in the least that George Benjamin is a Jew, others do. Benjamin's rival in Kingston, the editor of the *British Whig*, runs scurrilous articles denouncing the "Jew editor" and accompanies them with anti-Semitic verse. Benjamin keeps his head down, and proclaims his Orange loyalism, and for most of the people of Belleville that is enough.

Marrano? Crypto? Impossible to know. George Benjamin seemed to invent his own world religion. In it, he could lead Irish and British Protestants as one of them and still publicly give money to a Montreal synagogue. Interesting though, that all the print work was done on his paper by Friday night and that he had his sub-editor open the shop on Saturday and take full responsibility for the distribution of the rag.

DOURO TOWNSHIP, NORTH OF PETERBOROUGH, UPPER CANADA. JANUARY 1835

Writer in Residence

John Moodie scribbles and scribbles and scribbles. When she can find a moment away from the infants and restive young children, Susanna orders the serving girl to make him a pot of tea. With honey: he needs the encouragement.

The Moodies have moved to an uncleared farm in the back bush. It has the advantage of being near relatives, but beyond that it is a rough place to be. They're in bad financial shape and cannot reckon why. John has sold his half-pay commission, they have cashed in their original half-cleared farm, and Susanna has received a £700 inheritance from a distant relative.

But their funds keep dwindling and John, the successful writer in the family, works hard at completing his autobiographical volumes on life in South Africa. Bentley in London is pushing him hard for them: with the furore over the abolition of slavery in the empire, Africa is fashionable among English readers.

John has encouraged Susanna to send some of her old poems to North American publishers and she has done so. Mostly the items are repeats of her gift-book material, or from *Enthusiasm*. They have the uplifting and vaguely spiritual tone that family periodicals like. Both John and she write some original poems about Canada as well. Little things, they appear in local newspapers – *The Bytown Gazette*, *The Coburg Advertiser*, *The Kingston Spectator* – and occasionally in literary periodicals: the *Albion*, the *North American Quarterly Magazine*, and the *Lady's Magazine and Museum*. "I wish I could do more, John, really I do, but ..." He knows the end of the sentence and does not wish to hear it spoken yet again. "... but these children and this awful country ..."

John's work-in-progress has a title guaranteed to sell it: *Ten Years in South Africa, including a particular description of the Wild Sports of that Country.* If there's one thing the British armchair traveller likes more than hair-raising tales of encounters with wild peoples, it's some really skilful killing of large animals. This Moodie gives them all right, but he's much more artful than the usual British travel writer of the time. Without being seduced by overwriting, the Salome of most of his competitors, he gives the reader an understanding that southern Africa is not an undifferentiated hot, dry place. The subtle differences between regions, the shifting spectrum of colours, the changing texture of the air, he communicates. Somehow he does this in the middle of a Canadian winter, when the temperature frequently drops to forty degrees below freezing.

During most of the long evening, Susanna reads to the children. The servants listen too. Then, for an hour or two Master and Mistress (as they think of themselves) speak elliptically to each other. Their nightly puzzle is why they are doing so badly and running out of money. Because John has been speculating in farm land and in commercial paper is the answer they find most comforting. This is a comfortable answer because speculations can always come right. They avoid – in fact never face squarely – their real problem: they are too lazy to be frontier farmers. Susanna is physically incapable of the hard labour of a frontier farmer, and even if she had not been drained by successive childbirths, she would not have boiled her own wash or dug her kitchen garden. That's why she kept a servant girl. And John, though he would spend an occasional half-day in attacking the forest or scuffing the earth with a harrow, needed his hired man to do the heavy work. He was an officer, damn it, not an enlisted man. Organized in the Moodies' way, a frontier farm could be a financial siphon, nothing else. That's why John's book is so important. Writing is indoor work and requires no heavy lifting. It's genteel. And compared to being one's own draught animal in the backwoods, it's easy.

John gives the British reader Hottentots, Boers ("the Dutch are slow workers, sure gainers, and fast holders"), Xhosa, abused slaves, hardy British pioneers, baboons, snakes, antelope, hyenas, large quadrupeds of all sorts, and many of the items on the list are satisfyingly piked, shot, or spiritually redeemed. Whichever is appropriate. By some magic, in the snows of Upper Canada he produces a memoir of 300,000 words, one that makes the reader march with him through some of the driest, hottest, most hostile of worlds.

Bentley Publishers is delighted with the two volumes and has them out before the year 1835 is over. This project yields profits to the author equal to those of Moodie's writing on the 1814 campaign in Holland: another £65, which is still more than Susanna has made in her entire writing career. A good example to her.

This effort has left John Moodie's well empty. He's a military man, not a scribbler. Nevertheless he suggests for a second time to Richard Bentley that he do a similar book on settling in Upper Canada. His wife will include material from the woman's viewpoint.

Ten Years in South Africa is an easy pattern to follow, he says. But again Bentley says no, Canada's a bore.

Although *Ten Years in South Africa* is far-and-away the most successful piece of sustained non-fiction narrative to be written in Canada before Confederation (and, just maybe, during the entire nineteenth century), it is not included in the Canadian literary canon. John Moodie would not have minded. Writing was merely something any gentleman should be able to turn his hand to. His legacy, in literary terms, was to do for his dear Susanna what her father had done for the workers in his carriage manufactory: set down a basic pattern around which a bespoke conveyance could be framed.

"Susanna, dear one, I still believe there is money to be made in a book about our life here. I could help you get started."

UPPER CANADA. 1836–37

The Northern Light

She's a goddess. An iridescence in the gentle watercolours she paints during her all-too-brief visit. A European writer of craft and deserved reputation. A woman of great beauty: at age 42 she looks 22, slim, with genuine red hair and a complexion so white that touching it with a rose petal makes it blush. And a tongue like that of a fallen angel. She uses it on the bodies of men and women with a tormenting delicacy that leaves them wondering if they have been dreaming. And she also employs it to describe them and their provincial world, often to their faces, with a smile on her lips and a stiletto in her phrase. No one this supernally talented has yet been to Upper Canada and she is treated by her worshippers with a reverence usually reserved for members of the Trinity.

Anna Murphy – known to history as "Mrs. Jameson" – was the daughter of a Dublin portrait painter who was on the edge of events in 1798, and took his family to England to lower his chances of prosecution. Anna had a lady's education. Her wit and beauty served her and she became governess to one of the nieces of the Duke of Wellington. She married well in 1825: a literary lawyer. They agreed to be unhappy. When he, Robert Sympson Jameson, was appointed chief justice of Dominica in 1829 she refused to go along. When he became attorney general of Upper Canada, she agreed that she would visit him, but not to expect her to stay. She had a life.

And an excellent one. She was producing vivid travel writing, books on women in literature, and having a glorious affair with the widow Otillie Goethe, who was an aristocrat in her own right and the former daughter-in-law of the recently deceased Johann Wolfgang Goethe. The lovers spoke English and German together when they had to speak at all.

Anna Jameson turns her visit to Upper Canada into a year-long royal progress. Like a czarist princess, swathed in furs, she is transported by sleigh through the deep woods. As Cleopatra of the New World, she skims the inland waters in a giant birchbark canoe. As the second female Pope, she completes a rogation of holy sites, inspecting "Erindale" and the church of the Rev. James Magrath. And she declares herself to be a houseguest of the misanthrope Col. Thomas Talbot, and with a single touch of her hand turns him into a charming old gentleman.

I have not often in my life met with contented and cheerful-minded women, but I never met with so many repining and discontented woman as in Canada, Anna later wrote. Passing through as she was, she did not need to repine or face discontent. Her animated spirit made her a diamond in a pile of coal. And her skills a legend. Mrs. Jameson performed a few official acts for her husband, but reserved her private acts for others, mostly males. And they were of a type. *The men who have most interested me through life, were all self-educated, and what are called originals.* Here, they were all in the militia or some sort of military duty. Anna enjoyed youthful lieutenants for their energy and repeat-ability; captains and majors for their experience; colonels for their character and staying power. Her favourite colonel in bed-sport is James FitzGibbon, the hero of 1813. *Colonel FitzGibbon is a soldier of fortune – which phrase means, in his case at least, that he owes nothing whatever to fortune, but every thing to his own good heart, his own good sense, and his own good sword.* Especially the sword. Lovely phrasing, that.

Anna leaves Upper Canada in September 1837. Now she is legally separated from her husband and the recipient of an annual income from him, decent fellow. She writes an unforgivably delicate, and accurate reminiscence of her visit to the province. It reads as if done not with a pen, but with a diamond stylus, the sort employed in engraving glass.

In later years, the benefactors of her widely-cast intimacies would encounter each other and try to remember what her magic had been. Was it some physical characteristic, some trick of loveplay that only she knew? None can remember anything special: until one old stager offers up the answer, a single word, uttered like the answer to a prayer.

"Enthusiasm."

Fairly Good Wars

An early and enduring tradition of the Empire was Having a Good War. This involves not being killed and being given credit for something you or someone else has done.

Colonel James FitzGibbon was praised for suppressing William Lyon Mackenzie's rebellion (was it an attempted republican revolution? that's not clear) of December 1837. FitzGibbon was still tingling with the memory of Mrs. Jameson who, after leaving Upper Canada was writing of him: "With so much overflowing benevolence and fearless energy of character, and all the eccentricity, and sensibility, and poetry, and headlong courage of his country [she meant Ireland] you cannot wonder that this brave and worthy man interests me." And now, the frisson continued for FitzGibbon, for he saw, more clearly than his political masters, that there would be a Rising and he hoped to have the throbbing pleasure of commanding troops in battle. That, alas, was a problem. The last time he had commanded a body of men in battle array was when he had captured the Yankees at the battle of Beaver Dams in 1813. Since then he had stopped at least ten melées, riots, and near-riots all over Upper Canada. This he had done single-handedly, and by force of personality. Mostly the affrays involved Irish Catholics against Protestants, and his own background gave him an instinctive ability to choose the right words to calm each side. He was not incompetent to lead a large battle group, just out of practice.

When finally put in charge of suppressing the Toronto revolt he goes all wobbly for a moment and turns to prayer, a practice he usually approved only in theory. And then he puts the rebels to flight with as much ease as if he had been flicking away flies.

A good war: almost. His superior, the lieutenant-governor, does not mention him in reports to the London authorities. FitzGibbon is a local hero, but a grant of 5,000 acres from a grateful legislature is quashed in Westminster, and only in 1845 does he receive a long-promised financial reward: £1,000. FitzGibbon, bitter, only slowly recognized that the key to having a really Good War is to control the way it is talked about in the ensuing peace.

Captain George Benjamin. Undoubtedly the shortest, roundest captain in the Upper Canadian militia, he was a captain nonetheless: in the Belleville-area militia. This by virtue of his being an Orange master and of controlling the town's highly conservative newspaper.

After Mackenzie was defeated he fled to the United States. There Mackenzie fed the Americans' fantasy that most Canadians wanted to be freed from being Canadians, presumably so they could become Americans. Curious as the idea may sound, it played.

One result was that in February 1838 a small force of Americans secretly set up a base camp at Hickory Island, an easy enough walk from New York State when everything was frozen. Located about three miles below Gananoque, where Lake Ontario becomes the St. Lawrence River, Hickory Island lies mid-way between the U.S. and Canadian shores. Using it as a jumping-off point for invading Canada was the strategic equivalent of employing the Faroe Islands as the entry point for an invasion of Europe. Nothing important was close.

Warned, the Canadians drew together a force of men from the Brockville-Kingston corridor, and George Benjamin signed on as a private soldier in the new force: no insisting on being an officer. The Americans scattered upon sight of the Upper Canadian forces. Five prisoners captured, some muskets, ammunition and pikes. George Benjamin, when he returned to Belleville received credit for being plucky and loyal. His newspaper carried a detailed report of the action.

Lt-Colonel Ogle Gowan had his own unit. That put him at the head of loyalism in the Brockville area and vexed the descendants of the original loyalists. In November 1838, a force of 170–200 Americans under a former major in the Polish army, Nils Szoltevky von Schoultz, occupied a large windmill at Prescott, a dozen miles upstream from Brockville. This was a competent enemy. In wretched November weather, Gowan marched his men through mud and half-frozen roads. They merged with other loyal units and fought well, especially considering their enemy was inside an almost impregnable stone citadel. The battle took several days and Gowan was wounded twice: once by shot in the knee and once by bayonet in the posterior, a wound that, when peace came, he did not talk about a great deal.

Captain J.W.D. Moodie had the best war of all, if peacetime results are the standard of assessment. When news of the rebellion in Toronto reached him in December 1837, he immediately left for Port Hope where he joined a regiment of 200 volunteers. He was one of the few with real military experience, and he soon was a captain.

Leaving his wife (pregnant again) in the backwoods was a worry, but his officer's pay was more remunerative than farming. He served on the Niagara frontier for most of a year. He was a professional officer among amateurs and he could expect some reward. Here Susanna intervened and wrote to the lieutenant governor of Upper Canada asking for some prize for John. He probably would have received something on his own, though Susanna always took credit for the good things that followed: John was appointed temporary paymaster for all the militia regiments along Lake Ontario. And then, in late 1839, he was named sheriff of the Victoria district.

Escape! Susanna and John moved into Belleville in January 1840. No more bush farming. No more depending on rough neighbours in times of want. Money. Genteel status. Sheriffs in Upper Canada were not rough-hewn figures like those of the American States. No, they were modelled on the shire reeves of medieval England and that is something Susanna reminded John of frequently. He was to keep civil order, but constables did the disagreeable tasks. He was, she emphasized, to collect every penny due to him: a sheriff was paid by a lawyer or plaintiff every time he served a legal notice, and this would add up quickly. Susanna in her happiness dreamed of the day she would own a piano.

BELLEVILLE, UPPER CANADA ["CANADA WEST"].
NOVEMBER 1842

Pride and Prejudice

"That's lovely, my duchess. You're earning money for old rope. It will help our domestic economy no end."

Susanna had just received another $5.00 in Halifax-currency for a verse and a small story in the *Literary Garland* published in Montreal and every bit did help. John Moodie was not doing well as sheriff. He should have been earning more than £300 a year and was lucky to receive £200: he was too much of a gentleman to dun lawyers for fees he was owed. And he was not a very good sheriff.

Susanna did not wish to be patted on the head. "It's the riffraff." She quickly corrected her lapse. "I mean, the lower classes."

The Moodies had been conducting this conversation for a year-and-a-half. John nodded agreement as she continued. "They stick together, the new immigrants, even the English. And they join that evil order, the Orangemen, and they tyrannize decent people and they steal – everything, even elections."

"Perhaps you should write about it." Susanna's publishing career had been revitalized when she encountered John Lovell, the kind of Irishman she could accept – "a Protestant gentleman from Bandon" is how she described him. He had begun the *Literary Garland* in 1838 and in 1839, while John Moodie was away at war, she had sent Lovell some patriotic and landscape verses on Canada. He published these and happily republished material Susanna had done in England, sweet verses, little stories and serializations of tales she had never got quite right when at Home, some written as long ago as the early 1820s. She had yet to give him anything substantial.

"Yes, that's it: you should send Lovell something new. Cover our recent excitements. Make a good serial."

John Moodie was referring to a series of humiliations that he had borne as sheriff, embarrassments that he carried with the tired patience of a soldier accustomed to slogging through quagmire. The excitements arose because Upper and Lower Canada had been united in 1841 (renamed Canada West and Canada East, but the old terms continued in everyday usage). That necessitated elections and elections required that the sheriff of the district serve as returning officer and that officer had to keep order and ensure impartial balloting; no easy trick in the rough world of Upper Canadian politics and public voting. Belleville and its rural hinterland was a particularly nasty riding. Basically, the working class immigrants and small farmers and farm labourers were conservative. The better-sort and the Catholics were reformers. The names aren't important, the physics are: the conservatives were bonded by the Orange Order. The Moodies, being the better-sort themselves, favoured the reformers and John W.D. Moodie lost his credibility as an impartial electoral officer. The first election, April 1841, went to the reformers by thirty-six votes, and Moodie was charged by the losers, the everyday Protestant working class, with intimidation, partiality, and perjury. The Hastings County election was run again in October 1842 and this time Moodie called out the local militia to close the polls, as he saw a gang war in the making. At that time the conservatives were ahead.

An investigation voided this election. Without the central authorities saying so directly, Moodie was blamed.

"No, John, our local excitements won't be of much interest in Montreal or Toronto."

"I expect you are right."

"But that *Jew editor* will be!" Susanna was animated. "He's the author of the troubles! He's a demon puppeteer." She referred to George Benjamin, who had been the manager of the conservative candidate, and who, by using his Orange mastership and his *Belleville Intelligencer* had rallied the trash against the quality. "Him ... him ... I'll write about him and in such a way that they will remember him even in England!"

With remarkable speed, Susanna produces her first original work of note in Canada and John Lovell serializes it in four parts as "Richard Redpath" in 1843. An amazing work. So full of hatred, so lacking in self-knowledge, that it is an open window on the bile and noisome hatreds that boiled behind the facade of the Suffolk-lady Susanna tried so desperately to be in the cultural backwoods of Upper Canada.

Susanna writes a narrative set not in Upper Canada, but in Jamaica during the period before abolition. Canny strategy, for she is able to use material collected when she was working for Thomas Pringle in his anti-slavery agency; and also, she later explains, to use as a base for her own story, a tale she claimed to have heard from a West Indian planter she met on a steam boat in England in 1831. Susanna's plot is chaos, but the characters are right out of the costume-room of Victorian stage stereotypes. Mungo, the negro speakpiece, says things such as "Dem be queer customers, anyhow! Me nebber see de like oh dem." There's an Irish Jacobite: chevalier, gentleman, and Papist. And two ambitious brothers, the Redpaths, who are shipwrecked off the coast of Jamaica. To alleviate their poverty, one of the brothers in blackface allows himself to be sold into slavery to the benefit of the other. Rivetting stuff.

The true central character is irrelevant to the plot in Jamaica but central to the Moodie's life in Belleville. *He is a man whom all men hate; and were he to die tomorrow every decent person in the place would rejoice at the event.* Not perhaps the subtlest introduction of a character in Canadian fiction, but memorable. *Perhaps he is a wandering Jew ... He knows everybody and everything and must have a finger in every business. He is the most impudent blackguard that ever came to this town ... I believe the devil to be a gentleman when compared to him.* And, surprise, he is the editor of a newspaper, a rag run on evil principles. As editor, he is opposed to the abolition of slavery and when he isn't combatting virtue, this Jew Editor sells clothing on the side.

This is Benjamin Levi. ("Why not just call him George Benjamin?" John Moodie had asked Susanna, not with irony.) This terrible Jew is a perfect likeness of the Belleville Orangeman: *a short fat man with broad shoulders, a head and neck like a bull. He grinned a lot which though meant for a smile was but an acquired contortion to hide the evil workings of the spirit within.* Without consciously knowing that she is repeating most of the inflammatory and derogatory depictions of the Jews that Christendom had developed since the time of Constantine – Susanna thinks she is etching a brilliant character study – Mrs. Moodie produces a piece of work that could not be published in present-day Canada without criminal proceedings ensuing. *In short, sir, a more spiteful, unprincipled, malignant creature never received a commission from Satan to trouble the earth.* ("Do you think, dear one, that you should remind your readers that the Jews crucified Our Lord?" John asks.) Susanna is satisfied to dismiss this embodiment of Semitic perfidy by his going to an ignominious death through fright.

Susanna never backs away from her anti-Jewish principles, for she cannot see that she has them. The term anti-Semite had yet to be invented, so let her be simply hate-ridden. When in 1854 she packages "Richard Redpath" together with two shopworn novellas from her English years, Susanna finds some resistance from her publisher. Even in England, where being nasty to Jews is an art form, her views are a touch ripe. Jewish Emancipation was still being fought: the Commons favoured it, but the Lords believed that having Baron Rothschild sit in the Commons would be going down perdition's road. In 1858, a compromise let each house determine its own rules; but now, in the mid-1850s the Jewish issue was one a publisher of middle-class entertainment was leery of. Susanna tells Bentley that the Jew in this book of hers, *Matrimonial Speculations*, "is a true picture, drawn from life, which so closely resembles the original that it will be recognized by all who ever knew him, or fell under his lash. A man *detested* in his day and generation."

No self-knowledge; no reflection.

In the twentieth century, a wise observer remarked that anti-Semitism is the instinctive snobbery of the socially marginal.

ST. THOMAS'S (ANGLICAN) CHURCH, BELLEVILLE.
28 JUNE 1846

Grand Master

George and Isabella Benjamin stand at the back of the church. It is a private service. The rector is a person of sensitivity.

George Benjamin no longer wishes to be the Jew Editor: Susanna Moodie has made that a suit of clothes he can no longer wear. To effect the change in identity, the Benjamins offer up a child: they are having six months-old Harry Ansel Benjamin baptized in the Anglican faith. Neither George nor Isabella is willing to become a full converso, but this child sacrifice, when certified by the Church of England rector, will help them verify their trustworthiness in a Christian world.

There is some urgency. Since Mrs. Moodie's *Literary Garland* assassination of "Benjamin Levi" had appeared in November 1843, George Benjamin had moved into local government and politics, laying the basis for an escape from being the Jew Editor. He has become the first superintendent of common schools in Belleville, secretary of a small railroad corporation, and has been elected to various local councils. Now, two plums are coming up and he needs to look clean for the Christians.

He is appointed land registrar for Hastings county in August 1846.

And, better in the long run, in December he is elected Grand Master of the Orange Order of all of British North America!

Ogle Gowan has stepped aside, caught in one of his periodic bouts of depression, and from 1846 to 1853 (when he has a row with Gowan), George Benjamin is head heajin of lay Protestants in Canada. This in an organization whose character has been most strongly (but, in Canada, far from entirely) formed by Irish Protestants – and at a moment when the biggest outflow, ever, from Ireland is about to begin.

Stop the train!

What is going on here? Madness? No, not a touch. George Benjamin is exercising a privilege conferred on those who move to New Worlds: to re-invent himself, and those who follow him are not gulled. They find his re-invention useful to them. For, in truth, George Benjamin is a very good Grand Master and a boon to tens of thousands of Irish, new migrants and old.

Until the Great Famine, three-quarters of Irish migration to North America was to the Canadas and, if as much as a third of it was pass-through to the United States, there was a compensating flow from New York and Philadelphia to Canada, especially Upper Canada. The flow of the Irish had been in spate since the early 1830s and in the 1840s became a flood. That was before the Famine, and George Benjamin was head of an organization that claimed (perhaps with a bit of exaggeration) 50,000 adult males in Upper Canada alone.

When, in 1848 and after, the bulk of the Irish migrants begin travelling directly to the United States (cheaper fares), a healthy 20,000 Irish a year are still coming to Upper Canada. Two-thirds of them are Protestants and they are George Benjamin's special responsibility. These are people who, if not starving, are scared, afrighted of the future, diminished in resources, and needful of advice and a bit of encouragement. Benjamin uses the Order as a huge immigrant-assistance society. It's a sectarian one, no question: no Catholics need apply. The Order does what is crucial: gets immigrants out of the bigger cities (there are no really big ones) and into the small towns and farms where the real opportunities lie. Useful information, items such as where good bush land is still open, which land jobbers to avoid, how to obtain a mortgage in this new land, that is what the Order provides under Benjamin.

It's not the Boy Scouts and Benjamin is no saint. In the cities, Orange-Green riots are a stable of urban working-class culture for the next twenty years, and the countryside has its share of quiet sectarian nastiness.

Still, why do a group of hard-faced Prods follow this fat little Jew? Because he is special and in his own way, wise.

Consider an earlier event, when, in the first days of the Rebellion of 1837–38, George Benjamin is trying to drill a company of left-footed rurals, of whom he is captain. He looks silly enough on a horse, like a sphere on a pine table, and he makes it worse by wearing crimson overalls. Combined with the spectacles his extreme near-sightedness demands, he is the least military figure one can imagine. One drill day his entire militia company shows up wearing red stockings over their trousers and sporting cartoon spectacles that they have cut from scrap leather.

No yelling from Benjamin. He refuses to notice. He puts the men in drill order and marches them around for a bit until they are near a frog pond. They expect him to order halt. Instead he says "quick march" and soon they are up to their oxters in green slime. Then he calls halt and orders "About face, march!"

The men loved him for it and after that would have run through a stone wall for him: broad humour, all the better for being delivered straight-faced.

George Benjamin may have been Mrs. Moodie's Jew Editor, but he understood the heart of the rural Upper Canadians, by turns laconic, violent, helpful, hateful, and he knew intuitively that these people do not look up to someone who looks down upon them.

COMPRESSION AND EXPANSION.
THE UNITED STATES
1830–1845

All-Stars

At the same moment that Daniel O'Connell is achieving the goal of full civil liberty in Ireland – through the Catholic Emancipation Act – the American-Irish in the states that employ large numbers of slave labourers are on a mission of their own.

Unconsciously.

They are interweaving themselves into the genetic chain of many of the future members of the Halls of Fame of the National Football League, the National Basketball Association, Major League Baseball, professional boxing in all its dubious guises, and, not least, the Negro Leagues.

It is not a nice business. Coercion and petty bribery are more important than seduction, and most of the American-Irish do not recognize any duty to their milk-coffee-coloured offspring. The Irish of course are not the only ones, but as one-fifth to one-quarter of the population of the heaviest slave-holding states, they are a big part of the most intimate and unspoken swirl in the American melting pot. The Irish not only are slave holders, but are especially proficient as overseers; thus, cumulatively, they have access to thousands and thousands of African women in coercive situations. The business has been going on since the beginning of African slavery and will continue right up to the end of the American Civil War. Thereafter, it will become "voluntary."

In not acknowledging the African segment of their collective heritage, the American-Irish miss connection with some of the most extraordinarily gifted and strong-charactered people in the American tapestry.

Nate Archibald, Ernie Banks, Cool Papa Bell, Jim Brown, Rube Foster, Josh Gibson, Earvin Johnson, Judy Johnson, Buck Leonard, Willie Mays, Willie Lee McCovey, Lenny Moore, Calvin Murphy, Buck O'Neil, Walter Payton, Jack Roosevelt Robinson, Willis Reed, Nate Thurmond, Willie Wells.

And hundreds of others. No, these were not just convenience names taken at the time of Emancipation, but real bearers of a distant, but undeniable, paternity.

Only a tithe of the connections are thus recorded, and beneath other ethnic names are also Irish connections: woven into the DNA of America.

Did you forget Muhammad Ali? – and his great-grandfather Mr. Grady.

IRELAND AND NORTH AMERICA. 1830–45

Flood Tiding Beginning

For the record. The massive flood of Irish migration to the American portion of the New World does not begin with the Great Famine, but well before: 1830 is the start of the tidal wave.

For the record, until the later 1840s, the pathway is from Liverpool to the Canadas, mostly. Irish migrants sometimes live for years in Canada before crossing into the States. And many stay north.

For the record, now most Irish migrants are Catholics, but not overwhelmingly so: 40–50 percent are Protestants. The Catholics who go to the western frontier of the U.S. still are without Irish priests and generally become Protestants themselves. In the eastern cities, however, something new is happening. In Charleston, Baltimore, Philadelphia, New York, and even purblind Boston, churches are being built to serve Irish Catholics. The days of massive slippage from the One True Faith are just beginning to be numbered.

PARIS, TENNESSEE. 1831

King of the Wild Frontier

Reports vary, but there is no question that events of mid-1833 led David Crockett to transform himself into Davy Crockett, the forerunner of Buffalo Bill and of every Hollywood hick hero.

David Crockett, Tennessee state politician, had a noble dream. He wished to be president of the United States and since he had never found anything in life he could not conquer, circumvent, or castrate, this was not impossible: as long as he kept the goal to himself. Crockett dropped out of the legislature and in his second attempt, in 1827, was elected U.S. congressman for the ninth district of Tennessee. The Congressional Record (which admittedly cleaned things up a bit) shows him to be a sound debater. He can be amusing, as when he discusses the possible paths of the lunatic Buffalo-to-New Orleans Road, but mostly he is serious and hard-hitting. His logo, on which he hangs his future career, is land legislation to protect squatters who had gotten ahead of the formal laws of settlement. Mostly subsistence hunter-farmers, they would be broken if forced to pay for surveys and for quit-rents or for purchase. *The rich require but little legislation. We should, at least occasionally, legislate for the poor.* Shrewd and honestly felt as well.

Andrew Jackson gets in the way and Crockett turns on Jackson, formerly his hero. Unless he can get his signature-bill through congress, Crockett knows he has no big future in politics; and, at heart, he knows that Jackson is a nemesis not only in this instance but because he commands the Man of the West/Man of the People image that David Crockett himself will need to own if he is to rise to the top.

Thus, in 1831, Crockett is running in Tennessee against Andrew Jackson's candidate, William Fitzgerald, and the election swings on one debate. The *Nashville Banner* reports: *Fitzgerald spoke first. Upon mounting the stand he was noticed to lay something upon the pine table in front of him, wrapped in his handkerchief … He commenced his speech … When Fitzgerald reached the objectionable point, Crockett arose from his seat in the audience and advanced toward the stand. When he was within three or four feet of it, Fitzgerald suddenly removed a pistol from his handkerchief and, covering Colonel Crockett's breast, warned him that a step further and he would fire.*

This, in frontier politics was a moment of truth. *Crockett hesitated a second, turned around and resumed his seat.*

And, when his climb-down became well-known, he lost the election.

Crockett brooded, paid his electoral debts: he had to sell his cleared lands and a Negro girl, "Adaline," who was his sexual comfort since he and his second wife were separated and, in fact, living in separate counties. And he planned for the election of 1833. He entered into a partnership with a man who could spell and they produced the pseudonymous *Life and Adventures of Colonel David Crockett of West Tennessee*, one of America's first campaign biographies. It was in equal part lionization of Crockett and vilification of Andrew Jackson. David Crockett is transformed into Davy Crockett.

He wins the 1833 election and immediately joins another ghostwriter and produces his *Autobiography*, a collection of the Homeric adventures told with a winning, if calculated self-deprecation. Gosh, he's a modest hero, if a trifle hard on the wildlife and the indigène. Davy Crockett becomes a national figure and during the congressional session of 1834, instead of tending to his work in congress, he lets the Whigs parade him through the salons of Baltimore, New York, Newport, and Boston. This is a trial run, to see how he would do as a national candidate, and his backwoods speech and self-declared honesty go down a treat. Potentially a useful candidate, Davy Crockett.

Yet he still cannot force his signature land-bill through the house and he becomes increasingly bitter. No land bill, no political future. He'd kill Andrew Jackson if he could. With nothing concrete to show his West Tennessee electorate, Crockett loses to a one-legged Jackson supporter in 1835, and he decides to move to Texas. It's not as yet part of the United States and, in Davy Crockett's view, that might be a very good thing.

WASHINGTON, D.C. FEBRUARY, 1832

Cleansing the Land

No more than Sir Arthur Chichester had appreciated the O'Neills, did his wraith, the first American-Irish president, Andrew Jackson, honour his native American enemies.

Jackson, as president, re-kindles in his bowels the white-hot hatred of the Indians that had driven him through so many blood-thirsty months as a younger man. Of course he approves the policy of racial cleansing inaugurated by George Washington and accelerated by Thomas Jefferson after his purchase of Louisiana – clearing the savages to the far side of the Mississippi. Their presidential successors had all been tremblers, gumps, bench-legged milch-sticks who were soft on the heathen. Jackson will clear the lot, so he will.

Trouble is, the work to be done is not heroic. Most of the native Americans on the east side of the Mississippi live in small refugee bands, displaced from even further east, and they are not able to put up more than token resistance as white farmers flood in and strip the land of game and grab the best agricultural sites. The big blocs of savages, Jackson knows, are in the south, and they aren't really savages any more. Segments of the Five Civilized Tribes – Cherokee, Creek, Chickasaw, Chocktaw, and Seminole – have made treaties and were imitating the white man in the most unnerving way: farming, living in settled villages, buying African slaves and using them to build up their own local economies. They were doing as well or better than their slack-jawed neighbours who lusted after their land. No matter.

Goddamnthemtohell says Jackson and thus begins the Trail of Tears, the more reluctant native bands being driven like cattle by the U.S. cavalry until most of them find their designated spot of internal exile: eastern Oklahoma. Some escape. Some just filter away to empty spots on the map of the west, where they will slowly attenuate and leave only bones. But most settle in eastern Oklahoma, a gulag in a society that calls itself the land of freedom.

Among the hodge-podge of undistinguished souvenirs that were inventoried after Andrew Jackson's death was a mezzotint presented to him by an admirer: it was of Carrickfergus Castle, County Antrim. Tattered from having been rolled up and kept in a desk drawer, from whence, apparently, it had been removed frequently, it was a north-view of the castle. The engraving reproduced the protective sight that Jackson's parents had seen daily before their own migration to British North America in 1765. Carrickfergus, Jackson knew from family lore, was arranged the way things should be: big guns, clear boundaries, and only the most broken of native inhabitants permitted within its thick walls.

As so, God willing, Jackson's America will be.

ST. PETERSBURG, RUSSIA. 11 JUNE 1832

Spoiled

The American who presents his credentials to Nicholas I is garbed in full diplomatic regalia and speaks passable French. He tries not to be overwhelmed, but he has been dazzled since his arrival ten days earlier by the beauties of Peter the Great's creation; the Nevsky Prospekt, the Winter Palace, the display of wealth in every villa. And, heavens, the women, with their wonderfully deep décolletage. They evinced a willingness to flirt that, in Pennsylvania, would have led to anyone who dallied with them being challenged to a duel. Not here: their husbands just look on. The new American ambassador's only regret is that he does not speak German, for that language is used informally in St. Petersburg almost as much as is French.

James Buchanan II (he never used that designation), the spoiled son of James Buchanan I, is in his element. His father had denied him nothing and here, in St. Petersburg, he does not have to deny himself. James Buchanan, though the son of an adamantine Presbyterian mother, is no predestinarian or doom-sayer. In fact, he does not join the Presbyterian faith until he is in his mid-seventies and near death: Episcopalianism is much more appropriate for those living a Full Life. Here, on foreign soil, he acts much more like the younger son of

an Anglo-Irish gentleman than of an Ulster-American farmer and tavern keeper. His appreciation of wines grows nightly. He acquires
from several successive women of the court the names of the private
parts of the body in three languages, French, German, and Russian. In
winter, in the company of some portly aristocrats, he learns the difficult art of strapping blades to his boots and propelling himself along
the Neva River.

This is a pay-off from Andrew Jackson for having delivered Pennsylvania in the 1828 election. At that time, Pennsylvania was to national politics what New York and California later successively
became: a fulcrum on which national outcomes rest.

All James Buchanan has to do as ambassador is to complain in his
despatches home about how hard his life is and to conclude a commercial treaty with Russia and this was already in the bag before he
arrived. So Buchanan is able to relive his youth – his father having
paid for his tutoring at the Old Stone Academy, Mercersburg, and
then his two years at Dickinson College, where he drank and smoked
and was happy and was expelled and was re-admitted only when his
father posted a bond for his behaviour. Those were good days but
these were better.

The court of St. Petersburg makes up for James Buchanan's having
missed the brass ring earlier. In his late twenties he had won the hand
of one of America's first millionaires, the daughter of Robert Coleman of Castle Finn, County Donegal. Like the Russells, who had
raised James Buchanan I, the Colemans were Anglo-Irish of the
poorer-sort. The New World had made them rich.

Alas, Ann Coleman was as spoiled as was James Buchanan II, only
younger and more of a drama-queen. In 1819, misreading a courtesy
he paid on another woman as a slight to her dignity, she broke off
their engagement and took poison more successfully than she had intended. The suicide was put down to hysteria and no one talked of it.
From then on, James flirted with fashionable ladies, slept with prostitutes, conducted a few discreet liaisons with married women, but
never married. Instead, he married himself to politics. Willing to take
any side on any issue as long as the patronage was right, he became
the most important political fixer in Pennsylvania.

A tall man, but with a round face and the soft hands of a haber-
dasher's assistant, he was rewarded by James Polk for his knitting
and weaving of alliances during the 1844 election by being named
Secretary of State. Neither he nor Polk trusted each other, but Polk

worked like a dervish, producing a whirlwind of imperial expansion, and Buchanan merely went along with it. Not a hard job, really, though of course he complains.

Then, in 1848, having failed to be nominated by the Democrats for the presidency, Buchanan retires to his newly-purchased estate, Wheatland, in Lancaster County. He dresses like an Irish gentleman, with an ebony-topped cane, a high white collar, long frock coat and, usually, a top hat.

Nearly sixty, he waits: he intends to be elected president in 1852, and if not then, in 1856. White-haired, he takes on the guise of the Sage of Wheatland. He appears to be the embodiment of wisdom, but at heart he remains his father's spoiled son.

MIAMI, OHIO. 1833

The Nation's Tutor

Reluctantly, the professor of Greek, Latin and Hebrew at Miami University sits down to write a children's book. He is a realist and knows that it is easier to lecture on the subtleties of biblical philology than it is to write well for children. Nevertheless, William Holmes McGuffey sets to work, for he believes strongly in mass education. His *First Eclectic Reader* appears in 1836 and he continues at a considered pace, finishing the sixth in 1857.

These volumes teach more people (not just children) to read English than any other books in nineteenth-century America. And, outside the Bible, they sell more: by 1920, over 120 million copies have been sold.

REFUGIO AND SAN PATRICIO, MEXICAN TEXAS. 1834

Mirrors?

Empresario. What a fine title! Given by the Mexican government to James Power, James Hewetson, John McMullen and James McGloin, it let them become little Caesars in return for their bringing in Irish colonists as a buffer against American aggression. Two Irish Catholic colonies, Refugio and San Patricio (ah, dear St. Patrick) are formed on the coastal bend of Texas and by 1834 are nearly successful – this after amazingly bad luck having dogged the settlers, including cholera, shipwreck, robbery, and assassination.

The core of the Refugio colony is composed of Tipperary Catholics and the core of San Patricio is made up of Wexford Catholics. This at the very time that Tipperary Protestants and Wexford Protestants are migrating in clusters to Upper Canada. The two sets of migrations are virtual mirror images of each other. Taken together, they illustrate the immense hunger for land and the skill and ingenuity in its acquisition on the part of Irish people of all classes and all religions. In every New World, land hunger gnaws at the gut of almost all Irish emigrants.

And protection of land, once acquired, is a drive as deep as any except the most basic biological motives.

In Mexican Texas, the Irish install their own priests from the homeland, intermarry with Mexican Catholics, and look proudly over their massive holdings – with the Mexican government charging only £25 for a full league of land (4,428 acres), one could become very landproud very quickly.

The danger is the Americans. Nearly 20,000 illegal squatters saunter into Texas and, outnumbering the Mexicans ten-to-one, take land pretty much at will. The Irish colonists, who prefer Mexico to the United States, mostly because of the protection given to their religion and because of the generosity of the Mexican government in land grants, are caught on a hurdle. As war between the American squatters and Mexico looms, the colonists decide that they will cast their lot with the probable winners, the Americans. But they will stay on their lands while the combat rages: otherwise the Americans will strip them as naked as they do the Mexicans.

The Irish survival strategy is successful. To take one example: Thomas O'Connor, of County Wexford, arrived as San Patricio in 1833 as a fifteen-year-old. Before he died in 1887 he could plausibly claim to own lands equal in size to Ireland itself.

That, actually, was the same claim, equally valid, made in New South Wales, Australia by Edward Ryan of County Tipperary.

Another mirror, same picture: land hunger, land hunger, land hunger.

NEW YORK CITY. 1834

A Woman's Land

Muffled in the growl of male voices is a simple fact. That many Irish women from the small tenantry are as hungry for land in the New World as are the men.

When Minerva Padden comes down the gangplank in New York in 1834 she knows that, if she is lucky, she will find a job as a domestic servant in a nice well-run house. She is very lucky indeed, for she becomes a domestic servant with the widow of Gerard Beekman. Like many Irish young women, she saves prodigiously, but Minerva has no intention of staying in the city. Her life in Ireland taught her that secure holding of land and, of course, a husband, were the only true security. So, she leaves the Beekman family with her savings securely tied in a purse under her skirt, and looks for both land and husband in upstate New York.

A forgotten frontier in the rush westward, northern New York is only half cut-over, and has large patches of wild lands that were once reserved for Revolutionary War veterans and now are held by speculators. Bitter cold in winter, blanketed for four or five months a year by the massive snowfalls that drop south of the Great Lakes, frontier New York is a challenge.

Like a prospector, Minerva moves from town to town, earning her keep, maintaining her savings, learning about land prices and quietly selecting a husband. She finds another Irish migrant, Timothy Donovan, suitable. He is a bit dim, but very strong.

With Minerva in charge, the couple decides on a big gamble. For $77.00 they purchase a quit-claim deed to fifty acres of the Revolutionary Lands near Oswego. That's cheap, but the gamble is that the quit-claim is being sold by someone who actually has the right to the land – an heir of a revolutionary soldier, for example. The Donovans invest seven years of their lives in brutally hard labour: clearing land, building a log house, and having five children. Then, the sky falls. The land actually is owned by a large speculator, the couple's quit-claim is worthless. They are out on the road with their five children, one cow, and some sheep.

The cow died.

Minerva Padden Donovan must have been a fine domestic servant and her employers equally decent people: for she writes desperately to the Beekman family and they provide her, first, with a few dollars to get through the hard times, and, later, with enough money to buy another cow, with a bit left over. In two years, the family is back on a small piece of cleared land: they buy eleven acres from Gerrit Smith, later famous for funding John Brown's raid on Harper's Ferry.

Once the land is paid for, they are contracted to receive a New York State deed. *Then no body can turn us out doors.*

DUBUQUE, IOWA. 20 JUNE 1834

Duty

Father Charles J. Fitzmaurice rides on a casket that rests on a cart that is being pulled to a hanging.

St. Louis now has enough Catholics to be elevated to a diocese, and a huge area, including the not-yet-state of Iowa, comes under its bishop. Father Fitzmaurice is delegated to take the joint charge of Dubuque, a mercantile centre and Galena, a mining community. Soon after his arrival, one of his parishioners, Patrick O'Connor, is convicted of having committed the first murder in the Iowa territory: that of a fellow Irishmen named O'Keaf.

Doing his duty, the priest sits on the casket with the felon as it is drawn towards the scaffold. The murderer repents of his crime and asks for absolution for his sins, especially for the murder and for having brought scandal to his fellow Catholics. With Father Fitzmaurice's hand on his shoulder, he softly repeats the prayers for the dying that the priest whispers into his ear.

Father Fitzmaurice is in his charge only a little more than six months. Then the cholera takes him to join Pat O'Connor.

WASHINGTON, D.C. 8 JANUARY 1835

Miracle

The meal has eight wines, brandy, armagnac, and, for the backwoodsmen, whiskey. Eighteen courses of food, if one counts the two courses of native nuts and fruits as separate items. President Jackson, mid-way through his second term, has stage-managed this event himself. It is modelled on the formative meal of Jackson's political life, one given at Philadelphia in 1797 by Aaron Burr, champion of statehood for Tennessee. Several times in later years at The Hermitage, Jackson had unsuccessfully attempted to duplicate Burr's profligate hospitality and now, on the presidential budget, he finally makes it all come together.

The eighth of January is the anniversary of Jackson's triumph in the Battle of New Orleans. There he had outgeneralled the U.K. army and he is modest about it in a way that speaks anything but modesty. He praises his soldiers and he praises British gallantry. He is careful to use the word "British," though he in fact knows that the U.K. forces were under Irish generals and that half their troops were from Ireland. In the thinking of Jacksonian America, being English is a bad thing and being Irish is all right, especially given the power of the Irish on the American frontier. So "British" can cover a multitude of prejudices and keep the Irish out of it.

The dinner, held midway during Jackson's second term, is timed to coincide with a victory that Jackson holds to be as important as New Orleans. That afternoon, he has paid the final installment on the national debt.

The national government is free and clear.

Andrew Jackson permits himself the immodest luxury of suggesting to his guests that future presidents of the United States will be duty-bound to follow his example.

Near Miss

From behind a pillar on the portico of the Capitol, a delusionary lunatic steps towards President Andrew Jackson. From a distance of eight feet he fires two pistols. Each misfires and he is grabbed by members of Jackson's party.

Although now long in years, Jackson has to be restrained from beating the failed assassin with his ivory-handled cane.

Andrew Jackson has come within an ace of being the first American-Irish president to be assassinated.

NEW ORLEANS, LOUISIANA. AUTUMN, 1835

Ol' Side-Saddle

Sam Houston has a personal secret and it hurts, not least because he cannot be sure it is still a secret.

Houston has been appointed President Jackson's military leader in Mexican Texas. And the Committee of Vigilance of one local band of settlers has acclaimed him as Chief of the Forces of the Department of Nacogdoches. His real job is to lead an uncontrollable rabble, men proficient in all forms of violence and few forms of self-control, in conquering Texas for the United States. Part of his job is to avoid being crushed by the troops he is supposed to lead, and that gives Houston pause. Like his patron, Andrew Jackson, Houston makes a production of referring to his Irish Planter ancestors and goes on about how as their heirs, American frontiersmen must walk tall and not stoop while conquering.

Except that position hurts like hell.

Which is why Sam Houston is in New Orleans. He is acquiring a uniform of his own design. It has a general's stars on the shoulders, a sword with an engraved silver scabbard, and enough bogus campaign ribbons to prevent his alleged subordinates from mistaking him for one of themselves; and crucially, he is fitted for a special pair of trousers: high-rise with capacious front pleats.

Sam is drunk most of the time, but that is medically necessary. He is in pain and the opiates his doctors prescribe dull his mind too much. Alcohol he can handle.

Houston, surprisingly, spends even more time on being fitted for a special saddle than for his general's uniform. It's a unique design, with a special loop on the left side that Sam says is a fitting for his heavy carbine. Others who see it note that it is very similar to the fixtures on a lady's saddle.

And so it is. Whenever Sam Houston thinks he is out of the range of observers, he swings his right leg over the saddle pommel and rides side-saddle, like a Spanish lady. Whenever he does this, he breaths a long sigh of relief.

His secret is not entirely secret, but those who catch Houston in his female riding rig either think he is a frontier ferret or, usually, that he rides so stocioius that this keeps him from falling out of the saddle.

No one seems to remember that, while serving under Andrew Jackson, Sam Houston had taken a Cherokee arrow in his private parts and that no amount of stitching, clipping, and binding would set right his prospects or dull the pain that drives him almost blind.

THE ALAMO, MEXICAN TEXAS. MARCH 1836

Go Ahead?

"If you're sure you're right, go ahead," Sam Houston wrote to Davy Crockett, adding that he thought the whole idea ill-advised. The handwriting was hard to read as Houston was perpetually drunk, but the joke was not bad: a parody of one of the clichés Crockett was peddling in his self-initiated hagiographies. Despite Houston's being a protégé of Andrew Jackson, he and Crockett were civil to each other. As young men, each had fought under Jackson in the 1812–14 war and, separately, each had taken part in highly successful massacres: Crockett playing a leading role in obliterating about a thousand Creek in their surrounded village of Tullushatchee in November 1813 and Houston, fighting with a terrible wound, at Horseshoe Bend in March 1814, where 917 natives were killed. The latter number was so precise because the Americans cut off the nose of each corpse and placed them in rows of ten, to make accurate accounting possible. Men who had participated in big events like that respected each other.

Crockett read Houston's letter and laughed. "Well, Ol' Side-Saddle is still up to form." That form had been nicely defined in 1827 when Houston was elected governor of Tennessee (as a Jacksonian) at the same time as Crockett was keeping his seat in the congressional race. They got along and Crockett admired the younger man's style. Houston had himself inaugurated in the First Baptist Church, Nashville, in a flash outfit that would have done credit to a New Orleans pimp. Immediately he began to pay court to the teen-aged daughter of a large land-owner and he wed the young belle. The marriage lasted four months and ended in early 1829 with Houston resigning the governorship in disgrace. The newspapers dared not print the cause, but it was well known: Houston could not satisfy his wife and she complained to her family and they threatened to murder Houston. At the time, Crockett had thought Sam was harshly done by: the woman wasn't all that attractive, anyway.

Houston's implied permission to come to Texas was welcome. Davy wasn't going to be president of the U.S. any time soon and he needed a new world. Sam was Andrew Jackson's man in Mexico and, whether Davy liked it or not, the connection would make life easier. Houston had gone to Mexico soon after his disgrace in Tennessee and had become a Roman Catholic and a Mexican citizen, both as matters of convenience: he immediately bought one of the first divorces to be given by the Mexican government and bribed his way into several thousand acres of land. In doing this, he wasn't throwing around his own money: Andrew Jackson badly wanted Mexico to be annexed to the U.S. and eventually, the U.S. government spent about half a million dollars corrupting Mexican officials. Meanwhile, stocious most of the time, Sam Houston slides back and forth between Washington, D.C., where he preaches annexation, and his constantly-blurred Texas outpost, where he becomes the governor-in-waiting of an American Texas. "Wonderful that he could write me at all," Davy says, noting that Sam had spelled Crockett with three Ts.

Davy falls in love with Texas; big country, game, flowering hillsides in springtime, a beautiful land. He takes the oath of allegiance to the provisional Republic of Texas that American in-comers are forming and becomes a leader of a company of militia, mostly men formerly from Tennessee. The embryonic Texas republic is so democratic that it chooses, in two separate constitutional conventions, two separate governors (one of them is Sam Houston) and two separate Commanders in Chief (again, one of them is Houston).

Surprisingly, Davy sides with the anti-Houston forces because, finally, he cannot abide the hand of Andrew Jackson using drunken Sam as a glove puppet.

"Go ahead." Against the advice (it could scarcely be called an order) of Sam Houston, Crockett is among the band that sets out for the Rio Grande in January 1836. Despite trustworthy reports of a large Mexican army advancing, the force finds itself surrounded in a mud-walled compound near San Antonio. The 150, or so, able-bodied men were overrun at the Alamo. It is a punishment for hubris that could have been written by a Greek playwright. Nobody knows how Davy Crockett died, but there is no doubt that he died as Davy, not David: at least a dozen versions of his demise exist, and the only thing they have in common is that he dies as a hero, his heart beating to the last in the snare-drum rhythm of his political catch-phrase: Go-ahead, go-ahead, go-ahead.

BOSTON, MASSACHUSETTS. 1837;
PHILADELPHIA, PENNSYLVANIA. 1844

Not so Simple

Catholic-Protestant riots in Boston and Philadelphia: reflexively pigeon-holed by historians as Nativist vs. Irish-Catholic immigrants.

It is not so simple: for much of the trouble has little to do with bigotry within the USA and more to do with sectarian tensions in the homeland.

Well-known is the fact that Irish Catholic migrants to the New World carried with them memories of Protestant discrimination and violence in Ireland. What is almost totally forgotten is that, as the Catholics became more and more assertive after Catholic Emancipation, they did unto the Protestants as had been done unto them. The *Dublin University Magazine* was far from impartial, but it caught Protestant perceptions dead accurately. *There is nothing more common, during the last few years, than for some Roman Catholic who sees a Protestant possessed of a farm that would be a desirable acquisition, to resolve to make it his own; and in order to effect this object, a system of annoyance and persecution is resorted to, a threatening notice is posted on his house, his family is insulted, himself beaten at the fair or returning from market, and his life made so uncomfortable and, as he thinks, so insecure, that he proposes to free himself from all by emigration. This is the very object his persecutor was aiming at; and having succeeded in removing the occupant, the Roman Catholic gets possession of the farm.*

That hatred, Protestant for Catholic and Catholic for Protestant is imported directly into America and mingles with what is glibly called Nativism. Certainly the USA has its own deep bigotries, but not all of them are home made.

LOWELL, MASSACHUSETTS. 1837–1845

Neither Dark Nor Satanic

When explorers early in the twentieth century cleared the jungle from around Machu Picchu, they knew instantly that they were at the site of something breathtaking, some sort of temple to the past. That is the last emotion one has when entering a former New England mill-town and that is a shame: for at moments those mills were wonders of complex activity, an integration of inanimate force and human dexterity, and the light that glowed in the mill's windows was for many Irish people a beacon. The moment did not last long, but, then, nothing human does.

During the financial panic of 1837, the Yankee mill town of Lowell, Massachusetts almost stumbled to a halt. Then, like a big steam engine that only needs a valve to be cleared for it to roar into life, it ran faster than ever.

Recruitment was the key. The ring of factory owners realized that Yankee women, useful as they were as operatives, were in short supply and that very skilful Irish women were available. That was for the top-end jobs; anyone would do for the hauling and lifting. But to get disciplined and well-trained operatives for the finishing jobs – the tasks that allowed the owners to charge top-dollar for their product – the mill owners recruited from the Lancashire textile region of England. There they picked up English workers, but mostly Irish and mostly women.

These are a female elite. They have by virtue of daily application been promoted in the Lancashire factories until they reach the top of their trade. They know the latest techniques and they understand how to talk to mechanics about adjustments and fine tuning of the finishing machinery. Irish country girls originally; now as valuable as are the skilled tradesmen. They postpone marriage, save their money, and when they do marry, they make certain they situate themselves in the Irish respectable class.

Meanwhile, the skilled builders of the booming pre-Famine core of Lowell are mostly from Ireland. The major subcontractor in Lowell (he has his hand in every pie, but his name never appears on a brass plaque) is a Tyrone man who sweeps through the south and west of Ireland. There, in a swathe that runs from Cork City to Sligo, he tests, then employs, masons, carpenters, joiners, and, often coopers – anybody who can make a barrel can be turned into a top-class finishing carpenter. The contractor does not care if these men remain in America when Lowell is completed – many return to Ireland with money in their pocket and commercial knowledge in their head – all he wants is canals articulated, factory masonry set square, workers' housing done quickly and cheaply, and the occasional gentry home done in high style.

The male skilled tradesmen and the female skilled mill operatives are a natural labour aristocracy and have as much in common with the Yankee skilled class as they do with the other Irish. They frequently forsake their local home-country loyalties (still important in Lowell) and marry according to their social class. They support the very successful local temperance society and give to the church.

These self-proud people are the foundation of the successful urban Irish, a group larger and more varied than the dense foliage that later covers their abandoned temples of employment lets the casual passer-by discern.

DUBLIN. 1840

Mixed Views

Like an old dowager receiving courtesy-callers, the Liberator accepts the attentions of the leading American abolitionists: James G. Birney, William Lloyd Garrison, Ann Phillips, and others. They have been attending the World Anti-Slavery Convention in London and they want Daniel O'Connell to pull the American-Irish Catholics onto their side. Ever since 1829, the Liberator has been very strongly on record against slavery and very harsh on the hypocrisy of the United States, with its glorious Constitution and its inglorious practice. O'Connell has vowed that, though he would dearly love to visit America, he will not do so as long as slavery remains.

Yet, with the Repeal of the Union between Great Britain and Ireland paramount in his mind, he does not wish to distract his American followers from that main cause. Nevertheless, he puts his signature – along with those of 60,000 other Irish persons – on a thundering denunciation of American chattel slavery.

The Abolitionists think they are on to a winner: the Catholic Irish, who have experienced their own severe oppression, will certainly follow the Liberator in moving to destroy the Odious Institution.

Ah, naive hope. Mostly, the Irish document is greeted with disapproval. The Bishop of New York, John J. Hughes, declares it is the duty of every Irishman *to resist and repudiate the address with indignation*. Not because of its content, but because of its alien origin: *I am no friend of slavery, but I am still less friendly to any attempt of foreign origin to abolish it.* The most influential American-Irish nationalist newspapers also disapprove, for was not O'Connell a moral-force man, not a physical-force revolutionary? Then how, asks the Boston *Pilot*, could he join a cause that would *bathe the whole South [of the USA] in blood*? And some American-Irish writers suggest, with equal degrees of subtlety and fantasy, that the Abolition movement is actually part of an English plot to sap the strength of the American Republic and thus to prolong Albion's imperial rule over most of the earth's surface.

It is all very disappointing for the Abolitionists, and extremely confusing.

THE NORTH ATLANTIC. 12 MARCH 1841

Waves

The legendary Irish comic actor, Tyrone Power, having made his reputation in Dublin and London, added the United States to his list of venues. He toured for two years in the period 1833–35, not only playing New York and the east coast, but New Orleans and then going up the Mississippi. Like so many literary-cultural visitors of that age, he was fascinated by America and wrote a book about it: *Impressions of America*, published in London in 1836. He liked the place, and his broad humour and his signature theatrical wave – more a comic semaphoring, really – went down very well every place from Brooklyn to the hotel stages of still-wild middle America.

In fact, Power liked the USA so much that he came back for another tour in 1839–41. Though he did well everywhere, he was treated as family by that strand of Anglo-Irish radicals whose parents had been United Irish Protestants in 1798 or rebels in 1803 and who now, in the USA, were doing very well as establishment figures. Power was especially close with Judge Emmett, a nephew of the late Irish patriot. Judge Emmett was on hand to wave good-bye to Tyrone Power as he boarded the *President*, a steam-assisted vessel, for the trip back to the British Isles.

"You must come back, dear man," Emmett had said to Power.

"I shall, I will, I must," the actor replied. "I've left all my money here. With my lawyer. He's purchasing property for me." He did not mention the name of the lawyer.

The *President* sank beneath the waves off Martha's Vineyard on 12 March 1841, amidst a fierce gale.

Despite Judge Emmett's best efforts, he could not find any New York lawyer who would admit that he had accepted funds from the late comedian.

Family tradition, glorious genre, holds that the forever-invisible lawyer had been instructed to buy a large piece of land that encompassed the site of what is now Madison Square Garden.

THE GREAT SALT LAKE. SEPTEMBER 1843

Always Use Rubber?

When the gods decided not to make John C. Frémont a proctologist, they were being kind. Had they done so, we would all be walking on our tip-toes, for never has a man had as great a passion as his for investigating the bowels of everything. Lucky it was that he was made an explorer and that he worked out his fascination with interstices and convolutions by inserting himself into the most complex and forbidding portions of the unknown West. In what is now Kansas to Oregon, California, Nevada, Utah, he went to all the difficult places.

Still, his anatomist's instincts are obvious as he approaches the Great Salt Lake. He has seen it before and this time wishes to explore it more fully. He has brought with him the necessary rubber protection.

A boat. One that has no metal fasteners or copper keel-protectors. Metal would dissolve in the lake. And even a purely-wooden dinghy would soon sink, as the saline water would eat away at the caulking until the effort turned into one big leaky barrel.

Rubber's your man, so says Frémont. The small vessel, consisting of a series of bladders that are inflated by a hand bellows, is large enough to hold only four men and their surveying instruments. These include Frémont, naturally, and Kit Carson who would rather be buried in buffalo dung than caught on a large body of water. Land he understands, not waves.

The four men in the rubber tub paddle on waters that are crystal clear, yet sting their hands. They soon learn to apply force by gripping only the very top end of their paddles. The dinghy has no rudder, so that unless they stroke precisely, it goes forward in large, half-controlled arcs. They go ashore on a salt island and then make their way back against a rising wind. It is all they can do to keep moving against the waves while one crew member desperately works the hand bellows: the air bladders have begun to leak. The men barely make shore and after they have pulled the craft above the wave line, Kit Carson leads them in shooting holes in the unnatural device.

PRINCETON, NEW JERSEY. 1844

Fractured Equation

In the *Biblical Repertory and Princeton Review,* the Rev. Dr. Archibald Alexander, the most influential educator of Presbyterian clerics of the nineteenth and early twentieth centuries, states that *it is common to represent our church as having derived its origin from the Church of Scotland; and remotely this was the fact; but its immediate origin was from the Presbyterian Church of Ireland.*

He is of course correct; but he and his fellow Presbyterian ministers are living amidst the rubble of a fragmented equation. In Dr. Alexander's lifetime, it *is* true that the religion of mainline American Presbyterianism is still Irish Presbyterianism. But it is no longer true in the USA that most men and women of Irish Presbyterian background are of that faith. Most of them are Baptists, and Methodists, and Disciples of Christ: fragmented and therefore less civically effective.

This *before* the massive Irish migration of 1845–75 which, when its effects are fully worked out, yields almost as many Irish Catholics as Irish Protestants in the U.S. population.

LAWRENCE, MASSACHUSETTS. 1845

The Last Boat to Reach Shore
Before the Tsunami

Having saved a tidy packet as a builder of the mills and boarding houses of Lowell, Massachusetts, Andrew MacGowan goes home to Sligo. (A surprising number of men and women go back and forth between Ireland and the USA in the years before the Famine.) He rents a farm, marries, and has three children. Like many of the Irish, he has a network of former workmates, relatives, and lodge brothers in America and he keeps up on economic conditions there and on the opportunities for experienced tradesmen.

He learns that the Essex Company has been founded to create an entirely new community down river from Lowell on the Merrimack River. It will have a decent-sized common, streets that will be well-treed, a public library and schools, and the mill district will be strictly demarcated. Lawrence will not be a model town, but it will be liveable, and jobs for builders will be there in plenty.

So, by the autumn of 1845, Andrew MacGowan and his family are in Lawrence and he is at work. They have travelled on a good ship, with their own family cubicle and they arrive well-fed and in robust health. MacGowan does finishing carpentry for a time and, crucially, he buys a large lot on The Plains, well back from the river and near the Lawrence Common. There he builds a set of six row houses, for rental to the better sort of artisan, and sets his wife up in a shop and starts his own carpentry business.

This is an average story of Irish Catholic entrepreneurship.

It has salience only because of our own foreknowledge of the guillotine that is poised over the people of the Irish homeland.

Andrew MacGowan and his family are well settled before even a single potato has shrivelled with blight.

INDEX